For

Distinction

A Social Critique of the
Judgement of Taste

Pierre Bourdieu

Translated by Richard Nice

First published in French as
La Distinction, Critique sociale du jugement
by Les Editions de Minuit, Paris
© 1979 by Les Editions de Minuit

This English translation first published in Great Britain in 1984
by Routledge & Kegan Paul Ltd
First published in paperback in English 1986.

Reprinted 1989, 1992, 1994
by Routledge
11 New Fetter Lane, London EC4P 4EE

The preparation of this volume was assisted by grants from the
Translations Program of the National Endowment for the
Humanities, an independent federal agency, and from the
Cultural Exchange Service of the French Ministry of Foreign
Affairs. We also gratefully acknowledge the assistance of the
Maison de Sciences de l'Homme.

Printed in Great Britain by
T.J. Press (Padstow) Ltd., Padstow, Cornwall

British Library Cataloguing in Publication Data
A catalogue record for this book is available from the British Library.

ISBN 0-415-04546-0

Contents

Preface to the English-Language Edition   xi
Introduction   1

Part I | *A Social Critique of the Judgement of Taste*   9

   1 The Aristocracy of Culture   11
      The Titles of Cultural Nobility   18
      Cultural Pedigree   63

Part II | *The Economy of Practices*   97

   2 The Social Space and Its Transformations   99
      Class Condition and Social Conditioning   101
      A Three-Dimensional Space   114
      Reconversion Strategies   125

   3 The Habitus and the Space of Life-Styles   169
      The Homology between the Spaces   175
      The Universes of Stylistic Possibles   208

   4 The Dynamics of the Fields   226
      The Correspondence between Goods Production
      and Taste Production   230
      Symbolic Struggles   244

Part III | *Class Tastes and Life-Styles*   257

   5 The Sense of Distinction   260
      The Modes of Appropriation of the Work of Art   267
      The Variants of the Dominant Taste   283
      The Mark of Time   295
      Temporal and Spiritual Powers   315

6 Cultural Goodwill   318

Knowledge and Recognition   319
Education and the Autodidact   328
Slope and Thrust   331
The Variants of Petit-Bourgeois Taste   339
The Declining Petite Bourgeoisie   346
The Executant Petite Bourgeoisie   351
The New Petite Bourgeoisie   354
From Duty to the Fun Ethic   365

7 The Choice of the Necessary   372

The Taste for Necessity and the Principle
   of Conformity   374
The Effects of Domination   386

8 Culture and Politics   397

Selective Democracy   399
Status and Competence   405
The Right to Speak   411
Personal Opinion   414
The Modes of Production of Opinion   417
Dispossession and Misappropriation   426
Moral Order and Political Order   432
Class Habitus and Political Opinions   437
Supply and Demand   440
The Political Space   451
The Specific Effect of Trajectory   453
Political Language   459

Conclusion: Classes and Classifications   466

Embodied Social Structures   467
Knowledge without Concepts   470
Advantageous Attributions   475
The Classification Struggle   479
The Reality of Representation and the Representation
   of Reality   482

Postscript: Towards a 'Vulgar' Critique of 'Pure'
   Critiques   485

Disgust at the 'Facile'   486
The 'Taste of Reflection' and the 'Taste of Sense'   488
A Denied Social Relationship   491
Parerga and Paralipomena   494
The Pleasure of the Text   498

Appendices   503

   1.   Some Reflections on the Method   503
   2.   Complementary Sources   519
   3.   Statistical Data   525
   4.   Associations: A Parlour Game   546

Notes   561
Credits   605
Index   607

Tables

1   Class preferences for singers and music   15

2   Aesthetic disposition, by educational capital   36

3   Aesthetic disposition, by class and education   37

4   Knowledge of composers and musical works, by education and class of origin   64

5   Furniture purchases in the dominant class, by education and social origin   78

6   Some indicators of economic capital in different fractions of the dominant class, 1966   117

7   Some indicators of cultural practice in different fractions of the dominant class, 1966   118

8   Types of books preferred by different fractions of the dominant class, 1966   119

9   Social origin of members of the dominant class, by class fraction, 1970   121

10   Rate of employment of women aged 25–34, by education, 1962 and 1968   134

11   Changes in morphology and asset structure of the class fractions, 1954–1975   136

12   Changes in morphology and asset structure of the class fractions, 1954–1968   138

13   Morphological changes within the dominant class, 1954–1975   140

14   Morphological changes within the middle class, 1954–1975   140

15   Changes in class morphology and use of educational system, 1954–1968   158

16   Annual household expenditures on food: skilled manual workers, foremen and clerical workers, 1972   181

17   Yearly spending by teachers, professionals and industrial and commercial employers, 1972   184

18 Annual household expenditures on food: fractions of the dominant class, 1972   188

19 Variations in entertaining, by class fraction, 1978   198

20 Variations in value placed by Frenchwomen on body, beauty and beauty care, 1976   203

21 Class variations in sports activities and opinions on sport, 1975   216

22 Class-fraction variations in moral attitudes   312

23 Opinions on literary prizes, by class fraction, 1969   320

24 Chances of entering the dominant class, and fertility rates, by class fraction, 1970–71   332

25 Knowledge and preferences of established and new petite bourgeoisie, in Paris and in the provinces   364

26 Awareness of social factors in educational and social success, by class fraction, 1971   388

27 Views on ways of reducing inequality, by class fraction, 1970   389

28 'Don't know' responses to political questions, by sex, 1971   403

29 'Don't know' responses to questions on teaching, by educational level, 1970   404

30 The imposition effect: responses to question on the business world and politics, by class fraction, 1971   429

31 The imposition effect: responses to question on the new socialism, by sex, class fraction and party, 1971   430

32 Views on political order and moral order, by class fraction, 1959–1972   436

33 Newspaper reading by men, by educational level, 1975   445

34 Newspaper reading by men, by age, 1975   445

35 Newspaper reading by men and women, by class fraction, 1975   446

36 Percentage of each class fraction reading each daily and weekly paper   448

Figures

1 Distribution of preferences for three musical works   17

2 The aesthetic disposition in the petite bourgeoisie   59

3 The relationship between inherited cultural capital and educational capital   81

4 Specific competence and talk about art   90

5 The space of social positions   128

6 The space of life-styles   129

7 Displacement of schooling rates of 16- to 18-year-olds, 1954–1975   159

8 Conditions of existence, habitus and life-style 171

9 The food space 186

10 Ideal homes 248

11 Variants of the dominant taste: the space of properties 262

12 Variants of the dominant taste: the space of individuals 262

13 Variants of the dominant taste: simplified plane diagram of 1st and 3rd axes of inertia 266

14 Films seen: I 271

15 Variants of petit-bourgeois taste: the space of properties 340

16 Variants of petit-bourgeois taste: the space of individuals 340

17 Variants of petit-bourgeois taste: simplified plane diagram of 1st and 3rd axes of inertia 343

18 Films seen: II 361

19 Permissiveness and political preference 423

20 Opinions on foreign policy and political preference 427

21 The political space 452

Preface to the English-Language Edition

I have every reason to fear that this book will strike the reader as 'very French'—which I know is not always a compliment.

French it is, of course, by virtue of its empirical object, and it can be read as a sort of ethnography of France, which, though I believe it shows no ethnocentric indulgence, should help to renew the rather stereotyped image of French society that is presented by the American tradition. But I believe it is possible to enter into the singularity of an object without renouncing the ambition of drawing out universal propositions. It is, no doubt, only by using the comparative method, which treats its object as a 'particular case of the possible', that one can hope to avoid unjustifiably universalizing the particular case. With the aid of Norbert Elias's analyses, I do indeed emphasize the particularity of the French tradition, namely, the persistence, through different epochs and political regimes, of the aristocratic model of 'court society', personified by a Parisian *haute bourgeoisie* which, combining all forms of prestige and all the titles of economic and cultural nobility, has no counterpart elsewhere, at least for the arrogance of its cultural judgements.[1] It would, however, be a mistake to regard all that is said here about the social uses of art and culture as a collection of Parisian curiosities and frivolities—and not only because, as Erving Goffman once pointed out to me, the Parisian version of the art of living has never ceased to exert a sort of fascination in the 'Anglo-Saxon' world, even beyond the circle of snobs and socialites, thereby attaining a kind of universality.

The model of the relationships between the universe of economic and social conditions and the universe of life-styles which is put forward here, based on an endeavour to rethink Max Weber's opposition between class and *Stand,* seems to me to be valid beyond the particular French case and, no doubt, for every stratified society, even if the system of distinctive features which express or reveal economic and social differences (themselves variable in scale and structure) varies considerably from one period, and one society, to another.[2] For example, the slightest familiarity with the structural mode of thought tells one that the use of French words, proper names, preferably noble, or common nouns—Institut de Beauté, Confiseur, Haute couture, etc.—performs the same function for shops on Fifth Avenue or Madison Avenue as English words like hairdresser, shirtmaker or interior designer on shop fronts in the rue du Faubourg Saint-Honoré.[3] But, more broadly, the sense of distance, even strangeness, which scientific objectification itself produces and which is intensified by the differences in historical traditions, giving different contents to different realizations of the same structures, must not prevent the reader from reflecting onto his own society, onto his own position within it, in short, onto himself, the analyses he is offered.

That is why, though I am aware of the dangers of a facile search for partial equivalences which cannot stand in for a methodical comparison between systems, I shall take the risk of suggesting, within the limits of my knowledge of American society and culture, some guidelines for a reading that seeks to identify, behind the specific institution of a particular society, the structural invariant and, by the same token, the equivalent institution in another social universe. At the level of the 'international' pole of the dominant class the problem scarcely arises, since the cultural products are (relatively) international. One could replace *Les Temps Modernes* by *Partisan Review,*[4] France-Musique by educational television (Channel 13, WQXR, WGBH etc.) and perhaps ultra-leftism by sixties 'camp',[5] while the *New York Review of Books* would (alas) represent an unlikely combination of the weekly *Nouvel Observateur,* the review *Critique* and, especially in its successive enthusiasms, the journal *Tel Quel.* As regards bourgeois taste, the American professionals, executives and managers might ask of the film, book, art and music critics of the *New York Times* or magazines like *Time* and *Newsweek* the same balanced, subtly diversified judgements which their French opposite numbers expect from *Le Monde* or *Le Figaro* or weeklies like *L'Express* or *Le Point.* The titles and authors favoured by the best-seller readership will vary from country to country, but in each case there will be a preponderance of the life-stories and memoirs of exemplary heroes of bourgeois success or 'non-fiction novels'. The undemanding entertainment which Parisians expect from boulevard theatre, New Yorkers will seek in Broadway musicals.

But I believe I have said enough to encourage my readers to join in the game, at least so as to correct my mistakes and perhaps to pursue the search for equivalents, which would have to be sought in song and cinema (Is Brigitte Bardot like Marilyn Monroe? Is Jean Gabin the French

John Wayne, or Humphrey Bogart or Spencer Tracy?)—and also in dress, interior decoration, sport and cooking. For it is certain that on each side of the Channel or the Atlantic some things are compatible, others are not; and the preferences of a class or class fraction constitute coherent systems. To support this hypothesis, which all the empirical analyses confirm, I can invoke Edgar Allan Poe, who spells out the link between the most everyday choices, in decoration, for example, and choices in the 'fine arts', seeing in the ordinary arrangement of the wealthy apartments of his country the expression of a way of life and thought: 'We speak of the keeping of a room as we would of the keeping of a picture—for both the picture and the room are amenable to those undeviating principles which regulate all varieties of art; and very nearly the same laws by which we decide on the higher merits of a painting, suffice for decision on the adjustment of a chamber.'[6]

In its form, too, this book is 'very French'. This will be understood if the reader accepts that, as I try to show, the mode of expression character-istic of a cultural production always depends on the laws of the market in which it is offered.[7] Although the book transgresses one of the funda-mental taboos of the intellectual world, in relating intellectual products and producers to their social conditions of existence—and also, no doubt, *because* it does so—it cannot entirely ignore or defy the laws of academic or intellectual propriety which condemn as barbarous any attempt to treat culture, that present incarnation of the sacred, as an object of sci-ence. That is one of the reasons—along with the costs of book produc-tion—why I have only very partially reproduced the survey material and the statistical data used, and have not always given the exposition of the method as much prominence as the rhetoric of scientificity would de-mand. (As in the French edition, some passages of the text, containing detailed statistical material, illustrative examples or discussion of ancillary issues, are printed in small type so that the reader who seeks an overview of the main argument may pass over them on a first reading.) Likewise, the style of the book, whose long, complex sentences may offend—con-structed as they are with a view to reconstituting the complexity of the social world in a language capable of holding together the most diverse things while setting them in rigorous perspective—stems partly from the endeavour to mobilize all the resources of the traditional modes of ex-pression, literary, philosophical or scientific, so as to say things that were de facto or de jure excluded from them, and to prevent the reading from slipping back into the simplicities of the smart essay or the political po-lemic.[8]

Finally, I realize how much the specificity of the French intellectual field may have contributed to the conception of this book, in particular to its perhaps immoderate ambition of giving a scientific answer to the old questions of Kant's critique of judgement, by seeking in the struc-ture of the social classes the basis of the systems of classification which structure perception of the social world and designate the objects of aesthetic enjoyment. But in an age when the effects of a premature division of labour separate anthropology from sociology, and, within the latter, the sociology of knowledge from the sociology of culture, not to mention the sociology of food or sport, it is perhaps the advantage of a world still haunted by the ultimate and total questionings of the prophetic intellectual that one is led to refuse the self-induced myopia which makes it impossible to observe and understand everything that human practices reveal only when they are seen in their mutual relationships, that is, as a totality.[9]

At all events, there is nothing more universal than the project of objectifying the mental structures associated with the particularity of a social structure. Because it presupposes an epistemological break which is also a social break, a sort of estrangement from the familiar, domestic, native world, the critique (in the Kantian sense) of culture invites each reader, through the 'making strange' beloved of the Russian formalists, to reproduce on his or her own behalf the critical break of which it is the product. For this reason it is perhaps the only rational basis for a truly universal culture.

Distinction

Introduction

You said it, my good knight! There ought to be laws to
protect the body of acquired knowledge.
  Take one of our good pupils, for example: modest and
diligent, from his earliest grammar classes he's kept a little notebook full of phrases.
  After hanging on the lips of his teachers for twenty
years, he's managed to build up an intellectual stock in
trade; doesn't it belong to him as if it were a house, or
money?

Paul Claudel, *Le soulier de satin,* Day III, Scene ii

There is an economy of cultural goods, but it has a specific logic. Sociology endeavours to establish the conditions in which the consumers of
cultural goods, and their taste for them, are produced, and at the same
time to describe the different ways of appropriating such of these objects
as are regarded at a particular moment as works of art, and the social
conditions of the constitution of the mode of appropriation that is considered legitimate. But one cannot fully understand cultural practices
unless 'culture', in the restricted, normative sense of ordinary usage, is
brought back into 'culture' in the anthropological sense, and the elaborated taste for the most refined objects is reconnected with the elementary taste for the flavours of food.

  Whereas the ideology of charisma regards taste in legitimate culture as
a gift of nature, scientific observation shows that cultural needs are the
product of upbringing and education: surveys establish that all cultural
practices (museum visits, concert-going, reading etc.), and preferences in
literature, painting or music, are closely linked to educational level
(measured by qualifications or length of schooling) and secondarily to
social origin.[1] The relative weight of home background and of formal
education (the effectiveness and duration of which are closely dependent
on social origin) varies according to the extent to which the different
cultural practices are recognized and taught by the educational system,
and the influence of social origin is strongest—other things being
equal—in 'extra-curricular' and avant-garde culture. To the socially recognized hierarchy of the arts, and within each of them, of genres, schools or
periods, corresponds a social hierarchy of the consumers. This predisposes

tastes to function as markers of 'class'. The manner in which culture has been acquired lives on in the manner of using it: the importance attached to manners can be understood once it is seen that it is these imponderables of practice which distinguish the different—and ranked—modes of culture acquisition, early or late, domestic or scholastic, and the classes of individuals which they characterize (such as 'pedants' and *mondains*). Culture also has its titles of nobility—awarded by the educational system—and its pedigrees, measured by seniority in admission to the nobility.

The definition of cultural nobility is the stake in a struggle which has gone on unceasingly, from the seventeenth century to the present day, between groups differing in their ideas of culture and of the legitimate relation to culture and to works of art, and therefore differing in the conditions of acquisition of which these dispositions are the product.[2] Even in the classroom, the dominant definition of the legitimate way of appropriating culture and works of art favours those who have had early access to legitimate culture, in a cultured household, outside of scholastic disciplines, since even within the educational system it devalues scholarly knowledge and interpretation as 'scholastic' or even 'pedantic' in favour of direct experience and simple delight.

The logic of what is sometimes called, in typically 'pedantic' language, the 'reading' of a work of art, offers an objective basis for this opposition. Consumption is, in this case, a stage in a process of communication, that is, an act of deciphering, decoding, which presupposes practical or explicit mastery of a cipher or code. In a sense, one can say that the capacity to see (*voir*) is a function of the knowledge (*savoir*), or concepts, that is, the words, that are available to name visible things, and which are, as it were, programmes for perception. A work of art has meaning and interest only for someone who possesses the cultural competence, that is, the code, into which it is encoded. The conscious or unconscious implementation of explicit or implicit schemes of perception and appreciation which constitutes pictorial or musical culture is the hidden condition for recognizing the styles characteristic of a period, a school or an author, and, more generally, for the familiarity with the internal logic of works that aesthetic enjoyment presupposes. A beholder who lacks the specific code feels lost in a chaos of sounds and rhythms, colours and lines, without rhyme or reason. Not having learnt to adopt the adequate disposition, he stops short at what Erwin Panofsky calls the 'sensible properties', perceiving a skin as downy or lace-work as delicate, or at the emotional resonances aroused by these properties, referring to 'austere' colours or a 'joyful' melody. He cannot move from the 'primary stratum of the meaning we can grasp on the basis of our ordinary experience' to the 'stratum of secondary meanings', i.e., the 'level of the meaning of what is signified', unless he possesses the concepts which go beyond the sensible properties and which identify the specifically stylistic properties of the work.[3] Thus the encounter with a work of art is not 'love at first sight' as is generally supposed, and the act of empathy, *Einfühlung,* which is the art-lover's pleasure, presupposes an act of cognition, a decoding operation, which implies the implementation of a cognitive acquirement, a cultural code.[4]

This typically intellectualist theory of artistic perception directly contradicts the experience of the art-lovers closest to the legitimate definition; acquisition of legitimate culture by insensible familiarization within the family circle tends to favour an enchanted experience of culture which implies forgetting the acquisition.[5] The 'eye' is a product of history reproduced by education. This is true of the mode of artistic perception now accepted as legitimate, that is, the aesthetic disposition, the capacity to consider in and for themselves, as form rather than function, not only the works designated for such apprehension, i.e., legitimate works of art, but everything in the world, including cultural objects which are not yet consecrated—such as, at one time, primitive arts, or, nowadays, popular photography or kitsch—and natural objects. The 'pure' gaze is a historical invention linked to the emergence of an autonomous field of artistic production, that is, a field capable of imposing its own norms on both the production and the consumption of its products.[6] An art which, like all Post-Impressionist painting, is the product of an artistic intention which asserts the primacy of the mode of representation over the object of representation demands categorically an attention to form which previous art only demanded conditionally.

The pure intention of the artist is that of a producer who aims to be autonomous, that is, entirely the master of his product, who tends to reject not only the 'programmes' imposed a priori by scholars and scribes, but also—following the old hierarchy of doing and saying—the interpretations superimposed a posteriori on his work. The production of an 'open work', intrinsically and deliberately polysemic, can thus be understood as the final stage in the conquest of artistic autonomy by poets and, following in their footsteps, by painters, who had long been reliant on writers and their work of 'showing' and 'illustrating'. To assert the autonomy of production is to give primacy to that of which the artist is master, i.e., form, manner, style, rather than the 'subject', the external referent, which involves subordination to functions—even if only the most elementary one, that of representing, signifying, saying something. It also means a refusal to recognize any necessity other than that inscribed in the specific tradition of the artistic discipline in question: the shift from an art which imitates nature to an art which imitates art, deriving from its own history the exclusive source of its experiments and even of its breaks with tradition. An art which ever increasingly contains reference to its own history demands to be perceived historically; it asks to be referred not to an external referent, the represented or designated 'reality', but to the universe of past and present works of art. Like artistic production, in that it is generated in a field, aesthetic perception is necessarily historical, inasmuch as it is differential, relational, attentive to the deviations (*écarts*) which make styles. Like the so-called naive painter who, operating outside the field and its specific traditions, remains external to the history of the art, the 'naive' spectator cannot attain a specific grasp of works of art which only have meaning—or value—in relation to the specific history of an artistic tradition. The aesthetic disposition demanded by the products of a highly autonomous field of production is inseparable from a specific cultural competence. This historical culture functions as a principle of pertinence which enables one to identify, among the elements offered to the gaze, all the distinctive features and only these, by referring them, consciously or unconsciously, to the universe of possible alternatives. This mastery is, for the most part, acquired simply by contact with works of art—that is, through an implicit learning analogous to that which makes it possible to recognize familiar faces without explicit rules or criteria—and it generally remains at a practical level; it is what makes it possible to identify styles, i.e., modes of expression characteristic of a period, a civilization or a school, without having to distinguish clearly, or state explicitly, the features which constitute their originality. Everything seems to suggest that even among professional valuers, the criteria which define the stylistic properties of the 'typical works' on which all their judgements are based usually remain implicit.

The pure gaze implies a break with the ordinary attitude towards the world, which, given the conditions in which it is performed, is also a social separation. Ortega y Gasset can be believed when he attributes to modern art a systematic refusal of all that is 'human', i.e., generic, common—as opposed to distinctive, or distinguished—namely, the passions, emotions and feelings which 'ordinary' people invest in their 'ordinary' lives. It is as if the 'popular aesthetic' (the quotation marks are there to indicate that this is an aesthetic 'in itself' not 'for itself') were based on the affirmation of the continuity between art and life, which implies the subordination of form to function. This is seen clearly in the case of the novel and especially the theatre, where the working-class audience refuses any sort of formal experimentation and all the effects which, by introducing a distance from the accepted conventions (as regards scenery, plot etc.), tend to distance the spectator, preventing him from getting involved and fully identifying with the characters (I am thinking of Brechtian 'alienation' or the disruption of plot in the *nouveau roman*). In contrast to the detachment and disinterestedness which aesthetic theory regards as the only way of recognizing the work of art for what it is, i.e., autonomous, *selbständig,* the 'popular aesthetic' ignores or refuses the refusal of 'facile' involvement and 'vulgar' enjoyment, a refusal which is the basis of the taste for formal experiment. And popular judgements of paintings or photographs spring from an 'aesthetic' (in fact it is an ethos) which is the exact opposite of the Kantian aesthetic. Whereas, in order to grasp the specificity of the aesthetic judgement, Kant strove to distinguish that which pleases from that which gratifies and, more generally, to distinguish disinterestedness, the sole guarantor of the specifically aesthetic quality of contemplation, from the interest of reason which defines the Good, working-class people expect every image to explicitly perform a function, if only that of a sign, and their judgements make reference, often explicitly, to the norms of morality or agreeableness. Whether rejecting or praising, their appreciation always has an ethical basis.

Popular taste applies the schemes of the ethos, which pertain in the ordinary circumstances of life, to legitimate works of art, and so performs a systematic reduction of the things of art to the things of life. The very seriousness (or naivety) which this taste invests in fictions and representations demonstrates a contrario that pure taste performs a suspension of 'naive' involvement which is one dimension of a 'quasi-ludic' relationship with the necessities of the world. Intellectuals could be said to believe in the representation—literature, theatre, painting—more than in the things represented, whereas the people chiefly expect representations and the conventions which govern them to allow them to believe 'naively' in the things represented. The pure aesthetic is rooted in an ethic, or rather, an ethos of elective distance from the necessities of the natural and social world, which may take the form of moral agnosticism (visible when ethical transgression becomes an artistic *parti pris*) or of an aestheticism which presents the aesthetic disposition as a universally valid principle and takes the bourgeois denial of the social world to its limit. The detachment of the pure gaze cannot be dissociated from a general disposition towards the world which is the paradoxical product of conditioning by negative economic necessities—a life of ease—that tends to induce an active distance from necessity.

Although art obviously offers the greatest scope to the aesthetic disposition, there is no area of practice in which the aim of purifying, refining and sublimating primary needs and impulses cannot assert itself, no area in which the stylization of life, that is, the primacy of forms over function, of manner over matter, does not produce the same effects. And nothing is more distinctive, more distinguished, than the capacity to confer aesthetic status on objects that are banal or even 'common' (because the 'common' people make them their own, especially for aesthetic purposes), or the ability to apply the principles of a 'pure' aesthetic to the most everyday choices of everyday life, e.g., in cooking, clothing or decoration, completely reversing the popular disposition which annexes aesthetics to ethics.

In fact, through the economic and social conditions which they presuppose, the different ways of relating to realities and fictions, of believing in fictions and the realities they simulate, with more or less distance and detachment, are very closely linked to the different possible positions in social space and, consequently, bound up with the systems of dispositions (habitus) characteristic of the different classes and class fractions. Taste classifies, and it classifies the classifier. Social subjects, classified by their classifications, distinguish themselves by the distinctions they make, between the beautiful and the ugly, the distinguished and the vulgar, in which their position in the objective classifications is expressed or betrayed. And statistical analysis does indeed show that oppositions similar in structure to those found in cultural practices also appear in eating habits. The antithesis between quantity and quality, substance and form, corresponds to the opposition—linked to different distances from necessity—between the taste of necessity, which favours the most 'filling' and most economical foods, and the taste of liberty—or luxury—which shifts the emphasis to the manner (of presenting, serving, eating etc.) and tends to use stylized forms to deny function.

The science of taste and of cultural consumption begins with a transgression that is in no way aesthetic: it has to abolish the sacred frontier which makes legitimate culture a separate universe, in order to discover the intelligible relations which unite apparently incommensurable 'choices', such as preferences in music and food, painting and sport, literature and hairstyle. This barbarous reintegration of aesthetic consumption into the world of ordinary consumption abolishes the opposition, which has been the basis of high aesthetics since Kant, between the 'taste of sense' and the 'taste of reflection', and between facile pleasure, pleasure reduced to a pleasure of the senses, and pure pleasure, pleasure purified of pleasure, which is predisposed to become a symbol of moral excellence and a measure of the capacity for sublimation which defines the truly human man. The culture which results from this magical division is sacred. Cultural consecration does indeed confer on the objects, persons and situations it touches, a sort of ontological promotion akin to a transubstantiation. Proof enough of this is found in the two following quotations, which might almost have been written for the delight of the sociologist:

'What struck me most is this: nothing could be obscene on the stage of our premier theatre, and the ballerinas of the Opera, even as naked dancers, sylphs, sprites or Bacchae, retain an inviolable purity.'[7]

'There are obscene postures: the stimulated intercourse which offends the eye. Clearly, it is impossible to approve, although the interpolation of such gestures in dance routines does give them a symbolic and aesthetic quality which is absent from the intimate scenes the cinema daily flaunts before its spectators' eyes . . . As for the nude scene, what can one say, except that it is brief and theatrically not very effective? I will not say it is chaste or innocent, for nothing commercial can be so described. Let us say it is not shocking, and that the chief objection is that it serves as a box-office gimmick. . . . In *Hair,* the nakedness fails to be symbolic.'[8]

The denial of lower, coarse, vulgar, venal, servile—in a word, natural—enjoyment, which constitutes the sacred sphere of culture, implies an affirmation of the superiority of those who can be satisfied with the sublimated, refined, disinterested, gratuitous, distinguished pleasures forever closed to the profane. That is why art and cultural consumption are predisposed, consciously and deliberately or not, to fulfil a social function of legitimating social differences.

I | A Social Critique of the Judgement of Taste

And we do not yet know whether cultural life can survive
the disappearance of domestic servants

Alain Besançon, *Etre russe au XIXe siècle*

1 | The Aristocracy of Culture

Sociology is rarely more akin to social psychoanalysis than when it confronts an object like taste, one of the most vital stakes in the struggles fought in the field of the dominant class and the field of cultural production. This is not only because the judgement of taste is the supreme manifestation of the discernment which, by reconciling reason and sensibility, the pedant who understands without feeling and the *mondain*[1] who enjoys without understanding, defines the accomplished individual. Nor is it solely because every rule of propriety designates in advance the project of defining this indefinable essence as a clear manifestation of philistinism—whether it be the academic propriety which, from Alois Riegl and Heinrich Wölfflin to Elie Faure and Henri Focillon, and from the most scholastic commentators on the classics to the avant-garde semiologist, insists on a formalist reading of the work of art; or the upperclass propriety which treats taste as one of the surest signs of true nobility and cannot conceive of referring taste to anything other than itself.

Here the sociologist finds himself in the area par excellence of the denial of the social. It is not sufficient to overcome the initial self-evident appearances, in other words, to relate taste, the uncreated source of all 'creation', to the social conditions of which it is the product, knowing full well that the very same people who strive to repress the clear relation between taste and education, between culture as the state of that which is cultivated and culture as the process of cultivating, will be amazed that anyone should expend so much effort in scientifically proving that self-evident fact. He must also question that relationship, which only appears to be self-explanatory, and unravel the paradox whereby the relationship with educational capital is just as strong in areas which the educational system does not teach. And he must do this without ever being able to appeal unconditionally to the positivistic arbitration of what are called facts. Hidden behind the statistical relationships between educational capital or social origin and this or that type of knowledge or way of applying it, there are relationships between groups maintaining different, and even antagonistic, relations to culture, depending on the conditions in which they acquired their cultural capital and the markets in which they can derive most profit from it. But we have not yet finished with the self-evident. The question itself has to be questioned—in other words, the relation to culture which it tacitly privileges—in order to establish whether a change in the content and form of the question would not be sufficient to transform the relationships observed. There is no way out of the game of culture; and one's only chance of objectifying the true nature of the game is to objectify as fully as possible the very operations which one is obliged to use in order to achieve that objectification. *De te fabula narratur.* The reminder is meant for the reader as well as the sociologist. Paradoxically, the games of culture are protected against objectification by all the partial objectifications which the actors involved in the game perform on each other: scholarly critics cannot grasp the objective reality of society aesthetes without abandoning their grasp of the true nature of their own activity; and the same is true of their opponents. The same law of mutual lucidity and reflexive blindness governs the antagonism between 'intellectuals' and 'bourgeois' (or their spokesmen in the field of production). And even when bearing in mind the function which legitimate culture performs in class relations, one is still liable to be led into accepting one or the other of the self-interested representations of culture which 'intellectuals' and 'bourgeois' endlessly fling at each other. Up to now the sociology of the production and producers of culture has never escaped from the play of opposing images, in which 'right-wing intellectuals' and 'left-wing intellectuals' (as the current taxonomy puts it) subject their opponents and their strategies to an objectivist reduction which vested interests make that much easier. The objectification is always bound to remain partial, and therefore false, so long as it fails to include the point of view from which it speaks and so fails to construct the game as a whole. Only at the level of the field of positions is it possible to grasp both the generic interests associated with the fact of taking part in the game and the specific interests attached to the different positions, and, through this, the form and content of the self-positionings through which these interests are expressed. Despite the aura of objectivity they like to assume, neither the 'sociology of the intellectuals', which is traditionally the business of 'right-wing intellectuals', nor the critique of 'right-wing thought', the traditional speciality of 'left-wing intellectuals', is anything more than a series of symbolic aggressions which take on additional force when they dress themselves up in the impeccable neutrality of science. They tacitly agree in leaving hidden what is essential, namely the structure of objective positions which is the source, inter alia, of the view which the occupants of each position can have of the occupants of the other positions and which determines the specific form and force of each group's propensity to present and receive a group's partial truth as if it were a full account of the objective relations between the groups.

The analyses presented in this book are based on a survey by questionnaire, carried out in 1963 and 1967–68, on a sample of 1,217 people. (Appendix 1 gives full information concerning the composition of the sample, the questionnaire, and the main procedures used to analyze it. Appendix 3 contains the statistical data drawn from the survey, as well as data from other sources.) The survey sought to determine how the cultivated disposition and cultural competence that are revealed in the nature of the cultural goods consumed, and in the way they are consumed, vary according to the category of agents and the area to which they applied, from the most legitimate areas such as painting or music to the most 'personal' ones such as clothing, furniture or cookery, and, within the legitimate domains, according to the markets—'academic' and 'non-academic'—in which they may be placed. Two basic facts were thus established: on the one hand, the very close relationship linking cultural practices (or the corresponding opinions) to educational capital (measured by qualifications) and, secondarily, to social origin (measured by father's occupation); and, on the other hand, the fact that, at equivalent levels of educational capital, the weight of social origin in the practice- and preference-explaining system increases as one moves away from the most legitimate areas of culture.

The more the competences measured are recognized by the school system, and the more 'academic' the techniques used to measure them, the stronger is the relation between performance and educational qualification. The latter, as a more or less adequate indicator of the number of years of scholastic inculcation, guarantees cultural capital more or less completely, depending on whether it is inherited from the family or acquired at school, and so it is an unequally adequate indicator of this capital. The strongest correlation between performance and educational capital qua cultural capital recognized and guaranteed by the educational system (which is very unequally responsible for its acquisition) is observed when, with the question on the composers of a series of musical works, the survey takes the form of a very 'scholastic' exercise on knowledge very close to that taught by the educational system and strongly recognized in the academic market.

The interviewer read out a list of sixteen musical works and asked the respondent to name the composer of each. Sixty-seven percent of those with only a CEP or a CAP could not identify more than two composers (out of sixteen works), compared to 45 percent of those with a BEPC, 19 percent of those with the *baccalauréat*, 17 percent of those who had gone to a technical college (*petite école*) or started higher education and only 7 percent of those having a qualification equal or superior to a *licence*.[2] Whereas none of the manual or clerical workers questioned was capable of naming twelve or more of the composers of the sixteen works, 52 percent of the 'artistic producers' and the teachers (and 78 percent of the teachers in higher education) achieved this score.

The rate of non-response to the question on favourite painters or pieces of music is also closely correlated with level of education, with a strong opposition between the dominant class on the one hand and the working classes, craftsmen and small tradesmen on the other. (However, since in this case whether or not people answered the question doubtless depended as much on their dispositions as on their pure competence, the cultural pretensions of the new *petite bourgeoisie*—junior commercial executives, the medical and social services, secretaries, and the various cultural intermediaries (see Chapter 6)—found an outlet here.) Similarly, listening to the most 'highbrow' radio stations, France-Musique and France-Culture, and to musical or cultural broadcasts, owning a record-player, listening to records (without specifying the type, which minimizes the differences), visiting art-galleries, and knowledge of painting—features which are strongly correlated with one another—obey the same logic and, being strongly linked to educational capital, set the various classes and class fractions in a clear hierarchy (with a reverse distribution for listening to variety programmes). In the case of activities like the visual arts, or playing a musical instrument, which presupposes a cultural capital generally acquired outside the educational system and (relatively) independent of the level of academic certification, the correlation with social class, which is again strong, is established through social trajectory (which explains the special position of the new petite bourgeoisie).

The closer one moves towards the most legitimate areas, such as music or painting, and, within these areas, which can be set in a hierarchy according to their modal degree of legitimacy, towards certain genres or certain works, the more the differences in educational capital are associated with major differences (produced in accordance with the same principles) between genres, such as opera and operetta, or quartets and symphonies, between periods, such as contemporary and classical, between composers and between works. Thus, among works of music, the *Well-Tempered Clavier* and the *Concerto for the Left Hand* (which, as will become apparent, are distinguished by the modes of acquisition and consumption which they presuppose), are opposed to the Strauss waltzes and the *Sabre Dance,* pieces which are devalued either by belonging to a lower genre ('light music') or by their popularization (since the dialectic of distinction and pretension designates as devalued 'middle-brow' art those legitimate works which become 'popularized'),[3] just as, in the world of song, Georges Brassens and Léo Ferré are opposed to Georges Guétary and Petula Clark, these differences corresponding in each case to differences in educational capital (see table 1).

In fact, the weight of the secondary factors—composition of capital, vol-

Table 1 Class preferences for singers and music.[a]

Classes	Educational qualification	N	Singers				Music			
			Guétary	P. Clark	Brassens	Ferré	Blue Danube	Sabre Dance	Well-Tempered Clavier	Concerto for Left Hand
Working	None, CEP, CAP	143	33.0	31.0	38.0	20.0	65.0	28.0	1.0	0
	BEPC and above	18	17.0	17.0	61.0	22.0	62.5	12.5	0	0
Middle	None, CEP, CAP	243	23.0	29.0	41.0	21.0	64.0	26.0	1.5	1.5
	BEPC and above	335	12.5	19.0	47.5	39.0	27.0	16.0	8.0	4.0
	BEPC, bac	289	12.0	21.0	46.5	39.0	31.0	17.5	5.0	4.0
	higher education	46	17.0	9.0	54.0	39.0	3.0	5.0	21.0	4.0
Upper	None, CEP, CAP	25	16.0	44.0	36.0	12.0	17.0	21.0	8.0	8.0
	BEPC and above	432	5.0	17.0	74.0	35.0	16.0	8.0	15.0	13.0
	BEPC, bac	107	8.5	24.0	65.0	29.0	14.0	11.0	3.0	6.0
	higher education	325	4.0	14.5	77.0	39.0	16.5	7.0	19.0	15.0
	technical college	80	5.0	20.0	73.5	32.0	19.5	5.5	10.0	18.0
	licence	174	4.5	17.0	73.0	34.5	17.0	9.5	29.5	12.0
	agrég., grande école	71	0	3.0	90.0	49.5	11.5	3.0	29.5	12.0

a. The table (e.g., first row) is read as follows: out of every 100 working-class respondents with either no qualification, a CEP or a CAP, 33 choose Guétary and 31 Petula Clark among their three favourite singers (from a list of twelve); 65 choose the *Blue Danube* and 28 the *Sabre Dance* among their three favourite works of music (from a list of sixteen).

ume of inherited cultural capital (or social trajectory), age, place of residence—varies with the works. Thus, as one moves towards the works that are least legitimate (at the moment in question), factors such as age become increasingly important; in the case of *Rhapsody in Blue* or the *Hungarian Rhapsody,* there is a closer correlation with age than with education, father's occupational category, sex or place of residence.

Thus, of all the objects offered for consumers' choice, there are none more classifying than legitimate works of art, which, while distinctive in general, enable the production of distinctions ad infinitum by playing on divisions and sub-divisions into genres, periods, styles, authors etc. Within the universe of particular tastes which can be recreated by successive divisions, it is thus possible, still keeping to the major oppositions, to distinguish three zones of taste which roughly correspond to educational levels and social classes: (1) *Legitimate taste,* i.e., the taste for legitimate works, here represented by the *Well-Tempered Clavier* (see figure 1, histogram 1), the *Art of Fugue* or the *Concerto for the Left Hand,* or, in painting, Breughel or Goya, which the most self-assured aesthetes can combine with the most legitimate of the arts that are still in the process of legitimation—cinema, jazz or even song (here, for example, Léo Ferré, Jacques Douai)—increases with educational level and is highest in those fractions of the dominant class that are richest in educational capital. (2) *'Middle-brow' taste,* which brings together the minor works of the major arts, in this case *Rhapsody in Blue* (histogram 2), the *Hungarian Rhapsody,* or in painting, Utrillo, Buffet or even Renoir, and the major works of the minor arts, such as Jacques Brel and Gilbert Bécaud in the art of song, is more common in the middle classes (*classes moyennes*) than in the working classes (*classes populaires*) or in the 'intellectual' fractions of the dominant class. (3) Finally, *'popular' taste,* represented here by the choice of works of so-called 'light' music or classical music devalued by popularization, such as the *Blue Danube* (histogram 3), *La Traviata* or *L'Arlésienne,* and especially songs totally devoid of artistic ambition or pretension such as those of Luis Mariano, Guétary or Petula Clark, is most frequent among the working classes and varies in inverse ratio to educational capital (which explains why it is slightly more common among industrial and commercial employers or even senior executives than among primary teachers and cultural intermediaries).

The three profiles presented in figure 1 are perfectly typical of those that are found when one draws a graph of the distribution of a whole set of choices characteristic of different class fractions (arranged in a hierarchy, within each class, according to educational capital). The first one (the *Well-Tempered Clavier*) reappears in the case of all the authors or works named above, and also for such choices in the survey questionnaire (see appendix 1) as 'reading philosophical essays' and 'visiting museums' etc.; the second

Figure 1   Distribution of preferences for three musical works by class fraction.

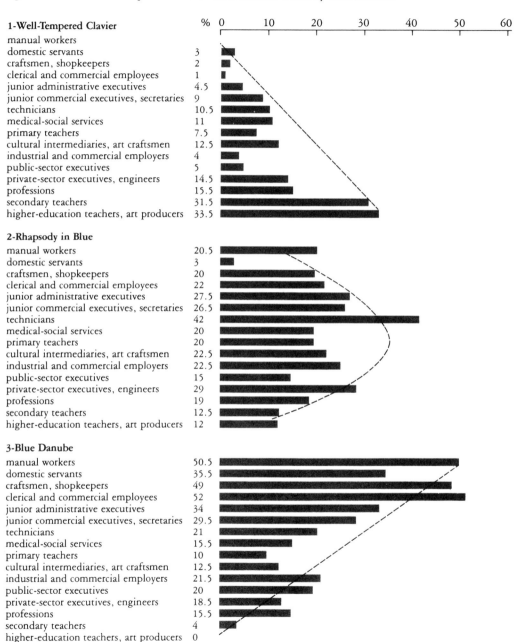

1-Well-Tempered Clavier	%
manual workers	
domestic servants	3
craftsmen, shopkeepers	2
clerical and commercial employees	1
junior administrative executives	4.5
junior commercial executives, secretaries	9
technicians	10.5
medical-social services	11
primary teachers	7.5
cultural intermediaries, art craftsmen	12.5
industrial and commercial employers	4
public-sector executives	5
private-sector executives, engineers	14.5
professions	15.5
secondary teachers	31.5
higher-education teachers, art producers	33.5

2-Rhapsody in Blue	%
manual workers	20.5
domestic servants	3
craftsmen, shopkeepers	20
clerical and commercial employees	22
junior administrative executives	27.5
junior commercial executives, secretaries	26.5
technicians	42
medical-social services	20
primary teachers	20
cultural intermediaries, art craftsmen	22.5
industrial and commercial employers	22.5
public-sector executives	15
private-sector executives, engineers	29
professions	19
secondary teachers	12.5
higher-education teachers, art producers	12

3-Blue Danube	%
manual workers	50.5
domestic servants	35.5
craftsmen, shopkeepers	49
clerical and commercial employees	52
junior administrative executives	34
junior commercial executives, secretaries	29.5
technicians	21
medical-social services	15.5
primary teachers	10
cultural intermediaries, art craftsmen	12.5
industrial and commercial employers	21.5
public-sector executives	20
private-sector executives, engineers	18.5
professions	15.5
secondary teachers	4
higher-education teachers, art producers	0

(*Rhapsody in Blue*) characterizes, in addition to all the works and authors mentioned (plus the *Twilight of the Gods*), 'photography', 'comfortable, cosy home' etc.; and the third (*Blue Danube*) is equally valid for 'love stories' and 'clean, tidy home' etc.

The Titles of Cultural Nobility

A relationship as close as that between academic capital (measured by duration of schooling) and knowledge or practices in areas as remote from academic education as music or painting, not to mention jazz or the cinema—like the correlation between museum visits and level of education—raises in the highest degree the question of the significance of the relationship, in other words, the question of the real identity of the two linked terms which are defined in their very relationship. One has explained nothing and understood nothing by establishing the existence of a correlation between an 'independent' variable and a 'dependent' variable. Until one has determined what is designated in the particular case, i.e., in each particular relationship, by each term in the relationship (for example, level of education and knowledge of composers), the statistical relationship, however precisely it can be determined numerically, remains a pure datum, devoid of meaning. And the 'intuitive' half-understanding with which sociologists are generally satisfied in such cases, while they concentrate on refining the measurement of the 'intensity' of the relationship, together with the *illusion of the constancy* of the variables or factors resulting from the *nominal identity* of the 'indicators' (whatever they may indicate) or of the terms which designate them, tends to rule out any questioning of the terms of the relationship as to the meaning they take on in that particular relationship and indeed receive from it.

Both terms of the relationship have to be queried in each case: the independent variable—occupation, sex, age, father's occupation, places of residence etc., which may express very different effects—and the dependent variable, which may manifest dispositions that themselves vary considerably depending on the classes divided up by the independent variables. Thus, for an adequate interpretation of the differences found between the classes or within the same class as regards their relation to the various legitimate arts, painting, music, theatre, literature etc., one would have to analyse fully the social uses, legitimate or illegitimate, to which each of the arts, genres, works or institutions considered lends itself. For example, nothing more clearly affirms one's 'class', nothing more infallibly classifies, than tastes in music. This is of course because, by virtue of the rarity of the conditions for acquiring the corresponding dispositions, there is no more 'classifactory' practice than concert-going or playing a 'noble' instrument (activities which, other things being equal, are less widespread than theatre-going, museum-going or even visits to modern-art galleries). But it is also because the flaunting of 'musical culture' is not a cultural display like others: as regards its social definition, 'musical culture' is something other than a quantity of knowledge and experiences combined with the capacity to talk about them. Music is the most 'spiritual' of the arts of the spirit and a love of music is a guarantee of 'spirituality'. One only has to think of the extraordinary value nowadays conferred on the lexis of 'listening' by the secularized (e.g., psychoanalytical) versions of religious language. As the countless variations on the soul of music and the music of the soul bear witness, music is bound up with 'interiority' ('inner music') of the 'deepest' sort and *all* concerts are sacred. For a bourgeois world which conceives its relation to the populace in terms of the relationship of the soul to the body, 'insensitivity to music' doubtless represents a particularly unavowable form of materialist coarseness. But this is not all. Music is the 'pure' art par excellence. It says nothing and has *nothing to say*. Never really having an expressive function, it is opposed to drama, which even in its most refined forms still bears a social message and can only be 'put over' on the basis of an immediate and profound affinity with the values and expectations of its audience. The theatre divides its public and divides itself. The Parisian opposition between right-bank and left-bank theatre, bourgeois theatre and avant-garde theatre, is inextricably aesthetic and political. Nothing comparable occurs in music (with some rare, recent exceptions). Music represents the most radical and most absolute form of the negation of the world, and especially the social world, which the bourgeois ethos tends to demand of all forms of art.

For an adequate interpretation of what would be implied in a table correlating occupation, age or sex with a preference for the *Well-Tempered Clavier* or the *Concerto for the Left Hand,* one has to break both with the blind use of indicators and with spurious, essentialist analyses which are merely the universalizing of a particular experience, in order to make completely explicit the multiple, contradictory meanings which these works take on at a given moment for the totality of social agents and in particular for the categories of individuals whom they distinguish or who differ with respect to them (in this particular case, the 'inheritors' and the 'newcomers'). One would have to take account, on the one hand, of the socially pertinent properties attached to each of them, that is, the social image of the works ('baroque'/'modern', harmony/dissonance, rigour/lyricism etc.), the composers and perhaps especially the corresponding instruments (the sharp, rough timbre of plucked strings/the warm, bourgeois timbre of hammered strings); and, on the other hand, the distributional properties acquired by these works in their relationship (perceived with varying clarity depending on the case) with the different classes or class fractions (*'ça fait . . .'*) and with the corresponding conditions of reception (belated knowledge through records/early knowledge through playing the piano, the bourgeois instrument par excellence).

The opposition found at the level of distributional properties is generally homologous to that found at the level of stylistic characteristics. This is because homology between the positions of the producers (or the works) in the field of production and the positions of the consumers in social space (i.e., in the overall class structure or in the structure of the dominant class) seems to be the most frequent case. Roughly speaking, the amateur of Mallarmé is likely to be to the amateur of Zola as Mallarmé was to Zola. Differences between works are predisposed to express differences between authors, partly because, in both style and content, they bear the mark of their authors' socially constituted dispositions (that is, their social origins, retranslated as a function of the positions in the field of production which these dispositions played a large part in determining); and partly because they remain marked by the social significance which they received from their opposition, and that of their authors, in the field of production (e.g., left/right, clear/obscure etc.) and which is perpetuated by the university tradition.

It is also clear what would be required for an adequate interpretation of the bourgeois predilection for the 'Impressionists', whose simultaneously lyrical and naturalistic adherence to natural or human nature contrasts both with realist or critical representation of the social world (doubtless one dimension of the opposition between Renoir and Goya, not to mention Courbet or Daumier) and with all forms of abstraction. Again, to understand the class distribution of the various sports, one would have to take account of the representation which, in terms of their specific schemes of perception and appreciation, the different classes have of the costs (economic, cultural and 'physical') and benefits attached to the different sports—immediate or deferred 'physical' benefits (health, beauty, strength, whether visible, through 'body-building' or invisible through 'keep-fit' exercises), economic and social benefits (upward mobility etc.), immediate or deferred symbolic benefits linked to the distributional or positional value of each of the sports considered (i.e., all that each of them receives from its greater or lesser rarity, and its more or less clear association with a class, with boxing, football, rugby or body-building evoking the working classes, tennis and skiing the bourgeoisie and golf the upper bourgeoisie), gains in distinction accruing from the effects on the body itself (e.g., slimness, sun-tan, muscles obviously or discreetly visible etc.) or from the access to highly selective groups which some of these sports give (golf, polo etc.).

Thus the only way of completely escaping from the intuitionism which inevitably accompanies positivistic faith in the nominal identity of the indicators would be to carry out a—strictly interminable—analysis of the social value of each of the properties or practices considered—a Louis XV commode or a Brahms symphony, reading *Historia* or *Le Figaro*, playing rugby or the accordion and so on. The statistics of the class distribution of newspaper reading would perhaps be interpreted less blindly if sociologists bore in mind Proust's analysis of 'that abominable, voluptuous act called "reading the paper"', whereby all the misfortunes and cataclysms suffered by the universe in the last twenty-four hours—battles which have cost the lives of fifty thousand men, murders, strikes, bankruptcies, fires, poisonings, suicides, divorces, the cruel emotions of statesman and actor, transmuted into a morning feast for our personal entertainment, make an excellent and particularly bracing accompaniment to a few mouthfuls of *café au lait*.'[4] This description of the aesthete's variant invites an analysis of the class variations and the invariants of the mediated, relatively abstract experience of the social world supplied by newspaper reading, for example, as a function of variations in social and spatial distance (with, at one extreme, the local items in the regional dailies—marriages, deaths, accidents—and, at the other extreme, international news, or, on another scale, the royal engagements and weddings in the glossy magazines) or in political commitment (from the detachment depicted in Proust's text to the activist's outrage or enthusiasm).

In fact, the absence of this kind of preliminary analysis of the social significance of the indicators can make the most rigorous-seeming surveys quite unsuitable for a sociological reading. Because they forget that the apparent constancy of the products conceals the diversity of the social uses they are put to, many surveys on consumption impose on them taxonomies which have sprung straight from the statisticians' social unconscious, associating things that ought to be separated (e.g., white beans and green beans) and separating things that could be associated (e.g., white beans and bananas—the latter are to fruit as the former are to vegetables). What is there to be said about the collection of products brought together by the apparently neutral category 'cereals'—bread, rusks, rice, pasta, flour—and especially the class variations in the consumption of these products, when one knows that 'rice' alone includes 'rice pudding' and *riz au gras,* or rice cooked in broth (which tend to be 'working-class') and 'curried rice' (more 'bourgeois' or, more precisely, 'intellectual'), not to mention 'brown rice' (which suggests a whole life-style)? Though, of course, no 'natural' or manufactured product is equally adaptable to all possible social uses, there are very few that are perfectly 'univocal' and it is rarely possible to deduce the social use from the thing itself. Except for products specially designed for a particular use (like 'slimming bread') or closely tied to a class, by tradition (like tea—in France) or price (like caviar), most products only derive their social value from the social use that is made of them. As a consequence, in these areas the only way to find the class variations is to introduce them from the start, by replacing words or things whose apparently univocal meaning creates no difficulty for the abstract classifications of the academic unconscious, with the social uses in which they become fully determined. Hence it is necessary to attend, for example, to *ways* of photographing and *ways* of cooking—in the casserole or the pressure-cooker, i.e., without counting time and money, or quickly and cheaply—or to the products of these operations—family snaps or photos of folk dancing, *boeuf bourguignon* or curried rice.

Appearances, need I repeat, always support appearances; and sociological science, which cannot find the differences between the social classes unless it introduces them from the start, is bound to appear prejudiced to those who dissolve the differences, in all good faith and with impeccable method, simply by surrendering to positivistic laisser-faire.

But the substantialist mode of thinking is perhaps most unrestrained when it comes to the search for 'explanatory factors'. Slipping from the substantive to the substance (to paraphrase Wittgenstein), from the constancy of the substantive to the constancy of the substance, it treats the properties attached to agents—occupation, age, sex, qualifications—as *forces* independent of the relationship within which they 'act'. This eliminates the question of what is determinant in the determinant variable and what is determined in the determined variable, in other words, the question of what, among the properties chosen, consciously or unconsciously, through the indicators under consideration, constitutes the *pertinent property* that is really capable of determining the relationship within which it is determined. Purely statistical calculation of the variations in the intensity of the relationship between a particular indicator and any given practice does not remove the need for the specifically sociological calculation of the *effects* which are expressed in the statistical relationship and which statistical analysis, when oriented towards the search for its own intelligibility, can help to discover. One has to take the relationship itself as the object of study and scrutinize its sociological significance (*signification*) rather than its statistical 'significantness' (*significativité*); only in this way is it possible to replace the relationship between a supposedly constant variable and different practices by a series of different *effects*—sociologically intelligible constant relationships which are simultaneously revealed and concealed in the statistical relationships between a given indicator and different practices. The truly scientific endeavour has to break with the spurious self-evidences of immediate understanding (to which the pseudo-refinements of statistical analysis—e.g., path analysis—bring unexpected reinforcement). In place of the phenomenal relationship between this or that 'dependent variable' and variables such as level of education or social origin, which are no more than *common-sense notions* and whose apparent 'explanatory power' stems from the mental habits of *common-sense knowledge* of the social world, it aims to establish 'an exact relation of well-defined concepts',[5] the rational principle of the effects which the statistical relationship records *despite everything*—for example, the relationship between the titles of nobility (or marks of infamy) awarded by the educational system and the practices they imply, or between the disposition required by works of legitimate art and the disposition which, deliberately and consciously or not, is taught in schools.

THE ENTITLEMENT EFFECT Knowing the relationship which exists between cultural capital inherited from the family and academic capital, by virtue of the logic of the transmission of cultural capital and the functioning of the educational system, one cannot impute the strong correlation, observed between competence in music or painting (and the practice it presupposes and makes possible) and academic capital, solely to the operation of the educational system (still less to the specifically artistic education it is supposed to give, which is clearly almost non-existent). Academic capital is in fact the guaranteed product of the combined effects of cultural transmission by the family and cultural transmission by the school (the efficiency of which depends on the amount of cultural capital directly inherited from the family). Through its value-inculcating and value-imposing operations, the school also helps (to a greater or lesser extent, depending on the initial disposition, i.e., class of origin) to form a general, transposable disposition towards legitimate culture, which is first acquired with respect to scholastically recognized knowledge and practices but tends to be applied beyond the bounds of the curriculum, taking the form of a 'disinterested' propensity to accumulate experience and knowledge which may not be directly profitable in the academic market.

The educational system defines non-curricular general culture (*la culture 'libre'*), negatively at least, by delimiting, within the dominant culture, the area of what it puts into its syllabuses and controls by its examinations. It has been shown that the most 'scholastic' cultural objects are those taught and required at the lowest levels of schooling (the extreme form of the 'scholastic' being the 'elementary'), and that the educational system sets an increasingly high value on 'general' culture and increasingly refuses 'scholastic' measurements of culture (such as direct, closed questions on authors, dates and events) as one moves towards the highest levels of the system.

In fact, the generalizing tendency of the cultivated disposition is only a necessary, not a sufficient, condition for the enterprise of cultural appropriation, which is inscribed, as an objective demand, in membership of the bourgeoisie and in the qualifications giving access to its rights and duties. This is why we must first stop to consider what is perhaps the best-hidden effect of the educational system, the one it produces by imposing 'titles',[6] a particular case of the attribution by status, whether positive (ennobling) or negative (stigmatizing), which every group produces by assigning individuals to hierarchically ordered classes. Whereas the holders of educationally uncertified cultural capital can always be required to prove themselves, because they *are* only what they *do*, merely a by-product of their own cultural production, the holders of titles of cultural nobility—like the titular members of an aristocracy, whose 'being', defined by their fidelity to a lineage, an estate, a race, a past, a fatherland or a tradition, is irreducible to any 'doing', to any know-how or function—only have to be what they are, because all their practices derive their value from their authors, being the affirmation and perpetuation of the essence by virtue of which they are performed. Defined by the titles which predispose and legitimate them in being what they are, which make what they do the manifestation of an essence earlier and greater than its manifestations, as in the Platonic dream of a division of functions based on a hierarchy of beings, they are separated by a difference in kind from the commoners of culture, who are consigned to the doubly devalued status of autodidact and 'stand-in'.[8]

Aristocracies are essentialist. Regarding existence as an emanation of essence, they set no intrinsic value on the deeds and misdeeds enrolled in the records and registries of bureaucratic memory. They prize them only insofar as they clearly manifest, in the nuances of their manner, that their one inspiration is the perpetuating and celebrating of the essence by virtue of which they are accomplished. The same essentialism requires them to impose on themselves what their essence imposes on them—noblesse oblige—to ask of themselves what no one else could ask, to 'live up' to their own essence.

This effect is one of the mechanisms which, in conditions of crisis, cause the most privileged individuals, who remain most attached to the former state of affairs, to be the slowest to understand the need to change strategy and so to fall victim to their own privilege (for example, ruined nobles who refuse to change their ways, or the heirs of great peasant families who remain celibate rather than marry beneath them). It could be shown, in the same way, that the ethic of noblesse oblige, still found in some fractions of the peasantry and traditional craftsmen, contributes significantly to the self-exploitation characteristic of these classes.

This gives us an insight into the effect of academic markers and classifications. However, for a full understanding we have to consider another property of all aristocracies. The essence in which they see themselves refuses to be contained in any definition. Escaping petty rules and regulations, it is, by nature, freedom. Thus, for the academic aristocracy it is one and the same thing to identify with an essence of the 'cultivated man' and to accept the demands implicitly inscribed in it, which increase with the prestige of the title.

So there is nothing paradoxical in the fact that in its ends and means the educational system defines the enterprise of *legitimate 'autodidacticism'* which the acquisition of 'general culture' presupposes, an enterprise that is ever more strongly demanded as one rises in the educational hierarchy (between sections, disciplines, and specialities etc., or between levels). The essentially contradictory phrase 'legitimate autodidacticism' is intended to indicate the difference in kind between the highly valued 'extra-curricular' culture of the holder of academic qualifications and the illegitimate extra-curricular culture of the autodidact. The reader of the popular-science monthly *Science et Vie* who talks about the genetic code or the incest taboo exposes himself to ridicule as soon as he ventures outside the circle of his peers, whereas Claude Lévi-Strauss or Jacques Monod can only derive additional prestige from their excursions into the field of music or philosophy. Illegitimate extra-curricular culture, whether it be the knowledge accumulated by the self-taught or the 'experience' acquired in and through practice, outside the control of the institution specifically mandated to inculcate it and officially sanction its acquisition, like the art of cooking or herbal medicine, craftsmen's skills or the stand-in's irreplaceable knowledge, is only valorized to the strict extent of its technical efficiency, without any social added-value, and is exposed to legal sanctions (like the illegal practice of medicine) whenever it emerges from the domestic universe to compete with authorized competences.

Thus, it is written into the tacit definition of the academic qualification *formally* guaranteeing a specific competence (like an engineering diploma) that it *really* guarantees possession of a 'general culture' whose breadth is proportionate to the prestige of the qualification;[9] and, conversely, that no real guarantee may be sought of what it guarantees formally and really or, to put it another way, of the extent to which it guarantees what it guarantees. This effect of symbolic imposition is most intense in the case of the diplomas consecrating the cultural élite. The qualifications awarded by the French *grandes écoles* guarantee, without any other guarantee, a competence extending far beyond what they are supposed to guarantee. This is by virtue of a clause which, though tacit, is firstly binding on the qualification-holders themselves, who are called upon really to procure the attributes assigned to them by their status.[10]

This process occurs at all stages of schooling, through the manipulation of aspirations and demands—in other words, of self-image and self-esteem—which the educational system carries out by channelling pupils towards prestigious or devalued positions implying or excluding legitimate practice. The effect of 'allocation', i.e., assignment to a section, a discipline (philosophy or geography, mathematics or geology, to take the extremes) or an institution (a *grande école* that is more or less *grande*, or a faculty), mainly operates through the social image of the position in question and the prospects objectively inscribed in it, among the foremost of which are a certain type of cultural accumulation and a certain image of cultural accomplishment.[11] The official differences produced by academic classifications tend to produce (or reinforce) real differences by inducing in the classified individuals a collectively recognized and supported belief in the differences, thus producing behaviours that are intended to bring real being into line with official being. Activities as alien to the explicit demands of the institution as keeping a diary, wearing heavy make-up, theatre-going or going dancing, writing poems or playing rugby can thus find themselves inscribed in the position allotted within the institution as a tacit demand constantly underlined by various mediations. Among the most important of these are teachers' conscious or unconscious expectations and peer-group pressure, whose ethical orientation is itself defined by the class values brought into and reinforced by the institution. This allocation effect and the status assignment it entails doubtless play a major role in the fact that the educational institution succeeds in imposing cultural practices that it does not teach and does not even explicitly demand, but which belong to the attributes attached by status to the position it assigns, the qualifications it awards and the social positions to which the latter give access.

This logic doubtless helps to explain how the legitimate disposition that is acquired by frequent contact with a particular class of works, namely, the literary and philosophical works recognized by the academic canon, comes to be extended to other, less legitimate works, such as avant-garde literature, or to areas enjoying less academic recognition, such as the cinema. The generalizing tendency is inscribed in the very principle of the disposition to *recognize* legitimate works, a propensity and capacity to recognize their legitimacy and perceive them as worthy of admiration in themselves, which is inseparable from the capacity to recognize in them something already known, i.e., the stylistic traits appropriate to characterize them in their singularity ('It's a Rembrandt', or even 'It's the *Helmeted Man*') or as members of a class of works ('It's Impressionist'). This explains why the propensity and capacity to accumulate 'gratuitous' knowledge, such as the names of film directors, are more closely and exclusively linked to educational capital than is mere cinemagoing, which is more dependent on income, place of residence and age.

Cinema-going, measured by the number of films seen among the twenty films mentioned in the survey, is lower among the less-educated than among the more highly educated, but also lower among provincials (in Lille) than among Parisians, among low-income than among high-income groups, and among old than among young people. And the same relationships are found in the surveys by the Centre d'études des supports de publicité (CESP): the proportion who say they have been to the cinema at least once in the previous week (a more reliable indicator of behaviour than a question on cinema-going in the course of the year, for which the tendency to overstate is particularly strong) is rather greater among men than women (7.8 percent compared to 5.3 percent), greater in the Paris area (10.9 percent) than in towns of over 100,000 people (7.7 percent) or in rural areas (3.6 percent), greater among senior executives and members of the professions (11.1 percent) than among junior executives (9.5 percent) or clerical and commercial employees (9.7 percent), skilled manual workers and foremen (7.3 percent), semi-skilled workers (6.3 percent), small employers (5.2 percent) and farmers and farm workers (2.6 percent). But the greatest contrasts are between the youngest (22.4 percent of the 21–24 year olds had been to the cinema at least once in the previous week) and the oldest (only 3.2 percent of the 35–49 year olds, 1.7 percent of the 50–64 year olds and 1.1 percent of the over-65s), and between the most and least highly educated (18.2 percent of those who had been through higher education, 9.5 percent of those who had had secondary education, and 2.2 percent of those who had had only primary education or none at all had been to the cinema in the previous week) (C.S. XIIIa).[12]

Knowledge of directors is much more closely linked to cultural capital than is mere cinema-going. Only 5 percent of the respondents who had an elementary school diploma could name at least four directors (from a list of twenty films) compared to 10 percent of holders of the BEPC or the *baccalauréat* and 22 percent of those who had had higher education, whereas the proportion in each category who had seen at least four of the twenty films was 22 percent, 33 percent and 40 percent respectively. Thus, although film-viewing also varies with educational capital (less so, however, than visits to museums and concerts), it seems that differences in consumption are not sufficient to explain the differences in knowledge of directors between holders of different qualifications. This conclusion would probably also hold good for jazz, strip cartoons, detective stories or science fiction, now that these genres have begun to achieve cultural consecration.[13]

Further proof is that, while increasing slightly with level of education (from 13 percent for the least educated to 18 percent for those with secondary education and 23 percent for the most qualified), knowledge of actors varies mainly—and considerably—with the number of films seen. This awareness, like knowledge of the slightest events in the lives of TV personalities, presupposes a disposition closer to that required for the acquisition of ordinary knowledge about everyday things and people than to the legitimate disposition. And indeed, these least-educated regular cinema-goers knew as many actors' names as the most highly educated. Among those who had seen at least four of the films mentioned, 45 percent of those who had had only a primary education were able to name four actors, as against 35 percent of those who had had a secondary education and 47 percent of those who had had some higher education. Interest in actors is greatest among office workers: on average they named 2.8 actors and one director, whereas the craftsmen and small shopkeepers, skilled workers and foremen named, on average, only 0.8 actors and 0.3 directors. (The secretaries and junior commercial executives, who also knew a large number of actors—average 2.4—were more interested in directors—average 1.4—and those in the social and medical services even named more directors—1.7—than actors—1.4). The reading of sensational weeklies (e.g., *Ici Paris*) which give information about the lives of stars is a product of a disposition similar to interest in actors; it is more frequent among women than men (10.8 percent had read *Ici Paris* in the last week, compared to 9.3 percent of the men), among skilled workers and foremen (14.5 percent), semi-skilled workers (13.6 percent), or office workers (10.3 percent) than among junior executives (8.6 percent) and especially among senior executives and members of the professions (3.8 percent) (C.S. XXVIII).

By contrast, although at equivalent levels of education, knowledge of directors increases with the number of films seen, in this area assiduous cinema-going does not compensate for absence of educational capital: 45.5 percent of the CEP-holders who had seen at least four of the films mentioned could not name a single director, compared to 27.5 percent of those with a BEPC or the *baccalauréat* and 13 percent of those with a higher education diploma.

Such competence is not necessarily acquired by means of the 'scholastic' labours in which some 'cinephiles' or 'jazz-freaks' indulge (e.g., transcribing film credits onto catalogue cards).[14] Most often it results from the unintentional learning made possible by a disposition acquired through domestic or scholastic inculcation of legitimate culture. This transposable disposition, armed with a set of perceptual and evaluative schemes that are available for general application, inclines its owner towards other cultural experiences and enables him to perceive, classify and memorize them differently. Where some only see 'a Western starring Burt Lancaster', others 'discover an early John Sturges' or 'the latest Sam Peckinpah'. In identifying what is worthy of being seen and the right way to see it, they are aided by their whole social group (which guides and reminds them with its 'Have you seen . . . ?' and 'You must see . . .') and by the whole corporation of critics mandated by the group to produce legitimate classifications and the discourse necessarily accompanying any artistic enjoyment worthy of the name.

It is possible to explain in such terms why cultural practices which schools do not teach and never explicitly demand vary in such close relation to educational qualifications (it being understood, of course, that we are provisionally suspending the distinction between the school's role in the correlation observed and that of the other socializing agencies, in particular the family). But the fact that educational qualifications function as a condition of entry to the universe of legitimate culture cannot be fully explained without taking into account another, still more hidden effect which the educational system, again reinforcing the work of the bourgeois family, exerts through the very conditions within which it inculcates. Through the educational qualification certain conditions of existence are designated—those which constitute the precondition for obtaining the qualification and also the aesthetic disposition, the most rigorously demanded of all the terms of entry which the world of legitimate culture (always tacitly) imposes. Anticipating what will be demonstrated later, one can posit, in broad terms, that it is because they are linked either to a bourgeois origin or to the quasi-bourgeois mode of existence presupposed by prolonged schooling, or (most often) to both of these combined, that educational qualifications come to be seen as a guarantee of the capacity to adopt the aesthetic disposition.

THE AESTHETIC DISPOSITION   Any legitimate work tends in fact to impose the norms of its own perception and tacitly defines as the only legitimate mode of perception the one which brings into play a certain disposition and a certain competence. Recognizing this fact does not mean constituting a particular mode of perception as an essence, thereby falling into the illusion which is the basis of recognition of artistic legitimacy. It does mean taking note of the fact that all agents, whether they like it or not, whether or not they have the means of conforming to them, find themselves objectively measured by those norms. At the same time it becomes possible to establish whether these dispositions and competences are gifts of nature, as the charismatic ideology of the relation to the work of art would have it, or products of learning, and to bring to light the hidden conditions of the miracle of the unequal class distribution of the capacity for inspired encounters with works of art and high culture in general.

Every essentialist analysis of the aesthetic disposition, the only socially accepted 'right' way of approaching the objects socially designated as works of art, that is, as both demanding and deserving to be approached with a specifically aesthetic intention capable of recognizing and constituting them as works of art, is bound to fail. Refusing to take account of the collective and individual genesis of this product of history which must be endlessly 're-produced' by education, it is unable to reconstruct its sole raison d'être, that is, the historical reason which underlies the arbitrary necessity of the institution. If the work of art is indeed, as Panofsky says, that which 'demands to be experienced aesthetically', and if any object, natural or artificial, can be perceived aesthetically, how can one escape the conclusion that it is the aesthetic intention which 'makes the work of art', or, to transpose a formula of Saussure's, that it is the aesthetic point of view that creates the aesthetic object? To get out of this vicious circle, Panofsky has to endow the work of art with an 'intention', in the Scholastic sense. A purely 'practical' perception contradicts this objective intention, just as an aesthetic perception would in a sense be a practical negation of the objective intention of a signal, a red light for example, which requires a 'practical' response: braking. Thus, within the class of worked-upon objects, themselves defined in opposition to natural objects, the class of art objects would be defined by the fact that it demands to be perceived aesthetically, i.e., in terms of form rather than function. But how can such a definition be made operational? Panofsky himself observes that it is virtually impossible to determine scientifically at what moment a worked-upon object becomes an art object, that is, at what moment form takes over from function: 'If I write to a friend to invite him to dinner, my letter is primarily a communication. But the more I shift the emphasis to the form of my script, the more nearly does it become a work of literature or poetry.'[15]

Does this mean that the demarcation line between the world of technical objects and the world of aesthetic objects depends on the 'intention' of the producer of those objects? In fact, this 'intention' is itself the product of the social norms and conventions which combine to define the always uncertain and historically changing frontier between simple technical objects and objets d'art: 'Classical tastes', Panofsky observes, 'demanded that private letters, legal speeches and the shields of heroes should be "artistic" . . . while modern taste demands that architecture and ash trays should be "functional".'[16]

But the apprehension and appreciation of the work also depend on the beholder's intention, which is itself a function of the conventional norms governing the relation to the work of art in a certain historical and social situation and also of the beholder's capacity to conform to those norms, i.e., his artistic training. To break out of this circle one only has to observe that the ideal of 'pure' perception of a work of art qua work of art is the product of the enunciation and systematization of the principles of specifically aesthetic legitimacy which accompany the constituting of a relatively auton ɔmous artistic field. The aesthetic mode of perception in the 'pure' form which it has now assumed corresponds to a particular state of the mode of artistic production. An art which, like all Post-Impressionist painting, for example, is the product of an artistic intention which asserts the *absolute primacy of form over function,* of the mode of representation over the object represented, *categorically* demands a purely aesthetic disposition which earlier art demanded only conditionally. The demiurgic ambition of the artist, capable of applying to *any* object the pure intention of an artistic effort which is an end in itself, calls for unlimited receptiveness on the part of an aesthete capable of applying the specifically aesthetic intention to any object, whether or not it has been produced with aesthetic intention.

This demand is objectified in the art museum; there the aesthetic disposition becomes an institution. Nothing more totally manifests and achieves the autonomizing of aesthetic activity vis-à-vis extra-aesthetic interests or functions than the art museum's juxtaposition of works. Though originally subordinated to quite different or even incompatible functions (crucifix and fetish, Pietà and still life), these juxtaposed works tacitly demand attention to form rather than function, technique rather than theme, and, being constructed in styles that are mutually exclusive but all equally necessary, they are a practical challenge to the expectation of realistic representation as defined by the arbitrary canons of an everyday aesthetic, and so lead naturally from stylistic relativism to the neutralization of the very function of representation. Objects previously treated as collectors' curios or historical and ethnographic documents have achieved the status of works of art, thereby materializing the omnipotence of the aesthetic gaze and making it difficult to ignore the fact that—if it is not to be merely an arbitrary and therefore suspect affirmation of this absolute power—artistic contemplation now has to include a degree of erudition which is liable to damage the illusion of immediate illumination that is an essential element of pure pleasure.

PURE TASTE AND 'BARBAROUS' TASTE In short, never perhaps has more been asked of the spectator, who is now required to 're-produce' the primary operation whereby the artist (with the complicity of his whole intellectual field) produced this new fetish.[17] But never perhaps has he been given so much in return. The naive exhibitionism of 'conspicuous consumption', which seeks distinction in the crude display of ill-mastered luxury, is nothing compared to the unique capacity of the pure gaze, a quasi-creative power which sets the aesthete apart from the common herd by a radical difference which seems to be inscribed in 'persons'. One only has to read Ortega y Gasset to see the reinforcement the charismatic ideology derives from art, which is 'essentially unpopular, indeed, antipopular' and from the 'curious sociological effect' it produces by dividing the public into two 'antagonistic castes', those who understand and those who do not'. 'This implies', Ortega goes on, 'that some possess an organ of understanding which others have been denied; that these are two distinct varieties of the human species. The new art is not for everyone, like Romantic art, but destined for an especially gifted minority.' And he ascribes to the 'humiliation' and 'obscure sense of inferiority' inspired by 'this art of privilege, sensuous nobility, instinctive aristocracy', the irritation it arouses in the mass, 'unworthy of artistic sacraments': 'For a century and a half, the "people", the mass, have claimed to be the whole of society. The music of Stravinsky or the plays of Pirandello have the sociological power of obliging them to see themselves as they are, as the "common people", a mere ingredient among others in the social structure, the inert material of the historical process, a secondary factor in the spiritual cosmos. By contrast, the young art helps the "best" to know and recognize one another in the greyness of the multitude and to learn their mission, which is to be few in number and to have to fight against the multitude.'[18]

And to show that the self-legitimating imagination of the 'happy few' has no limits, one only has to quote a recent text by Suzanne Langer, who is presented as 'one of the world's most influential philosophers': 'In the past, the masses did not have access to art; music, painting, and even books, were pleasures reserved for the rich. It might have been supposed that the poor, the "common people", would have enjoyed them equally, if they had had the chance. But now that everyone can read, go to museums, listen to great music, at least on the radio, the judgement of the masses about these things has become a reality and through this it has become clear that great art is not a direct sensuous pleasure. Otherwise, like cookies or cocktails, it would flatter uneducated taste as much as cultured taste.'[19]

It should not be thought that the relationship of distinction (which may or may not imply the conscious intention of distinguishing oneself from common people) is only an incidental component in the aesthetic disposition. The pure gaze implies a break with the ordinary attitude towards the world which, as such, is a social break. One can agree with Ortega y Gasset when he attributes to modern art—which merely takes to its extreme conclusions an intention implicit in art since the Renaissance—a systematic refusal of all that is 'human', by which he means the passions, emotions and feelings which *ordinary* people put into their *ordinary* existence, and consequently all the themes and objects capable of evoking them: 'People like a play when they are able to take an interest in the human destinies put before them', in which 'they participate as if they were real-life events.'[20] Rejecting the 'human' clearly means rejecting what is generic, i.e., *common,* 'easy' and immediately accessible, starting with everything that reduces the aesthetic animal to pure and simple animality, to palpable pleasure or sensual desire. The interest in the content of the representation which leads people to call 'beautiful' the representation of beautiful things, especially those which speak most immediately to the senses and the sensibility, is rejected in favour of the indifference and distance which refuse to subordinate judgement of the representation to the nature of the object represented.[21] It can be seen that it is not so easy to describe the 'pure' gaze without also describing the naive gaze which it defines itself against, and vice versa; and that there is no *neutral,* impartial, 'pure' description of either of these opposing visions (which does not mean that one has to subscribe to aesthetic relativism, when it is so obvious that the 'popular aesthetic' is defined in relation to 'high' aesthetics and that reference to legitimate art and its negative judgement on 'popular' taste never ceases to haunt the popular experience of beauty). Refusal or privation? It is as dangerous to attribute the coherence of a systematic aesthetic to the objectively aesthetic commitments of ordinary people as it is to adopt, albeit unconsciously, the strictly negative conception of ordinary vision which is the basis of every 'high' aesthetic.

THE POPULAR 'AESTHETIC'   Everything takes place as if the 'popular aesthetic' were based on the affirmation of continuity between art and life, which implies the subordination of form to function, or, one might say, on a refusal of the refusal which is the starting point of the high aesthetic, i.e., the clear-cut separation of ordinary dispositions from the specifically aesthetic disposition. The hostility of the working class and of the middle-class fractions least rich in cultural capital towards every kind of formal experimentation asserts itself both in the theatre and in painting, or still more clearly, because they have less legitimacy, in photography and the cinema. In the theatre as in the cinema, the popular audience delights in plots that proceed logically and chronologically towards a happy end, and 'identifies' better with simply drawn situations and characters than with ambiguous and symbolic figures and actions or the enigmatic problems of the theatre of cruelty, not to mention the suspended animation of Beckettian heroes or the bland absurdities of Pinteresque dialogue. Their reluctance or refusal springs not just from lack of familiarity but from a deep-rooted demand for participation, which formal experiment systematically disappoints, especially when, refusing to offer the 'vulgar' attractions of an art of illusion, the theatrical fiction denounces itself, as in all forms of 'play within a play'. Pirandello supplies the paradigm here, in plays in which the actors are actors unable to act— *Six Characters in Search of an Author, Comme ci (ou comme ça)* or *Ce soir on improvise*—and Jean Genet supplies the formula in the Prologue to *The Blacks:* 'We shall have the politeness, which you have taught us, to make communication impossible. The distance initially between us we shall increase, by our splendid gestures, our manners and our insolence, for we are also actors.' The desire to enter into the game, identifying with the characters' joys and sufferings, worrying about their fate, espousing their hopes and ideals, living their life, is based on a form of *investment,* a sort of deliberate 'naivety', ingenuousness, good-natured credulity ('We're here to enjoy ourselves'), which tends to accept formal experiments and specifically artistic effects only to the extent that they can be forgotten and do not get in the way of the substance of the work.

The cultural divide which associates each class of works with its public means that it is not easy to obtain working-class people's first-hand judgements on formalist innovations in modern art. However, television, which brings certain performances of 'high' art into the home, or certain cultural institutions (such as the Beaubourg Centre or the Maisons de la culture), which briefly bring a working-class public into contact with high art and sometimes avant-garde works, create what are virtually experimental situations, neither more nor less artificial or unreal than those necessarily produced by any survey on legitimate culture in a working-class milieu. One then observes the confusion, sometimes almost a sort of panic mingled with revolt, that is induced by some exhibits—I am thinking of Ben's heap of coal, on view at Beaubourg shortly after it opened—whose parodic intention, entirely defined in terms of an artistic field and its relatively autonomous history, is seen as a sort of aggression, an affront to common sense and sensible people. Likewise, when formal experimentation insinuates itself into their familiar entertainments (e.g., TV variety shows with sophisticated technical effects, such as those by Jean-Christophe Averty) working-class viewers protest, not only because they do not feel the need for these fancy games, but because they sometimes understand that they derive their necessity from the logic of a field of production which excludes them precisely by these games: 'I don't like those cut-up things at all, where you see a head, then a nose, then a leg. . . . First you see a singer all drawn out, three metres tall, then the next minute he's got arms two metres long. Do you find that funny? Oh, I just don't like it, it's stupid, I don't see the point of distorting things' (a baker, Grenoble).

Formal refinement—which, in literature or the theatre, leads to obscurity—is, in the eyes of the working-class public, one sign of what is sometimes felt to be a desire to keep the uninitiated at arm's length, or, as one respondent said about certain cultural programmes on TV, to speak to other initiates 'over the viewers' heads'.[22] It is part of the paraphernalia which always announces the sacred character, separate and separating, of high culture—the icy solemnity of the great museums, the grandiose luxury of the opera-houses and major theatres, the décor and decorum of concert-halls.[23] Everything takes place as if the working-class audience vaguely grasped what is implied in conspicuous formality, both in art and in life, i.e., a sort of censorship of the expressive content which explodes in the expressiveness of popular language, and by the same token, a distancing, inherent in the calculated coldness of all formal exploration, a refusal to communicate concealed at the heart of the communication itself, both in an art which takes back and refuses what it seems to deliver and in bourgeois politeness, whose impeccable formalism is a permanent warning against the temptation of familiarity. Conversely, popular entertainment secures the spectator's participation in the show and collective participation in the festivity which it occasions. If circus and melodrama (which are recreated by some sporting spectacles such as wrestling and, to a lesser extent, boxing and all forms of team games, such as those which have been televised) are more 'popular' than entertainments like dancing or theatre, this is not merely because, being less formalized (compare, for example, acrobatics with dancing) and less euphemized, they offer more direct, more immediate satisfactions. It is also because, through the collective festivity they give rise to and the array of spectacular delights they offer (I am thinking also of the music-hall, light opera or the big feature film)—fabulous sets, glittering costumes, exciting music, lively action, enthusiastic actors—like all forms of the comic and especially those working through satire or parody of the 'great' (mimics, chansonniers etc.), they satisfy the taste for and sense of revelry, the plain speaking and hearty laughter which liberate by setting the social world head over heels, overturning conventions and proprieties.

AESTHETIC DISTANCING   This popular reaction is the very opposite of the detachment of the aesthete, who, as is seen whenever he appropriates one of the objects of popular taste (e.g., Westerns or strip cartoons), introduces a distance, a gap—the measure of his distant distinction—vis-à-vis 'first-degree' perception, by displacing the interest from the 'content', characters, plot etc., to the form, to the specifically artistic effects which are only appreciated relationally, through a comparison with other works which is incompatible with immersion in the singularity of the work immediately given. Detachment, disinterestedness, indifference—aesthetic theory has so often presented these as the only way to recognize the work of art for what it is, autonomous, *selbständig,* that one ends up forgetting that they really mean disinvestment, detachment, indifference, in other words, the refusal to invest oneself and take things seriously. Worldly-wise readers of Rousseau's *Lettre sur les spectacles,*[24] who have long been aware that there is nothing more naive and vulgar than to invest too much passion in the things of the mind or to expect too much seriousness of them, tending to assume that intellectual creativity is opposed to moral integrity or political consistency, have no answer to Virginia Woolf when she criticizes the novels of Wells, Galsworthy and Bennett because 'they leave one with a strange sense of incompleteness and dissatisfaction' and the feeling that it is 'necessary to do something—to join a society, or, more desperately, to write a cheque', in contrast to works like *Tristram Shandy* or *Pride and Prejudice,* which, being perfectly 'self-contained', 'leave one with no desire to do anything, except indeed to read the book again, and to understand it better.'[25]

But the refusal of any sort of involvement, any 'vulgar' surrender to easy seduction and collective enthusiasm, which is, indirectly at least, the origin of the taste for formal complexity and objectless representations, is perhaps most clearly seen in reactions to paintings. Thus one finds that the higher the level of education,[26] the greater is the proportion of respondents who, when asked whether a series of objects would make beautiful photographs, refuse the ordinary objects of popular admiration—a first communion, a sunset or a landscape—as 'vulgar' or 'ugly', or reject them as 'trivial', silly, a bit 'wet', or, in Ortega y Gasset's terms, naively 'human'; and the greater is the proportion who assert the autonomy of the representation with respect to the thing represented by declaring that a beautiful photograph, and a fortiori a beautiful painting, can be made from objects socially designated as meaningless—a metal frame, the bark of a tree, and especially cabbages, a trivial object par excellence—or as ugly and repulsive—such as a car crash, a butcher's stall (chosen for the Rembrandt allusion) or a snake (for the Boileau reference)—or as misplaced—e.g., a pregnant woman (see tables 2 and 3).

Since it was not possible to set up a genuine experimental situation, we collected the interviewees' statements about the things they consider 'photogenic' and which therefore seem to them capable of being looked at aesthetically (as opposed to things excluded on account of their triviality or ugliness or for ethical reasons). The capacity to adopt the aesthetic attitude is thus measured by the gap (which, in a field of production that evolves through the dialectic of distinction, is also a time-lag, a backwardness) between what is constituted as an aesthetic object by the individual or group concerned and what is constituted aesthetically in a given state of the field of production by the holders of aesthetic legitimacy.

The following question was put to the interviewees: 'Given the following subjects, is a photographer more likely to produce a beautiful, interesting, meaningless or ugly photo: a landscape, a car crash etc.?' In the preliminary survey, the interviewees were shown actual photographs, mostly famous ones, of the objects which were merely named in the full-scale survey—pebbles, a pregnant woman etc. The reactions evoked by the mere idea of the image were entirely consistent with those produced by the image itself (evidence that the value attributed to the image tends to correspond to the

Table 2 Aesthetic disposition, by educational capital (%).[a]

Educational capital	N	First communion					Folk dance				
		No reply or incoherent	Ugly	Meaningless	Interesting	Beautiful	No reply or incoherent	Ugly	Meaningless	Interesting	Beautiful
No qualification, CEP	314	2.0	5.0	19.0	23.0	51.0	1.0	0.5	3.0	41.0	54.5
CAP	97	4.0	1.0	26.0	38.0	31.0	4.0	0	3.0	33.0	60.0
BEPC	197	2.5	7.0	27.0	31.0	32.5	3.5	0	7.0	33.5	56.0
Baccalauréat	217	2.0	12.0	43.0	24.0	19.0	2.0	0.5	13.0	47.5	37.0
Started higher education	118	4.0	13.0	45.0	23.0	15.0	6.0	2.5	13.0	37.0	41.5
Licence	182	1.0	11.0	53.0	28.0	7.0	2.0	1.0	11.0	49.5	36.5
Agrégation, grande école	71	4.0	15.5	49.0	6.0	25.5	4.0	6.0	22.5	28.0	39.5

Table 2 (continued).

Educational capital	N	Bark of a tree					Butcher's stall					Cabbages				
		No reply or incoherent	Ugly	Meaningless	Interesting	Beautiful	No reply or incoherent	Ugly	Meaningless	Interesting	Beautiful	No reply or incoherent	Ugly	Meaningless	Interesting	Beautiful
No qualification, CEP	314	2.0	14.5	46.5	21.5	15.5	1.5	31.0	46.0	16.5	5.0	2.0	28.0	56.0	10.0	4.0
CAP	97	5.0	1.0	20.0	37.0	37.0	6.0	15.5	48.5	24.0	6.0	5.0	16.5	63.0	7.0	8.5
BEPC	197	2.5	8.5	31.5	30.0	27.5	3.0	28.0	47.0	17.0	5.0	2.0	17.0	55.0	13.0	13.0
Baccalauréat	217	2.0	3.0	21.0	32.0	42.0	3.0	29.5	32.0	25.0	10.5	2.0	17.5	48.5	19.0	13.0
Started higher education	118	6.0	1.0	23.0	25.0	45.0	4.0	30.5	29.0	18.5	18.0	6.0	9.0	47.5	19.5	18.0
Licence	182	0	3.0	18.0	23.0	56.0	4.5	29.5	22.5	24.0	19.5	2.0	16.0	51.5	8.0	22.5
Agrégation, grande école	71	4.0	8.5	8.5	24.0	60.5	4.0	29.5	23.0	18.0	25.5	3.0	11.0	38.0	21.0	27.0

a. The respondents had to answer this question: 'Given the following subjects, is a photographer more likely to make a beautiful, interesting, meaningless, or ugly photo: a landscape, a car crash, a little girl playing with a cat, a pregnant woman, a still life, a woman suckling a child, a metal frame, tramps quarrelling, cabbages, a sunset over the sea, a weaver at his loom, a folk dance, a rope, the bark of a tree, a butcher's stall, a famous monument, a scrap-yard, a first communion, a wounded man, a snake, an "old master"? In each column, the italic figures indicate the strongest tendencies.

Table 3 Aesthetic disposition, by class and education (%).

Classes	Educational qualification	N	Pregnant woman					Cabbages				
			No reply or incoherent	Ugly	Meaningless	Interesting	Beautiful	No reply or incoherent	Ugly	Meaningless	Interesting	Beautiful
Working	None, CEP, CAP	143	1.5	40.0	36.5	14.0	8.0	1.5	28.0	57.0	8.5	5.0
	BEPC and above[a]	18	0	39.0	22.0	11.0	28.0	0	5.5	72.5	16.5	5.5
Middle	None, CEP, CAP	243	1.0	46.0	27.5	15.0	10.5	2.0	22.5	61.5	10.0	4.0
	BEPC and above[a]	335	3.5	34.0	30.0	13.5	19.0	2.5	17.5	49.5	14.5	16.0
	BEPC	149	3.5	39.0	35.0	9.0	13.5	2.0	21.0	56.0	8.5	12.5
	bac	140	3.5	37.0	21.0	17.5	21.0	3.0	15.5	45.0	19.5	17.0
	higher education	46	4.0	8.5	42.0	13.0	32.5	4.0	13.0	41.0	20.0	22.0
Upper	None, CEP, CAP	25	20.0	36.0	24.0	12.0	8.0	20.0	36.0	28.0	12.0	4.0
	BEPC and above[a]	432	3.0	36.0	22.0	19.0	20.0	3.0	14.5	48.0	15.5	19.0
	BEPC	31	6.5	48.5	38.5	0	6.5	6.5	6.5	38.5	32.5	16.0
	bac	76	0	60.5	16.0	5.0	18.5	0	21.0	55.5	17.0	6.5
	higher education	325	3.0	30.0	22.5	23.0	21.5	3.0	14.0	47.5	13.5	22.0
	technical college	80	7.5	17.5	30.0	32.5	12.5	6.5	6.5	52.0	20.0	15.0
	licence	174	0.5	36.0	21.5	19.5	22.5	2.0	18.5	49.0	7.5	23.0
	agrég., grande école	71	4.0	29.5	17.0	20.0	29.5	3.0	11.0	38.0	21.0	27.0

Table 3 (continued).

Classes	Educational qualification	N	Snake					Sunset over sea				
			No reply or incoherent	Ugly	Meaningless	Interesting	Beautiful	No reply or incoherent	Ugly	Meaningless	Interesting	Beautiful
Working	None, CEP, CAP	143	1.0	35.0	16.0	38.0	10.0	1.0	0	1.0	10.0	88.0
	BEPC and above	18	0	28.0	22.0	39.0	11.0	0	0	6.0	6.0	88.0
Middle	None, CEP, CAP	243	1.0	25.0	23.0	35.0	16.0	1.0	0.5	2.5	6.0	90.0
	BEPC and above	335	3.0	28.5	14.0	30.5	24.0	3.0	1.5	9.0	8.5	78.0
	BEPC	149	3.0	38.0	8.5	34.0	16.5	1.5	1.5	4.5	6.5	86.0
	bac	140	4.0	21.0	17.0	34.0	24.0	4.0	2.0	10.0	9.0	75.0
	higher education	46	2.0	19.5	24.0	9.0	45.5	2.0	2.0	20.0	13.0	63.0
Upper	None, CEP, CAP	25	20.0	36.0	4.0	24.0	16.0	20.0	0	8.0	8.0	64.0
	BEPC and above	432	3.0	18.0	13.0	38.0	28.0	2.0	3.0	15.0	17.0	63.0
	BEPC	31	6.5	19.5	16.0	29.0	29.0	0	0	22.5	0	77.5
	bac	76	0	22.5	8.0	50.0	19.5	0	0	14.5	8.0	77.5
	higher education	325	4.0	16.5	14.5	35.5	29.5	3.0	4.0	14.0	21.0	58.0
	technical college	80	5.0	14.0	20.0	36.0	25.0	6.0	5.0	10.0	26.5	52.5
	licence	174	2.5	20.0	14.5	35.0	28.0	0	5.0	13.0	24.0	58.0
	agrég, grande école	71	5.5	11.5	8.5	36.5	38.0	5.5	1.5	19.5	8.5	65.0

a. The category 'BEPC and above' (created for the sake of formal comparability) does not have the same content in the different social classes: the proportion of high qualifications within this category rises with social class. This essentially explains why the rarest choices—'beautiful' for the cabbages or the snake, 'ugly' or 'trivial' for the sunset—be- come more numerous as one moves up the social scale. The apparent exception in the case of the pregnant woman is due to the absence of women (who are known to be more likely to accept this subject) in this category.

value attributed to the thing). Photographs were used partly to avoid the legitimacy-imposing effects of paintings and partly because photography is perceived as a more accessible practice, so that the judgements expressed were likely to be less unreal.

Although the test employed was designed to collect statements of artistic intention rather than to measure the ability to put the intention into practice in doing painting or photography or even in the perception of works of art, it enables one to identify the factors which determine the capacity to adopt the posture socially designated as specifically aesthetic. Factorial analysis of judgements on 'photogenic' objects reveals an opposition within each class between the fractions richest in cultural capital and poorest in economic capital and the fractions richest in economic capital and poorest in cultural capital. In the case of the dominant class, higher-education teachers and artistic producers (and secondarily, teachers and the professions) are opposed to industrial and commercial employers; private-sector executives and engineers are in an intermediate position. In the petite bourgeoisie, the cultural intermediaries (distinctly separated from the closest fractions, the primary teachers, medical services and art craftsmen) are opposed to the small shopkeepers or craftsmen and the office workers.

In addition to the relationship between cultural capital and the negative and positive indices (refusal of 'wetness'; the capacity to valorize the trivial) of the aesthetic disposition—or, at least, the capacity to operate the arbitrary classification which, within the universe of worked-upon objects, distinguishes the objects socially designated as deserving and demanding an aesthetic approach that can recognize and constitute them as works of art—the statistics establish that the preferred objects of would-be aesthetic photography, e.g., the folk dance, the weaver or the little girl with her cat, are in an intermediate position. The proportion of respondents who consider that these things can make a beautiful photograph is highest at the levels of the CAP and BEPC, whereas at higher levels they tend to be judged either interesting or meaningless.

The proportion of respondents who say a first communion can make a beautiful photo declines up to the level of the *licence* and then rises again at the highest level. This is because a relatively large proportion of the highest-qualified subjects assert their aesthetic disposition by declaring that any object can be perceived aesthetically. Thus, in the dominant class, the proportion who declare that a sunset can make a beautiful photo is greatest at the lowest educational level, declines at intermediate levels (some higher education, a minor engineering school), and grows strongly again among those who have completed several years of higher education and who tend to consider that anything is suitable for beautiful photography.

The statistics also show that women are much more likely than men to manifest their repugnance toward repugnant, horrible or distasteful objects: 44.5 percent of them, as against 35 percent of the men, consider that there can only be an ugly photograph of a wounded man, and there are similar differences for the butcher's stall (33.5 and 27 percent), the snake (30.5 and 21.5 percent) or the pregnant woman (45 and 33.5 percent), whereas the gap disappears with the still life (6 and 6.5 percent) and the cabbages (20.5 and 19 percent). The traditional division of labour between the sexes assigns 'humane' or 'humanitarian' tasks and feelings to women and more readily allows them effusions and tears, in the name of the opposition between reason and sensibility; men are, ex officio, on the side of culture whereas women (like the working class) are cast on the side of nature. Women are therefore less imperatively required to censor and repress 'natural' feelings as the aesthetic disposition demands (which indicates, incidentally, that, as will be shown subsequently, the refusal of nature, or rather the refusal to surrender to nature, which is the mark of dominant groups—who start with *self*-control—is the basis of the aesthetic disposition).

Women's revulsion is expressed more overtly, at the expense of aesthetic neutralization, the more completely they are subject to the traditional model of the sexual division of labour and (in other words) the weaker their cultural capital and the lower their position in the social hierarchy. Women in the new petite bourgeoisie, who, in general, make much greater concessions to affective considerations than the men in the same category (although they are equally likely to say that there can be a beautiful photograph of cabbages), much more rarely accept that a photograph of a pregnant woman can only be ugly than women in any other category (31.5 percent of them, as against 70 percent of the wives of industrial and commercial employers, 69.5 percent of the wives of craftsmen and shopkeepers, 47.5 percent of the wives of manual workers, clerical workers or junior executives). In doing so they manifest simultaneously their aesthetic pretensions and their desire to be seen as 'liberated' from the ethical taboos imposed on their sex.

Thus, nothing more rigorously distinguishes the different classes than the disposition objectively demanded by the legitimate consumption of legitimate works, the aptitude for taking a specifically aesthetic point of view on objects already constituted aesthetically—and therefore put forward for the admiration of those who have learned to recognize the signs of the admirable—and the even rarer capacity to constitute aesthetically objects that are ordinary or even 'common' (because they are appropriated, aesthetically or otherwise, by the 'common people') or to apply the principles of a 'pure' aesthetic in the most everyday choices of everyday life, in cooking, dress or decoration, for example.

Statistical enquiry is indispensable in order to establish beyond dispute the social conditions of possibility (which will have to be made more explicit) of the 'pure' disposition. However, because it inevitably looks like a scholastic test intended to measure the respondents against a norm tacitly regarded as absolute, it may fail to capture the meanings which this disposition and the whole attitude to the world expressed in it have for the different social classes. What the logic of the test would lead one to describe as a deficiency (and that is what it is, from the standpoint of the norms defining legitimate perception of works of art) is *also* a refusal which stems from a denunciation of the arbitrary or ostentatious gratuitousness of stylistic exercises or purely formalistic experiments. A certain 'aesthetic', which maintains that a photograph is justified by the object photographed or by the possible use of the photographic image, is being brought into play when manual workers almost invariably reject photography for photography's sake (e.g., the photo of pebbles) as useless, perverse or bourgeois: 'A waste of film', 'They must have film to throw away', 'I tell you, there are some people who don't know what to do with their time', 'Haven't they got anything better to do with their time than photograph things like that?' 'That's bourgeois photography.'

It must never be forgotten that the working-class 'aesthetic' is a dominated 'aesthetic' which is constantly obliged to define itself in terms of the dominant aesthetics. The members of the working class, who can neither ignore the high-art aesthetic, which denounces their own 'aesthetic', nor abandon their socially conditioned inclinations, but still less proclaim them and legitimate them, often experience their relationship to the aesthetic norms in a twofold and contradictory way. This is seen when some manual workers grant 'pure' photographs a purely verbal recognition (this is also the case with many petit bourgeois and even some bourgeois who, as regards paintings, for example, differ from the working class mainly by what they know is the right thing to say or do or, still better, not to say): 'It's beautiful, but it would never occur to me to take a picture of a thing like that', 'Yes, it's beautiful, but you have to like it, it's not my cup of tea.'

AN ANTI-KANTIAN 'AESTHETIC' It is no accident that, when one sets about reconstructing its logic, the popular 'aesthetic' appears as the negative opposite of the Kantian aesthetic, and that the popular ethos implicitly answers each proposition of the 'Analytic of the Beautiful' with a thesis contradicting it. In order to apprehend what makes the specificity of aesthetic judgement, Kant ingeniously distinguished 'that which pleases' from 'that which gratifies', and, more generally, strove to separate 'disinterestedness', the sole guarantee of the specifically aesthetic quality of contemplation, from 'the interest of the senses', which defines 'the agreeable', and from 'the interest of Reason', which defines 'the Good'. By contrast, working-class people, who expect every image to fulfil a function, if only that of a sign, refer, often explicitly, to norms of morality or agreeableness in all their judgements. Thus the photograph of a dead soldier provokes judgements which, whether positive or negative, are always responses to the reality of the thing represented or to the functions the representation could serve, the horror of war or the denunciation of the horrors of war which the photographer is supposed to produce simply by showing that horror.[27] Similarly, popular naturalism recognizes beauty in the image of a beautiful thing or, more rarely, in a beautiful image of a beautiful thing: 'Now, that's good, it's almost symmetrical. And she's a beautiful woman. A beautiful woman always looks good in a photo.' The Parisian manual worker echoes the plain-speaking of Hippias the Sophist: 'I'll tell him what beauty is and I'm not likely to be refuted by him! The fact is, Socrates, to be frank, a beautiful woman, that's what beauty is!' (Plato, *Greater Hippias*, 287e).

This 'aesthetic', which subordinates the form and the very existence of the image to its function, is necessarily pluralistic and conditional. The insistence with which the respondents point out the limits and conditions of validity of their judgements, distinguishing, for each photograph, the possible uses or audiences, or, more precisely, the possible use for each audience ('As a news photo, it's not bad', 'All right, if it's for showing to kids') shows that they reject the idea that a photograph can please 'universally'. 'A photo of a pregnant woman is all right for me, not for other people', said a white-collar worker, who has to use his concern for propriety as a way of expressing anxiety about what is 'presentable' and therefore entitled to demand admiration. Because the image is always judged by reference to the function it fulfils for the person who looks at it or which he thinks it could fulfil for other classes of beholders, aesthetic judgement naturally takes the form of a hypothetical judgement implicitly based on recognition of 'genres', the perfection and scope of which are defined by a *concept*. Almost three-quarters of the judgements expressed begin with an 'if', and the effort to recognize culminates in classification into a genre, or, which amounts to the same thing, in the attribution of a social use, the different genres being defined in terms of their use and their users ('It's a publicity photo', 'It's a pure document', 'It's a laboratory photo', 'It's a competition photo', 'It's an educational photo' etc.). And photographs of nudes are almost always received with comments that reduce them to the stereotype of their social function: 'All right in Pigalle', 'It's the sort of photos they keep under the counter.' It is not surprising that this 'aesthetic', which bases appreciation on informative, tangible or moral interest, can only refuse images of the trivial, or, which amounts to the same thing in terms of this logic, the triviality of the image: judgement never gives the image of the object autonomy with respect to the object of the image. Of all the characteristics proper to the image, only colour (which Kant regarded as less pure than form) can prevent rejection of photographs of trivial things. Nothing is more alien to popular consciousness than the idea of an aesthetic pleasure that, to put it in Kantian terms, is independent of the charming of the senses. Thus judgements on the photographs most strongly rejected on grounds of futility (pebbles, bark, wave) almost always end with the reservation that 'in colour, it might be pretty'; and some respondents even manage to formulate the maxim governing their attitude, when they declare that 'if the colours are good, a colour photograph is always beautiful.' In short, Kant is indeed referring to popular taste when he writes: 'Taste that requires an added element of charm and emotion for its delight, not to speak of adopting this as the measure of its approval, has not yet emerged from barbarism.'[28]

Refusal of the meaningless (*insignifiant*) image, which has neither sense nor interest, or of the ambiguous image means refusing to treat it as a finality without purpose, as an image signifying itself, and therefore having no other referent than itself. The value of a photograph is measured by the interest of the information it conveys, and by the clarity with which it fulfils this informative function, in short, its legibility, which itself varies with the legibility of its intention or function, the judgement it provokes being more or less favourable depending on the expressive adequacy of the signifier to the signified. It therefore contains the expectation of the title or caption which, by declaring the signifying intention, makes it possible to judge whether the realization signifies or illustrates it adequately. If formal explorations, in avant-garde theatre or non-figurative painting, or simply classical music, are disconcerting to working-class people, this is partly because they feel incapable of understanding what these things must signify, insofar as they are signs. Hence the uninitiated may experience as inadequate and unworthy a satisfaction that cannot be grounded in a meaning transcendent to the object. Not knowing what the 'intention' is, they feel incapable of distinguishing a tour de force from clumsiness, telling a 'sincere' formal device from cynical imposture.

The confessions with which manual workers faced with modern pictures betray their exclusion ('I don't understand what it means' or 'I like it but I don't understand it') contrast with the knowing silence of the bourgeois, who, though equally disconcerted, at least know that they have to refuse—or at least conceal—the naive expectation of expressiveness that is betrayed by the concern to 'understand' ('programme music' and the titles foisted on so many sonatas, concertos and symphonies are sufficient indication that this expectation is not an exclusively popular one).

But formal refinement is also that which, by foregrounding form, i.e., the artist, his specific interests, his technical problems, his effects, his allusions and echoes, throws the thing itself into the background and precludes direct communion with the beauty of the world—a beautiful child, a beautiful girl, a beautiful animal or a beautiful landscape. The representation is expected to be a feast for the eyes and, like still life, to 'stir up memories and anticipations of feasts enjoyed and feasts to come.'[29] Nothing is more opposed to the celebration of the beauty and joy of the world that is looked for in the work of art, 'a choice which praises', than the devices of cubist or abstract painting, which are perceived and unanimously denounced as aggressions against the thing represented, against the natural order and especially the human form. In short, however perfectly it performs its representative function, the work is only seen as fully justified if the thing represented is worthy of being represented, if the representative function is subordinated to a higher function, such as that of capturing and exalting a reality that is worthy of being made eternal. Such is the basis of the 'barbarous taste' to which the most antithetical forms of the dominant aesthetic always refer negatively and which only recognizes realist representation, in other words, a respectful, humble, submissive representation of objects designated by their beauty or their social importance.

AESTHETICS, ETHICS AND AESTHETICISM   When faced with legitimate works of art, people most lacking the specific competence apply to them the perceptual schemes of their own ethos, the very ones which structure their everyday perception of everyday existence. These schemes, giving rise to products of an unwilled, unselfconscious systematicity, are opposed to the more or less fully stated principles of an aesthetic.[30] The result is a systematic 'reduction' of the things of art to the things of life, a bracketing of form in favour of 'human' content, which is barbarism par excellence from the standpoint of the pure aesthetic.[31] Everything takes place as if the emphasis on form could only be achieved by means of a neutralization of any kind of affective or ethical interest in the object of representation which accompanies (without any necessary cause-effect relation) mastery of the means of grasping the distinctive properties which this particular form takes on in its relations with other forms (i.e., through reference to the universe of works of art and its history).

Confronted with a photograph of an old woman's hands, the culturally most deprived express a more or less conventional emotion or an ethical complicity but never a specifically aesthetic judgement (other than a negative one): 'Oh, she's got terribly deformed hands! . . . There's one thing I don't get (the left hand)—it's as if her left thumb was about to come away from her hand. Funny way of taking a photo. The old girl must've worked hard. Looks like she's got arthritis. She's definitely crippled, unless she's holding her hands like that (imitates gesture)? Yes, that's it, she's got her hand bent like that. Not like a duchess's hands or even a typist's! . . . I really feel sorry seeing that poor old woman's hands, they're all knotted, you might say' (manual worker, Paris). With the lower middle classes, exaltation of ethical virtues comes to the forefront ('hands worn out by toil'), sometimes tinged with populist sentimentality ('Poor old thing! Her hands must really hurt her. It really gives a sense of pain'); and sometimes even concern for aesthetic properties and references to painting make their appearance: 'It's as if it was a painting that had been photographed . . . Must be really beautiful as a painting' (clerical worker, Paris). 'That reminds me of a picture I saw in an exhibition of Spanish paintings, a monk with his hands clasped in front of him and deformed fingers' (technician, Paris). 'The sort of hands you see in early Van Goghs, an old peasant woman or people eating potatoes' (junior executive, Paris). At higher levels in the social hierarchy, the remarks become increasingly abstract, with (other people's) hands, labour and old age functioning as allegories or symbols which serve as pretexts for general reflections on general problems:

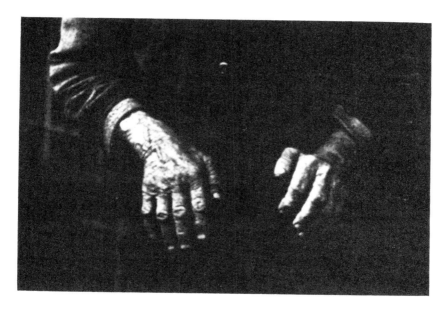

'Those are the hands of someone who has worked too much, doing very hard manual work . . . As a matter of fact it's very unusual to see hands like that' (engineer, Paris). 'These two hands unquestionably evoke a poor and unhappy old age' (teacher, provinces). An aestheticizing reference to painting, sculpture or literature, more frequent, more varied and more subtly handled, resorts to the neutralization and distancing which bourgeois discourse about the social world requires and performs. 'I find this a very beautiful photograph. It's the very symbol of toil. It puts me in mind of Flaubert's old servant-woman . . . That woman's gesture, at once very humble . . . It's terrible that work and poverty are so deforming' (engineer, Paris).

A portrait of a heavily made-up woman, taken from an unusual angle with unusual lighting, provokes very similar reactions. Manual workers, and even more so craftsmen and small shopkeepers, react with horror and disgust: 'I wouldn't like that photo in my house, in my room. It isn't very nice to look at. It's rather painful' (manual worker, provinces). 'Is she dead? Ghastly, enough to keep you awake at night . . . ghastly, horrible, I don't want to look at it' (shopkeeper, provinces). While most of the office workers and junior executives reject a photo which they can only describe as 'frightful' or 'unpleasant to look at', some of them try to characterize the technique: 'The photo is very well taken, very beautiful, but horrible' (clerical worker, Paris). 'What gives the impression of something monstrous is the expression on the face of the man or woman who is the subject of the photo and the angle from which it has been taken, that's to say looking up from below' (junior executive, Paris). Others appeal to aesthetic references, mainly drawn from the cinema: 'A rather fantastic sort of character, or at least rather bizarre . . . it could be a Dreyer character, Bergman at a pinch,

The Lacq gasworks by night

or perhaps even Eisenstein, in *Ivan the Terrible* . . . I like it a lot' (technician, Paris). Most of the senior executives and members of the professions
find the photograph 'beautiful' and 'expressive' and make reference not only
to the films of Bergman, Orson Welles, Dreyer, and others, but also to the
theatre, invoking Hamlet, Macbeth or Racine's Athalie.

When confronted with a photograph of the Lacq gas refinery, which is
likely to disconcert realist expectations both by its subject, an industrial
complex, normally excluded from the world of legitimate representation,
and by the treatment it receives (night photography), manual workers per-
plexed, hesitate, and eventually, in most cases, admit defeat: 'At first sight
it's a construction in metal but I can't make head or tail of it. It might be
something used in an electric power station . . . I can't make out what it is,
it's a mystery to me' (manual worker, provinces). 'Now, that one really
bothers me, I haven't got anything to say about it . . . I can't see what it
could be, apart from the lighting. It isn't car headlights, it wouldn't be all
straight lines like that. Down here I can see a railing and a goods lift, no,
really, I can't say' (manual worker, Paris). 'That's something to do with
electronics, I don't know anything about that' (manual worker, Paris).
Among small employers, who tend to be hostile to modern art experiments
and, more generally, to all art in which they cannot see the marks and
traces of work, a sense of confusion often leads to simple refusal: 'That is of
no interest, it may be all very fine, but not for me. It's always the same
thing. Personally that stuff leaves me cold' (craftsman, provinces). 'I've
tried to work out if it really is a photo. Perhaps it's a reproduction of a
drawing done with a few pencil lines . . . I wouldn't know what to do with
a photo like that. Perhaps it suits modern tastes. Up and down with the
pencil and they like it. And as for the photo and the photographer, they
don't deserve any credit, they've done nothing at all. The artist did it all,
he's the one who ought to take the credit, he's the one who drew it' (shop-

keeper, provinces). Office workers and junior executives, who are just as disconcerted as the manual workers and small employers, but are less inclined to admit it than the former and less inclined than the latter to challenge the legitimacy of what challenges them, less often decline to give a verdict:[32] 'I like it as a photo ... because it's all drawn out; they're just lines, it seems immense to me ... A vast piece of scaffolding ... It's just light, captured by the camera' (clerical worker, Paris). 'Buffet likes doing things like that' (technician, Paris). But only among members of the dominant class, who most often recognize the object represented, does judgement of form take on full autonomy vis-à-vis judgement of content ('It's inhuman but aesthetically beautiful because of the contrasts'), and the representation is apprehended as such, without reference to anything other than itself or realities of the same class ('abstract painting', 'avant-garde plays' etc.).

The variations in the attitude to a very comparable object, a metal frame, provide a numerical proof of this: the proportion of respondents who think it could make a beautiful photo is 6 percent among manual workers and domestic servants, 9 percent among craftsmen and small shopkeepers, 9.5 percent among the clerical workers and junior administrative executives, 24 percent among the primary teachers and technicians, 24.5 percent in the dominant class—and 50 percent among the secondary and higher-education teachers. (One may assume that the reactions aroused by the architecture of the Beaubourg Centre obey the same principles.)

The aestheticism which makes the artistic intention the basis of the 'art of living' implies a sort of moral agnosticism, the perfect antithesis of the ethical disposition which subordinates art to the values of the art of living. The aesthetic intention can only contradict the dispositions of the ethos or the norms of the ethic which, at each moment, define the legitimate objects and modes of representation for the different social classes, excluding from the universe of the 'representable' certain realities and certain ways of representing them. Thus the easiest, and so the most frequent and most spectacular way to 'shock (*épater*) the bourgeois' by proving the extent of one's power to confer aesthetic status is to *transgress* ever more radically the ethical censorships (e.g., in matters of sex) which the other classes accept even within the area which the dominant disposition defines as aesthetic. Or, more subtly, it is done by conferring aesthetic status on objects or ways of representing them that are excluded by the dominant aesthetic of the time, or on objects that are given aesthetic status by dominated 'aesthetics'.

One only has to read the index of contents recently published by *Art Vivant* (1974), a 'vaguely modern review run by a clique of academics who are vaguely art historians' (as an avant-garde painter nicely put it), which occupies a sort of neutral point in the field of avant-garde art criticism between *Flashart* or *Art Press* and *Artitude* or *Opus*. In the list of features and titles one finds: *Africa* (one title: 'Art Must Be for All'), *Architecture* (two titles, including 'Architecture without an Architect'), *Comic Strips* (five titles, nine pages out of the forty-six in the whole index), *Kids' Art, Kitsch* (three titles, five pages), *Photography* (two titles, three pages), *Street Art* (fifteen titles, twenty-three pages, including 'Art in the Street?', 'Art in the Street, First Episode', 'Beauty in the Back-Streets: You Just Have to Know How to Look', 'A Suburb Sets the Pace'), *Science-Fiction-Utopia* (two titles, three pages), *Underground* (one title), *Writing-Ideograms-Graffiti* (two titles, four pages). The aim of inverting or *transgressing,* which is clearly manifested by this list, is necessarily contained within the limits assigned to it a contrario by the aesthetic conventions it denounces and by the need to secure recognition of the aesthetic nature of the transgression of the limits (i.e., recognition of its conformity to the norms of the transgressing group). Hence the almost Markovian logic of the choices, with, for the cinema, Antonioni, Chaplin, cinémathèque, Eisenstein, eroticism-pornography, Fellini, Godard, Klein, Monroe, underground, Warhol.

This commitment to symbolic transgression, which is often combined with political neutrality or revolutionary aestheticism, is the almost perfect antithesis of petit-bourgeois moralism or of what Sartre used to call the revolutionary's 'seriousness'.[33] The ethical indifference which the aesthetic disposition implies when it becomes the basis of the art of living is in fact the root of the ethical aversion to artists (or intellectuals) which manifests itself particularly vehemently among the declining and threatened fractions of the petite bourgeoisie (especially independent craftsmen and shopkeepers), who tend to express their regressive and repressive dispositions in all areas of practice (especially in educational matters and vis-à-vis students and student demonstrations), but also among the rising fractions of that class whose striving for virtue and whose deep insecurity render them very receptive to the phantasm of 'pornocracy'.

The pure disposition is so universally recognized as' legitimate that no voice is heard pointing out that the definition of art, and through it the art of living, is an object of struggle among the classes. Dominated lifestyles (*arts de vivre*), which have practically never received systematic expression, are almost always perceived, even by their defenders, from the destructive or reductive viewpoint of the dominant aesthetic, so that their only options are degradation or self-destructive rehabilitation ('popular culture'). This is why it is necessary to look to Proudhon[34] for a naively systematic expression of the petit-bourgeois aesthetic, which subordinates art to the core values of the art of living and identifies the cynical perversion of the artist's life-style as the source of the absolute primacy given to form:

'Under the influence of property, the artist, *depraved* in his reason, *dissolute in his morals, venal and without dignity,* is the impure image of egoism. The idea of *justice* and *honesty* slides over his heart without taking root, and of all the classes of society, the artist class is the poorest in strong souls and noble characters.'[35]

'Art for art's sake, as it has been called, not having its legitimacy within itself, being based on nothing, is nothing. It is *debauchery* of the heart and *dissolution* of the mind. Separated from right and duty, cultivated and pursued as the highest thought of the soul and the supreme manifestation of humanity, art or the ideal, stripped of the greater part of itself, reduced to nothing more than an *excitement of fantasy and the senses,* is the source of *sin,* the origin of all servitude, the poisoned spring from which, according to the Bible, flow all the *fornications* and abominations of the earth ... Art for art's sake, I say, verse for verse's sake, style for style's sake, form for form's sake, fantasy for fantasy's sake, all the diseases which like a plague of lice are gnawing away at our epoch, are *vice* in all its refinement, the quintessence of evil.'[36]

What is condemned is the autonomy of form and the artist's right to the formal refinements by which he claims mastery of what ought to be merely a matter of 'execution': 'I have no quarrel with nobility, or elegance, or pose, or style, or gesture, or any aspect of what constitutes the execution of a work of art and is the usual object of traditional criticism.'[37]

Dependent on demand in the choice of their objects, artists take their revenge in the execution: 'There are church painters, history painters, genre painters (in other words, painters of anecdotes or farces), portrait painters, landscape painters, animal painters, seascape painters, painters of Venus, painters of fantasy. One specializes in nudes, another in drapery. Then each one endeavours to distinguish himself by one of the means which contribute to the execution. One goes in for sketching, another for colour; this one attends to composition, that one to perspective, a third to costume or local colour; one shines through sentiment, another through his idealized or realistic figures; yet another redeems the futility of his subject by the fineness of his detail. Each strives to have his own trick, his own 'je ne sais quoi', a personal manner, and so, with the help of fashion, reputations are made and unmade.'[38]

In contrast to this decadent art cut off from social life, respecting neither God nor man, an art worthy of the name must be subordinated to science, morality and justice. It must aim to arouse the moral sense, to inspire feelings of dignity and delicacy, to idealize reality, to substitute for the thing the ideal of the thing, by painting the true and not the real. In a word, it must educate. To do so, it must transmit not 'personal impressions' (like David in *The Tennis-Court Oath,* or Delacroix) but, like Courbet in *Les Paysans de Flagey,* reconstitute the social and historial truth which *all* may judge. ('Each of us only has to consult himself to be able, after brief consideration, to state a judgement on any work of art.')[39] And it would be a pity to conclude without quoting a eulogy of the small detached house which would surely be massively endorsed by the middle and working classes: 'I would give the Louvre, the Tuileries, Notre-Dame—and the Vendôme column into the bargain—to live in my own home, in a *little house of my own design,* where I would live alone, in

the middle of a little plot of ground, a quarter of an acre or so, where I'd
have water, shade, a lawn, and silence. And if I thought of putting a
statue in it, it wouldn't be a Jupiter or an Apollo—those gentlemen are
nothing to me—nor views of London, Rome, Constantinople or Venice.
God preserve me from such places! I'd put there what I lack—mountains,
vineyards, meadows, goats, cows, sheep, reapers and shepherds.'[40]

NEUTRALIZATION AND THE UNIVERSE OF POSSIBLES Unlike non-
specific perception, the specifically aesthetic perception of a work of art
(in which there are of course degrees of accomplishment) is armed with
a pertinence principle which is socially constituted and acquired. This
principle of selection enables it to pick out and retain, from among the
elements offered to the eye (e.g., leaves or clouds considered merely as
indices or signals invested with a denotative function—'It's a poplar',
'There's going to be a storm'), all the stylistic traits—and only those—
which, when relocated in the universe of stylistic possibilities, distinguish a particular manner of treating the elements selected, whether
clouds or leaves, that is, a style as a mode of representation expressing the
mode of perception and thought that is proper to a period, a class or class
fraction, a group of artists or a particular artist. No stylistic characteriza-
tion of a work of art is possible without presupposing at least implicit
reference to the compossible alternatives, whether simultaneous—to distinguish it from its contemporaries—or successive—to contrast it with
earlier or later works by the same or a different artist. Exhibitions devoted
to an artist's whole oeuvre or to a genre (e.g., the still-life exhibition in
Bordeaux in 1978) are the objective realization of the field of interchangeable stylistic possibilities which is brought into play when one
'recognizes' the singularities of the characteristic style of a work of art. As
E. H. Gombrich demonstrates, Piet Mondrian's *Broadway Boogie-Woogie*
only takes on its 'full meaning' in terms of a previous idea of Mondrian's
work and of the expectations it favours. The 'impression of gay abandon'
given by the play of bright, strongly contrasting patches of colour can
only arise in a mind familiar with 'an art of straight lines and a few primary colours in carefully balanced rectangles' and capable of perceiving
the 'relaxed style of popular music' in the distance from the 'severity'
which is expected. And as soon as one imagines this painting attributed
to Gino Severini, who tries to express in some of his paintings 'the
rhythm of dance music in works of brilliant chaos', it is clear that, measured by this stylistic yardstick, Mondrian's picture would rather suggest
the first *Brandenburg* Concerto.[41]
   The aesthetic disposition, understood as the aptitude for perceiving
and deciphering specifically stylistic characteristics, is thus inseparable
from specifically artistic competence. The latter may be acquired by explicit learning or simply by regular contact with works of art, especially
those assembled in museums and galleries, where the diversity of their

Piet Mondrian, *Broadway Boogie-Woogie*

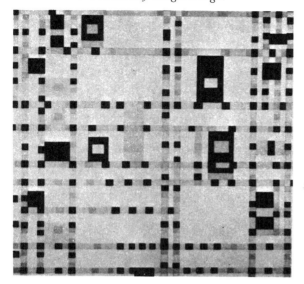

Piet Mondrian,
Painting I

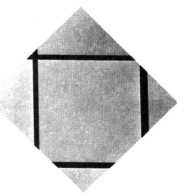

Gino Severini, *Dynamic Hieroglyphic of the Bal Tabarin*

original functions is neutralized by their being displayed in a place consecrated to art, so that they invite pure interest in form. This practical mastery enables its possessor to situate each element of a universe of artistic representations in a class defined in relation to the class composed of all the artistic representations consciously or unconsciously excluded. Thus, an awareness of the stylistic features which make up the stylistic originality of all the works of a period relative to those of another period, or, within this class, of the works of one school relative to another, or of the works of one artist relative to the works of his school or period, or even of an artist's particular period or work relative to his whole oeuvre, is inseparable from an awareness of the stylistic redundancies, i.e., the typical treatments of the pictorial matter which define a style. In short, a grasp of the resemblances presupposes implicit or explicit reference to the differences, and vice versa. Attribution is always implicitly based on reference to 'typical works', consciously or unconsciously selected because they present to a particularly high degree the qualities more or less explicitly recognized as pertinent in a given system of classification. Everything suggests that, even among specialists, the criteria of pertinence which define the stylistic properties of 'typical works' generally remain implicit and that the aesthetic taxonomies implicitly mobilized to distinguish, classify and order works of art never have the rigour which aesthetic theories sometimes try to lend them.

In fact, the simple placing which the amateur or specialist performs when he undertakes attribution has nothing in common with the genuinely scientific intention of grasping the work's immanent reason and raison d'être by reconstructing the perceived situation, the subjectively experienced problematic, which is nothing other than the space of the positions and self-positionings constituting the field and within which the artistic intention of the artist in question has defined itself, generally by opposition. The references which this reconstructing operation deploys have nothing to do with the kinds of semantic echo or affective correspondence which adorn celebratory discourse—they are the indispensable means of constructing the field of thematic or stylistic possibilities in relation to which, objectively and to some extent subjectively, the possibility selected by the artist presented itself. Thus, to understand why the early Romantic painters returned to primitive art, one would have to reconstitute the whole universe of reference of the pupils of David, with their long beards and Greek costumes, who, 'outdoing their master's cult of antiquity, wanted to go back to Homer, the Bible and Ossian, and condemned the style of classical antiquity itself as "rococo", "Van Loo" or "Pompadour".'[42] This would lead one back to the inextricably ethical and aesthetic alternatives—such as the identification of the naive with the pure and the natural—in terms of which their choices were made and which have nothing in common with the transhistorical oppositions beloved of formalist aesthetics.[43]

But the celebrant's or devotee's intention is not that of understanding, and, in the ordinary routine of the cult of the work of art, the play of academic or urbane references has no other function than to bring the work into an interminable circuit of inter-legitimation, so that a reference to Jan Breughel's *Bouquet of Flowers* lends dignity to Jean-Michel Picart's *Bouquet of Flowers with Parrot,* just as, in another context, reference to the latter can, being less common, serve to enhance the former. This play of cultured allusions and analogies endlessly pointing to other analogies, which, like the cardinal oppositions in mythical or ritual systems, never have to justify themselves by stating the basis of the relating which they perform, weaves around the works a complex web of factitious experiences, each answering and reinforcing all the others, which *creates* the enchantment of artistic contemplation. It is the source of the 'idolatry' to which Proust refers, which leads one to find 'an actress's robe or a society woman's dress beautiful ... not because the cloth is beautiful but because it is the cloth painted by Moreau or described by Balzac.'[44]

Analogy, functioning as a circular mode of thought, makes it possible to tour the whole area of art and luxury *without ever leaving it.* Thus Château Margaux wine can be described with the same words as are used to describe the château, just as others will evoke Proust apropos of Monet or César Franck, which is a good way of talking about neither: 'The house is in the image of the vintage. Noble, austere, even a little solemn. . . . Château Margaux has the air of an ancient temple devoted to the cult of wine. . . . Vineyard or dwelling, Margaux disdains all embellishments. But just as the wine has to be served before it unfolds all its charms, so the residence waits for the visitor to enter before it reveals its own. In each case the same words spring to one's lips: elegance, distinction, delicacy and that subtle satisfaction given by something which has received the most attentive and indeed loving care for generations. A wine long matured, a house long inhabited: Margaux the vintage and Margaux the château are the product of two equally rare things: *rigour and time.*'[45]

DISTANCE FROM NECESSITY   To explain the correlation between educational capital and the propensity or at least the aspiration to appreciate a work 'independently of its content', as the culturally most ambitious respondents put it, and more generally the propensity to make the 'gratuitous' and 'disinterested' investments demanded by legitimate works, it is not sufficient to point to the fact that schooling provides the linguistic tools and the references which enable aesthetic experience to be expressed and to be constituted by being expressed. What is in fact affirmed in this relationship is the dependence of the aesthetic disposition on the past and present material conditions of existence which are the precondition of both its constitution and its application and also of the accumulation of a cultural capital (whether or not educationally sanctioned) which can only be acquired by means of a sort of withdrawal from economic necessity. The aesthetic disposition which tends to bracket off the nature and function of the object represented and to exclude any 'naive' reaction—horror at the horrible, desire for the desirable, pious reverence for the sacred—along with all purely ethical responses, in order to concentrate solely upon the mode of representation, the style, perceived and appreciated by comparison with other styles, is one dimension of a total relation to the world and to others, a life-style, in which the effects of particular conditions of existence are expressed in a 'misrecognizable' form.[46] These conditions of existence, which are the precondition for all learning of legitimate culture, whether implicit and diffuse, as domestic cultural training generally is, or explicit and specific, as in scholastic training, are characterized by the suspension and removal of economic necessity and by objective and subjective distance from practical urgencies, which is the basis of objective and subjective distance from groups subjected to those determinisms.

To be able to play the games of culture with the playful seriousness which Plato demanded, a seriousness without the 'spirit of seriousness', one has to belong to the ranks of those who have been able, not necessarily to make their whole existence a sort of children's game, as artists do, but at least to maintain for a long time, sometimes a whole lifetime, a child's relation to the world. (All children start life as baby bourgeois, in a relation of magical power over others and, through them, over the world, but they grow out of it sooner or later.) This is clearly seen when, by an accident of social genetics, into the well-policed world of intellectual games there comes one of those people (one thinks of Rousseau or Chernyshevsky) who bring inappropriate stakes and interests into the games of culture; who get so involved in the game that they abandon the margin of neutralizing distance that the *illusio* (belief in the game) demands; who treat intellectual struggles, the object of so many pathetic manifestos, as a simple question of right and wrong, life and death. This is why the logic of the game has already assigned them rôles—eccentric or boor—which they will *play* despite themselves in the eyes of those who know how to stay within the bounds of the intellectual illusion and who cannot see them any other way.

The aesthetic disposition, a generalized capacity to neutralize ordinary urgencies and to bracket off practical ends, a durable inclination and aptitude for practice without a practical function, can only be constituted within an experience of the world freed from urgency and through the practice of activities which are an end in themselves, such as scholastic exercises or the contemplation of works of art. In other words, it presupposes the distance from the world (of which the 'rôle distance' brought to light by Erving Goffman is a particular case) which is the basis of the bourgeois experience of the world. Contrary to what certain mechanistic theories would suggest, even in its most specifically artistic dimension the pedagogic action of the family and the school operates at least as much through the economic and social conditions which are the precondition of its operation as through the contents which it inculcates.[47] The scholastic world of regulated games and exercise for exercise' sake is, at least in this respect, less remote than it might appear from the 'bourgeois' world and the countless 'disinterested' and 'gratuitous' acts which go to make up its distinctive rarity, such as home maintenance and decoration, occasioning a daily squandering of care, time and labour (often through the intermediary of servants), walking and tourism, movements without any other aim than physical exercise and the symbolic appropriation of a world reduced to the status of a landscape, or ceremonies and receptions, pretexts for a display of ritual luxuries, décors, conversations and finery, not to mention, of course, artistic practices and enjoyments. It is not surprising that bourgeois adolescents, who are both economically privileged and (temporarily) excluded from the reality of economic power, sometimes express their distance from the bourgeois world which they cannot really appropriate by a refusal of complicity whose most refined expression is a propensity towards aesthetics and aestheticism. In this respect they share common ground with the women of the bourgeoisie, who, being partially excluded from economic activity, find fulfilment in stage-managing the décor of bourgeois existence, when they are not seeking refuge or revenge in aesthetics.

Economic power is first and foremost a power to keep economic necessity at arm's length. This is why it universally asserts itself by the destruction of riches, conspicuous consumption, squandering, and every form of *gratuitous* luxury. Thus, whereas the court aristocracy made the whole of life a continuous spectacle, the bourgeoisie has established the opposition between what is paid for and what is free, the interested and the disinterested, in the form of the opposition, which Weber saw as characterizing it, between place of work and place of residence, working days and holidays, the outside (male) and the inside (female), business and sentiment, industry and art, the world of economic necessity and the world of artistic freedom that is snatched, by economic power, from that necessity.

Material or symbolic consumption of works of art constitutes one of the supreme manifestations of *ease,* in the sense both of objective leisure and subjective facility.[48] The detachment of the pure gaze cannot be separated from a general disposition towards the 'gratuitous' and the 'disinterested', the paradoxical product of a negative economic conditioning which, through facility and freedom, engenders distance vis-à-vis necessity. At the same time, the aesthetic disposition is defined, objectively and subjectively, in relation to other dispositions. Objective distance from necessity and from those trapped within it combines with a conscious distance which doubles freedom by exhibiting it. As the objective distance from necessity grows, life-style increasingly becomes the product of what Weber calls a 'stylization of life', a systematic commitment which orients and organizes the most diverse practices—the choice of a vintage or a cheese or the decoration of a holiday home in the country. This affirmation of power over a dominated necessity always implies a claim to a legitimate superiority over those who, because they cannot assert the same contempt for contingencies in gratuitous luxury and conspicuous consumption, remain dominated by ordinary interests and urgencies. The tastes of freedom can only assert themselves as such in relation to the tastes of necessity, which are thereby brought to the level of the aesthetic and so defined as vulgar. This claim to aristocracy is less likely to be contested than any other, because the relation of the 'pure', 'disinterested' disposition to the conditions which make it possible, i.e., the material conditions of existence which are rarest because most freed from economic necessity, has every chance of passing unnoticed. The most 'classifying' privilege thus has the privilege of appearing to be the most natural one.

THE AESTHETIC SENSE AS THE SENSE OF DISTINCTION   Thus, the aesthetic disposition is one dimension of a distant, self-assured relation to the world and to others which presupposes objective assurance and distance. It is one manifestation of the system of dispositions produced by the social conditionings associated with a particular class of conditions of existence when they take the paradoxical form of the greatest freedom conceivable, at a given moment, with respect to the constraints of economic necessity. But it is also a distinctive expression of a privileged position in social space whose distinctive value is objectively established in its relationship to expressions generated from different conditions. Like every sort of taste, it unites and separates. Being the product of the conditionings associated with a particular class of conditions of existence, it unites all those who are the product of similar conditions while distinguishing them from all others. And it distinguishes in an essential way, since taste is the basis of all that one has—people and things—and all that one is for others, whereby one classifies oneself and is classified by others.

Tastes (i.e., manifested preferences) are the practical affirmation of an inevitable difference. It is no accident that, when they have to be justified, they are asserted purely negatively, by the refusal of other tastes.[49] In matters of taste, more than anywhere else, all determination is negation;[50] and tastes are perhaps first and foremost distastes, disgust provoked by horror or visceral intolerance ('sick-making') of the tastes of others. 'De gustibus non est disputandum': not because 'tous les goûts sont dans la nature', but because each taste feels itself to be natural—and so it almost is, being a habitus—which amounts to rejecting others as unnatural and therefore vicious. Aesthetic intolerance can be terribly violent. Aversion to different life-styles is perhaps one of the strongest barriers between the classes; class endogamy is evidence of this. The most intolerable thing for those who regard themselves as the possessors of legitimate culture is the sacrilegious reuniting of tastes which taste dictates shall be separated. This means that the games of artists and aesthetes and their struggles for the monopoly of artistic legitimacy are less innocent than they seem. At stake in every struggle over art there is also the imposition of an art of living, that is, the transmutation of an arbitrary way of living into the legitimate way of life which casts every other way of living into arbitrariness.[51] The artist's life-style is always a challenge thrown at the bourgeois life-style, which it seeks to condemn as unreal and even absurd, by a sort of practical demonstration of the emptiness of the values and powers it pursues. The neutralizing relation to the world which defines the aesthetic disposition potentially implies a subversion of the spirit of seriousness required by bourgeois investments. Like the visibly ethical judgements of those who lack the means to make art the basis of their art of living, to see the world and other people through literary reminiscences and pictorial references, the 'pure' and purely aesthetic judgements of the artist and the aesthete spring from the dispositions of an ethos;[52] but because of the legitimacy which they command so long as their relationship to the dispositions and interests of a group defined by strong cultural capital and weak economic capital remains unrecognized, they provide a sort of absolute reference point in the necessarily endless play of mutually self-relativizing tastes. By a paradoxical reversal, they thereby help to legitimate the bourgeois claim to 'natural distinction' as difference made absolute.

Objectively and subjectively aesthetic stances adopted in matters like cosmetics, clothing or home decoration are opportunities to experience or assert one's position in social space, as a rank to be upheld or a distance to be kept. It goes without saying that the social classes are not equally inclined and prepared to enter this game of refusal and counter-refusal; and that the strategies aimed at transforming the basic dispositions of a life-style into a system of aesthetic principles, objective differences into elective distinctions, passive options (constituted externally by the logic of the distinctive relationships) into conscious, elective choices are in fact reserved for members of the dominant class, indeed the very top bourgeoisie, and for artists, who as the inventors and professionals of the 'stylization of life' are alone able to make their art of living one of the fine arts. By contrast, the entry of the petite bourgeoisie into the game of distinction is marked, inter alia, by the anxiety of exposing oneself to classification by offering to the taste of others such infallible indices of personal taste as clothes or furniture, even a simple pair of armchairs, as in one of Nathalie Sarraute's novels. As for the working classes, perhaps their sole function in the system of aesthetic positions is to serve as a foil, a negative reference point, in relation to which all aesthetics define themselves, by successive negations.[53] Ignoring or ignorant of manner and style, the 'aesthetic' (in itself) of the working classes and culturally most deprived fractions of the middle classes defines as 'nice', 'pretty', 'lovely' (rather than 'beautiful') things that are already defined as such in the 'aesthetic' of calendars and postcards: a sunset, a little girl playing with a cat, a folk dance, an old master, a first communion, a children's procession. The striving towards distinction comes in with petit-bourgeois aestheticism, which delights in all the cheap substitutes for chic objects and practices—driftwood and painted pebbles, cane and raffia, 'art' handicrafts and art photography.

This aestheticism defines itself against the 'aesthetic' of the working classes, refusing their favourite subjects, the themes of 'views', such as mountain landscapes, sunsets and woods, or souvenir photos, such as the first communion, the monument or the old master (see figure 2). In photography, this taste prefers objects that are close to those of the popular aesthetic but semi-neutralized by more or less explicit reference to a pictorial tradition or by a visible stylistic intention combining the human picturesque (weaver at his loom, tramps quarrelling, folk dance) with gratuitous form (pebbles, rope, tree bark).

Technicians seem to offer the purest form of 'middle-brow' taste. Their tastes in photography locate them centrally in the structure of the middle classes (see figure 2), with the craftsmen, small shopkeepers, clerical workers and junior executives inclining towards the working class and the primary teachers and new petit bourgeois inclining towards the upper classes. They are particularly drawn to the objects most typical of middle-brow photography—the weaver, the still life—whereas the new petit bourgeois prefer objects which they see as lying outside the repertoire of the traditional aesthetic and therefore more 'original' (rope, cabbages), and also those belonging to the 'social picturesque' (tramps quarrelling).

It is significant that this middle-brow art par excellence finds one of its preferred subjects in one of the spectacles most characteristic of middle-brow culture (along with the circus, light opera and bull-fights), the folk dance (which is particularly appreciated by skilled workers and foremen, junior executives, clerical and commercial employees) (C.S. VII). Like the photographic recording of the social picturesque, whose populist objectivism distances the lower classes by constituting them as an object of contemplation or even commiseration or indignation, the spectacle of the 'people' making a spectacle of itself, as in folk dancing, is an opportunity to experience the relationship of distant proximity, in the form of the idealized vision purveyed by aesthetic realism and populist nostalgia, which is a basic element in the relationship of the petite bourgeoisie to the working or peasant classes and their traditions. But this middle-brow aestheticism in turn serves as a foil to the most alert members of the new middle-class fractions, who reject its favoured subjects, and to the secondary teachers whose aestheticism (the aestheticism of consumers, since they are relatively infrequent practitioners of photography and the other arts) purports to be able to treat any object aesthetically, with the excep-

Figure 2 The aesthetic disposition in the petite bourgeoisie (the various objects are ranked for each class fraction according to the percentage saying they would make a beautiful photo).

	Independent craftsmen, shopkeepers	Clerical, junior admin. executives	Technicians	Primary teachers	New petite bourgeoisie
Most choices	sunset	sunset	sunset	sunset	sunset
	landscape	landscape	landscape	woman breast-feeding	landscape
	folk dance	folk dance	girl with cat	girl with cat	woman breast-feeding
	girl with cat	girl with cat	woman breast-feeding	landscape	girl with cat
	woman breast-feeding	woman breast-feeding	weaver	bark	bark
	weaver	old master	folk dance	weaver	weaver
	first communion	still life	still life	folk dance	still life
	old master	first communion	bark	snake	folk dance
	famous monument	bark	snake	pregnant woman	rope
	still life	monument	first communion	monument	snake
	bark of tree	weaver	monument	still life	old master
	pregnant woman	snake	metal structure	metal structure	cabbages
	metal structure	metal structure	old master	rope	pregnant woman
	snake	pregnant woman	scrap-yard	old master	metal structure
	tramps' quarrel	cabbages	rope	scrap-yard	tramps' quarrel
	wounded man	tramps' quarrel	pregnant woman	tramps' quarrel	monument
	scrap-yard	rope	cabbages	cabbages	first communion
	rope	butcher's stall	tramps' quarrel	butcher's stall	scrap-yard
	cabbages	scrap-yard	wounded man	wounded man	butcher's stall
	butcher's stall	wounded man	butcher's stall	first communion	wounded man
Fewest	car crash	car crash	car crash	car crash	car crash

tion of those so constituted by the middle-brow art of the petite bourgeoisie (such as the weaver and the folk dance, which are deemed merely 'interesting').[54] These would-be aesthetes demonstrate by their distinctive refusals that they possess the practical mastery of the relationships between objects and groups which is the basis of all judgements of the type 'Ça fait' ('It looks . . .') ('Ça fait petit-bourgeois', 'Ça fait nouveau riche' etc.), without being able to go so far as to ascribe beauty to the most marked objects of the popular aesthetic (first communion) or the petit-bourgeois aesthetic (mother and child, folk dance) which the relations of structural proximity spontaneously lead them to detest.

Explicit aesthetic choices are in fact often constituted in opposition to the choices of the groups closest in social space, with whom the competition is most direct and most immediate, and more precisely, no doubt, in relation to those choices most clearly marked by the intention (perceived as pretension) of marking distinction vis-à-vis lower groups, such as, for intellectuals, the primary teachers' Brassens, Jean Ferrat or Ferré. Thus the song, as a cultural property which (like photography) is almost universally accessible and genuinely common (since hardly anyone is not exposed at one moment or another to the 'successes' of the day), calls for particular vigilance from those who intend to mark their difference. The intellectuals, artists and higher-education teachers seem to hesitate between systematic refusal of what can only be, at best, a middle-brow art, and a selective acceptance which manifests the universality of their culture and their aesthetic disposition.[55] For their part, the employers and professionals, who have little interest in the 'intellectual' song, indicate their distance from ordinary songs by rejecting with disgust the most popular and most 'vulgar' singers, such as Les Compagnons de la Chanson, Mireille Mathieu, Adamo or Sheila, and making an exception for the oldest and most consecrated singers (like Edith Piaf or Charles Trénet) or those closest to operetta and bel canto. But it is the middle classes who find in song (as in photography) an opportunity to manifest their artistic pretension by refusing the favourite singers of the working classes, such as Mireille Mathieu, Adamo, Charles Aznavour or Tino Rossi, and declaring their preference for the singers who endeavour to dignify this 'minor' genre. That is why the primary teachers distinguish themselves most clearly from the other fractions of the petite bourgeoisie in this area, where, more easily than in the domain of legitimate art, they can invest their academic dispositions and assert their own taste in the choice of singers who offer populist poetry in the primary-school tradition, such as Jacques Douai or Brassens (who was on the syllabus of the Saint-Cloud entrance examination a few years ago).[56]

In addition to the data provided by the survey question, use was also made of the findings of a survey by the opinion research department of the

French broadcasting service (ORTF) (C.S. XIX) and of thirty in-depth interviews designed to grasp the constellation of preferences and refusals in conditions as close as possible to ordinary conversation. These interviews confirmed that, as the ORTF survey also shows, the more strongly a singer is preferred by the less cultivated, the more he or she is refused by the most cultivated—whose tastes in this area are almost exclusively expressed in rejections. These refusals, almost always expressed in the mode of distaste, are often accompanied by pitying or indignant remarks about the corresponding tastes ('I can't understand how anyone can like that!').

Similarly, one finds that the declining petite bourgeoisie systematically rejects the virtues that the new petite bourgeoisie most readily claims for itself (witty, refined, stylish, artistic, imaginative); whereas the latter signals its aesthetic pretension by a refusal of the most typically 'bourgeois' configurations and by a concern to go against common judgements, in which aesthetic commitments figure prominently. Thus, when asked to state the ideal qualities of a friend or a domestic interior, they produce motley combinations such as: 'artistic, sociable, amusing, comfortable, easy to maintain, imaginative' (sales representative, Paris), 'dynamic, pragmatic, stylish, studied, warm, imaginative' (gallery director, Lille), 'dynamic, refined, pragmatic, comfortable, harmonious, cosy' (radio presenter, Lille). It is again a similar process that leads the members of the professions to distinguish themselves from newcomers to the bourgeoisie by rejecting the qualities of ambition and upward mobility, such as 'pragmatic', 'dynamic' (often chosen by managerial executives), or the most 'pretentious' adjectives, such as 'stylish' or 'refined', which are much favoured by the new petite bourgeoisie.

It may also be assumed that the affirmation of the omnipotence of the aesthetic gaze found among higher-education teachers, the group most inclined to say that all the objects mentioned could make a beautiful photograph and to profess their recognition of modern art or of the artistic status of the photograph, stems much more from a self-distinguishing intention than from a true aesthetic universalism. This has not escaped the most knowing avant-garde producers, who carry sufficient authority to challenge, if need be, the very dogma of the omnipotence of art,[57] and are in a position to recognize this faith as a defensive manoeuvre to avoid self-exposure by reckless refusals: 'Who would say this: "When I look at a picture, I'm not interested in what it represents"? Nowadays, the sort of people who don't know much about art. Saying that is typical of someone who hasn't any idea about art. Twenty years ago, I'm not even sure that twenty years ago the abstract painters would have said that; I don't think so. It's exactly what a guy says when he hasn't a clue: "I'm not one of these old fogies, I know what counts is whether it's pretty" ' (avant-garde painter, age 35). They alone, at all events, can afford the audacious imposture of refusing all refusals by recuperating, in parody or sublimation, the very objects refused by the lower-degree aestheticism. The 'rehabilitation' of 'vulgar' objects is more risky, but also more 'profitable', the smaller the distance in social space or time, and the 'horrors' of popular kitsch are easier to 'recuperate' than those of petit-bourgeois imitation, just as the 'abominations' of bourgeois taste can begin to be found 'amusing' when they are sufficiently dated to cease to be 'compromising'.

Suffice it to point out that, in addition to those subjects which had already been constituted as aesthetic at the time of the survey, either by a pictorial tradition (e.g., the metal frame of Léger or Gromaire, the tramps quarrelling, a variant of an old theme of realist painting often taken up in photography, or the butcher's stall), or by the photographic tradition (e.g., the weaver, the folk dance, the bark), most of the 'banal' subjects have subsequently been constituted aesthetically by one avant-garde painter or another (for example, the sunset over the sea, by Richer, who paints typically romantic landscapes from photographs, or Long and Fulton, English painters who make 'conceptual' landscape photographs, or even Land Art; or the car crash, by Andy Warhol; or the tramps' quarrel, with the 'tramps sleeping in the Bowery' of the American hyper-realists; or the first communion, by Boltanski, who has even given artistic status to the family album etc.). The only 'unrecuperated' and, for the moment, 'irrecuperable' subjects are the favourite themes of first-degree aestheticism, the weaver at his loom, the folk dance, the tree-bark, and the woman suckling a child. They are too close to favour the flaunting of an absolute power of aesthetic constitution; and because they do not allow distance to be manifested, they are more liable to be mistaken for 'first-degree' intentions. Reappropriation is that much more difficult when the aesthetic-in-itself which it works on clearly manifests recognition of the dominant aesthetic so that the distinctive deviation is liable to go unnoticed.

The artist agrees with the 'bourgeois' in one respect: he prefers naivety to 'pretentiousness'. The essential merit of the 'common people' is that they have none of the pretensions to art (or power) which inspire the ambitions of the 'petit bourgeois'. Their indifference tacitly acknowledges the monopoly. That is why, in the mythology of artists and intellectuals, whose outflanking and double-negating strategies sometimes lead them back to 'popular' tastes and opinions, the 'people' so often play a role not unlike that of the peasantry in the conservative ideologies of the declining aristocracy.

In fact, their 'pretension' leaves the petit bourgeois particularly disarmed in the less legitimate or not-yet legitimate domains which the cultural 'elite' abandon to them, whether in photography or in cinema, in which their ambitions are often expressed (as is shown, for example, in the fact that the gap between the petite bourgeoisie and the bourgeoisie is much less wide regarding knowledge of cinema directors than of composers). The new-style petit bourgeois, who, confronted with objectively ranked judgements, are able to choose the 'right' answer, are almost as disarmed as the working classes when faced with an opportunity for aesthetic constitution of an object (not a single small art-dealer says that a car accident can make a beautiful photo, and the scrap-yard arouses similar responses).

Cultural Pedigree

While variations in educational capital are always very closely related to variations in competence, even in areas, like cinema or jazz, which are neither taught nor directly assessed by the educational system, the fact remains that, at equivalent levels of educational capital, differences in social origin (whose 'effects' are already expressed in differences in educational capital) are associated with important differences in competence. These differences become all the more striking (except at the highest educational levels, where over-selection tends to neutralize differences of trajectory), firstly, when one appeals less to a strict, and strictly assessable, competence and more to a sort of familiarity with culture; and, secondly, as one moves from the most 'scholastic' and 'classical' areas of culture to less legitimate and more 'outlandish' areas of the 'extra-curricular' culture, which is not taught in schools but is valued in the academic market and can often yield high symbolic profit. The relative weight of educational capital in the system of explanatory factors can even be much weaker than that of social origin when the respondents are only required to express a status-induced familiarity with legitimate or soon-to-be legitimated culture, a paradoxical relationship made up of that mixture of self-assurance and (relative) ignorance, expressing true bourgeois rights, which are measured by seniority.

At equal educational levels, the proportion who say they know at least twelve of the musical works mentioned increases more·sharply than the proportion who can attribute at least twelve of them to their composers, as one moves from the working class to the upper class (and the gap is very narrow among graduates) (see table 4). The same logic governs the differences by sex, except that they are less marked. Whereas, as regards composers, no differences are found between the sexes among individuals of the same class, strong differences appear in favour of women as regards familiarity with works, especially in the middle and upper classes (in the working class, this knowledge is very limited in both sexes); in the two most feminine occupational categories—the medical and social services and secretaries—all the persons questioned claimed to know at least three of the works. This difference in the experiential or stated relationship to music is no doubt partly explained by the fact that the traditional division of labour assigns to women familiarity with the things of art and literature.

The differences linked to social origin are also very strong as regards knowledge of film directors, which, at equal educational levels, rises with social origin. So too does the proportion who assert that 'ugly' or trivial

Table 4 Knowledge of composers and musical works by education and class of origin (%).

Educational qualification	Class of origin	Number of composers known				Number of works known			
		0–2	3–6	7–11	12+	0–2	3–6	7–11	12+
None, CEP, CAP	Working	69.5	23.5	5.5	1.5	32.5	48.5	17.5	1.5
	Middle	68.5	21.0	8.5	2.0	21.0	55.0	19.5	4.5
	Upper	46.0	25.0	8.5	20.5	12.5	33.5	29.0	25.0
	All classes	67.0	22.0	7.5	3.5	24.5	51.0	19.5	5.0
BEPC	Working	57.5	15.5	23.0	4.0	15.5	27.0	50.0	7.5
	Middle	48.5	35.5	9.5	6.5	8.5	43.0	34.5	14.0
	Upper	31.5	41.5	13.5	13.5	8.0	31.5	41.0	19.5
	All classes	44.5	34.0	13.0	8.5	9.5	37.0	39.0	14.5
Baccalauréat	Working	11.0	59.5	18.5	11.0	0	33.0	52.0	15.0
	Middle	19.0	32.0	38.0	11.0	3.5	26.5	51.0	19.0
	Upper	21.5	21.5	37.5	19.5	5.0	19.5	42.5	33.0
	All classes	18.5	32.5	35.5	13.5	3.5	25.5	48.5	22.5
Technical college, some higher education	Working	20.0	0	70.0	10.0	0	30.0	60.0	10.0
	Middle	16.0	22.5	51.5	10.0	13.0	19.5	54.5	13.0
	Upper	17.5	11.5	39.0	32.0	11.5	11.5	33.5	43.5
	All classes	17.5	13.5	45.5	23.5	11.0	15.5	42.0	31.5
Licence, agrégation, grande école	Working	0	35.0	32.5	32.5	0	7.0	66.5	26.5
	Middle	7.0	15.0	47.5	30.5	0	22.0	49.0	29.0
	Upper	7.5	15.5	44.5	32.5	8.0	13.5	38.5	40.0
	All classes	7.0	16.5	44.5	32.0	5.5	15.0	43.0	36.5

objects can make a beautiful photograph. Needless to say, corresponding to the different modes of acquisition, there are differences in the nature of the works preferred. The differences linked to social origin tend to increase as one moves away from the academic curriculum, from literature to painting or classical music and a fortiori jazz or avant-garde art.

An earlier survey showed that students of working-class or middle-class origin who had scores similar to those of students of bourgeois origin in classical culture fell back as the test moved towards 'extra-curricular' culture, i.e., both avant-garde theatre and Paris 'boulevard' (middle-brow) theatre. One finds an entirely analogous relation here between the artistic producers and the secondary teachers (or even the art teachers, who—as is evident in another survey now being analysed—especially when they are of working-class or middle-class origin, mostly have very 'classical' tastes and are much closer to the teachers than to the artists).

Those who have acquired the bulk of their cultural capital in and for school have more 'classical', safer cultural investments than those who have received a large cultural inheritance. For example, whereas the members of the dominant class with the highest qualifications (the *agrégation* or a diploma from a *grande école*) never mention certain works or certain painters typical of middle-brow culture, such as Buffet or Utrillo, have considerable knowledge of composers, and prefer the *Well-Tempered Clavier* or the *Firebird Suite,* the highly educated members of the working and middle classes more often make choices which indicate their respect for a more 'scholastic' culture (Goya, Leonardo, Breughel, Watteau, Raphael), and a significant proportion of them concur with the opinion that 'paintings are nice but difficult'. By contrast, those who originate from the dominant class know more works and more often choose works further from 'scholastic' culture (Braque, *Concerto for the Left Hand*). Similarly, those members of the established petite bourgeoisie (craftsmen, shopkeepers, clerical and commercial employees, junior executives) who have relatively low educational capital (BEPC or below) make choices clearly marked by their trajectory. Thus, those who are rising socially show their respect for legitimate culture in various ways (e.g., they are more likely to agree that 'paintings are nice but difficult') and choose works typical of middle-brow (Buffet, Utrillo) or even popular taste (*Blue Danube*). However, those whose fathers belonged to the upper classes manifest, at equivalent levels of educational capital, greater familiarity with musical works (although they are no more familiar with the composers' names), just as they more often say they like the Impressionists, visit museums more often and more often choose academically consecrated works (Raphael or Leonardo).

MANNERS AND MANNER OF ACQUISITION   Cultural (or linguistic) competence, which is acquired in relation to a particular field functioning both as a source of inculcation and as a market, remains defined by its conditions of acquisition. These conditions, perpetuated in the mode of utilization—i.e., in a given relationship to culture or language—function like a sort of 'trade-mark', and, by linking that competence to a particular market, help to define the value of its products in the various markets. In other words, what are grasped through indicators such as educational level or social origin or, more precisely, in the structure of the relationship between them, are *also* different modes of production of the cultivated habitus, which engender differences not only in the competences acquired but also in the manner of applying them. These differences in manner constitute a set of secondary properties, revealing different conditions of acquisition and predisposed to receive very different values in the various markets.

Knowing that 'manner' is a symbolic manifestation whose meaning and value depend as much on the perceivers as on the producer, one can see how it is that the manner of using symbolic goods, especially those regarded as the attributes of excellence, constitutes one of the key markers of 'class' and also the ideal weapon in strategies of distinction, that is, as Proust put it, 'the infinitely varied art of marking distances'. The ideology of natural taste contrasts two modalities of cultural competence and its use, and, behind them, two modes of acquisition of culture.[58] Total, early, imperceptible learning, performed within the family from the earliest days of life and extended by a scholastic learning which presupposes and completes it, differs from belated, methodical learning not so much in the depth and durability of its effects—as the ideology of cultural 'veneer' would have it—as in the modality of the relationship to language and culture which it simultaneously tends to inculcate.[59] It confers the self-certainty which accompanies the certainty of possessing cultural legitimacy, and the ease which is the touchstone of excellence; it produces the paradoxical relationship to culture made up of self-confidence amid (relative) ignorance and of casualness amid familiarity, which bourgeois families hand down to their offspring as if it were an heirloom.

The competence of the 'connoisseur', an unconscious mastery of the instruments of appropriation which derives from slow familiarization and is the basis of familiarity with works, is an 'art', a practical mastery which, like an art of thinking or an art of living, cannot be transmitted solely by precept or prescription. Learning it presupposes the equivalent of the prolonged contact between disciple and master in a traditional education, i.e., repeated contact with cultural works and cultured people. And just as the apprentice or disciple can unconsciously acquire the rules of the art, including those that are not consciously known to the master himself, by means of a self-abandonment, excluding analysis and selection of the elements of the exemplary conduct, so too the art-lover, in a sense surrendering himself to the work, can internalize its principles of construction, without these ever being brought to his consciousness and formulated or formulable as such; and this is what makes all the difference between the theory of art and the experience of the connoisseur, who is generally incapable of stating the principles of his judgements. By contrast, all institutionalized learning presupposes a degree of rationalization, which leaves its mark on the relationship to the goods consumed. The sovereign pleasure of the aesthete dispenses with concepts. It is opposed as much to the thoughtless pleasure of the 'naive' (glorified in ideology through the myth of childhood and the innocent eye) as to the supposedly pleasureless thought of the petit bourgeois and the 'parvenu', who are always exposed to those forms of aesthetic perversion which put knowledge above experience and sacrifice contemplation of the work to discussion of the work, *aisthesis* to *askesis,* like film-buffs who know everything there is to know about films they have not seen.[60] Not that the educational system ever entirely fulfils its rational function: the essential part of what schools communicate is again acquired incidentally, such as the system of classification which the school system inculcates through the order in which it inculcates knowledge or through the presuppositions of its own organization (the hierarchy of disciplines, sections, exercises etc.) or its operation (mode of assessment, rewards and punishments etc.). But, in order to transmit at all, it has to perform a degree of rationalization of what it transmits. Thus, for example, in place of practical schemes of classification, which are always partial and linked to practical contexts, it puts explicit, standardized taxonomies, fixed once and for all in the form of synoptic schemas or dualistic typologies (e.g., 'classical'/'romantic'), which are expressly inculcated and therefore conserved in the memory as knowledge that can be reproduced in virtually identical form by all the agents subjected to its action.

To avoid any absolutization of the culture in relation to which the autodidact's middle-brow culture is objectively defined, it has to be remembered that the higher one rises in the social hierarchy, the more one's tastes are shaped by the organization and operation of the educational system, which is responsible for inculcating the 'programme' (syllabus and intellectual schemes) which governs 'cultivated minds' even in their pursuit of the 'personal touch' and their aspiration to 'originality'. Discrepancies between educational qualifications and cultural competence (linked to social trajectory and largely attributable to the domestic transmission of non-scholastic cultural capital) are, however, sufficiently frequent to safeguard the irreducibility, recognized even by academics, of 'authentic' culture to 'scholastic' knowledge, which as such is devalued.

By providing the means of expression which enable practical preferences to be brought to the level of quasi-systematic discourse and to be consciously organized around explicit principles, the educational system makes possible a (more or less adequate) symbolic mastery of the practical principles of taste. As grammar does for linguistic competence, it rationalizes the 'sense of beauty', in those who already have it, giving them the means of referring to principles (of harmony or rhetoric, for example), precepts, formulae, instead of relying on improvisation; it substitutes the intentional quasi systematicity of a formal aesthetic for the objective systematicity of the 'aesthetic-in-itself' produced by the practical principles of taste. Thus academicism is potentially present in every rational pedagogy which tends to convey piecemeal, in a doctrinal set of explicit norms and formulae, explicitly taught, generally negative rather than positive, what traditional learning transmits in the form of a total style directly grasped in practice. But above all—and this is why aesthetes so abhor pedagogues and pedagogy—the rational teaching of art provides substitutes for direct experience, it offers short cuts on the long path of familiarization, it makes possible practices which are the product of concepts and rules instead of springing from the supposed spontaneity of taste, thereby offering a solution to those who hope to make up for lost time.

The ideology of natural taste owes its plausibility and its efficacy to the fact that, like all the ideological strategies generated in the everyday class struggle, it *naturalizes* real differences, converting differences in the mode of acquisition of culture into differences of nature; it only recognizes as legitimate the relation to culture (or language) which least bears the visible marks of its genesis, which has nothing 'academic', 'scholastic', 'bookish', 'affected' or 'studied' about it, but manifests by its ease and naturalness that true culture is nature—a new mystery of immaculate conception. This is clearly seen in the remarks of an aesthete of the culinary art, who writes no differently from Pierre Francastel when the latter, in a devastating confession for an art historian, rejects 'intellectualized knowledge', which can only 'recognize', in favour of 'visual experience', the sole means of access to 'true vision':[61]

'*Taste* must not be confused with *gastronomy*. Whereas taste is the *natural gift* of recognizing and loving perfection, gastronomy is the set of *rules* which govern the cultivation and *education* of taste. Gastronomy is to taste as *grammar* and literature are to the *literary sense*. And this brings us to the heart of the problem: if the gourmet is a delicate *connoisseur,* is the gastronome a *pedant?* . . . The gourmet is his own gastronome, just as the man of taste is his own grammarian . . . Not everyone is a gourmet; that is why we need gastronomes. We must look upon gastronomes as we look upon pedagogues in general: they are sometimes intolerable pedants, but they have their uses. They belong to the *lower, modest order,* and it is up to them to improve this *rather minor genre* by means of tact, restraint and elegant lightness . . . There is such a thing as bad taste . . . and persons of *refinement* know this *instinctively.* For those who do not, rules are needed.'[62]

Knowledge by experience, which, like Aquinas's *cognitio Dei experimentalis,* feels and deplores the essential inadequacy of words and concepts to express the reality 'tasted' in mystical union, rejects as unworthy the intellectual love of art, the knowledge which identifies experience of the work with an intellectual operation of deciphering.[63]

SCHOLARS AND GENTLEMEN   The differences in manner that indicate differences in mode of acquisition—i.e., in seniority of access to the dominant class—which are generally associated with differences in com-

Court Wit and Fusty Learning

TRISSOTIN
I'm not surprised to hear this
    gentleman say
The things he's said in this unpleas-
    ant fray.
He's much at court, and as one
    might expect,
He shares the court's mistrust of
    intellect,
And, as a courtier, defends with zest
The ignorance that's in his interest.

CLITANDRE
You're very hard indeed on the
    poor court,
Which hears each day how people
    of your sort,
Who deal in intellectual wares,
    decry it,
Complain that their careers are
    blighted by it,
Deplore its wretched taste, and
    blame their own
Unhappy failures on that cause
    alone.
Permit me, Mister Trissotin, with
    due

Respect for your great name, to say
    that you
And all your kind would do well
    to discuss
The court in tones less harsh and
    querulous;
That the court is not so short of
    wit and brain
As you and all your scribbling
    friends maintain;
That all things there are viewed
    with common sense,
That good taste, too, is much in
    evidence,
And that its knowledge of the
    world surpasses
The fusty learning of pedantic asses.

TRISSOTIN
It has good taste, you say? If only
    it had!

CLITANDRE
What makes you say, Sir, that its
    taste is bad?

J. B. P. de Molière, *Les femmes savantes*
(1672) in *The Learned Ladies*, translated
into English verse by Richard Wilbur
(New York and London, Harcourt Brace
Jovanovich, 1978), pp. 117–118.

position of capital, are predisposed to mark differences within the dominant class, just as differences in cultural capital mark the differences between the classes.[64] That is why manners, especially the manner of
relationship to legitimate culture, are the stake in a permanent struggle.
There can be no neutral statement in these matters: the terms designating the opposing dispositions can be taken as complimentary or pejorative depending on the point of view. It is no accident that the opposition
between the 'scholastic' (or 'pedantic') and the *mondain,* the effort-
lessly elegant, is at the heart of debates over taste and culture in every
age: behind two ways of producing or appreciating cultural works,
it very clearly designates two contrasting modes of acquisition, and,
in the modern period at least, two different relationships to the educational system.

In France, literary debate in the first half of the seventeenth century was dominated by the antagonism between the *doctes*—Chapelain, Balzac, La Mesnardière, Faret, Colletet, d'Aubignac etc., who looked to Italian theorists, and ultimately to Aristotle, for the rules they sought to impose on the construction of literary works,[65] and at the same time strove to ground these rules in reason—and the *mondains,* who refused to be bound by precept, made their pleasure their guide and pursued the infinitesimal nuances which make up the 'je ne sais quoi' and the delicate perfection of savoir vivre. The great debates over taste which literary works arouse or dramatize (such as the question of the précieux, who by codifying and rationalizing salon delicacy, an art of living defined as indefinable, changed its whole nature) involve not only the virtues with which the different fractions of the dominant class identify, but, as the Chevalier de Méré so well puts it, 'the manners of practising them, which are themselves kinds of virtues', and through which seniority in their class, and their way of getting there, are expressed or betrayed.

Innumerable illustrations could be cited from the vast literature designed to codify, inseparably, ordinary behaviour and the creation and perception of works of art, in short everything which falls under the absolute jurisdiction of taste, one of the key words of the age;[66] but one example will suffice, because it explicitly links manner, mode of acquisition and the group it designates: 'The author [Furetière, the bourgeois author of *Le Roman bourgeois* who had criticized La Fontaine and Benserade] shows clearly that he is neither of society nor of the court and that his taste is of a pedantry one cannot even hope to rectify. Certain things are never understood if they are not understood at once: some hard and rough minds will never be led into the charm and grace of Benserade's ballets and La Fontaine's fables. That door is closed to them, and so is mine ... One can only pray to God for such a man and hope never to have dealings with him' (Mme. de Sévigné, letter to Bussy-Rabutin, 14 May 1686).

Paradoxically, precocity is an effect of seniority: aristocracy is the form par excellence of precocity since it is nothing other than the seniority which is the birthright of the offspring of ancient families (at least in societies in which age and aristocracy—virtually equivalent notions—are recognized as values). And this initial status-derived capital is enhanced by the advantages which precocious acquisition of legitimate culture gives in learning cultural skills, whether table manners or the art of conversation, musical culture or the sense of propriety, playing tennis or pronunciation. The embodied cultural capital of the previous generations functions as a sort of advance (both a head-start and a credit) which, by providing from the outset the example of culture incarnated in familiar models, enables the newcomer to start acquiring the basic elements of

Ease or Cultivated Naturalness

'I would have a man know everything and yet, by his manner of speaking, not be convicted of having studied.' Antoine Gombaud, Chevalier de Méré (1607–1685), *De la conversation*.

'What needs correction in most teachers is something too composed, which reeks of art and study. The aim must be to make it seem natural.' Méré, *Des agrémens*.

'But kind words on all matters, agreeably uttered, will gratify every listener. Wit cannot go further, it is the masterpiece of intelligence. . . . Say to them nothing which savours of study or seems far-fetched. Above all, since they are well pleased with their own worth, refrain from instructing them on any matter, or correcting them, whatever mistakes you observe them to make.' Méré, *De la conversation*.

'This civility is perceived in the features, the manner, in the slightest actions of the body and mind; and the more one considers it, the more one is charmed by it, without realizing where it comes from. . . . For everything that is done out of constraint or servitude, or has any trace of coarseness, destroys it. And to render a person amiable in his ways, you should please him as much as you can and take care not to burden him with tedious instructions.' Méré, *Des agrémens*.

'Persons of refinement are sometimes obliged to turn a hand to many things, even the things of which they know least. In such a case, they should not behave like professional craftsmen, whose sole concern is to finish their task. A gentleman should seek, not so much to be expert in what he undertakes, as to undertake it like a gentleman . . . This air of ease which comes from a fortunate birth and an excellent habit is one of the amenities of a gentleman; he should set about even the most difficult task with such detachment that it seems to cost him no effort.' Méré, *Des agrémens*.

the legitimate culture, from the beginning, that is, in the most unconscious and impalpable way—and to dispense with the labour of deculturation, correction and retraining that is needed to undo the effects of inappropriate learning. Legitimate manners owe their value to the fact that they manifest the rarest conditions of acquisition, that is, a social power over time which is tacitly recognized as the supreme excellence: to possess things from the past, i.e., accumulated, crystallized history, aristocratic names and titles, châteaux or 'stately homes', paintings and collections, vintage wines and antique furniture, is to master time, through all those things whose common feature is that they can only be acquired in the course of time, by means of time, against time, that is, by inheritance or through dispositions which, like the taste for old things, are likewise only acquired with time and applied by those who can take their time.

Every group tends to set up the means of perpetuating itself beyond the finite individuals in whom it is incarnated. (This was one of Durkheim's fundamental insights.) In order to do so, it establishes a whole set of mechanisms, such as delegation, representation and symbolization, which confer ubiquity and eternity. The representative (e.g., the king) is eternal. As Kantarovitch has shown, the king has two bodies, a biological, mortal body, subject to biological infirmities, passion or imbecility, and a political body, immortal, immaterial and freed from infirmities or weaknesses.[67] He can secure ubiquity by delegating to others the authority with which he is invested. His taxes are levied by *fiscus ubique presens,* and, as Post observes, the delegate who holds *plena potestas agendi* 'can do everything that the mandator himself can do', thanks to his *procuratio ad omnia facienda.*[68] Again, *universitas non moritur.* Death, from the point of view of groups, is only an accident, and personified collectives organize themselves in such a way that the demise of the mortal bodies which once embodied the group—representatives, delegates, agents, spokesmen—does not affect the existence of the group or the function in which it is realized: *dignitas non moritur.*

If this is accepted (and it would need to be established more systematically), then capital makes it possible to appropriate the collectively produced and accumulated means of really overcoming anthropological limits. The means of escaping from generic alienations include representation, the portrait or statue which immortalizes the person represented (sometimes, by a sort of pleonasm, in his own lifetime); and memorials, the tombstone, the written word, *aere perennius,* which celebrates and 'hands on to posterity', and, in particular, historical writing, which gives a place in legitimate history—hence the particular status which the public, especially the bourgeois public, gives to historians, the masters of scientific eternization—and the commemorative ceremonies in which the group offers tributes of homage and gratitude to the dead, who are thereby shown to be still living and active. Thus it can be seen that eternal life is one of the most sought-after social privileges; the quality of the eternity depends, of course, on the quality and extent of the group providing it, and can range from a requiem mass organized by the family to an annual national holiday.

If the foregoing argument suggests an 'analysis of essence' (though far removed, it would seem, from Heidegger and his 'old chest'), that is because most groups have sought to lay down absolute, final differences by means of the irreversibility of time, which gives inflexible rigour to every form of social order based on the order of successions. The holders and claimants to succession—father and son, owner and heir, master and disciple, predecessor and successor—are separated by nothing, except time; but there is every sort of social mechanism to make this gap unbridgeable. Thus, in the struggle between the different 'manners', i.e., the different manners of acquiring, the dominant groups are always on the side of the most insensible and invisible mode of acquisition, that is, the oldest and most precious one. This is what provides the invariant elements of the dominant discourse and gives an air of eternal youth to certain themes, although they are in reality strictly situated and dated, like all the commonplaces of elegant disquisition on innate taste or the blundering of 'pedants'.

A practical mastery of social significance, based on functional and structural homology, underlies and facilitates everyday reading of the 'classics', and, even more, since it is a practical use, literary quotation, a quite special use of discourse which is a sort of summons to appear as advocate and witness, addressed to a past author on the basis of a social solidarity disguised as intellectual solidarity. The practical sense of meaning, which stops short of objectifying the social affinity which makes it possible—since that would nullify the desired effect, by relativizing both the reading and the text—provides simultaneously a social use and a denial of the social basis of that use.

Identifying the invariants must not, however, lead us to treat a particular state of the struggle as eternal, and a true comparative study would have to take account of the specific forms that the struggle and the themes in which it is expressed take on when the objective relations between the class fractions change. It seems, for example, that in the second half of the seventeenth century the growing authority of the mondains and of the court, combined with the tendency of high society to become more cultivated, reduced the distance between doctes and mondains; this led to the rise of a new species of man of letters, typified by the Jesuits Rapin and Bouhours,[69] masters of rhetoric who were themselves both doctes and mondains, who frequented artists and aristocrats and helped to produce a synthesis of the demands of the court and the academy (and did so by shifting the centre of the debate from the question of worthy subjects to that of the style in which they might be treated).

Similarly, nowadays, the fact that an increasingly large proportion of the business bourgeoisie is making intensive use of the educational system (and especially, in France, the *grandes écoles*) is tending to modify the form of the relationship between the mondain and the scholastic—cultural excellence increasingly belongs to those who combine the two modes of acquisition—and consequently the content of the ritual antitheses in which the opposition between 'scholars' and 'gentlemen' is expressed.[70]

The case of the relations between the nineteenth-century German universities and the princely courts represents another state of the power relation, resulting in a different configuration of the images of the scholarly virtues and the courtly virtues. As Norbert Elias very clearly shows, bourgeois intellectuals were much earlier and much more completely integrated into the world of the court in France than in Germany. The conventions of style and forms of civility which dominate the educational system and all its products, in particular the attention given to language and to intellectual propriety, derived, in the case of France, from court society, whereas in Germany the intelligentsia, especially in the universities, set itself up in opposition to the court and the French models it was importing, summing up its vision of 'high society' in the antithesis between 'Civilization', characterized by frivolity and superficiality, and 'Culture', defined by seriousness, profundity and authenticity.[71] In other words, there is the same basic opposition between doctes and mondains, with identical content, but with the values reversed: here the doctes could not assert their autonomy except by asserting their own virtues and their own 'manner of practising them', thereby devaluing high-society virtues.

The fact remains that the 'pedant's' situation is never entirely comfortable. Against the 'populace' and with the mondain aristocracy—who have every reason also to accept it, since they have an interest in birth-rights—he is inclined to accept the ideology of innate tastes, since it is the only absolute guarantee of his election; but against the mondain he is forced to assert the value of his acquirements, and, indeed, the value of the work of acquisition, the 'slow effort to improve the mind', as Kant put it, which is a blemish in the eyes of the mondain, but in his own eyes his supreme merit.

The embarrassment of academic minds, indebted and committed to acquisition, surfaces whenever it is a question of the adequate approach to a work of art and the right way to acquire it; and the contradiction is at the heart of all their aesthetic theories, not to mention their attempts to establish a pedagogy of art. The ideology of natural gifts is too potent, even within the educational system, for an expression of faith in the powers of a rational pedagogy aimed at reducing the practical schemes of familiarity to codified rules, despite the fact that this practical affirmation of the 'natural right' to art is the natural weapon of those who appeal to knowledge and ideas and aim to discredit the divine right of the advocates of immediate experience and pleasure. For example, there are all the debates over the teaching of art (more specifically, the teaching of drawing)—a contradiction in terms for some, who hold that beauty is neither taught nor learnt, but is a grace transmitted from invested masters to predestined disciples; for others, a field of pedagogy like any other. (One thinks, for example, of the polemics between the advocates of rational pedagogy, such as Guillaume, and the champions of the charismatic view, such as Ravaisson, over the introduction of drawing lessons into general education in the early years of the Third Republic.)

EXPERIENCE AND KNOWLEDGE   Ideology is an illusion consistent with interest, but a well-grounded illusion. Those who invoke experience against knowledge have a basis for their prejudice in the real opposition between the domestic learning and the scholastic learning of culture.

Bourgeois culture and the bourgeois relation to culture owe their inimitable character to the fact that, like popular religion as seen by Groethuysen, they are acquired, pre-verbally, by early immersion in a world of cultivated people, practices and objects. When the child grows up in a household in which music is not only listened to (on hi-fi or radio nowadays) but also performed (the 'musical mother' of bourgeois autobiography), and a fortiori when the child is introduced at an early age to a 'noble' instrument—especially the piano—the effect is at least to produce a more familiar relationship to music, which differs from the always somewhat distant, contemplative and often verbose relation of those who have come to music through concerts or even only through records, in much the same way as the relation to painting of those who have discovered it belatedly, in the quasi-scholastic atmosphere of the museum, differs from the relation developed by those born into a world filled with art objects, familiar family property, amassed by successive generations, testifying to their wealth and good taste, and sometimes 'home-made' (like jam or embroidered linen).

Differences linked to social origin are no doubt most marked in personal production of visual art or the playing of a musical instrument, aptitudes which, both in their acquisition and in their performance, presuppose not only dispositions associated with long establishment in the world of art and culture but also economic means (especially in the case of piano-playing) and spare time. At equal educational levels, they vary strongly by social origin. Thus, among holders of the *baccalauréat,* 11.5 percent of the respondents who originate from the dominant class say they often play a musical instrument, compared with 5 percent of those of middle-class or working-class origin. Among graduates, the corresponding proportions are 22.5 percent and 5 percent. Painting and sculpture, relatively neglected by those with the highest qualifications, are also, at equal educational levels, much more common among respondents of dominant-class origin.

Status-linked familiarity is manifested in, for example, knowledge of the opportunities and conditions for acquiring works of art, which depends not only on the material and cultural capacity to appropriate but also on long-standing membership in a social world in which art, being an object of appropriation, is present in the form of familiar, personal objects. Thus, in the survey commissioned by the Ministry of Culture (C.S. VII), the percentage of respondents able to give an answer when asked the lowest price at which 'one can now buy an original lithograph or serigraph by a contemporary professional artist' varies considerably by social class, ranging from 10.2 percent of agricultural workers, 13.6 percent of unskilled and semi-skilled workers and 17.6 percent of clerical and commercial employees to 66.6 percent of senior executives and professionals.

The choice of works such as the *Concerto for the Left Hand* (much more frequent among those who play an instrument—especially the piano—than among others) or *L'Enfant et les sortilèges* is much more strongly linked to social origin than to educational capital. By contrast, with works like the *Well-Tempered Clavier* or the *Art of Fugue*, there is a stronger correlation with educational capital than with social origin. Through these indicators, despite their imperfections, one can distinguish different relations to the hierarchical, hierarchizing world of cultural works, which are closely linked to a set of interrelated differences and which stem from different modes of acquisition—domestic *and* scholastic, or exclusively scholastic—of cultural capital. Thus, when Roland Barthes makes an aesthetic out of a particular relation to music, produced by early, domestic, 'practical' acquaintance, and describes aesthetic enjoyment as a sort of immediate communication between the listener's body and the performer's 'inner body', present in 'the grain of the singer's voice' or 'the pad of the pianist's fingers', he is in fact referring to the opposition between two modes of acquisition.

On the one hand, there is music for record collectors (linked to a demand arising from the 'growth of the number of listeners and the disappearance of practitioners'), an expressive, dramatic, sentimentally clear art of communication, of understanding: 'This culture ... wants art, wants music, provided they be clear, that they "translate" an emotion and represent a signified (the "meaning" of a poem): an art that inoculates pleasure (by reducing it to a known, coded emotion) and reconciles the subject to what in music *can be said:* what is said about it by Institution, Criticism, Opinion.'[72] On the other hand, there is an art which prefers the sensible to sense, which hates eloquence, grandiloquence, pathos and the pathetic, the expressive and the dramatic. This is French *mélodie,* Duparc, the later Fauré, Debussy, everything that in another age would have been called pure music, the intimism of the piano, the maternal instrument, and the intimacy of the bourgeois salon. In this antithesis between two relations to music which are aways defined, more unconsciously than consciously, in relation to each other—the taste for the artists of the past, Panzera or Cortot, loved even for their imperfections which evoke the freedom of the amateur, implies a distaste for modern performers and their impeccable recordings for mass production—one again finds the old opposition between the docte, who is bound to the code (in every sense), the rules, and therefore the Institution and Criticism, and the hedonistic mondain, who, being on the side of nature, the 'natural', is content to feel and enjoy, and who expels all trace of intellectualism, didacticism, pedantry from his artistic experience.

OBJECT LESSONS Every material inheritance is, strictly speaking, also a cultural inheritance. Family heirlooms not only bear material witness to the age and continuity of the lineage and so consecrate its social identity, which is inseparable from permanence over time; they also contribute in a practical way to its spiritual reproduction, that is, to transmitting the values, virtues and competences which are the basis of legitimate membership in bourgeois dynasties. What is acquired in daily contact with ancient objects, by regular visits to antique-dealers and galleries, or, more simply, by moving in a universe of familiar, intimate objects 'which are there', as Rilke says, 'guileless, good, simple, certain', is of course a certain 'taste', which is nothing other than a relation of immediate familiarity with the things of taste. But it is also the sense of belonging to a more polished, more polite, better policed world, a world which is justified in existing by its perfection, its harmony and beauty, a world which has produced Beethoven and Mozart and continues to produce people capable of playing and appreciating them. And finally it is an immediate adherence, at the deepest level of the habitus, to the tastes and distastes, sympathies and aversions, fantasies and phobias which, more than declared opinions, forge the unconscious unity of a class.

If a group's whole life-style can be read off from the style it adopts in furnishing or clothing, this is not only because these properties are the objectification of the economic and cultural necessity which determined their selection, but also because the social relations objectified in familiar objects, in their luxury or poverty, their 'distinction' or 'vulgarity', their 'beauty' or 'ugliness', impress themselves through bodily experiences which may be as profoundly unconscious as the quiet caress of beige carpets or the thin clamminess of tattered, garish linoleum, the harsh smell of bleach or perfumes as imperceptible as a negative scent.[73] Every interior expresses, in its own language, the present and even the past state of its occupants, bespeaking the elegant self-assurance of inherited wealth, the flashy arrogance of the nouveaux riches, the discreet shabbiness of the poor and the gilded shabbiness of 'poor relations' striving to live beyond their means; one thinks of the child in D. H. Lawrence's story 'The Rocking-Horse Winner' who hears throughout the house and even in his bedroom, full of expensive toys, an incessant whispering: 'There must be more money.' Experiences of this sort would be the material of a social psychoanalysis which set out to grasp the logic whereby the social relations objectified in things and also, of course, in people are insensibly internalized, taking their place in a lasting relation to the world and to others, which manifests itself, for example, in thresholds of tolerance of the natural and social world, of noise, overcrowding, physical or verbal violence—and of which the mode of appropriation of cultural goods is one dimension.[74]

The effect of mode of acquisition is most marked in the ordinary choices of everyday existence, such as furniture, clothing or cooking, which are particularly revealing of deep-rooted and long-standing dispositions because, lying outside the scope of the educational system, they have to be confronted, as it were, by naked taste, without any explicit prescription or proscription, other than from semi-legitimate legitimizing agencies such as women's weeklies or 'ideal home' magazines.

This means that, however imperfect it may be, given the present state of functioning of the educational system, the minimal rationalization implied by every institutionalized pedagogy, in particular the transformation of class 'sense', functioning in practical form, into partially codified knowledge (e.g., literary history, with its classifications by periods, genres and styles), has the effect of reducing, at least among the most over-selected survivors, the weight of what is abandoned to inherited 'senses' and, consequently, the differences linked to economic and cultural inheritance. It is also true that these differences continue to function in other areas, and that they recover their full force as soon as the logic of the struggle for distinction moves its real stakes into these areas—which it of course always tends to do.

The adjectives the respondents have chosen to describe an interior, and the source of their furniture, are more closely linked to their social origin than to their educational qualifications (unlike their judgement on photographs or their knowledge of composers), because nothing, perhaps, more directly depends on early learning, especially the learning which takes place without any express intention to teach, than the dispositions and knowledge that are invested in clothing, furnishing and cooking or, more precisely, in the way clothes, furniture and food are bought. Thus, the mode of acquisition of furniture (department store, antique-dealer, shop or Flea Market) depends at least as much on social origin as on schooling. At equal educational levels, those members of the dominant class who were also born into that class—who, more often than the others, inherited some of their furniture—acquired their furniture (especially those living in Paris) from an antique-dealer more often than those born into other classes, who tended to buy from a department store, a specialized shop or the Flea Market. (The last is especially frequented on

Table 5 Furniture purchases in the dominant class, by education and social origin (percentage of respondents who bought their furniture from each source).[a]

Educational qualification	Social origin	Department store	Specialized shop	Flea market	Auction	Antique-dealer
Lower than bac	Working and middle classes	25.5	41.5	11.0	14.5	33.5
	Upper classes	11.5	23.5	15.0	31.5	43.5
Technical college	Working and middle classes	13.5	36.5	4.5	32.0	4.5
	Upper classes	6.0	24.5	30.5	20.5	65.5
Licence	Working and middle classes	11.0	28.5	11.0	11.0	21.5
	Upper classes	4.5	21.5	21.5	14.5	49.0
Agrégation, grande école	Working and middle classes	21.5	46.5	32.0	21.5	43.0
	Upper classes	18.0	29.0	8.0	13.0	60.5

a. Some respondents indicated more than one source.

the one hand by the rising members of the dominant class who have most educational capital, and on the other hand by members of the dominant class, born into that class, who have less educational capital than their origin promised, i.e., those who have had one or two years of higher education—see table 5.)

And it is probably in tastes in *food* that one would find the strongest and most indelible mark of infant learning, the lessons which longest withstand the distancing or collapse of the native world and most durably maintain nostalgia for it. The native world is, above all, the maternal world, the world of primordial tastes and basic foods, of the archetypal relation to the archetypal cultural good, in which pleasure-giving is an integral part of pleasure and of the selective disposition towards pleasure which is acquired through pleasure.

While the aim was to identify preferences in food, the search for the most economical and 'synthetic' questions led me to question the respondents on the meals they served on special occasions, an interesting indicator of the mode of self-presentation adopted in 'showing off' a life-style (in which furniture also plays a part). For a complete understanding of choices in this area, a particularly complex set of factors has to be borne in mind: the style of meal that people like to offer is no doubt a very good indicator of the image they wish to give or avoid giving to others and, as such, it is the systematic expression of a system of factors including, in addition to the indicators of the position occupied in the economic and cultural hierarchies, economic trajectory, social trajectory and cultural trajectory.

This being so, it is not surprising that the effects are most visible in the petite bourgeoisie. The members of the established petite bourgeoisie more often serve their friends 'plentiful and good', 'simple but well-presented' meals than the new petite bourgeoisie, who prefer to serve 'original' meals or 'pot luck'. But one also finds strong differences linked to trajectory. Thus new petit bourgeois of middle or working-class origin more often offer 'plentiful and good' meals, which is *never* the case with those of upper-class origin, who, by contrast, are very inclined to the 'original and exotic'. In the established petite bourgeoisie, the propensity to offer 'plentiful and good' meals is as strong among those in decline as among those who are upwardly mobile and originate from the working classes. The former never say they offer 'pot luck' or 'original and exotic' meals, whereas the latter sometimes do (though not, of course, as often as the new petit bourgeois).

It is no accident that even the purest pleasures, those most purified of any trace of corporeality (such as the 'unique, pure note' of the *Philebus,* which already reserved them for the 'few'), contain an element which, as in the 'crudest' pleasures of the tastes of food, the archetype of all taste, refers directly back to the oldest and deepest experiences, those which determine and over-determine the primitive oppositions—bitter/sweet, flavourful/insipid, hot/cold, coarse/delicate, austere/bright—which are as essential to gastronomic commentary as to the refined appreciations of aesthetes. To different degrees, depending on the art, the genre and the style, art is never entirely the *cosa mentale,* the discourse intended only to be read, decoded, interpreted, which the intellectualist view makes of it. This product of an 'art' in Durkheim's sense, i.e., 'a pure practice without theory', and sometimes of a simple mimesis, a sort of symbolic gymnastics, always contains also something ineffable, not through excess, as the celebrants would have it, but by default, something which communicates, as it were, from body to body, like the rhythm of music or the flavour of colours, that is, falling short of words and concepts. Art is also a 'bodily thing', and music, the most 'pure' and 'spiritual' of the arts, is perhaps simply the most corporeal. Linked to *états d'âme* which are also states of the body or, as they were once called, humours, it ravishes, carries away, moves. It is pitched not so much beyond words as below them, in gestures and movements of the body, rhythms—which Piaget somewhere says characterize the functions located, like everything which governs taste, at the articulation of the organic and the mental—quickening and slowing, crescendo and decrescendo, tension and relaxation.[75] This is no doubt why, once it leaves the realm of pure technique, musical criticism scarcely speaks other than in adjectives and exclamations. As mystics speak of divine love in the language of human love, so the least inadequate evocations of musical pleasure are those which can replicate the peculiar forms of an experience as deeply rooted in the body and in primitive bodily experiences as the tastes of food.

INHERITED CAPITAL AND ACQUIRED CAPITAL Thus, the differences which the relationship to educational capital leaves unexplained, and which mainly appear in the relationship with social origin, may be due to differences in the mode of acquisition of the cultural capital now possessed. But they may also be due to differences in the degree to which this capital is recognized and guaranteed by academic qualifications: a certain proportion of the capital actually owned may not have received academic sanction, when it has been directly inherited and even when it has been acquired in school. Because of the long hysteresis of the mode of acquisition, the same educational qualifications may guarantee quite different relations to culture—but decreasingly so, as one rises in the educational hierarchy and as more value comes to be set on ways of using knowledge and less on merely knowing. If the same volume of educational capital (guaranteed cultural capital) may correspond to different volumes of socially profitable cultural capital, this is first because although the educational system, by its monopoly of certification, governs the conversion of inherited cultural capital into educational capital, it does not have a monopoly on the production of cultural capital. It gives its sanction to inherited capital to a greater or less extent (i.e., there is an unequal conversion of inherited cultural capital) because, at different moments and, at the same moment, at different levels and in different sectors, what it demands is more or less identical to what the 'inheritors' bring it, and because it acknowledges more or less value in other forms of embodied capital and other dispositions (such as docility towards the institution itself).

The possessors of strong educational capital who have also inherited strong cultural capital, and so enjoy a dual title to cultural nobility, the self-assurance of legitimate membership and the ease given by familiarity (point B in figure 3), are opposed, first, to those who lack both educational capital and inherited cultural capital (A) (and to all those who are situated lower down the axis representing perfect reconversion of cultural capital into educational capital). But they are also opposed, on the one hand, to those who, with equivalent inherited cultural capital, have obtained lower educational capital (C or C') (or who have an inherited cultural capital greater than their educational capital—e.g., C' relative to B', or D' relative to D) and who are closer to them, especially as regards 'general culture', than the holders of identical qualifications; and, on the other hand, to those who have similar educational capital but who started off with less cultural capital (D or D') and whose relation to culture, which they owe more to the school and less to the family, is less familiar and more scholastic. (These secondary oppositions occur at every level of the axis.)

Figure 3   The relationship between inherited cultural capital and educational capital.

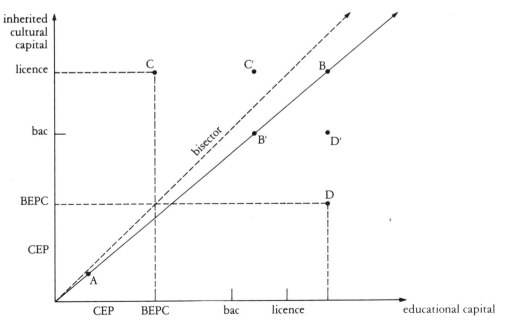

One could construct a similar diagram for each type of capital (economic, cultural and social) possessed initially and at the time of observation, and then define the set of possible cases for the relationship between initial capital (defined as regards volume and composition) and eventual capital, characterized in the same way. (There would be, for example, individuals declining in all types of capital, or declining in only one and rising in others—reconversion—etc.) If one sufficiently refined the analysis of the species of capital (dividing cultural capital, for example, into sub-species such as literary, scientific and legal-economic capital) or the analysis of the level, it would be possible to find all the cases empirically observed, in all their complexity but also in their quasi-infinite multiplicity.

To be entirely rigorous, one would have to allow for structural changes, such as the devaluation of nominal qualifications which occurs in periods (as in recent years) when the educational system is used more intensively. (This devaluation has been symbolized by placing the line indicating the real equivalents of qualifications below the bisector which marks the equivalents of the nominal value of qualifications.) One would also have to make allowance for the discrepancy between the number of years of study and the qualification obtained (which becomes more probable as initial capital rises and schooling becomes more widespread—so that it now affects even the working classes whose children often leave secondary school without any qualification). It would then be seen that, to explain certain practices adequately (in particular, autodidacticism) one has to consider not only the qualification and the number of years of schooling but also the relationship between the two (which may generate self-assurance or embarrassment, arrogance or resentment etc). One might also consider the relationship between age at the end of schooling and the legitimate age for a qualification, such as the *bac* (*baccalauréat*) at 17 or the age limits for the *concours* (entrance examinations for the *grandes écoles*). One of the mediations through which cultural capital is transformed into educational capital is speed of progress through the system.

The discrepancy between educational capital and the cultural capital actually possessed, which is the source of differences between holders of identical educational capital, can also result from the fact that the same educational qualification may correspond to schooling of very unequal duration (i.e., there is unequal conversion of scholastically acquired cultural capital). The direct or indirect effects of one or several years of study may in fact not be sanctioned by the award of a diploma—as is the case with all those who drop out in the two years leading to the baccalauréat or, at a higher level, those who have spent one or two years at university without obtaining a qualification. But in addition, because the frequency of this discrepancy has risen with the chances of access of the different classes to secondary and higher education, agents belonging to different generations (as identified by age-groups) are likely to have devoted a very different number of years of study (with all the related effects, including greater non-certified competence, of course, but also the acquisition of a different relation to culture—'studentification' effect—etc.) in educational institutions differing greatly in their teachers, their teaching methods, their social recruitment etc. in order to obtain an identical qualification. It follows from this that the differences connected with social trajectory and the volume of inherited cultural capital are reinforced by differences, mainly visible among members of the petite bourgeoisie who are themselves born into the petite bourgeoisie or drawn from the working classes (and particularly represented in the established petite bourgeoisie), which reflect changes in the state of the relations between the educational system and the class structure. To these different *modes of generation* correspond different relations to the educational system which are expressed in different strategies of cultural investment not guaranteed by the educational institution (i.e., autodidacticism).

In the absence of more precise indicators of the overall style of cultural consumption (e.g., the opposition between the satirical weeklies *Le Canard Enchaîné* and *Charlie Hebdo*, or, in the area of popular science, between *Science et Vie* and *Psychologie*), one can study the information the survey provides on favourite singers. It might be thought that the fact that, at all levels of educational capital, the youngest respondents choose the singers of the younger generation (Françoise Hardy or Johnny Hallyday) more often than the older respondents, who more often choose older singers (Guétary or Mariano), is adequately explained by the dates of the singers' first appearance in the field of cultural production. In fact, among baccalauréat-holders, the youngest more often choose Jacques Douai (who was born in 1920 and performed at the Vieux Colombier in 1963), Jacques Brel (who was born in 1929, made his Paris debut in 1953 at the Théâtre des Trois Baudets and performed at the Paris Olympia in 1958 and 1961) or even Léo Ferré (born 1916, degrees in Arts and Political Science, debut in Paris cabarets 1946), whereas the older ones more often choose Edith Piaf (born 1915, died 1963, debut at the ABC in 1937), Luis Mariano (born 1920, first success at Casino Montparnasse, 1945), Gilbert Bécaud (born 1927, first became known in right-bank cabarets and then at Olympia; consecrated in 1954, the 'Bécaud year') or even Petula Clark (born 1933, top of the bill at Olympia 1960, voted 'most likeable and popular star' in 1963).[76] It can be seen that to make sense of these relationships one has to take into account not only the singers' ages or the dates when they made their breakthroughs or even the places where they were performing at the time of the survey, but also—and especially—the degree of affinity between the style of their songs, more 'intellectual' in one case, closer to petit-bourgeois taste for light opera and realist song in the other, and the cultural dispositions of two educational generations produced by two very different states of the school system.

There are similar differences between educational generations within the 'technician' fraction of the class. The younger differ from the older not so much in their overall competence as in the extent and 'freedom' of their investments. Like their elders they read scientific and technical works, but they are slightly more interested in philosophical essays or poetry. They go no more frequently to museums, but when they do, they go more often to the Modern Art Museum. These tendencies are particularly pronounced amongst those of them (relatively more numerous than among the older ones) who originate from the middle or upper classes and who know a (relatively) very high number of musical works and composers, are interested in modern art and philosophy and often go to the cinema. But what perhaps most distinguish the two generations of technicians are the external signs—dress and hairstyle, in particular—and also their declared preferences; the younger ones, who seek to draw close to the student style, say they follow fashion and like clothes which 'suit their personality', whereas the older ones more often choose 'sober and correct' or 'classically cut' clothes (choices characteristic of established petit bourgeois).

The old-style autodidact was fundamentally defined by a reverence for culture which was induced by abrupt and early exclusion, and which led to an exalted, misplaced piety, inevitably perceived by the possessors of legitimate culture as a sort of grotesque homage.

The recognition of incompetence and cultural unworthiness which characterizes old-style autodidacticism is especially seen among members of the established petite bourgeoisie originating from the working or middle classes, who say very frequently (70 percent of them, compared with 31 percent of the new petite bourgeoisie originating from the same classes) that 'paintings are nice but difficult'. The clearest manifestation of the cultural alienation of old-style autodidacts is their readiness to offer proof of their culture even when it is not asked for, betraying their exclusion by their eagerness to prove their membership (in contrast to the well-born, who mask their ignorance by ignoring questions or situations which might expose it).

In these outsiders, who seek to use a deeply orthodox self-teaching as a way of continuing a brutally foreshortened trajectory by their own initiative, the whole relation to culture and cultural authorities bears the stamp of exclusion by a system that can get the excluded to recognize their exclusion. By contrast, new-style autodidacts have often kept a place in the educational system up to a relatively high level and in the course of this long, ill-rewarded association have acquired a relation to legitimate culture that is at once 'liberated' and disabused, familiar and disenchanted. It has nothing in common with the distant reverence of the old-style autodidact, although it leads to equally intense and passionate investments, but in quite different areas, disclaimed or abandoned by the educational system—strip cartoons or jazz rather than history or astronomy, psychology (even parapsychology) or ecology rather than archaeology or geology.[77] These are the categories which provide the audience for all the productions of the 'counter-culture' (*Charlie Hebdo, L'Echo des Sa-*

vanes, Sexpol etc.) which offer the products of the intellectual avant-garde in journalistic form, as others 'popularize' (i.e., transmit beyond the group of legitimate receivers) the products of the academic rear-guard (*Historia,* for example) or the consecrated avant-garde (*Le Nouvel Observateur*).

The holders of the monopoly of manipulation of the sacred, the literati of every church, never have much time for those who 'claim to discover within themselves the sources of traditional authority' and to have direct access to the treasure of which they are the guardians. As Gershom Scholem shows, 'They usually do their best to place obstacles in the path of the mystic. They give him no encouragement, and if in the end the obstacles frighten the mystic and bring him back to the old accustomed ways—so much the better from the standpoint of authority.'[78] But preventive censorship by the institution can take place without anyone having to apply controls or constraints. Whereas traditional autodidacts still expect the academic institution to indicate and open the short cuts of popularization and the vulgate, which are always, directly or indirectly, dominated by the institution,[79] the most liberated of the new autodidacts seek their gurus among the heresiarchs who still perform the function traditionally fulfilled by the authorities, namely, as Scholem also says, that of 'showing exactly what the novice has to expect at every step' and 'providing the symbols with which this experience can be described or interpreted.'

THE TWO MARKETS   The family and the school function as sites in which the competences deemed necessary at a given time are constituted by usage itself, and, simultaneously, as sites in which the *price* of those competences is determined, i.e., as markets which, by their positive or negative sanctions, evaluate performance, reinforcing what is acceptable, discouraging what is not, condemning valueless dispositions to extinction (jokes which 'fall flat' or, though acceptable in another context, in another market, here seem 'out of place' and only provoke embarrassment or disapproval, quotations—in Latin, for example—which sound 'pedantic' or 'laboured'). In other words, the acquisition of cultural competence is inseparable from insensible acquisition of a 'sense' for sound cultural investment.

This investment sense, being the product of adjustment to the objective chances of turning competence to good account, facilitates forward adjustment to these chances, and is itself a dimension of a relation to culture—close or distant, off-hand or reverential, hedonistic or academic—which is the internalized form of the objective relationship between the site of acquisition and the 'centre of cultural values'. The use of the phrase 'sense of investment', as in 'sense of propriety' or 'sense of balance', is intended to indicate that, when, for the purposes of objectification, terms are borrowed from the language of economics, it is in no way suggested that the corresponding behaviour is guided by rational calculation of maximum profit, as the ordinary usage of these concepts, no doubt mistakenly, implies. Culture is the site, par excellence, of misrecognition, because, in generating strategies objectively adapted to the objective chances of profit of which it is the product, the sense of investment secures profits which do not need to be pursued as profits; and so it brings to those who have legitimate culture as a second nature the supplementary profit of being seen (and seeing themselves) as perfectly disinterested, unblemished by any cynical or mercenary use of culture. This means that the term 'investment', for example, must be understood in the dual sense of economic investment—which it objectively always is, though misrecognized—and the sense of affective investment which it has in psychoanalysis, or, more exactly, in the sense of *illusio,* belief, an involvement in the game which produces the game. The art-lover knows no other guide than his love of art, and when he moves, as if by instinct, towards what is, at each moment, the thing to be loved, like some businessmen who make money even when they are not trying to, he is not pursuing a cynical calculation, but his own pleasure, the sincere enthusiasm which, in such matters, is one of the preconditions of successful investment.

So, for example, it is true that the effect of the hierarchies of legitimacy (the hierarchy of the arts, of genres etc.) can be described as a particular case of the 'labelling' effect well known to social psychologists. Just as people see a face differently depending on the ethnic label it is given,[80] so the value of the arts, genres, works and authors depends on the social marks attached to them at any given moment (e.g., place of publication). But the fact remains that the art-lover's sense of cultural investment which leads him always to love what is lovable, and only that, and always sincerely, can be supported by unconscious deciphering of the countless signs which at every moment say what is to be loved and what is not, what is or is not to be seen, without ever being explicitly oriented by pursuit of the associated symbolic profits. The specific competence (in classical music or jazz, theatre or film etc.) depends on the chances which the different markets, domestic, scholastic or occupational, together offer for accumulating, applying and exploiting it, i.e., the degree to which they encourage acquisition of this competence by promising or guaranteeing it profits which will reinforce it and induce new investments. The chances of using cultural competence profitably in the different markets play a part, in particular, in defining the propensity to make 'scholastic' investments and also the investments in extra-curricular 'general culture' which seem to owe nothing to the constraints or incentives of the institution.

The more legitimate a given area, the more necessary and 'profitable' it is to be competent in it, and the more damaging and 'costly' to be incompetent.[81] But this does not suffice to explain why it is that, as one moves towards the most legitimate areas, the statistical differences related to educational capital become increasingly important, whereas the more one moves towards the least legitimate areas, which might seem to be the realm of free and inexplicable choice, such as cooking or interior decoration, choice of friends or furniture, the more important are the statistical differences linked to social trajectory (and capital composition), with the areas that are undergoing legitimation, such as 'intellectual' song, photography or jazz, occupying an intermediate position. Here too, it is in the relationship between the properties of the field (in particular, the chances of negative or positive sanctions it offers 'on average', for any agent) and the properties of the agent, that the 'efficacy' of these properties is defined. Thus both the propensity towards 'non-academic' investments and the area to which they are directed depend, strictly speaking, not on the 'average' rate of profit offered by the area in question but on the rate of profit it offers each agent or particular category of agents in terms of the volume and composition of their capital.

The hierarchy of 'average' rates of profit broadly corresponds to the hierarchy of degrees of legitimacy, so that knowledge of classical or even avant-garde literature yields higher 'average' profits, in the scholastic market and elsewhere, than knowledge of cinema, or, a fortiori, strip cartoons, detective stories or sport. But the *specific* profits, and the consequent propensities to invest, are only defined in the relationship between a field and a particular agent with particular characteristics. For example, those who owe most of their cultural capital to the educational system, such as primary and secondary teachers originating from the working and middle classes, are particularly subject to the academic definition of legitimacy, and tend to proportion their investments very strictly to the value the educational system sets on the different areas.

By contrast, 'middle-ground' arts such as cinema, jazz, and, even more, strip cartoons, science fiction or detective stories are predisposed to attract the investments either of those who have entirely succeeded in converting their cultural capital into educational capital or those who, not having acquired legitimate culture in the legitimate manner (i.e., through early familiarization), maintain an uneasy relationship with it, subjectively or objectively, or both. These arts, not yet fully legitimate, which are disdained or neglected by the big holders of educational capital, offer a refuge and a revenge to those who, by appropriating them, secure the best return on their cultural capital (especially if it is not fully recognized scholastically) while at the same time taking credit for contesting the established hierarchy of legitimacies and profits. In other words, the propensity to apply to the middle-ground arts a disposition usually reserved for the legitimate arts—that measured, for example, by knowledge of film directors—depends less closely on educational capital than on a whole relationship to scholastic culture and the educational system which itself depends on the degree to which the cultural capital possessed consists solely of the capital acquired in and recognized by the educational system. (Thus, members of the new petite bourgeoisie have generally inherited more cultural capital than the primary teachers but possess much the same educational capital: they know many more directors but fewer composers.)

In fact, one can never entirely escape from the hierarchy of legitimacies. Because the very meaning and value of a cultural object varies according to the system of objects in which it is placed, detective stories, science fiction or strip cartoons may be entirely prestigious cultural assets or be reduced to their ordinary value, depending on whether they are associated with avant-garde literature or music—in which case they appear as manifestations of daring and freedom—or combine to form a constellation typical of middle-brow taste—when they appear as what they are, simple substitutes for legitimate assets.

Given that each social space—family or school, for example—functions both as one of the sites where competence is produced and as one of the sites where it is given its price, one might expect each field to set the highest price on the products created within it. Thus one might expect the scholastic field to give the highest value to scholastically certified cultural capital and the scholastic modality, whereas the markets dominated by extra-scholastic values—'society' salons and dinners, or all the occasions of professional life (appointment interviews, board meetings, conferences etc.) or even academic life (oral examinations at ENA or Sciences Po, for example), in which the whole person is evaluated—would set the highest value on the familiar relation to culture, devaluing all the dispositions and competences which bear the mark of scholastic acquisition. But this would be to ignore the effects of domination whereby the products of the scholastic mode of production may be devalued as 'scholastic' in the scholastic market itself.[82] Indeed, the clearest sign of the heteronomy of the scholastic market is seen in its ambivalent treatment of the products of the 'scholastic' habitus, which varies inversely with the autonomy of the educational system as a whole (variable at different times and in different countries) and of its constituent institutions, with respect to the demands of the dominant fraction of the dominant class.[83]

What is certain is that there exists an immediate affinity between the dispositions that are acquired by familiarization with legitimate culture and the 'high-society' market (or the most 'high-society' sectors of the educational market). The ordinary occasions of social life exclude tests as brutal as a closed questionnaire, the limiting case of the scholastic examination which the scholastic institution itself refuses whenever, implicitly accepting the high-society depreciation of the 'scholastic', it turns an examination intended to verify and measure competence into a variant of high-society conversation. In contrast to the most 'scholastic' of scholastic situations, which aim to disarm and discourage strategies of bluff, high-society occasions give unlimited scope to an art of playing with competence which is to competence what 'play' is to the 'hand' in card games. The accomplished socialite chooses his terrain, sidesteps difficulties, turns questions of knowledge into questions of preference, ignorance into disdainful refusal—a whole set of strategies which may manifest self-assurance or insecurity, ease or embarrassment, and which depend as much on mode of acquisition and the corresponding familiarity or distance as on educational capital. In other words, the lack of deep, methodical, systematic knowledge in a particular area of legitimate culture in no way prevents him from satisfying the cultural demands entailed by most social situations, even in the quasi-scholastic situation of a survey.[84]

In asking questions about painters in such a way that the knowledge claimed could not be verified in any way, the aim was not so much to measure the specific competence (which, one may assume, depends on the same factors as knowledge of composers) as to grasp indirectly the relationship to legitimate culture and the differential effects of the survey situation. Thus, respondents whose knowledge was not equal to their familiarity may have felt entitled to use strategies of bluff which are highly successful in the ordinary uses of culture (this is particularly the case with the new petite bourgeoisie). But bluff itself is only profitable if it is guided by the vague knowledge given by familiarity. Thus, while the room for manoeuvre in this question allowed the least competent to fasten on proper names which correspond neither to knowledge nor preference, such as Picasso (mentioned by 21 percent of the unskilled and semi-skilled workers) or Braque (10 percent), who was being celebrated in various ways at the time of the survey, it also functioned as a trap with Rousseau (10 percent), who was practically never mentioned by the other classes and was probably confused with the writer. (Breughel, by contrast, was never mentioned by the unskilled and semi-skilled, no doubt because they would not risk pronouncing a name they were not likely to have heard.)

To bring to light this 'society sense', generally associated with strong inherited cultural capital but irreducible to a sum of strictly verifiable knowledge, one only has to compare the variations in two dimensions of cultural capital—possession of specific knowledge of composers and the 'flair' which is needed to make it profitable, measured by the capacity to recognize what Flaubert would have called the 'smart opinions' among the statements offered. Figure 4 correlates the proportion of individuals in each category who know the composers of at least twelve of the musical works with the proportion who claim that 'abstract painting interests them as much as the classical schools'. On the one hand there are the fractions whose strict competence is greater than their sense of the 'right' answer (secondary and higher-education teachers), and on the other, those whose sense of the legitimate posture is incommensurate with their specific competence (new petite bourgeoisie, new bourgeoisie, artistic producers). The gap is smallest among the rising petit bourgeois or bourgeois (primary teachers, junior administrative executives, engineers, senior public-sector executives).

It was not possible to use the opinions selected on music because—unlike

Figure 4 Specific competence and talk about art.

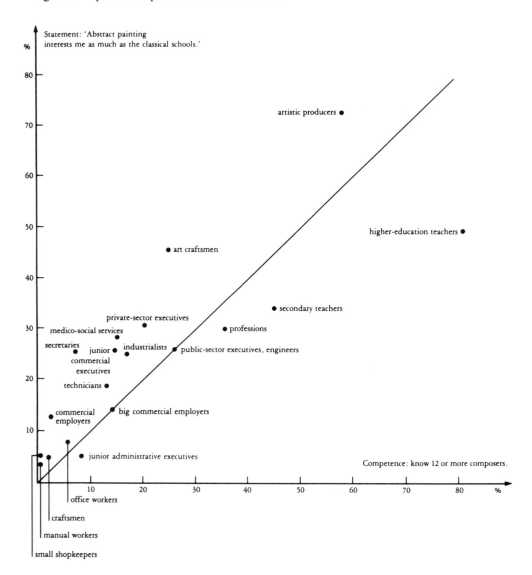

the set of statements on painting, which offered an intermediate opinion ('I love the Impressionists')—the range of possible judgements presented too great a discontinuity between the typically middle-brow opinion ('I like the Strauss waltzes') and the chic opinion ('All music of quality interests me'), so that the choice of the most legitimate judgement became more tempting for all those who refused to make do with a too visibly 'naive' judgement.

The distaste which bourgeois agents (especially those in decline) manifest for everything 'scholastic' is no doubt partly explained by the devaluation which the scholastic market inflicts, nonetheless, on the approximate knowledge and confused intuitions of familiarity. For example, the rejection of academic routine which underlies most of the innovations of the new cultural intermediaries (youth organizers, play leaders etc.) is more easily understood if one knows that the established petite bourgeoisie has relatively high educational capital and a relatively weak cultural inheritance, whereas the new petite bourgeoisie (of which artists are the limiting case) has a strong cultural inheritance and relatively low educational capital. The Parisian or even provincial primary teacher, who can beat the small employer, the provincial doctor or the Parisian antique-dealer in the tests of pure knowledge, is likely to appear incomparably inferior to them in all the situations which demand self-assurance or flair, or even the bluff which can cover lacunae, rather than the prudence, discretion and awareness of limits that are associated with scholastic acquisition. One can confuse Bernard Buffet with Jean Dubuffet and yet be quite capable of hiding one's ignorance under the commonplaces of celebration or the knowing silence of a pout, a nod or an inspired pose; one can identify philosophy with Saint-Exupéry, Teilhard de Chardin or even Leprince-Ringuet, and still hold one's own in today's most prestigious market-places—receptions, conferences, interviews, debates, seminars, committees, commissions—so long as one possesses the set of distinctive features, bearing, posture, presence, diction and pronunciation, manners and usages, without which, in these markets at least, all scholastic knowledge is worth little or nothing and which, partly because schools never, or never fully, teach them, define the essence of bourgeois distinction.

Educationally equivalent individuals (e.g., the students of the *grandes écoles*) may differ radically as regards bodily hexis, pronunciation, dress or familiarity with legitimate culture, not to mention the whole set of specific competences and capacities which function as admission tickets to the bourgeois world, such as dancing, the rare sports, or parlour games (especially bridge). These skills, through the encounters they provide and the social capital they help to accumulate, no doubt explain subsequent differences in career.

The manner which designates the infallible taste of the 'taste-maker' and exposes the uncertain tastes of the possessors of an 'ill-gotten' culture is so important, in all markets and especially in the market which decides the value of literary and artistic works, only because choices always owe part of their value to the value of the chooser, and because, to a large extent, this value makes itself known and recognized through the manner of choosing. What is learnt through immersion in a world in which legitimate culture is as natural as the air one breathes is a sense of the legitimate choice so sure of itself that it convinces by the sheer manner of the performance, like a successful bluff. It is not only a sense of the right area to invest in, directors rather than actors, the avant-garde more than the classical or, which amounts to the same thing, a sense of the right moment to invest or disinvest, to move into other fields, when the gains in distinction become too uncertain. It is, ultimately, the self-assurance, confidence, arrogance, which, normally being the monopoly of the individuals most assured of profit from their investments, has every likelihood—in a world in which everything is a matter of belief—of imposing the absolute legitimacy, and therefore the maximum profitability, of their investments.

The paradox of the imposition of legitimacy is that it makes it impossible ever to determine whether the dominant feature appears as distinguished or noble because it is dominant—i.e., because it has the privilege of defining, by its very existence, what is noble or distinguished as being exactly what itself is, a privilege which is expressed precisely in its self-assurance—or whether it is only because it is dominant that it appears as endowed with these qualities and uniquely entitled to define them. It is no accident that, to designate the legitimate manners or taste, ordinary language is content to say 'manners' or 'taste', 'in the absolute sense', as grammarians say. The properties attached to the dominant—Paris or Oxford 'accents', bourgeois 'distinction' etc.—have the power to discourage the intention of discerning what they are 'in reality', in and for themselves, and the distinctive value they derive from unconscious reference to their class distribution.

FACTORS AND POWERS   It is now clear that the difficulty of the analysis was due to the fact that what the very tools of analysis—educational level and social origin—designate is being fought out in struggles which have the object of analysis—art and the relation to the work of art—as their prize in reality itself. These struggles are fought between those who are identified with the scholastic definition of culture and the scholastic mode of acquisition, and those who defend a 'non-institutional' culture and relation to culture. The latter, though mainly recruited from the oldest sectors of the bourgeoisie, receive unquestioned support from writers and artists and from the charismatic conception of the production and consumption of art, of which they are the inventors and guarantors. Battles over authors and schools, which hold the limelight of the literary or artistic stage, conceal more important struggles, such as those which oppose teachers (from whose ranks, throughout the nineteenth century, critics were often recruited) and writers, who tend to be more closely linked, by origin and 'connections', to the dominant fractions of the dominant class; or the endless struggles between the dominated fractions as a whole and the dominant fractions over the definition of the accomplished man and the education designed to produce him.

For example, what is at stake in the late-nineteenth-century creation of a private education giving great importance to sport—with, among others, Edouard Demolins, the founder of the Ecole des Roches and disciple of Frédéric Le Play, like Baron de Coubertin, another advocate of a new style of education—is the imposition of an aristocratic definition of education within the academic institution itself. Knowledge, erudition, the 'scholastic' docility symbolized by 'barrack-like' lycée (this is where the much-repeated theme originates), and all the criteria of assessment favourable to the children of the petite bourgeoisie, through which the school affirms its autonomy, are contested in the name of such 'values' as 'energy', 'courage', 'will', the virtues of the leader (of the army or business—at that time it was almost the same thing) and, perhaps especially, (personal) initiative, baptized 'self-help' or 'enterprise', all virtues linked to sport. To put 'education' before 'instruction', 'character' before 'intelligence', sport before culture is to assert, within the scholastic world itself, the existence of a hierarchy irreducible to the specifically academic hierarchy which privileges the second term in each of these oppositions.[85]

These struggles are not confined to the past, as is shown by the existence of two routes to the senior positions in large firms, one leading from the Ecole des Roches or the major Jesuit colleges and great bourgeois lycées (in the 16th arrondissement) to the Law Faculty or, increasingly, to Sciences Po or HEC, the other running from the ordinary provincial or Parisian lycée to the Ecole Polytechnique.[86] It is still more clearly seen in the opposition, at the level of the grandes écoles, between two academic markets differing profoundly in the content of the cultural competence demanded, in the value set on manners and the criteria used to evaluate them, with at one extreme the Ecole Normale Supérieure (ENS) and Polytechnique and at the other Sciences Po and the Ecole Nationale d'Administration (ENA). These struggles over the legitimate definition of culture and the legitimate way of evaluating it are only one dimension of the endless struggles which divide every dominant class. Behind the virtues of the accomplished man the legitimate titles to the exercise of domination are at stake. Thus the glorification of 'character-building' sport and the valorization of economic and political culture, at the expense of literary or artistic culture, are just two of the strategies through which the dominant fractions of the dominant class aim to discredit the values recognized by the 'intellectual' fractions of the dominant class and the petite bourgeoisie—whose children compete dangerously with the children of the bourgeoisie on the terrain of the most academically defined academic competence. But more profoundly, these manifestations of anti-intellectualism are only one aspect of an antagonism which, far beyond the question of the legitimate uses of the body or culture, touches on every dimension of existence; the dominant fractions always tend to conceive their relationship to the dominated fractions in terms of the opposition between the male and the female, the serious and

the frivolous, the responsible and the irresponsible, the useful and the futile, the realistic and the unrealistic.

The principles of logical division which statistics uses to produce its
classes and the data it records about them are therefore also principles of
'socio-logical' division. The statistical variations associated with the (naively defined) two main variables—educational level and social origin—
can only be correctly interpreted so long as it is remembered that they are
bound up with antagonistic definitions of legitimate culture and of the
legitimate relation to culture, or, more precisely, with different markets,
in which the characteristics associated with one or the other are given different prices. It would be wholly mistaken to locate in any one of these
factors an 'efficacy' which only appears in a certain *relationship* and may
therefore be cancelled out or inverted in another field or another state of
the same field. The dispositions constituting the cultivated habitus are
only formed, only function and are only valid in a field, in the relationship with a field which, as Gaston Bachelard says of the physical field, is
itself a 'field of possible forces', a 'dynamic situation',[87] in which forces
are only manifested in their relationship with certain dispositions. This is
why the same practices may receive opposite meanings and values in different fields, in different configurations or in opposing sectors of the
same field.

So reflective analysis of the tools of analysis is not an epistemological
scruple but an indispensable pre-condition of scientific knowledge of the
object. Positivist laziness leads the whole, purely defensive, effort of verification to be focussed on the intensity of the relationships found, instead
of bringing questioning to bear on the very conditions of measurement
of the relationships, which may even explain the relative intensity of the
different relationships. In order to believe in the independence of the 'independent variables' of positivist methodology, one has to be unaware
that 'explanatory factors' are also 'powers' which are only valid and operative in a certain field, and that they therefore depend on the struggles
which are fought, within each field, to transform the price-forming
mechanisms which define it. If it is easy to imagine fields in which the
weight of the two dominant 'factors' would be inverted (and tests which
would be the experimental expression of this, giving greater prominence,
for example, to less 'scholastic' objects and forms of questioning), this is
because what is ultimately at stake in everyday struggles over culture is
the transformation of the price-forming mechanisms defining the relative
values of the cultural productions associated with educational capital
and social trajectory (and the primary variables through which they are
grasped).

If it is true that the statistical relationships between the properties attached to agents and their practices are only fully defined in the relationship between the dispositions of a habitus and a particular field, then the
limits within which the relations observed retain their validity—an ap-

parent restriction which is the pre-condition for full generalization—cannot be defined until one questions the relationship within which these relationships have been established. The relationship set up by a closed questionnaire mainly devoted to legitimate culture is akin to that of an examination (albeit without any institutional sanction at stake); and it is to the scholastic market what a market-place, as a real-world site of exchanges, is to the market of economic theory. Both in its subject matter and in the form of exchange it imposes (a questioning, which, as Charles Bally noted, always implies a form of intrusion, violence, challenge—hence the attenuations which normally accompany it), a survey by questionnaire, especially when it takes the form of methodical, asymmetrical interrogation,[88] is the complete opposite of ordinary conversation; it has nothing in common with the café or campus discussions in which the 'counter-culture' is constructed, or the high-society chatter which shuns pedantic precision and didactic insistence. The variations one observes in the relative weight of educational qualification and inherited cultural capital as one moves, within this quasi-scholastic situation, from what is more academic in form and content to what is less academic either in form (questions measuring familiarity without testing knowledge) or in content (questions on knowledge of the cinema or preferences in cooking) give some idea of this relationship between 'factors' and markets.

All the indices (difficult to obtain by questionnaire) of the manner of applying, showing or exploiting competence (self-assurance, arrogance, off-handedness, modesty, earnestness, embarrassment etc.) strictly depend, for their meaning and value, on the market in which they are placed, because they are the visible traces of a mode of acquisition (domestic or scholastic), i.e., a market; and also because all the markets which are able to assert their autonomy of scholastic control give them priority. The emphasis on manners, and through them on mode of acquisition, enables seniority within a class to be made the basis of the hierarchy within the class;[89] it also gives the recognized possessors of the legitimate manner an absolute, arbitrary power to recognize or exclude. Manner, by definition, only exists for others, and the recognized holders of the legitimate manner and of the power to define the value of manners—dress, bearing, pronunciation—have the privilege of indifference to their own manner (so they never have to *put on* a manner). By contrast, the 'parvenus' who presume to join the group of legitimate, i.e., hereditary, possessors of the legitimate manner, without being the product of the same social conditions, are trapped, whatever they do, in a choice between anxious hyper-identification and the negativity which admits its defeat in its very revolt: either the conformity of an 'assumed' behaviour whose very correctness or hyper-correctness betrays an imitation, or the ostentatious assertion of difference which is bound to appear as an admission of inability to identify.[90]

Because they are acquired in social fields which are also markets in which they receive their price, cultural competences are dependent on these markets, and all struggles over culture are aimed at creating the market most favourable to the products which are marked, in their manners, by a particular class of conditions of acquisition, i.e., a particular market. Thus, what is nowadays called the 'counter-culture' may well be the product of the endeavour of new-style autodidacts to free themselves from the constraints of the scholastic market (to which the less confident old-style autodidacts continue to submit, although it condemns their products in advance). They strive to do so by producing another market, with its own consecrating agencies, that is, like the high-society or intellectual markets, capable of challenging the pretension of the educational system to impose the principles of evaluation of competences and manners which reign in the scholastic market, or at least its most 'scholastic' sectors, on a perfectly unified market in cultural goods.

II | The Economy of Practices

But on things whose rules and principles had been instilled into her by her mother, on the way to make certain dishes, to play Beethoven's sonatas, to 'receive' with cordiality, she was quite sure that she had a right idea of perfection and of discerning how far others approximated to it. For these three things, moreover, perfection was almost the same, a kind of simplicity in the means, a sobriety and a charm. She repudiated with horror the introduction of spices in dishes that did not absolutely require them, affectation and abuse of the pedals in piano-playing, departure from perfect naturalness, and exaggerated talking of oneself in 'receiving.' From the first mouthful, from the first notes, from a simple letter she preened herself on knowing if she had to deal with a good cook, a real musician, a woman properly brought up. 'She may have many more fingers than I, but she lacks taste, playing that very simple *Andante* with so much emphasis.' 'No doubt a most brilliant woman full of parts, but it is a want of tact to speak of oneself in such a case.' 'Possibly a very knowing cook, but she does not know how to do steak and fried potatoes.' Steak and fried potatoes, an ideal competition-piece, a kind of culinary *Pathetic Sonata,* a gastronomic equivalent to what is in social life the visit of a lady who comes for a servant's 'character' and who, in an act as simple as that, can sufficiently display the presence or absence of tact and education.

Marcel Proust, *Days of Reading*

2 | The Social Space and Its Transformations

If the research had stopped at this point it would probably not raise great objections, so self-evident is the idea of the irreducibility of artistic taste. However, as has already been shown by the analysis of the social conditions of the aesthetic disposition, the dispositions which govern choices between the goods of legitimate culture cannot be fully understood unless they are reintegrated into the system of dispositions, unless 'culture', in the restricted, normative sense of ordinary usage, is reinserted into 'culture' in the broad, anthropological sense and the elaborated taste for the most refined objects is brought back into relation with the elementary taste for the flavours of food.[1] The dual meaning of the word 'taste', which usually serves to justify the illusion of spontaneous generation which this cultivated disposition tends to produce by presenting itself in the guise of an innate disposition, must serve, for once, to remind us that taste in the sense of the 'faculty of immediately and intuitively judging aesthetic values' is inseparable from taste in the sense of the capacity to discern the flavours of foods which implies a preference for some of them. The abstraction which isolates dispositions towards legitimate culture leads to a further abstraction at the level of the system of explanatory factors, which, though always present and active, only offers itself for observation through those elements (cultural capital and trajectory in the case analysed below) which are the principles of its efficacy in the field in question.

The consumption of the most legitimate cultural goods is a particular case of competition for rare goods and practices, whose particularity no doubt owes more to the logic of supply, i.e., the specific form of competition between the producers, than to the logic of demand and tastes, i.e., the logic of competition between the consumers. One only has to remove the magical barrier which makes legitimate culture into a separate universe, in order to see intelligible relationships between choices as seemingly incommensurable as preferences in music or cooking, sport or politics, literature or hairstyle. This barbarous reintegration of aesthetic consumption into the world of ordinary consumption (against which it endlessly defines itself) has, inter alia, the virtue of reminding us that the consumption of goods no doubt always presupposes a labour of appropriation, to different degrees depending on the goods and the consumers; or, more precisely, that the consumer helps to produce the product he consumes, by a labour of identification and decoding which, in the case of a work of art, may constitute the whole of the consumption and gratification, and which requires time and dispositions acquired over time.

Economists, who never jib at an abstraction, can ignore what happens to products in the relationship with the consumers, that is, with the dispositions which define their useful properties and real uses. To hypothesize, as one of them does, that consumers perceive the same decisive attributes, which amounts to assuming that products possess objective or, as they are known, 'technical' characteristics which can impress themselves as such on all perceiving subjects, is to proceed as if perception only seized on the characteristics designated by the manufacturers' brochures (and so-called 'informative' publicity) and as if social uses could be derived from the operating instructions. Objects, even industrial products, are not objective in the ordinary sense of the word, i.e., independent of the interest and tastes of those who perceive them, and they do not impose the self-evidence of a universal, unanimously approved meaning. The sociologist's task would be much easier if, when faced with each relationship between an 'independent variable' and a 'dependent variable', he did not have to determine how the perception and appreciation of what is designated by the 'dependent variable' vary according to the classes determined by the 'independent variable', or, in other words, identify the system of pertinent features on the basis of which each of the classes of agents was really determined.[2] What science has to establish is the objectivity of the object which is established in the relationship between an object defined by the possibilities and impossibilities it offers, which are only revealed in the world of social uses (including, in the case of a technical object, the use or function for which it was designed) and the dispositions of an agent or class of agents, that is, the schemes of perception, appreciation and action which constitute its objective utility in a practical usage.[3] The aim is not, of course, to reintroduce any form of what is called 'lived experience', which is most often merely a thinly disguised projection of the researcher's 'lived experience';[4] but to move beyond the abstract relationship between consumers with interchangeable tastes and products with uniformly perceived and appreciated properties to the relationship between tastes which vary in a necessary way according to their social and economic conditions of production, and the products on which they confer their different social identities. One only has to ask the question, which economists strangely ignore, of the economic conditions of the production of the dispositions demanded by the economy, i.e., in this case,[5] the question of the economic and social determinants of tastes, to see the necessity of including in the complete definition of the product the differential experiences which the consumers have of it as a function of the dispositions they derive from their position in economic space. These experiences do not have to be felt in order to be understood with an understanding which may owe nothing to lived experience, still less to sympathy. The habitus, an objective relationship between two objectivities, enables an intelligible and necessary relation to be established between practices and a situation, the meaning of which is produced by the habitus through categories of perception and appreciation that are themselves produced by an observable social condition.

Class Condition and Social Conditioning

Because it can only account for practices by bringing to light successively the series of effects which underlie them, analysis initially conceals the structure of the life-style characteristic of an agent or class of agents, that is, the unity hidden under the diversity and multiplicity of the set of practices performed in fields governed by different logics and therefore inducing different forms of realization, in accordance with the formula: [(habitus) (capital)] + field = practice. It also conceals the structure of the symbolic space marked out by the whole set of these structured practices, all the distinct and distinctive life-styles which are always defined objectively and sometimes subjectively in and through their mutual relationships. So it is necessary to reconstruct what has been taken apart, first by way of verification but also in order to rediscover the kernel of truth in the approach characteristic of common-sense knowledge, namely, the intuition of the systematic nature of life-styles and of the whole set which they constitute. To do this, one must return to the practice-unifying and practice-generating principle, i.e., class habitus, the internalized form of class condition and of the conditionings it entails. One must therefore construct the *objective class,* the set of agents who are placed in homogeneous conditions of existence imposing homogeneous conditionings and producing homogeneous systems of dispositions capable of generating similar practices; and who possess a set of common properties, objectified properties, sometimes legally guaranteed (as possession of goods and power) or properties embodied as class habitus (and, in particular, systems of classificatory schemes).[6]

VARIABLES AND SYSTEMS OF VARIABLES In designating these classes (classes of agents or, which amounts to the same thing in this context, classes of conditions of existence) by the name of an occupation, one is merely indicating that the position in the relations of production governs practices, in particular through the mechanisms which control access to positions and produce or select a particular class of habitus. But this is not a way of reverting to a pre-constructed variable such as 'socio-occupational category'. The individuals grouped in a class that is constructed in a particular respect (that is, in a particularly determinant respect) always bring with them, in addition to the pertinent properties by which they are classified, secondary properties which are thus smuggled into the explanatory model.[7] This means that a class or class fraction is defined not only by its position in the relations of production, as identified through indices such as occupation, income or even educational level, but also by a certain sex-ratio, a certain distribution in geographical space (which is never socially neutral) and by a whole set of subsidiary characteristics which may function, in the form of tacit requirements, as real principles of selection or exclusion without ever being formally stated (this is the case with ethnic origin and sex). A number of official criteria in fact serve as a mask for hidden criteria: for example, the requiring of a given diploma can be a way of demanding a particular social origin.

One needs to examine what the list of the criteria used by the analyst derives from the state of the struggle between the groups separated by these criteria, or more precisely from the capacity of groups defined by these criteria, to get themselves recognized as such. There would be less likelihood of forgetting that unskilled workers are to a large extent women and immigrants if groups based on sex or nationality of origin had constituted themselves as such within the working class. Furthermore, the fallacy of the apparent factor would not be so frequent if it were not the simple retranslation onto the terrain of science of the legitimating strategies whereby groups tend to put forward this or that legitimate property, the overt principle of their constitution, to camouflage the real basis of their existence. Thus the most selective groups (a concert audience or the students of a grande école) may doubly conceal the real principle of their selection: by declining to announce the real principles of their existence and their reproduction, they are obliged to rely on mechanisms which lack the specific, systematic rigour of an explicit condition of entry and therefore allow exceptions (unlike clubs and all 'elites' based on co-option, they cannot vet the whole set of properties of the 'elect', i.e., the total person).

The members of groups based on co-option, as are most of the corps protected by an overt or covert *numerus clausus* (doctors, architects, professors, engineers etc.) always have something else in common beyond the characteristics explicitly demanded. The common image of the professions, which is no doubt one of the real determinants of 'vocations', is less abstract and unreal than that presented by statisticians; it takes into account not only the nature of the job and the income, but those secondary characteristics which are often the basis of their social value (prestige or discredit) and which, though absent from the official job description, function as tacit requirements, such as age, sex, social or ethnic origin, overtly or implicitly guiding co-option choices, from entry into the profession and right through a career, so that members of the corps who lack these traits are excluded or marginalized (women doctors and lawyers tending to be restricted to a female clientele and black doctors and lawyers to black clients or research). In short, the property emphasized by the name used to designate a category, usually occupation, is liable to mask the effect of all the secondary properties which, although constitutive of the category, are not expressly indicated.

Similarly, when one is trying to assess the evolution of a social category (identified by occupation), crude errors are inevitable if, by considering only one of the pertinent properties, one ignores all the substitution effects in which the evolution is also expressed. The collective trajectory of a social class may be manifested in the fact that it is becoming 'feminized' or 'masculinized', growing older or young, getting poorer or richer. (The decline of a position may be manifested either in 'feminization'—which may be accompanied by a rise in social origin—or in 'democratization' or in 'ageing'.) The same would be true of any group defined by reference to a position in a field—e.g., a university discipline in the hierarchy of disciplines, a title of nobility in the aristocratic hierarchy, an educational qualification in the academic hierarchy.

The particular relations between a dependent variable (such as political opinion) and so-called independent variables such as sex, age and religion, or even educational level, income and occupation tend to mask the complete system of relationships which constitutes the true principle of the specific strength and form of the effects registered in any particular correlation. The most independent of 'independent' variables conceals a whole network of statistical relations which are present, implicitly, in its relationship with any given opinion or practice. Here too, instead of asking statistical technology to solve a problem which it can only displace, it is necessary to analyse the divisions and variations which the different secondary variables (sex, age etc.) bring into the class defined by the main variable, and consider everything which, though present in the real definition of the class, is not consciously taken into account in the nominal definition, the one summed up in the name used to designate it, or therefore in interpreting the relationship in which it is placed.

Typical of the false independence between so-called independent variables is the relationship between educational qualification and occupation. This is not only because, at least in some areas of social space (to which educational qualifications give some degree of access), occupation depends on qualification, but also because the cultural capital which the qualification is supposed to guarantee depends on the holder's occupation, which may presuppose maintenance or increase of the capital acquired within the family or at school (by and for promotion) or a diminishing of this capital (by

'de-skilling' or 'de-qualification'). To this effect of occupational condition—
in which one has to distinguish the specific effect of the work which, by its
very nature, may demand a more or less great, more or less constant investment of cultural capital, and therefore more or less continuous maintenance
of this capital, and the effect of the possible career which encourages or excludes cultural investments likely to assist or legitimate promotion—must
be added the effect of occupational milieu, i.e., the reinforcement of dispositions (especially cultural, religious or political dispositions) by a group that
is homogeneous in most of the respects which define it. Thus one would
have to examine in each case to what extent occupational conditions of existence assist or hinder this effect, which would mean taking into account
the characteristics of the work (unpleasantness etc.), the conditions in
which it is performed—noise, or silence permitting conversation etc.—the
temporal rhythms it imposes, the spare time it allows, and especially the
form of the horizontal or vertical relations it encourages at the workplace—
during work or in rest periods—or outside.

This effect no doubt explains a number of differences between office
workers (ledger clerks, bank clerks, agency clerks, typists) and commercial
employees (mainly shop assistants), which are not entirely accounted for
either by differences linked to class fraction of origin (office workers are
rather more often the children of farmers; commercial employees the children of small employers) or by differences in educational capital (the first
more often have the BEPC, the second a CAP).

The commercial employees and the office workers, who are distributed in
much the same way as regards sex, age and income, are separated by important differences in dispositions and practices. Office workers are more ascetic—they more often expect their friends to be conscientious or well
brought up, more often prefer a neat, clean and tidy interior and like Brel,
Guétary, Mariano, the *Hungarian Rhapsody, L'Arlésienne*, Raphael, Watteau
and Leonardo. By contrast, commercial employees more often look for
friends who are sociable, bons vivants, amusing and stylish, for a comfortable, cosy interior, and prefer Brassens, Ferré, Françoise Hardy, the *Twilight
of the Gods*, the *Four Seasons, Rhapsody in Blue*, Utrillo or Van Gogh.

Among the effects which the relationship between class fraction and practices simultaneously reveals and conceals, there is also the effect of the position in the distribution of the secondary properties attached to a class.
Thus, members of the class who do not possess all the modal properties—
e.g., men in a strongly feminized occupation or a worker's son at ENA—
have their social identity deeply marked by this membership and the social
image which it imposes and which they have to situate themselves in relation to, whether by acceptance or rejection.

Similarly, relationships such as those between educational capital, or age,
and income mask the relationship linking the two apparently independent
variables. Age determines income to an extent which varies according to educational capital and occupation, which is itself partly determined by educational capital and also by other, more hidden factors such as sex and inherited cultural or social capital. In another case, one of the variables is to a
degree merely a transformed form of the other. Thus, scholastic age (i.e.,
age at a given educational level) is a transformed form of inherited cultural

capital, and lost years are a step towards relegation or elimination. More generally, the educational capital held at a given moment expresses, among other things, the economic and social level of the family of origin. (This results from a long process which is no way a mechanical relationship, since initial cultural capital may be only partially converted into educational capital or may produce effects irreducible to those of educational qualification, as one finds whenever social origin distinguishes individuals whose qualifications are identical.)

Likewise, in every relationship between educational capital and a given practice, one sees the effect of the dispositions associated with gender which help to determine the logic of the reconversion of inherited capital into educational capital, that is, the 'choice' of the type of educational capital which will be obtained from the same initial capital, more often literary for girls, more often scientific for boys. Again, the relationship of a given practice to age may conceal a relationship to educational capital when age is in fact the key to different modes of access to the position—by qualification or internal promotion—and different school generations and different chances of access to the educational system (the oldest agents have lower educational capital than the youngest), or to social class, by virtue of the different social definitions of precociousness or backwardness in the various areas, particularly in schooling.

In fact, the change in chances of access is only one aspect of a more systematic change which also involves the very definition of competence, and tends to make comparisons between the generations increasingly difficult. The conflicts between holders of competences of different ages and different educational levels—old school-certificate holder versus new *bachêlier* (baccalauréat-holder)—centre precisely on the definition of competence, with the old generation complaining that the new generation does not possess the competences formerly defined as elementary and basic: 'They can't spell nowadays', 'They can't even add up'.

And finally, the variations in cultural practice by size of town of residence cannot be ascribed to the direct effect of spatial distance and the variations in the supply of culture, until it is confirmed that the differences persist after discounting the effect of the inequalities in educational capital concealed (even in the occupational category) by geographical distribution. The opposition between Paris and the provinces needs to be analysed in a way similar to that used for the notion of 'educational level'. Relationships involving the variable 'place of residence' manifest not only the effect of cultural supply, linked to the density of objectified cultural capital and so to the objective opportunities for cultural consumption and the related reinforcement of the aspiration to consume, but also all the effects of the unequal spatial distribution of properties and their owners (e.g., possessors of high educational capital), in particular the circular reinforcement each group performs on itself, for example, intensifying cultural practice if it is cultivated, discouraging it by indifference or hostility if it is not.

When, as often happens, the analysis is conducted variable by variable, there is a danger of attributing to one of the variables (such as sex or age, each of which may express in its own way the whole situation or trend of a class) the effect of the *set* of variables (an error which is encouraged by the conscious or unconscious tendency to substitute generic alienations, e.g., those linked to sex or age, for specific alienations, linked to class). Economic and social condition, as identified by occupation, gives a specific form to all the properties of sex and age, so that it is the efficacy of the whole structure of factors associated with a position in social space which is manifested in the correlations between age or sex and practices. The naivety of the inclination to attribute the differences recorded in relation to age to a generic effect of biological ageing becomes self-evident when one sees, for example, that the ageing which, in the privileged classes, is associated with a move to the right, is accompanied, among manual workers, by a move to the left. Similarly, in the relative precocity of executives, measured for example by the age at which they reach a given position, one sees in fact the expression of everything which divides them, despite the apparent identity of condition at a given moment, namely their whole previous and subsequent trajectory, and the capital volume and structure which govern it.

CONSTRUCTED CLASS   Social class is not defined by a property (not even the most determinant one, such as the volume and composition of capital) nor by a collection of properties (of sex, age, social origin, ethnic origin—proportion of blacks and whites, for example, or natives and immigrants—income, educational level etc.), nor even by a chain of properties strung out from a fundamental property (position in the relations of production) in a relation of cause and effect, conditioner and conditioned; but by the structure of relations between all the pertinent properties which gives its specific value to each of them and to the effects they exert on practices.[8] Constructing, as we have here, classes as homogeneous as possible with respect to the fundamental determinants of the material conditions of existence and the conditionings they impose, therefore means that even in constructing the classes and in interpreting the variations of the distribution of properties and practices in relation to these classes, one consciously takes into account the network of secondary characteristics which are more or less unconsciously manipulated whenever the classes are defined in terms of a single criterion, even one as pertinent as occupation. It also means grasping the principle of the objective divisions, i.e., divisions internalized or objectified in distinctive properties, on the basis of which the agents are most likely to divide and come together in reality in their ordinary practices, and also to mobilize themselves or be mobilized (in accordance with the specific logic, linked to a specific history, of the mobilizing organizations) by and for individual or collective political action.

The principles of logical division which are used to produce the classes are of course very unequally constituted socially in pre-existing social classifications. At one extreme, there is the simple existence of the name of a trade or 'social category', the product of classification by a governmental agency, such as INSEE (Institut national de la statistique et des études économiques), or of the social bargaining which leads to industrial 'collective agreements'; and at the other extreme, there are groups possessing a real social identity, recognized spokesmen and institutionalized channels for expressing and defending their interests etc. The secondary principles of division (such as country of origin or sex), which are likely to be ignored by an ordinary analysis until they serve as a basis for some form of mobilization, indicate potential lines of division along which a group socially perceived as unitary may split, more or less deeply and permanently. Because the different factors in the system of determinations constituting a class condition (which can function as real principles of division between objectively separate or actually mobilized groups) vary greatly in their functional weights and therefore in their structuring force, these principles of division are themselves set in a hierarchy; groups mobilized on the basis of a secondary criterion (such as sex or age) are likely to be bound together less permanently and less deeply than those mobilized on the basis of the fundamental determinants of their condition.

To account for the infinite diversity of practices in a way that is both unitary and specific, one has to break with *linear thinking,* which only recognizes the simple ordinal structures of direct determination, and endeavour to reconstruct the networks of interrelated relationships which are present in each of the factors.[9] The structural causality of a network of factors is quite irreducible to the cumulated effects of the set of linear relations, of different explanatory force, which the necessities of analysis oblige one to isolate, those which are established between the different factors, taken one by one, and the practice in question; through each of the factors is exerted the efficacy of all the others, and the multiplicity of determinations leads not to indeterminacy but to over-determination. Thus the superimposition of biological, psychological and social determinations in the formation of socially defined sexual identity (a basic dimension of social personality) is only a particular, but very important, case of a logic that is also at work in other biological determinations, such as ageing.

It goes without saying that the factors constituting the constructed class do not all depend on one another to the same extent, and that the structure of the system they constitute is determined by those which have the greatest functional weight. Thus, the volume and composition of capital give specific form and value to the determinations which the other factors (age, sex, place of residence etc.) impose on practices. Sexual properties are as inseparable from class properties as the yellowness of a lemon is from its acidity: a class is defined in an essential respect by the place and value it gives to the two sexes and to their socially constituted dispositions. This is why there are as many ways of realizing femininity as there are classes and class fractions, and the division of labour between the sexes takes quite different forms, both in practices and in representations, in the different social classes. So the true nature of a class or class fraction is expressed in its distribution by sex or age, and perhaps even more, since its future is then at stake, by the trend of this distribution over time. The lowest positions are designated by the fact that they include a large—and growing—proportion of immigrants or women (unskilled and semi-skilled workers) or immigrant women (charwomen).[10] Similarly, it is no accident that the occupations in personal services—the medical and social services, the personal-care trades, old ones like hairdressing, new ones like beauty care, and especially domestic service, which combine the two aspects of the traditional definition of female tasks, service and the home—are practically reserved for women.

Nor is it accidental that the oldest classes or class fractions are also the classes in decline, such as farmers and industrial and commercial proprietors; most of the young people originating from these classes can only escape collective decline by reconverting into the expanding occupations. Similarly, an increase in the proportion of women indicates the whole trend of an occupation, in particular the absolute or relative devaluation which may result from changes in the nature and organization of the work itself (this is the case with office jobs, for example, with the multiplication of repetitive, mechanical tasks that are commonly left to women) or from changes in relative position in social space (as in teaching, whose position has been affected by the overall displacement of the profession resulting from the overall increase in the number of positions offered).

One would have to analyse in the same way the relationship between marital status and class or class fraction. It has been clearly shown, for example, that male celibacy is not a secondary property of the small peasantry but an essential element of the crisis affecting this fraction of the peasant class. The breakdown of the mechanisms of biological and social reproduction brought about by the specific logic of symbolic domination is one of the mediations of the process of concentration which leads to a deep transformation of the class. But here too, one would have to subject the commonsense notion to close analysis, as has been done for educational level. Being married is not opposed to being unmarried simply as the fact of having a legitimate spouse to the fact of not having one. One only has to think of a few limiting cases (some much more frequent than others), the 'housewife', the artist supported by his wife, the employer or executive who owes his position to his father-in-law, to see that it is difficult to characterize an individual without including all the properties (and property) which are brought to each of the spouses, and not only the wife, through the other—a name (sometimes a distinguished 'de' as well), goods, an income, 'connections', a social status (each member of the couple being characterized by the spouse's social position, to different degrees according to sex, position and the gap between the two positions). The properties acquired or possessed through marriage will be omitted from the system of properties which may determine practices and properties if, as usually happens, one forgets to ask oneself who is the subject of the practices or, more simply, if the 'subject' questioned is really the subject of the practices on which he or she is questioned.

As soon as the question is raised, it can be seen that a number of strategies are concretely defined only in the relationship between the members of a domestic group (a household or, sometimes, an extended family), which itself depends on the relationship between the two systems of properties associated with the two spouses. The common goods, especially when they are of some economic and social importance, such as the apartment or furniture, or even personal goods, such as clothing, are—like the choice of a spouse for son or daughter in other societies—the outcome of these (denied) power relations which define the domestic unit. For example, there is every reason to suppose that, given the logic of the division of labour between the sexes, which gives precedence to women in matters of taste (and to men in politics), the weight of the man's own taste in choosing his clothes (and therefore the degree to which his clothes express his taste) depends not only on his own inherited cultural capital and educational capital (the traditional division of roles tends to weaken, here and elsewhere, as educational capital grows) but also on his wife's educational and cultural capital and on the gap between them. (The same is true of the weight of the wife's own preferences in politics: the effect of assignment by status which makes politics a man's business is less likely to occur, the greater the wife's educational capital, or when the gap between her capital and her husband's is small or in her favour.)

SOCIAL CLASS AND CLASS OF TRAJECTORIES   But this is not all. On the one hand, agents are not completely defined by the properties they possess at a given time, whose conditions of acquisition persist in the habitus (the hysteresis effect); and on the other hand, the relationship between initial capital and present capital, or, to put it another way, between the initial and present positions in social space, is a statistical relationship of very variable intensity. Although they are always perpetuated in the dispositions constituting the habitus, the conditions of acquisition of the properties synchronically observed only make themselves visible in cases of discordance between the conditions of acquisition and the conditions of use,[11] i.e., when the practices generated by the habitus appear as ill-adapted because they are attuned to an earlier state of the objective conditions (this is what might be called the Don Quixote effect). The statistical analysis which compares the practices of agents possessing the same properties and occupying the same social position at a given time but separated by their origin performs an operation analogous to ordinary perception which, within a group, identifies the parvenus and the déclassés by picking up the subtle indices of manner or bearing which betray the effect of conditions of existence different from the present ones or, which amounts to the same thing, a social trajectory different from the modal trajectory for the group in question.

Individuals do not move about in social space in a random way, partly because they are subject to the forces which structure this space (e.g., through the objective mechanisms of elimination and channelling), and partly because they resist the forces of the field with their specific inertia, that is, their properties, which may exist in embodied form, as dispositions, or in objectified form, in goods, qualifications etc. To a given volume of inherited capital there corresponds a band of more or less equally probable trajectories leading to more or less equivalent positions (this is the *field of the possibles* objectively offered to a given agent), and the shift from one trajectory to another often depends on collective events—wars, crises etc.—or individual events—encounters, affairs, benefactors etc.— which are usually described as (fortunate or unfortunate) accidents, although they themselves depend statistically on the position and disposition of those whom they befall (e.g., the skill in operating 'connections' which enables the holders of high social capital to preserve or increase this capital), when, that is, they are not deliberately contrived by institutions (clubs, family reunions, old-boys' or alumni associations etc.) or by the 'spontaneous' intervention of individuals or groups. It follows from this that position and individual trajectory are not statistically independent; all positions of arrival are not equally probable for all starting points. This implies that there is a strong correlation between social positions and the dispositions of the agents who occupy them, or, which amounts to the same thing, the trajectories which have led them to occupy them, and consequently that the modal trajectory is an integral part of the system of factors constituting the class. (The more dispersed the trajectories are—as in the petite bourgeoisie—the less are practices reducible to the effect of synchronically defined position.)

The homogeneity of the dispositions associated with a position and their seemingly miraculous adjustment to the demands inscribed in it result partly from the mechanisms which channel towards positions individuals who are already adjusted to them, either because they feel 'made' for jobs that are 'made' for them—this is 'vocation', the proleptic assumption of an objective destiny that is imposed by practical reference to the modal trajectory in the class of origin—or because they are seen in this light by the occupants of the posts—this is co-option based on the immediate harmony of dispositions—and partly from the dialectic which is established, throughout a lifetime, between dispositions and positions, aspirations and achievements. Social ageing is nothing other than the slow renunciation or disinvestment (socially assisted and encouraged) which leads agents to adjust their aspirations to their objective chances, to espouse their condition, become what they are and make do with what they have, even if this entails deceiving themselves as to what they are and what they have, with collective complicity, and accepting bereavement of all the 'lateral possibles' they have abandoned along the way.

The statistical character of the relationship between initial capital and present capital explains why practices cannot be completely accounted for solely in terms of the properties defining the position occupied in social space at a given moment. To say that the members of a class initially possessing a certain economic and cultural capital are destined, with a given probability, to an educational and social trajectory leading to a given position means in fact that a fraction of the class (which cannot be determined a priori within the limits of this explanatory system) will deviate from the trajectory most common for the class as a whole and follow the (higher or lower) trajectory which was most probable for members of another class.[12] The trajectory effect which then manifests itself, as it does whenever individuals occupying similar positions at a given time are separated by differences associated with the evolution over time of the volume and structure of their capital, i.e., by their individual trajectories, is very likely to be wrongly interpreted. The correlation between a practice and social origin (measured by the father's position, the real value of which may have suffered a decline concealed by constant nominal value) is the resultant of two effects (which may either reinforce or offset each other): on the one hand, the inculcation effect directly exerted by the family or the original conditions of existence; on the other hand, the specific effect of social trajectory,[13] that is, the effects of social rise or decline on dispositions and opinions, position of origin being, in this logic, merely the starting point of a trajectory, the reference whereby the slope of the social career is defined. The need to make this distinction is self-evident in all cases in which individuals from the same class fraction or the same family, and therefore presumably subject to identical moral, religious or political inculcations, are inclined towards divergent stances in religion or politics by the different relations to the social world which they owe to divergent individual trajectories, having, for example, succeeded or failed in the reconversion strategies necessary to escape the collective decline of their class.

This trajectory effect no doubt plays a large part in blurring the relationship between social class and religious or political opinions, owing to the fact that it governs the representation of the position occupied in the social world and hence the vision of its world and its future. In contrast to upwardly mobile individuals or groups, 'commoners' of birth or culture who have their future, i.e., their being, before them, individuals or groups in decline endlessly reinvent the discourse of all aristocracies, essentialist faith in the eternity of natures, celebration of tradition and the past, the cult of history and its rituals, because the best they can expect from the future is the return of the old order, from which they expect the restoration of their social being.[14]

This blurring is particularly visible in the middle classes and especially in the new fractions of these classes, which are grey areas, ambiguously located in the social structure, inhabited by individuals whose trajectories are extremely scattered. This dispersion of trajectories is even found here at the level of the domestic unit, which is more likely than in other classes to bring together spouses (relatively) ill matched not only as regards social origin and trajectories but also occupational status and educational level. (This has the effect, among other things, of foregrounding what the new vulgate calls 'the problems of the couple', i.e., essentially, the problems of the sexual division of labour and the division of sexual labour.)

In contrast to the effect of individual trajectory, which, being a deviation from the collective trajectory (that may have a zero slope), is immediately visible, the effect of collective trajectory may not be noticed as such. When the trajectory effect concerns a whole class or class fraction, that is, a set of individuals who occupy an identical position and are engaged in the same collective trajectory, the one which defines a rising or declining class, there is a danger of attributing to the properties synchronically attached to the class, effects (e.g., political or religious opinions) which are in reality the product of collective transformations. The analysis is complicated by the fact that some members of a class fraction may have embarked on individual trajectories running in the opposite direction to that of the fraction as a whole. This does not mean that their practices are not marked by the collective destiny. (It is questionable, for example, whether craftsmen or farmers whose individual success seems to run counter to the collective decline cease to be affected by that decline.)[15] But here too one must avoid substantialism. Thus, some of the properties associated with social class which may remain without efficacy or value in a given field, such as ease and familiarity with culture in an area strictly controlled by the educational system, can take on their full force in another field, such as high society, or in another state of the same field, like the aptitudes which, after the French Revolution, enabled the French aristocracy to become, in Marx's phrase, 'the dancing-masters of Europe'.

CAPITAL AND THE MARKET   But everything would still be too simple if it were sufficient to replace a factor, even a particularly powerful one such as socio-occupational category, which derives a major part of its effects from the secondary variables it governs, by a system of factors fundamentally defined by its structure.[16] In fact, what is determinant in a given area is a particular configuration of the system of properties constituting the constructed class, defined in an entirely theoretical way by the whole set of factors operating in all areas of practice—volume and structure of capital, defined synchronically and diachronically (trajectory), sex, age, marital status, place of residence etc. It is the specific logic of the field, of what is at stake and of the type of capital needed to play for it, which governs those properties through which the relationship between class and practice is established.

If this double correlation of each explanatory factor is not performed, every sort of error is likely, all of them resulting from ignoring the fact that what is 'operative' in the factor in question depends on the system it is placed in and the conditions it 'operates' in; or, more simply, from failing to raise the question of the real principle of the efficacy of the 'independent variable', by proceeding as if the relationship found between the factor—designated by what is usually no more than an indicator of it (e.g., educational level) —and this or that practice (e.g., the rate of response to political questions, or the capacity to adopt the aesthetic disposition, or museum-going etc.) did not itself have to be explained.

To understand why the same system of properties (which determines and is determined by the position occupied in the field of class struggles) always has the greatest explanatory power, whatever the area in question—eating habits, use of credit, fertility, political opinion, religion etc.—and why, simultaneously, the relative weight of the factors which constitute it varies from one field to another—educational capital being most important in one area, economic capital in another, and so on—one only has to see that, because capital is a social relation, i.e., an energy which only exists and only produces its effects in the field in which it is produced and reproduced, each of the properties attached to class is given its value and efficacy by the specific laws of each field. In practice, that is, in a particular field, the properties, internalized in dispositions or objectified in economic or cultural goods, which are attached to agents are not all simultaneously operative; the specific logic of the field determines those which are valid in this market, which are pertinent and active in the game in question, and which, in the relationship with this field, function as specific capital—and, consequently, as a factor explaining practices. This means, concretely, that the social rank and specific power which agents are assigned in a particular field depend firstly on the specific capital they can mobilize, whatever their additional wealth in other types of capital (though this may also exert an effect of contamination).

This explains why the relationship which analysis uncovers between class and practices appears to be established in each case through the mediation of a factor or particular combination of factors which varies according to the field. This appearance itself leads to the mistake of inventing as many explanatory systems as there are fields, instead of seeing each of them as a transformed form of all the others; or worse, the error of setting up a particular combination of factors active in a particular field of practices as a universal explanatory principle. The singular configuration of the system of explanatory factors which has to be constructed in order to account for a state of the distribution of a particular class of goods or practices, i.e., a balance-sheet, drawn up at a particular moment, of the class struggle over that particular class of goods or practices (caviar or avant-garde painting, Nobel prizes or state contracts, an enlightened opinion or a chic sport), is the form taken, in that field, by the objectified and internalized capital (properties and habitus) which defines social class and constitutes the principle of the production of classified and classifying practices. It represents a state of the system of properties which make class a universal principle of explanation and classification, defining the rank occupied in all possible fields.

A Three-Dimensional Space

Endeavouring to reconstitute the units most homogeneous from the point of view of the conditions of production of habitus, i.e., with respect to the elementary conditions of existence and the resultant conditionings, one can construct a space whose three fundamental dimensions are defined by volume of capital, composition of capital, and change in these two properties over time (manifested by past and potential trajectory in social space).[17]

The primary differences, those which distinguish the major classes of conditions of existence, derive from the overall volume of capital, understood as the set of actually usable resources and powers—economic capital, cultural capital and also social capital. The distribution of the different classes (and class fractions) thus runs from those who are best provided with both economic and cultural capital to those who are most deprived in both respects (see figure 5, later in this section). The members of the professions, who have high incomes and high qualifications, who very often (52.9 percent) originate from the dominant class (professions or senior executives), who receive and consume a large quantity of both material and cultural goods, are opposed in almost all respects to the office workers, who have low qualifications, often originate from the working or middle classes, who receive little and consume little, devoting a high proportion of their time to car maintenance and home improvement; and they are even more opposed to the skilled or semi-skilled workers, and still more to unskilled workers or farm labourers, who have the lowest incomes, no qualifications, and originate almost exclusively (90.5 percent of farm labourers, 84.5 percent of unskilled workers) from the working classes.[18]

The differences stemming from the total volume of capital almost always conceal, both from common awareness and also from 'scientific' knowledge, the secondary differences which, within each of the classes defined by overall volume of capital, separate class fractions, defined by different asset structures, i.e., different distributions of their total capital among the different kinds of capital.

Among the difficulties which this model aims to account for in a unitary and systematic way, the most visible is the observation, which others have often made (e.g., C.S. VII), that the hierarchies, both in the dominant class, between the executives and the employers, and in the middle class, between the junior executives and the craftsmen or shopkeepers, vary according to the activity or asset in question. This effect seems to support the relativistic critique of the social classes until it is seen that there is a relationship between the nature of these activities or assets, for example, theatre-going or possession of a colour TV, and the structure of each group's capital.

Once one takes account of the structure of total assets—and not only, as has always been done implicitly, of the dominant kind in a given structure, 'birth', 'fortune' or 'talents', as the nineteenth century put it— one has the means of making more precise divisions and also of observing the specific effects of the structure of distribution between the different kinds of capital. This may, for example, be symmetrical (as in the case of the professions, which combine very high income with very high cultural capital) or asymmetrical (in the case of higher-education and secondary teachers or employers, with cultural capital dominant in one case, economic capital in the other). One thus discovers two sets of homologous positions. The fractions whose reproduction depends on economic capital, usually inherited—industrial and commercial employers at the higher level, craftsmen and shopkeepers at the intermediate level—are opposed to the fractions which are least endowed (relatively, of course) with economic capital, and whose reproduction mainly depends on cultural capital—higher-education and secondary teachers at the higher level, primary teachers at the intermediate level.

The industrialists, who are grouped with the commercial employers in surveys by representative sample because of their small number, declare considerably higher incomes than the latter (33.6 percent say they earn more than 100,000 French francs, as against 14.5 percent of the commercial employers). Those classified as industrialists in the INSEE survey (C.S. I) are much closer to the new bourgeoisie than are the commercial employers: many more of them declare salaries and investment income, many fewer declare industrial, commercial or non-commercial profits. For the working classes, who are strongly ranked by overall capital volume, the data available do not enable one to grasp the differences in the second dimension (composition of capital). However, differences such as those between semi-skilled, educationally unqualified, provincial factory workers of rural origin, living in an inherited farmhouse, and skilled workers in the Paris region who have been in the working class for generations, who possess a 'trade' or technical qualifications, must be the source of differences in life-style and religious and political opinion.

Given that, as one moves from the artists to the industrial and commercial employers, volume of economic capital rises and volume of cultural capital falls, it can be seen that the dominant class is organized in a chiastic structure. To establish this, it is necessary to use various indicators borrowed from a survey which has the advantage of distinguishing between public-sector and private-sector executives (C.S. V) to examine, successively, the distribution of economic capital and the distribution of cultural capital among the fractions; the structures of these distributions must then be correlated.

Although it is self-evident when one considers indicators of wealth (as will be done later), the hierarchy of the class fractions as regards possession of economic capital, running from industrial and commercial employers to teachers, is already less visible when, as here, one is only dealing with indices of *consumption* (cars, boats, hotels) which are neither entirely adequate nor entirely unambiguous (see table 6). The first (cars) also depends on the type of professional activity, and the other two depend on spare time, which, as one learns in other ways, varies inversely with economic capital. Home ownership also depends on stability in the same place of residence (lower among executives, engineers and teachers). Incomes are very unevenly underestimated (the rate of non-declaration may be considered an indicator of the tendency to under-declare) and very unequally accompanied by fringe benefits such as expense-account meals and business trips (which are known to rise as one moves from teachers to private-sector executives and employers).

As regards cultural capital, except for a few inversions, which reflect secondary variables such as place of residence, with the corresponding supply of culture, and income, with the means it provides, the different fractions are organized in an opposite hierarchy (see table 7). (Differentiation according to the type of capital possessed, literary, scientific or economic and political, is mainly seen in the fact that engineers show more interest in music and 'intellectual' games such as bridge or chess than in literary activities—theatre-going or reading *Le Figaro Littéraire*.)

These indicators no doubt tend to minimize the gaps between the different fractions. Most cultural consumption also entails an economic cost: theatre-going, for example, depends on income as well as education. Moreover, equipment such as FM radios or hi-fi systems can be used in very different ways (e.g., classical music or dance music), whose values, in terms of the dominant hierarchy of possible uses, may vary as much as the different types of reading-matter or theatre. In fact, the position of the different fractions ranked according to their interest in the different types of reading-matter tends to correspond to their position when ranked according to volume of cultural capital as one moves towards the rarer types of reading, which are known to be those most linked to educational level and highest in the hierarchy of cultural legitimacy (see table 8).

One also finds (C.S. XIV, table 215a) that the over-representation of teachers (and students) in the audience of the different theatres steadily de-

Table 6 Some indicators of economic capital in different fractions of the dominant class, 1966.[a]

Indicators of economic capital	Teachers (higher and secondary)	Public-sector execs.	Professions	Engineers	Private-sector execs.	Industrial employers	Commercial employers
Homeowner	51%	38%	54%	44%	40%	70%	70%
Luxury car owner	12%	20%	28%	21%	22%	34%	33%
Boat owner	8%	8%	14%	10%	12%	14%	13%
Hotel holidays	15%	17%	23%	17%	21%	26%	32%
Median annual income (thousands of francs)	33	32	41	36	37	36	33
Rate of undeclared income	6	8	27	9	13	28	24

Source: C.S. V (1966).
a. In each row the italic figures indicate the strongest tendency.

Table 7 Some indicators of cultural practice in different fractions of the dominant class, 1966.[a]

Indicators	Teachers (higher and secondary)	Public sector execs.	Professions	Engineers	Private-sector execs.	Industrial employers	Commercial employers
Reading books other than for job[b]	21%	18%	18%	16%	16%	10%	10%
Theatre-going[c]	38%	29%	29%	28%	34%	16%	20%
Listening to classical music	83%	89%	86%	89%	89%	75%	73%
Museum visits	75%	66%	68%	58%	69%	47%	52%
Art gallery visits	58%	54%	57%	45%	47%	37%	34%
Own FM radio	59%	54%	57%	56%	53%	48%	48%
No TV	46%	30%	28%	33%	28%	14%	24%
Reading Le Monde[d]	410	235	230	145	151	82	49
Reading Le Figaro Littéraire[d]	168	132	131	68	100	64	24

Source: C.S. V (1966).
a. In each row the italic figures indicate the strongest tendency.
b. 15 hours or more per week.
c. At least once every two or three months.
d. Per thousand.

Table 8 Types of books preferred by different fractions of the dominant class (%), 1966.[a]

Type of book	Teachers (higher and secondary)	Public-sector execs.	Professions	Engineers	Private-sector execs.	Industrial employers	Commercial employers
Detective stories	25 (6)	29 (1)	27 (4)	28 (3)	29 (1)	27 (4)	25 (6)
Adventure stories	17 (7)	20 (3)	18 (6)	24 (1)	22 (2)	19 (4)	19 (4)
Historical	44 (4)	47 (2)	49 (1)	47 (2)	44 (4)	36 (6)	27 (7)
Illustrated art books	28 (2)	20 (3)	31 (1)	19 (5)	20 (3)	17 (6)	14 (7)
Novels	64 (2)	68 (1)	59 (5)	62 (3)	62 (3)	45 (6)	42 (7)
Philosophy	20 (1)	13 (3)	12 (5)	13 (3)	15 (2)	10 (7)	12 (5)
Politics	15 (1)	12 (2)	9 (4)	7 (5)	10 (3)	5 (6)	4 (7)
Economics	*10 (1)*	8 (3)	5 (6)	7 (5)	9 (2)	8 (3)	5 (6)
Science	15 (3)	14 (4)	18 (2)	*21 (1)*	9 (7)	10 (6)	11 (5)

Source: C.S. V (1966).

a. The figures in a given row show the percentage of each category of respondents who included that type of book among their favourite types (italic figures indicate the strongest tendency in the row). The figures in parentheses show the rank of each class fraction in that row. Books on economics and science are set apart on the grounds that interest in these types of reading-matter depends on secondary factors, in one case occupational activity (hence the rank of the private-sector executives and employers) and in the other, academic training (hence the rank of the engineers).

clines and the over-representation of the other fractions (employers, senior executives and members of the professions, unfortunately not distinguished in the statistics) increases as one moves from avant-garde or reputedly avant-garde theatre to classical theatre and especially from classical to boulevard theatre, which draws between a third and a quarter of its audience from the least 'intellectual' fractions of the dominant class.

Having established that the structure of the distribution of economic capital is symmetrical and opposite to that of cultural capital, we can turn to the question of the hierarchy of the two principles of hierarchization (without forgetting that this hierarchy is at all times a stake in struggles and that, in certain conjunctures, as in present-day France, cultural capital may be one of the conditions for access to control of economic capital). We may take as an indicator of the state of the power relation between these two principles of domination the frequency of intergenerational movements between the fractions.

If we use as indices of the rarity of a position (or, which amounts to the same thing, its degree of closure) the proportion of its occupants who originate from the dominant class as a whole and from the fraction in question, we find that the resulting hierarchy corresponds fairly exactly, for both indices, to the hierarchy by volume of economic capital (see table 9). The proportion of members of each fraction who originated from the dominant class, and the proportion of individuals who originated from the fraction to which they now belong, decline in parallel as one moves from the industrial employers to the teachers, with a clear break between the three higher-ranking fractions (industrial and commercial employers and the professions) and the three lower-ranking fractions (engineers, public-sector executives and teachers).

The use of these indicators may be contested on the grounds that the different fractions have very unequal control over the conditions of their social reproduction, so that the high proportion of endogenous employers may express nothing other than the capacity of these fractions (or at least of a proportion of their members) to transmit their powers and privileges without mediation or control. Indeed, this capacity is itself one of the rarest privileges, which, by giving greater freedom vis-à-vis academic verdicts, reduces the necessity or urgency of making the cultural investments which cannot be avoided by those who depend entirely on the education system for their reproduction. The fractions richest in cultural capital do in fact tend to invest in their children's education as well as in the cultural practices likely to maintain and increase their specific rarity; the fractions richest in economic capital set aside cultural and educational investments in favour of economic investments—industrial and commercial employers more so, however, than the new bourgeoisie of private-sector executives, who manifest the same concern for rational investment both in economic and in educational matters. The members of

Table 9 Social origin of members of the dominant class, by class fraction (%), 1970.[a]

Father's class fraction	Son's class fraction					
	Industrial employers	Commercial employers	Professions	Engineers	Public-sector executives	Teachers (higher and secondary)
Industrial employers	*33.5*	2.8	2.3	6.1	4.4	1.5
Commercial employers	1.9	*31.0*	0	1.8	5.0	0.8
Professions	0.6	0.9	*20.0*	0.9	2.4	7.6
Engineers	0	0	6.4	*6.7*	2.3	4.6
Public-sector executives	1.9	3.3	9.9	13.2	*14.2*	7.6
Teachers (higher and secondary)	0.6	0	2.9	2.7	0.3	*6.1*
Whole class	38.5	38.0	41.5	31.4	28.7	28.2

Source: C.S. II (1970).
a. In each row the italic figure indicates the strongest tendency.

the professions (especially doctors and lawyers), relatively well endowed with both forms of capital, but too little integrated into economic life to use their capital in it actively, invest in their children's education but also and especially in cultural practices which symbolize possession of the material and cultural means of maintaining a bourgeois life-style and which provide a social capital, a capital of social connections, honourability and respectability that is often essential in winning and keeping the confidence of high society, and with it a clientele, and may be drawn on, for example, in making a political career.

Given that scholastic success mainly depends on inherited cultural capital and on the propensity to invest in the educational system (and that the latter varies with the degree to which maintained or improved social position depends on such success), it is clear why the proportion of pupils in a given school or college who come from the culturally richest fractions rises with the position of that school in the specifically academic hierarchy (measured, for example, by previous academic success), reaching its peak in the institution responsible for reproducing the professorial corps (the Ecole Normale Supérieure). In fact, like the dominant class which they help to reproduce, higher-education institutions are organized in accordance with two opposing principles of hierarchy. The hierarchy dominant within the educational system, i.e., the one which ranks institutions by specifically academic criteria, and, correlatively, by the proportion of their students drawn from the culturally richest fractions, is diametrically opposed to the hierarchy dominant outside the educational system, i.e., the one which ranks institutions by the proportion of their students drawn from the fractions richest in economic capital or in power and by the position in the economic or power hierarchy of the occupations they lead to. If the offspring of the dominated fractions are less represented in the economically highest institutions (such as ENA or HEC) than might be expected from their previous academic success and the position of these schools in the specifically scholastic hierarchy, this is, of course, because these schools refuse to apply purely scholastic criteria, but it is also because the scholastic hierarchy is most faithfully respected (so that the science section of the ENS is preferred to Polytechnique, or the Arts faculty to Sciences Po), by those who are most dependent on the educational system. (Blindness to alternative ranking principles is most nearly complete in the case of teachers' children, whose whole upbringing inclines them to identify all success with academic success.)

The same chiastic structure is found at the level of the middle classes, where volume of cultural capital again declines, while economic capital increases, as one moves from primary teachers to small industrial and commercial employers, with junior executives, technicians and clerical workers in an intermediate position, homologous to that of engineers and executives at the higher level. Artistic craftsmen and art-dealers, who earn their living from industrial and commercial profits, and are close in those respects to other small businessmen, are set apart from them by their relatively high cultural capital, which brings them closer to the new petite bourgeoisie. The medical and social services, drawn to a relatively large extent from the dominant class,[19] are in a central position, roughly homologous to that of the professions (although slightly more tilted towards the pole of cultural capital); they are the only ones who receive not only wages or salaries but also, in some cases, non-commercial profits (like the professions).

It can immediately be seen that the homology between the space of the dominant class and that of the middle classes is explained by the fact that their structure is the product of the same principles. In each case, there is an opposition between owners (of their own home, of rural or urban property, of stocks and shares), often older, with little spare time, often the children of industrial or agricultural employers, and non-owners, chiefly endowed with educational capital and spare time, originating from the wage-earning fractions of the middle and upper classes or from the working class. The occupants of homologous positions, primary teachers and professors, for example, or small shopkeepers and commercial entrepreneurs, are mainly separated by the volume of the kind of capital that is dominant in the structure of their assets, i.e., by differences of degree which separate individuals unequally endowed with the same scarce resources. The lower positions—and, correlatively, the dispositions of their occupants—derive some of their characteristics from the fact that they are objectively related to the corresponding positions at the higher level, towards which they tend and 'pre-tend'. This is clearly seen in the case of the wage-earning petite bourgeoisie, whose ascetic virtues and cultural good intentions—which it manifests in all sorts of ways, taking evening classes, enrolling in libraries, collecting stamps etc.—very clearly express the aspiration to rise to the higher position, the objective destiny of the occupants of the lower position who manifest such dispositions.

To reconstruct the social conditions of production of the habitus as fully as possible, one also has to consider the social trajectory of the class or class fraction the agent belongs to, which, through the probable slope of the collective future, engenders progressive or regressive dispositions towards the future; and the evolution, over several generations, of the asset structure of each lineage, which is perpetuated in the habitus and introduces divisions even within groups that are as homogeneous as the fractions. To give an idea of the range of possibilities, it need only be pointed out that an individual's social trajectory represents the combination of: the lifelong evolution of the volume of his capital, which can be described, very approximately, as increasing, decreasing or stationary; the volume of each sort of capital (amenable to the same distinctions), and therefore the composition of his capital (since constant volume can conceal a change in structure);

and, in the same way, the father's and mother's asset volume and structure
and their respective weights in the different kinds of capital (e.g., father
stronger in economic capital and mother in cultural capital, or vice versa, or
equivalence); and therefore the volume and structure of the capital of both
sets of grandparents.

To account more fully for the differences in life-style between the different fractions—especially as regards culture—one would have to take
account of their distribution in a *socially ranked geographical space*. A
group's chances of appropriating any given class of rare assets (as measured by the mathematical probability of access) depend partly on its capacity for the specific appropriation, defined by the economic, cultural
and social capital it can deploy in order to appropriate materially or symbolically the assets in question, that is, its position in social space, and
partly on the relationship between its distribution in geographical space
and the distribution of the scarce assets in that space.[20] (This relationship
can be measured in average distances from goods or facilities, or in travelling time—which involves access to private or public transport.) In other
words, a group's real social distance from certain assets must integrate the
geographical distance, which itself depends on the group's spatial distribution and, more precisely, its distribution with respect to the 'focal
point' of economic and cultural values, i.e., Paris or the major regional
centres (in some careers—e.g., in the postal banking system—employment or promotion entails a period of exile).[21] Thus, the distance of farm
workers from legitimate culture would not be so vast if the specifically
cultural distance implied by their low cultural capital were not compounded by their spatial dispersion. Similarly, many of the differences
observed in the (cultural and other) practices of the different fractions of
the dominant class are no doubt attributable to the size of the town they
live in. Consequently, the opposition between engineers and private-
sector executives on the one hand, and industrial and commercial employers on the other, partly stems from the fact that the former mostly
live in Paris and work for relatively large firms (only 7 percent of private-sector executives work in firms employing from 1 to 5 people, as
against 34 percent in medium-sized firms and 40 percent in firms employing more than 50 people), whereas the latter mainly run small firms
(in the 1966 survey by SOFRES [Société française d'enquêtes par son-
dages]—C.S. V—6 percent of the industrialists had from 1 to 5 employees; 70 percent, 6 to 49; 24 percent, more than 50; in commerce, the
corresponding figures are 30 percent, 42 percent and 12 percent) and
mostly live in the provinces and even in the country (according to the
1968 census, 22.3 percent of the industrialists and 15.5 percent of the
commercial employers lived in a rural commune, 14.1 percent and 11.8
percent in communes of less than 10,000 inhabitants).

The model which emerges would not be so difficult to arrive at if it did not presuppose a break with the common-sense picture of the social world, summed up in the metaphor of the 'social ladder' and suggested by all the everyday language of 'mobility', with its 'rises' and 'falls'; and a no less radical break with the whole sociological tradition which, when it is not merely tacitly accepting the one-dimensional image of social space, as most research on 'social mobility' does, subjects it to a pseudo-scientific elaboration, reducing the social universe to a continuum of abstract strata ('upper middle class', 'lower middle class' etc.),[22] obtained by aggregating different forms of capital, thanks to the construction of indices (which are, par excellence, the destroyers of structures).[23] Projection onto a single axis, in order to construct the continuous, linear, homogeneous, one-dimensional series with which the social hierarchy is normally identified, implies an extremely difficult (and, if it is unwitting, extremely dangerous) operation, whereby the different types of capital are reduced to a single standard. This abstract operation has an objective basis in the possibility, which is always available, of converting one type of capital into another; however, the exchange rates vary in accordance with the power relation between the holders of the different forms of capital. By obliging one to formulate the principle of the convertibility of the different kinds of capital, which is the precondition for reducing the space to one dimension, the construction of a two-dimensional space makes it clear that the exchange rate of the different kinds of capital is one of the fundamental stakes in the struggles between class fractions whose power and privileges are linked to one or the other of these types. In particular, this exchange rate is a stake in the struggle over the dominant principle of domination (economic capital, cultural capital or social capital), which goes on at all times between the different fractions of the dominant class.

Reconversion Strategies

Reproduction strategies, the set of outwardly very different practices whereby individuals or families tend, unconsciously and consciously, to maintain or increase their assets and consequently to maintain or improve their position in the class structure, constitute a system which, being the product of a single unifying, generative principle, tends to function and change in a systematic way. Through the mediation of the disposition towards the future, which is itself determined by the group's objective chances of reproduction, these strategies depend, first, on the volume and composition of the capital to be reproduced; and, secondly, on the state of the instruments of reproduction (inheritance law and custom, the labour market, the educational system etc.), which itself depends on the state of the power relations between the classes. Any change in either the instruments of reproduction or the state of the capital to be reproduced therefore leads to a restructuring of the system of reproduc-

One of the difficulties of sociological discourse lies in the fact that, like all language, it unfolds in strictly linear fashion, whereas, to escape oversimplification and one-sidedness, one ought to be able to recall at every point the whole network of relationships found there. That is why it has seemed useful to present a diagram which has the property, as Saussure says, of being able to 'present simultaneous complications in several dimensions', as a means of grasping the correspondence between the structure of social space—whose two fundamental dimensions correspond to the volume and composition of the capital of the groups distributed within it—and the structure of the space of the symbolic properties attached to those groups. But this diagram does not aim to be the crystal ball in which the alchemists claimed to see at a glance everything happening in the world; and like mathematicians who also treat what they call 'imagery' as a necessary evil, I am tempted to withdraw it in the very act of presenting it. For there is reason to fear that it will encourage readings which will reduce the homologies between systems of differences to direct, mechanical relationships between groups and properties; or that it will encourage the form of voyeurism which is inherent in the objectivist intention, putting the sociologist in the role of the lame devil who takes off the roofs and reveals the secrets of domestic life to his fascinated readers.

To have as exact an idea as possible of the theoretical model that is proposed, it has to be imagined that three diagrams are superimposed (as could be done with transparent sheets). The first (here, figure 5) presents the space of social conditions, as organized by the synchronic and diachronic distribution of the volume and composition of the various kinds of capital; the position of each group (class fraction) in this space is determined by the set of properties characteristic in the respects thus defined as pertinent. The second (figure 6) presents the space of life-styles, i.e., the distribution of the practices and properties which constitute the life-style in which each of these conditions manifests itself. Finally, between the two previous diagrams one ought to insert a third, presenting the theoretical space of habitus, that is, of the generative formulae (e.g., for teachers, aristocratic asceticism) which underlie each of the classes of practices and properties, that is, the transformation into a distinct and distinctive life-style of the necessities and facilities characteristic of a condition and a position. The figures presented here are not plane diagrams of correspondence analyses, although various such analyses were drawn on in order to construct them, and although a number of these are organized in accordance with a similar structure (including the analyses of the survey data which are presented below).

Among the limitations of such a construct, the most important are due to the lacunae in the statistics, which are much better at measuring consumption or, at best, income (setting aside secondary and hidden profits) and property than capital in the strict sense (especially capital invested in the economy); others are due to the inadequacies of the analytical categories. These are very unequally homogeneous even as regards the pertinent criteria and, in the case of the industrial and commercial employers, make it impossible, for example, to identify the holders of a capital that can exert power over capital, i.e., big business. (For lack of rigorous indicators of the dispersion of the different categories, the economic and cultural dispersion of the most heterogeneous categories—farmers, industrial and commercial employers, craftsmen and shopkeepers—has been indicated by writing the corresponding names vertically between the extreme limits defining the group.) It has to be remembered that the position marked by the names always represents the central point in a space of variable extent which may in some cases be organized as a field of competition.

In the absence of a survey (perhaps impossible to carry out in practice) that would provide, with respect to the same representative sample, all the indicators of economic, cultural and social wealth and its evolution which are needed in order to construct an adequate representation of social space, a simplified model of that space has been constructed, based on information acquired through earlier research, and on a set of data taken from various surveys, all done by INSEE and therefore homogeneous at least as regards the construction of the categories (see appendix 3). From the INSEE survey of 1967 on leisure activities (tables relating to men) I have taken indicators of spare time such as length of the working week (C.S. IV); from the 1970 survey on vocational training (tables relating to men) I have taken data on the father's occupational category (social trajectory), the father's educa-

tional level (inherited cultural capital) and the subject's educational level (scholastic capital) (C.S. II); from the 1970 survey on incomes, I have taken information on total incomes, rural and urban property, shares, industrial and commercial profits, wages and salaries (economic capital) (C.S. I); from the 1972 survey on household consumption, data on the total amount spent, possession of a washing-machine and telephone, forms of tenancy of main and second residence (C.S. III); and from the 1968 census, data on the size of the town of residence.

For each of the groups represented, I have also indicated, firstly, the distribution of the occupants of each group according to the social trajectory which has brought them there, with histograms showing the proportion of each group having come from each of the different classes. For the sake of legibility, these histograms are reproduced only for a few illustrative categories. They suffice to show that the proportion of individuals from the dominant class (black) rises strongly, while the proportion from the working classes (white) declines, as one moves up the social hierarchy. (The histogram for the 'semi-skilled' workers, not reproduced here, is intermediate between those of the unskilled and skilled workers.) For the upper and middle classes at least, one really needs to be able to give the distribution by fraction of origin.

Secondly, I have indicated the history of the group as a whole. This is shown by the arrows, pointing up, down or horizontally, which indicate that between 1962 and 1968 the group in question expanded (by at least 25 percent), contracted or

Figure 5 (shown in black)

The space of social positions.

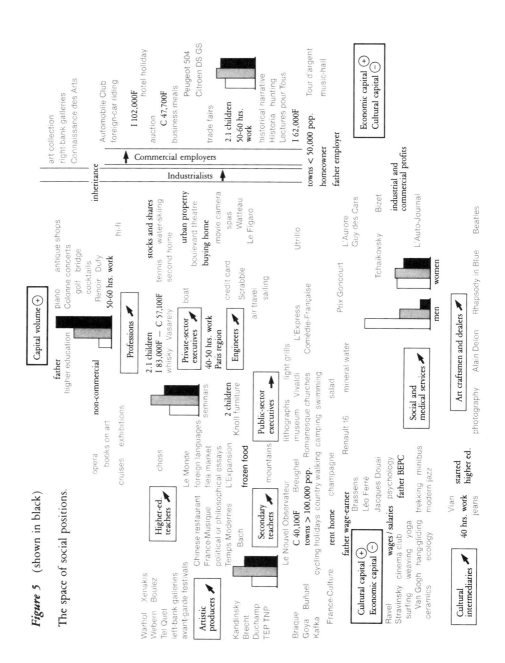

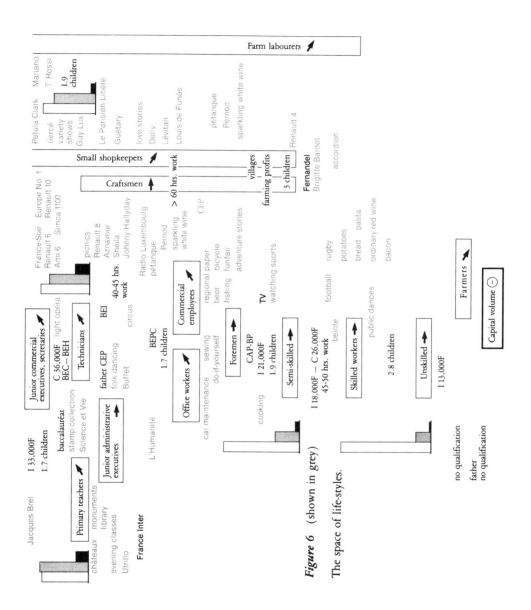

Figure 6 (shown in grey)

The space of life-styles.

remained stable. They thus make visible the opposition between the new, strongly growing fractions and the established, stable or declining fractions. I have thus endeavoured to show both the state of the power relation between the classes which constitutes the structure of the social space at a given moment and also something which is simultaneously an effect of and a factor in the transformation of that structure, namely the reconversion strategies whereby individuals (and groups) strive to maintain or improve their position in social space.

The synoptic schema, by bringing together information from areas which the usual classificatory systems separate—so much so that they make mere juxtaposition appear unthinkable or scandalous—and so making manifest the relationships among all the properties and practices characteristic of a group, which are perceived intuitively and which guide the classifications of everyday life, forces one to look for the basis of each of these systems of 'choices', on the one hand in the social conditions and conditionings characteristic of a given position in objective social space, which are expressed in those choices but in a misrecognizable form; and on the other hand, in their relationship to the other systems of 'choices', by reference to which their specifically symbolic meaning and value are defined. Because life-styles are essentially distinctive, a number of features do not take on their full significance until they are brought into relation not only with the social positions they express but also with features appearing at an opposite pole of this space. This is the case, for example, with the oppositions which are established primordially between the

positions most remote from each other in one or both of the fundamental dimensions of social space (i.e., with respect to volume and composition of capital): Goya and Renoir, avant-garde theatre and boulevard theatre, Jacques Brel and Tino Rossi, France-Musique and France-Inter or Radio Luxembourg, cinema clubs and variety shows and so forth.

In addition to the information gathered directly by the survey, I have used a number of indices of cultural consumption, such as possession of a piano or records, TV-viewing, visits to museums, exhibitions, variety shows and the cinema, membership in a library, evening classes, collections, sports, all taken from the 1967 INSEE survey on leisure activities (C.S. IV); information on the consumption and life-styles of members of the dominant class (hi-fi equipment, sailing, cruises, bridge, picture collections, champagne, whisky, sports etc.) from surveys by the SOFRES and CESP (C.S. V and VI); information on theatre-going from a survey by SEMA (Société d'économie et de mathématiques appliquées) (C.S. XIV); on favourite actors, from the surveys by IFOP (Institut français de l'opinion publique) (C.S. XIV); on the reading of daily and weekly newspapers and magazines, from the surveys by the CSE (Centre de sociologie européenne) and CESP (C.S. XXVIII); and on various cultural activities (ceramics, pottery, funfairs etc.) from the survey by the Ministry of Culture (C.S. VII).

In the resulting figure, each pertinent item appears only once and is therefore valid for a whole zone (of varying extent depending on the case) of social space, although it most strongly characterizes the category to which it is closest. (Thus the item 'wages/salaries', marked half-way up the left-hand side of figure 5 and opposed to 'industrial and commercial profits', is valid for the whole of the left-hand side of the social space, i.e., for the university and secondary teachers, senior executives and engineers and also the primary teachers, junior executives, technicians, clerical workers and manual workers. Similarly, the item 'stocks and shares'—top right—applies to employers, the professions, private-sector executives and engineers.) It can be seen immediately that possession of a piano and the choice of the *Concerto for the Left Hand* are most typical of members of the professions; that walking and mountaineering are particularly characteristic of secondary teachers and public-sector executives; or that swimming, placed half-way between the new petite bourgeoisie and the private-sector executives or the engineers, belongs to the life-style of both these sets of occupations. Thus, grouped around the name of each class fraction are those features of its life-style which are the most pertinent because they are the most distinctive—though it may in fact share them with other groups. This is the case, for example, with the use of a library, which appears in the area of the junior executives, primary teachers and technicians, although it is at least as frequent among secondary and university teachers; but the latter are less marked by the practice since it is part of their occupational role.

---

tion strategies. The reconversion of capital held in one form to another, more accessible, more profitable or more legitimate form tends to induce a transformation of asset structure.

These reconversions correspond to movements in a social space which has nothing in common with the unreal and yet naively realistic space of so-called 'social mobility' studies. The same positivistic naivety which sees 'upward mobility' in the morphological transformations of different classes or fractions is also unaware that the reproduction of the social structure may, in certain conditions, demand very little 'occupational heredity'. This is true whenever agents can only maintain their position in the social structure by means of a shift into a new condition (e.g., the shift from small landowner to junior civil servant, or from small craftsman to office worker or commercial employee).

The social space, being structured in two dimensions (overall capital volume and dominant/dominated capital), allows two types of movement which traditional mobility studies confuse, although they are in no way equivalent and are unequally probable: vertical movements, upwards or downwards, in the same vertical sector, that is, in the same field (e.g., from schoolteacher to professor, or from small businessman to big businessman); and transverse movements, from one field to another, which may occur either horizontally (a schoolteacher, or his son, becomes a small shopkeeper) or between different levels (a shopkeeper, or his son, becomes an industrialist). Vertical movements, the most frequent ones, only require an increase in the volume of the type of capital already dominant in the asset structure, and therefore a movement in the structure of the distribution of total capital which takes the form of a movement within a field (business field, academic field, administrative field, medical field etc.). Transverse movements entail a shift into another field and the reconversion of one type of capital into another or of one sub-type into another sub-type (e.g., from landowning to industrial capital or from literature to economics) and therefore a transformation of asset structure which protects overall capital volume and maintains position in the vertical dimension.

The probability of entering a given fraction of the dominant class from another class is, as we have seen, in inverse ratio to the position of that fraction in the hierarchy of economic capital. (The only exception is the 'liberal professions', which tend to transmit both economic and cultural capital and have the highest rate of endogenous recruitment.) Similarly, major sideways movements within the class (industrialists' sons becoming secondary or higher-education teachers, or vice versa) are extremely rare. Thus, in 1970, the probability of becoming an industrial or commercial employer was 1.9 percent for a professor's son, and the probability of becoming a teacher was 0.8 percent for an industrialist's son and 1.5 percent for a commercial entrepreneur's son. The probability of becoming a craftsman or shopkeeper was 1.2 percent for a primary teacher's son, and the probability of becoming a primary teacher was 2.4 percent for a craftsman's son and 1.4 percent for a small shopkeeper's son (C.S. II, secondary analysis).

CLASS MOBILITY AND MOBILE CLASSES The recent changes in the relationship between the different classes and the educational system—with the 'schooling boom' and the accompanying changes in the system itself—and also the changes in the social structure resulting from the new relationship between qualifications and jobs, are the consequences of intensified competition for academic qualifications. One important factor in intensifying this competition has doubtless been the fact that those fractions of the dominant class and middle class who are richest in economic capital (i.e., industrial and commercial employers, craftsmen and tradesmen) have had to make greatly increased use of the educational system in order to ensure their social reproduction.

The disparity between the scholastic capital of the adults of a class or class fraction (measured by the proportion who have a qualification equal or superior to the BÉPC) and the schooling rate of the corresponding adolescents is much more pronounced among craftsmen, shopkeepers and industrialists than among office workers and junior executives. This break in the usual correspondence between the children's educational participation rates and the parents' cultural capital indicates a profound change in dispositions towards scholastic investment. Many fewer small craftsmen and shopkeepers aged 45–54 than office workers have at least the BEPC (in 1962, 5.7 percent as against 10.1 percent), but their 18-year-old sons are equally likely to be in school (42.1 percent and 43.3 percent in 1962). Similarly industrialists and commercial entrepreneurs have less educational capital than technicians and junior executives (20 percent and 28.9 percent respectively have at least the BEPC), but their sons are equally likely to be in school (65.8 percent and 64.2 percent). The same process has begun among farm workers, as is shown by the rapid rise in their children's schooling rate between 1962 and 1975.[24]

When class fractions who previously made little use of the school system enter the race for academic qualifications, the effect is to force the groups whose reproduction was mainly or exclusively achieved through education to step up their investments so as to maintain the relative scarcity of their qualifications and, consequently, their position in the class structure. Academic qualifications and the school system which awards them thus become one of the key stakes in an interclass competition which generates a general and continuous growth in the demand for education and an inflation of academic qualifications.

To the effects of the competition between groups struggling for 'upclassing' and against 'downclassing' (*déclassement*), a competition that is organized around the academic qualification (*titre*) and more generally around all the 'entitlements' by which groups assert and constitute their own scarcity value vis-à-vis other groups, must be added the effect of what might be termed a *structural* factor. Generally increased schooling has the effect of increasing the mass of cultural capital which, at every moment, exists in an 'embodied' state. Since the success of the school's educative action and the durability of its effects depend on how much cultural capital has been directly transmitted by the family, it can be presumed that the efficiency of school-based educative action tends to rise constantly, other things being equal. In short, the same scholastic investment becomes more profitable, a fact which no doubt contributes to inflation by bringing diplomas within reach of a greater number of people.

Bearing in mind that the volume of corresponding jobs may also have varied over the same period, one may assume that a qualification is likely to have undergone devaluation if the number of diploma-holders has grown more rapidly than the number of suitable positions. Everything seems to suggest that the *baccalauréat* and lower qualifications are the ones most affected by such devaluation. To this must be added the less obvious devaluation resulting from the fact that if the number of corresponding jobs does keep pace, the positions themselves are likely to lose some of their scarcity value. This is what has happened, for example, to jobs at all levels of the teaching profession.

The very rapid growth in girls' and women's education has been a significant factor in the devaluing of academic qualifications. Because the image of the division of labour between the sexes has also changed, more women now bring academic qualifications onto the labour market which previously were partly held in reserve (and were 'invested' only in the marriage market); and the higher the diploma, the more marked this growth has been (see table 10). Just as all segregation (by sex or any other criterion) tends to slow down devaluation by its *numerus clausus* effect, so all desegregation tends to restore full strength to the devaluing mechanisms; and, as an American study of the effects of racial desegregation has shown, the least qualified are the ones who feel the effects most directly.

Indeed, it presents no paradox to suggest that the chief victims of the devaluing of academic qualifications are those who enter the labour market without such qualifications. The devaluation of diplomas is accompanied by the gradual extension of the monopoly held by academic-qualification-holders over positions previously open to the academically unqualified, which has the effect of limiting the devaluation of qualifications by limiting the competition, but only at the cost of restricting the career openings available to the unqualified and of reinforcing the academic predetermination of occupational opportunity. In certain areas, particularly the civil service, this leads to a decline both in the dispersal of the holders of the same qualifications among different jobs and in the dispersal of the qualifications of holders of equivalent jobs, or, in other words, a reinforced correlation between academic qualification and job occupied.

The market in jobs open to formally qualified candidates has grown constantly, inevitably at the expense of the formally unqualified. Universal recognition of academic qualifications no doubt has the effect of unifying the official set of qualifications for social positions and of eliminating local anomalies due to the existence of social spaces with their own rank-ordering principles. However, academic qualifications never achieve total, exclusive acceptance. Outside the specifically scholastic market, a diploma is worth what its holder is worth, economically and socially; the rate of return on educational capital is a function of the economic and social capital that can be devoted to exploiting it.

The change in the distribution of posts among qualification-holders

Table 10 Rate of employment of women aged 25–34, by education, 1962 and 1968.[a]

Year	CEP	CAP	BEPC	Bac	>Bac
1962	43.8	59.7	59.8	67.1	67.9
1968	46.3	60.6	63.5	74.3	77.5

Source: 1968 census.
a. It was not possible to isolate women without qualifications.

which results automatically from the increased number of formally qualified agents means that at every moment a proportion of the qualification-holders—starting, no doubt, with those who are least well endowed with the inherited means of exploiting their qualifications—are victims of devaluation. The strategies by which those who are most subject to devaluation endeavour to fight against it, in the short term (in the course of their own careers) or in the long term (through the strategies they employ for their children's schooling), constitute one of the decisive factors in the growth in the volume of qualifications awarded, which itself contributes to devaluation. The dialectic of devaluation and compensation thus tends to feed on itself.

RECONVERSION STRATEGIES AND MORPHOLOGICAL TRANSFORMATIONS
The strategies which individuals and families employ with a view to safeguarding or improving their position in social space are reflected in transformations which modify both the volume of the different class fractions and the structure of their assets.

Table 11 has been constructed so as to give at least an approximate idea of these transformations. Since it was not possible (though it would have been desirable) to establish in narrowly defined categories the changes in total income and income structure for the period 1954-1975 (instead, table 12 indicates these changes, in broad categories, for the period 1954-1968), I have indicated the distribution by source of income and the total income declared to the tax authorities, the source used by INSEE. It is known, however, that the degree of underestimation varies greatly. According to A. Villeneuve,[25] wages and salaries should be multiplied by 1.1, farmers' profits by 3.6, investment income by 2.9 and so forth. Once these corrections are applied, the members of the professions, and especially the farmers, craftsmen and small shopkeepers, return to their real places.

The categories (relatively) richest in economic capital (as represented by indicators such as stocks and shares, rural or urban property etc.) tend to regress very sharply, as is shown by the decline in their volume (in the case of the farmers, craftsmen, shopkeepers and industrialists) and by the fall or relatively small increase in the proportion of young people. (The fact that this has not occurred in the 'small shopkeeper' and 'craftsman' categories is explained by the coming of a new style of shopkeeper and craftsman.) Part of the apparent increase in the educational (and, no doubt, economic) capital of these categories is probably due to the fact that the reduction in their numbers chiefly concerns their lower strata.

By contrast, the fractions richest in cultural capital (measured by educational qualifications) have greatly expanded. They have acquired more young people, a higher proportion of women, and a higher rate of educational qualification. The categories most typical of this process are office workers and shop workers, technicians, junior and senior executives, primary teachers and especially secondary and tertiary teachers (in the last case the interlinked changes are particularly intense). Among engineers, how-

Table 11 Changes in morphology and asset structure of the class fractions, 1954–1975.

| Class fraction | Volume in 1975 | Proportion of men in 1975 (%) | Index of change in volume, 1954–1975 (1954 = 100) | | | | Change in educational capital, 1962–1975 (by % of qualification-holders) | | | | | | Economic Capital | | | | |
| | | | All ages | | Ages 20–34 | | In 1962 | | | In 1975 | | | Average household income (francs) in 1975 | Sources of income in 1970 (by % of households) | | | |
			Both sexes	Men only	Both sexes	Men only	BEPC	Bac	Higher-ed. diploma	BEPC	Bac	Higher-ed. diploma		Wages, salaries	Indust. and commercial profits	Urban property income	Stocks and shares income
Farm workers	375,480	88.4	32	33	27	27	0.5	0.2	0.1	2.7	0.6	0.3	27,740	86.0	1.5	0.8	6.3
Farmers	1,650,865	65.7	42	46	26	31	0.9	0.5	0.2	3.5	0.9	0.6	22,061	19.3	5.3	6.4	16.5
Unskilled	1,612,725	61.9	143	115	146	108	0.4	0.1	0	2.9	0.7	0.4	27,027	93.4	1.3	2.3	3.3
Semi-skilled	2,946,860	73.2	162	167	185	186	1.0	0.2	0.1	3.5	0.5	0.2	35,515	97.7	2.2	2.4	3.6
Skilled	2,985,865	86.5	112	126	120	128	2.1	0.5	0.1	5.5	0.7	0.3	39,527	98.2	2.2	2.7	3.6
Foremen	443,305	94.1					6.0	1.7	0.5	10.4	2.5	1.1	56,692	99.5	1.4	4.1	6.7
Office workers	3,104,105	35.0	191	141	218	168	11.5	2.9	1.2	19.6	5.3	2.6	42,785	98.8	2.1	5.1	8.6
Commercial employees	736,595	40.6	167	138	183	158	6.5	3.6	1.3	13.4	5.2	2.2	46,196	97.5	3.4	8.9	9.5
Craftsmen	533,635	88.1	71	77	81	88	2.8	1.0	0.5	6.1	1.8	1.3	50,335	34.1	96.9	12.9	14.2
Small shopkeepers	912,695	51.8	73	78	73	81	4.7	2.4	0.9	9.3	3.7	2.3	60,160	24.3	93.2	20.2	19.2
Junior admin. executives	970,185	55.1	182	132	218	152	20.1	11.6	5.3	26.5	12.8	9.0	73,478	99.3	4.0	11.1	17.5
Technicians	758,890	85.6	393	367	417	374	16.3	7.0	2.7	25.8	9.6	6.0	59,003	98.5	2.4	5.8	8.7
Social and medical services	298,455	21.0	269	261	345	340	9.7	7.7	6.1	17.7	18.1	20.3	53,450	84.2	0	10.0	12.4
Primary teachers	737,420	36.5					10.0	55.0	14.5	11.3	39.4	29.4	54,013	96.7	0.9	7.6	10.4
Industrialists	59,845	86.5	66	71	66	65	8.5	6.7	7.5	12.9	6.1	6.3	132,594	83.0	26.0	34.7	40.0
Commercial employers	186,915	69.2	103	100	98	95	9.0	7.3	5.7	14.6	9.1	6.3	132,435	64.0	47.5	29.7	30.2
Senior admin. executives	653,755	83.9	236	217	293	254	15.5	18.9	25.5	19.3	16.2	32.0	107,342	99.6	3.6	15.2	27.7
Engineers	256,290	95.6	338	305	272	263	7.3	9.0	59.8	10.0	18.1	63.2	105,989	98.7	3.1	15.5	30.4
Teachers (secondary, higher)	377,215	53.0	469	402	612	517	2.7	10.8	71.4	3.6	8.4	77.7	87,795	97.6	2.1	10.4	21.0
Professions	172,025	77.8	143	130	145	137	4.5	10.3	65.1	4.2	6.2	79.9	150,108	41.0	17.5	30.3	40.6

Sources: INSEE, Censuses, 1954, 1962, 1968, 1975. For changes in educational capital: INSEE, Recensement général de la population au 1/20ème pour la France entière: Formation (Paris, Imprimerie nationale, 1971) (this volume also gives data on education and training from the 1962 census); and INSEE, Tableau de la population totale de plus de 16 ans par catégorie socio-professionnelle, âge, sexe, diplôme d'enseignement général (forthcoming; data supplied by L. Thévenot). On incomes: INSEE, Enquêtes revenus 1975 et 1970 (data supplied by A. Villeneuve [1975 survey] and P. Ghigliazza [1970 survey]).

ever, the process seems to have stopped, since the rate of increase is lower for the youngest generation than for the group as a whole. Another remarkable feature is the relative stability of the 'liberal professions', whose deliberate policy of *numerus clausus* has prevented numerical growth and feminization and helped to maintain scarcity value.

The new reproduction strategies which underlie these morphological changes are seen partly in the increased importance of salaries in the income of the traditionally 'self-employed' categories and partly in the diversified assets and investments of the senior executives, who tend to hold their capital in both economic and cultural form, unlike the employers, who mainly hold economic capital. Salaries and pensions, as a proportion of employers' incomes, rise from 12.9 percent in 1956 to 16.4 percent in 1965; in 1975, with new classifications, they make up 19.2 percent of the income of craftsmen and small shopkeepers and 31.8 percent of the income of industrialists and commercial entrepreneurs. (By contrast, among farmers, the proportion remains much the same: 23.8 percent in 1956, 23.5 percent in 1965 and 24.8 percent in 1975.) In 1975, the proportion of income derived from investment in land, buildings, stocks and shares is much higher among private-sector than public-sector senior executives (5.9 percent and 2.7 percent respectively).

The reconversion of economic capital into educational capital is one of the strategies which enable the business bourgeoisie to maintain the position of some or all of its heirs, by enabling them to extract some of the profits of industrial and commercial firms in the form of salaries, which are a more discreet—and no doubt more reliable—mode of appropriation than 'unearned' investment income. Thus, between 1954 and 1975 the proportion of industrial and commercial entrepreneurs fell sharply, whereas there was a very strong rise in the proportion of salary-earners, who owed their position to their academic qualifications—executives, engineers, teachers and intellectuals (although, at least in the case of private-sector executives, a significant proportion of total income may be derived from shares, as table 13 indicates). Similarly, the disappearance of many small commercial or craft firms conceals the reconversion work which individual agents perform, with varying degrees of success, in accordance with the demands of their particular situation, and which results in a transformation of the relative weight of the different fractions of the middle classes (see table 14). Here, too, the decrease in the proportion of small shopkeepers, craftsmen, and farmers has been accompanied by an increase in the proportion of primary-school teachers, technicians, and the personnel of the medical and social services.

Furthermore, the relative morphological stability of an occupational group may conceal a transformation of its structure resulting from the conversion in situ of agents present in the group at the beginning of the period (or their children) or their replacement by agents from other groups. For example, the relatively small decline in the overall volume of

Table 12 Changes in morphology and asset structure of the class fractions, 1954-1968.

Class fraction	Volume in 1968		Index of change in volume, 1954-1968 (1954=100)		Index of change in number of under-35s, 1962-1968 (1962=100) (1)	Educational capital, 1968, by % of male qualification-holders			Annual income (francs), 1965 (primary income) (2)	Average household assets (francs), Jan. 1, 1966 (3)
	Both sexes (1)	Men only (1)	Both sexes (1)	Men only (1)		BEPC (1)	Bac (1)	Higher-ed. diploma (1)		
Farm workers	588,200	527,200	51	54	67	1.0	0.4	0.2	9,859	—
Farmers	2,459,840	1,527,780	62	65	72	1.6	0.7	0.4	23,854	—
Manual workers	7,698,600	6,128,840	119	123	116	2.3	0.4	0.2	14,811	35,000
Clerical and commercial	3,029,900	1,188,300	146	121	133	14.0	3.7	1.5	16,149	46,000
Junior executives	2,014,000	1,197,360	177	168	151	19.0	16.5	7.7	26,887	92,000
Craftsmen	622,800	532,340	85	88	109	4.1	1.5	1.0	—	—
Small shopkeepers	1,028,160	515,440	81	85	107	6.7	2.8	1.4	—	—
Big commercial employers	213,500	143,840	116	110	148	12.1	8.0	5.2	—	—
Industrialists	79,160	68,940	93	93	98	10.8	6.1	7.5	—	—
All industrial and commercial entrepreneurs	1,943,620	1,360,560	86	96	110	6.4	3.0	1.9	45,851	—
Professions	142,520	114,920	119	112	122	5.1	6.3	76.8	—	214,000
Senior executives	840,280	691,680	196	183	144	12.6	13.3	45.0	58,021	

Table 12 (continued).

Farm workers	10.2	2.3	—	59.5	29.8	9.2	1.5	96.7	95.9	1.4	1.8
Farmers	27.6	5.2	—	6.9	10.9	78.5	3.7	23.8	23.5	16.4	9.9
Manual workers	4.8	2.9	39.0	66.7	27.9	4.6	0.8	98.0	97.5	0.8	0.8
Clerical and commercial	11.8	6.0	40.8	69.6	23.2	5.4	1.8	95.9	95.9	2.6	2.1
Junior executives	14.0	8.1	50.3	73.1	18.5	6.8	1.8	91.6	94.4	4.9	2.1
Craftsmen	—	—	—	—	—	—	—	—	—	—	—
Small shopkeepers	—	—	—	—	—	—	—	—	—	—	—
Big commercial employers	—	—	—	—	—	—	—	—	—	—	—
Industrialists	—	—	—	—	—	—	—	—	—	—	—
All industrial and commercial entrepreneurs }	28.6	20.7	—	7.1	6.4	79.2	7.3	12.9	16.4	7.0	6.7
Professions	—	—	33.1	—	—	—	—	—	—	—	—
Senior executives	38.2	18.9	66.3	56.5	9.6	28.9	5.0	71.8	73.0	9.4	6.0

Sources: (1) INSEE, *Censuses*; (2) H. Roze, 'Prestations sociales, impôt direct et échelle des revenus', *Economie et Statistique*, February 1971; (3) P. L'Hardy, 'Les disparités du patrimoine', *Economie et Statistique*, February 1973; (4) G. Banderier, 'Les revenus des ménages en 1965,' *Collections de l'INSEE*, M 7, December 1970; (5) P. L'Hardy, 'Structure de l'épargne et du patrimoine des ménages en 1966,' *Collections de l'INSEE*, M 13, March 1972.

Table 13 Morphological changes within the dominant class, 1954–1975.

Class fraction	Structure (% of dominant class in each fraction)				Annual rate of variation (%)			Proportion of women per fraction (%)			
	1954	1962	1968	1975	1954–1962	1962–1968	1968–1975	1954	1962	1968	1975
Commercial employers	22.0	17.0	16.4	11.0	-1.5	0	-4.2	29.2	30.2	32.9	30.8
Industrialists	11.0	7.9	6.3	3.5	-0.6	3.3	-1.7	14.9	14.2	13.7	13.5
Professionals	14.6	12.3	10.9	10.1	0.5	2.0	2.9	15.6	17.3	19.3	22.2
Senior admin. executives	33.5	37.0	35.3	38.3	3.9	3.1	5.3	8.6	11.1	13.4	17.1
Engineers	9.2	13.5	14.5	15.0	7.8	5.1	4.7	2.1	3.2	3.4	4.4
Teachers, literary and scientific occupations	9.7	12.3	16.6	22.1	5.7	9.3	8.5	39.9	43.0	44.7	47.0

Table 14 Morphological changes within the middle class, 1954–1975.[a]

Class fraction	Structure (% of middle class in each fraction)				Annual rate of variation (%)			Proportion of women per fraction (%)			
	1954	1962	1968	1975	1954–1962	1962–1968	1968–1975	1954	1962	1968	1975
Craftsmen	14.6	11.2	9.3	6.6	-2.1	-0.5	-2.1	18.3	16.0	14.7	11.9
Small shopkeepers	24.1	20.0	15.4	11.3	-1.2	-1.7	-1.7	51.7	51.3	50.2	48.2
Commercial employees	8.5	9.0	9.4	9.1	1.9	3.4	2.4	52.0	57.0	57.7	59.4
Office workers	31.3	33.2	35.7	38.5	1.9	3.9	3.0	53.0	59.4	61.9	65.0
Junior admin. executives	10.2	11.0	11.1	12.0	2.0	2.8	3.9	24.6	31.9	34.9	44.9
Primary teachers	7.4[b]	7.4	8.4	9.1	4.1[b]	4.9	4.0	68.3[b]	65.1	62.7	63.5
Technicians	3.7	6.1	8.0	9.4	7.5	7.5	5.2	7.1	7.9	11.3	14.4
Social and medical services	c	1.9	2.6	3.7	c	7.8	8.1	c	84.8	83.2	79.0

Source: L. Thévenot, 'Les catégories sociales en 1975: l'extension du salariat,' Economie et Statistique, 91 (July–August 1977), 4–5.

a. It is known that the structure of the working population changed considerably between 1954 and 1975. The proportion of agricultural workers (farmers and wage-earners) fell from 26.7% to 9.3% and the proportion of industrial manual workers rose very slightly (from 33.8% to 37.7%), whereas the middle class increased considerably (from 27% to 37% of the wage-earning population)—as a result of the growth of the wage-earning sections of the class, as this table shows—and the dominant class rose from 4.3% to 7.8%.

b. Includes 'Social and medical services'.

c. Included under 'Primary teachers'.

the category 'shopkeepers', consisting very largely (93 percent) of the owners of small individual firms which have been able to withstand the crisis partly because of increased household consumption, conceals a change in the structure of this occupation. The stagnation or decline of small food stores, particularly hard hit by supermarket competition, and small clothing stores has almost been balanced by a growth in the retailing of automobiles, domestic equipment (including furniture, interior decorating and so on) and especially sports, leisure and cultural goods (books, records etc.) and pharmaceuticals. It may be assumed that, even within food retailing, the figures tend to conceal changes that have led to a progressive redefinition of the occupation: the closing-down of small grocery stores and rural bakeries may coexist with the opening of shops selling diet foods, 'natural' regional products and health foods, or of bakeries specializing in old-style bread.

These changes in the nature of retail firms—which are related to changes, over the same period, in the structure of household consumption, themselves related to the growth in incomes and above all to the increase in cultural capital resulting from the upward shift of the structure of educational opportunity—are dialectically linked to a rise in the cultural capital of their owners or managers.

Everything suggests that the 'craftsman' category has undergone changes very similar to the 'shopkeeper' category, with the decline of the most exposed strata of traditional craftsmanship being offset by the boom in luxury and 'aesthetic' crafts, which require economic assets but also cultural capital. This would explain why the fall in the volume of these middle-class categories is accompanied by a rise in cultural capital as measured by educational level.

Craftsmen and tradesmen specializing in luxury, cultural or artistic items, managers of fashion 'boutiques', retailers of 'famous maker' clothes, traders in exotic garments and jewels or rustic objects, record dealers, antique dealers, interior decorators, designers, photographers, restaurateurs, managers of trendy 'bistros', Provençal 'potters', avant-garde booksellers, all those vendors of cultural goods and services seeking to prolong the fusion of leisure and work, militancy and dilettantism, that characterizes the student life-style, use their ambiguous occupations, in which success depends at least as much on the subtly casual distinction of the salesman as on the nature and quality of his wares, as a way of obtaining the best return on a cultural capital in which technical competence is less important than familiarity with the culture of the dominant class and a mastery of the signs and emblems of distinction and taste. Because this new type of culture-intensive craftsmanship and commerce enables profit to be drawn from the cultural heritage transmitted directly by the family, it is predisposed to serve as a refuge for those sons and daughters of the dominant class who are eliminated by the educational system.

TIME TO UNDERSTAND   Among the effects of the inflation of qualifications and their associated devaluation, undoubtedly the most important are the set of strategies whereby the holders of devalued qualifications have sought to maintain their inherited positions or to obtain from their qualifications the real equivalent of what they guaranteed in an earlier state of the relationship between diplomas and jobs.

It is clear that what an academic qualification guarantees is much more than, and different from, the right to occupy a position and the capacity to perform the corresponding job. In this respect the diploma (*titre scolaire*) is more like a patent of nobility (*titre de noblesse*) than the title to property (*titre de propriété*) which strictly technical definitions make of it. So one can well understand that the victims of devaluation are disinclined to perceive and acknowledge the devaluing of qualifications with which they are closely identified, both objectively (they constitute an important part of these people's social identity) and subjectively. But the concern to preserve self-esteem, which encourages attachment to the nominal value of qualifications and jobs, would not be sufficient to maintain a misperception of this devaluation, if there were not also some complicity from objective mechanisms. The most important of these are, first, the hysteresis of habitus, which causes previously appropriate categories of perception and appreciation to be applied to a new state of the qualification market; and, second, the existence of relatively autonomous markets in which the value of qualifications declines at a slower rate.

The hysteresis effect is proportionately greater for agents who are more remote from the educational system and who are poorly or only vaguely informed about the market in educational qualifications. One of the most valuable sorts of information constituting inherited cultural capital is practical or theoretical knowledge of the fluctuations of the market in academic qualifications, the sense of investment which enables one to get the best return on inherited cultural capital in the scholastic market or on scholastic capital in the labour market, for example, by knowing the right moment to pull out of devalued disciplines and careers and to switch into those with a future, rather than clinging to the scholastic values which secured the highest profits in an earlier state of the market. By contrast, the hysteresis effect means that the holders of devalued diplomas become, in a sense, accomplices in their own mystification, since, by a typical effect of *allodoxia* ('misapprehension'), they bestow a value on their devalued diplomas which is not objectively acknowledged. This explains how those least informed about the diploma market, who have long been able to recognize a decline in real wages behind the maintenance of nominal wages, can nonetheless continue to accept and seek the paper certificates which they receive in payment for their years of schooling (despite the fact that they are the first victims of diploma devaluation, because of their lack of social capital).

This attachment to an anachronistic idea of the value of qualifications no doubt plays a part in the existence of markets in which diplomas can (apparently, at least) escape devaluation. The value objectively and subjectively placed on an academic qualification is in fact defined only by the totality of the social uses that can be made of it. Thus the evaluation of diplomas by the closest peer groups, such as relatives, neighbours, fellow students (one's 'class' or 'year') and colleagues, can play an important role in masking the effects of devaluation. These phenomena of individual and collective misrecognition are in no way illusory, since they can orient real practices, especially the individual and collective strategies aimed at establishing or re-establishing the objective reality of the value of the qualification or position; and these strategies can make a real contribution toward actual revaluation.

In the transactions in which the market value of academic qualifications is defined, the strength of the vendors of labour power depends—setting aside their social capital—on the value of their diplomas, especially when the relationship between qualifications and jobs is strictly codified (as is the case with established positions, as opposed to new ones). So it is clear that the devaluation of academic diplomas is of direct advantage to the suppliers of jobs, and that, while the interests of qualification-holders are bound up with the nominal value of qualifications, i.e., with what they guaranteed by right in the earlier situation, the interests of job suppliers are bound up with the real value of qualifications, in other words, the value that is determined at the moment in question in the competition among the candidates. (This is a structural de-skilling [*déqualification*] which aggravates the effects of the de-skilling strategies that firms have been using for a long time.) The greatest losers in this struggle are those whose diplomas have least relative value in the hierarchy of diplomas and are most devalued. In some cases the qualification-holder finds he has no other way to defend the value of his qualification than to refuse to sell his labour power at the price offered; the decision to remain unemployed is then equivalent to a one-man strike.[26]

THE CHEATING OF A GENERATION   In a period of 'diploma inflation' the disparity between the aspirations that the educational system produces and the opportunities it really offers is a structural reality which affects all the members of a school generation, but to a varying extent depending on the rarity of their qualifications and on their social origins. Newcomers to secondary education are led, by the mere fact of having access to it, to expect it to give them what it gave others at a time when they themselves were still excluded from it. In an earlier period and for other classes, these aspirations were perfectly realistic, since they corresponded to objective probabilities, but they are often quickly deflated by the verdicts of the scholastic market or the labour market. One of the paradoxes of what is called the 'democratization of schooling' is that only when the working classes, who had previously ignored or at best vaguely concurred in the Third Republic ideology of 'schooling as a liberating force' (*l'école libératrice*), actually entered secondary education, did they discover *l'école conservatrice,* schooling as a conservative force, by being relegated to second-class courses or eliminated. The collective disillusionment which results from the structural mismatch between aspirations and real probabilities, between the social identity the school system seems to promise, or the one it offers on a temporary basis, and the social identity that the labour market in fact offers is the source of the disaffection towards work, that *refusal of social finitude,* which generates all the refusals and negations of the adolescent counter-culture.

This discordance—and the disenchantment it engenders—takes forms that are objectively and subjectively different in the various social classes. Thus, for working-class youngsters, the transit through secondary schooling and through the ambiguous status of a 'student', temporarily freed from the demands of the world of work, produces misfirings of the dialectic of aspirations and probabilities which led their predecessors to accept their social destiny, almost always unquestioningly, and sometimes with positive eagerness (like the miners' sons who used to identify their entry into manhood with their first descent into the mine). The disenchantment with their work that is felt and expressed particularly acutely by the most obvious victims of downclassing, such as *baccalauréat*-holders obliged to take jobs as factory workers or postmen, is, in a way, common to a whole generation. It finds expression in unusual forms of struggle, protest and escapism that the organizations traditionally involved in industrial or political struggle find hard to understand, because something more than working conditions is at stake. These young people, whose social identity and self-image have been undermined by a social system and an educational system that have fobbed them off with worthless paper, can find no other way of restoring their personal and social integrity than by a total refusal. It is as if they felt that what is at stake is no longer just personal failure, as the educational system encourages them to believe, but rather the whole logic of the academic institution. The structural de-skilling of a whole generation, who are bound to get less out of their qualifications than the previous generation would have obtained, engenders a sort of collective disillusionment: a whole generation, finding it has been taken for a ride, is inclined to extend to all institutions the mixture of revolt and resentment it feels towards the educational system. This anti-institutional cast of mind (which draws strength from ideological and scientific critiques) points towards a denunciation of the tacit assumptions of the social order, a practical suspension of doxic adherence to the prizes it offers and the values it professes, and a withholding of the investments which are a necessary condition of its functioning.

So it is understandable that, not only within families but also in educational institutions and political or union organizations, and above all

*The new
production lines*

Disenchanted

'First I did market research surveys. I had a friend in L. who was into that. I got a list of all the research firms in Paris. After two months phoning and writing, finally I got something. Then, several months later, they still hadn't got in touch with me. They weren't doing any more surveys. I was entitled to unemployment benefit, a thousand francs a month. We lived on that for seven months, then we did two months' grape-picking. Then I went back to surveys for seven months, working free-lance. Then I quit; the place was full of lesbians and they gave out the work to their favourites, so I got out. Anyway, we each work a bit in turns. In this sort of society, work isn't the main thing in life. Now, if things were run the way they are in China, I might want to work ten hours a day' (F., age 24, baccalauréat and a few months in an Arts faculty; father: private means).

'Once you've flunked your bac, you're already in the shit. There are no possible careers and the jobs you *can* find are completely useless.
'All the jobs I did were boring, so I saved up some money so I could stop working for a few months. Anyway, I prefer to stop once in a while so I don't get into a rut.
'After I failed the bac, I spent the summer working as a monitor in a vacation camp. Then I got a job with a newspaper in Dreux. I was a trainee sub-editor but after two months it was time to take out my union card so I went free-lance. But I didn't seem to fit in. Everything I wrote, they went through with a fine-tooth comb. I did photos, too. But there was a power struggle in the paper. I couldn't be bothered to fight. After six months, they stopped giving me work, so I left. I got taken in by the "public service" myth and I signed on at the Post Office. I was on sorting for three weeks. I couldn't take any more. It was a work environment I'd never known before. It wasn't so much the people that got up my nose as the relations between them, the tale-telling. There was no solidarity. After three weeks I chucked it in. There were five of us auxiliaries, one was fired on the spot for taking fifteen minutes' extra break, so we all walked out. The worst of it is that you flunk your exams, you hated school, and you end up being treated as an intellectual.
'Next I got a job through the employment agency, as a clerk in an office dealing with wholesale beef. There was a row about a bonus that wasn't given to everyone. There was a slanging-match and I got out. I'd been there two and a half months. In September I picked grapes and then I went back to the employment agency. I was a courier on a scooter for six months. That was the craziest thing I've ever done. It's a ghastly job, you get completely paranoid on your scooter, imagining they're all trying to run you down. I chucked it in, I couldn't take any more.
'After two months on the dole, I got a temporary job, just for the holiday period, on the railways. I was on electronic reservations, "operator" they called it, or something like that, and I stayed for four

months. I left because I wanted to live in the country, and that's how I ended up here' (G., age 21, failed baccalauréat; father: policeman; mother: charwoman).

Extracts from C. Mathey, *L'entrée dans la vie active*, Cahiers du Centre d'études de l'emploi, 15 (Paris, PUF, 1977), 479–658 passim (interviews with 50 unemployed young people).

in the work situation, whenever old-style autodidacts, who started out thirty years earlier with a *certificat d'études* (CEP) or a BEPC and boundless respect for culture, come into contact with young *bacheliers* or new-style autodidacts, who bring their anti-institutional stance with them into the institution, the clash of generations often takes the form of a showdown over the very foundations of the social order. More radical, less self-confident than the usual form of political contestation, and reminiscent of the mood of the first Romantic generation, this disenchanted temperament attacks the fundamental dogmas of the petit-bourgeois order—'career', 'status', 'promotion' and 'getting on.'

THE STRUGGLE TO KEEP UP   The specific contradiction of the scholastic mode of reproduction lies in the opposition between the interests of the class which the educational system serves *statistically* and the interests of those class members whom it sacrifices, that is, the 'failures' who are threatened with *déclassement* for lack of the qualifications formally required of rightful members. Nor should one forget those holders of qualifications which 'normally'—i.e., in an earlier state of the relationship between diplomas and jobs—gave access to a bourgeois occupation, who, because they do not originate from that class, lack the social capital to extract the full yield from their academic qualifications. The overproduction of qualifications, and the consequent devaluation, tend to become a structural constant when theoretically equal chances of obtaining qualifications are offered to all the offspring of the bourgeoisie (regardless of birth rank or sex) while the access of other classes to these qualifications also increases (in absolute terms). The strategies which one group may employ to try to escape downclassing and to return to their class trajectory, and those which another group employs to rebuild the interrupted path of a hoped-for trajectory, are now one of the most important factors in the transformation of social structures. The individual substitution strategies which enable the holders of a social capital of inherited 'connections' to make up for their lack of formal qualifications or to get the maximum return from those they have, by moving into relatively unbureaucratized areas of social space (where social dispositions count for more than academically guaranteed 'competences'), are combined with collective strategies aimed at asserting the value of formal qualifications and obtaining the rewards they secured in an earlier state of the market.

Whereas in 1962 only 1.5 percent of semi-skilled workers aged 15–24 had the BEPC, and 0.2 percent the baccalauréat or a higher diploma, in 1975 the corresponding percentages were 8.2 and 1.0. Among white-collar workers, where by 1962 even in the oldest age-group there was a relatively high percentage of diploma-holders, the proportion of the very highly qualified rose faster among the young, so that by 1975 a larger proportion of them had higher qualifications than did the older workers (in 1962, 25.0 percent of office workers aged 15–24 had the BEPC, 2.0 percent the baccalauréat, and 0.2 percent a higher education degree, compared with 38.0 percent, 8.0 percent and 1.0 percent in 1975; the corresponding figures in 1975 for older staff members were 16.1 percent, 3.3 percent and 1.4 percent). In addition to all the changes in the relations between colleagues of different generations that are implied in these statistics, one has to bear in mind the changed relation to work which results from putting agents with higher qualifications into jobs that are often de-skilled (by automation and all the forms of job mechanization which have turned white-collar staff into the production-line workers of the great bureaucracies). There is every reason to think that the opposition between the somewhat strict and even stuffy rigour of the older staff and the casual style of the younger workers, which is doubtless perceived as sloppiness, especially when it includes long hair and a beard (the traditional emblems of the bohemian artist or intellectual), expresses rather more than a simple generation gap.

The combined effect is to encourage the creation of a large number of *semi-bourgeois* positions, produced by redefining old positions or inventing new ones, and designed to save unqualified 'inheritors' from downclassing and to provide parvenus with an approximate pay-off for their devalued qualifications.

The strategies agents use to avoid the devaluation of their diplomas are grounded in the discrepancy between opportunities objectively available at any given moment and aspirations based on an earlier structure of objective opportunities. This discrepancy, which is particularly acute at certain moments and in certain social positions, generally reflects a failure to achieve the individual or collective occupational trajectory which was inscribed as an objective potentiality in the former position and in the trajectory leading to it. When this 'broken trajectory' effect occurs—for example, in the case of a man whose father and grandfather were *polytechniciens* and who becomes a sales engineer or a psychologist, or in the case of a law graduate who, for lack of social capital, becomes a community cultural worker—the agent's aspirations, flying on above his real trajectory like a projectile carried on by its own inertia, describe an ideal trajectory that is no less real, or is at any rate in no way imaginary in the ordinary sense of the word. This impossible objective potentiality, inscribed at the deepest level of their dispositions as a sort of blighted hope or frustrated promise, is the common factor, behind all their differences, between those sons and daughters of the bourgeoisie to whom the educational system has not given the means of pursuing the trajectory most likely for their class and those sons and daughters of the middle and working classes who have not obtained the rewards which their academic qualifications would have guaranteed in an earlier state of the market —two categories who are particularly likely to try to move into the new positions.

Agents who seek to avoid downclassing can either produce new occupations more closely matching their pretensions (which were socially justified in an earlier state of relations between qualifications and jobs) or can refurbish the occupations to which their qualifications do give access, redefining and upgrading them in accordance with their pretensions. When agents start to arrive in a job who possess qualifications different from those of the usual occupants, they bring hitherto unknown aptitudes, dispositions and demands with them into their relation with that job, in terms of both its technical and social definition; and this necessarily causes changes in the job itself. Among the most visible changes observed when the newcomers have high qualifications are an intensified division of labour, with autonomous status being given to some of the tasks previously performed, in principle or in practice, by less qualified jacks-of-all-trades (e.g., the diversification of the education and social welfare fields); and, often, a redefinition of careers, related to the emergence of expectations and demands that are new in both form and content.

To make clear the break with the realist, static model implied in certain traditions of the sociology of work, it has to be emphasized that the post cannot be reduced either to the theoretical post, i.e., as described in regulations, circulars or organization charts, or to the real post, i.e., as described on the basis of observation of the occupant's real function, or even to the relationship between the two. In fact, posts, as regards both their theoretical definition and their practical reality, are the site of permanent struggles, in which position-holders may clash with their superiors or their subordinates, or with the occupants of neighbouring and rival positions, or amongst themselves (old-timers and newcomers, graduates and non-graduates and so on). Those aspiring to or holding a position may have an interest in redefining it in such a way that it cannot be occupied by anyone other than the possessors of properties identical to their own. (Consider the struggles between graduates of ENA and Polytechnique or, in the middle classes, between different generations of nurses.)

There is every reason to suppose that the job redefinition resulting from a change in the scholastic properties of the occupants—and all their associated properties—is likely to be more or less extensive depending on the *elasticity* of the technical and social definition of the position (which is probably greater at higher levels in the hierarchy of positions) and on the *social origin* of the new occupants, since the higher their origin, the less inclined they will be to accept the limited ambitions of petit-bourgeois agents looking for modest, predictable progress over a lifetime. These factors are probably not independent. Whether led by their sense of a good investment and their awareness of the opportunities awaiting their capital, or by the refusal to demean themselves by entering one of the established occupations whose elementary definition makes them invidious, those sons and daughters of the bourgeoisie who are threatened with downclassing tend to move, if they possibly can, into the most indeterminate of the older professions and into the sectors where the new professions are under construction. This 'creative redefinition' is therefore found particularly in the most ill-defined and professionally unstructured occupations and in the newest sectors of cultural and artistic production, such as the big public and private enterprises engaged in cultural production (radio, TV, marketing, advertising, social science research and so on), where jobs and careers have not yet acquired the rigidity of the older bureaucratic professions and recruitment is generally done by co-option, that is, on the basis of 'connections' and affinities of habitus, rather than formal qualifications.

This means that the sons and daughters of the Paris bourgeoisie, rather than directly entering a well-defined and lifelong profession (e.g., teaching), are more likely to enter and to succeed in positions, half-way between studenthood and a profession, that are offered by the big cultural bureaucracies, occupations for which the specific qualifications (e.g., a diploma in photography or filmmaking, or a sociology or psychology degree) are a genuine ticket of entry only for those who are able to supplement the official qualifications with the real—social—qualifications.[27]

The relative weight of the different categories involved in the cultural production system has radically changed in the last two decades. The new categories of wage-earning producers created by the development of radio and television and the public and private research bodies (especially in the social sciences) have considerably expanded, as has the teaching profession, especially in its lower strata, whereas the artistic and legal professions, that is, intellectual craftsmanship, have declined. These changes, together with new ways of organizing intellectual life (research committees, brain trusts, think tanks etc.) and new institutionalized modes of communication (conferences, debates, etc.) tend to encourage the emergence of intellectual producers more directly subordinated to economic and political demands, bringing new modes of thought and expression, new themes and new ways of conceiving intellectual work and the role of the intellectual. The main effect of these developments—together with the considerable growth in the student population, placed in the position of apprentice intellectuals, and the emergence of a whole set of semi-intellectual occupations—may well be to have provided 'intellectual production' with something once reserved for 'bourgeois art', namely, an audience sufficiently large to justify the existence of specific agencies for production and distribution, and the appearance, on the edges of the university field and intellectual field, of a sort of superior popularization—of which the *nouveaux philosophes* are an extreme case.[28]

But the site par excellence of this type of transformation is to be found in the group of occupations whose common factor is that they ensure a maximum return on the cultural capital most directly transmitted by the family: good manners, good taste or physical charm. This group includes the aesthetic and semi-aesthetic, intellectual and semi-intellectual occupations, the various consultancy services (psychology, vocational guidance, speech therapy, beauty advice, marriage counselling, diet advice and so on), the educational and para-educational occupations (youth leaders, runners of day-care centres, cultural programme organizers) and jobs involving presentation and representation (tour organizers, hostesses, ciceroni, couriers, radio and TV announcers, news anchormen and quiz show hosts, press attachés, public relations people and so on).

Public and, especially, private bureaucracies are now obliged to perform representational and 'hosting' functions which are very different in both scale and style from those traditionally entrusted to men (diplomats, ministerial attachés and so on) often drawn from those fractions of the dominant class (the aristocracy and the old bourgeoisie) who were richest in social capital and in the socializing techniques essential to the maintenance of that capital. The new requirements have led to the emergence of a whole set of female occupations and to the establishment of a legitimate market in physical properties. The fact that certain women derive occupational profit from their charm(s), and that beauty thus acquires a value on the labour market, has doubtless helped to produce not only a number of changes in the norms of clothing and cosmetics, but also a whole set of changes in ethics and a redefinition of the legitimate image of femininity. Women's magazines and all the acknowledged authorities on the body and the legitimate ways to use it transmit the image of womanhood incarnated by those professional manipulators of bureaucratic charm, who are rationally selected and trained, in accordance with a strictly programmed career-structure (with specialized schools, beauty contests and so on), to fulfil the most traditional feminine functions in conformity with bureaucratic norms.

The most indeterminate sectors of the social structure offer the most favourable ground for the operations which, by transforming old positions or 'creating' new ones ex nihilo, aim to produce areas of specialist expertise, particularly in the field of 'consultancy', the performance of which requires no more than a rationalized form of competence in a class culture. The constitution of a socially recognized corps of experts specializing in advice on sexuality, which is now coming about through the gradual professionalization of voluntary, philanthropic or political associations, is the paradigmatic form of the process whereby agents tend, with that deep conviction of disinterestedness which is the basis of all missionary zeal, to satisfy their group interests by deploying the legitimate culture with which they have been endowed by the education system to win the acquiescence of the classes excluded from legitimate culture, in producing the need for and the rarity of their class culture.

From marriage counsellors to the vendors of slimming aids, all those who now make a profession of supplying the means of bridging the gap between 'is' and 'ought' in the realm of the body and its uses would be nothing without the unconscious collusion of all those who contribute to producing an inexhaustible market for the products they offer, who by imposing new uses of the body and a new bodily *hexis*—the *hexis* which the new bourgeoisie of the sauna bath, the gymnasium and the ski slope has discovered for itself—produce the corresponding needs, expectations and dissatisfactions. Doctors and diet experts armed with the authority of science, who impose their definition of *normality* with height-weight tables, balanced diets or models of sexual adequacy; couturiers who confer the sanction of good taste on the unattainable measurements of fashion models; advertisers for whom the new obligatory uses of the body provide scope for countless warnings and reminders ('Watch your weight!' 'Someone isn't using . . .'); journalists who exhibit and glorify their own life-style in women's weeklies and magazines for well-heeled executives—all combine, in the competition between them, to advance a cause which they can serve so well only because they are not always aware of serving it or even of serving themselves in the process.

And the emergence of this new petite bourgeoisie, which employs new means of manipulation to perform its role as an intermediary between the classes and which by its very existence brings about a transformation of the position and dispositions of the old petite bourgeoisie, can itself be understood only in terms of changes in the mode of domination, which, substituting seduction for repression, public relations for policing, advertising for authority, the velvet glove for the iron fist, pursues the symbolic integration of the dominated classes by imposing needs rather than inculcating norms.

CHANGES IN THE EDUCATIONAL SYSTEM   Clearly it would be naive to see a merely *mechanical* process of inflation and devaluation at work. The massive increase in the school population has caused a whole set of transformations, both inside and outside the educational system, modifying its organizations and operation partly through morphological transformations at all its levels but also through defensive manoeuvres by its traditional users, such as the multiplication of subtly ranked paths through it and skilfully disguised 'dumping grounds' which help to blur perception of its hierarchies. For the sake of clarity, one may contrast two states of the secondary school system. In the older state, the organization of the institution, the pathways it offered, the courses it taught and the qualifications it awarded were all based on sharp divisions, clear-cut boundaries; the primary/secondary division produced systematic differences in all dimensions of the culture taught, the teaching methods used and the careers promised. (It is significant that the division has been maintained or even strengthened at the points where access to the dominant class is now decided—that is, at the point of streaming for the baccalauréat, and in higher education, with the division between the grandes écoles and the rest.) In the present state of the system, the exclusion of the great mass of working-class and middle-class children takes place not at the end of primary schooling but steadily and impalpably, all through the early years of secondary schooling, through hidden forms of elimination such as repeated years (equivalent to a deferred elimination); relegation into second-class courses, entailing a stigma that tends to induce proleptic recognition of scholastic and social destiny; and finally, the awarding of devalued certificates. (It is remarkable that just when the division into two streams—strictly speaking, there were always three, with 'higher primary' education and the whole set of internal training courses and competitions offered by all the major government departments—was tending to disappear and to be reconstituted at another level, Christian Baudelot and Roger Establet discovered this dichotomy, which no one would have thought of denying since it was the clearest manifestation of the scholastic mechanisms of reproduction.)[29]

Whereas the old system with its strongly marked boundaries led to the internalizing of scholastic divisions clearly corresponding to social divisions, the new system with its fuzzy classifications and blurred edges encourages and entertains (at least among the new 'intermediaries' in social space) aspirations that are themselves blurred and fuzzy. Aspiration levels are now adjusted to scholastic hurdles and standards in a less strict and also a less harsh manner than under the old system, which was characterized by the remorseless rigour of the national competitive examination. It is true that the new system fobs off a good number of its users with devalued qualifications, playing on the faulty perceptions that are encouraged by the anarchic profusion of courses and diplomas which are difficult to compare and yet subtly ranked in prestige. However, it does not force them into such abrupt disinvestment as the old system: the blurring of hierarchies and boundaries between the elected and the rejected, between true and false qualifications, plays a part in 'cooling out' and in calm acquiescence in being cooled out. The new system favours the development of a less realistic, less resigned relationship to the future than the old sense of proper limits, which was the basis of an acute sense of hierarchy. The *allodoxia* which the new system encourages in innumerable ways is the reason why relegated agents collaborate in their own relegation by overestimating the studies on which they embark, overvaluing their qualifications, and banking on possible futures which do not really exist for them; but it is also the reason why they do not truly accept the objective reality of their position and qualifications. And the reason for the attractiveness of the new or renewable positions lies in the fact that, being vague and ill-defined, uncertainly located in social space, often offering (like the occupations of 'artist' or 'intellectual' in the past) none of the material or symbolic criteria—promotion, benefits, increments—whereby social time, and also social hierarchies, are experienced and measured, they leave aspirations considerable room for manoeuvre.

They thus make it possible to avoid the sudden, final disinvestment imposed by occupations that are clearly delimited and defined from recruitment to retirement. The indeterminate future which they offer, a privilege hitherto reserved for artists and intellectuals, makes it possible to treat the present as a sort of endlessly renewed provisional status and to regard one's 'station' as an accidental detour, like the painter who works in advertising but continues to consider himself a 'true' artist and insists that this mercenary trade is only a temporary expedient that will be abandoned as soon as he has put by enough money to be independent.[30] These ambiguous occupations exempt their practitioners from the work of disinvestment and reinvestment that is implied, for example, in switching from a 'vocation' as a philosopher to a 'vocation' as a philosophy teacher, or from artist to publicity designer or art teacher—or at least allow them to defer their transfer indefinitely. It is not surprising that such people should be drawn to schemes of 'continuing education' (*éducation permanente*), a perpetual studenthood which offers an open, unlimited future and contrasts diametrically with the system of national competitions designed to demonstrate, once and for all, and as early as possible, that what is done cannot be undone.[31]

Again, it is understandable that, like artists, they should so readily embrace the aesthetic and ethical modes and models of youth: it is a way of showing to oneself and others that one is not finite, finished, defined. In place of abrupt, all-or-nothing breaks, between study and work, between work and retirement, there is an impalpable, infinitesimal slippage (consider all the temporary or semi-permanent occupations, often taken by students approaching the end of their course, which cluster around the established positions in scientific research or higher education or, at another level, consider the phased retirement now offered by the most 'advanced' firms). Everything takes place as if the new logic of the educational system and economic system encouraged people to defer for as long as possible the moment of ultimate crystallization toward which all the infinitesimal changes point, in other words, the final balance-sheet which sometimes takes the form of a 'personal crisis'.

It goes without saying that the adjustment between objective chances and subjective aspirations that is thereby established is both more subtle and more subtly extorted, but also more risky and unstable. Maintaining vagueness in the images of the present and future of one's position is a way of accepting limits, but it is also a way to avoid acknowledging them, or to put it another way, a way of refusing them. But it is a refusal in bad faith, the product of an ambiguous cult of revolution which springs from resentment at the disappointment of unrealistic expectations. Whereas the old system tended to produce clearly demarcated social identities which left little room for social fantasy but were comfortable and reassuring even in the unconditional renunciation which they demanded, the new system of structural instability in the representation of social identity and its legitimate aspirations tends to shift agents from the terrain of social crisis and critique to the terrain of personal critique and crisis.

COMPETITIVE STRUGGLES AND DISPLACEMENT OF THE STRUCTURE   It can be seen how naive it is to claim to settle the question of 'social change' by locating 'newness' or 'innovation' in a particular *site* in social space. For some, this site is at the top; for others, at the bottom; and it is always elsewhere, in all the 'new', 'marginal', 'excluded' or 'dropped-out' groups, for all those sociologists whose chief concern is to bring 'newness' into the discussion at all costs. But to characterize a class as 'conservative' or 'innovating' (without even specifying in what respect it is so), by tacit recourse to an ethical standard which is necessarily situated socially, produces a discourse which states little more than the site it comes from, because it sweeps aside what is essential, namely, the field of struggles, the system of objective relations within which positions and postures are defined relationally and which governs even those struggles aimed at transforming it. Only by reference to the space in the game which defines them and which they seek to maintain or redefine, can one understand the strategies, individual or collective, spontaneous or organized, which are aimed at conserving, transforming or transforming so as to conserve.

Reconversion strategies are nothing other than an aspect of the permanent actions and reactions whereby each group strives to maintain or change its position in the social structure, or, more precisely—at a stage in the evolution of class societies in which one can conserve only by changing—to change so as to conserve. Frequently the actions whereby each class (or class fraction) works to win new advantages, i.e., to gain an advantage over the other classes and so, objectively, to reshape the structure of objective relations between the classes (the relations revealed by the statistical distributions of properties), are compensated for (and so cancelled out ordinally) by the reactions of the other classes, directed toward the same objective. In this particular (though very common) case, the outcome of these opposing actions, which cancel each other out by the very countermovements which they generate, is an overall displacement of the structure of the distribution, between the classes or class fractions, of the assets at stake in the competition (as has happened in the case of the chances of university entrance—see table 15 and figure 7).

Table 15 shows the relationship between morphological change in the different classes and class fractions and the extent to which the members of these classes and class fractions make use of the educational system. The volume of the groups whose social reproduction was based, at the beginning of the period, on economic inheritance tends to decline or remain stationary, while, over the same period, their children—who will, to a large extent, join the wage-earning categories at the same level of the social hierarchy—make increasing use of the educational system. Those class fractions which are expanding, which are mainly rich in cultural capital and which used the educational system as their main means of reproduction (junior and senior executives, clerical workers) tend to increase their children's schooling in much the same proportion as the self-employed categories occupying an equivalent position in the class structure. The reversal of the relative positions of the commercial employers and clerical workers, and also of the farm workers and industrial manual workers, is explained both by the intensified schooling that is forced on the numerically declining categories (commercial employers, farm workers) and by the rise in the overall statistical characteristics of these categories (seen, for example, in their educational qualifications), resulting from change in their internal structure—towards less dispersion—and, more precisely, from the fact that their lower strata have been particularly hard hit and have disappeared or reconverted.

The schooling rates shown in the graph are probably overestimates, since the statistics only take account of young people living at home, more especially, no doubt, at lower levels of the social hierarchy. The slight narrowing of the range which is apparent in the most recent period is due partly to a saturation effect in the highest categories and partly to the fact that the statistics ignore the distribution of adolescents from different classes between academic courses that are themselves strongly ranked. Between 1968 and 1977, the proportion of industrial workers' children (who made up to 40.7 percent of the 17-year-old age groups in 1977) in the fifth grade of

Table 15 Changes in class morphology and use of educational system, 1954–1968.

Class fraction	Index of morphological change (1954=100)	% of men holding BEPC and above		Chances of access to higher education (%)		% of 16–18-year-olds receiving education		
		1962	1968	1961–1962	1965–1966	1954	1962	1968
Farm workers	53.7	0.8	1.6	0.7	2.7	8.0	23.3	29.7
Farmers	65.2	1.6	2.7	3.6	8.0	7.5	22.5	38.8
Manual workers	122.8	2.0	2.9	1.4	3.4	16.3	26.1	35.4
Industrial and commercial employers	89.0	8.5	11.3	16.4	23.2	30.0	45.0	51.7
Clerical and commercial	120.4	14.7	19.2	9.5	16.2	34.9	47.0	54.3
Junior executives	168.3	39.9	43.3	29.6	35.4	42.6	71.0	74.6
Senior executives, professions	167.8	69.5	73.4	48.5	58.7	59.3	87.0	90.0

Sources: INSEE, *Censuses 1954, 1962, 1968*; INSEE, *Données sociales*, 1973, p. 105; P. Bourdieu and J. C. Passeron, *The Inheritors* (Chicago and London, University of Chicago Press, 1979), p. 4; Bourdieu and Passeron, *Reproduction* (London and Beverly Hills, Sage Publications, 1977), p. 225.

Figure 7   Displacement of schooling rates of 16- to 18-year-olds, 1954–1975.

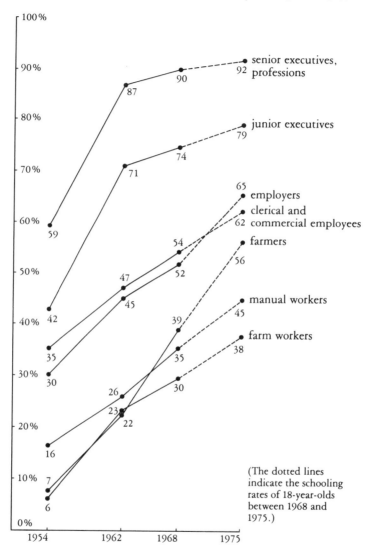

Sources: INSEE, *Censuses 1954, 1962, 1968, 1975;* INSEE, *Données sociales,* 1973, p. 105; P. Bourdieu and J.C. Passeron, *The Inheritors* (Chicago and London, University of Chicago Press, 1979), p. 4; Bourdieu and Passeron, *Reproduction* (London and Beverly Hills, Sage Publications, 1977), p. 225.

state secondary schooling remained constant (25.7 percent and 25.9 percent respectively), whereas the proportion of senior executives' and professionals' children rose from 15.4 percent to 16.8 percent. Moreover, in 1977, in this grade, 57.6 percent of the senior executives' and professionals' children were in section C (scientific), compared to 20.6 percent of the farm workers' children and 23.5 percent of the industrial workers' children. Conversely, only 9.8 percent of the senior executives' and professionals' children were in a 'technical' section, as against 24.6 percent of the farm workers' children and 28.7 percent of the industrial workers' children. Similar tendencies are found in higher education, where students of working-class origin are increasingly relegated to the arts and science faculties or to short technical courses, whereas the upper-class students tend to be in the grandes écoles, the medical faculties or, if academically less successful, in the minor business schools.

In the case of the social sciences, scientific discourse cannot ignore the conditions of its own reception. This depends at all times on the state of the prevailing social problematic, which is itself at least partly defined by the reactions to an earlier form of that discourse. Those who oversimplify the arguments of my earlier works, *The Inheritors* and *Reproduction*—which subsequent research has shown to err on the side of simplification—share with those who criticize them without understanding them a taste for simple truths and an inability to think relationally. Ideological stubbornness is not a sufficient explanation for naiveties such as that of referring to a 'rise in middle-class recruitment' to universities between 1950 and 1960 and concluding that the bourgeois university had been transformed into one 'dominated by the middle classes'.[32] One only has to look at the position of the faculties—especially those of arts and science—in the hierarchy of higher-education institutions by social origin of their students to know what to think of such a statistical analysis (highly praised by Alain Peyrefitte, who regrets that it has not had the success it deserves, thereby giving further proof of his great knowledge of university matters).[33] These faculties, which are situated at the lowest point of a field naturally dominated by the grandes écoles—and now even lower, to judge from the economic and social value of their diplomas, than the least prestigious and most recent of the business schools that have proliferated in recent years—have all the characteristics of dumping grounds, not least their level of 'democratization' (and feminization). It is as if the 'democratization' of secondary education were to be measured in a technical high school in an industrial suburb. Nor could anyone speak of a 'middle-class-dominated' university unless he had, consciously or unconsciously, confused the level of representation of the middle classes in the faculty-student population with the chances of faculty entrance for the middle classes—in other words, confused change in the social composition of the faculties with change in the structure of probabilities of schooling, a structure which has been shifted upwards without real transformation.

A similar process of homothetic development seems to take place whenever the strengths and efforts of the groups competing for a given type of asset or entitlement tend to balance one another out, as in a race in which, after a series of bursts in which various runners forge ahead or catch up, the initial gaps are maintained; in other words, whenever the attempts of the initially most disadvantaged groups to come into possession of the assets previously possessed by groups immediately above them in the social hierarchy or immediately ahead of them in the race are more or less counterbalanced, at all levels, by the efforts of better-placed groups to maintain the scarcity and distinctiveness of their assets. One thinks of the struggle which the sale of letters of nobility provoked among the English aristocracy in the second half of the sixteenth century, triggering a self-sustaining process of inflation and devaluation of these titles. The lowest titles, such as esquire or arms, were the first to be affected, followed by the rank of knight, which was devalued so fast that the oldest holders had to press for the creation of a new title, that of baronet. But this new title, which filled the gap between knight and peer of the realm, was seen as a threat by the holders of the higher rank, whose value depended on maintaining a certain distance.[34] Thus the newcomers conspire to ruin the existing holders by acquiring the titles which made them rare; the surest way to devalue a title of nobility is to purchase it as a commoner. The existing holders, for their part, objectively devalue the newcomers either by abandoning their titles to them in order to pursue rarer ones, or by introducing differences among the title-holders linked to seniority in accession to the title (such as the manner of possessing it). It follows that all the groups involved in the race, whatever rank they occupy, cannot conserve their position, their rarity, their rank except by running to keep their distance from those immediately behind them, thus jeopardizing the difference which distinguishes the group immediately in front; or, to put it another way, by aspiring to possess that which the group just ahead already have, and which they themselves will have, but later.

The holders of the rarest titles can also protect themselves from competition by setting up a numerus clausus. Such measures generally become necessary whenever the statistical mechanisms 'normally' protecting the group are found to be inadequate. The laisser-faire which is maintained so long as it discreetly protects the interests of the privileged group is replaced by a conscious protectionism, which calls on institutions to do openly what seemingly neutral mechanisms did invisibly. To protect themselves against excessive numbers, the holders of rare titles and rare jobs must defend a definition of the job which is nothing other than the definition of those who occupy the position at a given state of the relationship between titles and jobs. Declaring that the doctor, the architect or the professor of the future must be what they are today, i.e., what they themselves are, they write into the definition of the post, for all eternity, all the properties it derives from its small number of occupants (such as the secondary properties associated with severe selection, including high social origin), that is, the limits placed on competition and on the changes it would bring.

In place of statistical boundaries, which leave groups surrounded by the 'hybrid' zone of which Plato speaks apropos of the boundary of being and non-being, and which challenge the discriminatory power of social taxonomies (Young or old? Urban or rural? Rich or poor? 'Middle-class' or 'lower-middle'?), the numerus clausus, in the extreme form it receives from discriminatory law, sets sharp, arithmetical limits. In place of principles of selection, of inclusion and exclusion, based on a number of fairly closely interrelated and normally implicit criteria, it sets up an institutionalized and therefore conscious and organized process of segregation and discrimination, based on a single criterion (no women, or no Jews, or no blacks) which leaves no room for misclassification. In fact, the most select groups prefer to avoid the brutality of discriminatory measures and to combine the charms of the apparent absence of criteria, which allows the members the illusion of election on grounds of personal uniqueness, with the certainties of selection, which ensures maximum group homogeneity.

Smart clubs preserve their homogeneity by subjecting aspirants to very strict procedures—an act of candidature, a recommendation, sometimes presentation (in the literal sense) by sponsors who have themselves been members for a certain number of years, election by the membership or by a special committee, payment of sometimes very high initial subscriptions (5,000 francs per person at the Cercle du Bois de Boulogne in 1973, 9,500 francs at the Saint-Cloud Golf Club in 1975), plus the annual subscription (2,050 francs at Saint Cloud) and so on. In fact, it would be pointless to seek to discover whether the formal rules, which aim above all to protect the group against outsiders (not so much other classes, which are excluded from the start, as other fractions of the same class, or even parvenu members of the same fraction) and which generally prove superfluous, are intended to disguise the arbitrariness of election, or whether, on the contrary, the conspicuous arbitrariness which makes election a matter of indefinable flair is intended to disguise the official rules. 'We take you if we like the look of you (*C'est à la tête du client*),' said one club chairman; and another: 'There are clubs where you need two sponsors and they accept almost anyone; there are others with two sponsors where they're very choosy.' Besides, everything depends on the quality of the sponsors: 'Normally you have to wait two or three years; with good sponsors, you don't wait at all' (a member of the management committee, Cercle du Bois de Boulogne). Similarly, although membership is not officially hereditary, a young woman who applies to join the Cercle du Bois de Boulogne will be asked if her father or elder brother is a member. All the evidence suggests that although a number of them are officially organized around some rare, selective activity, which is often a mere pretext (golf, polo, hunting, riding, pigeon-shooting, sailing etc.), smart clubs (*les clubs chics*) are opposed to specialized clubs, whose members are defined by possession of a common property (for example, a yacht in the case of the Cercle de la Voile de Paris), in that they take account of the whole social person; and the more prestigious they are, and the more concerned they are to achieve a total harmony of interests and values (for example, the Jockey Club, the Cercle du Bois de Boulogne or Le Nouveau Cercle), the more this is the case.

Because the social reality of the criteria of selection can only come from outside, that is, from an objectification of what is refused in advance as reductive and vulgar, the group is able to persuade itself that its own assembly is based on no other principle than an indefinable sense of propriety which only membership can procure. The miracle of mutual election achieves perfection with groups of intellectuals, who are not so naive as to concede the minimal objectification required to form a club. Because they place their trust in the quasi-mystical sense of participation which does indeed define the participants, the excluded outsiders (who cannot even prove the existence of the exclusive group except involuntarily, through their denunciations of it), end up tilting against windmills when they attempt to point out the invisible barriers which separate them from the elect. Intellectual groups, particularly the most prestigious ones, are extraordinarily immune to objectification. This is not only because one has to belong in order to have a practical mastery of the mechanisms of membership; it is also because one cannot objectify the intellectual game without putting at stake one's own stake in the game—a risk which is at once derisory and absolute.

The dialectic of downclassing and upclassing which underlies a whole set of social processes presupposes and entails that all the groups concerned run in the same direction, toward the same objectives, the same properties, those which are designated by the leading group and which, by definition, are unavailable to the groups following, since, whatever these properties may be intrinsically, they are modified and qualified by their distinctive rarity and will no longer be what they are once they are multiplied and made available to groups lower down. Thus, by an apparent paradox, the maintenance of order, that is, of the whole set of gaps, differences, 'differentials', ranks, precedences, priorities, exclusions, distinctions, ordinal properties, and thus of the relations of order which give a social formation its structure, is provided by an unceasing change in substantial (i.e., non-relational) properties. This implies that the social order established at any given moment is also necessarily a temporal order, an 'order of successions', as Leibniz put it, each group having as its past the group immediately below and for its future the group immediately above (one sees the attraction of evolutionist models). The competing groups are separated by differences which are essentially located in the order of time.

It is no accident that *credit* is so important in this system. The imposition of legitimacy which occurs through the competitive struggle and is enhanced by the gentle violence of cultural missionary work tends to produce pretension, in the sense of a need which pre-exists the means of adequately satisfying. And in a social order which acknowledges that even the most deprived have the right to every satisfaction, but only in the long run, the only alternatives are credit, which allows immediate enjoyment of the promised goods but implies acceptance of a future which is merely the continuation of the past, or the 'imitation'—mock luxury cars, mock luxury holidays and so on.

But the dialectic of downclassing and upclassing is predisposed to function also as an ideological mechanism, whose effects conservative discourse strives to intensify. Especially when they compare their present conditions with their past, the dominated groups are exposed to the illusion that they have only to wait in order to receive advantages which, in reality, they will obtain only by struggle. By situating the difference between the classes in the order of successions, the competitive struggle establishes a difference which, like that which separates predecessor from successor in a social order governed by well-defined rules of succession, is not only the most absolute and unbridgeable (since there is nothing to do but wait, sometimes a whole lifetime, like the petit bourgeois who acquire their own houses at the moment of retirement, sometimes several generations, like the petit bourgeois who extend their own foreshortened trajectories through their children) but also the most unreal and evanescent (since a person knows that if he can wait, he will in any case get what he is promised by the ineluctable laws of evolution). In short, what the competitive struggle makes everlasting is not different conditions, but the difference between conditions.

Collective and individual delay has social consequences which further complicate this process. Relatively late arrival not only reduces the duration of enjoyment; it also implies a less familiar, less 'easy' relationship to the activity or asset in question, which may have technical consequences—e.g., in the use of a car—or symbolic ones—in the case of cultural goods. It may also represent the disguised equivalent of pure and simple privation when the value of the asset or activity lies in its distinguishing power (which is clearly linked to exclusive or priority access) rather than in the intrinsic satisfactions it gives. The vendors of goods and services, who have an interest in these effects of allodoxia, exploit these lags, offering, out-of-season (e.g., in the case of holidays), or when they are out of fashion (clothes, activities), things which have their full value only at the 'right' time.

Once this mechanism is understood, one perceives the futility of the abstract debates which arise from the opposition of permanence and change, structure and history, reproduction and the 'production of society'. The real basis of such debates is the refusal to acknowledge that social contradictions and struggles are not all, or always, in contradiction with the perpetuation of the established order; that, beyond the antitheses of 'thinking in pairs', permanence can be ensured by change and the structure perpetuated by movement; that the 'frustrated expectations' which are created by the time-lag between the imposition of legitimate needs ('musts', as the marketing men put it) and access to the means of satisfying them, do not necessarily threaten the survival of the system; that the structural gap and the corresponding frustrations are the very source of the reproduction through displacement which perpetuates the structure of positions while transforming the 'nature' of conditions.

It also becomes clear that those who point to what might be called 'cardinal' properties and speak of the 'embourgeoisement' of the working class, and those who try to refute them by pointing to ordinal properties, are equally unaware that the contradictory aspects of reality which they isolate are in fact indissoluble dimensions of a single process. The reproduction of the social structure can take place in and through a competitive struggle leading to a simple displacement of the structure of distributions, so long and only so long as the members of the dominated classes enter the struggle in extended order, that is, through actions and reactions which are compounded only statistically, by the external effects which the actions of some exert on the actions of others, in the absence of any interaction or transaction, and consequently in conditions of objectivity, without collective or individual control and generally against the agents' individual and collective interests.

The limiting case of these processes of statistical action is panic or rout, in which each agent helps to produce what he fears by performing actions inspired by the feared effect (as in financial panics). In all these cases, the collective action, the mere statistical sum of uncoordinated individual actions, leads to a collective result irreducible or hostile to the collective interests and even to the particular interests pursued by the individual actions. This is seen clearly when the demoralization produced by a pessimistic picture of the future of a class contributes to the decline of that class; in a number of ways, the members of a declining class contribute to the collective decline, like the craftsmen who push their children through school while complaining that the educational system discourages young people from entering the trade.

Competitive struggle is the form of class struggle which the dominated classes allow to be imposed on them when they accept the stakes offered by the dominant classes. It is an integrative struggle and, by virtue of the initial handicaps, a reproductive struggle, since those who enter this chase, in which they are beaten before they start, as the constancy of the gaps testifies, implicitly recognize the legitimacy of the goals pursued by those whom they pursue, by the mere fact of taking part.

Having established the logic of the processes of competition (or rout) which condemn each agent to react in isolation to the effect of the countless reactions of other agents, or, more precisely, to the result of the statistical aggregation of their isolated actions, and which reduce the class to the state of a mass dominated by its own number, one can pose

the question, much debated at present among historians,[35] of the conditions (economic crisis, economic crisis following a period of expansion and so on) in which the dialectic of mutually self-reproducing objective chances and subjective aspirations may break down. Everything suggests that an abrupt slump in objective chances relative to subjective aspirations is likely to produce a break in the tacit acceptance which the dominated classes—now abruptly excluded from the race, objectively and subjectively—previously granted to the dominant goals, and so to make possible a genuine inversion of the table of values.

3 | The Habitus and the Space of Life-Styles

The mere fact that the social space described here can be presented as a diagram indicates that it is an abstract representation, deliberately constructed, like a map, to give a bird's-eye view, a point of view on the whole set of points from which ordinary agents (including the sociologist and his reader, in their ordinary behaviour) see the social world. Bringing together in simultaneity, in the scope of a single glance—this is its heuristic value—positions which the agents can never apprehend in their totality and in their multiple relationships, social space is to the practical space of everyday life, with its distances which are kept or signalled, and neighbours who may be more remote than strangers, what geometrical space is to the 'travelling space' (*espace hodologique*) of ordinary experience, with its gaps and discontinuities.

But the most crucial thing to note is that the question of this space is raised within the space itself—that the agents have points of view on this objective space which depend on their position within it and in which their will to transform or conserve it is often expressed. Thus many of the words which sociology uses to designate the classes it constructs are borrowed from ordinary usage, where they serve to express the (generally polemical) view that one group has of another. As if carried away by their quest for greater objectivity, sociologists almost always forget that the 'objects' they classify produce not only objectively classifiable practices but also classifying operations that are no less objective and are themselves classifiable. The division into classes performed by sociology leads to the common root of the classifiable practices which agents produce and of the classificatory judgements they make of other agents' practices and their own. The habitus is both the generative principle of objectively classifiable judgements and the system of classification (*principium divisionis*) of these practices. It is in the relationship between the two capacities which define the habitus, the capacity to produce classifiable practices and works, and the capacity to differentiate and appreciate these practices and products (taste), that the represented social world, i.e., the space of life-styles, is constituted.

The relationship that is actually established between the pertinent characteristics of economic and social condition (capital volume and composition, in both synchronic and diachronic aspects) and the distinctive features associated with the corresponding position in the universe of life-styles only becomes intelligible when the habitus is constucted as the generative formula which makes it possible to account both for the classifiable practices and products and for the judgements, themselves classified, which make these practices and works into a system of distinctive signs. When one speaks of the aristocratic asceticism of teachers or the pretension of the petite bourgeoisie, one is not only describing these groups by one, or even the most important, of their properties, but also endeavouring to name the principle which generates all their properties and all their judgements of their, or other people's, properties. The habitus is necessity internalized and converted into a disposition that generates meaningful practices and meaning-giving perceptions; it is a general, transposable disposition which carries out a systematic, universal application—beyond the limits of what has been directly learnt—of the necessity inherent in the learning conditions. That is why an agent's whole set of practices (or those of a whole set of agents produced by similar conditions) are both systematic, inasmuch as they are the product of the application of identical (or interchangeable) schemes, and systematically distinct from the practices constituting another life-style.

Because different conditions of existence produce different habitus— systems of generative schemes applicable, by simple transfer, to the most varied areas of practice—the practices engendered by the different habitus appear as systematic configurations of properties expressing the differences objectively inscribed in conditions of existence in the form of systems of differential deviations which, when perceived by agents endowed with the schemes of perception and appreciation necessary in order to identify, interpret and evaluate their pertinent features, function as life-styles (see figure 8).[1]

The habitus is not only a structuring structure, which organizes practices and the perception of practices, but also a structured structure: the principle of division into logical classes which organizes the perception of the social world is itself the product of internalization of the division into social classes. Each class condition is defined, simultaneously, by its intrinsic properties and by the relational properties which it derives from its position in the system of class conditions, which is also a system of

Figure 8 Conditions of existence, habitus and life-style.

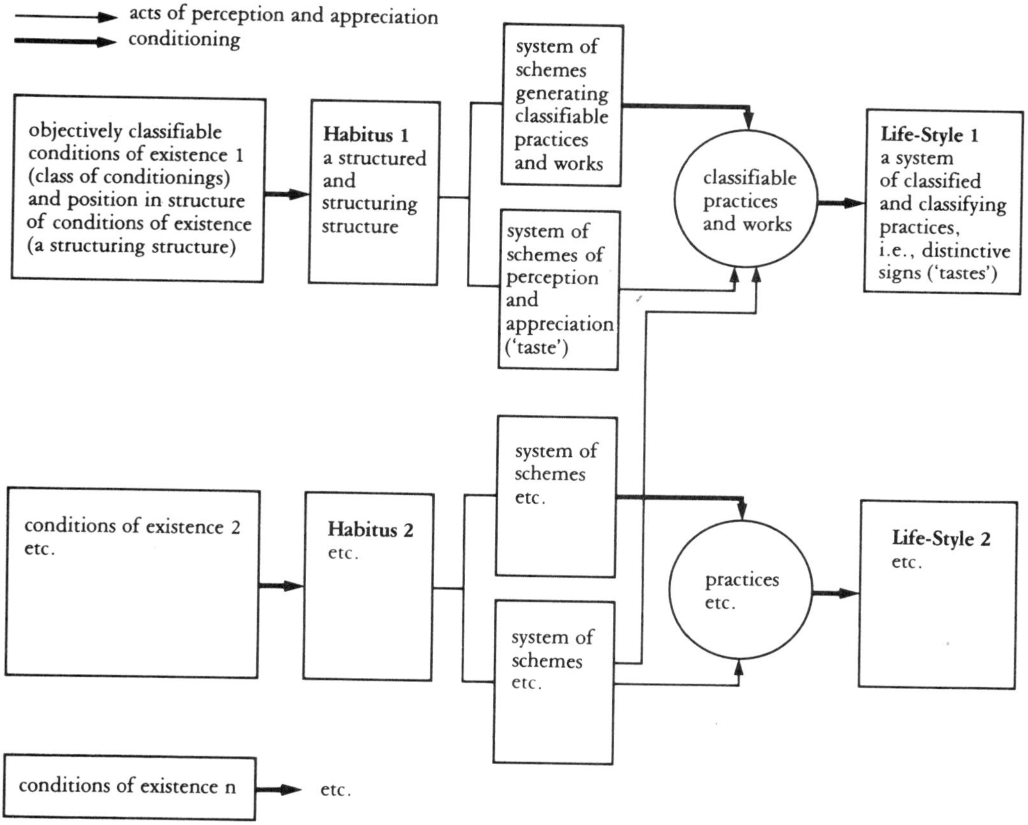

differences, differential positions, i.e., by everything which distinguishes it from what it is not and especially from everything it is opposed to; social identity is defined and asserted through difference. This means that inevitably inscribed within the dispositions of the habitus is the whole structure of the system of conditions, as it presents itself in the experience of a life-condition occupying a particular position within that structure. The most fundamental oppositions in the structure (high/low, rich/poor etc.) tend to establish themselves as the fundamental structuring principles of practices and the perception of practices. As a system of practice-generating schemes which expresses systematically the necessity and freedom inherent in its class condition and the difference constituting that position, the habitus apprehends differences between conditions, which it grasps in the form of differences between classified, classifying practices (products of other habitus), in accordance with principles of differentiation which, being themselves the product of these differences, are objectively attuned to them and therefore tend to perceive them as natural.

The observer who divides a population into classes performs an operation which has its equivalent in social practice. If he is not aware of this, he is likely to present a more or less modified form of a native classification as a scientific classification (a number of 'typologies' are precisely this). In addition, he has no chance of bringing to the level of consciousness the true status of his classifying operations which, like native knowledge, presuppose connections and comparisons and which, even when they seem to belong to the realm of social physics, in fact produce and interpret signifying distinctions, in short, belong to the order of the symbolic.

While it must be reasserted, against all forms of mechanism, that ordinary experience of the social world is a cognition, it is equally important to realize—contrary to the illusion of the spontaneous generation of consciousness which so many theories of the 'awakening of class consciousness' (*prise de conscience*) amount to—that primary cognition is misrecognition, recognition of an order which is also established in the mind. Life-styles are thus the systematic products of habitus, which, perceived in their mutual relations through the schemes of the habitus, become sign systems that are socially qualified (as 'distinguished', 'vulgar' etc.). The dialectic of conditions and habitus is the basis of an alchemy which transforms the distribution of capital, the balance-sheet of a power relation, into a system of perceived differences, distinctive properties, that is, a distribution of symbolic capital, legitimate capital, whose objective truth is misrecognized.

As structured products (*opus operatum*) which a structuring structure (*modus operandi*) produces through retranslations according to the specific logic of the different *fields,* all the practices and products of a given agent are objectively harmonized among themselves, without any deliberate pursuit of coherence, and objectively orchestrated, without any conscious concertation, with those of all members of the same class. The habitus continuously generates practical metaphors, that is to say, transfers (of which the transfer of motor habits is only one example) or, more precisely, systematic transpositions required by the particular conditions in which the habitus is 'put into practice' (so that, for example, the ascetic ethos which might be expected always to express itself in saving may, in a given context, express itself in a particular way of using credit). The practices of the same agent, and, more generally, the practices of all agents of the same class, owe the stylistic affinity which makes each of them a metaphor of any of the others to the fact that they are the product of transfers of the same schemes of action from one field to another. An obvious paradigm would be the disposition called 'handwriting', a singular way of tracing letters which always produces the same writing, i.e., graphic forms which, in spite of all the differences of size, material or colour due to the surface (paper or blackboard) or the instrument (pen or chalk)—in spite, therefore, of the different use of muscles—present an immediately perceptible family resemblance, like all the features of style or manner whereby a painter or writer can be recognized as infallibly as a man by his walk.

True pastiche, as Proust does it, for example, reproduces not the most striking features of a style—like parody or caricature—but the habitus, which Jacques Rivière calls 'the hearth of mental activity', in which the original discourse is generated: 'We are amused to see each writer "resurrected" with his whole personality and, faced with an event he has never experienced, react just as he did to those which life brought him. The hearth of his mental activity is rekindled, the lamp relit in his brain.'[2]

Systematicity is found in the opus operatum because it is in the modus operandi.[3] It is found in all the properties—and property—with which individuals and groups surround themselves, houses, furniture, paintings, books, cars, spirits, cigarettes, perfume, clothes, and in the practices in which they manifest their distinction, sports, games, entertainments, only because it is in the synthetic unity of the habitus, the unifying, generative principle of all practices. Taste, the propensity and capacity to appropriate (materially or symbolically) a given class of classified, classifying objects or practices, is the generative formula of life-style, a unitary set of distinctive preferences which express the same expressive intention in the specific logic of each of the symbolic sub-spaces, furniture, clothing, language or body hexis. Each dimension of life-style 'symbolizes with' the others, in Leibniz's phrase, and symbolizes them. An old cabinetmaker's world view, the way he manages his budget, his time or his body, his use of language and choice of clothing are fully present in his ethic of scrupulous, impeccable craftsmanship and in the aesthetic of work for work's sake which leads him to measure the beauty of his products by the care and patience that have gone into them.

The system of matching properties, which includes people—one speaks of a 'well-matched couple', and friends like to say they have the same tastes—is organized by taste, a system of classificatory schemes which may only very partially become conscious although, as one rises in the social hierarchy, life-style is increasingly a matter of what Weber calls the 'stylization of life'. Taste is the basis of the mutual adjustment of all the features associated with a person, which the old aesthetic recommended for the sake of the mutual reinforcement they give one another; the countless pieces of information a person consciously or unconsciously imparts endlessly underline and confirm one another, offering the alert observer the same pleasure an art-lover derives from the symmetries and correspondences produced by a harmonious distribution of redundancies. The over-determination that results from these redundancies is felt the more strongly because the different features which have to be isolated for observation or measurement strongly interpenetrate in ordinary perception; each item of information imparted in practice (e.g., a judgement of a painting) is contaminated—and, if it deviates from the probable feature, corrected—by the effect of the whole set of features previously or simultaneously perceived. That is why a survey which tends to isolate features—for example, by dissociating the things said from the way they are said—and detach them from the system of correlative features tends to minimize the deviation, on each point, between the classes, especially that between the petit bourgeois and the bourgeois. In the ordinary situations of bourgeois life, banalities about art, literature or cinema are inseparable from the steady tone, the slow, casual diction, the distant or self-assured smile, the measured gesture, the well-tailored suit and the bourgeois salon of the person who pronounces them.

Thus, lacunae can turn into disdainful refusals and confusion into absent-mindedness. Bourgeois respondents particularly distinguish themselves by their ability to control the survey situation (and any analysis of survey data should take this into account). Control over the social situation in which culture operates is given to them by the very unequally distributed capacity to adopt the relation to language which is called for in all situations of polite conversation (e.g., chatter about cinema or travel), and which presupposes an art of skimming, sliding and masking, making abundant use of all the hinges, fillers and qualifiers identified by linguists as characteristic of bourgeois language.

Taste is the practical operator of the transmutation of things into distinct and distinctive signs, of continuous distributions into discontinuous oppositions; it raises the differences inscribed in the physical order of bodies to the symbolic order of significant distinctions. It transforms objectively classified practices, in which a class condition signifies itself (through taste), into classifying practices, that is, into a symbolic expression of class position, by perceiving them in their mutual relations and in terms of social classificatory schemes. Taste is thus the source of the system of distinctive features which cannot fail to be perceived as a systematic expression of a particular class of conditions of existence, i.e., as a distinctive life-style, by anyone who possesses practical knowledge of the relationships between distinctive signs and positions in the distributions—between the universe of objective properties, which is brought to light by scientific construction, and the no less objective universe of life-styles, which exists as such for and through ordinary experience.

This classificatory system, which is the product of the internalization of the structure of social space, in the form in which it impinges through the experience of a particular position in that space, is, within the limits of economic possibilities and impossibilities (which it tends to reproduce in its own logic), the generator of practices adjusted to the regularities inherent in a condition. It continuously transforms necessities into strategies, constraints into preferences, and, without any mechanical determination, it generates the set of 'choices' constituting life-styles, which derive their meaning, i.e., their value, from their position in a system of oppositions and correlations.[4] It is a virtue made of necessity which continuously transforms necessity into virtue by inducing 'choices' which correspond to the condition of which it is the product. As can be seen whenever a change in social position puts the habitus into new conditions, so that its specific efficacy can be isolated, it is taste—the taste of necessity or the taste of luxury—and not high or low income which commands the practices objectively adjusted to these resources. Through taste, an agent has what he likes because he likes what he has, that is, the properties actually given to him in the distributions and legitimately assigned to him in the classifications.[5]

The Homology between the Spaces

Bearing in mind all that precedes, in particular the fact that the generative schemes of the habitus are applied, by simple transfer, to the most dissimilar areas of practice, one can immediately understand that the practices or goods associated with the different classes in the different areas of practice are organized in accordance with structures of opposition which are homologous to one another because they are all homologous to the structure of objective oppositions between class conditions. Without presuming to demonstrate here in a few pages what the whole of the rest of this work will endeavour to establish—but lest the reader fail to see the wood for the trees of detailed analysis—I shall merely indicate, very schematically, how the two major organizing principles of the social space govern the structure and modification of the space of cultural consumption, and, more generally, the whole universe of life-styles.

In cultural consumption, the main opposition, by overall capital value, is between the practices designated by their rarity as distinguished, those of the fractions richest in both economic and cultural capital, and the practices socially identified as vulgar because they are both easy and common, those of the fractions poorest in both these respects. In the intermediate position are the practices which are perceived as pretentious, because of the manifest discrepancy between ambition and possibilities. In opposition to the dominated condition, characterized, from the point of view of the dominant, by the combination of forced poverty and unjustified laxity, the dominant aesthetic—of which the work of art and the aesthetic disposition are the most complete embodiments—proposes the combination of ease and asceticism, i.e., self-imposed austerity, restraint, reserve, which are affirmed in that absolute manifestation of excellence, relaxation in tension.

This fundamental opposition is specified according to capital composition. Through the mediation of the means of appropriation available to them, exclusively or principally cultural on the one hand, mainly economic on the other, and the different forms of relation to works of art which result from them, the different fractions of the dominant class are oriented towards cultural practices so different in their style and object and sometimes so antagonistic (those of 'artists' and 'bourgeois')[6] that it is easy to forget that they are variants of the same fundamental relationship to necessity and to those who remain subject to it, and that each pursues the exclusive appropriation of legitimate cultural goods and the associated symbolic profits. Whereas the dominant fractions of the dominant class (the 'bourgeoisie') demand of art a high degree of denial of the social world and incline towards a hedonistic aesthetic of ease and facility, symbolized by boulevard theatre or Impressionist painting, the dominated fractions (the 'intellectuals' and 'artists') have affinities with the ascetic aspect of aesthetics and are inclined to support all artistic revolutions conducted in the name of purity and purification, refusal of ostentation and the bourgeois taste for ornament; and the dispositions towards the social world which they owe to their status as poor relations incline them to welcome a pessimistic representation of the social world.

While it is clear that art offers it the greatest scope, there is no area of practice in which the intention of purifying, refining and sublimating facile impulses and primary needs cannot assert itself, or in which the stylization of life, i.e., the primacy of form over function, which leads to the denial of function, does not produce the same effects. In language, it gives the opposition between popular outspokenness and the highly censored language of the bourgeois, between the expressionist pursuit of the picturesque or the rhetorical effect and the choice of restraint and false simplicity (litotes). The same economy of means is found in body language: here too, agitation and haste, grimaces and gesticulation are opposed to slowness—'the slow gestures, the slow glance' of nobility, according to Nietzsche[7]—to the restraint and impassivity which signify elevation. Even the field of primary tastes is organized according to the fundamental opposition, with the antithesis between quantity and quality, belly and palate, matter and manners, substance and form.

FORM AND SUBSTANCE   The fact that in the realm of food the main opposition broadly corresponds to differences in income has masked the secondary opposition which exists, both within the middle classes and within the dominant class, between the fractions richer in cultural capital and less rich in economic capital and those whose assets are structured in the opposite way. Observers tend to see a simple effect of income in the fact that, as one rises in the social hierarchy, the proportion of income spent on food diminishes, or that, within the food budget, the proportion spent on heavy, fatty, fattening foods, which are also cheap—pasta, potatoes, beans, bacon, pork—declines (C.S. XXXIII), as does that spent on wine, whereas an increasing proportion is spent on leaner, lighter (more digestible), non-fattening foods (beef, veal, mutton, lamb, and especially fresh fruit and vegetables).[8] Because the real principle of preferences is taste, a virtue made of necessity, the theory which makes consumption a simple function of income has all the appearances to support it, since income plays an important part in determining distance from necessity. However, it cannot account for cases in which the same income is associated with totally different consumption patterns. Thus, foremen remain attached to 'popular' taste although they earn more than clerical and commercial employees, whose taste differs radically from that of manual workers and is closer to that of teachers.

For a real explanation of the variations which J. F. Engel's law merely records, one has to take account of all the characteristics of social condition which are (statistically) associated from earliest childhood with possession of high or low income and which tend to shape tastes adjusted to these conditions.[9] The true basis of the differences found in the area of consumption, and far beyond it, is the opposition between the tastes of luxury (or freedom) and the tastes of necessity. The former are the tastes of individuals who are the product of material conditions of existence defined by distance from necessity, by the freedoms or facilities stemming from possession of capital; the latter express, precisely in their adjustment, the necessities of which they are the product. Thus it is possible to deduce popular tastes for the foods that are simultaneously most 'filling' and most economical[10] from the necessity of reproducing labour power at the lowest cost which is forced on the proletariat as its very definition. The idea of taste, typically bourgeois, since it presupposes absolute freedom of choice, is so closely associated with the idea of freedom that many people find it hard to grasp the paradoxes of the taste of necessity. Some simply sweep it aside, making practice a direct product of economic necessity (workers eat beans because they cannot afford anything else), failing to realize that necessity can only be fulfilled, most of the time, because the agents are inclined to fulfil it, because they have a taste for what they are anyway condemned to. Others turn it into a taste of freedom, forgetting the conditionings of which it is the product, and so reduce it to pathological or morbid preference for (basic) essentials, a sort of congenital coarseness, the pretext for a class racism which associates the populace with everything heavy, thick and fat.[11] Taste is *amor fati,* the choice of destiny, but a forced choice, produced by conditions of existence which rule out all alternatives as mere daydreams and leave no choice but the taste for the necessary.

One only has to describe the tastes of necessity as if they were tastes of luxury (which inevitably happens whenever one ignores the modality of practices)[12] to produce false coincidences between the two extreme positions in social space: fertility or celibacy (or which amounts to the same thing, late marriage) is an elective luxury in one case, an effect of privation in the other. In this respect, Nicole Tabard's analysis of women's attitudes to 'working wives' is exemplary: for working-class women, 'employment is a constraint which weakens as the husband's income rises'; for the women of the privileged classes, work is a choice, as is shown by the fact that 'the rate of female employment does not decline as status rises.'[13] This example should be borne in mind when reading statistics in which the nominal identity imposed by uniform questioning conceals totally different realities, as often happens when one moves from one extreme of social space to the other. If in one case women who work say they are in favour of women working, whereas in the other they may work while saying they are against it, this is because the work to which working-class women are tacitly referring is the only sort they can expect, i.e., unpleasant, poorly paid work, which has nothing in common with what 'work' implies for bourgeois women. To give an idea of the ideological effects which the essentialist and anti-genetic dominant vision produces when, consciously or unconsciously, it naturalizes the taste of necessity (Kant's 'barbarous taste'), converting it into a natural inclination simply by dissociating it from its economic and social raisons d'être, one only has to recall a social psychology experiment which showed that the same act, that of giving blood, is seen as voluntary or forced depending on whether it is performed by members of the privileged classes or the working classes.[14]

The taste of necessity can only be the basis of a life-style 'in-itself', which is defined as such only negatively, by an absence, by the relationship of privation between itself and the other life-styles. For some, there are elective emblems, for others stigmata which they bear in their very bodies. 'As the chosen people bore in their features the sign that they were the property of Jehovah, so the division of labour brands the manufacturing worker as the property of capital.'[15] The brand which Marx speaks of is nothing other than life-style, through which the most deprived immediately betray themselves, even in their use of spare time; in so doing they inevitably serve as a foil to every distinction and contribute, purely negatively, to the dialectic of pretension and distinction which fuels the incessant changing of taste. Not content with lacking virtually all the knowledge or manners which are valued in the markets of academic examination or polite conversation nor with only possessing skills which have no value there, they are the people 'who don't know how to live', who sacrifice most to material foods, and to the heaviest, grossest and most fattening of them, bread, potatoes, fats, and the most vulgar, such as wine; who spend least on clothing and cosmetics, appearance and beauty; those who 'don't know how to relax', 'who always have to be doing something', who set off in their Renault 5 or Simca 1000 to join the great traffic jams of the holiday exodus, who picnic beside major roads, cram their tents into overcrowded campsites, fling themselves into the prefabricated leisure activities designed for them by the engineers of cultural mass production; those who by all these uninspired 'choices' confirm class racism, if it needed to be confirmed, in its conviction that they only get what they deserve.

The art of eating and drinking remains one of the few areas in which the working classes explicitly challenge the legitimate art of living. In the face of the new ethic of sobriety for the sake of slimness, which is most recognized at the highest levels of the social hierarchy, peasants and especially industrial workers maintain an ethic of convivial indulgence. A bon vivant is not just someone who enjoys eating and drinking; he is someone capable of entering into the generous and familiar—that is, both simple and free—relationship that is encouraged and symbolized by eating and drinking together, in a conviviality which sweeps away restraints and reticence.

Sixty-four percent of senior executives, professionals and industrialists and 60 percent of junior executives, clerical and commercial employees consider that 'the French eat too much'. Farm workers (who are by far the most inclined to think the quantity 'about right'—54 percent as against 32 percent in the upper classes) and industrial workers are the categories who least often accept the new cultural norm (40 percent and 46 percent), which is recognized more by women than men and more by young people than old. As regards drink, only farm workers stand out clearly against the dominant view (32 percent of them consider that 'French people drink about the right amount'), though industrial workers also accept it less frequently than the other categories. Sixty-three percent of the industrial workers (and 50 percent of the farm workers, as against 48 percent of the executives, professionals and industrialists) say they have a favourable opinion of someone who enjoys eating and drinking. Another index of their willingness to stand up in this area for heterodox practices which in cultural matters they would try to disguise is that they say that, in a restaurant, they would choose a substantial dish rather than a light grill (favoured by the senior executives) or that they would have both cheese *and* a dessert. This is understandable when it is remembered that, by its very rarity, a visit to a restaurant is, for most of them—51 percent of the farm workers and 44 percent of the industrial workers hardly ever eat in a restaurant, as against only 6 percent of the upper classes—something extraordinary, associated with the idea of abundance and the suspension of ordinary restrictions. Even as regards alcohol consumption, where the weight of legitimacy is no doubt greater, the working classes are the least inclined (35 percent of farm workers, 46 percent of industrial workers, 55 percent of the upper classes) to set the minimum age for drinking alcohol above fifteen (C.S. XXXIV).

The boundary marking the break with the popular relation to food runs, without any doubt, between the manual workers and the clerical and commercial employees (see table 16). Clerical workers spend less on food than skilled manual workers, both in absolute terms (9,376 francs as against 10,347 francs) and in relative terms (34.2 percent as against 38.3 percent); they consume less bread, pork, pork products (*charcuterie*), milk, cheese, rabbit, poultry, dried vegetables and fats, and, within a smaller food budget, spend as much on meat—beef, veal, mutton and lamb—and slightly more on fish, fresh fruit and aperitifs. These changes in the structure of spending on food are accompanied by increased spending on health and beauty care and clothing, and a slight increase in spending on cultural and leisure activities. When it is noted that the reduced spending on food, especially on the most earthly, earthy, down-to-earth foods, is accompanied by a lower birth-rate, it is reasonable to suppose that it constitutes one aspect of an overall transformation of the relationship to the world. The 'modest' taste which can defer its gratifications is opposed to the spontaneous materialism of the working classes, who refuse to participate in the Benthamite calculation of pleasures and pains, benefits and costs (e.g., for health and beauty). In other words, these two relations to the 'fruits of the earth' are grounded in two dispositions towards the future which are themselves related in circular causality to two objective futures. Against the imaginary anthropology of economics, which has never shrunk from formulating universal laws of 'temporal preference', it has to be pointed out that the propensity to subordinate present desires to future desires depends on the extent to which this sacrifice is 'reasonable', that is, on the likelihood, in any case, of obtaining future satisfactions superior to those sacrificed.[16]

Among the economic conditions of the propensity to sacrifice immediate satisfactions to expected satisfactions one must include the probability of these future satisfactions which is inscribed in the present condition. There is still a sort of economic calculation in the unwillingness to subject existence to economic calculation. The hedonism which seizes day by day the rare satisfactions ('good times') of the immediate present

Table 16 Annual household expenditures on food: skilled manual workers, foremen and clerical workers, 1972.

	Skilled manual		Foremen		Clerical workers	
Average number persons per household	3.61		3.85		2.95	
Average total household expenditure (francs)	26,981		35,311		27,376	
Average total household expenditure on food (francs)	10,347		12,503		9,376	
Expenditure on food as % of total expenditure	38.3		35.4		34.2	
	Average exp.		Average exp.		Average exp.	
Type of food	Francs	As % of all food exp.	Francs	As % of all food exp.	Francs	As % of all food exp.
Cereals	925	8.9	1,054	8.4	789	8.4
bread	464	4.5	512	4.1	349	3.7
cakes, pastries	331	3.2	439	3.5	322	3.4
rusks	27	0.3	28	0.2	24	0.2
rice	65	0.6	46	0.4	49	0.5
flour	37	0.3	27	0.2	45	0.5
Vegetables	858	8.3	979	7.8	766	8.2
potatoes	141	1.4	146	1.2	112	1.2
fresh vegetables	556	5.4	656	5.2	527	5.6
dried or canned	162	1.6	177	1.4	127	1.3
Fruit	515	5.0	642	5.1	518	5.5
fresh fruit	248	2.4	329	2.6	278	3.0
citrus fruit, bananas	202	1.9	229	1.8	177	1.9
dried	65	0.6	86	0.7	62	0.7
Butcher's meat	1,753	16.9	2,176	17.4	1,560	16.5
beef	840	8.1	1,086	8.7	801	8.5
veal	302	2.9	380	3.0	296	3.1
mutton, lamb	169	1.6	170	1.3	154	1.6
horse	88	0.8	112	0.9	74	0.8
pork	354	3.4	428	3.4	235	2.5
Pork products, delicatessen	893	8.6	1,046	8.4	758	8.0
Fish, shellfish	268	2.6	330	2.6	280	3.0

Table 16 (continued)

	Skilled manual		Foremen		Clerical workers	
Average number persons per household	3.61		3.85		2.95	
Average total household expenditure (francs)	26,981		35,311		27,376	
Average total household expenditure on food (francs)	10,347		12,503		9,376	
Expenditure on food as % of total expenditure	38.3		35.4		34.2	
	Average exp.		Average exp.		Average exp.	
Type of food	Francs	As % of all food exp.	Francs	As % of all food exp.	Francs	As % of all food exp.
Poultry	389	3.7	403	3.2	317	3.4
Rabbit, game	173	1.7	156	1.2	131	1.4
Eggs	164	1.6	184	1.5	146	1.5
Milk	342	3.3	337	2.7	252	2.7
Cheese, yogurt	631	6.1	700	5.6	521	5.5
Fats	547	5.3	629	5.0	439	4.7
butter	365	3.5	445	3.5	292	3.1
oil	149	1.4	146	1.2	125	1.3
margarine	30	0.3	37	0.3	21	0.2
lard	2	0	0	0	1	0
Sugar, confectionery, cocoa	345	3.3	402	3.2	290	3.1
Alcohol	883	8.6	1,459	11.7	771	8.2
wine	555	5.4	1,017	8.1	466	5.0
beer	100	1.0	109	0.9	68	0.7
cider	13	0	5	0	8	0
apéritifs, liqueurs	215	2.1	328	2.6	229	2.4
Non-alcoholic drinks	236	2.3	251	2.0	224	2.4
Coffee, tea	199	1.9	252	2.0	179	1.9
Restaurant meals	506	4.9	583	4.7	572	6.1
Canteen meals	457	4.4	559	4.5	473	5.0
Miscellaneous	263	2.5	359	2.9	389	4.1

Source: C.S. III (1972).

is the only philosophy conceivable to those who 'have no future' and, in any case, little to expect from the future.[17] It becomes clearer why the practical materialism which is particularly manifested in the relation to food is one of the most fundamental components of the popular ethos and even the popular ethic. The being-in-the-present which is affirmed in the readiness to take advantage of the good times and take time as it comes is, in itself, an affirmation of solidarity with others (who are often the only present guarantee against the threats of the future), inasmuch as this temporal immanentism is a recognition of the limits which define the condition. This is why the sobriety of the petit bourgeois is felt as a break: in abstaining from having a good time and from having it with others, the would-be petit bourgeois betrays his ambition of escaping from the common present, when, that is, he does not construct his whole self-image around the opposition between his home and the café, abstinence and intemperance, in other words, between individual salvation and collective solidarities.

The café is not a place a man goes to for a drink but a place he goes to in order to drink in company, where he can establish relationships of familiarity based on the suspension of the censorships, conventions and proprieties that prevail among strangers. In contrast to the bourgeois or petit-bourgeois café or restaurant, where each table is a separate, appropriated territory (one asks permission to borrow a chair or the salt), the working-class café is a site of companionship (each new arrival gives a collective greeting, 'Salut la compagnie!' etc.). Its focus is the counter, to be leaned on after shaking hands with the landlord—who is thus defined as the host (he often leads the conversation)—and sometimes shaking hands with the whole company; the tables, if there are any, are left to 'strangers', or women who have come in to get a drink for their child or make a phone call. In the café free rein is given to the typically popular art of the joke—the art of seeing everything as a joke (hence the reiterated 'Joking apart' or 'No joke', which mark a return to serious matters or prelude a second-degree joke), but also the art of making or playing jokes, often at the expense of the 'fat man'. He is always good for a laugh, because, in the popular code, his fatness is more a picturesque peculiarity than a defect, and because the good nature he is presumed to have predisposes him to take it in good heart and see the funny side. The joke, in other words, is the art of making fun without raising anger, by means of ritual mockery or insults which are neutralized by their very excess and which, presupposing a great familiarity, both in the knowledge they use and the freedom with which they use it, are in fact tokens of attention or affection, ways of building up while seeming to run down, of accepting while seeming to condemn—although they may also be used to test out those who show signs of stand-offishness.[18]

THREE STYLES OF DISTINCTION The basic opposition between the tastes of luxury and the tastes of necessity is specified in as many oppositions as there are different ways of asserting one's distinction vis-à-vis the working class and its primary needs, or—which amounts to the same thing—different powers whereby necessity can be kept at a distance. Thus, within the dominant class, one can, for the sake of simplicity, distinguish three structures of the consumption distributed under three items: food, culture and presentation (clothing, beauty care, toiletries, domestic servants). These structures take strictly opposite forms—like the structures of their capital—among the teachers as against the industrial and commercial employers (see table 17). Whereas the latter have exceptionally high expenditure on food (37 percent of the budget), low cultural costs and medium spending on presentation and representation, the former, whose total spending is lower on average, have low expenditure on food (relatively less than manual workers), limited expenditure on presentation (though their expenditure on health is one of the highest) and relatively high expenditure on culture (books, papers, entertainments, sport, toys, music, radio and record-player). Opposed to both these groups are the members of the professions, who devote the same proportion of their budget to food as the teachers (24.4 percent), but out of much greater total expenditure (57,122 francs as against 40,884 francs), and who spend much more on presentation and representation than all other fractions, especially if the costs of domestic service are included, whereas their cultural expenditure is lower than that of the teachers (or even the engineers and senior executives, who are situated between the teachers and the professionals, though nearer the latter, for almost all items).

The system of differences becomes clearer when one looks more closely at the patterns of spending on food. In this respect the industrial and commercial employers differ markedly from the professionals, and a fortiori from the teachers, by virtue of the importance they give to cereal-based products (especially cakes and pastries), wine, meat preserves (foie

Table 17 Yearly spending by teachers, professionals and industrial and commercial employers, 1972.

Type of spending	Teachers (higher and secondary)		Professionals		Industrial and commercial employers	
	Francs	% of total	Francs	% of total	Francs	% of total
Food[a]	9,969	24.4	13,956	24.4	16,578	37.4
Presentation[b]	4,912	12.0	12,680	22.2	5,616	12.7
Culture[c]	1,753	4.3	1,298	2.3	574	1.3

Source: C.S. III (1972).

a. Includes restaurant or canteen meals.

b. Clothes, shoes, repairs and cleaning, toiletries, hairdressing, domestic servants.

c. Books, newspapers and magazines, stationery, records, sport, toys, music, entertainments.

gras, etc.) and game, and their relatively low spending on meat, fresh fruit and vegetables. The teachers, whose food purchases are almost identically structured to those of office workers, spend more than all other fractions on bread, milk products, sugar, fruit preserves and non-alcoholic drinks, less on wine and spirits and distinctly less than the professions on expensive products such as meat—especially the most expensive meats, such as mutton and lamb—and fresh fruit and vegetables. The members of the professions are mainly distinguished by the high proportion of their spending which goes on expensive products, particularly meat (18.3 percent of their food budget), and especially the most expensive meat (veal, lamb, mutton), fresh fruit and vegetables, fish and shellfish, cheese and aperitifs.[19]

Thus, when one moves from the manual workers to the industrial and commercial employers, through foremen, craftsmen and small shopkeepers, economic constraints tend to relax without any fundamental change in the pattern of spending (see figure 9). The opposition between the two extremes is here established between the poor and the rich (nouveau riche), between *la bouffe* and *la grande bouffe*;[20] the food consumed is increasingly rich (both in cost and in calories) and increasingly heavy (game, foie gras). By contrast, the taste of the professionals or senior executives defines the popular taste, by negation, as the taste for the heavy, the fat and the coarse, by tending towards the light, the refined and the delicate (see table 18). The disappearance of economic constraints is accompanied by a strengthening of the social censorships which forbid coarseness and fatness, in favour of slimness and distinction. The taste for rare, aristocratic foods points to a traditional cuisine, rich in expensive or rare products (fresh vegetables, meat). Finally, the teachers, richer in cultural capital than in economic capital, and therefore inclined to ascetic consumption in all areas, pursue originality at the lowest economic cost and go in for exoticism (Italian, Chinese cooking etc.)[21] and culinary populism (peasant dishes). They are thus almost consciously opposed to the (new) rich with their rich food, the buyers and sellers of *grosse bouffe*, the 'fat cats',[22] gross in body and mind, who have the economic means to flaunt, with an arrogance perceived as 'vulgar', a life-style which remains very close to that of the working classes as regards economic and cultural consumption.

Eating habits, especially when represented solely by the produce consumed, cannot of course be considered independently of the whole life-style. The most obvious reason for this is that the taste for particular dishes (of which the statistical shopping-basket gives only the vaguest idea) is associated, through preparation and cooking, with a whole conception of the domestic economy and of the division of labour between the sexes. A taste for elaborate casserole dishes (pot-au-feu, *blanquette, daube*), which demand a big investment of time and interest, is linked to a traditional conception of woman's role. Thus there is a particularly

Figure 9 The food space.

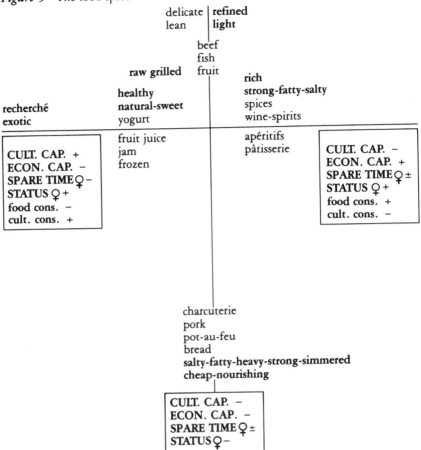

delicate | refined
lean | light

beef
fish
fruit

raw grilled

healthy
natural-sweet
yogurt

recherché
exotic

rich
strong-fatty-salty
spices
wine-spirits

fruit juice
jam
frozen

apéritifs
pâtisserie

CULT. CAP. +
ECON. CAP. −
SPARE TIME ♀ −
STATUS ♀ +
food cons. −
cult. cons. +

CULT. CAP. −
ECON. CAP. +
SPARE TIME ♀ ±
STATUS ♀ +
food cons. +
cult. cons. −

charcuterie
pork
pot-au-feu
bread
salty-fatty-heavy-strong-simmered
cheap-nourishing

CULT. CAP. −
ECON. CAP. −
SPARE TIME ♀ ±
STATUS ♀ −

strong opposition in this respect between the working classes and the dominated fractions of the dominant class, in which the women, whose labour has a high market value (and who, perhaps as a result, have a higher sense of their own value) tend to devote their spare time rather to child care and the transmission of cultural capital, and to contest the traditional division of domestic labour. The aim of saving time and labour in preparation combines with the search for light, low-calorie products, and points towards grilled meat and fish, raw vegetables (*'salades composées'*), frozen foods, yogurt and other milk products, all of which are diametrically opposed to popular dishes, the most typical of which is pot-au-feu, made with cheap meat that is boiled (as opposed to grilled or roasted), a method of cooking that chiefly demands time. It is no accident that this form of cooking symbolizes one state of female existence

and of the sexual division of labour (a woman entirely devoted to housework is called 'pot-au-feu'), just as the slippers put on before dinner symbolize the complementary male rôle.

Small industrial and commercial employers, the incarnation of the 'grocer'
traditionally execrated by artists, are the category who most often (60 percent) say they change into their carpet slippers every day before dinner,
whereas the professions and the senior executives are most inclined to reject
this petit-bourgeois symbol (35 percent say they never do it). The particularly high consumption of carpet slippers by working-class women (both
urban and rural) no doubt reflects the relation to the body and to self-
presentation entailed by confinement to the home and to domestic life.
(The wives of craftsmen, shopkeepers and manual workers are those who
most often say that their choice of clothes is mainly guided by a concern to
please their husbands.)
It is among manual workers that most time and interest is devoted to
cooking: 69 percent of those questioned say they like doing elaborate cooking (*la grande cuisine*), as against 59 percent of the junior executives, 52
percent of the small shopkeepers and 51 percent of the senior executives,
professionals and industrialists (C.S. XXXIVa). (Another indirect index of
these differences as regards the sexual division of labour is that whereas the
teachers and senior executives seem to give priority to a washing machine
and a dishwasher, for the professionals and industrial or commercial employers priority seems to go rather to a TV set and a car—C.S. III.) Finally,
when invited to choose their two favourite dishes from a list of seven, the
farm workers and manual workers, who, like all other categories, give the
highest rank to roast leg of lamb, are the most inclined (45 percent and 34
percent, as against 28 percent of the clerical workers, 20 percent of the senior executives and 19 percent of the small employers) to choose pot-au-feu
(the farm workers are almost the only ones who choose *andouillette*—pork
tripe sausage—14 percent of them, as against 4 percent of the manual workers, clerical workers and junior executives, 3 percent of the senior executives
and 0 percent of the small employers). Manual workers and small employers also favour coq au vin (50 percent and 48 percent), a dish typical of
small restaurants aiming to be 'posh', and perhaps for this reason associated
with the idea of 'eating out' (compared with 42 percent of the clerical
workers, 39 percent of the senior executives and 37 percent of the farm
workers). The executives, professionals and big employers clearly distinguish themselves solely by choosing—from a list which for them is particularly narrow—the dish which is both relatively 'light' and symbolically
marked (in contrast to the ordinary routine of petit-bourgeois cooking),
bouillabaisse (31 percent, as against 22 percent of the clerical workers, 17
percent of the small employers, 10 percent of the manual workers, 7 percent of the farm workers), in which the opposition between fish and meat
(especially the pork in sauerkraut or *cassoulet*) is clearly strengthened by
regionalist and touristic connotations (C.S. XXXIV). It is obvious that the
imprecise classifications used in this survey prevent one from seeing the effects of the secondary opposition between the fractions, and that the ten-

Table 18 Annual household expenditures on food: fractions of the dominant class, 1972.

	Teachers (higher and secondary)		Senior executives		Professions		Engineers		Industrial and commercial employers	
Average number persons per household	3.11		3.6		3.5		3.6		3.6	
Average total household expenditure (francs)	40,844		52,156		57,122		49,822		44,339	
Average total household expenditure on food (francs)	9,969		13,158		13,956		12,666		16,578	
Expenditure on food as % of total expenditure	24.4		25.2		24.4		25.4		37.4	
	Average exp.		Average exp.		Average exp.		Average exp.		Average exp.	
Type of Food	Francs	As % of all food exp.	Francs	As % of all food exp.	Francs	As % of all food exp.	Francs	As % of all food exp.	Francs	As % of all food exp.
Cereals	865	8.7	993	7.5	1,011	7.2	951	7.5	1,535	9.2
bread	322	3.2	347	2.6	326	2.3	312	2.5	454	2.5
cakes, pastries	452	4.5	552	4.1	548	4.0	539	4.2	989	5.6
rusks	16	0.2	27	0.2	33	0.2	28	0.2	29	0.1
rice	35	0.3	32	0.2	62	0.4	41	0.3	33	0.1
flour	40	0.4	35	0.2	41	0.3	31	0.2	28	0.1
Vegetables	766	7.7	1,015	7.7	1,100	7.9	899	7.1	1,222	7.4
potatoes	81	0.8	94	0.7	95	0.7	98	0.7	152	0.8
fresh vegetables	555	5.6	729	5.5	811	5.8	647	5.1	915	5.1
dried or canned	131	1.3	191	1.4	216	1.5	154	1.2	153	0.8
Fruit	632	6.3	871	6.6	990	7.2	864	6.8	877	5.2
fresh fruit	295	2.9	405	3.1	586	4.2	424	3.3	547	3.1
citrus fruit, bananas	236	2.4	343	2.6	303	2.2	324	2.5	256	1.4
dried	102	1.0	122	0.9	98	0.7	116	0.9	72	0.4
Butcher's meat	1,556	15.6	2,358	18.0	2,552	18.3	2,073	16.4	2,323	14.0
beef	814	8.1	1,291	9.8	1,212	8.7	1,144	9.0	1,273	7.2
veal	335	3.4	452	3.4	630	4.5	402	3.1	377	2.3
mutton, lamb	156	1.6	315	2.3	438	3.2	242	1.9	390	2.2
horse	31	0.3	49	0.3	31	0.2	37	0.3	94	0.5
pork (fresh)	221	2.2	251	1.7	239	1.7	247	1.9	187	1.3

Pork products	634	6.3	741	5.6	774	5.5	705	5.6	812	4.9
Meat preserves	336	3.4	350	2.6	233	1.7	310	2.4	1,362	8.0
Fish, shellfish	336	3.4	503	3.8	719	5.1	396	3.1	588	3.5
Poultry	235	2.3	311	2.4	399	2.8	310	2.4	333	2.0
Rabbit, game	36	0.3	97	0.7	148	1.1	89	0.7	289	1.7
Eggs	149	1.4	172	1.3	190	1.4	178	1.4	185	1.1
Milk	299	3.0	271	2.0	249	1.8	287	2.3	309	1.9
Cheese, yogurt	692	6.9	776	5.9	843	6.0	785	6.1	1,090	6.5
Fats	399	4.0	564	4.3	525	3.8	504	4.0	551	3.3
butter	320	3.2	408	3.1	379	2.7	371	2.9	405	2.4
oil	66	0.6	136	1.0	132	1.0	103	0.8	112	0.6
margarine	12	0.1	17	0.1	12	0.1	29	0.2	19	0.1
lard	1	0	2	0	1	0	1	0	13	0.1
Sugar, confectionery, cocoa	304	3.0	395	3.0	265	1.9	327	2.6	407	2.4
Alcohol	711	7.1	1,365	10.3	1,329	9.5	937	7.4	2,218	13.4
wine	457	4.6	869	6.6	899	6.4	392	3.1	1,881	11.8
beer	82	0.8	91	0.7	40	0.3	184	1.4	93	0.5
cider	13	0.1	12	0	0	0	8	0	5	0
apéritifs, liqueurs etc.	157	1.6	391	3.0	389	2.8	352	2.8	237	1.4
Non-alcoholic drinks	344	3.4	342	2.6	267	1.9	295	2.3	327	2.0
Coffee, tea	152	1.5	215	1.5	291	2.1	178	1.4	298	1.8
Restaurant meals	829	8.3	1,863	13.0	1,562	11.2	1,372	10.8	1,179	7.1
Canteen meals	745	7.5	562	4.0	221	1.6	773	6.1	299	1.8
Miscellaneous	264	2.6	379	2.7	258	1.8	432	3.4	324	1.9

Source: C.S. III (1972).

dencies observed would have been more marked if, for example, it had been possible to isolate the teachers or if the list of dishes had been more diversified in the sociologically pertinent respects.

Tastes in food also depend on the idea each class has of the body and of the effects of food on the body, that is, on its strength, health and beauty; and on the categories it uses to evaluate these effects, some of which may be important for one class and ignored by another, and which the different classes may rank in very different ways. Thus, whereas the working classes are more attentive to the strength of the (male) body than its shape, and tend to go for products that are both cheap and nutritious, the professions prefer products that are tasty, health-giving, light and not fattening. Taste, a class culture turned into nature, that is, *embodied,* helps to shape the class body. It is an incorporated principle of classification which governs all forms of incorporation, choosing and modifying everything that the body ingests and digests and assimilates, physiologically and psychologically. It follows that the body is the most indisputable materialization of class taste, which it manifests in several ways. It does this first in the seemingly most natural features of the body, the dimensions (volume, height, weight) and shapes (round or square, stiff or supple, straight or curved) of its visible forms, which express in countless ways a whole relation to the body, i.e., a way of treating it, caring for it, feeding it, maintaining it, which reveals the deepest dispositions of the habitus. It is in fact through preferences with regard to food which may be perpetuated beyond their social conditions of production (as, in other areas, an accent, a walk etc.),[23] and also, of course, through the uses of the body in work and leisure which are bound up with them, that the class distribution of bodily properties is determined.

The quasi-conscious representation of the approved form of the perceived body, and in particular its thinness or fatness, is not the only mediation through which the social definition of appropriate foods is established. At a deeper level, the whole body schema, in particular the physical approach to the act of eating, governs the selection of certain foods. For example, in the working classes, fish tends to be regarded as an unsuitable food for men, not only because it is a light food, insufficiently 'filling', which would only be cooked for health reasons, i.e., for invalids and children, but also because, like fruit (except bananas) it is one of the 'fiddly' things which a man's hands cannot cope with and which make him childlike (the woman, adopting a maternal role, as in all similar cases, will prepare the fish on the plate or peel the pear); but above all, it is because fish has to be eaten in a way which totally contradicts the masculine way of eating, that is, with restraint, in small mouthfuls, chewed gently, with the front of the mouth, on the tips of the teeth (because of the bones). The whole masculine identity—what is called virility—is involved in these two ways of eating, nibbling and picking, as befits a

The body for the job

woman, or with whole-hearted male gulps and mouthfuls, just as it is involved in the two (perfectly homologous) ways of talking, with the front of the mouth or the whole mouth, especially the back of the mouth, the throat (in accordance with the opposition, noted in an earlier study, between the manners symbolized by *la bouche* and *la gueule*).[24]

This opposition can be found in each of the uses of the body, especially in the most insignificant-looking ones, which, as such, are predisposed to serve as 'memory joggers' charged with the group's deepest values, its most fundamental 'beliefs'. It would be easy to show, for example, that Kleenex tissues, which have to be used delicately, with a little sniff from the tip of the nose, are to the big cotton handkerchief, which is blown into sharply and loudly, with the eyes closed and the nose held tightly, as repressed laughter is to a belly laugh, with wrinkled nose, wide-open mouth and deep breathing ('doubled up with laughter'), as if to amplify to the utmost an experience which will not suffer containment, not least because it has to be shared, and therefore clearly manifested for the benefit of others.

And the practical philosophy of the male body as a sort of power, big and strong, with enormous, imperative, brutal needs, which is asserted in every male posture, especially when eating, is also the principle of the division of foods between the sexes, a division which both sexes recognize in their practices and their language. It behooves a man to drink and eat more, and to eat and drink stronger things. Thus, men will have two rounds of aperitifs (more on special occasions), big ones in big glasses (the success of Ricard or Pernod is no doubt partly due to its being a drink both strong and copious—not a dainty 'thimbleful'), and they leave the tit-bits (savoury biscuits, peanuts) to the children and the women, who have a small measure (not enough to 'get tipsy') of home-made aperitif (for which they swap recipes). Similarly, among the hors d'oeuvres, the *charcuterie* is more for the men, and later the cheese, especially if it is strong, whereas the *crudités* (raw vegetables) are more for the women, like the salad; and these affinities are marked by taking a second helping or sharing what is left over. Meat, the nourishing food par excellence, strong and strong-making, giving vigour, blood, and health, is the dish for the men, who take a second helping, whereas the women are satisfied with a small portion. It is not that they are stinting themselves; they really don't want what others might need, especially the men, the natural meat-eaters, and they derive a sort of authority from what they do not see as a privation. Besides, they don't have a taste for men's food, which is reputed to be harmful when eaten to excess (for example, a surfeit of meat can 'turn the blood', over-excite, bring you out in spots etc.) and may even arouse a sort of disgust.

Strictly biological differences are underlined and symbolically accentuated by differences in bearing, differences in gesture, posture and behaviour which express a whole relationship to the social world. To these are added all the deliberate modifications of appearance, especially by use of the set of marks—cosmetic (hairstyle, make-up, beard, moustache, whiskers etc.) or vestimentary—which, because they depend on the economic and cultural means that can be invested in them, function as social markers deriving their meaning and value from their position in the system of distinctive signs which they constitute and which is itself homologous with the system of social positions. The sign-bearing, sign-wearing body is also a producer of signs which are physically marked by the relationship to the body: thus the valorization of virility, expressed in a use of the mouth or a pitch of the voice, can determine the whole of working-class pronunciation. The body, a social product which is the only tangible manifestation of the 'person', is commonly perceived as the most natural expression of innermost nature. There are no merely 'physical' facial signs; the colour and thickness of lipstick, or expressions, as well as the shape of the face or the mouth, are immediately read as indices of a 'moral' physiognomy, socially characterized, i.e., of a 'vulgar' or 'distinguished' mind, naturally 'natural' or naturally 'cultivated'. The signs constituting the perceived body, cultural products which differentiate groups by their degree of culture, that is, their distance from nature, seem grounded in nature. The legitimate use of the body is spontaneously perceived as an index of moral uprightness, so that its opposite, a 'natural' body, is seen as an index of *laisser-aller* ('letting oneself go'), a culpable surrender to facility.

Thus one can begin to map out a universe of class bodies, which (biological accidents apart) tends to reproduce in its specific logic the universe of the social structure. It is no accident that bodily properties are perceived through social systems of classification which are not independent of the distribution of these properties among the social classes. The prevailing taxonomies tend to rank and contrast the properties most frequent among the dominant (i.e., the rarest ones) and those most frequent among the dominated.[25] The social representation of his own body which each agent has to reckon with,[26] from the very beginning, in order to build up his subjective image of his body and his bodily hexis, is thus obtained by applying a social system of classification based on the same principle as the social products to which it is applied. Thus, bodies would have every likelihood of receiving a value strictly corresponding to the positions of their owners in the distribution of the other fundamental properties—but for the fact that the logic of social heredity sometimes endows those least endowed in all other respects with the rarest bodily properties, such as beauty (sometimes 'fatally' attractive, because it threatens the other hierarchies), and, conversely, sometimes denies the 'high and mighty' the bodily attributes of their position, such as height or beauty.

UNPRETENTIOUS OR UNCOUTH?   It is clear that tastes in food cannot be considered in complete independence of the other dimensions of the relationship to the world, to others and to one's own body, through which the practical philosophy of each class is enacted. To demonstrate this, one would have to make a systematic comparison of the working-class and bourgeois ways of treating food, of serving, presenting and offering it, which are infinitely more revelatory than even the nature of the products involved (especially since most surveys of consumption ignore differences in quality). The analysis is a difficult one, because each life-style can only really be constructed in relation to the other, which is its objective and subjective negation, so that the meaning of behaviour is totally reversed depending on which point of view is adopted and on whether the common words which have to be used to name the conduct (e.g., 'manners') are invested with popular or bourgeois connotations.

Considerable misunderstanding can result from ignorance of this mechanism in all surveys by questionnaire, which are always an exchange of words. The confusions are made even worse when the interviewer tries to collect opinions about words or reactions to words (as in the 'ethical test' in which the respondents were presented with the same lists of adjectives to describe an ideal friend, garment or interior). The responses he records in this case have in fact been defined in relation to stimuli which, beyond their nominal identity (that of the words offered), vary in their perceived reality, and therefore their practical efficacy, in accordance with the very principles of variation (and firstly, social class) whose effects one is seeking to measure (which can lead to literally meaningless encounters between opposing classes). Groups invest themselves totally, with everything that opposes them to other groups, in the common words which express their social identity, i.e., their difference. Behind their apparent neutrality, words as ordinary as 'practical', 'sober', 'clean', 'functional', 'amusing', 'delicate', 'cosy', 'distinguished' are thus divided against themselves, because the different classes either give them different meanings, or give them the same meaning but attribute opposite values to the things named. Some examples: *soigné* (neat, trim, careful, well-groomed, well-kept), so strongly appropriated by those who use it to express their taste for a job well done, properly finished, or for the meticulous attention they devote to their personal appearance, that it no doubt evokes for those who reject it the narrow or 'up-tight' rigour they dislike in the petit-bourgeois style; or *drôle* (amusing, funny, droll), whose social connotations, associated with a socially marked pronunciation, bourgeois or snobbish,[27] clash with the values expressed, putting off those who would certainly respond to a popular equivalent of *drôle*, such as *bidonnant, marrant* or *rigolo;* or, again, *sobre*, which, applied to a garment or an interior, can mean radically different things when expressing the prudent, defensive strategies of a small craftsman, the aesthetic asceticism of a teacher or the austerity-in-luxury of the old-world *grand bourgeois*. It can be seen that every attempt to produce an ethical organon common to all classes is condemned from the start, unless, like every 'universal' morality or religion, it plays systematically on the fact that language is both common to the different classes and capable of receiving different, even opposite, meanings in the particular, and sometimes antagonistic, uses that are made of it.

Plain speaking, plain eating: the working-class meal is characterized by plenty (which does not exclude restrictions and limits) and above all by freedom. 'Elastic' and 'abundant' dishes are brought to the table—soups or sauces, pasta or potatoes (almost always included among the vegetables)—and served with a ladle or spoon, to avoid too much measuring and counting, in contrast to everything that has to be cut and divided, such as roasts.[28] This impression of abundance, which is the norm on special occasions, and always applies, so far as is possible, for the men, whose plates are filled twice (a privilege which marks a boy's accession to manhood), is often balanced, on ordinary occasions, by restrictions which generally apply to the women, who will share one portion between two, or eat the left-overs of the previous day; a girl's accession to womanhood is marked by doing without. It is part of men's status to eat and to eat well (and also to drink well); it is particularly insisted that they should eat, on the grounds that 'it won't keep', and there is something suspect about a refusal. On Sundays, while the women are on their feet, busily serving, clearing the table, washing up, the men remain seated, still eating and drinking. These strongly marked differences of social status (associated with sex and age) are accompanied by no practical differentiation (such as the bourgeois division between the dining room and the kitchen, where the servants eat and sometimes the children), and strict sequencing of the meal tends to be ignored. Everything may be put on the table at much the same time (which also saves walking), so that the women may have reached the dessert, and also the children, who will take their plates and watch television, while the men are still eating the main dish and the 'lad', who has arrived late, is swallowing his soup.

This freedom, which may be perceived as disorder or slovenliness, is adapted to its function. Firstly, it is labour-saving, which is seen as an advantage. Because men take no part in housework, not least because the women would not allow it—it would be a dishonour to see men step outside their rôle—every economy of effort is welcome. Thus, when the coffee is served, a single spoon may be passed around to stir it. But these short cuts are only permissible because one is and feels at home, among the family, where ceremony would be an affectation. For example, to save washing up, the dessert may be handed out on improvised plates torn from the cake-box (with a joke about 'taking the liberty', to mark the transgression), and the neighbour invited in for a meal will also receive his piece of cardboard (offering a plate would exclude him) as a sign of familiarity. Similarly, the plates are not changed between dishes. The soup plate, wiped with bread, can be used right through the meal. The hostess will certainly offer to 'change the plates', pushing back her chair with one hand and reaching with the other for the plate next to her, but everyone will protest ('It all gets mixed up inside you') and if she were to insist it would look as if she wanted to show off her crockery (which she is allowed to if it is a new present) or to treat her guests as strangers, as is sometimes deliberately done to intruders or 'scroungers' who never return the invitation. These unwanted guests may be frozen out by changing their plates despite their protests, not laughing at their jokes, or scolding the children for their behaviour ('No, no, *we* don't mind', say the guests; 'They ought to know better by now', the parents respond). The common root of all these 'liberties' is no doubt the sense that at least there will not be self-imposed controls, constraints and restrictions—especially not in eating, a primary need and a compensation—and especially not in the heart of domestic life, the one realm of freedom, when everywhere else, and at all other times, necessity prevails.

In opposition to the free-and-easy working-class meal, the bourgeoisie is concerned to eat with all due form. Form is first of all a matter of rhythm, which implies expectations, pauses, restraints; waiting until the last person served has started to eat, taking modest helpings, not appearing over-eager. A strict sequence is observed and all coexistence of dishes which the sequence separates, fish and meat, cheese and dessert, is excluded: for example, before the dessert is served, everything left on the table, even the salt-cellar, is removed, and the crumbs are swept up. This extension of rigorous rules into everyday life (the bourgeois male shaves and dresses first thing every morning, and not just to 'go out'), refusing the division between home and the exterior, the quotidian and the extra-quotidian, is not explained solely by the presence of strangers—servants and guests—in the familiar family world. It is the expression of a habitus of order, restraint and propriety which may not be abdicated. The relation to food—*the* primary need and pleasure—is only one dimension of the bourgeois relation to the social world. The opposition between the immediate and the deferred, the easy and the difficult, substance (or function) and form, which is exposed in a particularly striking fashion in bourgeois ways of eating, is the basis of all aestheticization of practice and every aesthetic. Through all the forms and formalisms imposed on the immediate appetite, what is demanded—and inculcated—is not only a disposition to discipline food consumption by a conventional structuring which is also a gentle, indirect, invisible censorship (quite different from enforced privations) and which is an element in an art of living (correct eating, for example, is a way of paying homage to one's hosts and to the mistress of the house, a tribute to her care and effort). It is also a whole relationship to animal nature, to primary needs and the populace who indulge them without restraint; it is a way of denying the meaning and primary function of consumption, which are essentially common, by making the meal a social ceremony, an affirmation of ethical tone and aesthetic refinement. The manner of presenting and consuming the food, the organization of the meal and setting of the places, strictly differentiated according to the sequence of dishes and arranged to please the eye, the presentation of the dishes, considered as much in terms of shape and colour (like works of art) as of their consumable substance, the etiquette governing posture and gesture, ways of serving oneself and others, of using the different utensils, the seating plan, strictly but discreetly hierarchical, the censorship of all bodily manifestations of the act or pleasure of eating (such as noise or haste), the very refinement of the things consumed, with quality more important than quantity—this whole commitment to stylization tends to shift the emphasis from substance and function to form and manner, and so to deny the crudely material reality of the act of eating and of the things consumed, or, which amounts to the same thing, the basely material vulgarity of those who indulge in the immediate satisfactions of food and drink.[29]

The main findings of an extremely detailed survey of the art of entertaining (C.S. XLIII) are brought together in a synoptic table (see table 19) which confirms and extends these arguments. It can be seen first that, in the working class, the world of reciprocal invitations, spontaneous or organized, is restricted to the family and the world of familiars who can be treated as 'one of the family', people 'you feel at home with', whereas 'acquaintances', 'connections', in the sense of professional or business connections who are useful in one's work, appear in the middle classes but are essentially a feature of the dominant class. One sign of this informality is that working-class invitations tend to be for coffee, dessert or an aperitif (whereas, at the other end of the social space, invitations are more often for tea, lunch or dinner, or to go out to a restaurant). If working-class people prefer to limit their spontaneous invitations to the offer of a drink or coffee, this is because there can be no 'half-measures' in giving a meal, no 'quick and easy solutions' (as recommended by the women's weeklies) to save time and effort, such as a buffet or a single course.[30]

This refusal to skimp (the main thing is to make sure that the guests have enough to eat and that the food 'goes down well', secondarily that they are not bored) is even more clearly seen when the composition of the meals is analysed. For manual workers, a real meal is a meal with nothing left out, from the aperitif through to the dessert (whereas the other classes are often willing to 'simplify' by omitting the hors d'oeuvre, the salad or the dessert.[31] Because substance takes priority over form, if anything has to be 'simplified' it can only be in the order of form, etiquette, which is seen as inessential, purely symbolic. No matter that the tableware is ordinary, so long as the food is 'extra-ordinary': this is a commonplace underlined by many ritual remarks. No matter that the guests are not seated as etiquette dictates, nor dressed for the occasion. No matter that the children are present at a meal which is in no way a ritual—so long as they do not chip into the conversation, which is adults' business. Since informality is the order of the day, there is no reason not to keep an eye on the television, to break into song at the end of the meal or even organize games; here too, since the function is clearly recognized—'We're here to have fun'—fun will be had, using every available means (drinks, games, funny stories etc.). And the primacy of substance over form, the refusal of the denial implied in formality, is again expressed in the content of the goods exchanged on arrival: flowers, which are seen as gratuitous, as art, art for art's sake (there are jokes to the effect that 'you can't eat them') are discarded in favour of earthly foods, wines or desserts, presents that 'always go down well' and which can be unpretentiously offered and accepted in the name of a realistic view of the costs of the meal and a willingness to share in them.

Given the basic opposition between form and substance, one could re-generate each of the oppositions between the two antagonistic approaches to the treatment of food and the act of eating. In one case, food is claimed as a material reality, a nourishing substance which sustains the body and gives strength (hence the emphasis on heavy, fatty, strong foods, of which the paradigm is pork—fatty and salty—the antithesis of

Table 19 Variations in entertaining, by class fraction (%), 1978.[a]

Variations in ways of entertaining	Manual workers	Clerical, junior execs.	Executives, industrialists, professions
Spontaneous invitations reserved for:			
close family	51.7	34.7	32.5
close friends	20.9	35.9	33.2
children's friends	2.8	3.4	8.3
colleagues/associates	1.9	3.1	4.2
Invite in advance:			
close family	41.2	33.1	30.2
colleagues/associates	2.6	8.4	18.9
Invite fairly or very often for:			
coffee	49.2	48.4	38.2
dessert	23.7	24.7	15.1
dinner	51.3	67.8	70.2
Make spontaneous invitations for:			
apéritif	52.8	46.3	39.2
a meal	23.9	31.9	40.0
Most important thing in spontaneous invitations:			
successful cooking	10.1	5.9	9.4
enough to eat	33.6	28.4	26.0
guests not bored	33.4	46.6	47.9
Prefer to offer guests:			
buffet or single dish	19.4	25.3	26.1
a full meal	77.2	71.6	70.9
When entertaining, use (reg. and often):			
silverware	27.8	40.7	61.5
crystal glasses	29.3	49.7	57.3
china crockery	39.6	46.3	60.0
ordinary glasses	84.8	56.5	55.4
earthenware crockery	60.6	55.9	54.8
Like their guests to dress:			
elegantly	10.8	15.9	30.6
casually	79.7	70.9	58.5
Seating—prefer:			
to indicate guest's place	29.7	31.3	46.0
guests to choose places	65.7	63.1	46.8
to separate couples	22.8	35.0	50.6
not to separate couples	26.0	38.4	26.0
Children welcome (avg. min. age in years):			
at meal	6.5	7.5	8.8
at end of evening	10.9	11.9	12.9
in conversation	12.0	12.2	12.1
Guests bring:			
flowers	41.8	56.3	68.3
dessert	24.6	16.6	9.8
wine	18.6	16.9	14.0

Table 19   (continued)

Variations in ways of entertaining	Manual workers	Clerical, junior execs.	Executives, industrialists, professions
When entertaining, like:			
background music	48.1	56.6	*57.7*
to keep an eye on TV	*14.4*	4.7	4.2
singing after meal	*64.9*	55.3	45.3
organizing games	*66.4*	59.7	50.9

Source: C.S. XLIII (1978).
a. This table is read as follows: 51.7% of manual workers restrict their spontaneous invitations to their close family, 20.9% to close friends etc.; 34.7% of clerical workers and junior executives restrict such invitations to their close family, 35.9% to close friends etc. For each question the total of the percentages may be greater or less than 100, since for each question the respondents could choose several answers or none. Italic figures indicate the strongest tendency in each row.

fish—light, lean and bland); in the other, the priority given to form (the shape of the body, for example) and social form, formality, puts the pursuit of strength and substance in the background and identifies true freedom with the elective asceticism of a self-imposed rule. And it could be shown that two antagonistic world views, two worlds, two representations of human excellence are contained in this matrix. Substance—or matter—is what is substantial, not only 'filling' but also real, as opposed to all appearances, all the fine words and empty gestures that 'butter no parsnips' and are, as the phrase goes, purely symbolic; reality, as against sham, imitation, window-dressing; the little eating-house with its marble-topped tables and paper napkins where you get an honest square meal and aren't 'paying for the wallpaper' as in fancy restaurants; being, as against seeming, nature and the natural, simplicity (pot-luck, 'take it as it comes', 'no standing on ceremony'), as against embarrassment, mincing and posturing, airs and graces, which are always suspected of being a substitute for substance, i.e., for sincerity, for feeling, for what is felt and proved in actions; it is the free-speech and language of the heart which make the true 'nice guy', blunt, straightforward, unbending, honest, genuine, 'straight down the line' and 'straight as a die', as opposed to everything that is pure form, done only for form's sake; it is freedom and the refusal of complications, as opposed to respect for all the forms and formalities spontaneously perceived as instruments of distinction and power. On these moralities, these world views, there is no neutral viewpoint; what for some is shameless and slovenly, for others is straightforward, unpretentious; familiarity is for some the most absolute form of recognition, the abdication of all distance, a trusting openness, a relation of equal to equal; for others, who shun familiarity, it is an unseemly liberty.

The popular realism which inclines working people to reduce practices to the reality of their function, to do what they do, and be what they are ('That's the way I am'), without 'kidding themselves' ('That's the way it is'), and the practical materialism which inclines them to censor the expression of feelings or to divert emotion into violence or oaths, are the near-perfect antithesis of the aesthetic disavowal which, by a sort of essential hypocrisy (seen, for example, in the opposition between pornography and eroticism) masks the interest in function by the primacy given to form, so that what people do, they do as if they were not doing it.

THE VISIBLE AND THE INVISIBLE   But food—which the working classes place on the side of being and substance, whereas the bourgeoisie, refusing the distinction between inside and outside or 'at home' and 'for others', the quotidian and the extra-quotidian, introduces into it the categories of form and appearance—is itself related to clothing as inside to outside, the domestic to the public, being to seeming. And the inversion of the places of food and clothing in the contrast between the spending patterns of the working classes, who give priority to being, and the middle classes, where the concern for 'seeming' arises, is the sign of a reversal of the whole world view. The working classes make a realistic or, one might say, functionalist use of clothing. Looking for substance and function rather than form, they seek 'value for money' and choose what will 'last'. Ignoring the bourgeois concern to introduce formality and formal dress into the domestic world, the place for freedom—an apron and slippers (for women), bare chest or a vest (for men)—they scarcely mark the distinction between top clothes, visible, intended to be seen, and underclothes, invisible or hidden—unlike the middle classes, who have a degree of anxiety about external appearances, both sartorial and cosmetic, at least outside and at work (to which middle-class women more often have access).

Thus, despite the limits of the data available, one finds in men's clothing (which is much more socially marked, at the level of what can be grasped by statistics on purchases, than women's clothing) the equivalent of the major oppositions found in food consumption. In the first dimension of the space, the division again runs between the office workers and the manual workers and is marked particularly by the opposition between grey or white overalls and blue dungarees or boiler-suits, between town shoes and the more relaxed moccasins, kickers or sneakers (not to mention dressing-gowns, which clerical workers buy 3.5 times more often than manual workers). The increased quantity and quality of all purchases of men's clothing is summed up in the opposition between the suit, the prerogative of the senior executive, and the blue overall, the distinctive mark of the farmer and industrial worker (it is virtually unknown in other groups, except craftsmen); or between the overcoat, always much rarer among men than women, but much more frequent among senior executives than the other classes, and the fur-lined jacket or lumber jacket, mainly worn by agricultural and industrial workers. In between are the junior executives, who now scarcely ever wear working clothes but fairly often buy suits.

Among women, who, in all categories (except farmers and farm labourers), spend more than men (especially in the junior and senior executive, professional and other high-income categories), the number of purchases increases as one moves up the social hierarchy; the difference is greatest for suits and costumes—expensive garments—and smaller for dresses and especially skirts and jackets. The top-coat, which is increasingly frequent among women at higher social levels, is opposed to the 'all-purpose' raincoat, in the same way as overcoat and lumber jacket are opposed for men. The use of the smock and the apron, which in the working classes is virtually the housewife's uniform, increases as one moves down the hierarchy (in contrast to the dressing-gown, which is virtually unknown among peasants and industrial workers).

Every year, on average, manual workers buy more handkerchiefs, vests and underpants, and about as many socks, sweat shirts, sweaters etc. as the other classes, but fewer pyjamas (like dressing-gowns, a typically bourgeois garment) and shirts. Among women, the class differences in underwear purchases, which are clearly marked as regards price, are less strong as regards number (and are even inverted for slips, nightdresses, stockings, tights and handkerchiefs). By contrast, among both men and women, purchases of top clothes increase in number and value as one moves up the social hierarchy.

The transverse oppositions are harder to determine because the survey on household living conditions, which would show variations by five categories, makes only very rough divisions by item. However, expenditure on clothing (almost entirely devoted to top clothes) varies strongly between the fractions of the dominant class, rising steadily from teachers, who devote least to this item in both absolute and relative terms (1,523 francs per annum, or 3.7 percent), through the industrial and commercial employers (4.5 percent), senior executives (5.7 percent) and engineers (6.1 percent) to the members of the professions (4,361 francs or 7.6 percent). These differences in the value placed on these means of self-presentation (shoe consumption varies like that of clothes) can be traced back to the generative formulae which retranslate the necessities and facilities characteristic of a position and a condition into a particular life-style, determining the value and importance accorded to social 'connections'—smallest, it seems, among teachers, who are close in this respect to the petite bourgeoisie, and greatest in the professions or the bourgeoisie of big business, which is not isolated in the statistics—as an opportunity to accumulate social capital. But in order to characterize completely the specific form which the basic principles of each life-style take in this particular area, one would need to have close descriptions of the *quality* of the objects in question, cloth (e.g., the English associate tweeds with the 'country gentleman'), colour, cut, enabling one to grasp the taxonomies used and the conscious or unconscious expressive intentions ('young' or 'classical', 'sporty' or 'smart' etc.). There is, however, every reason to think that clothing and hairstyles become 'younger' as one moves away from the dominant pole, more and more 'serious' (i.e., dark, severe, classical) as one moves towards it.[32] The younger one is socially, that is, younger in biological age, and the closer, within the space of the fractions, to the dominated pole or to the new sectors of occupational space, the greater the affinities with all the new forms of dress (unisex garments of 'junior fashion', jeans, sweat shirts and so forth) which are defined by a refusal of the constraints and conventions of 'dressing up'.

The interest the different classes have in self-presentation, the attention they devote to it, their awareness of the profits it gives and the investment of time, effort, sacrifice and care which they actually put into it are proportionate to the chances of material or symbolic profit they can reasonably expect from it (see table 20). More precisely, they depend on the existence of a labour market in which physical appearance may be valorized in the performance of the job itself or in professional relations; and on the differential chances of access to this market and the sectors of this market in which beauty and deportment most strongly contribute to occupational value. A first indication of this correspondence between the propensity to cosmetic investments and the chances of profit may be seen in the gap, for all forms of beauty care, between those who work and those who do not (which must also vary according to the nature of the job and the work environment). It can be understood in terms of this

Table 20 Variations in value placed by Frenchwomen on body, beauty and beauty care, 1976.[a]

Aspect of body, beauty or beauty care	Positive responses (%) by occupation of head of respondent's household				Positive responses (%) by activity of respondent	
	Farm worker	Manual	Clerical, junior exec.	Executive, industrialist, professions	Does not work	Works
Waist is over 33"	33.7	24.2	20.4	11.4	24.7	17.3
Thinks self below average in beauty	40.2	36.0	33.2	24.2	34.2	31.0
Thinks looks older than she is	13.0	14.0	10.1	7.6	13.6	9.8
Average rating of her own:						
hair	5.22	5.47	5.40	5.88	5.47	5.62
face	5.36	5.53	5.51	5.67	5.54	5.58
eyes	6.18	6.44	6.30	6.48	6.35	6.41
skin	5.88	5.63	5.64	5.75	5.63	5.74
teeth	5.24	5.45	5.40	5.74	5.40	5.59
body	5.35	5.78	5.75	5.91	5.76	5.83
nose	5.94	5.48	5.56	5.65	5.41	5.74
hands	5.88	5.99	6.10	5.82	5.78	6.17
Often or sometimes wishes face was different	45.7	60.8	68.2	64.4	60.1	64.6
Beauty depends on:						
care you take	33.7	46.9	52.0	54.7	45.8	53.1
income	15.2	18.8	9.2	8.9	16.7	10.3
Care with looks increases chances of success	75.0	68.8	72.9	74.5	70.1	72.1

Table 20 (continued)

Aspect of body, beauty or beauty care	Positive responses (%) by occupation of head of respondent's household				Positive responses (%) by activity of respondent	
	Farm worker	Manual	Clerical, junior exec.	Executive, industrialist, professions	Does not work	Works
Would rather look:						
natural	69.6	69.8	62.8	57.6	68.8	61.6
raffinée	12.0	15.6	22.9	25.0	16.8	22.3
Thinks husband prefers woman to be:						
natural	65.2	65.0	51.4	50.8	60.6	54.1
raffinée	6.5	8.1	15.1	16.1	10.6	12.3
Thinks it is better to be:						
beautiful	52.2	58.5	59.2	61.9	59.5	58.7
rich	39.1	35.4	33.5	27.5	32.7	33.9
Thinks it is better to be:						
beautiful	9.8	14.0	17.5	17.4	15.7	14.4
lucky	83.7	83.3	76.8	75.8	80.2	80.3
Thinks it is normal to use make-up to look younger	53.3	51.9	62.3	67.8	52.1	63.6
To lose weight, uses:						
diet	23.9	19.8	28.8	23.3	23.9	23.1
sport, exercise	4.3	8.3	14.0	16.9	10.6	11.8
drugs	2.2	4.6	3.6	3.0	3.8	3.6
nothing	69.6	71.7	60.6	66.1	68.3	66.4

Approves of plastic surgery to look younger	50.0	56.4	52.0	51.3	53.4
Bath or shower at least once a day	9.8	36.6	43.2	23.2	32.0
Puts on make-up every day	12.0	45.0	54.7	30.1	44.8
Puts on make-up never or rarely	48.9	21.2	17.3	35.1	22.9
Spends more than half an hour on grooming	12.3	48.9	45.3	42.1	48.2
Uses make-up to feel good	45.6	25.9	27.8	21.0	22.1
Hairdresser at least once a fortnight	15.9	16.9	20.8	9.8	13.5
Cleanses face every night:					
with soap	34.8	20.1	15.7	28.1	25.7
with make-up remover	47.8	86.0	91.4	67.5	78.8
etc.					

Source: C.S. XLIV (1976).

a. Italic figures indicate the strongest tendency or tendencies in each row.

logic why working-class women, who are less likely to have a job and much less likely to enter one of the occupations which most strictly demand conformity to the dominant norms of beauty, are less aware than all others of the 'market' value of beauty and much less inclined to invest time and effort, sacrifices and money in cultivating their bodies.

It is quite different with the women of the petite bourgeoisie, especially the new petite bourgeoisie, in the occupations involving presentation and representation, which often impose a uniform (*tenue*) intended, among other things, to abolish all traces of heterodox taste, and which always demand what is called *tenue*, in the sense of 'dignity of conduct and correctness of manners', implying, according to the dictionary, 'a refusal to give way to vulgarity or facility'. (In the specialized 'charm schools' which train hostesses, the working-class girls who select themselves on the basis of 'natural' beauty undergo a radical transformation in their way of walking, sitting, laughing, smiling, talking, dressing, making-up etc.) Women of the petite bourgeoisie who have sufficient interests in the market in which physical properties can function as capital to recognize the dominant image of the body unconditionally without possessing, at least in their own eyes (and no doubt objectively) enough body capital to obtain the highest profits, are, here too, at the site of greatest tension.

The self-assurance given by the certain knowledge of one's own value, especially that of one's body or speech, is in fact very closely linked to the position occupied in social space (and also, of course, to trajectory). Thus, the proportion of women who consider themselves below average in beauty, or who think they look older than they are, falls very rapidly as one moves up the social hierarchy. Similarly, the ratings women give themselves for the different parts of their bodies tend to rise with social position, and this despite the fact that the implicit demands rise too. It is not surprising that petit-bourgeois women—who are almost as dissatisfied with their bodies as working-class women (they are the ones who most often wish they looked different and who are most discontented with various parts of their bodies), while being more aware of the usefulness of beauty and more often recognizing the dominant ideal of physical excellence—devote such great investments, of self-denial and especially of time, to improving their appearance and are such unconditional believers in all forms of cosmetic voluntarism (e.g., plastic surgery).

As for the women of the dominant class, they derive a double assurance from their bodies. Believing, like petit-bourgeois women, in the value of beauty and the value of the effort to be beautiful, and so associating aesthetic value and moral value, they feel superior both in the intrinsic, natural beauty of their bodies and in the art of self-embellishment and everything they call *tenue*, a moral and aesthetic virtue which defines 'nature' negatively as sloppiness. Beauty can thus be simultaneously a gift of nature and a conquest of merit, as much opposed to the abdications of vulgarity as to ugliness.

Thus, the experience par excellence of the 'alienated body', embarrassment, and the opposite experience, ease, are clearly unequally probable for members of the petite bourgeoisie and the bourgeoisie, who grant the same recognition to the same representation of the legitimate body and legitimate deportment, but are unequally able to achieve it. The chances of experiencing one's own body as a vessel of grace, a continuous miracle, are that much greater when bodily capacity is commensurate with recognition; and, conversely, the probability of experiencing the body with unease, embarrassment, timidity grows with the disparity between the ideal body and the real body, the dream body and the 'looking-glass self' reflected in the reactions of others (the same laws are also true of speech).

The mere fact that the most sought-after bodily properties (slimness, beauty etc.) are not randomly distributed among the classes (for example, the proportion of women whose waist measurement is greater than the modal waist rises sharply as one moves down the social hierarchy) is sufficient to exclude the possibility of treating the relationship which agents have with the social representation of their own body as a generic alienation, constitutive of the 'body for others'. The 'alienated body' described by Sartre is a generic body, as is the 'alienation' which befalls each body when it is perceived and named, and therefore objectified by the gaze and the discourse of others.[33] The phenomenologists' 'body-for-others' is doubly a social product: it derives its distinctive properties from its social conditions of production; and the social gaze is not a universal, abstract, objectifying power, like the Sartrian gaze, but a social power, whose efficacy is always partly due to the fact that the receiver recognizes the categories of perception and appreciation it applies to him or her.

Although it is not a petit-bourgeois monopoly, the petit-bourgeois experience of the world starts out from timidity, the embarrassment of someone who is uneasy in his body and his language and who, instead of being 'as one body with them', observes them from outside, through other people's eyes, watching, checking, correcting himself, and who, by his desperate attempts to reappropriate an alienated being-for-others, exposes himself to appropriation, giving himself away as much by hypercorrection as by clumsiness. The timidity which, despite itself, realizes the objectified body, which lets itself be trapped in the destiny proposed by collective perception and statement (nicknames etc.), is betrayed by a body that is subject to the representation of others even in its passive, unconscious reactions (one feels oneself blushing). By contrast, ease, a sort of indifference to the objectifying gaze of others which neutralizes its powers, presupposes the self-assurance which comes from the certainty of being able to objectify that objectification, appropriate that appropriation, of being capable of imposing the norms of apperception of one's own body, in short, of commanding all the powers which, even when they reside in the body and apparently borrow its most specific weapons, such as 'presence' or charm, are essentially irreducible to it. This is the real meaning of the findings of the experiment by W. D. Dannenmaier and F. J. Thumin, in which the subjects, when asked to assess the height of familiar persons from memory, tended to overestimate most the height of those who had most authority or prestige in their eyes.[34] It would seem that the logic whereby the 'great' are perceived as physically greater than they are applies very generally, and that authority of whatever sort contains a power of seduction which it would be naive to reduce to the effect of self-interested servility. That is why political contestation has always made use of caricature, a distortion of the bodily image intended to break the charm and hold up to ridicule one of the principles of the effect of authority imposition.

Charm and charisma in fact designate the power, which certain people have, to impose their own self-image as the objective and collective image of their body and being; to persuade others, as in love or faith, to abdicate their generic power of objectification and delegate it to the person who should be its object, who thereby becomes an absolute subject, without an exterior (being his own Other), fully justified in existing, legitimated. The charismatic leader manages to be for the group what he is for himself, instead of being for himself, like those dominated in the symbolic struggle, what he is for others. He 'makes' the opinion which makes him; he constitutes himself as an absolute by a manipulation of symbolic power which is constitutive of his power since it enables him to produce and impose his own objectification.

The Universes of Stylistic Possibles

Thus, the spaces defined by preferences in food, clothing or cosmetics are organized according to the same fundamental structure, that of the social space determined by volume and composition of capital. Fully to construct the space of life-styles within which cultural practices are defined, one would first have to establish, for each class and class fraction, that is, for each of the configurations of capital, the generative formula of the habitus which retranslates the necessities and facilities characteristic of that class of (relatively) homogeneous conditions of existence into a particular life-style. One would then have to determine how the dispositions of the habitus are specified, for each of the major areas of practice, by implementing one of the stylistic possibles offered by each field (the field of sport, or music, or food, decoration, politics, language etc.). By superimposing these homologous spaces one would obtain a rigorous representation of the space of life-styles, making it possible to characterize each of the distinctive features (e.g., wearing a cap or playing the piano) in the two respects in which it is objectively defined, that is, on the one hand by reference to the set of features constituting the area in question (e.g., the system of hairstyles), and on the other hand by reference to the set of features constituting a particular life-style (e.g., the working-class life-style), within which its social significance is determined.

For example, the universe of sporting activities and entertainments presents itself to each new entrant as a set of ready-made choices, objectively instituted possibles, traditions, rules, values, equipment, symbols, which receive their social significance from the system they constitute and which derive a proportion of their properties, at each moment, from history.

A sport such as rugby presents an initial ambiguity. In England, at least, it is still played in the elite 'public schools', whereas in France it has become the characteristic sport of the working and middle classes of the regions south of the Loire (while preserving some 'academic' bastions such as the Racing Club or the Paris Université Club). This ambiguity can only be understood if one bears in mind the history of the process which, as in the 'elite schools' of nineteenth-century England, leads to the transmutation of popular games into elite sports, associated with an aristocratic ethic and world view ('fair play', 'will to win' etc.), entailing a radical change in meaning and function entirely analogous to what happens to popular dances when they enter the complex forms of 'serious' music; and the less well-known history of the process of popularization, akin to the diffusion of classical or 'folk' music on LPs, which, in a second phase, transforms elite sport into mass sport, a spectacle as much as a practice.

The distributional properties which are conferred on the different practices when they are evaluated by agents possessing a practical knowledge of their distribution among agents who are themselves distributed into ranked classes, or, in other words, of the probability, for the different classes, of practising them, do indeed owe much to past patterns of distribution, because of the effects of hysteresis. The 'aristocratic' image of sports like tennis, riding or golf can persist beyond a—relative—transformation of the material conditions of access, whereas *pétanque* (a form of bowls), doubly stigmatized by its popular and southern origins and connections, has a distributional significance very similar to that of Ricard or other strong drinks and all the cheap, strong foods which are supposed to give strength.

But distributional properties are not the only ones conferred on goods by the agents' perception of them. Because agents apprehend objects through the schemes of perception and appreciation of their habitus, it would be naive to suppose that all practitioners of the same sport (or any other practice) confer the same meaning on their practice or even,

Strength and Silhouette

'I was no weakling for my age when I started, but all the same I've put 5 inches on my shoulders, 3 inches on my chest and 1½ inches on my arms, and all that in just three months. It's beyond my wildest hopes. My muscles are several inches bigger and my strength has doubled. I feel like a new man. My parents and friends used to make fun of me, but now my father gets me to take off my shirt and show visitors what I've achieved, thanks to you.'

Prospectus for *Sculpture Humaine*

'The President's tennis lesson, Paris, July 1978. Like a growing number of people in France, President Valéry Giscard d'Estaing is interested in tennis. To improve his style, he now takes regular early-morning lessons in a club on the outskirts of Paris, where our photographer surprised him.'

Tennis-Magazine/Sygma

' "An aesthete of fashion cannot fail to be sensitive to the harmony of his body," Karl Lagerfeld explains. The Paris fashion designer spends at least thirty minutes a day keeping in trim. His bedroom, which he has turned into a home gymnasium, contains all sorts of apparatus: an exercise bicycle, wall bars, a rowing machine, a massage machine etc. Back from his holidays in Saint-Tropez (where he did a lot of swimming), he uses this panoply of equipment to keep himself looking the way he wants. "I want to be free to choose my silhouette." '

La Maison de Marie-Claire (October 1971).

strictly speaking, that they are practising the same practice. It can easily be shown that the different classes do not agree on the profits expected from sport, be they specific physical profits, such as effects on the external body, like slimness, elegance or visible muscles, and on the internal body, like health or relaxation; or extrinsic profits, such as the social relationships a sport may facilitate, or possible economic and social advantages. And, though there are cases in which the dominant function of the practice is reasonably clearly designated, one is practically never entitled to assume that the different classes expect the same thing from the same practice. For example, gymnastics may be asked—this is the popular demand, satisfied by body-building—to produce a strong body, bearing the external signs of its strength, or a healthy body—this is the bourgeois demand, satisfied by 'keep-fit' exercises or 'slimnastics'—or, with the 'new gymnastics', a 'liberated' body—this is the demand characteristic of women in the new fractions of the bourgeoisie and petite bourgeoisie.[35] Only a methodical analysis of the variations in the function and meaning conferred on the different sporting activities will enable one to escape from abstract, formal 'typologies' based (it is the law of the genre) on universalizing the researcher's personal experience; and to construct the table of the sociologically pertinent features in terms of which the agents (consciously or unconsciously) choose their sports.

The meaning of a sporting practice is linked to so many variables—how long ago, and how, the sport was learnt, how often it is played, the socially qualified conditions (place, time, facilities, equipment), how it is played (position in a team, style etc.)—that most of the available statistical data are very difficult to interpret. This is especially true of highly dispersed practices, such as pétanque, which may be played every weekend, on a prepared pitch, with regular partners, or improvised on holiday to amuse the children; or gymnastics, which may be simple daily or weekly keep-fit exercises, at home, without special equipment, or performed in a special gymnasium whose 'quality' (and price) vary with its equipment and services (not to mention athletic gymnastics and all the forms of 'new gymnastics'). But can one place in the same class, given identical frequency, those who have skied or played tennis from early childhood and those who learnt as adults, or again those who ski in the school holidays and those who have the means to ski at other times and off the beaten track? In fact, it is rare for the social homogeneity of the practitioners to be so great that the populations defined by the same activity do not function as fields in which the very definition of the legitimate practice is at stake. Conflicts over the legitimate way of doing it, or over the resources for doing it (budget allocations, equipment, grounds etc.) almost always retranslate social differences into the specific logic of the field. Thus sports which are undergoing 'democratization' may cause to coexist (generally in separate spaces or times) socially different sub-populations which correspond to different ages of the sport. In the case of tennis, the members of private clubs, long-standing practitioners who are more than ever attached to strict standards of dress (a Lacoste shirt, white shorts or skirt, special shoes) and all that this implies, are opposed in every respect to the new practitioners in municipal clubs and holiday clubs who demonstrate that the ritual of clothing is no superficial aspect of the legitimate practice. Tennis played in Bermuda shorts and a tee shirt, in a track suit or even swimming trunks, and Adidas running-shoes, is indeed another tennis, both in the way it is played and in the satisfactions it gives. And so the necessary circle whereby the meaning of a practice casts light on the class distribution of practices and this distribution casts light on the differential meaning of the practice cannot be broken by an appeal to the 'technical' definition. This, far from escaping the logic of the field and its struggles, is most often the work of those who, like physical-education teachers, are required to ensure the imposition and methodical inculcation of the schemes of perception and action which, in practice, organize the practices, and who are inclined to present the explanations they produce as grounded in reason or nature.

In any case, one only needs to be aware that the class variations in sporting activities are due as much to variations in perception and appreciation of the immediate or deferred profits they are supposed to bring, as to variations in the costs, both economic and cultural and, indeed, bodily (degree of risk and physical effort), in order to understand in its broad outlines the distribution of these activities among the classes and class fractions. Everything takes place as if the probability of taking up the different sports depended, within the limits defined by economic (and cultural) capital and spare time, on perception and assessment of the intrinsic and extrinsic profits of each sport in terms of the dispositions of the habitus, and more precisely, in terms of the relation to the body, which is one aspect of this.

The relationship between the different sports and age is more complex since it is only defined—through the intensity of the physical effort called for and the disposition towards this demand, which is a dimension of class ethos— in the relationship between a sport and a class. The most important property of the 'popular' sports is that they are tacitly associated with youth— which is spontaneously and implicitly credited with a sort of temporary licence, expressed, inter alia, in the expending of excess physical (and sexual) energy—and are abandoned very early (generally on entry into adult life, symbolized by marriage). By contrast, the common feature of the 'bourgeois' sports, mainly pursued for their health-maintaining functions and their social profits, is that their 'retirement age' is much later, perhaps the more so the more prestigious they are (e.g., golf).

The instrumental relation to their own bodies which the working classes express in all practices directed towards the body—diet or beauty care, relation to illness or medical care—is also manifested in choosing sports which demand a high investment of energy, effort or even pain (e.g., boxing) and which sometimes endanger the body itself (e.g., motor cycling, parachute jumping, acrobatics, and, to some extent, all the 'contact sports').

Rugby, which combines the popular features of the ball-game and a battle involving the body itself and allowing a—partially regulated—expression of physical violence and an immediate use of 'natural' physical qualities (strength, speed etc.), has affinities with the most typically popular dispositions, the cult of manliness and the taste for a fight, toughness in 'contact' and resistance to tiredness and pain, and sense of solidarity ('the mates') and revelry ('the third half') and so forth. This does not prevent members of the dominant fractions of the dominant class (or some intellectuals, who consciously or unconsciously express their values) from making an aesthetico-ethical investment in the game and even sometimes playing it. The pursuit of toughness and the cult of male values, sometimes mingled with an aestheticism of violence and man-to-man combat, bring the deep dispositions of first-degree practitioners to the level of discourse. The latter, being little inclined to verbalize and theorize, find themselves relegated by the managerial discourse (that of trainers, team managers and some journalists) to the rôle of docile, submissive, brute force ('gentle giant', etc.), working-class strength in its approved form (self-sacrifice, 'team spirit' and so forth). But the aristocratic reinterpretation which traditionally hinged on the 'heroic' virtues associated with the three-quarter game encounters its limits in the reality of modern rugby, which, under the combined effects of modernized tactics and training, a change in the social recruitment of the players and a wider audience, gives priority to the 'forward game', which is increasingly discussed in metaphors of the meanest industrial labour ('attacking the coal-face') or trench warfare (the infantryman who 'dutifully' runs headlong into enemy fire).[36]

Everything seems to indicate that the concern to cultivate the body appears, in its elementary form—that is, as the cult of health—often associated with an ascetic exaltation of sobriety and controlled diet, in the middle classes (junior executives, the medical services and especially schoolteachers, and particularly among women in these strongly feminized categories). These classes, who are especially anxious about appearance and therefore about their body-for-others, go in very intensively for gymnastics, the ascetic sport par excellence, since it amounts to a sort of training (*askesis*) for training's sake. We know from social psychology that self-acceptance (the very definition of ease) rises with unselfconsciousness, the capacity to escape fascination with a self possessed by the gaze of others (one thinks of the look of questioning anxiety, turning the looks of others on itself, so frequent nowadays among bourgeois women who *must not* grow old); and so it is understandable that middle-class women are disposed to sacrifice much time and effort to achieve the sense of meeting the social norms of self-presentation which is the pre-condition of forgetting oneself and one's body-for-others (C.S. LXI).

But physical culture and all the strictly health-oriented practices such as walking and jogging are also linked in other ways to the dispositions of the culturally richest fractions of the middle classes and the dominant class. Generally speaking, they are only meaningful in relation to a quite theoretical, abstract knowledge of the effects of an exercise which, in gymnastics, is itself reduced to a series of abstract movements, decom-posed and organized by reference to a specific, erudite goal (e.g., 'the ab-dominals'), entirely opposed to the total, practically oriented movements of everyday life; and they presuppose a rational faith in the deferred, often intangible profits they offer (such as protection against ageing or the ac-cidents linked to age, an abstract, negative gain). It is therefore under-standable that they should find the conditions for their performance in the ascetic dispositions of upwardly mobile individuals who are prepared to find satisfaction in effort itself and to take the deferred gratifications of their present sacrifice at face value. But also, because they can be per-formed in solitude, at times and in places beyond the reach of the many, off the beaten track, and so exclude all competition (this is one of the differences between running and jogging), they have a natural place among the ethical and aesthetic choices which define the aristocratic as-ceticism of the dominated fractions of the dominant class.

Team sports, which only require competences ('physical' or acquired) that are fairly equally distributed among the classes and are therefore equally accessible within the limits of the time and energy available, might be expected to rise in frequency, like individual sports, as one moves through the social hierarchy. However, in accordance with a logic observed in other areas—photography, for example—their very accessibil-ity and all that this entails, such as undesirable contacts, tend to discredit them in the eyes of the dominant class. And indeed, the most typically popular sports, football and rugby, or wrestling and boxing, which, in France, in their early days were the delight of aristocrats, but which, in becoming popular, have ceased to be what they were, combine all the features which repel the dominant class: not only the social composition of their public, which redoubles their commonness, but also the values and virtues demanded, strength, endurance, violence, 'sacrifice', docility and submission to collective discipline—so contrary to bourgeois 'rôle distance'—and the exaltation of competition.

Regular sporting activity varies strongly by social class, ranging from 1.7 percent for farm workers, 10.1 percent for manual workers and 10.6 percent for clerical workers to 24 percent for junior executives and 32.3 percent for members of the professions. Similar variations are found in relation to edu-cational level, whereas the difference between the sexes increases, as else-where, as one moves down the social hierarchy.[37] The variations are even more marked in the case of an individual sport like tennis, whereas in the case of soccer the hierarchy is inverted: it is most played among manual workers, followed by the craftsmen and shopkeepers. These differences are partly explained by the encouragement of sport in schools, but they also result from the fact that the decline in sporting activity with age, which occurs very abruptly and relatively early in the working classes, where it coincides with school-leaving or marriage (three-quarters of the peasants and manual workers have abandoned sport by age 25), is much slower in the dominant class, whose sport is explicitly invested with health-giving functions (as is shown, for example, by the interest in children's physical development). (This explains why, in the synoptic table—table 21—the proportion who regularly perform any sporting activity at a given moment rises strongly with position in the social hierarchy, whereas the proportion who no longer do so but used to at one time is fairly constant, and is even highest among craftsmen and shopkeepers.)

Attendance at sporting events (especially the most popular of them) is most common among craftsmen and shopkeepers, manual workers, junior executives and clerical workers (who often also read the sports paper *L'Equipe*); the same is true of interest in televised sport (soccer, rugby, cycling, horse-racing). By contrast, the dominant class watches much less sport, either live or on TV, except for tennis, rugby and skiing.

Just as, in an age when sporting activities were reserved for a few, the cult of 'fair play', the code of play of those who have the self-control not to get so carried away by the game that they forget that it is 'only a game', was a logical development of the distinctive function of sport, so too, in an age when participation is not always a sufficient guarantee of the rarity of the participants, those who seek to prove their excellence must affirm their disinterestedness by remaining aloof from practices devalued by the appearances of sheep-like conformism which they acquired by becoming more common. To distance themselves from common amusements, the privileged once again need only let themselves be guided by the horror of vulgar crowds which always leads them elsewhere, higher, further, to new experiences and virgin spaces, exclusively or firstly theirs, and also by the sense of the legitimacy of practices, which is a function of their distributional value, of course, but also of the degree to which they lend themselves to aestheticization, in practice or discourse.[38]

All the features which appeal to the dominant taste are combined in sports such as golf, tennis, sailing, riding (or show-jumping), skiing (especially its most distinctive forms, such as cross-country) or fencing. Practised in exclusive places (private clubs), at the time one chooses, alone or with chosen partners (features which contrast with the collective discipline, obligatory rhythms and imposed efforts of team sports), demanding a relatively low physical exertion that is in any case freely determined, but a relatively high investment—and the earlier it is put in,

Table 21 Class variations in sports activities and opinions on sport, 1975.

Sports characteristics of respondents	Positive responses (%) by class fraction					Positive responses (%) by sex	
	Farm workers	Manual workers	Craftsmen, small shopkeepers	Clerical, junior execs.	Senior execs., professions	Men	Women
Attend sports events fairly or very often	20	22	24	18	16	26	10
Watch or listen to sports events (on TV or radio) often or fairly often	50	62	60	60	50	71	47
Would like their child to become sports champion	50	61	55	44	33	52	47
Think that physical education ought to have a bigger place in the school curriculum	23	48	41	60	71	47	39
Regularly practise one or more sports (other than swimming if only on holiday)	17	18	24	29	45	25	15
Practise no sport now but used to	26	34	41	34	33	42	21
Have never regularly practised any sport	57	48	35	37	22	33	64
Regularly practise:							
tennis	0	1.5	2.5	2.5	15.5	2	2.5
riding	1.5	0.5	1	1.5	3.5	1	1
skiing	3.5	1.5	6.5	4.5	8	3	3
swimming	2.0	2.5	3.5	6.5	10	4	3
gymnastics	0.5	3	0.5	5	7	1.5	4
athletics	0	1.5	0.5	2.5	4	2	0.5
football	2.5	6	4.5	4	4	7	0.5

Source: C.S. XXXVIII (1975).

a. The statistics available (see app. 2, Complementary Sources) only indicate the most general tendencies, which are confirmed in all cases, despite variations due to vague definition of the practice, frequency, occasions etc. (It may also be assumed that the rates are over-estimated, to an unequal extent in the different classes, since all the surveys are based on the respondents' statements and are no substitute for surveys of the actual practitioners or spectators.) For this reason a synoptic table is used to show the proportion of each class or sex of agents who present a given characteristic according to the most recent survey on sporting activities and opinions on sport (C.S. XXXVIII). Italic figures indicate the strongest tendency in each row.

the more profitable it is—of time and learning (so that they are relatively independent of variations in bodily capital and its decline through age), they only give rise to highly ritualized competitions, governed, beyond the rules, by the unwritten laws of fair play. The sporting exchange takes on the air of a highly controlled social exchange, excluding all physical or verbal violence, all anomic use of the body (shouting, wild gestures etc.) and all forms of direct contact between the opponents (who are often separated by the spatial organization and various opening and closing rites). Or, like sailing, skiing and all the Californian sports, they substitute man's solitary struggle with nature for the man-to-man battles of popular sports (not to mention competitions, which are incompatible with a lofty idea of the person).

Thus it can be seen that economic barriers—however great they may be in the case of golf, skiing, sailing or even riding and tennis—are not sufficient to explain the class distribution of these activities. There are more hidden entry requirements, such as family tradition and early training, or the obligatory manner (of dress and behaviour), and socializing techniques, which keep these sports closed to the working class and to upwardly mobile individuals from the middle or upper classes and which maintain them (along with smart parlour games like chess and especially bridge) among the surest indicators of bourgeois pedigree.

In contrast to belote (and, even more so, manille), bridge is a game played more at higher levels of the social hierarchy, most frequently among members of the professions (IFOP, 1948). Similarly, among students of the grandes écoles, bridge, and especially intensive playing, with tournaments, varies very strongly by social origin. Chess (or the claim to play it) seems less linked than bridge to social traditions and to the pursuit of the accumulation of social capital. This would explain why it increases as one moves up the social hierarchy, but chiefly towards the area of social space defined by strong cultural capital (C.S. VII).

The simple fact that, at different times, albeit with a change in meaning and function, the same practices have been able to attract aristocratic or popular devotees, or, at the same time, to assume different meanings and forms for the different groups, should warn us against the temptation of trying to explain the class distribution of sports purely in terms of the 'nature' of the various activities. Even if the logic of distinction is sufficient to account for the basic opposition between popular and bourgeois sports, the fact remains that the relationships between the different groups and the different practices cannot be fully understood unless one takes account of the objective potentialities of the different institutionalized practices, that is, the social uses which these practices encourage, discourage or exclude both by their intrinsic logic and by their positional and distributional value. We can hypothesize as a general law that a sport is more likely to be adopted by a social class if it does not contradict that class's relation to the body at its deepest and most unconscious level, i.e., the body schema, which is the depository of a whole world view and a whole philosophy of the person and the body.

Thus a sport is in a sense predisposed for bourgeois use when the use of the body it requires in no way offends the sense of the high dignity of the person, which rules out, for example, flinging the body into the rough and tumble of 'forward-game' rugby or the demeaning competitions of athletics. Ever concerned to impose the indisputable image of his own authority, his dignity or his distinction, the bourgeois treats his body as an end, makes his body a sign of its own ease. Style is thus foregrounded, and the most typically bourgeois deportment can be recognized by a certain breadth of gesture, posture and gait, which manifests by the amount of physical space that is occupied the place occupied in social space; and above all by a restrained, measured, self-assured tempo. This slow pace, contrasting with working-class haste or petit-bourgeois eagerness, also characterizes bourgeois speech, where it similarly asserts awareness of the right to take one's time—and other people's.

The affinity between the potentialities objectively inscribed in practices and dispositions is seen most clearly of all in flying, and especially military aviation. The individual exploits and chivalrous ethic of the Prussian aristocrats and French nobles who joined the Air Force from cavalry school (everything that *La Grande Illusion* evokes) are implied in the very activity of flying which, as all the metaphors of skimming and high flying suggest, are associated (*per ardua ad astra*) with elevated society and high-mindedness, 'a certain sense of altitude combining with the life of the spirit', as Proust says apropos of Stendhal.[39] The whole opposition between a bellicose, jingoistic bourgeoisie, which identified the virtues of leadership with the gallant, risk-taking, stiff-upper-lipped man of action, and a free-trading, multinational bourgeoisie which derives its power from its decision-making, organizational (in a word, cybernetic) capacities is contained in the opposition between the horse-riding, fencing, boxing or flying aristocrats and bourgeois of the Belle Epoque and the modern skiing, sailing or gliding executive.

And just as a history of the sporting practices of the dominant class would no doubt shed light on the evolution of its ethical dispositions, the bourgeois conception of the human ideal and in particular the form of reconciliation between the bodily virtues and the supposedly more feminine intellectual virtues, so too an analysis of the distribution at a given moment of sporting activities among the fractions of the dominant class would bring to light some of the most hidden principles of the opposition between these fractions, such as the deep-rooted, unconscious conception of the relationship between the sexual division of labour and the division of the work of domination. This is perhaps truer than ever now that the gentle, invisible education by exercise and diet which is appropriate to the new morality of health is tending to take the place of the explicitly ethical pedagogy of the past in shaping bodies and minds. Because the different principles of division which structure the dominant class are never entirely independent—such as the oppositions between the economically richest and the culturally richest, between inheritors and parvenus, old and young (or seniors and juniors)—the practices of the different fractions tend to be distributed, from the dominant fractions to the dominated fractions, in accordance with a series of oppositions which are themselves partially reducible to each other: the opposition between the most expensive and smartest sports (golf, sailing, riding, tennis) or the most expensive and smartest ways of doing them (private clubs) and the cheapest sports (rambling, hiking, jogging, cycling, mountaineering) or the cheapest ways of doing the smart sports (e.g., tennis on municipal courts or in holiday camps); the opposition between the 'manly' sports, which may demand a high energy input (hunting, fishing, the 'contact' sports, clay-pigeon shooting), and the 'introverted' sports, emphasizing self-exploration and self-expression (yoga, dancing, 'physical expression') or the 'cybernetic' sports (flying, sailing), requiring a high cultural input and a relatively low energy input.

Thus, the differences which separate the teachers, the professionals and the employers are, as it were, summed up in the three activities which, though relatively rare—about 10 percent—even in the fractions they distinguish, appear as the distinctive feature of each of them, because they are much more frequent there, at equivalent ages, than in the others (C.S. V and VII, secondary analysis). The aristocratic asceticism of the teachers finds an exemplary expression in mountaineering, which, even more than rambling, with its reserved paths (one thinks of Heidegger) or cycle-touring, with its Romanesque churches, offers for minimum economic costs the maximum distinction, distance, height, spiritual elevation, through the sense of simultaneously mastering one's own body and a nature inaccessible to the many.[40] The health-oriented hedonism of doctors and modern executives who have the material and cultural means of access to the most prestigious activities, far from vulgar crowds, is expressed in yachting, open-sea swimming, cross-country skiing or underwater fishing; whereas the employers expect the same gains in distinction from golf, with it aristocratic etiquette, its English vocabulary and its great exclusive spaces, together with extrinsic profits, such as the accumulation of social capital.[41]

Since age is obviously a very important variable here, it is not surprising that differences in social age, not only between the biologically younger and older in identical social positions, but also, at identical biological ages, between the dominant and the dominated fractions, or the new and the established fractions, are retranslated into the opposition between the traditional sports and all the new forms of the classic sports (pony trekking, cross-country skiing, and so on), or all the new sports, often imported from America by members of the new bourgeoisie and petite bourgeoisie, in particular by all the people working in fashion—designers, photographers, models, advertising agents, journalists—who invent and market a new form of poor-man's elitism, close to the teachers' version but more ostentatiously unconventional.

The true nature of this counter-culture, which in fact reactivates all the traditions of the typically cultivated cults of the natural, the pure and the authentic, is more clearly revealed in the equipment which one of the new property-rooms of the advanced life-style—the FNAC ('executive retail' shops), Beaubourg, *Le Nouvel Observateur,* holiday clubs etc.— offers the serious trekker: parkas, plus-fours, *authentic* Jacquard sweaters in *real* Shetland wool, *genuine* pullovers in *pure natural* wool, Canadian trappers' jackets, English fishermen's pullovers, U.S. Army raincoats, Swedish lumberjack shirts, fatigue pants, U.S. work shoes, rangers, Indian moccasins in supple leather, Irish work caps, Norwegian woollen caps, bush hats—not forgetting the whistles, altimeters, pedometers, trail guides, Nikons and other essential gadgets without which there can be no natural return to nature. And how could one fail to recognize the dynamics of the dream of social weightlessness as the basis of all the new sporting activities—foot-trekking, pony-trekking, cycle-trekking, motorbike trekking, boat-trekking, canoeing, archery, windsurfing, cross-country skiing, sailing, hang-gliding, microlights etc.—whose common feature is that they all demand a high investment of cultural capital in the activity itself, in preparing, maintaining and using the equipment, and especially, perhaps, in verbalizing the experiences, and which bear something of the same relation to the luxury sports of the professionals and executives as symbolic possession to material possession of the work of art?

In the opposition between the classical sports and the Californian sports, two contrasting relations to the social world are expressed, as clearly as they are in literary or theatrical tastes. On the one hand, there is respect for forms and for forms of respect, manifested in concern for propriety and ritual and in unashamed flaunting of wealth and luxury, and on the other, symbolic subversion of the rituals of bourgeois order by ostentatious poverty, which makes a virtue of necessity, casualness towards forms and impatience with constraints, which is first marked in clothing or cosmetics since casual clothes and long hair—like the minibus or camping-car, or folk and rock, in other fields—are challenges to the standard attributes of bourgeois rituals, classically styled clothes, luxury cars, boulevard theatre and opera. And this opposition between two relations to the social world is perfectly reflected in the two relations to the natural world, on the one hand the taste for natural, wild nature, on the other, organized, signposted, cultivated nature.

The Catalogue of New Sporting Resources

Physical expression

Gazelle

She is deeply imbued with the teaching of L'Arche, where she lived for ten years. Lanza del Vasto has written of her: 'Her art is not just in her legs, it has matured for a long time in her head and heart ... if I bring her out from time to time, it's so that this precious art, inspired by Hindu dance as much as by mediaeval Christian imagery, should not be lost.'

The approaches to the inner life are made through activities throughout the day's session, and are subsequently pursued in life; indeed, the search for inner unity is the central theme. Dance has the place of honour, be it folk, religious or creative dance. It is not a goal in itself, but a support for the inner life. Technique is worked on, certainly, but never at the expense of the relaxation that is essential for the harmony of the self.

*Women discover their bodies
through dance*

For women, dance is above all a way of becoming aware of their bodies, and, in this sense, it is a self-discovery. Awareness of the body is sometimes accompanied by awareness of the body as a particular means of expression. Women experience dance as a new language through which they can express themselves.... Moreover, for around half of the interviewees, this activity seems to awaken a primary eroticism, even a primary auto-eroticism; heightened consciousness of the body is experienced as a pleasure....

'That's when I feel I have a body.... I think that dancing can give me harmony with myself....' 'A search for myself, discovering myself physically....' 'Sensations running through my body ... a way of talking, you can say a lot!' 'It's a self-affirmation....' 'I feel good when dancing. I become aware of myself. Once, I stopped for two years; there was something missing.... It's a need.'

Wheels

*Four girls, two guys, a hired horse,
a second-hand cart and a bike*

We started out from La Charité-sur-Loire in the Nièvre, with no precise destination. In the course of a month we did 300 kilometres to Montaigut-en-Combraille (Puy-de-Dôme), along the minor roads of the Bourbonnais. Average speed 3 kilometres an hour (the horse didn't feel like going any faster). Fifteen or 20 kilometres a day. Because we were just ambling along we had time to do all sorts of things you can't do in a car: blackberrying, cycling, talking to the locals, climbing up on the cart, bathing, making love.... After a few days, we'd completely lost the sense of time (the time of the rat-race).

Free flight

A hang-glider is a sail stretched between aluminum tubes, a big kite without a string but with a bloke hanging in a harness; you take it somewhere high, jump off, and FLY.

You start with little hills, grassy slopes, sand-pits, just a few yards above the ground. Geographically speaking, you can do it anywhere: from the Pyrenees to the Vosges, from the slag-heaps and cliffs of the Nord to the Jura and the Alps, not forgetting the Puy-de-Dôme.

Walking

To think there are people who don't know that you only have to leave the claustrophobic world of the *métro* at Porte de Saint-Cloud to find yourself on the route of National Trail No. 1!!! Yes indeed!!! Sounds like the blurred breakfast-time account of a dream? And yet it's true: at the end of the Avenue de Versailles, there's the start of 565 kilometres, no less, of footpaths, WITHOUT ENTERING A SINGLE TOWN!

Groovy football

Alternative soccer is on the up-and-up. Spontaneity is the word: no clubs, no championships, often no grounds. The traditional team colours give way to multi-coloured tee shirts, even Indian shirts. Not many shorts to be seen, but lots of jeans. Heavy boots with studs and laces all over them are rare in the extreme, and when they do appear a crowd gathers to gawk at them before the match. Sneakers and desert boots are more like it.

The number of players is very variable and rarely reaches the symbolic eleven. The players aren't even always men and I can remember some matches in the winter mud of the Parc de Sceaux in which each team included three or four girls whose high heels made their mark on a few ankles and shins, and not just their opponents'!

They were epic struggles, with two or three intervals, during which the least out of breath would have a quick joint or two. A typical score would be 32–28.

Age is pretty variable, too. No categories like kiddies, juniors, minors, seniors, veterans. And kids of eleven or twelve are the sort of mosquitoes you can't easily shake off.

Naturally, the rules are liberally interpreted. Besides, most of the time there's no referee. The off-side rule only applies in cases of flagrant violation (for example, when a player hangs around the opposite goal throughout the match in case a pass comes his way). There are no touch-lines, so the pitches are often wider than they're long! Corners are taken, because they're a real gas. The teams expand during the match as more players arrive.

Competitiveness isn't entirely ruled out, but we're a long way from the fanaticism of 'pro' teams. In fact the people who come along to kick the ball aren't out there to win at all costs, given that there are no prizes, it's rarely the same teams, the length of the match is very elastic, and the scoring is very approximate (to within a goal or two). And when one team is obviously stronger, you balance it out by 'transferring' players between the two teams. . . . It's a far cry from the gamesmanship they teach you most of the time at school.

What's the answer? Perhaps it comes from games masters like the one who gave each player a ball so there would be no competitive spirit (a true story—the teacher in question even got into trouble for not observing the usual rule).

Next weekend, if you see a couple of gangs of hairy louts chasing after a ball, don't hesitate, just ask if you can join in. They won't eat you.

Extracts from *Catalogue des ressources* (Paris, Librairies Alternative and Parallèles, 1977).

Thus, the system of the sporting activities and entertainments that offer themselves at a given moment for the potential 'consumers' to choose from is predisposed to express all the differences sociologically pertinent at that moment: oppositions between the sexes, between the classes and between class fractions. The agents only have to follow the leanings of their habitus in order to take over, unwittingly, the intention immanent in the corresponding practices, to find an activity which is entirely 'them' and, with it, kindred spirits. The same is true in all areas of practice: each consumer is confronted by a particular state of the supply side, that is, with objectified possibilities (goods, services, patterns of action etc.) the appropriation of which is one of the stakes in the struggles between the classes, and which, because of their probable association with certain classes or class fractions, are automatically classified and classifying, rank-ordered and rank-ordering. The observed state of the distribution of goods and practices is thus defined in the meeting between the possibilities offered at a given moment by the different fields of production (past and present) and the socially differentiated dispositions which—associated with the capital (of determinate volume and composition) of which, depending on the trajectory, they are more or less completely the product and in which they find their means of realization—define the interest in these possibilities, that is, the propensity to acquire them and (through acquisition) to convert them into distinctive signs.

Thus, a study of the toy market undertaken along these lines would first have to establish the specific structuring principles of a field of production in which, as in other such fields, there coexist firms differing in 'age' (from small workshops producing wooden toys to large modern companies), in volume (turnover, number of employees) and, perhaps especially, in the extent to which production is guided by psychological as well as technological research. Secondly, on the basis of an analysis of the conditions in which toy purchases are made, and in particular of the degree (probably varying with class) to which they are linked to traditional, seasonal, gift exchanges (Christmas, New Year), one could try to determine the meaning and function which the different classes consciously or unconsciously confer on toys according to their own schemes of perception and appreciation and, more precisely, according to their educational strategies. (The latter in turn have to be seen in terms of their whole system of reproduction strategies: the propensity to confer an educational function on toys no doubt rises with the degree to which the reproduction of social position depends exclusively on transmission of cultural capital, i.e., with the weight of cultural capital in the asset structure.) It would also be necessary to examine how the logic of the competition between firms of different types, having different strengths and therefore inclined to defend different products, is in a sense decided by the different categories of clients. Craft firms may get a new lease on life when wooden toys encounter the taste for natural materials and simple shapes among the intellectual fractions, who are also attracted by all forms of logical games which are supposed to 'awaken' and 'develop' the intelligence; and the cultural-capital-intensive firms benefit not only from the intensified competition for educational qualifications and the general rise in educational investments, but also from the unsolicited advertising given to products which suit their taste by those who present their own life-style as an example to others and elevate the inclinations of their own ethos into a universal ethic. The producers of cultural toys, who have every interest in 'de-seasonalizing' their sales by creating a continuous need for their products, can count on the proselytism of all those who are inclined to believe and persuade others to believe in the (strictly unverifiable) educational value of toys and play—psychologists, psychoanalysts, nursery teachers, 'toy bank' organizers, and everyone else with a stake in a definition of childhood capable of producing a market for goods and services aimed at children.[42]

There is no clearer indication of the existence, in all areas, of a legitimacy and a definition of legitimate practice than the careless, but socially corroborated, assurance with which the new taste-makers measure all practices against the yardstick of their own taste, the acid test of modernity (as opposed to all that is archaic, rigid, old-fashioned). The naivety of some of the comments embroidering the statistics on consumption they produce for the purposes of marketing reveals, for example, that they classify all eating habits in terms of their distance from the American ideal of eggs and bacon for breakfast or a light lunch washed down with mineral water, just as others adjudicate what is 'in' in politics or the latest 'must' in philosophical fashion in terms of what is (or is not) being done at Harvard, Princeton or Stanford.

It follows that it is only by increasing the number of empirical analyses of the relations between relatively autonomous fields of production of a particular class of products and the market of consumers which they assemble, and which sometimes function as fields (without ceasing to be determined by their position in the field of the social classes), that one can really escape from the abstraction of economic theories, which only recognize a consumer reduced to his purchasing power (itself reduced to his income) and a product characterized, equally abstractly, by a technical function presumed to be equal for all; only in this way is it possible to establish a genuine scientific theory of the economy of practices.

The abstract notion of the 'labour market' requires a similar critique which would describe both the invariants and the variations in the relationship between the owner of the means of production—and therefore of jobs—and the seller of labour power, according to the power relations between the two parties. These depend, among other things, on the rarity of the post and the material and symbolic advantages it gives and on the rarity of the labour power supplied or of the qualifications which guarantee it; in other words, on the degree to which the job supplier can withstand individual or collective withdrawal of labour power (refusal of the job, a strike etc.) and the extent to which the possessor of labour power is able to refuse the job (depending, for example, on his qualifications, age and family responsibilities, with the unmarried young being least vulnerable).

4 | The Dynamics of the Fields

There are thus as many fields of preferences as there are fields of stylistic possibles. Each of these worlds—drinks (mineral waters, wines and aperitifs) or automobiles, newspapers or holiday resorts, design or furnishing of house or garden, not to mention political programmes—provides the small number of distinctive features which, functioning as a system of differences, differential deviations, allow the most fundamental social differences to be expressed almost as completely as through the most complex and refined expressive systems available in the legitimate arts; and it can be seen that the total field of these fields offers well-nigh inexhaustible possibilities for the pursuit of distinction.

If, among all these fields of possibles, none is more obviously predisposed to express social differences than the world of luxury goods, and, more particularly, cultural goods, this is because the relationship of distinction is objectively inscribed within it, and is reactivated, intentionally or not, in each act of consumption, through the instruments of economic and cultural appropriation which it requires. It is not only a matter of the affirmations of difference which writers and artists profess ever more insistently as the autonomy of the field of cultural production becomes more pronounced,[1] but also of the intention immanent in cultural objects. One could point to the socially charged nature of legitimate language and, for example, the systems of ethical and aesthetic values deposited, ready for quasi-automatic reactivation, in pairs of contrasting adjectives; or the very logic of literary language, whose whole value lies in an *écart,* i.e., a distance from simple, common ways of speaking. Rhetorical figures, as modifications of ordinary usage, are in a sense the objectifications of the social relationship in which they are produced and function, and it is futile to seek, in the intrinsic nature of the tropes catalogued in the 'Arts of Rhetoric', properties which, like all properties of distinction, exist only in and through the relationship,. in and through difference. A figure of words or style is always only an alteration of usage, and consequently a distinctive mark which may consist in the absence of any mark when the intention of distinguishing oneself from a would-be distinction that is held to be 'excessive' (the vulgarity of 'pretension') or simply 'worn out' or 'outmoded' leads to the double negations which underlie so many spurious encounters between the opposite extremes of social space. It is well known that all dominant aesthetics set a high value on the virtues of sobriety, simplicity, economy of means, which are as much opposed to first-degree poverty and simplicity as to the pomposity or affectation of the 'half-educated'.

It is scarcely necessary to establish that the work of art is the objectification of a relationship of distinction and that it is thereby explicitly predisposed to bear such a relationship in the most varied contexts. As soon as art becomes self-conscious, in the work of Alberti, for example, as Gombrich demonstrates, it is defined by a negation, a refusal, a renunciation, which is the very basis of the refinement in which a distance is marked from the simple pleasure of the senses and the superficial seductions of gold and ornaments that ensnare the vulgar taste of the Philistines: 'In the strict hierarchic society of the sixteenth and seventeenth centuries the contrast between the "vulgar" and the "noble" becomes one of the principal preoccupations of the critics. . . . Their belief was that certain forms or modes are "really" vulgar, because they please the low, while others are inherently noble, because only a developed taste can appreciate them.'[2] The aim of distinction, expressing the specific interest of the artists, who are increasingly inclined to claim exclusive control over form at the risk of disappointing their clients' 'bad taste', is far from incompatible with the functions really conferred on works of art by those who commission them or conserve them in their collections: these 'cultural creations which we usually regard purely aesthetically, as variants of a particular style, were perceived by their contemporaries', as Norbert Elias reminds us, referring to the society of the Grand Siècle, as 'the highly differentiated expression of certain social qualities.'[3]

This means that, like art as defined by Yeats ('Art is a social act of a solitary man'), every appropriation of a work of art which is the embodiment of a relation of distinction is itself a social relation and, contrary to the illusion of cultural communism, it is a relation of distinction. Those who possess the means of symbolically appropriating cultural goods are more than willing to believe that it is only through their economic dimension that works of art, and cultural goods in general, acquire rarity. They like to see symbolic appropriation—the only legitimate sort, in their view—as a kind of mystical participation in a common good of which each person has a share and which everyone has entirely, as a paradoxical appropriation, excluding privilege and monopoly, unlike material appropriation, which asserts real exclusivity and therefore exclusion. 'If I contemplate a painting by Poussin or read a Platonic dialogue, that doesn't imply that I am depriving anyone and that we need to produce as many Poussins and Platos as there are possible beholders or readers' (Philosophy teacher, age 30).

The love of art is conceived as a secularized form of the 'intellectual love of God', a love, according to Spinoza, that is 'the greater as more men enjoy it.' There is no doubt that the works of art inherited from the past and deposited in museums and private collections and, beyond them, all objectified cultural capital, the product of history accumulated in the form of books, articles, documents, instruments, which are the trace or materialization of theories or critiques of these theories, problematics or conceptual systems, present themselves as an autonomous world which, although it is the product of historical action, has its own laws, transcending individual wills, and remains irreducible to what each agent or even the whole population of agents can appropriate (i.e., to internalized cultural capital), just as the language objectified in dictionaries and grammars remains irreducible to the language really appropriated, that is, to what is internalized by each speaker or even the whole population. However, contrary to theories of the autonomy of the world of ideas or of 'objective knowledge without a knowing subject' and 'subjectless processes' (in which Louis Althusser and Karl Popper concur), it has to be pointed out that objectified cultural capital only exists and subsists in and through the struggles of which the fields of cultural production (the artistic field, the scientific field etc.) and, beyond them, the field of the social classes, are the site, struggles in which the agents wield strengths and obtain profits proportionate to their mastery of this objectified capital, in other words, their internalized capital.[4]

Because the appropriation of cultural products presupposes dispositions and competences which are not distributed universally (although they have the appearance of innateness), these products are subject to exclusive appropriation, material or symbolic, and, functioning as cultural capital (objectified or internalized), they yield a profit in distinction, proportionate to the rarity of the means required to appropriate them, and a profit in legitimacy, the profit par excellence, which consists in the fact of feeling justified in being (what one is), being what it is right to be.[5] This is the difference between the legitimate culture of class societies, a product of domination predisposed to express or legitimate domination, and the culture of little-differentiated or undifferentiated societies, in which access to the means of appropriation of the cultural heritage is fairly equally distributed, so that culture is fairly equally mastered by all members of the group and cannot function as cultural capital, i.e., as an instrument of domination, or only so within very narrow limits and with a very high degree of euphemization.

The symbolic profit arising from material or symbolic appropriation of a work of art is measured by the distinctive value which the work derives from the rarity of the disposition and competence which it demands and which determines its class distribution.[6] Cultural objects, with their subtle hierarchy, are predisposed to mark the stages and degrees of the initiatory progress which defines the enterprise of culture, according to Valéry Larbaud. Like 'Christian's progress towards the heavenly Jerusalem', it leads from the 'illiterate' to the 'literate', via the 'non-literate' and 'semiliterate', or the 'common reader' (*lecteur*)—leaving aside the 'bibliophile'—to the truly cultivated reader (*liseur*). The mysteries of culture have their catechumens, their initiates, their holy men, that 'discrete elite' set apart from ordinary mortals by inimitable nuances of manner and united by 'a quality, something which lies in the man himself, which is part of his happiness, which may be indirectly very useful to him but which will never win him a sou, any more than his courtesy, his courage or his goodness.'[7]

Hence the incessant revisions, reinterpretations and rediscoveries which the learned of all religions of the book perform on their canonical texts: since the levels of 'reading' designate hierarchies of readers, it is necessary and sufficient to change the hierarchy of readings in order to overturn the hierarchy of readers.

It follows from what has been said that a simple upward displacement of the structure of the class distribution of an asset or practice (i.e., a virtually identical increase in the proportion of possessors in each class) has the effect of diminishing its rarity and distinctive value and threatening the distinction of the older possessors. Intellectuals and artists are thus divided between their interest in cultural proselytism, that is, winning a market by widening their audience, which inclines them to favour popularization, and concern for cultural distinction, the only objective basis of their rarity; and their relationship to everything concerned with the 'democratization of culture' is marked by a deep ambivalence which may be manifested in a dual discourse on the relations between the institutions of cultural diffusion and the public.

When asked in a survey how they thought works of art in museums might be better presented, and whether the 'supply level' ought to be made more accessible by providing technical, historical or aesthetic explanations, members of the dominant class—and especially the teachers and art specialists—endeavour to escape from the contradiction by dissociating what is desirable for others from what is desirable for themselves. It is because the museum is as it is that it is their exclusive privilege; so it is as it should be for people like them, i.e., people made for it. But they cannot fail to be sensitive to the fact that they, the habitués, are being consulted first about what should be done, because this recognizes their privilege of granting part of their privilege to others. In accepting educational improvements, it is *their* museum, the one that they alone can enjoy, austere, ascetic and noble, which they graciously open to others. (An analysis of the debates which occurred when cheap paperbacks came onto the market—a promise of popularity for the author, a threat of vulgarization for the reader—would reveal the same ambivalence).

Because the distinctive power of cultural possessions or practices—an artifact, a qualification, a film culture—tends to decline with the growth in the absolute number of people able to appropriate them, the profits of distinction would wither away if the field of production of cultural goods, itself governed by the dialectic of pretension and distinction, did not endlessly supply new goods or new ways of using the same goods.

The Correspondence between Goods Production and Taste Production

In the cultural market—and no doubt elsewhere—the matching of supply and demand is neither the simple effect of production imposing itself on consumption nor the effect of a conscious endeavour to serve the consumers' needs, but the result of the objective orchestration of two relatively independent logics, that of the fields of production and that of the field of consumption. There is a fairly close homology between the specialized fields of production in which products are developed and the fields (the field of the social classes or the field of the dominant class) in which tastes are determined. This means that the products developed in the competitive struggles of which each of the fields of production is the site, and which are the source of the incessant changing of these products, meet, without having expressly to seek it, the demand which is shaped in the objectively or subjectively antagonistic relations between the different classes or class fractions over material or cultural consumer goods or, more exactly, in the competitive struggles between them over these goods, which are the source of the changing of tastes. This objective orchestration of supply and demand is the reason why the most varied tastes find the conditions for their realization in the universe of possibles which each of the fields of production offers them, while the latter find the conditions for their constitution and functioning in the different tastes which provide a (short- or long-term) market for their different products.[8]

The field of production, which clearly could not function if it could not count on already existing tastes, more or less strong propensities to consume more or less clearly defined goods, enables taste to be realized by offering it, at each moment, the universe of cultural goods as a system of stylistic possibles from which it can select the system of stylistic features constituting a life-style. It is always forgotten that the universe of products offered by each field of production tends in fact to limit the universe of the forms of experience (aesthetic, ethical, political etc.) that are objectively possible at any given moment.[9] It follows from this, among other things, that the distinction recognized in all dominant classes and in all their properties takes different forms depending on the state of the distinctive signs of 'class' that are effectively available. In the case of the production of cultural goods at least, the relation between supply and demand takes a particular form: the supply always exerts an effect of symbolic imposition. A cultural product—an avant-garde picture, a political manifesto, a newspaper—is a constituted taste, a taste which has been raised from the vague semi-existence of half-formulated or unformulated experience, implicit or even unconscious desire, to the full reality of the finished product, by a process of objectification which, in present circumstances, is almost always the work of professionals. It is consequently charged with the legitimizing, reinforcing capacity which objectification always possesses, especially when, as is the case now, the logic of structural homologies assigns it to a prestigious group so that it functions as an authority which authorizes and reinforces dispositions by giving them a collectively recognized expression.[10] Taste, for its part, a classification system constituted by the conditionings associated with a condition situated in a determinate position in the structure of different conditions, governs the relationship with objectified capital, with this world of ranked and ranking objects which help to define it by enabling it to specify and so realize itself.[11]

Thus the tastes actually realized depend on the state of the system of goods offered; every change in the system of goods induces a change in tastes. But conversely, every change in tastes resulting from a transformation of the conditions of existence and of the corresponding dispositions will tend to induce, directly or indirectly, a transformation of the field of production, by favouring the success, within the struggle constituting the field, of the producers best able to produce the needs corresponding to the new dispositions. There is therefore no need to resort to the hypothesis of a sovereign taste compelling the adjustment of production to needs, or the opposite hypothesis, in which taste is itself a product of production, in order to account for the quasi-miraculous correspondence prevailing at every moment between the products offered by a field of production and the field of socially produced tastes. The producers are led by the logic of competition with other producers and by the specific interests linked to their position in the field of production (and therefore by the habitus which have led them to that position) to produce distinct products which meet the different cultural interests which the consumers owe to their class conditions and position, thereby offering them a real possibility of being satisfied. In short, if, as they say, 'There is something for everyone', if each fraction of the dominant class has its own artists and philosophers, newspapers and critics, just as it has its hairdresser, interior decorator or tailor, or if, as an artist put it, 'Everyone sells', meaning that paintings of the most varied styles always eventually find a purchaser, this is not the result of intentional design but of the meeting between two systems of differences.

The functional and structural homology which guarantees objective orchestration between the logic of the field of production and the logic of the field of consumption arises from the fact that all the specialized fields (haute couture or painting, theatre or literature) tend to be governed by the same logic, i.e., according to the volume of the specific capital that is possessed (and according to seniority of possession, which is often associated with volume), and from the fact that the oppositions which tend to be established in each case between the richer and the less rich in the specific capital—the established and the outsiders, veterans and newcomers, distinction and pretension, rear-guard and avant-garde, order and movement etc.—are mutually homologous (which means that there are numerous invariants) and also homologous to the oppositions which structure the field of the social classes (between dominant and dominated) and the field of the dominant class (between the dominant fraction and the dominated fraction).[12] The correspondence which is thereby objectively established between the classes of products and the classes of consumers is realized in acts of consumption only through the mediation of that sense of the homology between goods and groups which defines tastes. Choosing according to one's tastes is a matter of identifying goods that are objectively attuned to one's position and which 'go together' because they are situated in roughly equivalent positions in their respective spaces, be they films or plays, cartoons or novels, clothes or furniture; this choice is assisted by institutions—shops, theatres (left- or right-bank), critics, newspapers, magazines—which are themselves defined by their position in a field and which are chosen on the same principles.

For the dominant class, the relationship between supply and demand takes the form of a pre-established harmony. The competition for luxury goods, emblems of 'class', is one dimension of the struggle to impose the dominant principle of domination, of which this class is the site; and the strategies it calls for, whose common feature is that they are oriented towards maximizing the distinctive profit of exclusive possessions, must necessarily use different weapons to achieve this common function. On the supply side, the field of production need only follow its own logic, that of distinction, which always leads it to be organized in accordance with a structure analogous to that of the symbolic systems which it produces by its functioning and in which each element performs a distinctive function.

THE LOGIC OF HOMOLOGIES Thus, the case of fashion, which might seem to justify a model which locates the motor of changing sartorial styles in the intentional pursuit of distinction (the 'trickle-down effect') is an almost perfect example of the meeting of two spaces and two relatively autonomous histories. The endless changes in fashion result from the objective orchestration between, on the one hand, the logic of the struggles internal to the field of production, which are organized in terms of the opposition old/new, itself linked, through the oppositions expensive/(relatively) cheap and classical/practical (or rear-guard/avant-garde), to the opposition old/young (very important in this field, as in sport); and, on the other hand, the logic of the struggles internal to the field of the dominant class which, as we have seen, oppose the dominant and the dominated fractions, or, more precisely, the established and the challengers, in other words—given the equivalence between power (more specifically, economic power) and age, which means that, at identical biological ages, social age is a function of proximity to the pole of power and duration in that position—between those who have the social properties associated with accomplished adulthood and those who have the social properties associated with the incompleteness of youth. The couturiers who occupy a dominant position in the field of fashion only have to follow through the negative strategies of discretion and understatement that are forced on them by the aggressive competition of the challengers to find themselves directly attuned to the demands of the old bourgeoisie who are oriented towards the same refusal of emphasis by a homologous relation to the audacities of the new bourgeoisie; and, similarly, the newcomers to the field, young couturiers or designers endeavouring to win acceptance of their subversive ideas, are the 'objective allies' of the new fractions and the younger generation of the dominant fractions of the bourgeoisie, for whom the symbolic revolutions of which vestimentary and cosmetic outrages are the paradigm, are the perfect vehicle for expressing the ambiguity of their situation as the 'poor relations' of the temporal powers.

Just as the ready-to-wear 'revolution' arose when the dispositions of a designer occupying a particular position in the field of fashion encountered the 'modern', 'dynamic', 'casual' life-style of the new bourgeoisie which brings the traditional functions of representation into professional life, so the new fashion based on the 'authentic' and 'genuine' (real Chinese clothes, real Army surplus—parkas, combat trousers, light raincoats etc.— Canadian trappers' jackets, Japanese martial-art kimonos, safari jackets), which the most 'in' boutiques sell at inflated prices to a clientele of 'beautiful people'—models, photographers, advertising agents, journalists—owes its success to the fact that it meets the demands of the young counter-culture.[13]

The logic of the functioning of the fields of cultural-goods production, together with the distinction strategies which determine their dynamics, cause the products of their functioning, be they fashion designs or novels, to be predisposed to function differentially, as means of distinction, first between the class fractions and then between the classes. The producers can be totally involved and absorbed in their struggles with other producers, convinced that only specific artistic interests are at stake and that they are otherwise totally disinterested, while remaining un- aware of the social functions they fulfil, in the long run, for a particular audience, and without ever ceasing to respond to the expectations of a particular class or class fraction.

This is especially clear in the case of the theatre, where the correspon- dence between several relatively autonomous spaces—the space of the producers (playwrights and actors), the space of the critics (and through them the space of the daily and weekly press), and the space of the audi- ences and readerships (i.e., the space of the dominant class), is so perfect, so necessary and yet so unforeseeable that every actor can experience his encounter with the object of his preference as a miracle of predestina- tion.[14]

In the same way, it would be easy to show how much newspapers owe, even in an age of market research, to the logic of competition for adver- tisers and for readers. Like political parties, newspapers must endlessly work to maximize their clientele, at the expense of their closest competitors in the field of production, through more or less disguised borrowings of themes, formulae and even journalists, without losing the core readership which defines them and gives them their distributional value.

Boulevard theatre, which offers tried and tested shows (adaptations of foreign plays, revivals of boulevard 'classics' etc.), written to reliable for- mulae and performed by consecrated actors, and which caters to a mid- dle-aged, 'bourgeois' audience that is disposed to pay high prices, is opposed in every respect to experimental theatre, which attracts a young, 'intellectual' audience to relatively inexpensive shows that flout ethical and aesthetic conventions. This structure of the field of production oper- ates both in reality, through the mechanisms which produce the opposi- tions between the playwrights or actors and their theatre, the critics and their newspapers, and in people's minds, in the form of a system of cate- gories shaping perception and appreciation which enable them to classify and evaluate playwrights, works, styles and subjects. Thus, critics occu- pying opposed positions in the field of cultural production will assess plays in terms of the very same oppositions which engender the objective differences between them, but they will set the terms of these oppositions in opposite hierarchies.

Thus in 1973 Françoise Dorin's play *Le Tournant* (*The Turning*), which dramatizes a boulevard playwright's attempt to start a new career as an avant-garde playwright, aroused reactions which varied in form and content according to the position of the publication in which they ap- peared, that is, according to how distant the critic and his readership were from the 'bourgeois' pole and consequently from Dorin's play. They range from unconditional approval to disdainful silence, via a neutral point (occupied by *Le Monde*), as one moves from right to left, from the Right Bank to the Left Bank, through the field of newspapers and week-lies, from *L'Aurore* to *Le Nouvel Observateur,* and, simultaneously, through the field of readership, which is itself organized in accordance with oppositions corresponding fairly exactly to those defining the field of the theatre. When confronted with an object so clearly organized in terms of the basic opposition, the critics, who are themselves distributed in the field of the press in accordance with the structure which shapes both the classified object and the classification system they apply to it, re-produce—in the space of the judgements whereby they classify both it and themselves—the space within which they are themselves classified. (The whole process constitutes a perfect circle from which the only es-cape is to objectify it sociologically.)

In the play itself, Françoise Dorin sets 'bourgeois' drama (her own), which applies technical skill to produce gaiety, lightness and wit, 'typi-cally French' qualities, in opposition to the 'pretentiousness' and 'bluff,' camouflaged under 'ostentatious starkness', the dull solemnity and drab decor, which characterize 'intellectual' drama. The series of contrasted properties which the right-bank critics pick out—technical skill, joie de vivre, clarity, ease, lightness, optimism, as opposed to tedium, gloom, ob-scurity, pretentiousness, heaviness and pessimism—reappears in the col-umns of the left-bank critics, but here the positives are negatives and vice versa, because the hierarchy of qualities is reversed.

As in a set of facing mirrors, each of the critics located at either ex-treme can say exactly what the critic on the other side would say, but he does so in conditions such that his words take on an ironic value and stigmatize by antiphrasis the very things that are praised by his opposing counterpart. Thus, the left-bank critic credits Mme. Dorin with the quali-ties on which she prides herself; but when *he* mentions them, to *his* read-ership, they automatically become derisory (so that her 'technique' becomes 'a box of tricks', and 'common sense' is immediately understood as synonymous with bourgeois stupidity). In so doing, he turns against Mme. Dorin the weapon she herself uses against avant-garde theatre when, exploiting the structural logic of the field, she turns against avant-garde theatre the weapon it likes to use against 'bourgeois' chatter and the 'bourgeois' theatre which reproduces its truisms and clichés (e.g., Ionesco's descriptions of *The Bald Prima Donna* or *Jacques* as 'a sort of parody or caricature of boulevard theatre, boulevard theatre falling apart and going mad').

In each case the same device is used: the critic's relationship of ethical and aesthetic connivance with his readers supplies the leverage to break the connivance of the parodied discourse with its own audience and to turn it into a series of 'misplaced' remarks which are shocking and

A Sociological Test

Moving from right to left or from right bank to left bank, we start with *L'Aurore:* 'Cheeky Françoise Dorin is going to be in hot water with our *toffee-nosed, Marxist* intelligentsia (the two things go together). The author of *Un sale égoïste* shows no respect for the solemn *boredom,* profound emptiness and vertiginous nullity which characterize so many so-called 'avant-garde' theatrical productions. She dares to profane with sacrilegious laughter the notorious "incommunicability" which is the alpha and omega of the contemporary stage. And this perverse *reactionary,* who flatters the lowest appetites of consumer society, far from acknowledging the error of her ways and wearing her boulevard playwright's reputation with humility, has the impudence to prefer the jollity of Sacha Guitry, or Feydeau's bedroom farces, to the darkness visible of Marguerite Duras or Arrabal. This is a crime for which she will not easily be forgiven. Especially since she commits it with cheerfulness and gaiety, using all the dreadful devices which make lasting successes' (Gilbert Guilleminaud, *L'Aurore,* 12 January 1973).

Situated at the fringe of the intellectual field, at a point where he already has to speak of it as an outsider ('our intelligentsia'), the *L'Aurore* critic does not mince his words (he calls a reactionary a reactionary) and does not hide his strategies. The rhetorical effect of putting words into the opponent's mouth, in conditions in which his discourse, functioning ironically, objectively signifies the opposite of what he means, presupposes and brings into play the very structure of the field of criticism and his relationship of immediate connivance with his readership based on homology of position.

From *L'Aurore* we move to *Le Figaro.* In perfect harmony with the author of *Le Tournant*—the harmony of orchestrated habitus—the *Figaro* critic cannot but experience absolute delight at a play which so perfectly corresponds to his categories of perception and appreciation, his view of the theatre and his view of the world. However, being forced into a higher degree of euphemization, he excludes overtly political judgements and limits himself to the language of aesthetics and ethics: 'How grateful we should be to Mme. Françoise Dorin for being a *courageously light* author, which means to say that she is *wittily* dramatic, and *smilingly serious,* irreverent without fragility, pushing her comedy into outright vaudeville, *but* in the *subtlest* way imaginable; an author who wields satire *with elegance,* who at all times demonstrates astounding virtuosity.... Françoise Dorin knows *much more than any of us* about the *tricks of the dramatist's art,* the *springs of comedy,* the *potential of a situation,* the comic or biting force of the mot juste.... Yes, what skill in taking things apart, what irony in her deliberate sidestepping, what mastery in the way she lets you see her pulling the strings! *Le Tournant* gives every sort of enjoyment without a hint of self-indulgence or vulgarity. And without ever being facile, since it is quite clear that in this day and age, *it is entirely the avant-garde which is conformist,* it is gravity which is ridiculous and boredom which is the imposture. Mme. Françoise Dorin will *relieve a well-balanced audience* by bringing it back into *balance* with healthy laughter. . . . Hurry along and see for yourselves and I'm sure you will *laugh so heartily* that you will forget to think how anguishing it can be for a writer to wonder if she is still in tune with the times in which she lives. . . . In the end it is a question everyone asks himself and only humour and *incurable optimism* can rid him of it!' (Jean-Jacques Gautier, *Le Figaro,* 12 January 1973).

From *Le Figaro* one moves naturally to *L'Express,* which balances between endorsement and distance, thereby attaining a distinctly higher degree of euphemization: 'It *ought* to be a runaway success. . . . A witty and amusing play. A character. An actor made for the part: Jean Piat. . . . With an *unfailing virtuosity that is only occasionally overdone,* with *a sly cunning, a perfect mastery of the tricks of the trade,* Françoise Dorin has written a play on the 'turning points' in the Boulevard which is, ironically, the most traditional of Boulevard plays. *Only morose pedants will probe too far into the contrast between two types of theatre and the contrast between two conceptions of political life and the private life behind it.* The *brilliant* dialogue, full of *wit* and *epigrams,* is often bitingly sarcastic. But Romain is not a caricature, he is much less stupid than your run-of-the-mill avant-gardist. Philippe has the *plum rôle,* because he is on his own ground. What the author of *Comme au théâtre* gently wants to suggest is that the Boulevard stage is where people speak and behave 'as in real life', and this is true, but it is only a partial truth, and not just because it is a class truth' (Robert Kanters, *L'Express,* 15–21 January 1973).

Here the approval, which is still total, begins to be coloured by sys-

tematic use of formulations that are ambiguous even as regards the oppositions involved: "It ought to be a runaway success', 'a sly cunning, a perfect mastery of the tricks of the trade', 'Philippe has the plum rôle', all formulae which could equally be taken pejoratively. And we even find, surfacing through its denial, a hint of the other truth ('Only morose pedants will probe too far . . .') or even of the plain truth, but doubly neutralized by ambiguity and denial ('and not just because it is a class truth').

Le Monde offers a perfect example of ostentatiously neutral discourse, even-handedly dismissing both sides, both the overtly political discourse of *L'Aurore* and the disdainful silence of *Le Nouvel Observateur:* 'The simple, or simplistic, argument is complicated by a very subtle "two-tier" structure, as if there were two plays overlapping. One by Françoise Dorin, a conventional author, the other invented by Philippe Roussel, who tries to take "the turning" towards modern theatre. This conceit performs a circular movement, like a boomerang. Françoise Dorin deliberately exposes the Boulevard clichés which Philippe attacks and, through his voice, delivers a violent denunciation of the bourgeoisie. On the second floor, she contrasts this language with that of a young author whom she assails with equal vigour. Finally, the trajectory brings the weapon back onto the Boulevard stage, and the futilities of the mechanism are unmasked by the devices of the traditional theatre, which are shown to have lost nothing of their value. Philippe can declare himself a "courageously light" playwright, inventing "characters who talk like real people"; he can claim that his art is "without frontiers" and therefore non-political. However, the demonstration is entirely distorted by the model avant-garde author chosen by Françoise Dorin. Vankovicz is an epigone of Marguerite Duras, a vaguely militant, belated existentialist. He is parodic in the extreme, like the theatre that is denounced here ("A black curtain and a scaffold certainly help!" or the title of the play: "Do take a little angst in your coffee, Mr. Karsov"). The audience sniggers at this derisive picture of modern drama; the denunciation of the bourgeoisie is an amusing provocation inasmuch as it rebounds onto an odious victim and finishes him off. . . . To the extent that it reflects the state of bourgeois theatre and reveals its systems of defence, *Le Tournant* can be regarded as an *important work*. Few plays let slip so much anxiety about an "external" threat and *recuperate* it with so much *unconscious* fury' (Louis Dandrel, *Le Monde*, 13 January 1973).

The ambiguity which Robert Kanters was already beginning to cultivate here reaches its peak. The argument is 'simple *or* simplistic', take your pick; the play is split in two, offering two works for the reader's choice, a 'violent' but 'recuperatory' critique of the bourgeoisie and a defence of non-political art. For anyone naive enough to ask whether the critic is 'for or against', whether he finds the play 'good or bad', there are two answers: first, the observation by an 'objective informant' with a duty towards truth that the avant-garde author portrayed is 'parodic in the extreme' and that 'the audience sniggers' (but without our knowing where the critic stands in relation to this audience, and therefore what the sniggering signifies); and then, after a series of judgements that are held

in ambiguity by many reservations, nuances and academic attenuations ('insofar as . . .', 'can be regarded as . . .'), the assertion that *Le Tournant* is 'an important work', but be it noted, as a document illustrating the crisis of modern civilization, as they would no doubt say at Sciences Po.

This art of conciliation and compromise achieves the virtuosity of art for art's sake with the critic of the Catholic paper *La Croix*, who laces his unconditional approval with such subtly articulated justifications, understatements through double negation, nuances, reservations and self-corrections that the final *conciliatio oppositorum*, so naively Jesuitical 'in form and substance', as he would say, almost seems to go without saying: '*Le Tournant*, as I have said, seems to me an admirable work, in both form and substance. This is not to say it would not put many people's teeth on edge. I happened to be sitting next to an unconditional supporter of the avant-garde and throughout the evening I was aware of his suppressed anger. However, I by no means conclude that Françoise Dorin is unfair to certain very respectable—albeit often tedious—experiments in the contemporary theatre . . . And if she concludes—her preference is delicately hinted—with the triumph of the "Boulevard"—but a boulevard that is itself avant-garde—that is precisely because for many years a master like Anouilh has placed himself as a guide at the crossroads of these two paths' (Jean Vigneron, *La Croix*, 21 January 1973).

Although the silence of *Le Nouvel Observateur* no doubt signifies something in itself, we can form an approximate idea of what its position might have been by reading its review of Félicien Marceau's play *La Preuve par quatre,* or the review of *Le Tournant* which Philippe Tesson, then editor of *Combat,* wrote for *Le Canard Enchaîné:*

'Theatre seems to me the wrong term to apply to these *society gatherings of tradesmen and businesswomen* in the course of which a famous and much loved actor recites the laboriously witty text of an equally famous author in the middle of an elaborate stage set, even a revolving one decorated with Folon's measured humour . . . No "ceremony" here, no "catharsis" or "revelation" either, still less improvisation. Just a plateful of bourgeois cuisine for stomachs that have seen it all before. . . . The audience, like all boulevard audiences in Paris, bursts out laughing, on cue, in the most conformist places, as and when this spirit of easy-going rationalism inspires them. The connivance is perfect and the actors are all in on it. This play could have been written ten, twenty, or thirty years ago' (M. Pierret, *Le Nouvel Observateur,* 12 February 1964, reviewing Félicien Marceau's *La Preuve par quatre*).

'Françoise Dorin really *knows a thing or two.* She's a first-rate *recuperator* and terribly *well-bred.* Her *Tournant* is an excellent Boulevard comedy, which runs mainly on bad faith and demagogy. The lady wants to prove that avant-garde theatre is a dog's dinner. To do so, she takes a *big bag of tricks* and, needless to say, as soon as she pulls one out the *audience* rolls in the aisles and calls for more. Our author, *who was just waiting for that,* does it again. She gives us a young trendy leftist playwright called Vankowicz—get it?—and puts him in various ridiculous, uncomfortable and rather shady situations, to show that this young gentleman is no more disinterested, no less bourgeois, than you and I. What *common sense,* Mme. Dorin, what *lucidity,* what *honesty!* You at least have the courage to stand by your opinions, and very healthy, red-white-and-blue ones they are too' (Philippe Tesson, *Le Canard Enchaîné,* 17 March 1973 [italics in all foregoing quotations are mine]).

laughable because they are not uttered in the appropriate place and before the right audience. Instead, they become a 'mockery', a parody, establishing with their audience the immediate complicity of laughter, because they have persuaded their audience to reject (if it had ever accepted) the presuppositions of the parodied discourse.

As this exemplary case clearly shows, it is the logic of the homologies, not cynical calculation, which causes works to be adjusted to the expectations of their audience. The partial objectifications in which intellectuals and artists indulge in the course of their battles omit what is essential by describing as the conscious pursuit of success with an audience what is in fact the result of the pre-established harmony between two systems of interests (which may coincide in the person of the 'bourgeois' writer), or, more precisely, of the structural and functional homology between a given writer's or artist's position in the field of production and the position of his audience in the field of the classes and class fractions. By refusing to recognize any other relationship between the producer and his public than cynical calculation or pure disinterestedness, writers and artists give themselves a convenient device for seeing themselves as disinterested, while exposing their adversaries as motivated by the lust for success at any price, provocation and scandal (the right-bank argument) or mercenary servility (the left-bank argument). The so-called 'intellectual lackeys' are right to think and profess that they, strictly speaking, serve no one. They serve objectively only because, in all sincerity, they serve their own interests, specific, highly sublimated and euphemized interests, such as 'interest' in a form of theatre or philosophy which is logically associated with a certain position in a certain field and which (except in crisis periods) has every likelihood of concealing, even from its advocates, the political implications it contains.

Between pure disinterestedness and cynical servility, there is room for the relationships established, objectively, without any conscious intention, between a producer and an audience, by virtue of which the practices and artifacts produced in a specialized and relatively autonomous field of production are necessarily over-determined; the functions they fulfil in the internal struggles are inevitably coupled with external functions, those which they receive in the symbolic struggles between the fractions of the dominant class and, in the long run, between the classes. 'Sincerity' (which is one of the pre-conditions of symbolic efficacy) is only possible—and real—in the case of perfect, immediate harmony between the expectations inscribed in the position occupied (in a less consecrated area, one would say 'job description') and the dispositions of the occupant; it is the privilege of those who, guided by their 'sense of their place,' have found their natural site in the field of production. In accordance with the law that one only preaches to the converted, a critic can only 'influence' his readers insofar as they grant him this power because they are structurally attuned to him in their view of the social world, their tastes and their whole habitus. Jean-Jacques Gautier, for a long time literary critic of *Le Figaro,* gives a good description of this elective affinity between the journalist, his paper and his readers: a good *Figaro* editor, who has chosen himself and been chosen through the same mechanisms, chooses a *Figaro* literary critic because 'he has the right tone for speaking to the readers of the paper', because, without making a deliberate effort, 'he naturally speaks the language of *Le Figaro'* and is the paper's 'ideal reader'. 'If tomorrow I started speaking the language of *Les Temps Modernes,* for example, or *Saintes Chapelles des Lettres,* people would no longer read me or understand me, so they would not listen to me, because I would be assuming a certain number of ideas or arguments which our readers don't give a damn about.'[15] To each position there correspond presuppositions, a *doxa,* and the homology between the producers' positions and their clients' is the precondition for this complicity, which is all the more strongly required when fundamental values are involved, as they are in the theatre.

ELECTIVE AFFINITIES   This limiting case forces one to question the appearances of the direct effect of demand on supply or of supply on demand, and to consider in a new light all the encounters between the logic of goods production and the logic of taste production through which the universe of appropriate, appropriated things—objects, people, knowledge, memories etc.—is constituted. The limit of these coincidences of homologous structures and sequences which bring about the concordance between a socially classified person and the socially classified things or persons which 'suit' him is represented by all acts of co-option in fellow-feeling, friendship or love which lead to lasting relations, socially sanctioned or not. The social sense is guided by the system of mutually reinforcing and infinitely redundant signs of which each body is the bearer—clothing, pronunciation, bearing, posture, manners—and which, unconsciously registered, are the basis of 'antipathies' or 'sympathies'; the seemingly most immediate 'elective affinities' are always partly based on the unconscious deciphering of expressive features, each of which only takes on its meaning and value within the system of its class variations (one only has to think of the ways of laughing or smiling noted by ordinary language). Taste is what brings together things and people that go together.

The most indisputable evidence of this immediate sense of social compatibilities and incompatibilities is provided by class and even class-fraction endogamy, which is ensured almost as strictly by the free play of sentiment as by deliberate family intervention. It is known that the structure of the circuit of matrimonial exchanges tends to reproduce the structure of the social space as described here;[16] it is probable that the homogeneity of couples is still underestimated and that better knowledge of the 'secondary' properties of the spouses and their families would further reduce the apparent random element. For example, a survey in 1964 of the matrimonial strategies of six classes (1948–1953) of arts graduates of the Ecole Normale showed that of those who were married by then (85 percent of the total), 59 percent had married a teacher, and of these 58 percent had married an *agrégée*.[17] Among the directors of the central administration, who occupy an intermediate position between the civil service and business, 22.6 percent of whose fathers are civil servants and 22 percent businessmen, 16.6 percent of those who are married have a civil-servant father-in-law and 25.2 percent a businessman father-in-law.[18] Among the alumni of INSEAD (European Institute of Business Administration), which trains future top executives for the private sector, 28 percent of whose fathers are industrial or commercial employers and 19.5 percent executives or engineers, 23.5 percent of those who are married have an employer for father-in-law and 21 percent an executive or engineer; very rarely are they the sons (2 percent) or sons-in-law (5 per-

cent) of a teacher.[19] And the decisive contribution of the logic of matrimonial exchanges to the reproduction of the *grande bourgeoisie* has been demonstrated in an earlier study.[20]

Taste is a match-maker; it marries colours and also people, who make 'well-matched couples', initially in regard to taste. All the acts of co-option which underlie 'primary groups' are acts of knowledge of others qua subjects of acts of knowledge or, in less intellectualist terms, sign-reading operations (particularly visible in first encounters) through which a habitus confirms its affinity with other habitus. Hence the astonishing harmony of ordinary couples who, often matched initially, progressively match each other by a sort of mutual acculturation.[21] This spontaneous decoding of one habitus by another is the basis of the immediate affinities which orient social encounters, discouraging socially discordant relationships, encouraging well-matched relationships, without these operations ever having to be formulated other than in the socially innocent language of likes and dislikes.[22] The extreme improbability of the particular encounter between particular people, which masks the probability of interchangeable chance events, induces couples to experience their mutual election as a happy accident, a coincidence which mimics transcendent design ('made for each other') and intensifies the sense of the miraculous.

Those whom we find to our taste put into their practices a taste which does not differ from the taste we put into operation in perceiving their practices. Two people can give each other no better proof of the affinity of their tastes than the taste they have for each other. Just as the art-lover finds a raison d'être in his discovery, which seems to have been waiting for all eternity for the discoverer's eye, so lovers feel 'justified in existing', as Sartre puts it, 'made *for* each other', constituted as the end and raison d'être of another existence entirely dependent on their own existence, and therefore accepted, recognized in their most contingent features, a way of laughing or speaking, in short, legitimated in the arbitrariness of a way of being and doing, a biological and social destiny. Love is also a way of loving one's own destiny in someone else and so of feeling loved in one's own destiny. It is no doubt the supreme occasion of a sort of experience of the *intuitus originarius* of which the possession of luxury goods and works of art (made *for* their owner) is an approximate form and which makes the perceiving, naming subject (we know the role of name-giving in love relations), the cause and the end, in short, the raison d'être, of the perceived subject.

> Le Maître, par un oeil profond, a, sur ses pas,
> Apaisé de l'éden l'inquiète merveille
> Dont le frisson final, dans sa voix seule, éveille
> Pour la Rose et le Lys le mystère d'un nom.[23]

Taste is the form par excellence of *amor fati*. The habitus generates representations and practices which are always more adjusted than they seem to be to the objective conditions of which they are the product. To say with Marx that 'the petit bourgeois cannot transcend the limits of his mind' (others would have said the limits of his understanding) is to say that his thought has the same limits as his condition, that his condition in a sense doubly limits him, by the material limits which it sets to his practice and the limits it sets to his thought and therefore his practice, and which make him accept, and even love, these limits.[24] We are now better placed to understand the specific effect of the 'raising of consciousness': making explicit what is given presupposes and produces a suspension of immediate attachment to the given so that the knowledge of probable relationships may become dissociated from recognition of them; and *amor fati* can thus collapse into *odium fati,* hatred of one's destiny.

Symbolic Struggles

To escape from the subjectivist illusion, which reduces social space to the conjunctural space of interactions, that is, a discontinuous succession of abstract situations,[25] it has been necessary to construct social space as an objective space, a structure of objective relations which determines the possible form of interactions and of the representations the interactors can have of them. However, one must move beyond this provisional objectivism, which, in 'treating social facts as things', reifies what it describes. The social positions which present themselves to the observer as places juxtaposed in a static order of discrete compartments, raising the purely theoretical question of the limits between the groups who occupy them, are also strategic emplacements, fortresses to be defended and captured in a field of struggles.

Care must be taken to avoid the objectivist inclination (which is expressed and reinforced in a spatial diagram) to mark out regions of this space that are defined once and for all in a single respect and delimited by clearly drawn frontiers. For example, as has been shown in the case of industrial employers and as will subsequently be shown in the exemplary case of the new middle-class fractions, a particularly indeterminate zone in that site of relative indeterminacy represented by the petite bourgeoisie, each of the classes of positions which the ordinary classifications of statistics require us to construct can itself function as a relatively autonomous field. One only has to substitute more strictly defined occupational positions for the relatively abstract categories imposed by the necessities of statistical accumulation in order to see the emergence of the network of competitive relations which give rise, for example, to conflicts of competence—conflicts over the qualifications for legitimate practice of the occupation and the legitimate scope of the practice—between agents possessing different qualifications, such as doctors, anaesthetists, nurses, midwives, physiotherapists and healers (each of these universes itself functioning as a field of struggles); or between the occupations, mostly of recent creation, offering 'social' guidance (social workers, domestic-economy counsellors, child-care services, mother's helpers etc.), educational services (special teachers, remedial teachers, approved schools etc.), cultural services (play leaders, youth leaders, adult tutors etc.), or medico-psychological services (marriage guidance consultants, paediatric nurses, physiotherapists etc.), whose common feature is that they are only defined in and by the competition between them and in the antagonistic strategies through which they seek to transform the established order so as to secure a recognized place within it.

The model of social space that has been put forward here is not only limited by the nature of the data used (and usable), particularly by the practical impossibility of including in the analysis structural features such as the power which certain individuals or groups have over the economy, or even the innumerable associated hidden profits. If most of those who carry out empirical research are often led to accept, implicitly or explicitly, a theory which reduces the classes to simple ranked but non-antagonistic strata, this is above all because the very logic of their practice leads them to ignore what is objectively inscribed in every distribution. A distribution, in the statistical but also the political-economy sense, is the balance-sheet, at a given moment, of what has been won in previous battles and can be invested in subsequent battles; it expresses a state of the power relation between the classes or, more precisely, of the struggle for possession of rare goods and for the specifically political power over the distribution or redistribution of profit.

Thus, the opposition between theories which describe the social world in the language of stratification and those which speak the language of the class struggle corresponds to two ways of seeing the social world which, though difficult to reconcile in practice, are in no way mutually exclusive as regards their principle. 'Empiricists' seem locked into the former, leaving the latter for 'theorists', because descriptive or explanatory surveys, which can only manifest classes or class fractions in the form of a punctual set of distributions of properties among individuals, always arrive after (or before) the battle and necessarily put into parentheses the struggle of which this distribution is the product. When the statistician forgets that *all* the properties he handles, not only those he classifies and measures but also those he uses to classify and measure, are weapons and prizes in the struggle between the classes, he is inclined to abstract each class from its relations with the others, not only from the oppositional relations which give properties their distinctive value, but also from the relations of power and of struggle for power which are the very basis of the distributions. Like a photograph of a game of marbles or poker which freezes the balance sheet of assets (marbles or chips) at a given stage, the survey freezes a moment in a struggle in which the agents put back into play, at every moment, the capital they have acquired in early phases of the struggle, which may imply a power over the struggle itself and therefore over the capital held by others.

The structure of class relations is what one obtains by using a synchronic cross-section to fix a (more or less steady) state of the field of struggles among the classes. The relative strength which the individuals can put into this struggle, or, in other words, the distribution at that moment of the different types of capital, defines the structure of the field; but, equally, the strength which the individuals command depends on the state of the struggle over the definition of the stake of the struggle. The definition of the legitimate means and stakes of struggle is in fact one of the stakes of the struggle, and the relative efficacy of the means of controlling the game (the different sorts of capital) is itself at stake, and therefore subject to variations in the course of the game. Thus, as has constantly been emphasized here (if only by use of quotation marks), the notion of 'overall volume of capital', which has to be constructed in order to account for certain aspects of practice, nonetheless remains a theoretical artifact; as such, it could produce thoroughly dangerous effects if everything that has to be set aside in order to construct it were forgotten, not least the fact that the conversion rate between one sort of capital and another is fought over at all times and is therefore subject to endless fluctuations.

Dispositions are adjusted not only to a class condition, presenting itself as a set of possibilities and impossibilities, but also to a relationally defined position, a rank in the class structure. They are therefore always related, objectively at least, to the dispositions associated with other positions. This means that, being 'adapted' to a particular class of conditions of existence characterized by a particular degree of distance from necessity, class 'moralities' and 'aesthetics' are also necessarily situated with respect to one another by the criterion of degree of banality or distinction, and that all the 'choices' they produce are automatically associated with a distinct position and therefore endowed with a distinctive value. This occurs even without any conscious intention of distinction or explicit pursuit of difference. The genuinely intentional strategies through which members of a group seek to distinguish themselves from the group immediately below (or believed to be so), which they use as a foil, and to identify themselves with the group immediately above (or believed to be so), which they thus recognize as the possessor of the legitimate life-style, only ensure full efficacy, by intentional reduplication, for the automatic, unconscious effects of the dialectic of the rare and the common, the new and the dated, which is inscribed in the objective differentiation of conditions and dispositions. Even when it is in no way inspired by the conscious concern to stand aloof from working-class laxity, every petit-bourgeois profession of rigour, every eulogy of the clean, sober and neat, contains a tacit reference to uncleanness, in words or things, to intemperance or improvidence; and the bourgeois claim to ease or discretion, detachment or disinterestedness, need not obey an intentional search for distinction in order to contain an implicit denunciation of the 'pretensions', always marked by excess or insufficiency, of the 'narrow-minded' or 'flashy', 'arrogant' or 'servile', 'ignorant' or 'pedantic' petite bourgeoisie.

It is no accident that each group tends to recognize its specific values in that which makes its value, in Saussure's sense, that is, in the latest difference which is also, very often, the latest conquest,[26] in the structural and genetic deviation which specifically defines it. Whereas the working classes, reduced to 'essential' goods and virtues, demand cleanness and practicality, the middle classes, relatively freer from necessity, look for a warm, 'cosy', comfortable or neat interior, or a fashionable and original garment.[27] These are values which the privileged classes relegate to second rank because they have long been theirs and seem to go without saying; having attained intentions socially recognized as aesthetic, such as the pursuit of harmony and composition, they cannot identify their distinction with properties, practices or 'virtues' which no longer *have* to be claimed or which, because they have become commonplace and lost their distinctive value, no longer *can* be claimed.

As is shown in figure 10 by the series of histograms indicating the class-fraction variations of the adjectives applied to the ideal domestic interior (except for three of them, classical, neat—*soigné*—and sober, which proved to be ambiguous), the proportion of choices emphasizing overtly aesthetic properties (studied, imaginative, harmonious) grows as one moves up the social hierarchy, whereas the proportion of 'functionalist' choices (clean, practical, easy to maintain) declines. The steady distortion of the histogram in fact points towards three relatively incommensurable extremes: the small shopkeepers lead to the industrial and commercial employers, the primary teachers to the secondary teachers and the 'cultural intermediaries' to the artistic producers. The same logic is found in the refusal of adjectives. The working classes never reject 'clean and tidy', 'easy to maintain' or 'practical'. In the middle classes, the established fractions (office workers, junior administrative executives, craftsmen and shopkeepers) reject 'imaginative' much more often than 'classical', in contrast to the new petite bourgeoisie (except the 'art craftsmen'), who, like most fractions of the dominant class (especially the teachers and members of the professions), reject 'classical' more often than 'imaginative'.

Tastes thus obey a sort of generalized Engel's law. At each level of the distribution, what is rare and constitutes an inaccessible luxury or an absurd fantasy for those at an earlier or lower level becomes banal and common, and is relegated to the order of the taken-for-granted by the appearance of new, rarer and more distinctive goods; and, once again, this

Figure 10 Ideal homes.

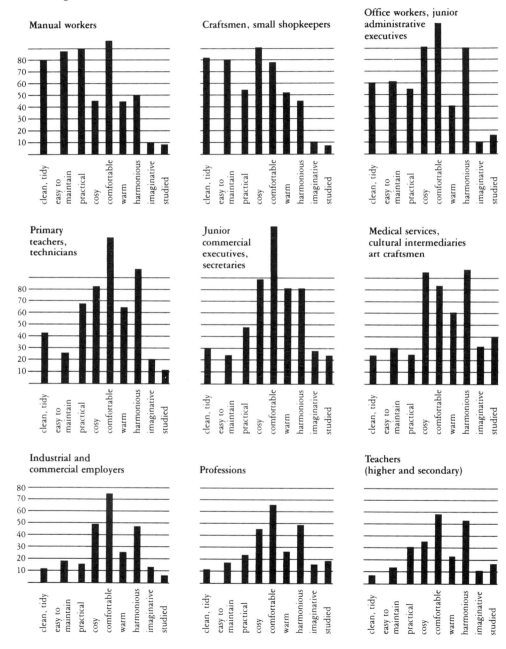

happens without any intentional pursuit of distinctive, distinguished rarity.[28] The sense of good investment which dictates a withdrawal from outmoded, or simply devalued, objects, places or practices and a move into ever newer objects in an endless drive for novelty, and which operates in every area, sport and cooking, holiday resorts and restaurants, is guided by countless different indices and indications, from explicit warnings ('Saint-Tropez'—or the Buffet de la gare de Lyon, or anywhere else—'has become impossible') to the barely conscious intuitions, which, like the awareness of popularization or overcrowding, insidiously arouse horror or disgust for objects or practices that have become common. (It is no accident that tastes in painting or music so often follow paths which, revivals and rehabilitations apart, reproduce history in biography.) So the search for distinction has no need to see itself for what it is, and all the intolerances—of noise, crowds etc.—inculcated by a bourgeois upbringing are generally sufficient to provoke the changes of terrain or object which, in work as in leisure, lead towards the objects, places or activities rarest at a given moment. Those who are held to be distinguished have the privilege of not worrying about their distinction; they can leave it to the objective mechanisms which provide their distinctive properties and to the 'sense of distinction' which steers them away from everything 'common'. Where the petit bourgeois or nouveau riche 'overdoes it', betraying his own insecurity, bourgeois discretion signals its presence by a sort of ostentatious discretion, sobriety and understatement, a refusal of everything which is 'showy', 'flashy' and pretentious, and which devalues itself by the very intention of distinction.

When asked how they would dress if 'invited to dinner by their husband's boss', 33 percent of the wives of junior executives or office workers (32 percent of manual workers' wives, 29 percent of farm workers' wives) say they would 'wear their best clothes', as against only 19 percent of the wives of industrial and commercial employers, senior executives and professionals, of whom 81 percent say they would change their clothes 'but without putting on their Sunday best', compared with 67 percent of the middle-class wives and 68 percent of the working-class wives (C.S. XLII).

Struggles over the appropriation of economic or cultural goods are, simultaneously, symbolic struggles to appropriate distinctive signs in the form of classified, classifying goods or practices, or to conserve or subvert the principles of classification of these distinctive properties. As a consequence, the space of life-styles, i.e., the universe of the properties whereby the occupants of different positions differentiate themselves, with or without the intention of distinguishing themselves, is itself only the balance-sheet, at a given moment, of the symbolic struggles over the imposition of the legitimate life-style, which are most fully developed in the struggles for the monopoly of the emblems of 'class'—luxury goods, legitimate cultural goods—or the legitimate manner of appropriating them. The dynamic of the field in which these goods are produced and reproduced and circulate while yielding profits of distinction lies in the strategies which give rise to their rarity and to belief in their value, and which combine—in their very opposition—to bring about these objective effects. 'Distinction', or better, 'class', the transfigured, misrecognizable, legitimate form of social class, only exists through the struggles for the exclusive appropriation of the distinctive signs which make 'natural distinction'.

Culture is a stake which, like all social stakes, simultaneously presupposes and demands that one take part in the game and be taken in by it; and interest in culture, without which there is no race, no competition, is produced by the very race and competition which it produces. The value of culture, the supreme fetish, is generated in the initial investment implied by the mere fact of entering the game, joining in the collective belief in the value of the game which makes the game and endlessly remakes the competition for the stakes. The opposition between the 'authentic' and the 'imitation', 'true' culture and 'popularization', which maintains the game by maintaining belief in the absolute value of the stake, conceals a collusion that is no less indispensable to the production and reproduction of the *illusio,* the fundamental recognition of the cultural game and its stakes. Distinction and pretension, high culture and middle-brow culture—like, elsewhere, high fashion and fashion, haute coiffure and coiffure, and so on—only exist through each other, and it is the relation, or rather, the objective collaboration of their respective production apparatuses and clients which produces the value of culture and the need to possess it. It is in these struggles between objectively complicit opponents that the value of culture is generated, or, which amounts to the same thing, belief in the value of culture, interest in culture and the interest of culture—which are not self-evident, although one of the effects of the game is to induce belief in the innateness of the desire to play and the pleasure of playing. It is barbarism to ask what culture is for; to allow the hypothesis that culture might be devoid of intrinsic interest, and that interest in culture is not a natural property—unequally distributed, as if to separate the barbarians from the elect—but a simple social artifact, a particular form of fetishism; to raise the question of the interest of activities which are called disinterested because they offer no intrinsic interest (no palpable pleasure, for example), and so to introduce the question of the interest of disinterestedness.

The struggle itself thus produces effects which tend to disguise the very existence of the struggle. If the relationship of the different classes with culture can be described indifferently either in the language (favoured by Maurice Halbwachs) of distance from the centres of cultural values or in the language of conflict, this is because the symbolic struggles between the classes have no chance of being seen and organized as such, and are bound to take the form of competitive struggles helping to reproduce the gaps which are the essence of the race. It is no accident that—apart from Proudhon, who is inspired by his petit-bourgeois horror of the dissolute, slovenly life-style of artists, and by what Marx calls his 'irae hominis probi', to dare to expose the hidden, repressed face of the petite bourgeoisie's ambivalent idea of art—there is practically no questioning of art and culture which leads to a genuine objectification of the cultural game, so strongly are the dominated classes and their spokesmen imbued with a sense of their cultural unworthiness.

Nothing is further from such objectification than the artistic denunciation of the art which some artists go in for,[29] or the activities grouped under the term counter-culture. The latter merely contest one culture in the name of another, counterposing a culture dominated within the relatively autonomous field of cultural production and distribution (which does not make it the culture of the dominated) to a dominant culture; in so doing they fulfil the traditional role of a cultural avant-garde which, by its very existence, helps to keep the cultural game functioning.

The dominated classes intervene in the symbolic struggles to appropriate the distinctive properties which give the distinctive life-styles their physiognomy and especially in the struggles to define the legitimate properties and the legitimate mode of appropriation, only as a passive reference point, a foil. The nature against which culture is here constructed is nothing other than what is 'popular', 'low', 'vulgar', 'common'. This means that anyone who wants to 'succeed in life' must pay for his accession to everything which defines truly humane humans by a change of nature, a 'social promotion' experienced as an ontological promotion, a process of 'civilization' (Hugo speaks somewhere of the 'civilizing power of Art'), a leap from nature to culture, from the animal to the human; but having internalized the class struggle, which is at the very heart of culture, he is condemned to shame, horror, even hatred of the old Adam, his language, his body and his tastes, and of everything he was bound to, his roots, his family, his peers, sometimes even his mother tongue, from which he is now separated by a frontier more absolute than any taboo.

The struggles to win everything which, in the social world, is of the order of belief, credit and discredit, perception and appreciation, knowledge and recognition—name, renown, prestige, honour, glory, authority, everything which constitutes symbolic power as a recognized power—always concern the 'distinguished' possessors and the 'pretentious' challengers. Pretension, the recognition of distinction that is affirmed in the effort to possess it, albeit in the illusory form of bluff or imitation, inspires the acquisition, in itself vulgarizing, of the previously most distinctive properties; it thus helps to maintain constant tension in the symbolic goods market, forcing the possessors of distinctive properties threatened with popularization to engage in an endless pursuit of new properties through which to assert their rarity. The demand which is generated by this dialectic is by definition inexhaustible since the dominated needs which constitute it must endlessly redefine themselves in terms of a distinction which always defines itself negatively in relation to them.

Nietzsche's 'enlightened elitism' comes close to the scientific truth of the mechanisms of the production of belief in the value of culture: 'You were wont to say that no one would strive for culture if he knew how unbelievably small the number of truly cultured men is and indeed can only be; and yet that even this small number of truly cultured men was not possible unless a great mass, determined, fundamentally, against their nature and only by a seductive illusion, engaged in the pursuit of culture; that therefore nothing should be publicly divulged of the ridiculous disproportion between the number of truly cultivated men and the vast apparatus of culture; that the peculiar secret of culture was this: that countless people work for culture, apparently for themselves, but ultimately only to make a few people possible.'[30]

The symbolic struggles over being and seeming, over the symbolic manifestations which the sense of appropriateness, as strict as the old sumptuary laws, assigns to the different social conditions ('Who does he think he is?'), separating, for example, natural 'grace' from usurped 'airs and graces', are both based and focussed on the degree of freedom from one's 'station' that is allowed by the specific logic of symbolic manifestations. Countless social arrangements are designed to regulate the relations between being and seeming, from the laws on the illegal wearing of uniforms and decorations and all forms of usurpation of titles, to the gentlest forms of repression aimed at recalling to reality, to the 'sense of reality', of limits, those who, by exhibiting the external signs of a wealth associated with a condition higher than their own, show that they 'think themselves' something better than they are, the pretentious pretenders, who betray by their poses, their postures, their 'presentation' that they have a self-image too far out of line with the image others have of them, to which they ought to cut down their self-image ('climb down').

The relation to one's own body which is expressed in a certain manner and bearing—the 'natural' self-confidence, ease and authority of someone who feels authorized, the awkwardness or arrogance of someone who brings suspicion upon his legitimacy by his too patent need to assert it—is one of the most visible traces of early and recurrent exposure to archetypal situations which are very unequally probable for the different social classes. It is one of the most powerful social markers, and for this reason the forced or affected ease of the bluffer is always exposed to the demystifying irony of an interlocutor who 'sees through' it and refuses to be 'taken in'.

This does not mean that the strategies of pretension are lost in advance. Since the surest sign of legitimacy is self-assurance, bluff—if it succeeds (first by impressing the bluffer)—is one of the few ways of escaping the limits of social condition by playing on the relative autonomy of the symbolic (i.e., of the capacity to make and perceive representations) in order to impose a self-representation normally associated with a higher condition and to win for it the acceptance and recognition which make it a legitimate, objective representation. Without subscribing to the interactionist—and typically petit-bourgeois—idealism which conceives the social world as will and representation, it would nonetheless be absurd to exclude from social reality the representation which agents form of that reality. The reality of the social world is in fact partly determined by the struggles between agents over the representation of their position in the social world and, consequently, of that world.

As is shown by the inversion of the relationship between spending on food and on clothing, and more generally, on substance and on appearance, as one moves from the working class to the petite bourgeoisie, the middle classes are *committed* to the symbolic. Their concern for appearance, which may be experienced as unhappy consciousness, sometimes disguised as arrogance,[31] is also a source of their pretension, a permanent disposition towards the bluff or usurpation of social identity which consists in anticipating 'being' by 'seeming', appropriating the appearances so as to have the reality, the nominal so as to have the real, in trying to modify the positions in the objective classifications by modifying the representation of the ranks in the classification or of the principles of classification. Torn by all the contradictions between an objectively dominated condition and would-be participation in the dominant values, the petit bourgeois is haunted by the appearance he offers to others and the judgement they make of it. He constantly overshoots the mark for fear of falling short, betraying his uncertainty and anxiety about belonging in his anxiety to show or give the impression that he belongs. He is bound to be seen—both by the working classes, who do not have this concern with their being-for-others, and by the privileged classes, who, being sure of what they are, do not care what they seem—as the man of appearances, haunted by the look of others and endlessly occupied with being seen in a good light.

Being so linked to appearance—the one he has to give, not only to do his job, that is, play his role, to 'make believe', to inspire confidence or respect and present his social character, his 'presentation', as a guarantee of the products or services he offers (as is the case with salespeople, business representatives, hostesses etc.), but also to assert his pretensions and demands, to advance his interests and upward aspirations—the petit bourgeois is inclined to a Berkeleian vision of the social world, reducing it to a theatre in which being is never more than perceived being, a mental representation of a theatrical performance (*représentation*).[32] His ambiguous position in the social structure, sometimes compounded by the ambiguity inherent in all the roles of intermediary between the classes—manipulated manipulators, deceived deceivers—often his very trajectory, which leads him to the positions of second-in-command, second officer, second lead, second fiddle, éminence grise, agent, deputy or stand-in, deprived of the symbolic profits associated with the recognized status and official delegation which allow legitimate imposture (and well-placed to suspect its true foundation): everything predisposes him to perceive the social world in terms of appearance and reality, and the more he has personally had to 'climb down', the more inclined he is to observe manipulations and impostures with the suspicious eyes of resentment.[33]

But the site par excellence of symbolic struggles is the dominant class itself. The conflicts between artists and intellectuals over the definition of culture are only one aspect of the interminable struggles among the different fractions of the dominant class to impose the definition of the legitimate stakes and weapons of social struggles; in other words, to define the legitimate principle of domination, between economic, educational or social capital, social powers whose specific efficacy may be compounded by specifically symbolic efficacy, that is, the authority conferred by being recognized, mandated by collective belief. The struggle between the dominant fractions and the dominated fractions (themselves constituting fields organized in a structure homologous to that of the dominant class as a whole) tends, in its ideological retranslation—and here the dominated fractions have the initiative and the upper hand—to be organized by oppositions that are almost superimposable on those which the dominant vision sets up between the dominant class and the dominated classes: on the one hand, freedom, disinterestedness, the 'purity' of sublimated tastes, salvation in the hereafter; on the other, necessity, self-interest, base material satisfactions, salvation in this world. It follows that all the strategies which intellectuals and artists produce against the 'bourgeois' inevitably tend, quite apart from any explicit intention, and by virtue of the structure of the space in which they are generated, to be dual-action devices, directed indifferently against all forms of subjection to material interests, popular as much as bourgeois: 'I call bourgeois whoever thinks basely', as Flaubert put it. This essential over-determination explains how the 'bourgeois' can so easily use the art produced against them as a means of demonstrating their distinction, whenever they seek to show that, compared to the dominated, they are on the side of 'disinterestedness', 'freedom', 'purity' and the 'soul', thus turning against the other classes weapons designed for use against themselves.

It is clearly no accident that the dominant art and the dominant art of living agree on the same fundamental distinctions, which are all based on the opposition between the brutish necessity which forces itself on the vulgar, and luxury, as the manifestation of distance from necessity, or asceticism, as self-imposed constraint, two contrasting ways of defying nature, need, appetite, desire; between the unbridled squandering which only highlights the privations of ordinary existence, and the ostentatious freedom of gratuitous expense or the austerity of elective restriction; between surrender to immediate, easy satisfactions and economy of means, bespeaking a possession of means commensurate with the means possessed. Ease is so universally approved only because it represents the most visible assertion of freedom from the constraints which dominate ordinary people, the most indisputable affirmation of capital as the capacity to satisfy the demands of biological nature or of the authority which entitles one to ignore them.

Thus linguistic ease may be manifested either in the tours de force of going beyond what is required by strictly grammatical or pragmatic rules, making optional liaisons, for example, or using rare words and tropes in place of common words and phrases, or in the freedom from the demands of language or situation that is asserted in the liberties taken by those who are known to know better. These opposing strategies, which place one above the rules and proprieties imposed on ordinary speakers, are in no way mutually exclusive. The two forms of conspicuous freedom, unconventional constraint and deliberate transgression, can coexist at different moments or different levels of the same discourse; lexical 're-laxation' may, for example, be counterbalanced by increased tension in syntax or diction, or the reverse (this is clearly seen in condescension strategies, in which the gap thus maintained between the levels of language is the symbolic equivalent of the double game of asserting distance by appearing to negate it). Such strategies—which may be perfectly unconscious, and thereby even more effective—are the ultimate riposte to the hyper-correction strategies of pretentious outsiders, who are thrown into self-doubt about the rule and the right way to conform to it, paralyzed by a reflexiveness which is the opposite of ease, and left 'without a leg to stand on'.

The speaker who can 'take the liberty' of standing outside rules fit only for pedants or grammarians—who, not surprisingly, are disinclined to write these games with the rules into their codifications of the linguistic game—puts himself forward as a maker of higher rules, i.e., a taste-maker, an *arbiter elegantium* whose transgressions are not mistakes but the annunciation of a new fashion, a new mode of expression or action which will become a model, and then modal, normal, the norm, and will call for new transgressions by those who refuse to be ranked in the mode, to be included, absorbed, in the class defined by the least classifying, least marked, most common, least distinctive, least distinguishing property. Thus we see that, contrary to all naively Darwinian convictions, the (sociologically well-founded) illusion of 'natural distinction' is ultimately based on the power of the dominant to impose, by their very existence, a definition of excellence which, being nothing other than their own way of existing, is bound to appear simultaneously as distinctive and different, and therefore both arbitrary (since it is one among others) and perfectly necessary, absolute and natural.

Ease in the sense of 'natural facility' is no more than ease in the sense of a 'comfortable situation ensuring an easy life': the proposition is self-destructive, since there would be no need to point out that ease is only what it is, if it were really not something else, which is also part of its truth. This is the error of objectivism, which forgets to include in the complete definition of the object the representation of the object that it has had to destroy in order to arrive at the 'objective' definition; which forgets to perform the final reduction of its reduction that is indispensable in order to grasp the objective truth of social facts, objects whose being *also* consists in their being perceived.[34] One has to put back into a complete definition of ease what is destroyed by recalling that ease, like Aristotle's virtue, requires a certain ease (or, conversely, that embarrassment arises from embarrassment), that is, the effect of imposition which those who only have to be in order to be excellent achieve by their mere existence. This perfect coincidence is the very definition of ease which, in return, bears witness to this coincidence of 'is' and 'ought' and to the self-affirming power it contains.

The value placed on casualness and on all forms of distance from self stems from the fact that, in opposition to the anxious tension of the challengers, they manifest both the possession of a large capital (linguistic or other capital) and a freedom with respect to that capital which is a second-order affirmation of power over necessity. Verbal virtuosities or the gratuitous expense of time or money that is presupposed by material or symbolic appropriation of works of art, or even, at the second power, the self-imposed constraints and restrictions which make up the 'asceticism of the privileged' (as Marx said of Seneca) and the refusal of the facile which is the basis of all 'pure' aesthetics, are so many repetitions of that variant of the master-slave dialectic through which the possessors affirm their possession of their possessions. In so doing, they distance themselves still further from the dispossessed, who, not content with being slaves to necessity in all its forms, are suspected of being possessed by the desire for possession, and so potentially possessed by the possessions they do not, or do not yet, possess.[35]

III | Class Tastes and Life-Styles

Our pride is more offended by attacks on our tastes than on our opinions

La Rochefoucauld, *Maxims*

In order that the description of life-styles may constitute a valid *empirical verification,* we must go back to the survey and compare the unities that are brought to light by the method which seems best suited to grasp the whole set of observations in simultaneity and to draw out the immanent structures without imposing any presuppositions—namely, analysis of the correspondences—with the unities that can be *constructed* on the basis of the principles of division which objectively define the major classes of homogeneous conditions and conditionings, and therefore habitus and practices. Such an operation reproduces, in reverse, the transformation which ordinary perception performs when it applies socially constituted schemes of perception and assessment to the practices and properties of agents, constituting them as distinctive life-styles through which it intuits social conditions.

In restricting ourselves to the survey data (as a linguist may limit himself to the finite corpus of sentences produced in response to a finite set of triggers), we deny ourselves the possibility of evoking the infinite richness of each life-style. This possibility is in fact purely theoretical since, to avoid the positivist temptation, which Jorge Luis Borges describes, of making a map as big as the country, one would have to find the style most capable of evoking the features which (as a differential equation condenses a curve) condense a whole universe of practices. To avoid the monotony of references limited to the indicators used in the survey, it would have been possible to substitute numerous equivalents for the works and composers actually offered (for example, the *Goldberg Variations* or the *Little Notebook for Anna Magdalena Bach* for the *Well-Tempered Clavier,* or, among the singers, Reggiani, Ferrat, Barbara or Juliette Greco for Brel and Douai, or Marcel Amont, Adamo or Mireille Mathieu for Aznavour). This procedure, though perfectly consistent with the logic of taste, which constantly makes such substitutions within classes of equivalents vaguely perceived on the basis of social cues, was rejected on the grounds that the very nature of classes of equivalents depends on the system of classification put into operation: where one person will only see interchangeable elements of the category 'classical music', another will refuse the seemingly most justified substitutions (same composer or period, similar form and style).

As Aristotle said, it is because bodies have colour that we observe that some are a different colour from others; different things differentiate themselves through what they have in common. Similarly, the different fractions of the dominant class distinguish themselves precisely through that which makes them members of the class as a whole, namely the type of capital which is the source of their privilege and the different manners of asserting their distinction which are linked to it.

And just as, to borrow an example from Anatol Rapaport, we speak of a cloud or a forest, although in each case the density of the trees or droplets is a continuous function and the limit does not exist as a clear-cut line, so we can speak of a class fraction although it is nowhere possible to draw a demarcation line such that we can find no one on either side who possesses all the properties most frequent on one side and none of the properties most frequent on the other. In this universe of continuity, the work of construction and observation is able to isolate (relatively) homogeneous sets of individuals characterized by sets of properties that are statistically and 'socio-logically' interrelated, in other words, groups separated by systems of differences.

5 | The Sense of Distinction

If it is true, as I have endeavoured to establish, that, first, the dominant class constitutes a relatively autonomous space whose structure is defined by the distribution of economic and cultural capital among its members, each class fraction being characterized by a certain configuration of this distribution to which there corresponds a certain life-style, through the mediation of the habitus; that, second, the distribution of these two types of capital among the fractions is symmetrically and inversely structured; and that, third, the different inherited asset structures, together with social trajectory, command the habitus and the systematic choices it produces in all areas of practice, of which the choices commonly regarded as aesthetic are one dimension—then these structures should be found in the space of life-styles, i.e., in the different systems of properties in which the different systems of dispositions express themselves.[1] To endeavour to establish this, the whole set of survey data was subjected to correspondence analysis.[2]

As a first stage, after a methodical reading of the tables expressing the results of the survey (see appendix 3), the answers given by the members of the dominant class (n = 467) to various sets of questions (see the questionnaire, appendix 1) were analyzed in order to determine whether the structures and explanatory factors varied according to the area of practice. These included: all the questions on knowledge or preferences in painting and music and on museum-going, which all measure legitimate competence; all the questions on the likelihood of producing a beautiful, interesting, meaningless or ugly photograph from each of the twenty-one subjects, which measure the aesthetic disposition; all the questions on the preferred singers, radio programmes and books, on knowledge of film actors and directors and on personal photography, which all measure middle-brow culture; all the choices as regards domestic interior, furniture, cooking, clothes, the qualities of friends, through which ethical dispositions are more directly expressed, and so on. In all these analyses, the first factor opposes the fractions richest in economic capital to the fractions richest in cultural capital: the commercial employers and the higher-education teachers or cultural producers are situated at the two opposite extremes of the axis (see figures 11, 12), while the members of the professions, the executives and the engineers occupy intermediate positions. In the analysis based on the indicators of preference in middle-brow culture, the commercial employers are opposed most strongly to the secondary teachers (rather than the higher-education teachers or the artistic producers), in accordance with a logic already observed in the primary teachers' preferences for singers. In the analysis based on the indicators of ethical disposition, the artistic producers, who thereby assert their casualness and indifference to convention, are opposed to the teachers, the engineers and the public-sector executives, and occupy positions very close to those of the commercial employers (to whom they are very strongly opposed in other respects, identified in this case by the second factor).

Having thus identified the most pertinent indicators in each case, it was necessary, in order to avoid the over-loading resulting from the abundance of information gathered (see questionnaire, appendix 1), to eliminate from the final analysis—only the results of which are presented here—the questions which proved to be badly phrased (such as the questions on clothing or on types of books) or less classifying, in favour of questions (such as that on cooking) measuring much the same dispositions (the questions on photographic subjects were also excluded, and analysed separately). The data retained (for disjunctive coding) were thus those which concerned the qualities of an interior (twelve adjectives), the qualities of a friend (twelve adjectives), the style of meals served to friends (six possibilities), furniture purchases (six possibilities), preferred singers (twelve), preferred works of classical music (fifteen), visits to the Modern Art Museum or the Louvre, knowledge of composers (classified into four levels), opinions on art (five). To give the demonstration its full force, the characteristics treated as illustrative variables were age, father's occupation, qualifications and income; class fraction, which constitutes the most powerful explanatory factor, was not used as such in the analysis. (Exactly the same operations were applied in analysing the responses of the middle and working classes; see chapters 6 and 7.)

Analysis of the correspondences makes it possible to isolate, through successive divisions, different coherent sets of preferences stemming from distinct and distinctive systems of dispositions, defined as much by their interrelationship as by the relationship between each of them and its social conditions of production. The indicators measuring cultural capital (which vary, of course, in approximately inverse ratio to the indicators of

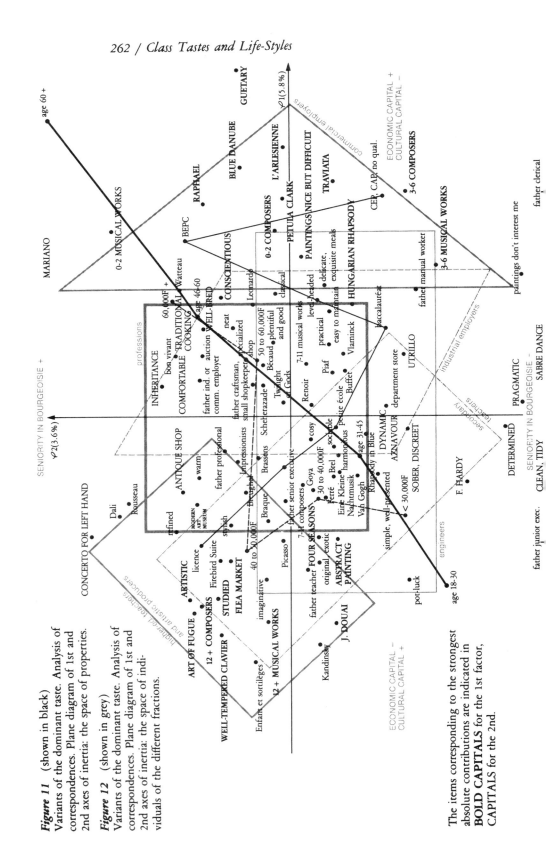

Figure 11 (shown in black)
Variants of the dominant taste. Analysis of correspondences. Plane diagram of 1st and 2nd axes of inertia: the space of properties.

Figure 12 (shown in grey)
Variants of the dominant taste. Analysis of correspondences. Plane diagram of 1st and 2nd axes of inertia: the space of individuals: the space of the different fractions.

The items corresponding to the strongest absolute contributions are indicated in **BOLD CAPITALS** for the 1st factor, CAPITALS for the 2nd.

economic capital) make the strongest contribution to the constitution of the first factor (which represents 5.8 percent of the total inertia as against 3.6 percent and 3.2 percent respectively for the second and third factors).[3] Thus on the left side of figures 11 and 12 are those who, with the lowest incomes, have the greatest competence, who know the largest number of musical works (6 percent) and composers (7.7 percent), who prefer the works demanding the 'purest' aesthetic disposition, such as the *Well-Tempered Clavier* (1.8 percent) or the *Art of Fugue* (1.7 percent), who are most capable of applying this aesthetic disposition to less consecrated areas, such as song or cinema or even cooking or interior decoration, who are interested in abstract painting, visit the Modern Art Museum and expect their friends to be artistic (2.4 percent). On the right side are those who receive the highest incomes and have the lowest competence, who know few musical works or composers, like their friends to be conscientious (1.5 percent) and whose tastes run to second-rank, déclassé or classical works of bourgeois culture—*L'Arlésienne* (3 percent), the *Blue Danube* (2.9 percent), *La Traviata* (2.1 percent), the *Hungarian Rhapsody*, Buffet, Vlaminck, Utrillo, Raphael (2.3 percent), Watteau, Leonardo—and to light opera—Guétary (1.8 percent), Mariano—or the most 'popular' singers—Petula Clark (2.2 percent).[4]

It can be seen intuitively that these indicators of the different life-styles fall into a pattern which corresponds to the structure of the space of life-styles as it has been established, and therefore to the structure of positions. And indeed, in terms of individuals, the most clear-cut opposition is set up between the commercial and, to a lesser extent, the industrial employers, and the higher-education teachers and artistic producers, who are virtually indistinguishable at this level of analysis. The clusters of points representing the members of the same fraction are distributed in the expected pattern.[5] Projection of the determinants of position (income, qualifications, social origin, age) as supplementary variables confirms that this structure corresponds to the structure of the distribution of the types of capital; educational capital is distributed along the first axis, from zero qualification to post-*licence* degrees, while incomes have an opposite (but less dispersed and non-linear) distribution.

The industrial and commercial employers closest to the extremity of the first axis are those in whose overall capital cultural capital has least weight; those situated close to the professions are heads of businesses handling cultural goods (antique-dealers, record-dealers, the book trade etc.), all possessing greater cultural capital than the average for their fraction (*licence* or *grande école*). Except for those who sell cultural goods, the commercial employers are very close to middle-brow culture in another respect (brought out by the third factor) in their cultural preferences (*Blue Danube*, Guétary, Petula Clark) and also in the choices most strongly involving ethical dispositions (in their ideal interior or friend they seek qualities often chosen by the working and middle classes, such as 'easy to maintain', 'practical', and 'conscientious', 'level-headed'); in this respect they are opposed to the industrial employers, who are closer overall to bourgeois taste.

It is certain that, with respect to culture, language and life-style, the boundary with the working classes is much less marked, and situated much higher, in the self-employed sector (especially in the commercial occupations) than among wage-earners, where it appears at the level of clerical workers. As in their eating habits, small employers are much closer to the working class in their speech, their tastes (for sport, music-hall etc.) and their values than clerical workers, who are much more strongly opposed to the working class in all these respects but much closer in their political positions.

The higher-education teachers, who have very high competence even in less consecrated areas, such as cinema, occupy the other extremity of the first axis. Their preferences are balanced between a certain audacity and a prudent classicism; they refuse the facile pleasures of right-bank taste without venturing into the artistic avant-garde, exploring 'rediscoveries' rather than 'discoveries', the rarest works of the past rather than the contemporary avant-garde (warm, studied, imaginative interior, Braque, Picasso, Breughel and sometimes Kandinsky, *Firebird Suite, Art of Fugue, Well-Tempered Clavier*).

The members of the professions occupy an intermediate position and divide into two sub-groups differing mainly in respect of cultural capital. The larger group, situated near the pole occupied by the artistic producers, mainly includes Parisian architects, barristers (*avocats*), doctors (and only a few dentists or pharmacists); the second sub-set, closer to the employers' pole, largely consists of relatively old provincials, dentists, solicitors (*notaires*) etc. The former choose, for example, the rarest works, Braque, Kandinsky, the *Concerto for the Left Hand,* the most 'intellectual' films (*Exterminating Angel, Salvatore Giuliano*), and very often know the directors of the films mentioned, whereas the latter declare the most banal preferences of middle-brow taste, Vlaminck, Renoir, the *Blue Danube,* and see 'wide audience' films (*Les dimanches de Ville d'Avray*) or historical spectaculars (*The Longest Day*).

Thus, given that the differences linked to the overall volume of capital are partially neutralized (by the fact that the analysis is applied to the members of the same class, who are roughly equal in this respect), each individual's position in the space defined by the first two factors depends essentially on the structure of his assets, that is, on the relative weights of the economic capital and cultural capital he possesses (axis 1), and his social trajectory (axis 2), which, through the corresponding mode of acquisition, governs his relationship to those assets.[6] The greatest absolute contributions to the second factor are made by the indicators of the dispositions associated with more or less seniority in the bourgeoisie; mainly manifested in the relation to legitimate culture and in the nuances of the art of living, they separate individuals who have much the same volume of cultural capital. Within each fraction, the second factor opposes those individuals whose families have long been members of the bourgeoisie to those who have recently entered it, the parvenus: those who have the supreme privilege, seniority in privilege, who acquired their cultural capital by early, daily contact with rare, 'distinguished' things, people, places and shows, to those who owe their capital to an acquisitive effort directed by the educational system or guided by the serendipity of the autodidact, and whose relationship to it is more serious, more severe, often more tense.

This (second) factor naturally distributes the fractions according to the proportion of their members who originate from the bourgeoisie or from another class: on one side the professions and the higher-education teachers (and, to a lesser extent, the private-sector executives), and on the other the engineers, the public-sector executives and the secondary teachers, categories which represent the main routes (via academic success) into the dominant class, while the employers divide fairly equally between the two poles. The former, grouped on the positive side of the second factor, have in common the fact that they (initially) acquired their capital by familiarization within the family, and they present signs of long-standing membership of the bourgeoisie such as inherited furniture (3.1 percent), purchases from antique-dealers (2.4 percent), a predilection for a comfortable interior and traditional cooking (1.5 percent), visits to the Louvre and the Modern Art Museum (1.8 percent), and a taste for the *Concerto for the Left Hand,* which proves to be almost always associated with piano-playing. The others, who owe the essential part of their culture to the educational system and the relatively late learning encouraged and entailed by a high scholastic culture, are opposed to them by their preference for friends who are 'determined' (2.6 percent) and 'pragmatic' (3.6 percent), rather than, as at the opposite pole, cultivated or artistic, their taste for clean and tidy (3.2 percent), sober and discreet (1.6 percent) interiors, and works of mainstream bourgeois culture, such as the *Sabre Dance* (1.5 percent), Utrillo and Van Gogh or, in another order, Jacques Brel or Aznavour, Buffet and *Rhapsody in Blue,* all indices of upward mobility. They are characterized by prudent and therefore relatively homogeneous choices. Never stooping to works suspected of banality or vulgarity, such as *L'Arlésienne* or the *Blue Danube,* they rarely venture into the slightly less 'canonical' works, such as *L'Enfant et les sortilèges,* which are often chosen by the cultural intermediaries and artistic producers.

Projection of the father's occupation, the respondent's age, qualification, income etc. as illustrative variables shows that the principle of division is indeed social trajectory. The opposition is established between

Figure 13 Variants of the dominant taste. Analysis of correspondences: simplified plane diagram of 1st and 3rd axes of inertia.

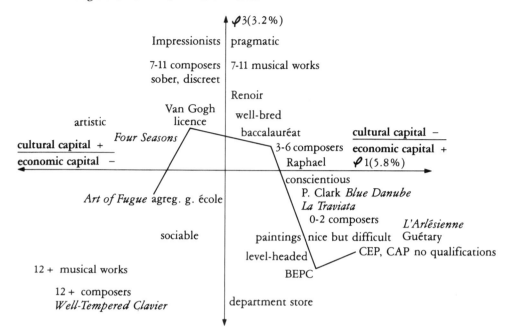

This simplified diagram only includes variables which make an absolute contribution equal to or greater than 1.5%. The only illustrative variable represented is educational qualification.

those members of the dominant class who are both older and drawn from the oldest or economically richest fractions (professionals, industrial and commercial employers), and those whose father was a clerical worker, junior executive or manual worker, who are relatively less rich in economic capital and younger (see figure 13). The complex relationship which emerges between the positions of the fractions in social space, seniority in the bourgeoisie and age (also linked to the first two factors), and which is very important in understanding a number of ethical or aesthetic differences between members of the dominant class—for example, differences in sports or clothing—becomes clear when one knows that the proportion of parvenus rises as one moves from the dominant to the dominated fractions (and, a fortiori, the proportion of those who owe their entry to the accumulation of scholastic capital—the dispersion of the executives is no doubt partly due to the fact that the lower their social origin, the more likely they are to achieve these positions at a relatively advanced age).[7]

The third factor which, at the level of individuals, sets the majority of the teachers and especially the artists—who are even more inclined than the teachers to mark their refusal of bourgeois taste—and also the commercial employers, in opposition to the most typically bourgeois (by origin, place of residence and education) of the professionals, industrialists and executives tends chiefly to characterize the 'bourgeois taste' of these latter categories by opposing it to the tastes of all the other fractions, principally to the better equipped and more daring 'intellectual taste', but also, secondarily, to a taste defined negatively and combining features of middle-brow taste and popular taste (that of the commercial employers). 'Bourgeois' taste, a modal taste or taste à la mode—as is shown by the strength of the preference for the Impressionist painters (4.2 percent), confirmed by the choice of Van Gogh (2.1 percent) or Renoir (2.1 percent)—is based on an average competence (knowledge of 7 to 11 works, 3.3 percent, and 7 to 11 composers, 3.2 percent). It is fundamentally a taste for tradition (with a preference for traditional French meals, 1.3 percent, for furniture from antique shops, 1.0 percent, for 'well-bred' friends, 1.5 percent) and a sort of temperate hedonism (e.g., its favourite interior is comfortable but also sober and discreet, 1.8 percent, and cosy, 1.2 percent), moderate even in its audacities (with the choice of the *Firebird Suite* or *Rhapsody in Blue*, 1.3 percent, or the preference for 'pragmatic' friends, 1.7 percent—as opposed to 'artistic'). It is chiefly defined by opposition to a set of indicators which characterize a culture that is both more 'scholastic' (knowledge of 12 or more composers, 3 percent, knowledge of 12 or more works, 1.9 percent, preference for Leonardo, 1.6 percent etc.) and—relatively—more daring (with Kandinsky, 1.4 percent, and Picasso, 1.3 percent), but also more ascetic (Goya or the *Well-Tempered Clavier*, furniture from the Flea Market etc.).

The Modes of Appropriation of the Work of Art

But this statistical analysis would not really fulfil its purpose of verification if it did not help one to understand the underlying logic of the distributions it establishes; if, having proved that volume and structure of capital, synchronically and diachronically defined, constitute the principle of division of practices and preferences, it were not possible to bring to light the intelligible, 'socio-logical' relationship between, for example, an asymmetric asset structure biased towards culture and a particular relation to the work of art, and to explain, that is, understand completely, why the most ascetic form of the aesthetic disposition and the culturally most legitimate and economically cheapest practices, e.g., museumgoing, or, in sport, mountain-climbing or walking, are likely to occur particularly frequently among the fractions (relatively) richest in cultural capital and (relatively) poorest in economic capital.

A Cosy Samovar-Style Bedroom

Isabelle d'Ornano, the Minister's sister-in-law, has made her bedroom the centre-piece of her apartment. A baroque masterpiece.

'I know how I want to live. Decoration is a way of expressing it.' Scorning fashion and its conventions, she has applied this principle throughout her apartment—a rhapsody of colours, imitation green marble and Venetian blinds—and especially in her bedroom. An almost timeless and yet very up-to-date room, which also serves as Isabelle's study when she is working (marketing the 'Sisley' range of cosmetics her husband launched three years ago), as a TV room for her five children and sometimes, since it communicates with the reception rooms, as a second salon for big dinner parties. Originally it was a big dull library, sumptuous and boring; she has turned it into something warm and 'cosy', as she puts it.

First, by having a circular balcony built around the walls almost halfway up. . . . By organizing movement in the room around a centre-piece: the bed. And quite a bed it is! . . . Isabelle d'Ornano likes 'muscular' furniture and wanted 'a bed which suggests a gondola.' Her upholsterer had his work cut out for a year and a half!

By flouting all the classical rules and combining different styles of furniture—in fact, every style. A Louis XVI inlaid roll-top desk, upholstered 'tub' easy-chairs and Second Empire fireside chairs, an enormous eighteenth-century crystal chandelier from the La Granja works, bought from a Madrid antique-dealer, one or two little late-nineteenth-century English stands holding plants, books and an orchid ('the only flower that lasts'), two glass lamps bought for a song at Drouot, with modern shades, two tiered bedside tables recently ordered from a cabinet-maker.

By mingling colours and fabrics with a certain audacity....

By sprinkling the *ensemble,* not with knick-knacks ('they're pointless') but with dozens of photos ... With wicker baskets full of bric-à-brac. With children's mugs bristling with pencils. With novels, exhibition catalogues, magazines on interior decoration (she cuts out the useful addresses and sticks them in scrap-books), scattered all over the place. And other very personal details, such as the painted *faïence* tiles surrounding the chimney-piece ... In short, by adopting an original, personal style of decoration. So much so that designer Henri Samuel, who acted as technical adviser, replied, when I asked him to define this bedroom: 'It's pure d'Ornano, and that's a compliment!'

D. de Saint-Sauveur, *Le Figaro-Magazine* (*Madame Figaro*), 7 October, 1978.

One's immediate intuition should be followed—for the purpose of testing it—when it sees in the teachers' taste for the austerity of pure works, Bach or Braque, Brecht or Mondrian, the same ascetic disposition that is expressed in all their practices, and when it senses in these seemingly innocent choices the symptom of a similar, but merely better-hidden, relationship to sexuality or money; or when it divines the whole view of the world and of existence that is expressed in the taste for the delights of boulevard theatre or the Impressionists, for Renoir's rosy women, Boudin's sunlit beaches or Dufy's stage sets.

As is clearly seen in theatre or painting (but the same is true of the other arts), what emerge through the discontinuous or disparate indices which have to be used to take measurements are two antagonistic relations to the work of art or, more precisely, two modes of aesthetic appropriation expressing two opposite asset structures. Thus, how is one to explain why the median price paid for a theatre ticket rises from 4.17 francs among teachers (less than is paid by junior executives in the private sector, 4.61, and the public sector, 4.77) to 6.09 for public-sector senior executives, 7.00 for the professions, 7.58 for private-sector executives, 7.80 for commercial employers and 9.19 for industrialists—which gives one the ordinary hierarchy of the fractions distributed by volume of economic capital?[8] And how does one explain why the hierarchy of the fractions is inverted if their rate of representation in the cheapest theatres is considered? If the elective affinity between relatively inexpensive avant-garde theatre and the intellectual fractions, or between the much more expensive boulevard theatre and the dominant classes is understood superficially—i.e., as simply a direct effect of the relationship between economic cost and economic means—one is liable to forget that through the price they are willing to pay for access to a work of art, or, more precisely, through the relationship between the material cost and the expected 'cultural' benefit, each fraction expresses its conception of what specifically makes the value of the work of art and of the legitimate way of appropriating it.

The same logic explains why the desired price makes the strongest absolute contribution to the first factor brought to light by analysis of the correspondences of a set of characteristics of a sample of Parisian theatres and their audiences (C.S. XIV). Or again, why the propensity to judge the admission charge of a museum as being cheap or very cheap rises very strongly, in relation to the ordinary hierarchy, as one moves from the fractions (relatively) rich in cultural capital to those rich in economic capital, with the professions being distinguished only by a bi-modal distribution (reasonable—very cheap).

For certified or apprentice intellectuals, activities such as theatre-going, visits to exhibitions or 'art' cinemas, performed with a frequency and regularity which take away any 'extra-ordinary' quality, are in a sense governed by the pursuit of maximum 'cultural profit' for minimum economic cost, which implies renunciation of all ostentatious expense and all gratifications other than those given by symbolic appropriation of the work ('You go to the theatre to see the play, not to show off your wardrobe,' as one of them said). They expect the symbolic profit of their practice from the work itself, from its rarity and from their discourse about it (after the show, over a drink, or in their lectures, their articles or their books), through which they will endeavour to appropriate part of its distinctive value. By contrast, for the dominant fractions a 'night out' at the theatre is an occasion for conspicuous spending. They 'dress up to go out' (which costs both time and money), they buy the most expensive seats in the most expensive theatres just as in other areas they buy 'the best there is'; they go to a restaurant after the show.[9] Choosing a theatre is like choosing the right shop,[10] marked with all the signs of 'quality' and guaranteeing no 'unpleasant surprises' or 'lapses of taste': a playwright who knows his job, who commands 'the springs of comedy, the potential of a situation, the comic or biting force of the mot juste', in short, a goldsmith or jeweller, a past master in the 'art of construction' who has 'the tricks of the dramatist's art' at his fingertips;[11] actors known for their ability to enter the 'twenty-four carat' role he offers them and to place the eager docility of a perfect thespian technician at the 'service' of the polytechnician playwright;[12] and a play which 'gives every sort of enjoyment, without a hint of self-indulgence or vulgarity', which is designed to 'relieve a well-balanced audience by bringing it back into balance with healthy laughter', because it only asks questions which 'everyone asks himself', from which 'the only escape' is 'humour and incurable optimism'.

Figure 14 Films seen (in order of preference): I.

Secondary teachers	Professions	Industrial and commercial employers
Divorce Italian Style	Divorce Italian Style	The Longest Day
Exterminating Angel	The Trial	Divorce Italian Style
Rocco and His Brothers	Les dim. de V. d'Avray	55 Days at Peking
Salvatore Giuliano	Rocco and His Brothers	The Trial
Singing in the Rain	Exterminating Angel	Vice and Virtue
The Suitor	The Leopard	Rocco and His Brothers
The Trial	The Magnificent Seven	Le glaive et la balance
Les dim. de V. d'Avray	The Longest Day	Singing in the Rain
Le glaive et la balance	Singing in the Rain	The Suitor
The Leopard	The Suitor	Les dim. de V. d'Avray
The Longest Day	Ballade pour un voyou	The Leopard
The Magnificent Seven	Le glaive et la balance	Exterminating Angel
Ballade pour un voyou	Salvatore Giuliano	L'abominable homme
L'abominable homme	Vice and Virtue	Ballade pour un voyou
55 Days at Peking	Imperial Venus	The Magnificent Seven
Voyage à Biarritz	55 Days at Peking	Voyage à Biarritz
Le boucanier des îles	Voyage à Biarritz	Salvatore Giuliano
Vice and Virtue	L'abominable homme	Le boucanier des îles
Imperial Venus	Le boucanier des îles	Imperial Venus

These are the films chosen by the Parisians. The respondents from the Lille area were offered a different list (based on the films then showing); their choices were organized in a similar structure.

The implications of the opposition between bourgeois theatre and avant-garde theatre have already been explored (see chapter 4). To remain within the limits of the data provided directly by the survey, we may glance at the oppositions found in the field of the cinema (see figure 14), where the taste for 'ambitious' works that demand a large cultural investment is opposed to the taste for the most spectacular feature films, overtly designed to entertain (differences which are often accompanied by differences in admission prices and in the geographical location of the cinemas). No doubt there are some 'all-purpose' films which gain the unanimous approval of the various fractions of the dominant class (and their critics)—in the list offered, *The Trial*, 'a strong, solemn work of intellectual courage, not to be missed' (*Le Monde*, 25 December 1962), *Rocco and His Brothers*, by Visconti, with Alain Delon, and *Divorce Italian Style*, with Mastroianni, an 'honest commercial film' for *Combat* (2 June 1962), a comedy 'of astonishing cynicism, cruelty and audacity' for *Le Monde* (22 May 1962). However, there are very marked divergences of cinematic taste between the two extremities, with the professions, as usual, in the middle. Thus the industrial and commercial employers choose historical films, like *The Longest Day*, a 'colossal reconstruction' of the 'most spectacular battle' of World War II (*Le Monde*, 12 October 1962), 'blockbusters' like *55 Days at Peking*, 'an excellent example of box-office movie-making', 'sumptuous spectacles, deliberately stripped of intellectual content, which show to packed audiences because they know how to appeal to the public's capacity for wonderment' (*Le Monde*, 17 May 1963), 'commercially successful' films like Vadim's *Vice and Virtue,* a 'solidly constructed film of undeniable virtuosity' which 'makes a moderate sadism available to all' (*France-Soir,* 2 March 1963), and comic films and actors, Fernandel, Darry Cowl etc. By contrast, the secondary teachers, who can almost always name the directors and actors of the films they have seen, systematically exclude popular comedies and big commercial successes, and give their preference to 'classic' films (almost all consecrated in histories of the cinema) such as Buñuel's *Exterminating Angel,* which the *Le Monde* critic (4 May 1963) compares to Sartre's *Huis Clos, Salvatore Giuliano,* 'an enthralling and very beautiful film by Francesco Rosi which retraces a moment in Sicilian life with the rigour of an historian and the lyricism of an artist' (*Le Monde,* 6 March 1963) and finally *The Suitor,* a comedy by Pierre Étaix, which the critic predicts will 'one day take its place in the great tradition which runs from Mack Sennett to Tati, via Max Linder, Chaplin, Keaton and a few others' (*Le Monde,* 16 February 1963). It is significant that in order to justify the injunctions which alert readers expect from 'serious' newspapers ('essential viewing', 'not to be missed' etc.), a phrase can be used in one place ('certainly not a harmless entertainment'—*Le Monde,* 25 December 1962—about *The Trial*) which in another would be an irrevocable condemnation.

In contrast to 'bourgeois' theatre, the opera or exhibitions (not to mention premieres and gala nights), which are the occasion or pretext for social ceremonies enabling a select audience to demonstrate and experience its membership of high society in obedience to the integrating and distinguishing rhythms of the 'society' calendar, the art museum admits anyone (who has the necessary cultural capital), at any moment, without any constraints as regards dress, thus providing none of the social gratifications associated with great 'society' occasions. Moreover, unlike the theatre and, especially, music-hall and variety shows, it always offers the purified, sublimated pleasures demanded by the pure aesthetic and, rather like the library in this respect, it often calls for an austere, quasi-scholastic disposition, oriented as much towards the accumulation of experience and knowledge, or the pleasure of recognition and deciphering, as towards simple delight.

The middle-class visitors and the teachers—and secondarily the engineers—are those most inclined to associate the museum with a library ('What do I like most? A library. It contains works of value and you need to want to go there.' Engineer, Cambrai, age 44, Lille Museum). The same groups are most inclined to combine contemplation with acts of recording (e.g., taking notes) and accumulation (e.g., buying reproductions). One also finds that the teachers are those who most often refuse to dissociate direct experience of the work from erudite knowledge (they are the ones who most often refuse the judgement, 'I don't need to know who painted the picture or how; what counts is whether it is pleasurable to look at').

Behind the obligatory exaltation of the austere severity of the musem and the 'meditation' it encourages, there are sometimes glimpses of the true nature of the visit—an always somewhat laborious task which the devotees set themselves and duly perform with methodical determination, rewarded as much by the sense of a duty done as by the immediate pleasure of contemplation. 'The museum left me with an impression of silence. Emptiness, too, but perhaps because of the silence. That helps you concentrate on the works, helps them sink into you. I wasn't bowled over by it, it's very tedious. Looking at everything systematically is tiring. It was a self-imposed discipline. It's constraining and you get indigestion. I think I got through it quickly because I wanted to be able to tell myself I'd done that museum. It was very monotonous, one picture after another. They ought to put something different in between the paintings to break it up a bit' (engineer, Amiens, age 39, Lille Museum). These comments are reminiscent of those of the conservator of the New York Metropolitan Museum, who sees his museum as 'a gymnasium in which the visitor is able to develop his eye muscles.'[13]

It is understandable that as one moves from avant-garde concerts or plays, museums with a high transmission level and low tourist appeal or avant-garde exhibitions to spectacular exhibitions, major concerts or the 'classical' theatres, and finally to the boulevard theatre and variety shows, the rate of representation of the different fractions distributed in order of decreasing cultural capital and increasing economic capital—i.e., teachers, administrative executives, engineers, professionals, industrial and commercial employers—tends to change systematically and continuously, so that the hierarchy of the fractions distributed by their weight in the public tends to be inverted.[14] The teachers and the industrial or commercial employers occupy symmetrically opposite positions in the diagrams of correlation between the rates of attendance at two categories of shows presenting opposite properties: on the one hand, concerts and art exhibitions, on the other, variety shows and trade exhibitions. In each case the members of the professions and the senior executives are in an intermediate position. The professions, under-represented in use of libraries and museums, are more represented among exhibition visitors than museum visitors, and go to the theatre relatively frequently (to 'boulevard' plays or musicals rather than classical or avant-garde theatre).

The museum, a consecrated building presenting objects withheld from private appropriation and predisposed by economic neutralization to undergo the 'neutralization' defining the 'pure' gaze, is opposed to the commercial art gallery which, like other luxury emporia ('boutiques', antique shops etc.) offers objects which may be contemplated but also bought, just as the 'pure' aesthetic dispositions of the dominated fractions of the dominant class, especially teachers, who are strongly over-represented in museums, are opposed to those of the 'happy few' in the dominant fractions who have the means of materially appropriating works of art. The whole relation to the work of art is changed when the

A *Grand Bourgeois* 'Unique among His Kind'*

S., a lawyer aged 45, is the son of a lawyer and his family belongs to the Parisian *grande bourgeoisie*. His wife, the daughter of an engineer, studied at the Paris Political Science Institute and does not work. Their four children are at the 'best' private Catholic secondary schools in Paris. They live in a very big apartment (more than 300 square metres) in the 16th arrondissement: a very large entrance-hall, a spacious living-room, a dining-room, a study, and the bedrooms (his office is not in the apartment).

In the living-room, modern furniture (big cushions, a large couch, armchairs), antiquities, 'a Greek head in stone, authentic and rather beautiful' (a wedding present), an object which the head of the household calls his 'personal altar' ('a rather attractive religious thing I managed to get off my parents'—his father collects all sorts of objets d'art, and has bought, among other things, 'all sorts of stuff, enamel-work, chalices, crosses . . . from a sort of Russian, a dealer'), 'a terra-cotta thing from the Tang dynasty', bought from an antique shop in Formosa where he went accompanied by ten specialists, several paintings, a Paul Sérusier ('It is rather charming but, that said, I'd just as soon put a modern picture in its place'), in the dining-room a Dutch still life.

'Unique among its kind'

When he buys objets d'art, 'it's in no way an investment.' What

counts for him is 'first of all the beauty of the thing, the object, and secondly, not whether it is unique, but whether it's made in a crafts-manlike way': 'you can make it again, but you can also make a mess of it. So it becomes unique among its kind, because you can't copy the same object, the same subject, twice . . . What makes the beauty of a face, the beauty of a sculpture, is the smile, the look. . . . You can't do it twice. You can make a plaster copy but you can't do it again in the same material, the material counts more, anyway as much as the mass . . . I'd love to own a very fine bronze. There are bronzes that are absolutely extraordinary.'

'The nouveau-riche approach'

He does not often visit commercial galleries and does not 'systemati-cally' inspect antique shops or the

* All these interviews (this one and those of the same type that follow) were carried out in 1974, with the aim of collecting, as systematically as possible, the most signifi-cant features of each of the life-styles that had emerged from analysis of the survey, which had already reached a fairly advanced stage. Given previous knowledge of the generative formula of his or her properties and practices, it was decided to lead the in-terviewee (who was often a relation or ac-quaintance of the interviewer) methodically towards the most central areas of his or her life-style (hence the heterogeneity of the themes discussed, which contrasts with the forced homogeneity of statistical survey data). This was done by supplying all the reassurances and reinforcements that are ex-pected in ordinary life from someone in whom one 'confides'. Finally, by tightening the discourse, through alternating use of direct, semi-direct and indirect quotation, the aim has been to intensify and so make palpable the concrete image of the system-atic totality, the life-style, which statistical analysis dissolves even as it brings it to light.

Drouot auction rooms. He buys (an objet d'art, a piece of furniture ...) because it 'pleases him at that moment'. He is somewhat condescending about people who 'want to invest and haven't got the time': 'They haven't got the time to be personally interested. What essentially interests them is not what pleases them but what has value.' So they club together and 'pay in __ francs a year. They delegate other people to purchase for them. On the one hand, investment, and on the other, total incompetence. If you stuck a piece of shit on the wall, it would be all the same to them as long as someone tells them the shit is worth money. That's the nouveau-riche approach, wanting to show off that you've got something ... or that you're capable of having something. It's like hiring an interior designer, delegating someone.'

'You've looked for it for a long time and at last you've found it'

'The object has an inward value, an emotional value, when you've wanted it, looked for it, for a long time. That was what you wanted and at last, by a stroke of luck, you've found it ... it's a revelation.... When it's for my pleasure, price doesn't come into it, it's like the organ (a gadget, it's electronic), I want it and I have it ... Once again, you normally keep within your means; I wouldn't buy Chartres Cathedral.' (He would have 'loved to own a church and renovate it ... What I find beautiful is stone, the shape of the stones, vaults, stone is beautiful.' He comes from a Catholic family but no longer practices; he makes frequent, half-ironic religious references.)

'For my personal enjoyment'

For his country house in Burgundy, a very big one ('a thousand square metres to furnish, after all!'), almost a 'mistress', he bought furniture from 'a rag-and-bone man': 'I came across a chap, a junk dealer, who had solid wood furniture, real country-style, and I bought other bits and pieces, stuffed animals', including stuffed boars 'which outraged everyone, except me ... because they are funny. Pleasure is what is fun.

'I'm irritated by people who buy things just to show them off, to say they've got them or put them in a particular place. The value isn't what counts, it's the pleasure it gives you.... I bought the boars for my personal enjoyment, or simply because I found it was funny, a joke, or because it annoyed other people.' The house is 'too damp to put a decent piano in it' but he is 'going to get a grand piano.... At the casino, they are throwing out old grand pianos ... perhaps they have a note or two missing.'

'Heirlooms? Don't make me laugh'

The inherited objects with which he has furnished the house are of little interest to him. When his wife reminds him that there are some, he replies: 'Heirlooms? Don't make me laugh, there have been three bits of furniture.' She enumerates them: "When we were getting married, Aunt X. popped off. I inherited a certain amount of silver: first legacy. Then there was Madame C.: second legacy. Then Mademoiselle L.: third legacy.' 'So we have a certain amount of china, old bits and pieces and furniture. Furniture has never been much of a problem for us because we inherited a certain amount. Fourth legacy, my in-laws got rid of some of their property. We got some armchairs. . . .'

If he does not like this furniture, he 'chucks it out': 'not too much clutter'. 'You need a big enough apartment, rooms which allow you a certain inner silence, uncluttered, and then on the other hand, you need rooms containing all the personal objects which are never souvenirs—they can go into the dustbin—but objects you like to have around you.' He 'detests travel souvenirs' and never brings any back ('except the thing I just mentioned, the Chinese terracotta. . . . I've bought little knick-knacks and trinkets that we've distributed to all and sundry, but we've never cluttered ourselves up. . . . Looking around, you wouldn't know we'd travelled. The local souvenir, bought on the spot, has no interest whatsoever'). Besides, when you're travelling, it's better to keep an open mind, 'walk around with your hands in your pockets and look around you, but without having one eye glued to a view-finder' (in the Far East, his wife recalls, 'we took photos', but, she adds, 'we looked at them, showed them round once or twice', and now they are 'at the bottom of the cupboard').

'Many hours in museums, for the pleasure of it, in Holland and Italy'

He has a painting studio in which he spends a lot of time ('He likes twirling a brush', his wife emphasizes), but he considers his efforts 'of no interest' and prefers not to talk about them. On the other hand, he readily confesses to having spent 'many hours in museums, for the pleasure of it, in Holland and

Italy.' He was 'very struck, educated, by Italian painting . . . Leonardo, Venetian and Sienese paintings, all the pictures in the Villa Borghese, Botticelli.' He is also 'very responsive to Dutch painting because of its character, Franz Hals, Rembrandt. It's a totally different sort of painting, laid on much thicker. . . . There are also some Matisse and Cocteau drawings.' Painting 'doesn't have to be' figurative for him to appreciate it. But he is 'left completely cold by practical-joke painting', for example, a white canvas 'slashed this way and that.' His wife says bluntly that 'she doesn't call that sort of thing painting', whereas he is less forthright: 'Well, no, it isn't painting, but it's a sort of art, of expression.'

'Loving something means having it with you'

For him, 'a painting is something which can be dreamt of for a long time and which is always looked at with the same pleasure. Perhaps the pleasure varies depending on what you are or what your mood is.' 'The criterion is whether I'd want to have it in my home. . . . Loving something means having it with you.' And he adds: 'Pleasant things are non-necessary things. I don't live to hoard things . . . I live for the sake of living. And, so far as possible, I try to live for the present moment; it isn't always easy.'

'As necessary as a cooking stove'

He could not live without his hi-fi system, bought more than ten years ago for about eight thousand francs. ('No one brand, it's a combination of several. I asked around and that was that. Same thing for the organ, I asked around and that was that.')

'It's something which is as necessary to me as a cooking stove. . . . Everyone, even someone who earns nothing at all, needs music. It's a need, like food.' Among his records: 'Vivaldi, Bach, a lot of Bach cantatas, masses, requiems, Monteverdi.' Modern music 'doesn't mean much' to him, 'not because I deliberately reject it, but it's a question of attuning one's ears to it.' 'Mahler, Jolivet, Messiaen, I can cope with', but 'in a lot of purely serial music, electronic music, there are some things that are rather beautiful, and others which, again, sound to me like practical jokes, the same thing as in painting.'

'When there's an important work, you always know'

He rarely goes to concerts and is not one of those people who 'go and see things because they have to be seen'; he does not read the reviews in *Le Monde* (his daily paper), but would rather trust the judgement and recommendation of a friend: 'When there's something on that's an important work, you always know. You know because you're in contact with loads of people; that's why I don't bother to read the critics. If you read one, you'd have to read all of them.' He recently went to see *One Man Show,* 'some Italian Maoist alone on stage. We left at the interval because it was lousy.' When he does go to the theatre, he does not necessarily go out for dinner as well: 'You can't do umpteen things at the same time . . . you have to enjoy things to the full.'

'I have a high opinion of myself'

He refuses any sartorial 'refinement': 'If people want to see me, it's not for the socks I'm wearing, my pocket handkerchief or the flower in my buttonhole, or my tie. If people want to see me or invite me to dinner, they invite me as I am. In other words, I have a high opinion of myself,' he explains, taking the opportunity to indicate once again his distance both from bourgeois taste and from the questions put to him by the sociologist (who belongs to his wife's family). He adds: 'I think that five hundred francs is quite enough for a suit, there's no point in spending a thousand francs on a suit when personally I don't give a damn.'

'Cooking is a state of mind'

He is a busy man and does not have much time in the middle of the day; he 'almost wishes they'd invent a pill so you didn't have to eat in the daytime. . . . Cooking is a state of mind.' To appreciate it, you have to be 'relaxed': 'Sturgeons' eggs, some Russian cooking, is quite delicious. Cooking isn't just a matter of food, there's also the setting. If you're going to eat smoked eel, it's more agreeable to eat it in the Amsterdam fish market than in some tacky restaurant . . . Real cooking, the sort where it takes two days to make a madeira sauce, where you keep things simmering away for ages, that's what I call cooking, and it's an art. But when people talk about cooking nowadays, they just mean throwing a few things together, pulling them out of the freezer, sticking them under the grill—that's not cooking. There's no preparation, it isn't an art any more.'

'A certain liturgy'

He likes 'hunting out restaurants' with the aid of the *Guide Michelin* or *Gault et Millau* and remembers 'wines drunk three years ago, a bouquet, a Port, a rather special Saint-Estèphe from a particular year': 'I have very clear memories of bottles from 1923 to 1929 . . . Bordeaux . . . I still have ten bottles of wine from 1923 here. And four bottles of liqueur dated 1870.' A good bottle 'isn't to be drunk with just anyone . . . It requires a certain liturgy: a liturgy to get the temperature right, and a liturgy to drink it. It's a communion', to be celebrated 'only with certain people, who are capable of enjoying it in the same way . . . I'd rather drink it on my own than with people who don't appreciate it.' 'A dinner with champagne is rather quaint . . . A wine is varied, different; comparing champagne with wine is rather like comparing a sort of little flute with an orchestra.'

'I prefer pleasure'

Among the books in his library, 'left by a grandmother' or 'bought in a sort of shop in the rue de Provence', there are leather-bound '17th-century-ish' books, 'more for the beauty of the edition than the interest of the text . . . Bossuet's *Sermons,* Pascal's *Pensées* . . . a 17th-century book considered pornographic in its day, quite amusing.' The only books he now keeps in Paris are 'sort of philosophical or religious, and a bit of poetry'; his 'novels and so on' (about two thousand books) are in his country house. He also has books on German history, the Algerian war. . . . Setting aside 'the leather-bound stuff, the artsy-craftsy shelves', 'for me books are a tool to work with, not books for the sake of it.' He does not belong to any clubs. ('Some people love wearing uniforms, belonging to this or that team or club; I'm my own man, an individualist at all costs.') He no longer hunts 'because you have to go a long way, it's rather tiring and it's also rather expensive.' He plays tennis occasionally, on holiday, and goes skiing 'for pleasure'. 'I'm not going to struggle up a mountain with skis over my shoulder when there's a ski-tow beside me. I like coming down more than going up. I prefer pleasure.'

---

painting, the statue, the Chinese vase or the piece of antique furniture belongs to the world of objects available for appropriation, thus taking its place in the series of the luxury goods which one possesses and enjoys without needing to prove the delight they give and the taste they illustrate, and which, even when not personally possessed, belong to the status attributes of one's group, decorating the offices one works in or the salons one frequents.

In the pages of a journal like *Connaissance des Arts,* we discover the series into which the dominant fractions insert the work of art: the universe of luxury objects, distinguished and distinctive, selected and selective. In a single issue (November 1973) we find advertised: jewels, furs, perfumes, carpets, tapestries, antique furniture, clocks, chandeliers, bronzes, porcelains, faience, silverware, leather-bound books, luxury cars (Volvo, SM, Mercedes,

Rolls etc.), luxury cigarettes (Craven, Benson and Hedges, Kent, Roth-
mans), haute couture (Dior Boutique and Old England), châteaux,
manors, estates, 'residences of character', 'parks with lake', Champagne, Bordeaux, Burgundy, brandy, cruises, movie cameras. A lavishly illustrated an-
nouncement of auctions at the Hôtel Drouot or the Palais Galliera, beside
two advertisements for antique-dealers on the quai Voltaire and in the Faubourg Saint-Honoré, offering 'furniture and objets d'art', 'antique faience
and porcelain', 'paintings, statues, furniture and objets d'art'. An advertisement for the Galerie Arditti, featuring American hyper-realists, next to one
for 'Curiosités', offering 'nineteenth-century French and English furniture';
the Galerie Martin-Caille (Faubourg Saint-Honoré), presenting Max Agos-
tini (a Post-Impressionist born in 1914), opposite Dupont cigarette-
lighters.[15]

In a series of advertisements ranging all the way from Cognac to watches,
the combination of material and symbolic appropriation confers on the possession of luxury goods a second-order rarity and a legitimacy which make
it the supreme symbol of excellence. First, Cognac: 'Princes de Cognac: to
talk about it, you need to use the ancient words of the language of Cognac.
Charnu: The quality of the body of a Cognac. Princes de Cognac has
charnu, but a *charnu* with no fat, a svelte *charnu* which is all muscle. What
a Botticelli is to a Rubens. *Fleur:* The scent of the flower of the *fine champagne* vine, the aristocrat of Cognac. Princes de Cognac has *fleur,* an elegant,
purified *fleur* with eloquence and breeding. *Fûts roux:* very old, very civilized
casks that have sown their wild oats, shed their excess tannin. Princes de
Cognac has aged in *fûts roux.* Hence its taste, dry, clean, discreetly wooded.
Paradis: that's what we call the cellar containing the oldest reserves of
Cognac. Princes de Cognac was brought up in the *paradis* of Maison Otard,
at the Château de Cognac. Princes de Cognac is produced in limited quantities—only a few thousand bottles a year—and is only found in selected
stores and restaurants' (*Connaissance des Arts,* November 1973, p. 16).

Burgundy is treated to the same esoteric archaism: 'Down in Burgundy,
it's *épondage* time. The last echo of the vintage has scarcely died away, and
already the vines are being attended to. Deftly wielding their secateurs,
skilled craftsmen snip off the unwanted shoots and prepare the stocks to receive the next season's dressing; this is *épondage,* a delicate operation, which
demands much dexterity and which Moillard supervises on your behalf. Selected for your pleasure from the most highly considered vineyards, Moillard Burgundies are only entrusted to qualified distributors' (ibid., p. 200).

Through his mastery of a verbal accompaniment, preferably technical,
archaic and esoteric, which separates informed tasting from mere passive
consumption, the connoisseur shows himself worthy of symbolically appropriating the rarities he has the material means of acquiring: 'For some connoisseurs, there is only one beer in France. That's not many. But a real
connoisseur is hard to please. Exclusive. And if some connoisseurs will only
grant their favour to 1664, that's quite simply because 1664 gives a unique
pleasure ... And a pleasure three hundred years old ... Sometimes it's good
to rediscover the taste of the authentic' (ibid., p. 187). 'Few people would
dare to explain what makes a good Cognac. The Baron of the Château de
Cognac has that right. In 1795 Baron Otard made the Château de Cognac

his home ... He also found, under the vaults of the château, the ideal place to mature his Cognac. And you realize the importance of that, when you know that a great Cognac has to age for many long years before becoming a V.S.O.P. Since 1795, nothing has changed at the Château de Cognac. The same vaults, the same ageing, the same care devoted to this great Cognac' (ibid., p. 155).

The ostentatious, gratuitous expense implied in the purchase of a 'priceless' object is the most indisputable way of showing the price one is prepared to set on things that have no price, an absolute testimony of the irreducibility of love to money which only money can buy: 'What is true luxury? Refinement; a necessity for those who can afford it, and a key for those who, when they see it, train their eye, their taste, and can find it in the simplest object, a scarf, a skirt, a pair of shoes, a garment, if it is beautiful. But expensive? Haute couture is absolute rigour and the absolute has no price' (Marc Bohan, artistic director of the Christian Dior company, interview).

'You have to be Perrier-Jouet and own the finest vineyard on the slopes of Cramant to afford this folly and to offer it to others: a Champagne made from the most expensive grapes in the world. But the 78 centilitres in this 18th century bottle have no price for a lover of Champagne for its own sake. Especially when it's an exceptional vintage' (*Connaissance des Arts,* November 1973, p. 14). 'To highlight your personality, we create luxurious, delicate watches ... made only in limited editions. Each of our watches brings out the personality of the discriminating purchaser ... You will become the owner of an exclusive, precious timepiece' (ibid., p. 81).

One might be reading Marx, who writes: 'Man is initially posited as a private property owner, i.e., an exclusive owner whose exclusive ownership permits him both to preserve his personality and to distinguish himself from other men, as well as relate to them ... private property is man's personal, distinguishing and hence essential existence.'[16] The appropriation of symbolic objects with a material existence, such as paintings, raises the distinctive force of ownership to the second power and reduces purely symbolic appropriation to the inferior status of a symbolic substitute. To appropriate a work of art is to assert oneself as the exclusive possessor of the object and of the authentic taste for that object, which is thereby converted into the reified negation of all those who are unworthy of possessing it, for lack of the material or symbolic means of doing so, or simply for lack of a desire to possess it strong enough to 'sacrifice everything for it'.

The consumption of works of art, an almost too obvious illustration of this argument, is only one, among others, of these distinctive practices. Consider the new cult of nature which the fashion for second homes and the refusal of petit-bourgeois tourism have brought back into favour and which has a deep affinity with the *'vieille France'* life-style of the most 'ancient' fraction among the dominant fractions. Animals, flowers, hunting, gastronomy, environment, riding, gardening, fishing, 'oenology', rambling, the regular topics of the Parisian journal *Connaissance de la Campagne* (which is to the distinguished tasting of nature as *Connaissance des Arts* is to the distinguished tasting of culture), present an exhaustive programme of the legitimate objects and modes of appropriation. Appropriating 'nature'—birds, flowers, landscapes—presupposes a culture, the privilege of those who have ancient roots. Owning a château, a manor house or grange is not only a question of money; one must also appropriate it, appropriate the cellar and learn the art of bottling, described as 'an act of deep communion with the wine' which every 'believer' should have performed 'at least once', acquire trophies, the secrets of fishing, the skills of gardening, competences which are both ancient and slowly learned, like cooking or knowledge of wines, appropriate, in a word, the art of living of the aristocrat, or country gentleman, indifferent to the passage of time and rooted in things which last. 'There's nothing easier than pickling gherkins, my mother claims. As long as you pick them by a new moon, as long as you sweat them in cooking salt for twenty-four hours in a stoneware pot after rubbing them with a linen cloth, the only sort that is rough enough. As long as you add dried but not bone dry tarragon and bend them to pack them in tightly ... etc.' (*Connaissance de la Campagne*, September 1973). A pot of 'home-made gherkins', 'made to grandma's recipe' and brought to the table with the appropriate verbal accompaniment—as when exhibiting the 'little picture by an eighteenth-century French master' spotted at the antique-dealer's, or the 'exquisite little piece of furniture' unearthed in a junk shop—symbolizes a squandering of time and a competence which can only be acquired by long frequentation of old, cultivated people and things, that is, membership of an ancient group, the sole guarantee of possession of all the properties which are endowed with the highest distinctive value because they can only be accumulated over time.

What is at stake is indeed 'personality', i.e., the quality of the person, which is affirmed in the capacity to appropriate an object of quality.[17] The objects endowed with the greatest distinctive power are those which most clearly attest the quality of the appropriation, and therefore the quality of their owner, because their possession requires time and capacities which, requiring a long investment of time, like pictorial or musical culture, cannot be acquired in haste or by proxy, and which therefore appear as the surest indications of the quality of the person. This explains the importance which the pursuit of distinction attaches to all those activities which, like artistic consumption, demand pure, pointless expenditure, especially of the rarest and most precious thing of all—particularly for those whose market value gives them least of it to waste—namely, time, time devoted to consumption or time devoted to the cultural acquisition which adequate consumption presupposes.

One has to bear in mind, firstly, that time, despite the possibility of appropriating other people's time or of saving time by rationalization and by exploiting the freedom to avoid the effects of overcrowding by using unusual times and places, is one of the most rigorous anthropological limits, and, secondly, that the market value of time—more or less directly experienced, depending on the mode of remuneration (consultation fees, monthly salary or profits)—increases as one rises in the social hierarchy, in order to understand the value of the potlatch of time. This term can be applied to all the practices involving the 'granting' or 'giving' of time to others—an important dimension of what is offered at receptions—and, of course, to all leisure activities whose symbolic value always lies partly in the capacity to dominate time and money that is affirmed in 'taking one's time', i.e., expending such valuable time to no purpose.

Of all the conversion techniques designed to create and accumulate symbolic capital, the purchase of works of art, objectified evidence of 'personal taste', is the one which is closest to the most irreproachable and inimitable form of accumulation, that is, the internalization of distinctive signs and symbols of power in the form of natural 'distinction', personal 'authority' or 'culture'. The exclusive appropriation of priceless works is not without analogy to the ostentatious destruction of wealth; the irreproachable exhibition of wealth which it permits is, simultaneously, a challenge thrown down to all those who cannot dissociate their 'being' from their 'having' and attain disinterestedness, the supreme affirmation of personal excellence. And as is shown, for example, by the primacy given to literary and artistic culture over scientific or technical culture, the exclusive possessors of a 'vast culture' behave no differently when they fling into the potlatch of social encounters the time they have spent without thought for immediate profit in exercises as prestigious as they are useless.

The dominant fractions do not have a monopoly of the uses of the work of art that are objectively—and sometimes subjectively—oriented towards the exclusive appropriation which attests the owner's unique 'personality'. But in the absence of the conditions of material possession, the pursuit of exclusiveness has to be content with developing a unique mode of appropriation. Liking the same things differently, liking different things, less obviously marked out for admiration—these are some of the strategies for outflanking, overtaking and displacing which, by maintaining a permanent revolution in tastes, enable the dominated, less wealthy fractions, whose appropriations must, in the main, be exclusively symbolic, to secure exclusive possessions at every moment. Intellectuals and artists have a special predilection for the most risky but also most profitable strategies of distinction, those which consist in asserting the power, which is peculiarly theirs, to constitute insignificant objects as works of art or, more subtly, to give aesthetic redefinition to objects already defined as art, but in another mode, by other classes or class fractions (e.g., kitsch). In this case, it is the manner of consuming which creates the object of consumption, and a second-degree delight which transforms the 'vulgar' artifacts abandoned to common consumption, Westerns, strip cartoons, family snapshots, graffiti, into distinguished and distinctive works of culture.

The Variants of the Dominant Taste

The ascetic colouring of the teachers' and intellectuals' cultural practices stands out clearly when they are replaced in the system to which they belong, and when it becomes necessary to raise the question of the very meaning of culture and symbolic appropriation—the sublimated substitutes for all material appropriations and all the fruits of the earth which the division of the labour of domination leaves for the poor relations. The antagonism between the life-styles corresponding to the opposing poles of the field of the dominant class is clear-cut, total, and the opposition between the teachers and the employers (particularly between the lower and middle ranks of the two categories) is comparable to the gap between two 'cultures' in the anthropological sense. On one side, reading, and reading poetry, philosophical and political works, *Le Monde,* and the (generally leftish) literary or artistic magazines; on the other, hunting or betting, and, when there is reading, reading *France-Soir* or *l'Aurore, Auto-Journal* or *Lectures pour tous.*[18] On one side, classic or avant-garde theatre (with, for example, Roger Planchon's productions of *Tartuffe* or *La remise,* Lorca's *Blood Wedding* or Turgenev's *A Month in the Country*), museums, classical music, France-Musique, the Flea Market, camping, mountaineering or walking; on the other, business trips and expense-account lunches, boulevard theatre (Robert Lamoureux, Marcel Achard, Françoise Dorin) and music-hall, variety shows on TV, commercial exhibitions, the auction room and 'boutiques', luxury cars and a boat, three-star hotels and spas (C.S. V). And the style itself of the different cultural practices, the social philosophies and world views they imply, are seen much more clearly if one bears in mind the universes of practices to which they belong; if one knows, for example, that avant-garde theatre, or reading poetry or philosophy, is opposed to bourgeois theatre or the music-hall, to the reading of historical or adventure novels or glossy magazines, as the teachers' walking, camping, mountain or country holidays are opposed both to the set of luxury activities and goods which characterize the old bourgeoisie—Mercedes or Volvo, yachts, hotel holidays in spa towns—and to the constellation of the most expensive and prestigious cultural and material possessions and practices—art books, movie cameras, tape recorders, motorboats, skiing, golf, riding or water-skiing—which distinguish the liberal professions.

The clearest indication that aesthetic choices belong to the set of ethical choices which constitutes a life-style is the opposition which emerges, in the aesthetic area itself, between two categories as close to each other with respect to cultural capital as the members of the professions and the

Luxury Trade Directory from le goût du luxe

ANIMALS
Retail
Oisellerie du Pont-Neuf
Oisellerie Vilmorin

Taxidermist
Nérée, Boubée et Cie

ANTIQUES
Aaron
Bensimon
Hagnauer
Jansen
Kugel
Lagrand
Laroussilhe
Lévy
Litybur
Mallie de Fonfais
Mancel
Perrin
Taillemas

ARTISTS (HIRE)
Marouani et Tavel

ASTROLOGERS
Belline
Criss
Delya
Martinez
Sabato

BATHROOM
Au Bain de Diane
Juif-Delepine

BEAUTY PARLOURS
Elizabeth Arden
Carita
Guerlain
Harriet Hubbard Ayer
Lancôme
Germaine Monteil
Helena Rubinstein

BOOTS
Roger Vivier

CARPETS
Benadava
Catan

CATERERS
Battendier
Casimir
Lenotre
Marquise de Presles

Pons
Potel et Chablot
Scott

CHATEAUX (HIRE)
Préfecture d'Indre-et Loire

CHILDREN
Clothes
Baby Dior
Dominique
Enfantillage
Petit Faune
Petite Gaminerie
Minimômes

Furniture
Bonnichon
Thireau

Toys
Le Nain Bleu

CLINICS
Clinique du Belvédère

Veterinary clinics
Clinique du Dr. Neienat
Clinique vétérinaire de
    Maisons-Alfort
Fondation Windsor
Hôpital Frégis

DOCTORS
Boivin
Chartier
Dolto
Dubost
Hervé
Lacan
Lagache
Leibovici
Nacht
Vellay

DOMESTIC STAFF
Bons Secours

DRY CLEANING
Billard
Bobin
Pouyanne
Starisky

EMBALMING
Ets Marette
Roblot

FIREWORKS
Ruggieri

FLORISTS
Boullet
Lachaume
Lambert
Moreux
Veyrat

FURS
Révillon

HAIRDRESSERS
Alexandre
Arden
Carita
Jean-Louis David

HAUTE COUTURE
Balmain
Cardin
Courrèges
Dior
Hermès
Lapidus
Rabanne
Saint-Laurent
Ungaro

INTERIOR
DECORATORS
Carlhian
Demachy
Jansen

JEWELLERY
Boucheron
Cartier
Chaumet
Van Cleef & Arpels
Mauboussin

LEATHER GOODS
Hermès
Morabito

PROVISIONS
Côte-de France
Dominique
Fauchon
Godiva
Hédiard
Petrossian
Maison de la Truffe

SILVERWARE, CHINA
Andrieux
Helft
Kugel
Nicolier

TRAVEL
Car Hire
Murdoch

Cruises
International Sea Service

Rail
SNCF—DCP

S. Schroeder and J. Matignon, *Le goût du luxe* (Paris, Balland, 1972).

Pascal then took her to the drug store for an ice cream. Sipping a Pimm's, he undertook to complete her education. He enumerated his domestic servants—butler, major-domo, chauffeur, nanny, chamber-maid, valet, cook, gardener—and solemnly indicated their wages.

Domestic servants

Butler	per month	1,500F
Majordomo	"	1,500F
Chauffeur	"	1,500F
Nanny	"	1,200F
Chambermaid	"	1,100F
Valet	"	1,000F
Cook	"	1,000F
Gardener according to region	"	800F

He regretted that there were no boxes for life at the Comédie-Française and disdained, mischievously no doubt, the price of season tickets for evening-dress performances.

Comédie-Française

Season tickets	
Evening-dress	108F
Classical matinées	85F

He spoke of fashionable doctors, with mysterious honoraria, whether obstetricians, such as Drs. Hervé, Dubost, Velley or Chartier, or psychoanalysts, such as Drs. Lacan, Daniel Lagache, Sacha Nacht, Leibovici, Mme. Dolto.

Doctors

Psychoanalyst, little known		
	per session	60F
Psychoanalyst, famous		
	per session, from	200F

He described a suite overlooking the garden at the Belvedere Clinic in Boulogne-sur-Seine, where it was only forbidden to plug in film projection equipment so as to avoid endangering the electrical system—but this restriction could be lifted by special permission of the management.

Clinics

Most expensive: Belvedere Clinic
Confinement
including: maternity ward, treatment, meals and usual medicines.

Small room overlooking courtyard	800F
Small room overlooking garden	800F
Medium room overlooking garden	950F
Large room overlooking garden	1,000F
Suite overlooking garden	1,250F

Not included:
Service and taxes, special medicines, drinks, laundry, telephone etc.

Le goût du luxe, pp. 187–189.

teachers.[19] Based on the opposition between ethical dispositions corresponding to different trajectories, it is reinforced and brought to fruition by very different economic conditions.

Once one considers, in addition to the differences in respect to capital composition, those deriving from trajectory, and in particular the fact that the proportion of individuals who owe their place in the dominant class to the accumulation of educational capital rises as one moves from the dominant fractions to the dominated fractions, it is clear why teachers and, secondarily, engineers and executives are those most inclined to direct the ascetic dispositions developed by and for previous cultural accumulation towards further such accumulation—all the more readily since their low economic capital does not lead them to expect many alternative pleasures and profits. By contrast, the members of the professions have the means to realize the dispositions towards indulgence in luxury which are associated with a bourgeois origin and which are encouraged by the requirements of occupations presupposing a large accumulation of symbolic capital. The ascetic aristocratism of the teachers (and public-sector executives), who are systematically oriented towards the least expensive and most austere leisure activities and towards serious and even somewhat severe cultural practices—visiting museums, for example, especially in the provinces (rather than major exhibitions, galleries and foreign museums, like the members of the professions)—is opposed to the luxury tastes of the members of the professions, who amass the (culturally or economically) most expensive and most prestigious activities, reading expensive glossy magazines, visiting antique-dealers, galleries and concert-halls, holidaying in spa towns, owning pianos, illustrated art books, antique furniture, works of art, movie cameras, tape recorders, foreign cars, skiing, playing tennis and golf, riding, hunting and water-skiing.

As in our survey, the third factor brought out by analysis of the correspondences in the SOFRES survey separates all other fractions from the members of the professions. The latter are particularly inclined to luxury goods and activities, as is shown by simply listing (in order of importance) the characteristics which make the highest absolute contributions to this factor: subscriptions to glossy monthly magazines, possession of a movie camera, water-skiing, possession of a tape recorder, art books, playing tennis, spa holidays, bridge, hunting, skiing, riding, business cocktails etc. Since one knows that magazines like *Connaissance des Arts* or *La Maison Française* have a high proportion of professionals among their readers (15.5 percent and 18.5 percent) one may, in addition, on the basis of the 1970 CESP survey, attribute to this fraction properties particularly frequent among the readers of these journals, such as possession of antique furniture and works of art, visits to auction rooms and galleries. One also knows from the INSEE 'leisure' survey that the members of the professions give a particularly large number of receptions.

The members of the professions, possessing neither the competence nor the dispositions needed to reinvest effectively in the economy the high economic profits they derive from their cultural capital, and being attached to 'intellectual values' by education and life-style (they provide a high proportion of the amateur writers),[20] find in smart sports and games, in receptions, cocktails and other society gatherings not only intrinsic satisfactions and edification but also the select society in which they can make and keep up their 'connections' and accumulate the capital of honourability they need in order to carry on their professions. This is only one of the cases in which luxury, 'a conventional degree of prodigality', becomes, as Marx observed, 'a business necessity' and 'enters into capital's expenses of representation' as 'an exhibition of wealth and consequently as a source of credit.'[21]

These generic tendencies take different forms depending on the profession, the speciality and the place of residence. Thus, doctors, who have a savings rate much higher than the national average (30 percent of disposable income, as against 15 percent) but with an incomparably higher income, spend a very high percentage of their very high income, particularly on holidays (10 percent of disposable income), cars and 'consumer durables'. Very often owning their own homes (two-thirds of them do), they often own second homes, investment property, agricultural property, woods and land (hardly ever industrial companies) and also shares. Property purchases are most frequent among rural general practitioners, whereas financial investments, which generally increase with age, are more frequent among surgeons and specialists.[22] One may assume that surgeons and other specialists—especially in Paris—devote a particularly high proportion of their income to luxury expenditure, particularly the purchase of works of art.

By contrast, each of the teachers' choices (their preference for a harmonious, sober, discreet interior, for example, or for simple but well-presented meals) can be understood as a way of making a virtue of necessity by maximizing the profit they can draw from their cultural capital and their spare time (while minimizing their financial outlay). If the professionals do not always have the tastes to match their means, the teachers hardly ever have the means to match their tastes, and this disparity between cultural and economic capital condemns them to an ascetic aestheticism (a more austere variant of the 'artist' life-style) which 'makes the most' of what it has, substituting 'rustic' for antique, Romanian carpets for Persian carpets, a converted barn for an ancestral manor-house, lithographs (or reproductions) for paintings—unavowed substitutes which, like really poor people's leatherette or 'sparkling white' wine, are the tributes deprivation pays to possession.[23] The disparity between economic capital and cultural capital, or, more precisely, the educational capital which is its certified form, is undoubtedly one of the

A 'Truly Classical' University Teacher

Jean L., aged 36, an alumnus of the Ecole Normale Supérieure, has the *agrégation* in physics. He is now a *maître-assistant* (senior lecturer or assistant professor) in one of the Paris universities and lives in the north-western suburbs. His father (an *agrégé* in grammar) was a lycée teacher and his grandfather a primary teacher. His wife, a pharmacist's daughter, is a dentist. She teaches at the Paris Dental School and also runs her own practice.

'A Louis XIII convent table from the Flea Market'

Preferring 'sobriety' and 'discretion', Jean dislikes 'fat cushions and heavy curtains', and 'apartments done up by interior designers.' He is 'quite sensitive to the overall harmony of an interior': 'If you're lucky enough to come across a really fine piece of furniture, you put that one piece in a corner. That's all you need for a whole room.' 'At home, until recently, we had cheap furniture that we bought when we married. A quietly modern style that wasn't unattractive. Veneered teak, quite cheap, but now the chairs are giving up the ghost ... Now we have one or two old bits of furniture that we've picked up, real antiques ... a Louis XIII convent table that someone spotted for us in the Flea Market, a Louis XIII chest that isn't bad', found in an antique shop in Amiens. 'Of course, we won't be getting any Louis XIII chairs—for one thing they're terribly expensive, and anyway, if they're genuine, they're not even solid. So we'll get some made for us in the same style

but without pretending to be antique.' The decorating and furnishing of the house are mainly left to his wife, who attaches a great deal of importance to them. 'She's quite expert at that, I'm not, especially as regards prices ... I enjoy it, but when all's said and done, if I were on my own I don't think I'd devote much time to it. I haven't got much of a taste for it, but my wife certainly has and in the end I do appreciate it, all the same.' His wife is very fond of old *faïence:* 'I'm always willing to accompany her if she says, "Come along, let's go and look at some porcelain." I know I'll enjoy it, I know she's much more sensitive to it than I am.... There's one thing I'd really like to buy, I haven't done so yet, but I sometimes look: it's old scientific instruments, because they used to make some remarkable things in the last century and three or four centuries back.'

'I'd rather read something more concentrated'

At home, he does a bit of amateur carpentry, 'out of duty'. 'My wife's the one who says this or that needs doing, and I do it, taking quite unnecessary trouble over it. I could do it quicker if I did it less carefully, but I enjoy designing things, working them out and then making them.'

He does not have a TV set at home but manages to watch from time to time. 'The interest of the things they're dealing with often gets diluted. On any given subject, I'd rather read something more concentrated. Still, there are some things for which it's irreplaceable. I have to admit, I went to my mother's to see the first moon land-ing, things like that. . . . I remember seeing Ivan Illich for five minutes; it was unforgettable, I'm glad I saw what he looks like instead of just reading him.'

'All my reading used to be based on *Le Monde*'

He subscribes to *Tribune Socialiste*— 'it's not bad'—and occasionally reads *Le Nouvel Observateur*. His wife takes *L'Express:* 'It gives a superficial view of events, though some of the interviews are good. All my reading used to be based on *Le Monde*. I used to receive it regularly. But now I don't read it every day.' His reading is somewhat austere, no detective stories or novels: 'Solzhenitsyn's *First Circle*, all the same, because my wife said I ought to read it.' He has also recently read *Deschooling Society* by Illich ('It made a great impression on me'), *Chance and Necessity* (Monod), and Konrad Lorenz's *On Aggression*. He owns a UNESCO history of world cultures in seven or eight volumes: 'It's marvellous, it isn't a narrative, certainly not a narrative; if there are characters and so on, that doesn't interest me. Archaeology, now, that interests me a lot. . . . Something I browse in a good deal is the *Dictionary of Archaeology*.'

'Truly classical, restrained things'

'A Vermeer is something I can gaze at for two hours and I feel really satisfied, whereas that [a book of drawings by 'a guy called Escher'] not at all.' He much appreciates a history of art in the series edited by Francastel. 'The text is outstanding. There aren't many reproductions, and they're not brilliant, though they're relatively original, but they're good because they analyse the painters' ideas, not just anecdotically but the way they connect with the economic and social structures of the period.' He 'doesn't "do" museums exhaustively,' but is 'always willing to go': 'I'm quite prepared to go along if a friend says "Look, there's something I want to go and see", or if I've seen or read something. . . . I'm always willing to go, and I spend a certain amount of time there.' He has been to Tuscany several times: 'I love everything there is to be seen there . . . I enjoy situating the painters of the period in relation to one another; I say to myself, Angelico was still painting like this while someone else was doing that.' He particularly likes 'the Quattrocento, Botticelli, Piero della Francesca and also Vermeer and Watteau.' 'I don't quite know how to put it, whether it's the subject, or the technique. . . . I like the surfaces, and that sort of grace, charm, melancholy.' He realizes that painters cannot dispense with stylistic devices, but he dislikes those of Rousseau: 'There's something unnatural, over-deliberate, over-sophisticated about his technique.' 'Matisse, now, truly classical, restrained things, those I do like. I like a lot of Picasso's work, and Villon, the little I know of it. To be honest, I'm not well up on modern painting. . . . There's one thing which to me is *not* painting, and that's the whole of Surrealism. In my view it's a purely intellectual exercise. Dali and company are something I detest.'

'I prefer *The Art of Fugue* on the organ'

He has no hi-fi ('I'd quite like to have one, but for me it's not essential'), but he does have 'a record-player that isn't bad' ('mono, I bought it for 600 francs four or five years ago'). 'In my view, music is something you ought to go and see done by the people who make it. That's the best way. Otherwise, at home, you just need something reasonable to play the records on and some good performances. . . . I'm not enormously sensitive to the performance, but still, I do appreciate it.' His 'sense of the economy of means', his taste of 'sobriety' and 'also his scientific training' incline him to appreciate 'pure music'. *'The Art of Fugue,* for example, I prefer that on the organ rather than an orchestral version, it really is pure music, it's not a question of timbre.' He dislikes 'Romantic music, it's too emphatic, too grandiloquent. For example, I like Berlioz, but the *Fantastic Symphony* is too rhetorical.' Although he has 'all sorts of minor activities', he is 'busy four evenings a week with meetings, choir rehearsals' (with a choral society he joined ten years ago): 'and nowadays, with a group of opera-lovers, you do a bit of opera, a bit of *lieder,* it takes up a lot of time in the end.' 'For me, the summit of music is Mozart . . . *Così fan tutte* . . . I adore all of Poulenc, I like Delalande . . . I really enjoyed *Wozzeck* when Boulez conducted it at the Paris Opera. It was the first time I'd heard it.' He goes to concerts four or five times a year. 'Earlier this week I went to hear Fischer-Dieskau; for me he's the god of singing.' He scarcely ever listens to light music or non-classical singers, and has never bought any of their records ('I like Brassens, but I don't listen to him').

'Effective use of limited means'

He is 'not really a connoisseur of films'; he often 'just goes to the local cinema in D. to see the current releases if they're not too bad.'

He likes Truffaut but 'is impervious to the American arts' ('I find a lot of American films a bit puerile, except Woody Allen'). He doesn't watch many historical films, but, 'Obviously Abel Gance's *Napoleon,* that was something not to be missed, or *The Battleship Potemkin,* or *Alexander Nevsky.'* 'I'm very allergic to anything that strikes me as overdone. I like someone to show me something he feels very strongly, making effective use of limited means.'

He is neither a 'gastronome' nor a 'connoisseur', but he is 'fairly sensitive' to the food he is offered. 'When friends invite me for a meal, it's a pleasure I take notice of, I appreciate it.' He 'tries to keep a few presentable wines in the house' ('I've found a little dealer specializing in Beaujolais. I like some of the things he has to offer, and that's how I stock my cellar').

'I rush out walking'

He 'would like to be able to play chess' and sometimes plays scrabble. He does a bit of photography: 'I end up using two rolls of thirty-six pictures a year, mainly on holiday. One thing I typically do when I'm on holiday in the mountains is to take pictures of landscapes . . . then I spend hours poring over a map working out what can be seen.' On holiday 'I rush out walking and then, like an idiot, I do forty kilometres at top speed on the first day and then my feet are swollen for a fortnight. When I go walking, I do it fairly intensively, but unfortunately there are long periods when I don't do any. . . . For the last year I've had a dog, and she has to be taken for walks. I do that at a furious pace. . . . I take her out on Saturdays and we run half the time. We cover ten kilometres at full speed.'

foundations of their propensity to contest a social order which does not fully recognize their merits because it recognizes other principles of classification than those of the educational system which has classified them. This meritocratic (and therefore, in a sense, aristocratic) revolt is intensified when it is combined with the loyalties, refusals and impossibilities, or refusals of the impossible, which are linked to a petit-bourgeois or working-class origin and which, together with purely economic constraints, prevent full membership in the bourgeoisie.

One of the subjectively acceptable ways of escaping from the contradictions resulting from the fact that cultural capital is a dominated principle of domination lies in participation as a cadre in the organizations claiming to express and defend the interests of the dominated classes. Thus the distribution of the members of the different dominant-class fractions who aspire (with unequal chances of success) to positions as political representatives (which can be gauged by analysing the social characteristics of parliamentary candidates) corresponds fairly strictly to the distribution of their respective fractions in the field of the dominant class. It follows from this that political struggles are one of the arenas of the struggle to impose the legitimate (i.e., dominant) principle of domination.

By contrast, for those who, like the professionals, live on the sale of cultural services to a clientele, the accumulation of economic capital merges with the accumulation of symbolic capital, that is, with the acquisition of a reputation for competence and an image of respectability and honourability that are easily converted into political positions as a local or national *notable*. It is therefore understandable that they should identify with the established (moral) order to which they make daily contributions, of which their political positions and actions, or the declarations of the national medical association, are only the most visible form.

According to a SOFRES survey of a national sample of two hundred doctors made before the first round of the 1974 presidential election, 59 percent said they would vote for Giscard, 16 percent for Mitterrand, 9 percent for Chaban-Delmas (the Gaullist candidate) and 11 percent for another candidate, and 5 percent were undecided. Asked who they thought was most likely to win, 71 percent said Giscard, 16 percent Mitterrand, 9 percent Chaban-Delmas and 1 percent another candidate, and 13 percent would not predict.[24] One can get an idea of what the doctors were voting for in Giscard by reading the interview with him in the same issue of *Le Quotidien du Médecin* that reports the survey, in which he declares himself in favour of highly selective recruitment, the maintenance of the 'liberal profession', the family practitioner and the coexistence of public and private hospital treatment, promises to eliminate 'wastage' in the Social Security system and sees no need for any reform of the Ordre des médecins.

So the contrast that is usually drawn between 'intellectual' or left-bank taste and 'bourgeois' or right-bank taste is not only an opposition between the preference for contemporary works (here, within the limits of the lists offered, Picasso, Kandinsky, Boulez) and the taste for older, more consecrated works (the Impressionists and especially Renoir, Watteau, the *Hungarian Rhapsody,* the *Four Seasons, Eine Kleine Nachtmusik*), between the taste for solid values, in painting and music, as in cinema and theatre, and the commitment to novelty. It is also an opposition between two world views, two philosophies of life, symbolized, for example, by Renoir and Goya (or Maurois and Kafka), the centres of two constellations of choices, *la vie en rose* and *la vie en noir,* rose-coloured spectacles and dark thoughts, boulevard theatre and avant-garde theatre, the social optimism of people without problems and the anti-bourgeois pessimism of people with problems—the opposition between material and mental comfort, with intimate, discreet interiors and traditional French cooking, and aesthetic and intellectual invention, with the taste for exotic dishes or (by inversion) pot-luck, 'studied' interiors, or (by inversion) those that are easy to maintain, furniture from the Flea Market and avant-garde shows.[25]

The oppositions between systems of purely aesthetic preferences that are symbolized by the antithesis Kandinsky/Renoir can be replaced in the sets of choices constituting life-styles simply by considering the characteristics of an audience such as that of *Connaissance des Arts.* This relatively expensive, luxury cultural journal, which is at the same time an advertising medium for the luxury goods trade, especially in objets d'art, no doubt gives a fairly accurate picture of the groups who are united by 'bourgeois taste' and who are brought together by the most select and also most expensive cultural events—smart exhibitions, gala performances at the Paris Opera, premieres, major concerts etc. The common features of the private-sector executives and professionals—and the many fewer, and therefore strongly over-selected, teachers and industrial employers—who make up this readership are a liking for expensive, prestigious activities (golf, riding) and for cultural practices oriented at least as much towards material appropriation as towards merely symbolic appropriation, frequenting theatres and galleries (predominantly right-bank), auction rooms, antique shops and luxury boutiques. The 'bourgeois taste' which characterizes them is opposed not only to 'intellectual' taste but also (essentially by possession of works of art, gallery- and theatre-going) to the 'middling' taste of the great majority of the industrial and especially the commercial employers, great readers of *Auto-Journal,* who appropriate only those rare goods to which money gives direct access, such as luxury cars (C.S. VI).

To measure the distance between the 'bourgeois' public and the 'intellectual' public, one only has to observe that the proportion of students, teachers and artists is 53 percent at the Saintes ancient music festival, 60 percent at the La Rochelle contemporary arts festival, 66 percent at the Nancy international (avant-garde) theatre festival, 83 percent at the Royan contemporary music festival; and that rate of attendance varies in the same way, rising from an average of 3.5 shows per person at Saintes to 5 at La Rochelle and 7 at Nancy and Royan (C.S. XXIX, XXX).

Whereas the 'intellectual' fractions expect rather from the artist a symbolic challenging of social reality and of the orthodox representation of it in 'bourgeois' art, the 'bourgeois' fractions expect their artists, their writers, their critics, like their couturiers, jewellers or interior designers, to provide emblems of distinction which are at the same time means of denying social reality. Luxury goods and works of art are only the most visible aspect of this décor enveloping bourgeois existence, or at least, the private, domestic part of a fundamentally dual life, spuriously unified in and through a spurious division against itself, disinterestedness against interest, art against money, the spiritual against the temporal. Polite political newspapers, discreetly politicized or ostentatiously depoliticized, decorative journals and coffee-table art books, Blue Guides and travel stories, regional novels and biographies of great men are so many screens to hide social reality. 'Bourgeois' theatre, a scarcely 'de-realized' representation of one of the forms of bourgeois existence, with its beautiful stage sets, pretty women, facile adventures, frivolous conversation and reassuring philosophy (any other combination of the nouns and adjectives is equally valid), is no doubt the form par excellence of the art the 'bourgeois' recognizes because he recognizes himself in it. The bourgeoisie expects from art (not to mention what it calls literature or philosophy) a reinforcement of its self-assurance, and, as much out of sufficiency as insufficiency, it can never really recognize the audacities of the avant-garde, even in the most highly neutralized arts, such as music. And for every enlightened amateur who has understood that it costs nothing to be, like Proust's Mme. de Cambremer, 'in art, always on the left', there are many present-day admirers of Flaubert or Mahler who have the same impatience with disorder, even symbolic, and the same horror of 'movement', even artistically sublimated, as their counterparts in the past.

In fact, a class or class fraction is defined not so much by its overall judgement of intellectuals or artists in general (although anti-intellectualism is a determinant characteristic of some fractions of the bourgeoisie and petite bourgeoisie) as by the artists and intellectuals it chooses from the range offered by the field of production. Thus the anti-intellectualism of the dominant fraction of the dominant class may be expressed in the choice of intellectuals who are inclined to anti-intellectualism by their own position in the intellectual field. The further one moves from the 'purest' genres, i.e., those most completely purified of all reference to the social world and politics (first music, then poetry, philosophy and painting), the wider the gap between the producers recognized by the dominant fractions—playwrights and theatre critics or philosophers and political essayists—and those recognized by the producers themselves. Furthermore, as one is reminded by the reaction it arouses among the declining petit bourgeois, the artist's lifestyle, in particular everything in it which challenges the ordinary relationships between age (or social status) and symbolic attributes, such as clothing, or behaviour, such as sexual or political conduct, contains a denunciation of the practical postulates which are the basis of the bourgeois life-style. Like the old women in Australian myths, who overthrow the structure of relations between the generations by magically conserving a smooth, youthful skin, artists and intellectuals (like Sartre refusing a Nobel prize or frequenting young revolutionaries at an age when others pursue honours and cultivate the powerful) can sometimes call into question one of the most deeply buried foundations of the social order, Spinoza's *obsequium*, the disposition of those who have 'self-respect' and feel entitled to command respect.

One has to take into account the whole logic of the field of artistic production and its relationship to the field of the dominant class to understand why avant-garde artistic production is bound to disappoint bourgeois expectations—unequally, and always in the short term.[26] It is no accident that the taste for the artistic avant-garde appears in the analysis only at the end of a series of oppositions. In fact, everything takes place as if, although it embodies artistic legitimacy, the artistic producers' taste for the avant-garde defined itself in a quasi-negative way, as the sum of the refusals of all socially recognized tastes: refusal of the middle-of-the-road taste of the big shopkeepers and parvenu industrialists, the 'grocers' pilloried by Flaubert and others as one incarnation of the 'bourgeois', and especially, perhaps, at present, the petite bourgeoisie, led by their cultural pretension to the products of middle-brow culture or the most accessible products of legitimate culture (such as light opera or the easiest boulevard theatre), which are immediately devalued by their new audience; refusal of bourgeois taste, i.e., the typically right-bank luxury taste, which has some accomplices among the artists; and, finally, refusal of the teachers' 'pedantic taste',[27] which though opposed to bourgeois taste is, in the eyes of the artists, merely a variant of it, disdained for its heavy, pettifogging, passive, sterile didacticism, its 'spirit of seriousness', and most of all for its prudence and backwardness. And so the logic of double negation can lead the artists back, as if in defiance, to some of the preferences characteristic of popular taste. For example, they concur with the working classes and the lower fractions of the middle classes, from which they differ in every other way, in choosing an interior that is 'practical and functional', 'easy to maintain', the antithesis of 'bourgeois comfort'; just as they may rehabilitate, but at the second degree, the most derided forms of popular taste (kitsch, pop art). The 'artist' life-style which is defined by this distance from all other life-styles and their temporal attachments presupposes a particular type of asset structure in which time functions as an independent factor, partly interchangeable with economic capital. But spare time and the disposition to defend it, by renouncing what it could be used to earn, presuppose both the (inherited) capital needed to make renunciation materially possible and the—highly aristocratic—disposition to renounce.

Artists, by an almost complete inversion of the ordinary world view, frequently consider money (often earned through activities external to their craft) as a means of buying time to work and to lead the 'artist's life' which is an integral part of their specific activity.[28] Thus artists (and intellectuals) exchange money, which they could otherwise earn, for time, the time which has to be spent without counting to produce objects which often (in the short term) have no markets, and to 'discover' objects and places whose rarity and value they help to produce, antiques, back-street restaurants, new shows etc.; and they quasi-exclusively appropriate collective goods or services (museums, galleries, cultural broadcasts). Variations in spare time and in the relation to time are, together with unequal propensity to consume, among the factors which make patterns of expenditure very unequal guides to the resources of each class.

The Mark of Time

In no other class is the opposition between the young and old, the challengers and the possessors—and also the opposition between the senior members of the class and the newcomers, which cannot always be superimposed upon it (since, in some sectors at least, the most senior are also the most precocious)—more determinant than in the dominant class, which can ensure its own perpetuation only if it is capable of overcoming the crises that are liable to arise from the competition between the fractions to impose the dominant principle of domination and from the succession struggles within each fraction. The differences between the generations (and the potential for generation conflicts) increase with the magnitude of the changes that have occurred in the definitions of occupational positions or in the institutionalized means of access to them, i.e., the modes of generation of the individuals appointed to them.[29] Consequently, the differences due to the diversity of routes into a given job at a given moment (particularly visible in populations which are highly dispersed in this respect, like the executives and engineers) are coupled with the differences resulting from the variations over time in the job description and in the conditions of access to the job, in particular the variations in the relative importance of the different routes which are linked to changes in the educational system and its relation to industry.

The opposition between the oldest, who valorize the most ascetic ethical dispositions, and the youngest, who identify with the values most typical of the modern executive, is particularly marked among the executives and engineers (and secondarily among the teachers and professionals). For example, in the dominant class as a whole, 51.5 percent of the over-45s choose a 'conscientious' friend, as against 24.5 percent of the under-45s, 39 percent of whom choose 'dynamic' as against 19.5 percent of the over-45s; among the executives and engineers, 42.5 percent of the under-45s and 8 percent of the over-45s choose 'dynamic', while 15 percent of the under-45s and 54 percent of the over-45s choose 'conscientious'. (Similar variations, always more marked among executives and engineers, are observed for 'determined', which varies like 'dynamic', or 'well-bred', which varies like 'conscientious'.) A similar evolution (no doubt linked to a general increase in cultural capital) is found in tastes in legitimate culture: thus, the younger executives and engineers more often choose *Rhapsody in Blue* (32 percent as against 17.5 percent) or the *Four Seasons* (47 percent and 24 percent), less often *L'Arlésienne* (14.5 percent and 28 percent), *Hungarian Rhapsody* (32 percent and 58.5 percent), *Blue Danube* (13 percent and 30.5 percent).

These historical variations are particularly significant in the case of the fractions most directly linked to the economy, the engineers and executives, but they have, in a more insidious way, affected the whole of the dominant class. They are likely to pass unnoticed because they always manifest themselves in combination with age, so that they can easily be taken for an effect of biological or even social age rather than generation, and because they are translated into trajectories, i.e., individual histories which are so many responses to a given state of the chances objectively offered to a whole generation by collective history.

The 'liberal professions' (doctors, at least) have succeeded in maintaining the traditional definition of their job and the competence it requires by defending, among other things, the most Malthusian conditions of access, thus in a sense escaping from history and the divisions between the generations. By contrast, categories such as those of the executives and engineers bring together individuals separated both in trajectory and in generation, in the sense of the set of products of a single mode of generation associated with a similar pattern of objective chances. In fact, because of the duality of the modes of access, by qualification and by promotion, and the corresponding divisions which prevented an organized defence of the modes of access and of the corresponding privileges, these categories have been much more directly affected by educational expansion, which, by increasing the number of formally qualified candidates entitled to jobs, has transformed the de facto relationship between titles and jobs and the form of the competition for jobs between formally qualified and non-qualified candidates.[30]

Furthermore, changes in the economy have been reflected in new numerical and hierarchical relationships between the different managerial and executive functions, thereby transforming the system of opportunities open to the products of the different types of training—autodidact candidates for promotion, engineers from the minor engineering schools, engineers from the scientific grandes écoles (Polytechnique, l'Ecole des Mines etc.), graduates of the various Instituts des sciences politiques or HEC etc. (It must, of course, always be remembered that the different responses of the various groups to the new situations arising from economic changes can be traced back to the differences in social and educational origin which have always determined important differences between individuals occupying formally identical positions at a given moment.) For example, the strengthening of finance and marketing departments relative to technical departments, resulting from the increased power of banks over industry and the growing internationalization of industrial groups, their capital, their management and their patents, has caused a revaluation of the qualifications and institutions leading to these positions, Sciences Po, ENA or HEC on the one hand, Polytechnique and the other engineering schools on the other hand, and, simultaneously, redistributed the chances available to the fractions of the bourgeoisie who use these institutions. Thus, as a result of changes in the economic structures, and chiefly through its use of the Paris Instituts des sciences politiques, situated at the bottom of the specifically academic hierarchy of the 'schools of power', the Parisian *grande bourgeoisie* has reappropriated, perhaps more completely than ever, the commanding positions in the economy and the civil service (provoking collective and individual ripostes by Polytechnique graduates, more and more of whom are taking a detour through Harvard, Columbia or M.I.T.).

In addition, the emergence of a large number of new positions, which promise profits at least equivalent to those of the established positions and strictly predictable career targets, but without offering the same guarantees of security, is tending to subvert the system of differential chances of profit. At least in the phase when both their risks and their profits are greatest, these new positions situated at critical points in the social structure are most attractive to those whose social origin has provided them with an inclination towards risky investments, the social connections needed in order to make them and the information needed in order to succeed in them.

Thus, within a category such as that of the engineers, it is possible to distinguish families of taste corresponding to sub-sets of individuals separated both with respect to cultural and educational capital and to seniority within the bourgeoisie. At one extreme is found the petit-bourgeois taste of the older engineers, originating from the middle or working classes and promoted from the ranks or trained in second-rank schools; at the other extreme, the bourgeois taste of the young engineers who have recently graduated from the grandes écoles and are at least second-generation members of the bourgeoisie.

The same divisions reappear a fortiori in the catch-all category of the

A Young Executive Who 'Knows How to Live'

Michel R., an advertising executive working in a Paris agency, the son of the managing director of the French subsidiary of a leading multinational corporation, studied in a private Catholic secondary school in the 17th arrondissement and then at the Paris Political Science Institute; his wife, Isabelle, the daughter of a provincial industrialist, also went to Sciences Po and works for a weekly news-magazine. He is 30, she is 28; they have two children. They live in Paris, in a modern five-roomed apartment in the 15th arrondissement. They like things to be 'snug and cosy'. They have no interest in 'home-improvement' and have kept their apartment as they found it. 'The decoration is all the work of our predecessor. I didn't much like the green in the dining-room, it was rather gloomy, but we got used to it, and I get bored working on the place I live in.' 'I hate that beading on the doors, I'd like to get rid of it. The pseudo 16th- or 18th-century veneering or whatever it is all over this modern apartment is ghastly; I put up with it but it gets on my nerves,' says Michel, who has removed some of it but 'couldn't face the rest.'

'The world of my grandparents'

Their flat 'is partly the world of my grandparents, my great-grandparents, who were *grands bourgeois*': pictures by Michel's grandfather, 'who spent his whole life painting and never did a day's work'; other pictures which they have been given—a Boudin, a Bissière, and a Folon. But Michel, who 'adores the Impressionists in general and especially Bonnard, and Monet or Manet, the one who does a lot of landscapes, and Pissarro', does not like them.

Nor does he like still lifes, or 'problem pictures': 'Fernand Léger, and stuff like that, is horrible, it's thick and heavy . . . two or three Braques can be interesting to look at, but when you see two hundred of them, all done the same way, it gets a bit repetitive, a bit nightmarish. . . . I tend to go for landscapes . . . My grandmother's got a Bonnard in her apartment, the one really valuable picture she owns. *We* won't inherit it because there are lots of relatives. But it would be wonderful to own it. I go for things that are outside fashion, sort of timeless.'

Isabelle doesn't entirely agree with her husband: 'There are some things I like a lot in modern art, but that's because I like the colours . . . For example, Vieira da Silva (she hesitates over the name), Boudin, who is behind you, I like a lot.' They both occasionally visit galleries, and exhibitions two or three times a year. They went to the Braque exhibition and expect to see the Impressionists at Durand-Ruel.

'We'd seen a lot of mediocre stuff'

The dining-room tables and chairs, mahogany, 18th-century English style, were bought in London as soon as they were married. 'I don't know if we'd do the same thing today . . . I can't remember why we bought them, but from a bourgeois point of view they must be a good investment.' After visiting many antique shops, they 'finally chose something very expensive. It would have cost twice as much in Paris. We'd seen a lot of mediocre stuff and decided we didn't like it. Importing the furniture 'was no problem. It's exempt from customs duties. You just have to pay VAT [value-added tax].' In the living-room they have some modern and some old furniture, a bookcase from Roche-Bobois, a sofa from a shop in Le village suisse. . . .

Michel's car is 'only an old Peugeot 404', whereas his bosses 'have got Jaguars, the director of the agency has an Alfa-Romeo, a Lancia'. 'From time to time, they say, "So you aren't trading it in?" They'd be relieved if I got a new car. They're afraid I'll visit clients in my car.'

'The right sort of clothes for people in advertising'

Though at weekends, at home, he wears 'a filthy pair of trousers', for work he dresses with great care and elegance. He buys his suits at Barnes, the advertising man's tailor, in the rue Victor Hugo in Paris. 'They're the right sort of clothes for people who make it in advertising— English cloth, Prince of Wales checks with a touch of luxury. Not the sort of thing civil servants could wear, and bank managers couldn't get away with it either. In banking you need a plain shirt; banking isn't showy, whereas in advertising, people put every penny they earn into clothes . . . In my business we're constantly classifying people, there are social classes, castes, and it's a matter of fitting a product to the right caste. When someone new comes to the agency, we size them up at a glance. . . . A guy with a velvet suit and big lapels is compensating for something, he's not very

sure of himself, he wants to make an impression.' For a while, the agency had 'a finance manager from a very modest background; when he arrived he was so badly dressed that it was bad for business . . . he was dressed like a junior clerk.' 'Wearing a suit with narrow lapels, narrow bottoms, a bit short, in a loud colour with a shirt that doesn't match and a narrow tie, for example, by our standards, that's grotty.'

'Not the way some secretaries do it'

'On the other hand, being too fashionable is not much better,' adds Isabelle, who dresses their children 'in fairly classic style', paying particular attention to the colours. 'I like a pretty smocked dress from time to time, and English overcoats. Of course it's done with an eye to fashion, but not in the silly way some secretaries at *L'Express* do it, dressing their children in the new kiddy-boutiques, Mini-this and Mini-that, with things that cost a fortune and are a miniature copy of the parents' clothes.' These secretaries 'are all well dressed, by my standards, they have perfect colour sense. . . . There were some girls who arrived, who dressed with terrible taste, it was vulgar, cheap, tacky, just awful . . . and then, after four years, they finally got it right.' Isabelle has a friend who is 'always exquisitely dressed . . . the effect is always stunning, I mean, it's chic, it's got real class . . . She pays attention to every little detail.' Michel's father is also 'very well-dressed, nothing is ever over-done, his colours are always perfect. Refinement without the slightest ostentation. He has a tailor in London.' Michel's mother is 'equally restrained. Always a beautifully cut fur coat.' She, too, often buys her clothes in London.

'Provincial clerks who fill their gardens with gnomes'

'The *petits bourgeois* have no taste, it's a phrase we often use, though we're well aware it's racist.' (Michel and Isabelle constantly indicate in this way their 'distance' from the ways of the older generation of the *grande bourgeoisie*—perhaps especially when speaking to a sociologist, albeit a friend's sister.) Isabelle's parents, provincial industrialists, are more severe or less tolerant: 'About the *petit-bourgeois* phenomenon—provincial clerks who fill their gardens with gnomes, windmills and similar rubbish, Mummy used to say, "It's outrageous; making things like that ought to be banned." It was terribly authoritarian, really fascist, whereas we spoke up for everyone's right to have their own tastes.'

'A very light meal, a vegetable dish and some cheese'

In cooking, as in clothing and furnishing, they manifest the same refusal of pretension, of 'excess', the same sense of 'distinction'. Without being 'a wine-buff who can tell one year from another', Michel is 'something of an expert'. His father-in-law, who has a huge cellar, has slowly initiated them. When they visit him, they drink 'Margaux 1926, amazing things that they don't stock in restaurants any more . . . With colleagues, for example, I'm the one who chooses the wine. They can see I know what I'm doing. I don't go for some miserable Cahors, for example. I know it doesn't taste the same as a Saint-Estèphe or a Saint-Emilion. . . . Hardly anyone knows how to

choose wine, so as soon as you know a little bit about it, you look like someone who knows how to live.' At home, they have a few magnums of Veuve Clicquot 1926 which they bought: 'good-quality things; we drink some two or three times a month and then there are the Christmas presents . . . If it's whisky, we drink Chivas, we're rather demanding.' They buy their claret direct from the producer 'at fifteen or eighteen francs a bottle, forty francs in the shops, a very good wine.' In the evening, when they are alone, they eat 'a very light meal, a vegetable dish and some cheese.' They like to invite friends for *'escalopes à la crème, sauté de veau*, curry, salmon that we buy occasionally.' Michel is particularly partial to *'foie de canard frais aux raisins* cooked in the coals, and *confit d'oie.'* He has eaten in 30 of the 100 best restaurants in Paris listed in the *Gault et Millau* guide, often business lunches ('I only paid for ten of them'). He also likes traditional French food ('plain home cooking, in other words') but is not keen on little local restaurants or 'foreign dishes, Italian or Chinese cooking'.

'Healthy exercise'

Michel and Isabelle are members of a golf club: 'it's marvellous, but the people aren't. They're mostly gaga. In France it's always a certain type of people, whereas in Japan 30 percent of the population belong to a golf club.' Their initial subscription cost them 10,000 francs; they no longer go, because of the children, but they have kept up their membership. Michel no longer plays tennis: 'It's very stressful . . . you have to keep moving all the time, running up to the net. It gives me backache ... Golf is less hard on the muscles.' 'Victims of fashion, everyone's talking about it this year,' they are going to go cross-country skiing. They have also bought second-hand racing bicycles and last summer they went for long rides: 'It's healthy exercise.'

When he was a student, Michel used to go to the TNP (Théâtre National Populaire) in Aubervilliers, to see Gombrowicz or Brecht, but he no longer goes; they have recently been to the Cartoucherie de Vincennes and the Paris Opera: they go to the cinema fairly often. They have a hi-fi system and a tape-recorder; they listen to the classical record reviews on France-Musique. Michel particularly likes Mozart (*The Marriage of Figaro*), Schubert Quartets, Bach, and the Beethoven Quartets. 'I haven't learnt to appreciate purely modern stuff, Webern and so on.' Michel does not read many novels but intends to read Tony Duvert (he likes books that are 'a bit stimulating'; he read Robbe-Grillet's *Les Gommes* but 'couldn't get into it'). He mainly reads 'anything in social studies'—psychology, economics.

---

cadres (executives), a sort of junction where one encounters former engineers, endowed with a traditional cultural capital (usually scientific), who exercise a (delegated) managerial authority; administrative executives who have achieved promotion (in the public sector, by internal examination) by dint of a great effort to catch up scholastically (evening classes etc.) that is rarely sanctioned by diplomas (except purely 'internal' titles); young graduates of the grandes écoles (Polytechnique and ENA), trained for the public sector but destined, in many cases, to move to high positions in the private sector; and, finally, executives of a new type, generally in marketing or management, deriving their educational capital (when they have any) from the business schools or political science institutes, and inclined to a life-style which differs from that of the 'old bourgeoisie' from which many of them originate.

Everything seems to indicate that the different modes of access (from the ranks or by qualification) lead to very different careers. The possessors of qualifications move much further and faster, especially in the second half of their careers (all observers agree that autodidacts have their best chance in the period from entry to mid-career, i.e., to about age 35–40). But occupational life-cycles also depend on firms: the possessors of qualifications have affinities with the largest firms, the only ones which can provide career-structures of the bureaucratic type. And it is among the executives of large companies in the private sector that all the features of the new bourgeois life-style are most strongly developed.

Although executives and engineers have the monopoly of the means of symbolic appropriation of the cultural capital objectified in the form of instruments, machines and so forth which are essential to the exercise of the power of economic capital over this equipment, and derive from their monopoly a real managerial power and relative privileges within the

Model Executives

A rapid analysis of the 'executive opportunities' advertised in Le Monde in the course of a single week (in July 1973) is sufficient to identify the set of characteristic features of the new breed of marketing-oriented managers required by the new forms of business organization:

Whether 'product manager', 'sales engineer' [these two terms are in English in the original text], 'deputy sales director', 'assistant financial manager' or 'general sales manager', he must above all be a 'negotiator' and a 'communicator', and be

skilled in 'top-level contacts': able to act with 'diplomacy'; adaptable to 'contacts at all levels'; 'accustomed to contacts with senior civil servants, excellent negotiator'; 'capacity for high-level contacts'; 'top-level contacts and negotiation'; 'negotiation with banks'; 'take charge of relations with Government departments, represent the firm on national negotiating bodies'; 'taste for contacts and motivation'; 'taste for problem-solving and human relations, highly articulate';

and in internal negotiations, which means, for a head of sales management: 'an on-going co-ordination function between sales division and general management'; for a chief buyer, 'this position entails full control of liaison between a marketing [English in original] department and a production unit'; for a sales engineer, 'the negotiations he will have to conduct will require an understanding attitude and the creativity which his competence justifies'; 'co-ordinator between clients, sales personnel, senior management, after-sales service and manufacturing';

a graduate of one of the new business schools, HEC, INSEAD, Ecole Supérieure de Commerce (ESC) or Institut Supérieur des Affaires (ISA), generally listed together— perhaps rounded off by a 'period of study in an American university';

endowed with the aptitudes and attitudes implied in working for multinational or strongly export-oriented firms ('English absolutely indispensable'; English vocabulary: 'marketing', 'merchandising' [last two terms in English] etc., and Anglicisms: 'opportunité' etc.);

having a 'taste for team-work' and a capacity for 'animating' others (the substitute for authority): 'dynamic and adaptable ... he must be prepared to join a team'; 'to direct and motivate a staff of twenty';

creative and dynamic (like the firm itself, which is 'rapidly expanding into the export field'): 'lead, animate, form a team'; 'dynamism, drive, capacity for synthesis and team-work';

young ('young executive');

mobile: he must expect to travel frequently, particularly to the USA.

A similar profile emerges from a typical report in L'Expansion—no. 64 (June 1973), p. 139)—entitled 'The New Rare Birds', on 'new executive positions' that 'are well paid, for lack of applicants': 'A director of forward planning will always start at 70,000–80,000 francs a year; a management controller at between 60,000 and 90,000. There's a strong demand for internal auditors, recruited if possible from Peat Marwick,

Arthur Andersen or Price Waterhouse. A "junior" will pick up 70,000 to 80,000, a "senior" 110,000 to 120,000. The *financial analyst* still gets at least 60,000. The *director of staff development* has come up strongly: 45,000 to 70,000 last year, 50,000 to 80,000 this year. In the major banks there are even some at 110,000–130,000. *Hypermarket* [shopping center] *managers* have been moving up in the same way. This year, five challengers have broken away: the *servicing manager,* the *hotel director,* the *merchandising* [in English] *manager* (within the marketing [English] plan, he endeavours to improve his product's position in the new distribution circuits; the basic merchandiser [English] goes round the hypermarket shelves trying to get the maximum display "footage" for his company's products), the *business methods analyst* (he analyses the company's system and standards; like auditors, his starting salary depends to a large extent on the practices he has been trained in), and the *plant manager* (the Anglo-American origin of this position means that the ideal candidate is one who has experience in a charter-accounting [*sic*] firm). And what of the future? Two new rare birds are on the horizon:

the *marketing auditor* and the *public-relations auditor.'*

The portrait of the modern manager, as drawn in 1973, seems to have changed recently, no doubt because the recession is creating conditions more favourable to the old style of management (there is again a demand for the 'leader of men'—someone who, as an informant put it, 'can say no without explaining'— and an increased demand for production specialists and sales managers trained 'on the ground') and also because the engineering schools have reacted to the rise of the management schools (for example, the creation of the Institute for the Sciences of Action at Polytechnique in 1977). According to a survey published in *Le Nouvel Économiste* (November 8, 1976), which questioned the personnel directors of 5,000 companies, firms still look for 'open-mindedness', 'dynamism', 'capacity to adapt and relate', 'ability to synthesize' and 'self-motivation', but they also insist on 'loyalty' (at Saint-Gobain) and 'team spirit' (BSN and Oréal). Some 49 percent said they attached importance to candidates' views on politics and trade unions, 33 percent said they did not (18 percent did not reply).

---

firm, the profits accruing from their cultural capital are at least partially appropriated by those who have power over this capital, i.e., those who possess the economic capital needed to ensure the concentration and utilization of cultural capital. It follows from this that their position in the dominant class is an ambiguous one which leads them to a highly ambivalent adherence both to the firm and to the 'social order'. When making demands or rising in protest, they are actuated as much by their concern to maintain the legitimate distance, established by academic verdicts, between themselves and ordinary workers, or by meritocratic indignation at being treated like them, as by the sense of a real solidarity of condition;

and, conversely, their anxious search for integration into the dominant class, either for themselves or for their children, always includes (to a greater or lesser extent, depending on the current state of their interests) an element of ambivalent resentment towards prizes they can neither completely possess nor completely ignore and refuse.

All these dispositions characteristic of the 'cadre' category as a whole are perhaps most intensely developed among those, who, for lack of educational capital, or of the educational capital most valuable at a given moment or of the social capital needed to invest it profitably, are relegated to the position of *technicians*, i.e., executants without economic, political or cultural power. Bringing into the lower positions of the dominant class the petit-bourgeois dispositions which have brought them to those positions, they are opposed in almost all respects to the young executives from the grandes écoles and often from bourgeois families, who occupy a large proportion of the new positions created in the private sector.[31]

The dispersion of this fraction, a simple category of bureaucratic statistics, but also a movement of corporate defence which is affirmed in the representation it has and gives of itself, expresses the objective ambiguity of the position of the 'cadres', who are condemned to oscillate between collaboration and distance and therefore to be the object of annexation strategies which enable them to use their solidarity as a bargaining counter; it also stems from the fact that the term cadre is one of the *titles* which, as rewards attached to the occupation of a position, are important weapons and prizes in the games which are played in and on the gap between the nominal and the real.

Although the opposition between the new positions, with the corresponding life-style, and the established positions does not exactly coincide with the opposition between the private sector and the public sector, it is mainly among the private-sector executives that one finds the life-style characteristic of the 'new bourgeoisie'.[32] And, although our survey only imperfectly captures the distinctive features of the new bourgeoisie,[33] it does register a set of slight but systematic oppositions between the public-sector executives—more often originating from the working and lower classes, and closer to the engineers—and the private-sector executives—younger, generally of higher social origin, often graduates of HEC or Sciences Po and closer to the professions. Private-sector executives buy slightly more often from antique dealers; choose Dali and Kandinsky rather than Vlaminck, Renoir and Van Gogh, who are preferred by the private-sector executives; choose the *Art of Fugue* and the *Concerto for the Left Hand* rather than *L'Arlésienne*, *La Traviata*, the *Twilight of the Gods*, *Eine Kleine Nachtmusik* and *Scheherazade;* Aznavour, Françoise Hardy and Brassens rather than Bécaud, Piaf and Jacques Brel; philosophical essays and poetry rather than travel, history and the classics. They describe the ideal friend as artistic and stylish rather than conscientious, bon vivant and level-headed; the ideal interior as studied, imaginative and warm, rather than sober, harmonious and discreet. In short, differing little with respect to strict cultural competence (knowledge of composers), private- and public-sector executives are clearly opposed in all the areas which depend on ethos.

These differences would be even more marked did not each of the two categories contain a proportion of individuals whose characteristics are those dominant in the opposing category: graduates of the grandes écoles, of bourgeois origin, passing through high positions in the public sector and very close to *polytechnicien* engineers and the professions; private-sector executives from the working or middle classes, with low qualifications, who are very close to the public-sector executives and ordinary engineers.

But the new bourgeoisie is mainly characterized by its opposition to the old business bourgeoisie. Having achieved positions of power at an earlier age, more often being graduates, more often belonging to bigger, more modern firms, the private-sector executives are distinguished from the industrial and commercial employers, a traditional bourgeoisie with its spa holidays, its receptions and its 'society' obligations, by a more 'modernist', 'younger' life-style, certainly one that is more consistent with the new dominant definition of the dynamic manager (although the same opposition is found among the owner-employers).

Thus, they much more often read the financial daily *Les Echos* (penetration index 126, industrial employers 91) and economic weeklies (224, industrial employers 190); they seem less inclined to invest their capital in property; they much more often indulge in the sports that are at once smart, active and often 'cybernetic', such as sailing, skiing, water-skiing and tennis, followed by riding and golf; they more often play parlour games that are both 'intellectual' and smart, such as bridge and especially chess. Above all, they identify more fully with the role of the modern executive who is oriented towards the outside world (along with the public-sector executives and the engineers, they have the highest rate of foreign travel) and is open to modern ideas (as shown by their very frequent attendance at professional conferences or seminars). A final, apparently minor but very significant index of this opposition may be seen in the fact that private-sector executives far more often keep whisky in the house whereas the industrial and commercial employers remain most attached to champagne, the drink of tradition par excellence.[34]

This combination of 'luxurious' and 'intellectual' properties, which seem incompatible because they are ordinarily associated with diametrically opposed positions in the dominant class, opposes the new business bourgeoisie both to the teachers and to the traditional industrialists, whose comfortable cars, hotel holidays, yachts and golf evoke ethical dispositions now regarded as rather *vieux jeu* ('old hat'). But it is also opposed to the professions, and their somewhat different combination of luxury and culture, by a strong integration into economic life, seen in the reading of economic and financial publications (*Les Echos, L'Expansion, Entreprise*) and by an occupational activity which implies a modern-

‗‗

Business Tourism

'Reward seminars' and 'prestige seminars', as they are called in the native language, are part of the range of hidden profits which modern firms offer their executives. 'Residential seminars' (those which last longer than one day and take place away from company premises) provide business for one of the most flourishing industries. (It is estimated that 25,000 such 'seminars' were organized in 1973.) They involve the hotel chains which specialize in 'business tourism' (such as Novotel, Frantel, Sofitel, P.L.M., Méridien, Mercure and Motellerie); the agencies (such as Seminotel) which promote a set of hotels specializing in seminars and conferences in exchange for 4 percent of turnover; consultancy firms (such as CEGOS or SEMA) and their social psychologists, who offer à la carte (see the CEGOS 'catalogue' with its 294 'formats' at rates ranging from 200 to 600 francs per day) 'creativity seminars' together with 'facilita-tors' to organize them. 'Séminarc' is the invention of an INSEAD graduate who has turned the mountain resort of Les Arcs into a seminar centre so as to keep it running during the six 'dead' months of spring and autumn. The economic weekly in which this information was found explains that 'spring and fall are ideal times for executive meditation' (*L'Expansion,* December 1973). The winter low season is reserved for 'updating-reward seminars for successful sales teams', while the high season receives the prestige seminars of 'top management' and big clients. Gilbert Trigano [president of Club Méditerranée], who can be regarded as an authority on these matters, says that 'in twenty years' time, the Club will be providing 50 percent pseudo-conferences and 50 percent real holidays.' Those who inquire into the causes of inflation would do well to take account (among other hidden factors) of the fact that businessmen, with their 'business tourism', their 'company gifts' and their company cars, are good business for businessmen.

A Seminarist Confesses

Your seminar is our business. Club Méditerranée.

The angelic smiles of the Club hostesses, a smooth check-in, punctual take-off (did I tell you we were going to Tunisia?)—it has to be said, the journey was most agreeable, and so was our welcome at the village. 'Djerba la Douce' is a real little paradise. The groups from Lyons and Brussels arrived soon after, on special charter flights, like us. There was just time to slip into something more suited to the weather, and then we were introduced to the programme and the Club. After which, off we went to the Club's 'table of plenty', which, take it from a connoisseur, certainly deserves its name. Next thing, I was in Bermuda shorts—how else would you go water-skiing?

Next day we got down to work, just in the morning, and that was the pattern each day. And the facilities are excellent: an attractive, well-equipped conference room with all the audio-visual aids, individual microphones and so on. The Club scores again.

Everyone responded to the atmosphere, and the debates and presentations were lively and positive. The rest of the time was taken up with excursions, concerts, sport (never compulsory!), dolce far niente and shows, evening events and then, of course, the night club. And it was all rounded off with a gala farewell dinner.

So there you are: a great seminar. And productive, too. Everyone works better in congenial surroundings, where they can really relax. Forgive me for preaching, but is there anything *better* than the Club?

L'Expansion, no. 63, May 1973.

Three-Star Seminars*

Five hotels:
Hôtel des Trois Arcs (very comfortable)
Hôtel de la Cascade (luxury)
Hôtel Pierre Blanche (very comfortable)
Hôtel de la Cachette (top class)
Hotel du Golf (top class)

All rooms have *en suite* bathroom and W.C., telephone (automatic dialling within the resort), radio etc. Twelve restaurants at Arc Pierre Blanche and on the peak. Two restaurants at Arc Chantel.

Seminars Where You Can Breathe

Nature has laid on everything at Les Arcs. The resort overlooks the valley of the Isère, which is here just a rushing mountain torrent. The valley enjoys long hours of sunlight. Our bedrooms and seminar rooms alike offer a magnificent view of Mont Blanc.

Documentation Séminarc.

* The French word *séminaire,* translated as 'seminar', denotes here a business training conference; it retains its academic connotations, and, as in 'A Seminarist Confesses', the original meaning—a religious seminary—can be revived with humorous intention (translator).

Prices, 1975–1976

(1 December 1975—30 November 1976) 600 'three-star' hotel rooms. Prices per day, per participant (francs).

Number of participants	Low season	High season (school holidays, 24 January—20 March)		
		2 d. 1 night 3 d. 2 nights	4 d. 3 nights	5 d. 4 nights 6 d. 4 nights 7 d. 6 nights
10 to 25	170	250	235	205
26 to 50	165	245	230	200
51 to 75	160	240	225	195
76 to 100	155	235	220	190
101 to 200	145	230	195	185
201 to 300	135	225	190	180

I Have Met Happy Seminarists

If you're looking for the perfect venue for a successful conference or seminar, the place you want is Mont d'Arbois near Megève (Haute Savoie), in the heart of the Mont Blanc Massif.

There I met seminarists and conference-goers who were tanned, relaxed and happy to be there. They were there to work, of course, but in a setting that helped them unwind and relax at the same time.

On the work side, the Mont d'Arbois Hotel meets the particular requirements of each firm. It's fully equipped with conference and committee rooms for groups from 20 to 200, audio-visual facilities, simultaneous translation booths. . . . The arrangement is always 'made to measure.'

There is easy access by air (Mont d'Arbois is 90 minutes from Paris by Air Alpes), by rail (night trains from Paris) and by road (a choice of routes).

On the entertainment side, it's Paradise. Depending on the time of year, you can ski in the heart of the fantastic Mont Blanc Massif or enjoy one of the most beautiful golf courses in France. Other facilities include tennis courts, an indoor swimming pool with a sauna and a gym.

For the less energetic, there are delightful walks in outstanding countryside and the charming village of Megève with its many amenities. In the hotel itself, gala evenings are organized on request, with decorations, a band and even visiting stars. At meal times, enjoy the impeccable cuisine and attentive service offered by this top-class hotel.

And how much does it cost? The prices are actually very competitive, especially in September and December. Mr. Thommen or Mr. Ziegler at the Mont d'Arbois Hotel (tel. 50/ 21 25 03) will be glad to supply details to help you compare.

One final point: it has been proved that altitude stimulates the mental faculties. Mont d'Arbois is at 1,300 metres . . . so everyone will be in top form.

Entreprise, 31 May 1974 (advertisement).

istic, cosmopolitan life-style, with its frequent foreign business trips (by air), its business lunches and cocktails, its conferences and seminars.

In view of the decisive role of the reading of economic daily and weekly papers in defining the new bourgeoisie, it is important to recall that, according to a 1973 IFOP survey, 20 percent of the readers of *Entreprise* belong to firms employing more than 1,000 people; that 20 percent of them work in the chemical, aeronautical, automobile, engineering or electronics industries, although the corresponding firms numerically represent only 2.6 percent of French firms, and that only 6 percent of them work in construction or public works firms, whereas 13.5 percent of French firms are in this category; that there is a relatively high proportion of subscribers in financial establishments, services and distribution, in contrast to commercial firms, hotels, cafés and restaurants (which represent a very high proportion of French firms); that, within their firms, 4.6 percent of the readers are company heads or directors; that 15 percent of them are sales executives, 12 percent administrators and only 10 percent involved in production.[35] It is also clear (C.S. VI) that the readers of *Entreprise,* of *L'Expansion* (who would present similar, but no doubt still more accentuated, characteristics) and of *Les Echos* differ from the readers of other publications in that they enjoy talking about economics and business, they make frequent business trips within France and abroad, they use credit cards, they read foreign-language journals and they have contemporary furniture—a very equivocal indicator, although one does observe elsewhere a systematic link between the new bourgeoisie and new urban areas, modern buildings and modern furniture. Further features of this new bourgeoisie are indicated by the characteristics of the alumni of INSEAD: drawn to a large extent from the traditional *patronat* (owner-employer class), they have acquired in this Atlantic-oriented institution (the teaching is largely given in English by an international teaching staff often trained in the USA) the capacities needed to achieve a successful reconversion towards executive positions (especially in sales and administration) in multinational companies, many of them U.S.-based. These 'dynamic young executives' read *L'Expansion* (63.5 percent), *L'Express* (53 percent) and *Entreprise* (33 percent), followed by *Le Nouvel Observateur* (22.5 percent); they ski (71.5 percent), play tennis (58 percent), go sailing (37 percent) and riding (23.5 percent). Their wives often work in the new occupations (10 percent of those who work are journalists, 6 percent interpreters, 12 percent doctors or psychologists); they share the same cosmopolitan dispositions (84 percent speak at least one foreign language) but remain more attached to the traditional forms of culture (28 percent go to a museum or exhibition at least once a month).[36]

The classification struggle which is waged initially within firms, a struggle for supremacy between production and publicity, between engineering and marketing, in which each category of managers seeks to advance its occupational interests by imposing a scale of values which sets at the top of the hierarchy the functions for which it feels itself best equipped, and all the similar struggles which are fought out within the dominant fraction of the dominant class, are inseparable from conflicts of values which involve the participants' whole world views and arts of living,[37] because they oppose not only different sectional interests but different scholastic and occupational careers and, through them, different social recruitment areas and therefore ultimate differences in habitus. Thus, for example, the financial managers of the largest firms,[38] who are almost all Sciences Po or HEC graduates, who possess a large social capital (family connections, their respective 'old-boy networks'), often belong to clubs, are almost all in *Who's Who* and very often in the *Bottin mondain* (the *Who's Who* of the French aristocracy), are no doubt opposed in every aspect of life-style to the 'research and development' managers, who are generally engineering-school graduates, are more often of working- or middle-class origin and have pastimes very similar to those of the teachers (mountaineering, walking etc.).

This means that changes in posts (and their occupants) are inevitably accompanied by a whole effort at symbolic restructuring aimed at winning recognition in representations and therefore by a permanent struggle between those who seek to impose the new system of classification and those who defend the old system. Taste is at the heart of these symbolic struggles, which go on at all times between the fractions of the dominant class and which would be less absolute, less total, if they were not based on the primary belief which binds each agent to his life-style. A materialist reduction of preferences to their economic and social conditions of production and to the social functions of the seemingly most disinterested practices must not obscure the fact that, in matters of culture, investments are not only economic but also psychological. Conflicts over art or the art of living, in which what is really at stake is the imposition of the dominant principle of domination within the dominant class—or, to put it another way, the securing of the best conversion rate for the type of capital with which each group is best provided—would not be so dramatic (as they are, for example, in debates over the school curriculum) if they did not involve the ultimate values of the person, a highly sublimated form of interests.

The new bourgeoisie is the initiator of the ethical retooling required by the new economy from which it draws its power and profits, whose functioning depends as much on the production of needs and consumers as on the production of goods. The new logic of the economy rejects the ascetic ethic of production and accumulation, based on abstinence, sobriety, saving and calculation, in favour of a hedonistic morality of consumption, based on credit, spending and enjoyment. This economy demands a social world which judges people by their capacity for consumption, their 'standard of living', their life-style, as much as by their capacity for production. It finds ardent spokesmen in the new bourgeoisie of the vendors of symbolic goods and services, the directors and executives of firms in tourism and journalism, publishing and the cinema, fashion and advertising, decoration and property development. Through their slyly imperative advice and the example of their consciously 'model' life-style, the new taste-makers propose a morality which boils down to an art of consuming, spending and enjoying. Through injunctions masquerading as advice or warnings, they maintain, especially among women, the privileged consumer subjects and objects, the fear of not living up to the innumerable duties entailed by the 'liberated' life-style, and the awareness of not possessing the dispositions needed to fulfil them, a new form of the sense of moral unworthiness.

Composed of members of the dominant fractions who have reconverted to adapt to the new mode of profit appropriation, the new bourgeoisie is in the vanguard of the transformation of ethical dispositions and world views occurring within the bourgeoisie as a whole, which (as table 22 shows) is itself in the vanguard of a general transformation of life-style which is particularly manifest in the division of labour between the sexes and the method of imposing domination. This is the fraction which imports (from the USA) the new mode of domination, based on 'velvet glove' methods, at school, in church or in industry, and on the 'relaxed' life-style which starts by euphemizing all the manifestations of social distance (especially sartorial ones) and by studiously rejecting the aristocratic stiffness that tends to create distance. After so much historical work on the symbolism of power, it would be naive not to see that fashions in clothing and cosmetics are a basic element in the mode of domination. And the whole opposition between the *vieux jeu* and the *nouveau jeu*, between the old-style authoritarian industrialist and the modern manager, tuned in to the latest techniques of business administration, public relations and group dynamics, can be read in the opposition between the pot-bellied, pompous *patron* and the slim, sun-tanned cadre, who is as 'casual' in his dress as in his manner, as 'relaxed' at cocktail parties as in his relations with those he calls his 'social partners'.

Bourgeois distinction is still defined, both in speech and bearing, by relaxation in tension, ease within restraint, a rare and highly improbable combination of antagonistic properties. Everything takes place as if what was at stake in the struggle between the old bourgeoisie and the new was the primacy given to one or the other of the contraries which distinction has to reconcile. Whereas the juniors of the dominant class and the new bourgeoisie denounce the 'up-tight', 'stuffed-shirt' rigour of the old bourgeoisie and preach 'relaxation' and a 'laid-back' life-style, the old bourgeoisie condemns the 'sloppy' life-style of the new bourgeoisie and calls for more restraint in language and morals.

A sort of composite picture of the bodily hexis of the new bourgeoisie could be drawn from the portraits of 'the property development men' presented by the magazine *Entreprise* (no. 894, 27 October 1972). Here are two exemplary specimens: 'Tall, slim, tanned W.S., age 32, with grey suit and

Table 22 Class-fraction variations in moral attitudes.[a]

Moral attitude	Positive responses, by class fraction (%)				
	Farm workers	Indust. and comm. employers	Manual workers	Clerical, junior execs.	Senior execs., professions
A boy can go out alone before age 18 (1959)	39	29	42	40	62
A girl can go out alone before age 18 (1959)	12	5	14	14	26
Boys of 18 should be allowed to see any films they want to (1971)	56	62	69	70	69
Girls of 18 should be allowed to see any film they want to (1971)	55	58	63	66	66
Mixed schools are a good thing for boys' upbringing (1971)	59	64	75	81	87
Mixed schools are a good thing for girls' upbringing (1971)	55	64	74	78	86
Unmarried minors should be allowed to buy the pill without parental authorization (1967)	8	18	13	20	32
Abortion is not murder (1971)	24	b	44	56	47
It is better to trust one's children and leave them plenty of scope for initiative (1972)	60	60	58	65	70
Young people cannot live without spending a certain amount of money (1972)	34	41	42	48	41
A boy should not go out alone until at least age 18 (1959)	58	71	56	58	38
A girl should not go out alone until at least age 18 (1959)	83	88	82	82	70
Boys of 18 should not be allowed to see all the films they want to (1971)	38	33	25	26	26
Girls of 18 should not be allowed to see all the films they want to (1971)	38	38	31	30	28
Mixed schools are a bad thing for boys' upbringing (1971)	21	22	18	13	8
Mixed schools are a bad thing for girls' upbringing (1971)	24	24	20	15	9
Unmarried minors should be allowed to buy the pill only with parental authorization (1967)	74	70	78	76	62
Abortion is murder (1971)	59	b	43	36	43
It is better to tell children what to do and avoid appearing weak-minded (1972)	36	34	40	29	25
Young people spend too much money (1971)	50	47	45	37	37

Source: Institut français d'opinion publique (IFOP). Dates of surveys as indicated.

b. In this survey, the employers were grouped with the senior executives and members of the professions.

a. Italic figures indicate the strongest tendency in each row

The objects are not there to fulfil a technical or even aesthetic function, but quite simply to symbolize that function and to solemnize it by their age, to which their patina bears witness. Being defined as the instruments of a ritual, they are never questioned as to their function or convenience. They are part of the 'taken for granted' necessity to which their users must adapt themselves.

'In a bourgeois block . . . a resolutely modern, but not revolutionary, apartment': the home of Jean-Jacques Servan-Schreiber, as described by the magazine *Maison et Jardin*. 'Everything is subordinated to comfort and efficiency: The Servan-Schreiber bedroom. The silver-papered walls are lit by a battery of three spotlights. . . . On either side of the bed, aeronautical-style hatches lead to the bathroom. As an ultimate refinement, a bedside switch operates the bathroom lights.'

Maison et Jardin, April 1970.

horn-rimmed spectacles, law degree, a graduate of the Paris Ecole Supérieure de Commerce, son of an industrialist, tells us he loves his work but makes time to play golf and tennis and read the occasional modern novel.' 'Tall, slim, receding hairline, smiling J.C.A., 55, law degree, son of a Paris stock-market financier, is as much at ease with his peers as when negotiating with ministers . . . He has not played poker for several years, but in his moments of leisure he liked to"breathe" on a golf course or play the organ.' Thus, the ideal or ideal-typical property developer originates from the big business bourgeoisie, has attended a major Paris lycée followed by higher education, loves art or classical music and goes in for at least one of the smart sports, often skiing, golf or tennis, but also riding, underwater fishing, sailing, hunting or flying—as indicated by his 'athletic looks', his 'sun-tanned face', and negatively, by his 'slimness'. As for his use of clothing, which, as I have shown in another study,[39] is bound up with this relation to the body and the ethical dispositions it expresses, I need only quote an article in *Le Figaro* (1 December 1975) which, after telling us that Antoine Riboud, managing director of BSN, likes relaxed, sporty clothes and that Gilbert Trigano (Club Méditerranée) rarely wears a tie, confirms that clothing, like language or any other property, enters the quasi-conscious strategies of ma-nipulation: 'A young French businessman told us: "I have three styles. When I go to Regional Development Council meetings, where I meet bankers and civil servants, I have to dress very correctly. For normal busi-ness, my clothes are fairly 'way-out', because I work in furnishings, which is close to decoration. To visit factories, I *clock in* in a leather jacket and a polo-neck" ' (italics mine).

The life-style of the new ethical avant-garde very directly expresses the asset structure which is the basis of its power and its conditions of exis-tence. Executives in major national firms, public or private (a somewhat artificial distinction, at this level), or heads of large, modern, often mul-tinational companies, they are not attached to a place like the proprietors of small local firms, local *notables* whose prestige is inseparable from a world of real interactions and personal representation. The new execu-tives look to a 'centre', their headquarters, for directives and promotion; a large part of their prestige and power derives from academic qualifica-tions which are themselves national or international; they are much less dependent on local privilege and prestige, which are increasingly deval-ued as the economic and symbolic markets are unified, setting them in the national or international hierarchy. Convinced that they owe their position solely to their qualifications and to the technical and 'human' competence ('dynamism', 'competitive spirit') which they are believed to guarantee, imbued with the economic-political culture taught in the po-litical science institutes or business schools and with the modernistic eco-nomic and social world view which is bound up with it and which they help to produce in their conferences, commissions and seminars, these 'cadres dynamiques' have abandoned the champagne of the *vieille France* industrialists (and the whole view of the world, and of France, and of

France in the world, which went with it) for the whisky of American-style managers, the cult of 'literature' (delegated to their wives) and economic news which they read in English. Being both the negation and the future of the old-style *patrons,* of whom they are often the heirs, and from whom they are only separated, in the end, by time, and therefore often by age—which can make it seem like a question of generation in the ordinary sense—they are the ones who transcend, the better to conserve.

Not only the internal structure of the dominant fractions, but also the structure of the relations between the dominant and the dominated fractions tend to be profoundly changed when a growing proportion of the ruling fraction derives, if not its power, at least the legitimacy of its power from educational capital acquired in formally pure and perfect academic competition, rather than directly from economic capital. The new culture of the new masters of the economy, a rationalization of their world view which tends to be ever more widely accepted as 'management science' is developed within the discipline of economics, provides them with the sense of possessing an authority of intellectual right over the conduct of society.[40] Thus the opposition between the 'disinterested' culture of the intellectual and the 'philistinism' of the bourgeois, preoccupied with the mundane interests of his practice, gives way, and not only among the new bourgeoisie, to the opposition between the gratuitous, unreal, unrealistic culture of the intellectual and the economic or poly-technical culture of 'modern managers', which sees itself as action-oriented but irreducible to the triviality of mere 'practice'.

If old-style intellectuals continue to preserve an apparent monopoly over legitimate cultural practices, or at least over the definition of these practices, this is perhaps due to the inertia of the institutions of cultural production and diffusion (in particular, the educational system) and the hysteresis of habitus, which are continuously reinforced by the fact that literary and artistic culture remains the form par excellence of disinterested culture, and consequently the most legitimate of the marks of distinction from other classes; and also, no doubt, to the division of labour between the sexes, which confines women to the privilege of judging taste and the tasks of maintaining cultural capital in its traditional form, reserving the new culture, turned towards action, business and power, for men. This only confirms the tendency of the ruling fractions to conceive the opposition between the 'man of action' and the 'intellectual' as a variant of the opposition between male and female.

Temporal and Spiritual Powers

The different forms of capital, the possession of which defines class membership and the distribution of which determines position in the power relations constituting the field of power and also determines the strategies available for use in these struggles—'birth', 'fortune' and 'talent' in a past age, now economic capital and educational capital—are simultaneously instruments of power and stakes in the struggle for power; they are unequally powerful in real terms and unequally recognized as legitimate principles of authority or signs of distinction, at different moments and, of course, by the different fractions. The definition of the hierarchy between the fractions, or, which amounts to the same thing, the definition of the legitimate hierarchizing principles, i.e., the legitimate instruments and stakes of struggle, is itself a stake in struggles between the fractions.[41]

Because those who take part in a game agree on the stakes, at least sufficiently to fight for them, one may choose to emphasize either the complicities which unite them in hostility or the hostilities which separate them in complicity. One only needs to consider, for example, the highly ambivalent relations between artists and the patrons of art, who, at least in the nineteenth century, are often also *patrons* of business. The latter respond with a sort of paternalistic patronage to the symbolic provocations of the artists, in the name of a not-so-unrealistic image of what the producers of cultural goods really are, that is, deviant children of the bourgeoisie or 'poor relations' forced into alternative trajectories; the patrons may even find a pretext for their exploitation of the artists in their conspicuous concern to protect them from the consequence of their 'idealism' and their lack of 'practical' sense.[42] For their part, intellectuals and especially artists may find in the structural homology between the relationship of the dominated classes to the dominant class and the relationship of the dominated fractions to the dominant fractions the basis of a felt and sometimes real solidarity with the dominated classes. At the same time they are able to play on the symbolic licence which the 'bourgeois' are in a sense obliged to grant them, if only because they are obliged to recognize the supreme affirmation of their spiritual point of honour in the negation of popular materialism implied in the artistic negation of 'bourgeois' materialism.

Those who occupy the temporally dominant position within the dominant class are in fact placed in a contradictory situation, which inclines them to maintain an ambivalent relationship with cultural goods and those who produce them. Castigated by the intellectuals and artists for philistine materialism and anti-intellectual machismo, when they define themselves in relation to the dominated classes they have to invoke the very terms used against them by the intellectuals and artists. And they cannot be entirely satisfied with the solution offered by 'their' intellectuals and 'their' artists (i.e., the intellectuals and artists who occupy within the field of cultural production a temporally—and temporarily—dominant position, homologous to their own position in the dominant class); the very relationship to temporal power and to the associated profits which defines the 'bourgeois' intellectual or artist compromises the 'disinterestedness' which, even in the eyes of the dominant fraction, specifically defines intellectuals and artists.

Intellectuals and artists are so situated in social space that they have a particular interest in disinterestedness and in all the values that are universal and universally recognized as highest (the more so the closer they are to the dominated pole of the field of cultural production). The ideological strategies they use to discredit the activities of the opposing fraction in the space of the dominant class (of which the left-bank critics' remarks about right-bank theatre give a fair idea) owe their quasi-automatic perfection to the fact that, given the chiastic structure of the distribution of the different sorts of capital, whereby the first in one order are likely to be the last in another, they only have to make a virtue of necessity in order to discredit as arbitrary the 'virtues' corresponding to other necessities. The hope of an apocalyptic reversal of the temporal hierarchies which arises from the lived experience of the scandalous disparity between the hierarchy of 'temporal' greatness and the hierarchy of 'spiritual' greatness impresses itself as a practical self-evidence on cultural producers, especially those whose position in the field of cultural production is homologous to the position of cultural producers as a whole in the field of the dominant class. Because they are opposed to those producers who offer products directly adjusted to the dominant taste and who are therefore temporally most recognized, just as the whole group of cultural producers is opposed to the dominant fractions, those writers and artists who are temporally—and temporarily—dominated, because their products must produce their own markets, are the predestined bearers of the eschatological hopes which, insofar as they support their 'inner-worldly asceticism' and their sense of 'mission', are the true opium of the intellectuals. The analogy with religion is not artificial: in each case the most indubitable transcendence with respect to strictly temporal interest springs from the immanence of struggles of interest.

6 | Cultural Goodwill

The members of the different social classes differ not so much in the extent to which they acknowledge culture as in the extent to which they know it. Declarations of indifference are exceptional, and hostile rejection even rarer—at least in the legitimacy-imposing situation set up by a cultural questionnaire reminiscent of an examination. One of the surest indications of the recognition of legitimacy is the tendency of the most deprived respondents to disguise their ignorance or indifference and to pay homage to the cultural legitimacy which the interviewer possesses in their eyes, by selecting from their cultural baggage the items which seem to them closest to the legitimate definition, for example, works of so-called light music, Viennese waltzes, Ravel's *Bolero,* or some great name, more or less timidly pronounced.[1]

Recognition of legitimate works or practices always asserts itself in the end, at least in the relationship with the interviewer, who, because of the dissymmetry of the survey situation and his social position, is invested with an authority which encourages the imposition of legitimacy. It may take the form of a simple profession of faith—'I like it'—a declaration of good intentions—'I wish I knew it'—or a confession of indifference—'I'm not interested in that'—which in fact attributes the lack of interest to the speaker rather than the object. Picasso, or even 'the Picasso', a generic term covering all forms of modern art, especially what is actually known of it, i.e., a certain style of decoration, incurs the only explicit denunciations—as if the impossible refusal of the dominant culture could only be confessed in the guise of an objection limited to what is seen as its weakest point. The imposition of legitimacy in the course of the survey is such that, if one is not careful, one may, as many cultural surveys have done, *produce* declarations of principle which correspond to no real practice. Thus, in one survey on theatre-going, 74 percent of the respondents with only primary schooling endorse ready-made judgements such as 'Theatre elevates the mind', and speak enthusiastically of the 'positive', 'educational' and 'intellectual' virtues of the theatre, as opposed to the cinema, a mere pastime, facile, factitious and even vulgar. However artificial, these declarations have a kernel of reality, and it is no accident that it is the culturally most deprived, the oldest, those furthest from Paris, in short those least likely really to go to the theatre, who most often acknowledge that 'the theatre *elevates* the mind'. It would be equally mistaken either to take these extorted credos at face value (as so many well-meaning cultural evangelists have done) or to ignore them. They give an idea of the power to impose which cultural capital and cultural institutions can exert, far beyond the specifically cultural sphere. One finds, for example, that literary institutions are most recognized by those furthest from them, those who are therefore least likely really to conform to the standards they impose and guarantee (see table 23).

While the propensity and capacity to form opinions on book prizes vary with reading and with knowledge of the prizes, a good number of those who do not read books (especially not prize-winning books), and who have no knowledge of literary prizes, nonetheless state an opinion about them, and on the whole a favourable one (e.g., for question 5, 54 percent of those questioned and 67 percent of those answering). This acknowledgement without knowledge is increasingly frequent as one moves down the social hierarchy (as is shown by the widening gap between the proportion who buy neither prize books nor any books and the proportion who express no opinion on prizes or juries). Similarly, the proportion of opinions explicitly affirming the legitimacy of the prizes increases as one moves down the hierarchy by occupation and education (columns 4b and 5b), variations which cannot be attributed to a direct imposition of legitimacy by the question itself (since question 4, which offers a negative view, varies in the same way and only receives fewer answers than question 5, no doubt because it more clearly appears as appealing to competence and presupposing specific knowledge of the literary world).

Knowledge and Recognition

The whole relationship of the petite bourgeoisie to culture can in a sense be deduced from the considerable gap between knowledge and recognition, the source of the cultural goodwill which takes different forms depending on the degree of familiarity with legitimate culture, that is, on social origin and the associated mode of cultural acquisition. The rising petite bourgeoisie invests its good intentions in the minor forms of the legitimate cultural goods and practices—monuments and châteaux (as opposed to museums and art collections), journals of popularized science or history, photography, film or jazz culture—just as it deploys prodi-

Table 23 Opinions on literary prizes, by class fraction (%), 1969.[a]

Class fraction	Questions 1 & 2 on practices — Do not buy		Question 3 on knowledge of prizes	Questions 4 & 5 on opinions concerning prizes			
	prize books	any books	Do not know names	Juries suspect? don't know	Good books? don't know	Juries suspect? no	Good books? yes
Agricultural workers	95	88	65	50	26	44	81
Manual workers	90	75	59	43	20	46	71
Indus. and comm. employers	82	63	45	39	16	37	64
Clerical, junior exec.	74	53	36	28	10	35	56
Professions, senior exec.	29	46	16	18	16	33	64
Primary education	94	85	68	51	27	48	78
Secondary education	66	67	30	23	8	40	53
Higher education	55	21	9	18	5	25	37

Source: IFOP, *Attitudes des Français a l'égard des prix littéraires*, November 1969.

a. Since these data are only meaningful when the complete system of relationships has been constructed, this table endeavours to present synoptically all the pertinent facts derived from a series of questions on literary prizes:

1. Have you ever bought a book after it had won a literary prize?

2. In the last year, have you bought any general books for adults, i.e., apart from textbooks or children's books?

3. A certain number of literary prizes are awarded each year. Can you name any of these awards, or at least the most important ones?

4. What do you think of this statement: 'The way the major prizes are decided is often suspect'?

5. What do you think of this statement: 'The major prizes are generally awarded to very good books'?

gious energy and ingenuity in 'living beyond its means'. In the home this is done by devising 'nooks' and 'corners' (the 'kitchen-corners', 'dining areas', 'bedroom-corners' etc. recommended by the women's magazines) intended to multiply the rooms, or the 'space-saving ideas' designed to enlarge them, 'storage areas', 'moveable partitions', 'bed-settees' etc., not to mention all the forms of 'imitation' and all the things that can be made to 'look like' something they are not, so many ways in which the petit bourgeois makes his home and himself 'look' bigger than they are.

Cultural goodwill is expressed, inter alia, in a particularly frequent choice of the most unconditional testimonies of cultural docility (the choice of 'well-bred' friends, a taste for 'educational' or 'instructive' entertainments), often combined with a sense of unworthiness ('paintings are nice but difficult') commensurate with the respect that is accorded. The petit bourgeois is filled with *reverence* for culture: one thinks of Djuna Barnes's character, Felix,[2] who, as Joseph Frank points out, shares with Leopold Bloom, that other Wandering Jew of modern literature, 'a vain striving for integration into a culture to which he is essentially

---

For Today's Career-Woman, Entertaining Means Planning

Because, for her, entertaining means getting home just in time to arrange the flowers, check the table setting or slip into some new clothes before the first ring of the doorbell. Setting aside all thoughts of her working life, the busy career-woman turns back into a smiling, attentive hostess.

To bring it off—a welcoming apartment full of flowers, service appropriate to the style of the occasion, good cheer with nothing left out, from the first cigarette to the farewell glass—the woman who spends her life away from home must make up for her absence by possessing the talents of a domestic-science consultant.

Above all, her home must not give the impression of being a place she just passes through, but look like a comfortable, refined retreat, as lively as her own personality. She considers herself the first guest in her home. And as she hasn't much time to give to it, she wants it always to be ready to receive people, even when she's out all day long or goes off on long journeys. Result: a cosy, warm, congenial apartment which testifies to her presence and her preferences.

If she has a favourite colour, the décor makes it no secret. If she travels a lot, every homecoming brings some improvement. If she loves painting or reading, the walls and shelves proclaim her tastes. Through her home, a woman whose job often requires her to adapt to other people's opinions, rediscovers the very feminine pleasure of saying, 'What *I* like is . . .'

How does she entertain? That, of course, depends on the layout of her home, whether she has a dining room or a *fixed or fold-away dining-bar*. That, plus her domestic potential, will decide whether she'll give dinner parties in the traditional style or offer an elegant, humorous 'ready-to-serve' or 'self-service' buffet.

As for the cooking, the work is often remote-controlled, notebook in hand, with everything planned in advance. She knows all the *time-saving* advantages of modern techniques; she has a well-rehearsed repertoire of dishes that can be prepared the night before; she's expert at using the services of a caterer without depersonalizing her menus.

That's how today's career-woman, a strategist of hospitality, combines charm with efficiency to give the illusion of being 100 percent devoted to her home!

An Up-to-the-Minute Welcome

Here, the working woman has worked for herself. . . . The creator of the décor is none other than Françoise Sée, designer and interior decorator. She lives in a three-room apartment overlooking the Seine, and entertains in a big living-room divided into two parts: the *'salon-salon'* and the *'salon-dining-room'*. A simple arrangement but without severity, and it shows that peculiarly feminine gift of drawing attention to a detail without insisting. . . . A lacquer partition can be drawn across to separate the reception area from the dining area. On either side, the walls are upholstered with light mustard-yellow fabric; the car-

pet is olive-green, the curtains white natural silk and the ceiling white. In the *part-time dining-room*, in front of a white sofa she pulls out a white lacquer table with a mat chrome support, and *folding* white leather chairs by McGuire. When *folded back*, the table *becomes* a console, the perfect dining-room piece with its white *side-chairs*. In the main living-room the comfort is more emphatic, dominated by the big corner sofa in velvet calfskin. In front of it stands a simple green lacquer coffee-table with steel trimmings.

Hostess in Paris

Susan Train, a journalist with *Vogue* and a great traveller, has made her home on the Left Bank, in a quiet three-room apartment in a modern block. Her experience of beauty gives her decoration a virtuosity in the play of colours and materials, in successful contrasts of style. It's all done with subtlety and a classically elegant taste. . . . Although Susan entertains in a relaxed way, she has set aside a little dining-room, to avoid the discomfort of buffets or coffee-table picnics. So, even with no one to help with the serving, she can shut the door on it after the meal and forget the mess. During the meal, she uses a wicker basket to stack the dirty plates and cutlery. The first course is served in advance and the rest of the meal is ready on a *trolley* with dish-warmers. Simplified but refined menus, for, being American and a globe-trotter, she collects delicious recipes and exotic ideas wherever she goes.

Maison et Jardin, April 1970.

alien';[3] Jewish and petit bourgeois, and therefore doubly excluded, doubly anxious to be included, he bows, just in case, to everything which
looks as if it might be culture and uncritically venerates the aristocratic
traditions of the past. This pure but empty goodwill which, for lack of
the guidelines or principles needed to apply it, does not know which way
to turn, exposes the petit bourgeois to cultural allodoxia, that is, all the
mistaken identifications and false recognitions which betray the gap
between acknowledgement and knowledge. Allodoxia, the heterodoxy
experienced as if it were orthodoxy that is engendered by this undifferentiated reverence, in which avidity combines with anxiety, leads the petit
bourgeois to take light opera for 'serious music', popularization for science, an 'imitation' for the genuine article, and to find in this at once
worried and over-assured false recognition the source of a satisfaction
which still owes something to the sense of distinction.[4]

This middle-brow culture (*culture moyenne*) owes some of its charm, in
the eyes of the middle classes who are its main consumers, to the references to legitimate culture it contains and which encourage and justify
confusion of the two—accessible versions of avant-garde experiments or
accessible works which pass for avant-garde experiments, film 'adaptations' of classic drama and literature, 'popular arrangements' of classical
music or 'orchestral versions' of popular tunes, vocal interpretations of
classics in a style evocative of scout choruses or angelic choirs, in short,
everything that goes to make up 'quality' weeklies and 'quality' shows,
which are entirely organized to give the impression of bringing legitimate culture within the reach of all, by combining two normally exclusive characteristics, immediate accessibility and the outward signs of
cultural legitimacy.

Unlike legitimate, i.e., scholastic, popularization, which overtly proclaims its pedagogic objectives and can therefore unashamedly reveal the
means it uses to lower the transmission level, ordinary popularization
cannot, by definition, admit to being what it is, and the imposture it
presupposes would necessarily fail if it could not rely on the complicity
of the consumers. This complicity is guaranteed in advance since, in culture as elsewhere, the consumption of 'imitations' is a kind of unconscious bluff which chiefly deceives the bluffer, who has most interest in
taking the copy for the original, like the purchasers of 'seconds', 'rejects',
cut-price or second-hand goods, who need to convince themselves that
'it's cheaper and creates the same effect'.[5]

Although they are situated at very different points in the space of the
middle classes, the producers and consumers of middle-brow culture
share the same fundamental relationship to legitimate culture and to its
exclusive possessors, so that their interests are attuned to each other as if
by a pre-established harmony. Faced with the double competition of the
producers, *auctores,* and the legitimate reproducers, *lectores,* against whom
they would have no chance if they did not have the specific power given

A 'Very Modest' Nurse

Mme. B., whose parents had a small farm in the department of the Lot, is 48. She has worked at the Saint-Louis Hospital in Paris for almost twenty years. She 'used to love school' and would have liked to become a teacher, but had to leave a year after her CEP because her parents 'couldn't afford to keep her'. Divorced at 28, with two children, she had to take a job in a hospital. While working, she studied to become a nurse. Her son, aged 26, is married; her daughter, aged 20, a biology student, lives with her. Mme. B., who 'loves children', is 'horrified by large families' ('a lot of worry').

I'm always shocked when I see a mistake'

She very much regrets 'not having a higher level' (of education): 'I make do with what I've got but I wish I knew more . . . It's very important to be educated.' Education starts with knowing the rules of grammar and spelling. 'The girls who work with me don't speak properly, they make words feminine when they're masculine and vice versa, which proves they've no notion of grammar. It just shows you how primitive they are.' 'I'm always shocked when I see a mistake. Yesterday someone had written *examens amener* with *er* . . . I'd be really ashamed if I made mistakes as obvious as that. . . . Personally I would have written *apportés,* but at a pinch . . . I'd say *amener* a child, but *apporter* a test.'

'I hate pretentious people'

She likes 'simple, unpretentious people': 'I hate pretentious people, I can't stand people who don't know how to behave . . . people who don't say "Good morning", and then just stride in without so much as a by-your-leave. And why? Because perhaps you're not up to their level. I don't like being trodden on by superiors.' (She 'respects the people below her'.) She also detests 'people who are dirty': 'I think that even if you're not rich, at least you can be poor and clean. I see patients coming in with dirty feet, it's disgusting. Why don't they go to the public baths?'

'It's very modest'

Her flat is 'very modest', two rooms plus kitchen; she lives in one room, her daughter in the other. There is no dining room. 'It's very modest. There's no washing machine, because I don't like washing machines. I do my washing by hand, I haven't got many clothes to wash anyway, and then I wash things in the boiler, I find that gets them very clean . . . Anyway, you can't get the same temperature in a washing machine . . . I've got my fridge, my cooking stove with oven, I paid cash for them, I'm not keen on hire purchase (installment buying). For big things, yes, a dining-room suite or a bedroom, then I might get them on credit, but for a little cook-stove, or a washing machine or a fridge, I don't think it's necessary.'

'I like things to be tidy'

In her room, 'a wardrobe bought from the Samaritaine department store for 700 francs, a table from a small local shop, a small bench.' 'I'm very comfortable here, it suits me fine, it's very modest.' On the walls are a few family photos; the trinkets and souvenirs she has been given are put away in a box: 'They take up a lot of room, clutter the place up . . . I like things to be tidy . . . of course, if you've got a glass case, you can put knick-knacks inside it, they're out of the way and don't get dusty.'

'Classic clothes, little suits, little cotton dresses'

In her choice of clothes, the same 'sobriety', the same concern for propriety: 'There isn't a vast amount of money to throw around . . . You just have to be able to budget properly, that's what counts.' She cannot see herself 'strolling around in jeans' (considering that more suitable for her daughter), but wears 'classic clothes, little suits, little cotton dresses.' 'Right now, I have a navy-blue skirt from Gérard Pasquier, a little shop in the suburbs which does some famous names, Cacharel and so on. I really feel comfortable in it, more than with those flared skirts they make.' She goes to the hairdresser's every week: 'It's a relaxation, certainly. I love having my hair done. A set takes no time at all. There's a nice calm atmosphere, I read a quiet magazine, things on fashion.'

She does not buy magazines, because 'they are full of advertisements, they're expensive and there's not much in them.' The television is in her daughter's room; she does not often watch, except 'to pass the time' or 'to relax', with variety shows and especially singers. In fact she 'hasn't really got time': 'I'd rather have hours of sleep, for example, than eat a lot' (mostly she eats grilled meat, salads, fruit). 'I find that it's better for my constitution. I need my eight hours' sleep.' She has not been to the cinema for two or three years: 'The last time I saw a film, I don't remember the names, it was a story about doctors.'

She 'listens to the radio, mainly France-Inter, for the music', she likes Frédéric François: 'I find that his songs . . . the words are very meaningful, some of them . . . Enrico Macias is quite good, he's modern, I find his songs are very nostalgic. I like Hugues Aufray, his songs are terrific, he's got an amazing philosophy . . . What I like in songs is words that mean something, mainly I listen to the words.'

For her summer holiday she rents a small flat or villa at the seaside (Hendaye, Arcachon, Les Sables d'Olonne—on the Atlantic coast). She rests, goes to the beach 'a little bit', plays 'a bit of miniature golf', does 'a little bit of knitting but not a vast amount when it's hot', 'doesn't do much.'

(An interview with another nurse, younger and better qualified, is presented later in this chapter. A comparison of the two will show in a very concrete way that the oppositions between age-groups which divide a number of occupations in fact correspond to differences in scholastic generation and social trajectory, and consequently in life-style.)

---

by control over the mass media, the new cultural intermediaries (the most typical of whom are the producers of cultural programmes on TV and radio or the critics of 'quality' newspapers and magazines and all the writer-journalists and journalist-writers) have invented a whole series of genres half-way between legitimate culture and mass production ('letters', 'essays', 'eye-witness accounts'). Assigning themselves the impossible, and therefore unassailable, role of divulging legitimate culture—in which they resemble the legitimate popularizers—without possessing the specific competence of the legitimate simplifiers, they have to make themselves, as Kant puts it, 'the apes of genius' and seek a substitute for the charismatic *auctoritas* of the *auctor* and the lofty freedom in which it asserts itself, in an 'arty' off-handedness (seen for example in the casual facility of their style) and in a conspicuous refusal of the heavy didacticism and grey, impersonal, tedious pedantry which are the counterpart or external sign of institutional competence—and all this must be done while living in the unease of the inherently contradictory role of a 'presenter' devoid of intrinsic value. The partial revolutions in the hierarchies which the intermediaries' low position in the field of intellectual production and their ambivalent relation to the intellectual or scientific authorities encourage them to carry out, such as canonization of not-yet-legitimate arts or of minor, marginal forms of legitimate art, combine with the effects of the allodoxia resulting from their distance from the centre of cultural values to produce, through the mixture of 'genres', 'styles' and 'levels', those objectified images of petit-bourgeois culture, juxtaposing 'easy' or 'old-fashioned' (i.e., devalued) legitimate products with the most ambitious products of the field of mass production—anthologies of 'poetic' songs, wide-circulation 'intellectual' weeklies bringing together would-be authoritative popularizers and self-popularizing authorities, television programmes uniting jazz and symphonic extracts, music-hall and chamber music, string quartets and gypsy orchestras, violinists and fiddlers, bel canto and cantata, prima donnas and songsters, the 'Pas de deux' from *Swan Lake* and Rossini's 'Cat Duet'. Nothing could be less subversive than these controlled transgressions which are inspired by a concern to rehabilitate and ennoble when they are not simply the expression of a misplaced recognition of the hierarchies, as anarchic as it is eager. The petit-bourgeois spectators know they have no need to be alarmed: they can recognize the 'guarantees of quality' offered by their moderately revolutionary taste-makers, who surround themselves with all the institutional signs of cultural authority—Academician contributors to painless history magazines, Sorbonne professors debating on TV, Menuhins gracing 'quality' variety shows.[6] Middle-brow culture is resolutely against vulgarity.

Uncertain of their classifications, divided between the tastes they incline to and the tastes they aspire to, the petit bourgeois are condemned to disparate choices (which the new petite bourgeoisie, with its concern to rehabilitate folklore and exotic music, actively pursues); and this is seen as much in their preferences in music or painting as in their everyday choices.[7] In radio programmes, they combine a taste for light music with an interest in cultural programmes, two classes of goods which, at the two ends of the social space, are mutually exclusive: manual workers almost exclusively listen to culturally heterodox programmes, and the dominant-class fractions closest to the intellectual pole—senior executives and members of the professions—rank their preferences in accordance with the established hierarchy of legitimacy (if one takes account of the unequally devaluing effect of broadcasting). The petit bourgeois also distinguish themselves from the other categories by the importance they give to the minor forms of legitimate culture, like light opera, or to the substitutes for legitimate practices, such as radio plays, science programmes or poetry readings. This is, of course, the category which contains most of the keen photographers, jazz and cinema specialists, and its members are (relatively) much better informed about film directors than composers. Similarly, in the most legitimate arts, their preferences go with particular frequency to 'accessible' (*moyen*) or 'déclassé' works, Buffet or Vlaminck, *Scheherazade*, *Rhapsody in Blue*, *La Traviata*, *L'Arlésienne* or the *Sabre Dance*.

It is not difficult to find in these works the properties which, at a given moment, predispose them to the treatment they receive from the new cultural intermediaries and their petit-bourgeois audience, when they are not specially produced for this use. But it would be a mistake to locate in the works which enter into middle-brow culture at a given moment the properties conferred on them by a particular form of consumption. As is shown by the fact that the same object which is today typically middle-brow—'average' (*moyen*)—may yesterday have figured in the most 're-fined' constellations of tastes and may be put back there at any moment by one of those taste-maker's coups which are capable of rehabilitating the most discredited object, the notion of an 'average' culture (*culture moyenne*) is as fictitious as that of an 'average', universally acceptable language. What makes middle-brow culture is the middle-class relation to culture—mistaken identity, misplaced belief, allodoxia. Equally, one must avoid treating this objectively and subjectively 'unhappy' relation in substantialist fashion, although it always betrays itself, in the eyes of the dominant, by the most incontestable and objective indices of a manner and mode of acquisition (such as, nowadays, the typically 'record-shop' air of certain systems of musical preferences). What makes the petit-bourgeois relation to culture and its capacity to make 'middle-brow' whatever it touches, just as the legitimate gaze 'saves' whatever it lights upon, is not its 'nature' but the very position of the petit bourgeois in social space, the social nature of the petit bourgeois, which is constantly impressed on the petit bourgeois himself, determining his relation to legitimate culture and his avid but anxious, naive but serious way of clutching at it. It is, quite simply, the fact that legitimate culture is not made for him (and is often made against him), so that he is not made for it; and that it ceases to be what it is as soon as he appropriates it—as would happen tomorrow to the melodies of Fauré or Duparc if the devel-

opment of suburban and provincial Conservatoires caused them to be
sung, well or badly, in petit-bourgeois living rooms.

Education and the Autodidact

The relation to culture characteristic of those fractions of the petite
bourgeoisie whose position is based on possession of a small cultural capital accumulated at least partly through autodidacticism can only be understood in the context of the effects produced by the mere existence of
an educational system offering (very unequally) the possibility of learning by institutionalized stages in accordance with standardized levels and
syllabuses. The correspondence between the hierarchy of knowledge and
the hierarchy of certificates means, for example, that possession of the
highest educational qualifications is assumed, by implication, to guarantee possession of all the knowledge guaranteed by all the lower qualifications. Similarly, two individuals doing the same job and endowed with
the same useful competences (i.e., those directly necessary for doing the
job), but holding different qualifications, are likely to be separated by a
difference in status (and also, of course, in pay), the justification for this
being the idea that only the competence certified by the higher qualifications can guarantee possession of the 'basic' knowledge which underlies
all practical know-how.

So it presents no paradox to see the autodidact's relation to culture,
and the autodidact himself, as *products of the educational system,* the sole
agency empowered to transmit the hierarchical body of aptitudes and
knowledge which constitutes legitimate culture, and to consecrate arrival
at a given level of initiation, by means of examinations and certificates.[8]
Because he has not acquired his culture in the legitimate order established by the educational system, the autodidact constantly betrays, by
his very anxiety about the right classification, the arbitrariness of his classifications and therefore of his knowledge—a collection of unstrung
pearls, accumulated in the course of an uncharted exploration, un-
checked by the institutionalized, standardized stages and obstacles, the
curricula and progressions which make scholastic culture a ranked and
ranking set of interdependent levels and forms of knowledge.[9] The ab-
sences, lacunae and arbitrary classifications of the autodidact's culture
only exist in relation to a scholastic culture which has the power to induce misrecognition of its arbitrariness and recognition of a necessity
which includes its lacunae. The apparent heterogeneity of his preferences,
his confusion of genres and ranks, operetta and opera, popularization and
science, the unpredictability of his ignorance and knowledge, with no
other connections than the sequence of biographical accidents, all stem
from the particularities of a heretical mode of acquisition. For lack of
that sense of cultural investment which only needs external signs like the
name of the publisher, the director or the venue to pick out a 'top quality' cultural offering, just as it reads the quality of other products from

the 'guarantees' implied in certain trade-marks or shops, the petit bourgeois, always liable to know too much or too little, like the heroes of TV
quiz games whose misplaced erudition makes them ridiculous in 'cultivated' eyes, is condemned endlessly to amass disparate, often devalued information which is to legitimate knowledge as his stamp collection is to
an art collection, a miniature culture.

But above all, the autodidact, a victim by default of the effects of educational entitlement, is ignorant of the right to be ignorant that is conferred by certificates of knowledge, and it would no doubt be futile to
seek elsewhere than in the manner in which it is affirmed the difference
between the forced eclecticism of this culture, picked up in the course of
unguided reading and accidental encounters, and the elective eclecticism
of aesthetes who use the mixing of genres and the subversion of hierarchies as an opportunity to manifest their all-powerful aesthetic disposition. One only has to think of the Camus of *The Rebel,* that breviary of
edifying philosophy having no other unity than the egoistic melancholy
which befits an intellectual adolescence and infallibly wins a reputation
for beauty of soul; or the Malraux of *The Voices of Silence,* which envelops
a cultural patchwork with Spenglerian metaphysical bric-à-brac, imper-
turbably associating the most contradictory intuitions, hasty borrowings
from Schlosser or Worringer, rhetorically exalted platitudes, purely in-
cantatory litanies of proper names and insights which are called brilliant
because they are not even false.[10] In fact—but who will say so, since those
who could will not, if they even still know it, because so much of themselves is at stake, and those who would have an interest in saying so don't
know it?—nothing truly separates that other materialized image of petit-
bourgeois culture, Postman Cheval's Ideal Palace—a ramshackle fairyland
straight out of the engravings of *La Veillée des Chaumières,*[11] with its laby-
rinths and galleries, grottoes and waterfalls, Inize and Velleda the
Druidess, the Saracen tomb and the mediaeval castle, the Virgin Mary's
grotto and the Hindu temple, the Swiss chalet, the White House and the
Algiers mosque—from the tawdry pathos of Malraux when he marshals
in a single sentence the 'innumerable laughter of the waves', and the
horsemen of the Parthenon, Rubens's *Kermesse* and Khmer sculpture,
Sung painting and the Dance of Siva, the Romanesque tympanum and
'Antigone's immortal cry', all in the name of communion with the cosmos.[12] Nothing, except the loftiness of the references and, above all, the
arrogance, the complacency, the insolence, in a word, the self-assurance,
the certainty of having which is grounded in the certainty of having always had, as if by an immemorial gift, and which is the exact opposite of
the naivety, innocence, humility, seriousness which betray illegitimacy.
'If there be more stubborn than I, let him set to work'; 'To a valiant
heart, nothing is impossible'; 'On the field of toil I await my better':
these avowals of pure love of work for work's sake are of course not by
Malraux.[13]

Here, no doubt, one touches on the principle of the opposition between all rising classes, the bourgeoisie in an earlier period, now the petite bourgeoisie, and the established classes, the aristocracy or bourgeoisie. On the one hand, thrift, acquisition, accumulation, an appetite for possession inseparable from permanent anxiety about property, especially about women, the object of a tyrannical jealousy which is the effect of insecurity; on the other, not only the ostentation, big spending and generosity which are some of the conditions for the reproduction of social capital, but also the self-assurance which is manifested, in particular, in aristocratic gallantry and elegant liberalism, forbidding the jealousy which treats the loved object as a possession[14]—as if the essential privilege conferred on the possessors of inherited wealth were freedom from the insecurity which haunts self-made men, Harpagon as much as Arnolphe,[15] who are perhaps too aware that 'property is theft' not to fear the theft of their property.

The stockpiling avidity which is the root of every great accumulation of culture is too visible in the perversion of the jazz-freak or cinema-buff who carries to the extreme, i.e., to absurdity, what is implied in the legitimate definition of cultivated contemplation, and replaces consumption of the work with consumption of the circumstantial information (credits, exact composition of the band, recording dates etc.); or in the acquisitive intensity of all collectors of inexhaustible knowledge on socially minuscule subjects. In his symbolic class struggle with the certified holders of cultural competence, the 'pretentious' challenger—nurse against doctor, technician against engineer, promoted executive against business-school graduate—is likely to see his knowledge and techniques devalued as too narrowly subordinated to practical goals, too 'self-interested', too marked, in their style, by the haste of their acquisition, in favour of more 'fundamental' and also more 'gratuitous' knowledge. In a whole host of markets, from the major state examinations to editorial boards, from job interviews to garden parties, the cultural productions of the petit-bourgeois habitus are subtly discredited because they recall their acquisition in matters in which, more than anywhere else, the important thing is to know without ever having learnt, and because the seriousness with which they are offered reveals the ethical dispositions from which they flow, which are the antithesis of the legitimate relation to culture.

The petit bourgeois do not know how to play the game of culture as a game. They take culture too seriously to go in for bluff or imposture or even for the distance and casualness which show true familiarity; too seriously to escape permanent fear of ignorance or blunders, or to sidestep tests by responding with the indifference of those who are not competing or the serene detachment of those who feel entitled to confess or even flaunt their lacunae. Identifying culture with knowledge, they think that the cultivated man is one who possesses an immense fund of knowledge and refuse to believe him when he professes, in one of those impious jests allowed to a Cardinal, who can take liberties with the faith forbidden to the parish priest, that, brought down to its simplest and most sublime expression, it amounts to a *relation* to culture ('Culture is what remains when you've forgotten everything').[16] Making culture a matter of life and death, truth and falsehood, they cannot suspect the irresponsible self-assurance, the insolent off-handedness and even the hidden dishonesty presupposed by the merest page of an inspired essay on philosophy, art or literature. Self-made men, they cannot have the familiar relation to culture which authorizes the liberties and audacities of those who are linked to it by birth, that is, by nature and essence.

Slope and Thrust

The dispositions manifested in the relation to culture, such as the concern for conformity which induces an anxious quest for authorities and models of conduct and leads to a choice of sure and certified products (such as classics and prize winners), or in the relation to language, with the tendency to hyper-correction, a viligance which overshoots the mark for fear of falling short and pounces on linguistic incorrectness, in oneself and others (as it does elsewhere with moral incorrectness), are the very same ones which are manifested in relation to ethics, with an almost insatiable thirst for rules of conduct which subjects the whole of life to rigorous discipline, or in relation to politics, with the respectful conformism or prudent reformism which are the despair of aesthete revolutionaries. The true nature of the cultural accumulation strategies of upwardly mobile petit bourgeois, or their educational strategies, is most clearly seen in the context of their whole set of strategies, which clearly expresses the necessity underlying the characteristic dispositions of the petit-bourgeois habitus—asceticism, rigour, legalism, the propensity to accumulation in all its forms. Thus their fertility strategies are those of people who can only achieve their initial accumulation of economic and cultural capital by restricting their consumption, so as to concentrate all their resources on a small number of descendants, whose role is to continue the group's upward trajectory.

It is well known that fertility is high among low-income groups, falls to its lowest point in the middle-income groups, and rises again among high-income groups. If this is so, it is because the relative cost of child-rearing—which is small for both low-income and high-income groups, since the former cannot see a future for their children that is different from their present, and therefore restrict their investments, while the latter have incomes to match their commitments—is highest for those with middle incomes, i.e., the middle classes, whose social ambitions lead them to make high educational investments relative to their resources. This relative cost is defined by the ratio between the family's resources and the monetary or non-monetary investments it has to make in order to reproduce, through its off-

Table 24 Chances of entering the dominant class, and fertility rates, by class fraction, 1970–71.

Class fraction	Chances of access to dominant class[a]	Fertility rate[b]
Farm workers	1.8	3.00
Unskilled	2.3	2.77
Farmers	2.9	2.83
Semi-skilled	3.7	2.42
Skilled	4.3	2.10
Foremen	9.6	1.94
Craftsmen	10.6	c
Office workers	10.9	1.97
Commercial employees	12.0	1.68
Small shopkeepers	15.6	c
Junior executives	19.2	1.71
Technicians	20.4	1.67
Primary teachers	32.5	1.68
Industrial employers	35.0	2.09
Big commercial employers	35.6	—
Engineers	38.7	—
Senior executives	42.0	2.00
Secondary and higher-ed. teachers	52.7	—
Professions	54.5	2.06

a. From C.S. II (1970). Percentage probability, for men, of entering dominant class, by father's occupation.

b. Average number of children per complete family: from G. Calot and J. C. Deville, 'Nuptialité et fécondité selon le milieu socio-culturel', *Economie et Statistique,* 27 (October 1971), 28.

c. Calot and Deville give a fertility rate of 1.92 for craftsmen and shopkeepers taken together. But it can be shown that the fertility of craftsmen is considerably higher than that of shopkeepers. Analysis of the 1968 census (which confirms the distribution found here) shows that the craftsmen are much closer to manual workers than are the shopkeepers: the average number of children under 16 per household is 1.35 for manual workers, 1.01 for craftsmen, 0.88 for office and shop workers and 0.78 for shopkeepers.

spring, its—dynamically defined—position in the social structure, that is, to achieve the future it expects, by giving its children the means of fulfilling the effective ambitions it has for them. This explains the form of the relationship observed between the fertility of the different classes or fractions and the chances of upward mobility objectively available to their members (see table 24). The working classes, whose chances of entering the dominant class within two generations are virtually nil, have very high fertility rates, which slightly decline as the chances of inter-generational mobility increase. As soon as the chances of access to the dominant class (or, which amounts to the same thing, to the instruments which can provide it, such as the higher-education system) reach a certain threshold, among foremen and office workers, fertility rates fall markedly (the fertility rate of those categorized as public-sector 'office workers', among whom there is a higher proportion of manual workers, is 2.04 as against only 1.83 for private-sector 'office workers', who are almost all non-manual). In the middle classes, whose chances of mobility are incomparably greater (and much more dispersed than their incomes), fertility rates remain at a minimum (oscillating between 1.67 and 1.71); in the dominant class, the fertility rate rises strongly again, showing that biological reproduction does not fulfil the same function in the system of reproduction strategies of these categories, who only have to *maintain* their position.

It is a paradoxical characteristic of the petit bourgeois that their practice is adjusted to objective chances which they would not have if they did not have the pretension of having them and if they did not thereby add a 'psychological' boost to the force of their economic and cultural capital. Having succeeded in escaping from the proletariat, their past, and aspiring to enter the bourgeoisie, their future, in order to achieve the accumulation necessary for this rise they must somewhere find the resources to make up for the absence of capital. This additional force, a thrust inscribed in the slope of the past trajectory which is the precondition for achievement of the future implied in that trajectory, can only be exerted negatively, as a limiting and restricting power, so that its effects can only be measured in the form of 'negative magnitudes', as Kant would have put it, whether 'savings'—refused expenditure—or birth control. If rising petit bourgeois can act as if they had better chances than they have (or, at least, better than they would be if they did not believe them to be better) and so actually improve them, this is because their dispositions tend to reproduce not the position of which they are the product, but the slope of their individual or collective social trajectory, transformed into an inclination whereby this upward trajectory tends to be continued and completed. A sort of *nisus perseverandi,* as Leibniz put it, in which past trajectory is conserved in the form of a striving towards the future which prolongs it, it delimits 'reasonable' ambitions and therefore the price to be paid to realize this realistic ambition. The rising petite bourgeoisie endlessly remakes the history of the origins of capitalism; and to do so, like the Puritans, it can only count on its asceticism. In social exchanges, where other people can give real guarantees, money, culture or connections, it can only offer moral guarantees; (relatively) poor in economic, cultural and social capital, it can only 'justify its pretensions', and get the chance to realize them, by paying in sacrifices, privations, renunciations, goodwill, recognition, in short, virtue.

If the fractions richest in economic capital, i.e., small- and medium-sized shopkeepers, craftsmen or small landowners, concentrate their efforts (or at least, did so until fairly recently) on saving, whereas the fractions richest in cultural capital (junior executives and clerical workers) mainly make use of the educational system, in both cases they invest in their economic and educational strategies the ascetic dispositions which

A Technician Who 'Tries to Get on'

Jacques C., aged 29, is a draughts-man in an engineering consultancy. At secondary school he studied in the technical stream and left school at 17 after obtaining the equivalent of the probationary industrial training diploma ('It isn't an examination'). He started as a junior draughtsman, at 450 francs a month, in the firm where his father was a senior technician. He was not taken back after his military service, and he joined another firm, still as a draughtsman.

'Another five years to go at the CNAM'

He has changed firms several times: 'I would spend two years in a firm to learn all there was to be learnt, and then I'd move on. That's how I've worked my way up.' In the last three years, he has specialized in building design. In 1966 he started to follow courses at the CNAM (Centre National des Arts et Métiers)—'A colleague gave me the idea.' As he had always wanted to do interior decoration (his father had been against it when he was younger), he decided 'to try and get into architecture' and 'began to take courses in architectural design': 'That's how I moved into the building trade . . .' His sister, who is studying to be an architectural secretary, told him about 'lots of architects' offices and the atmosphere in them.' So he has studied architecture, the history of architecture, construction ('thanks to which I got a place in an engineering consultancy') and has 'another five years to go' at the CNAM.

His wife (whose father is a policeman and her mother a department-store sales assistant) is 26; for the last five years she has been a secretary with Renault. She got the baccalauréat (technical and economic options), followed by a management secretary's diploma (BTS) and then started work as a 'secretary'. ('Shall we say it's a long way from what we were promised. . . . The bosses don't know how to make use of our qualifications and training. We've studied law. You don't stay at school until you're 21 without learning a thing or two, and then we're taken on as shorthand typists.')

'Comfortable, cosy, homey'

They live in an apartment in the western suburbs of Paris; they do not often entertain ('apart from the family . . . we haven't got many friends'). He likes his home to be 'comfortable, that's the main thing', 'cosy', 'homey' ('I like a nice warm cosy atmosphere'). He would like to have 'a bit more room, all the same', but 'there are limits to what we can afford.' Their furniture (a big divan 'from Roche-Bobois, 7,000 francs in the sales', a sideboard bought from an interior decorator who reduced the price for them, 3,000 francs) was bought on hire-purchase (installment plan) over the course of two years. He likes 'modern things' and would have liked 'white furniture' but does not like the English style his wife favours (she would like to own 'a big dresser with a collection of plates').

As regards painting, he 'has no preconceptions . . . it just has to be something that pleases me.' He's 'very fond of Modigliani, his very pure forms': 'I haven't seen all his paintings, but those I have, I liked a lot . . . they were reproductions in magazines, or maybe I've seen some of them in Paris . . . I've been to a good number of exhibitions at the Grand Palais. . . . I remember, one was on modern painting, I didn't like it . . . Another painter I really like is Van Gogh, his pictures are terrifying, you can feel something boiling up in them.' (His wife also likes the Impressionists. She went to the Picasso exhibition and 'loved the first part, the whole of the Blue Period.')

'To try to get on, achieve something'

The courses he is taking, to 'try to get on, to achieve something', absorb much of the little spare time he has. He leaves for work at eight in the morning and gets back at seven in the evening. Two or three evenings a week, and Saturday mornings, he studies (as well as his CNAM courses, he is taking private math lessons at home). So he 'doesn't have much time for reading, especially reading for pleasure'; what he does read 'tends to be technical or scientific, and so on, to learn something.' He likes 'books with lots of action' and has read some 'adventure stories' ('Cousteau, I don't know if you can call that scientific'), 'war stories' ('books about the Second World War, air battles'). He 'used to enjoy history lessons' but 'hasn't got many historical books.' 'Love stories don't interest me at all, I couldn't say why.' Since he enrolled at the CNAM, he 'has lost the taste for reading': 'you read other things, you can't relax, relax with something different, you haven't got the time.' (His wife,

who likes books that 'have something to do with medicine' or 'raise moral questions', has recently been reading Boris Vian. She found *L'ecume des jours* 'very funny' but was less keen on *L'arrache-coeur;* her husband 'didn't like it at all.')

'What with the night-classes and the exams', they 'hardly went out at all last winter'; a bit more, recently. Occasionally they go to the cinema because 'it's easy, you can go to the pictures whenever you feel like it, and it isn't too expensive, just ten francs. We try to choose good films, all the same, we don't just turn up like that, we read up a bit before we go.' He 'likes Westerns, adventure films, films with an exciting plot' but 'doesn't have any real preference, so long as it's a good film, well made, well directed.' He recently saw 'an Italian film that was totally absurd, a nun on a roof trying to fly into the air, an industrialist selling off everything he owned . . . Perhaps it's a psychological image, but it only means something to a certain type of person.' Besides, 'the economics students and mathematicians, and people like that' with whom he saw the film 'didn't understand any more than I did . . . I don't really see *who* can understand films like that.' They have seen *The Sting:* 'What we liked about it was the acting, the characters,' his wife explains; she also enjoyed *The Godfather,* 'especially Marlon Brando's performance.'

In some ways he is 'conservative', with a taste for 'classical things'; yet he 'has an anti-conformist streak, too': 'When you're young, you don't give a damn, you're anti-conformist . . . you're always a little bit, I wouldn't say revolutionary, but you wouldn't mind seeing a thing or two changed.' He reads *Le Can-*

ard Enchaîné because he 'likes the revelations about people in government, the scandals and so on, in politics and the property market and high finance', *Le Nouvel Observateur* 'particularly for foreign news', but he does not regularly read a daily paper.

'They'd certainly put some work in'

Until this year, they had season tickets at the Théâtre de la Ville: 'It's not expensive, that's important; the Opera, all the theatres in fact, are out of our price-range.' ('I wanted to go and see Nureyev and I found it was more than 90 francs for two. We had second thoughts and didn't go', his wife adds. Before she took the bac she used to go to the Théâtre National Populaire, and saw *Hamlet, The Madwoman of Chaillot, The Executioner's Song.* . . .) They enjoy ballet (especially 'classical dance'): 'The Moisseyev Ballet, now, we really liked that. They'd certainly put some work in.' They have also been to ballets at the Théâtre de la Musique (near the CNAM: 'It wasn't classical dance, but it was very good.' 'It was *The Firebird,*' his wife explains, adding 'You felt they'd worked at it, the work really stood out' (she also likes 'French provincial folklore . . . in fact, folk dances from every country'). At the theatre, he likes plays to be 'well-acted'. He would like to go and see the Grand Magic Circus; he has seen extracts on TV.

Almost every year they take their holidays in Spain ('It's cheap'; his father is Spanish and has a seaside apartment). On holiday, he 'reads quite a lot' and, his wife reminds him, 'goes to nightclubs every night.' He has tried water-skiing (his wife does it a lot): 'But I'm no good at it, I haven't got enough strength in my legs. You need to keep fit all year to do it. I don't, I arrive on holiday completely whacked. If I had a shorter working week I'd have more leisure time; and then I use the time I've got to get better at my job . . . You have to be crazy to carry on the way I do.' 'Right now I really feel I want to live like a millionaire, I'm sick of the daily routine, even sick of holidays of the sort we have. I want to be a millionaire, with a vast estate, a forest, a swimming pool, a big villa, sports facilities, tennis.' His wife 'would like to go on a cruise': 'We'd do some fishing, have a laugh with friends, lie around in the sun, dance, read.' She particularly enjoyed their Club Méditerranée holiday in Rumania. They chose the 'motel format': 'It's comfortable but at the same time you feel part of things, you make friends easily, it's not like a hotel where you can't get to know people . . . Everything is within easy reach.' While they were there, they did a bit of tourism, because 'when you're in a foreign country, you have to look around', he adds. He didn't at all like 'the organizers' attitude': 'Most evenings, there was a show put on by the "Friendly Organizers", who are generally students who are there on holiday. Well, they didn't put any effort into it at all, it wasn't even improvisation, they just didn't give a damn!'

make them the ideal clientele of the bank or the school: cultural goodwill and financial prudence, seriousness and hard work. These are guarantees which the petit bourgeois offers to these institutions while putting himself entirely at their mercy (as opposed to the owner of *real* economic or cultural capital) since they represent his only hope of deriving profits from fundamentally negative assets. Pretension could be written 'pre-tension': the thrust to continue along the upward inclination has its reverse side in the economizing mentality and in all the 'small-mindedness' associated with the petit-bourgeois virtues. If pre-tension forces the petit bourgeois to enter the competition of antagonistic pretensions and pushes him to live always beyond his means, at the cost of a permanent *tension* that is always liable to explode into aggressivity, it is also what gives him the necessary strength to extract from himself, through every form of self-exploitation (in particular, asceticism and Malthusianism), the economic and cultural means he needs in order to rise.

It is in the area of sociability and the corresponding satisfactions that the petit bourgeois makes the greatest, if not the most obvious, sacrifices. He is convinced that he owes his position solely to his own merit, and that for his salvation he only has himself to rely on: 'Every man for himself', 'A man's home is his castle.' To concentrate his efforts and reduce his costs, he will break the ties, even the family ties, which hinder his individual ascension. The bonds of solidarity which help to chain the (relatively) least deprived to the most deprived can make poverty an eternal vicious circle. 'Taking off' always presupposes a break, and the disowning of former companions in misfortune is only one aspect of this. The solitary renegade has to reverse his whole table of values, convert his whole attitude. Thus, substituting a small family or a single child for the large family (which the negative causes, such as inadequate mastery of the techniques of birth control do not entirely explain) means renouncing the popular conception of family relations and the functions of the domestic unit, abandoning not only the satisfactions of the extended family and a whole traditional mode of sociability, with its exchanges, its festivities, its conflicts, but also the guarantees which it offers, the one almost infallible protection, especially for mothers, against the uncertainties of old age, in a world haunted by domestic instability and social and economic insecurity. For the petit bourgeois, kinship and friendship can no longer be an insurance against misfortune and disaster, a network of support and protection which will always provide a helping hand, a loan or a job; but they are not yet 'connections', i.e., the social capital that is needed to make the most of economic and cultural capital. They are merely hindrances, which have to be removed whatever the cost, because the gratitude, the mutual aid, the solidarity and the material and symbolic satisfactions they give, in the short or long term, are among the forbidden luxuries.

In limiting his family, often to an only son, on whom all hopes and efforts are concentrated, the petit bourgeois is simply obeying the system of constraints implied in his ambition. If he cannot increase his income, he must limit his expenditure, the number of mouths he has to feed. But in so doing, he additionally conforms to the dominant representation of legitimate fertility, that is, procreation subordinated to the imperatives of social reproduction. Birth control is one form (no doubt the most elementary form) of numerus clausus. The petit bourgeois is a proletarian who makes himself small to become bourgeois.

If the petit bourgeois is a small bourgeois in reality and not just in the sociologist's mind, then it is clear what would be lost by abandoning the concept 'petit bourgeois' in the name of an objectivist definition of objectivity. Here as elsewhere, native concepts concentrate the maximum number of sociologically pertinent properties in a particularly evocative form. Furthermore, an objectifying reduction, however brutal, has nothing in common with class contempt, which is flagrant in so much writing on the petite bourgeoisie, the traditional whipping boys of aestheticizing prophecy and the favourite target for political anathemas (one only has to think of Marx's attacks on Proudhon): it relates the properties of the habitus, those most often picked on by class racism, such as 'pretension' or 'narrowness', to the objective conditions of which they are the product. Those who can afford less surly virtues and present a more prepossessing face forget that the traits they condemn are the inevitable counterpart of the mechanisms providing for individual mobility, i.e., the selective extraction of appropriate individuals, and they speak as if the 'vices' and 'virtues' of the petit bourgeois (which—need one repeat?—are only defined as such in relation to the dominant ethic) were, in this case, to be imputed to the individuals and not to the structures, on the grounds that the structures have left them free to 'choose' their alienation.

Renouncing the prolificity of the proletariat, the petit bourgeois 'chooses' restricted, selective reproduction, often limited to a single product, conceived and shaped for the rigorously selective expectations of the importing class. He encloses himself in a tightly knit but narrow and somewhat oppressive nuclear family. It is no accident that the adjective *petit* (small) or one of its synonyms can be applied to everything the petit bourgeois says, thinks, does, has or is, even to his morality, although that is his strong point: strict and rigorous, its formalism and scruples always make it somewhat tense, susceptible and rigid. With his petty cares and petty needs, the petit bourgeois is indeed a bourgeois 'writ small'. Even his bodily hexis, which expresses his whole objective relation to the social world, is that of a man who has to make himself small to pass through the strait gate which leads to the bourgeoisie: strict and sober, discreet and severe, in his dress, his speech, his gestures and his whole bearing, he always lacks something in stature, breadth, substance, largesse.

The Variants of Petit-Bourgeois Taste

Thus, given a sufficiently high level of statistical aggregation, one can contrast a bourgeois ethos of ease, a confident relation to the world and the self, which are thus experienced as necessary, that is, as a materialized coincidence of 'is' and 'ought', which supports and authorizes all the inner or manifest forms of *certitudo sui,* casualness, grace, facility, elegance, freedom, in a word, naturalness, with a petit-bourgeois ethos of restriction through pretension, the voluntaristic rigour of the 'called' but not yet 'chosen', who base their pretension to embody one day what 'ought to be' on a permanent invocation of 'ought'. However, as soon as the analysis is refined, it is seen that this system of dispositions takes on as many modalities as there are ways of attaining, staying in or passing through a middle position in the social structure, and that this position itself may be steady, rising or declining.

The survey data collected for the middle classes (n = 583 individuals) were analysed for correspondences, applying the same sequence of operations and using the same active and illustrative variables as for the dominant class (see chapter 5). The first factor has a greater relative weight than in the analysis of the dominant class (7 percent as against 3.4 percent for the second factor and 3 percent for the third). This is no doubt because the composition of this factor includes not only the structure of the capital possessed but also the overall volume of capital, the effect of which is not completely neutralized by the difficulty and relative arbitrariness of defining the limits of the class, both on the side of the cultural pole, where the cultural intermediaries, very close to the secondary teachers, might have been excluded, and on the side of the economic pole, where it is never easy, with the available information, to draw the line between 'big' and 'small' shopkeepers or craftsmen. (Because of this, the plane diagram—figures 15 and 16—presents itself as a systematic skewing of the social space as it appears in the theoretical schema—figures 5 and 6—in which volume and structure of capital correspond to two different dimensions, whereas here the first factor corresponds to the second dimension but also, to some extent, to the first dimension, with the second factor corresponding to the third dimension.)

This first factor brings to light a structure of oppositions very similar to that brought out by the first factor in the analysis of the dominant class. On one side we find the ability to identify at least twelve composers (2.0 percent), knowledge of at least twelve of the works of music (2.4 percent), visits to the Louvre and the Modern Art Museum, the choice of works of classical music typical of the 'discophile' disposition, such as the *Four Seasons* (2.4 percent), the *Art of Fugue* (1.6 percent) and the *Well-Tempered Clavier* (1.6 percent), 'intellectual' singers like Jacques Douai (1.8 percent) and Leo Ferré, painters who are the equivalent of Bach or Vivaldi in the space of pictorial tastes, like Breughel (1.8 percent), ambitious judgements on painting, such as 'Abstract painting interests me as much as the classical

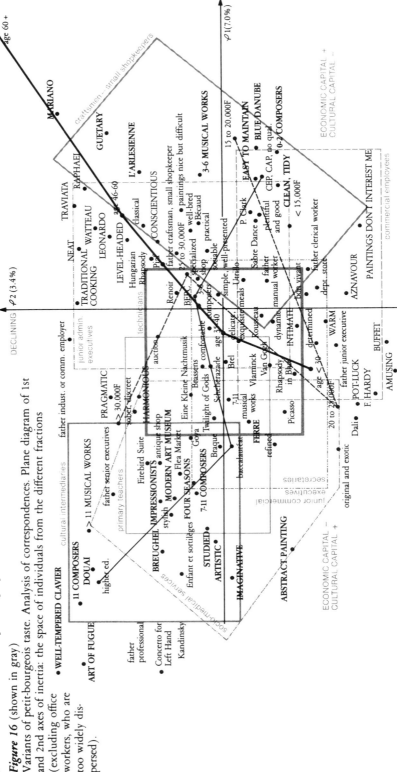

Figure 15 (shown in black)
Variants of petit-bourgeois taste. Analysis of correspondences. Plane diagram of 1st and 2nd axes of inertia: the space of properties.

Figure 16 (shown in gray)
Variants of petit-bourgeois taste. Analysis of correspondences. Plane diagram of 1st and 2nd axes of inertia: the space of individuals from the different fractions (excluding office workers, who are too widely dispersed).

The items corresponding to the strongest absolute contributions are indicated in **BOLD CAPITALS** for the 1st factor, CAPITALS for the 2nd.

schools' (2.4 percent), 'artistic' friends (2.0 percent), and a 'studied', 'imaginative' interior. On the other side, low (0 to 6) knowledge of composers (2.9 percent) and works (2.7 percent), the choice of works capable of being perceived as legitimate through an allodoxia effect, such as the *Blue Danube* (2.8 percent) or *L'Arlésienne* (1.5 percent), singers associated with light opera, such as Guétary (1.6 percent), and the most 'common' preferences (such as for a 'clean and tidy', 'easy to maintain' interior). (As regards the relative contributions, we find that the adjectives chosen for the ideal interior are more strongly explained by the first factor than by the other two: in particular, 'harmonious', 'studied' and 'imaginative', associated with the cultural pole, and 'clean and tidy', 'easy to maintain' associated with the economic pole. This also applies to the choice of painters like Renoir and Kandinsky.)

Projection of the illustrative variables shows that, as with the dominant class, educational qualifications are distributed in linear fashion along the first axis (which is not the case with incomes). In terms of individuals, the first factor opposes the craftsmen and small shopkeepers to the members of the new petite bourgeoisie richest in cultural capital (cultural intermediaries, medical and social services) and, secondarily, to the primary teachers, with the technicians and junior executives occupying intermediate positions.

The second factor systematically characterizes the most traditional or conservative ethical or aesthetic dispositions: attachment to the old, consecrated values in painting, with Raphael (2.6 percent), Leonardo (2.3 percent), or Watteau (1.6 percent), as in classical music, with *La Traviata* (2.4 percent), or song, with Mariano, and also in life-style, with the taste for traditional French cooking (2.3 percent), a 'neat' (2.3 percent) and 'harmonious' (1.6 percent) interior. It does so by opposing them to dispositions which seem to have nothing in common except ignorance or refusal of the established values (with preferences for Hallyday—4.4 percent—Aznavour—3.3 percent—Buffet—2.3 percent—for a 'warm' interior—1.6 percent—and 'amusing' friends—2.9 percent). (Among the indicators more strongly explained by the second factor, one finds the same opposition: on one side the 'conscientious' or 'pragmatic' friend, on the other the 'determined' friend, department-store furniture, Françoise Hardy, or the judgement, 'Paintings don't interest me.')

When the 'objective' characteristics are projected as illustrative variables, they show that, as in the case of the dominant taste, the second factor expresses an opposition by age (the oldest are at the top of the second axis and towards the economic pole, the youngest at the bottom of this axis and towards the cultural pole) and, inseparable from this, an opposition by social origin: the children of big or small employers, senior executives or professionals are situated on the positive-value side, the children of manual workers, clerical workers or junior executives on the negative-value side. In other words, within each fraction, the second factor contrasts those who are tending to decline and those who are tending to rise; the overall distribution of the different categories corresponds to the proportions of the two categories within each of them, with the opposition between the cultural intermediaries or the junior administrative executives, who incline towards the positive side, and the commercial employees or the secretaries, who incline towards the negative side.

Finally, as in the case of the dominant class where it opposed the professionals, in whom 'bourgeois taste' is fully developed, to the two fractions which represent the extremes of the dominant cultural space (teachers and intellectuals on one hand, industrial and commercial employers on the other), the third factor opposes the fractions which most, and most completely, possess the modal characteristics of the whole class, the ones which best contrast it with the other classes, in short, the most typically 'middle-range' ones, to the fractions with least cultural capital, i.e., the craftsmen and shopkeepers, and to those who have most, i.e., the cultural intermediaries and primary teachers (see figure 17). The indices of average cultural competence, such as average knowledge (7 to 11) of musical works (4.0 percent) and average knowledge (3 to 6) of composers (2.9 percent), or the taste for the most typically middle-brow cultural goods, such as Brel (2.9 percent), Buffet (1.7 percent), Van Gogh (1.9 percent), Leonardo (2.2 percent), *Eine Kleine Nachtmusik* (1.9 percent), are opposed, on the one hand, to the indices of high knowledge (12 or more) of works (2.2 percent) and composers (4.0 percent) and a taste for more legitimate works like the *Art of Fugue* (2.2 percent), and on the other hand to the indices of low knowledge (0 to 2) of works (3.3 percent) and composers (3.3 percent) and a taste for the least legitimate works and singers, such as Guétary (2.4 percent) or Hallyday (1.9 percent). (The indicators strongly explained by this third factor are all among those which make high absolute contributions and so have already been mentioned.)

Projection of the illustrative variables brings out, as one might expect, an opposition between the holders of medium qualifications (BEPC or baccalauréat) and those with lower (CEP or CAP) or higher qualifications; this is combined with an opposition between those originating predominantly from the middle class and those from the working or upper classes. 'Average culture' is thus most characteristic of the primary teachers, technicians, people in the medical and social services, and junior administrative executives.

The whole set of facts which correspondence analysis brings to light in systematic form cannot be adequately explained simply by observing that, although phenomenally very different (since they are applied to generally less legitimate objects), the choices of the members of the petite bourgeoisie are organized in a structure similar to the one which organizes the tastes of the members of the dominant class, with the craftsmen and small shopkeepers, whose position is based on possession of a certain economic capital, being opposed to the primary teachers and cultural intermediaries in accordance with principles entirely analogous to those which distinguish the industrial and commercial employers from the teachers and artistic producers. The problem brought to light by the second factor, that of the link between the sets of aesthetic and ethical dispositions roughly definable as 'conservative' or 'innovating', and social origin and age, which are themselves related in a complex way

Figure 17 Variants of petit-bourgeois taste. Analysis of correspondences: simplified plane diagram of 1st and 3rd axes of inertia.

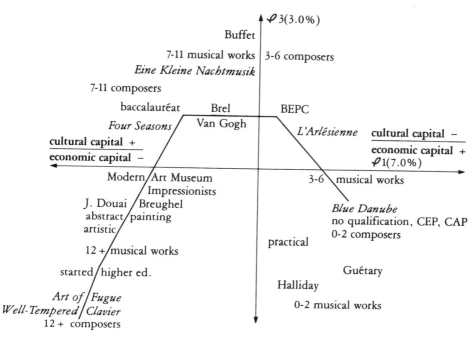

This simplified diagram only indicates variables which make an absolute contribution of 1.5% or more. The only illustrative variable included is educational qualification.

to position in the horizontal dimension of space, can only be tackled by systematically examining the relationship which is established between positions (or jobs) situated in social space-time and agents also situated in this space.

If what goes on in this central area of social space is generally so little understood, this is because, at best, in order to understand and measure (by using, for example, codes which are, by definition, definite), one has to freeze the movements in the same direction or in opposite directions which transport both the positions and the agents, turning the middle region of social space, a site of relative uncertainty and indeterminacy between the two poles of the social classes, into a set of mobile crossing-points, or rather, a set of shifting crossing-points where agents meet for a certain time as they are carried along by similar or opposite, rising or falling trajectories. We are still closer to reality if we characterize the middle positions as mobile crossing-points which move—in a relatively indeterminate region of a social space-time which is nothing other than the structure of these ordered but partially disordering movements—partly at least because the people who meet there for a shorter or longer time, whose practices and trajectories are partially determined by the determinations attached to these places, help to make them move by their own movements or, more precisely, by the transformations they induce in the reality or the representation of the positions which they occupy and which in some cases they carry off in their movement. This is as valid in cases in which the agents are 'coming up' in social space by 'upgrading' their positions as in cases in which they are going down, 'dragging down' their positions with them in their decline (the process of 'rout'). It can be seen, incidentally, that the mechanical metaphors one is obliged to use in order to refer to a reality which is not easily named are liable to obscure the fact that the agent's representation of his or her own position, which depends not only on the objective future of the position but also on the representation other agents have of it, helps to determine the objective future of that position.[17] In fact, an adequate description of such a universe would presuppose a questioning, at every moment, of all the dispositions, inclinations or propensities towards substantialist realism that are inscribed both in ordinary modes of thought and ordinary language and in the ordinary expectations of social science, which is led to demand strict classifications, groups with strict frontiers, clearly defined as regards their name—a petit bourgeois has to be called petit-bourgeois—and their number (precise numbers look so much more 'scientific': thus one learns on good authority that 'there are at the very most 4,311,000 petit bourgeois in France').[18] (This is said here to invite the reader's indulgence for all the—perhaps provisionally inevitable—relapses into the realist mode of thought which are bound to appear in the rest of this text.)

Thus the middle positions in the social field may be defined synchronically as situated in an intermediate region—characterized by its relative indeterminacy (the first, i.e., vertical, dimension of social space)—of one or the other of the sub-fields (the second, i.e., horizontal, dimension), economic or cultural, of the field of the social classes; but also diachronically, as having a history (which may be the collective history of the successive occupants of that position) relatively independent of that of the individuals occupying that position at a given moment, in other words, a past and future trajectory, a past and a future. This future, that is, the collective future which the position has in store for its occupants, may be relatively predetermined, in which case it may be more or less favourable, i.e., may promise with relative certainty a more or less marked rise or fall or a stagnation; or it may be almost indeterminate, open.

Among the properties common to all the occupants of these intermediate or neutral positions, the most characteristic are no doubt those which stem from this structural indeterminacy. Equidistant from the two extreme poles of the field of the social classes, at a neutral point where the forces of attraction and repulsion are evenly balanced, the petit bourgeois are constantly faced with ethical, aesthetic or political dilemmas forcing them to bring the most ordinary operations of existence to the level of consciousness and strategic choice. In order to survive in the world of their aspirations they are condemned to 'live beyond their means' and to be constantly attentive and sensitive, hypersensitive, to the slightest signs of the reception given to their self-representation. Constantly exposed to snubs and refusals intended to 'put them in their place', they are always on their guard, ready to turn docility into aggressivity.

Among the relatively predetermined positions, one can thus distinguish declining positions, such as those of craftsmen or small shopkeepers, which have suffered a considerable reduction in numbers, linked to a rapid economic and social decline, and stable or rising positions, such as those of office workers, junior administrative executives or commercial employees, which have undergone a moderate increase in numbers, accompanied by few changes in the associated economic and social advantages.[19] On the other side, in the most indeterminate zone of an indeterminate region, that is, mainly towards the cultural pole of the middle class, one finds positions that are still ill-determined as regards both the present they offer and the very uncertain, and therefore very open, i.e., both risky and scattered, future they promise (as opposed to the predictable but closed future of the strongly predetermined positions).[20] Some of these new or renovated positions result from the recent changes in the economy (in particular, the increasing role of the symbolic work of producing needs, even in the production of goods—design, packaging, sales promotion, public relations, marketing, advertising etc.). Others have been in a sense 'invented' and imposed by their occupants, who, in order to be able to sell the symbolic products they had to offer, had to produce the need for them in potential consumers by a symbolic action (usually referred to by euphemisms such as 'social work', 'cultural facilitation' etc.) tending to impose norms and needs, particularly in the areas of lifestyle and material or cultural consumption.

Everything takes place as if the synchronic and diachronic properties of positions were linked by a sufficiently close statistical relation to the synchronic and diachronic properties of the individuals, that is, to the capital volume and composition which govern their position at a given moment and to the evolution of these two properties which define their past and potential trajectories, for it to be equally possible (as has been done here) to characterize the positions in terms of the properties of their occupants or these properties in terms of the positions. This can be (and constantly has been) shown for the synchronic properties: capital volume and composition are so clearly linked to position that one may, in some cases, fail to question the relationship between the occupants and the position and the mechanisms through which it occurs. But the middle classes offer a particularly favourable opportunity to show that the same is true of diachronic properties. We thus return to the starting point of the analysis, namely, the relationship established by observation between the broad classes of positions defined in terms of their diachronic properties and individual properties which are obviously linked to time, like age, which expresses the relationship to the past (the past of the economic system, at the economic pole, the past of the educational system, at the cultural pole) and to the future, or like social origin, an (imperfect) indicator of the evolution of capital volume and composition and also of a whole relationship to past and future as well as to the other social classes.

This link between the future and social ascent or between the past and social decline is strongly emphasized in the dominant world view (an individual or a position is said to 'have a future', meaning the promise of social ascension, i.e., embourgeoisement). It is based on and constantly reinforced by all the social mechanisms of competition (the most exemplary of which is, of course, fashion), in which the differences between the classes are retranslated into time-lags in a race aiming at the same objective. It functions in the political or even scientific unconscious through all the normative uses of the evolutionary scheme which identifies the 'people' with the superseded past or which, more subtly, turns the revolutionary world view, a reversal of the dominant view which gives the future to the 'people', into the form par excellence of archaism. (This scheme of thought is particularly potent in universes which, like the intellectual field, are based on the opposition between the new and the old.)

The Declining Petite Bourgeoisie

The positions whose numerical decline expresses their economic decline are occupied by individuals whose objective properties, practices and opinions can be seen as linked to a past age. Situated at the extreme point of the first axis, relatively elderly on the whole and under-endowed with educational capital (at most they have the CEP or CAP), the craftsmen and small shopkeepers manifest in all their preferences regressive dispositions which are no doubt the source of their repressive inclinations, particularly visible in their reactions to every sign of departure from the old order, not least, of course, the behaviour of young people. Thus, reacting against all inclinations towards modernism or comfort, which they can only see as moral decadence, on every question concerned with the everyday art of living they make choices which can be called regressive inasmuch as they are very close to those of the manual workers, without having been forced on them to the same extent by necessity (they say, for example, that they prefer a 'clean and tidy', 'easy to maintain', or 'practi-

A Baker's Wife Who Gets It 'Just About Right'

Madame D. and her husband run a bakery business in Grenoble. She lost both parents by the time she was twelve, and was sent to an orphanage. She went to school until age fourteen but did not take the CEP. Her husband first worked at night in a dairy. Then he was employed as a baker for eight years. Twelve years ago he set up his own bakery business. They have one married daughter, aged 22, who works in a pharmacy. They own a small bakery (employing one other person), which they will soon be selling so as to acquire another small shop, but this time a business that is less demanding, 'less of a bind'. They have recently bought a house in the suburbs of Grenoble; it has a living-room, dining-room, several bedrooms, kitchen and bathroom and is surrounded by a large, well-kept garden.

'I do like things to be clean'

Inside, everything is brightly polished. 'I don't want to boast, but I do like things to be clean, so I like keeping my house nice and tidy, doing the dusting and sweeping, perhaps too much, because if I was here all the time, that's all I'd be doing.' The concern to be 'reasonable', to be 'just about right', never conspicuous, is apparent in everything she says. She says of their house that 'in a way it's what we've worked for . . . a sort of reward.' 'It's nice but of course there are much nicer houses. Let's say it's not bad. . . . Just an ordinary little

house. Not that I'm boasting. If it had been a little bit smaller, I would still have taken it. The fact is, it's just about right. Not super-luxurious, no, but not just run-of-the-mill either.' 'We were brought up to be very economical. . . . Working the way we worked, we didn't have time to spend money. . . . We don't have time to go out, so we're almost forced to save money. Often I say, "There are folks that have money and the time to spend it; I've got the money but I haven't got the time." It's a sad fact but it's true.'

'Something intermediate between old and very modern'

Choosing their furniture—eventually bought from the chain-store Lévitan—was 'a real headache'. 'I went round no end of shops . . . so as not to make a mistake. . . . I wanted something that was right for my age because I can't really see a 50-year-old with ultra-modern furniture. . . . I was looking for something intermediate between old and very modern.' When buying the house, she preferred to 'take her time' rather than 'rush into it'. 'Some folks get a house straight away, but we wouldn't have been able to enjoy it, it wouldn't have been any use to us. We waited quite a few years and that way I got something more comfortable.'

'Not the most ordinary, but not the most beautiful either'

In the living room—'it's not the most ordinary furniture in the world, but it isn't the most beautiful either—I went for something classic.' As for the big grey settee, 'with that shade, you can sit on it', 'you're not a slave to it' (for fear of marking it) 'and at the same time it's quite comfortable.' She had to choose all these things on her own; her husband had no time and no inclination to accompany her. 'He couldn't have cared less, he just said "Get whatever you like." ' She looked for something 'that would go with the style of the rooms. I don't claim to be very competent but you do have to respect a certain style in the rooms.'

'Those things are worth a bit now they're cleaned up'

On the wall there is a painting given to her by her brother-in-law and one she bought from a 'picture artist'. 'I would like to have more paintings but I can't afford it.' She thinks she might also like to listen to records but has never bought any and cannot imagine herself doing so. Her sense of economy, the refusal to waste anything, has led her to 'rescue' knick-knacks for her house. 'I've got lots of trinkets and odds and ends that I found in aunts' and uncles' attics. They were terribly tarnished and rusty but I polished them up. All those things are worth a bit now they're cleaned up. . . . When I rescued them, nobody would have bothered to pick them up, they were so dirty.'

'I don't like showing off'

Her home means a lot to her. When she has money to spare, she would rather 'spend it on furniture or something for the house', buy curtains or a carpet that she can 'keep for a long time', rather than a dress that will be out of fashion next year or jewellery that she will hardly ever wear. 'Some people are constantly buying new clothes. I don't feel the need. Sometimes you end up buying things you never

even wear. You liked the look of them in the shop and then somehow, overnight, you decide you don't like them any more. Take shoes; they only have to pinch a little bit, you wear them once for an hour or two and then you think, "No, they hurt too much, I won't wear them", and then they stay in the box. I'm sure I'm not the only person that happens to.' She likes 'real jewellery', 'gold jewellery', but does not wear what she owns. 'I don't like showing off, putting all my jewellery on; people would say, "Look at her, dressed up in all her jewellery!" I don't like flaunting my wealth, if that's the word for it.'

'Just a trim to tidy myself up'

She 'never splurges' on clothes: 'I'm not one to spend a lot on my wardrobe.' Anyway, 'fashion is constantly changing . . . whatever you do, you can never keep up with it.' Instead, she goes more for 'classic' clothes. She is not sure whether to accept a wedding invitation: 'I'm not keen because it means buying a lot of expensive new things and then you only wear them once.' She occasionally goes to the hairdresser's and regards it as a 'chore': 'just a trim to tidy myself up.' In the country, where she spent her childhood, 'you didn't sit for hours in front of a mirror putting make-up on.' Normally, Madame D. does not do much real cooking 'just for the two of us'; but when they have guests, she 'enjoys cooking traditional things'—quiche lorraine, *gratin dauphinois,* all sorts of roasts, stuffed tomatoes.

'People who throw their money away'

She gets on very well with people who have 'the same tastes' as herself; she likes 'dealing with decent people.' Being 'quite economical without being, shall we say, mean' ('but we really don't like to waste money'), she thinks she could not get on with 'people who throw their money away.' She cannot understand people who 'haven't two pennies to rub together and yet as soon as they get any money they spend it. . . . It's not always the best-off people who stint themselves least; often it's middle-class people who won't deny themselves anything. They go and buy fancy cakes or a bottle of good wine whenever they feel like it, and when the money runs out they put it on their account.' She extends the same disapproval to those 'who don't know how to manage their budget' and who ask for credit towards the end of the month—meaning, no doubt, although she is not explicit, working-class people.

'Cheerful programmes you don't have to think about'

She has not been to the cinema 'for at least ten years', and says she doesn't have time to read either a daily paper or weekly magazines, like *Paris Match* or *Jours de France,* which customers sometimes leave behind in the shop: 'a lot of pages with not much on them and a lot of advertisements.' She watches television a little, but 'not too much', mainly on Sundays, but never after ten at night. She is not 'a TV fanatic' but likes 'cheerful programmes' that 'you don't have to think about', especially light entertainment so long as the producer doesn't 'try to be clever': 'Nowadays I find they're always trying to be clever with their variety programmes; it was much better the

way it used to be.' She refuses all formal experimentation and special effects, and has not liked Averty's recent experimental productions: 'I don't like those cut-up things at all, where you see a head, then a nose, then a leg. It just seems plain silly to me; I must be old-fashioned. . . . First you see a singer all drawn out, three metres tall, then he's got arms two metres long. Do you find that funny? Oh, I just don't like it, it's stupid; I don't see the point of distorting things.' But she does like to watch a 'traditional' singer, 'a singer who just sings, who sings normally, who's normal size and not all distorted.'

'My husband doesn't like hotels'

Every year, they go on holiday in their caravan for two or three weeks. Two or three times they have been to a caravan camp site on the Riviera and last year they stayed beside a lake in the Grenoble region. Until they got the caravan, they did not go on holiday; her husband 'doesn't like hotels at all, or restaurants.' On holiday, her husband plays bowls and cards and 'makes a lot of friends.' She doesn't like doing nothing, so she relaxes and knits or makes tapestry: 'it's a nice hobby, the time goes quicker.' They spend a bit of time on the beach and drink pastis with friends. Apart from the summer holidays, their work is so demanding that they have no time to go out. Her husband, who starts work at nine every Sunday evening, catches up on his sleep Sunday afternoon. At most, they go out 'once a year, on Easter Monday or Whit Monday. Because it was a public holiday, we used to shut up shop for two days, Sunday and Monday.'

cal' interior). Similarly, in music and song, they systematically opt for the déclassé works of bourgeois culture (such as *L'Arlésienne* or the *Blue Danube*) and particularly for the most old-fashioned and traditional singers (Guétary, Mariano).

By a logic which is also valid for the other positions, it is in the sub-category whose diachronic properties of age and trajectory are most in harmony with the diachronic properties of the position, that is, which is most directly in line with the collective history, and therefore most disposed to express its objective truth and announce its future, that the preferences characteristic of the fraction as a whole are expressed with the highest degree of density and intensity. Thus the group (situated above the second axis) of small craftsmen and small shopkeepers, most of whose fathers were also small craftsmen or small shopkeepers, and who, for lack of the economic and especially the cultural capital they would need in order to attempt a reconversion, are condemned to carry on at all costs at the head of particularly threatened small businesses (food shops, small traditional crafts etc.) which will not outlive them (they are even older than the others), is distinguished by systematically retrograde choices from the rest of the fraction, which contains a fair proportion of modern craftsmen (electricians, mechanics etc.), possessing the BEPC or even the baccalauréat, who, especially when young and Parisian, are very close to the technicians in their ethical and aesthetic, and no doubt also their political, choices.[21]

Convinced that they owe their position, albeit diminished, to a 'simple', 'serious', 'honest' life, the declining petit bourgeois express in all areas the most austere and traditional values (a 'neat' [*soigné*], 'classical' interior, a 'conscientious', 'level-headed' friend, traditional French cooking, the most canonical painters, Raphael, Leonardo, Watteau, and the longest-consecrated singers, Piaf, Mariano, Guétary). Their refusals, expressing resentment against the new morality, its showy pretension, its laxity in matters of money (use of credit), child-rearing or sex, are no less significant. Rejecting the most characteristic elements of the life-style favoured by manual workers (e.g., the quality 'bon vivant'), they systematically exclude all the virtues cultivated by the members of the professions ('artistic', 'amusing', 'stylish', 'refined') and all the 'modernist' tastes the latter so readily exhibit (they *never* choose either Picasso, who is one of the whipping-boys of petit-bourgeois resentment against artists, or those exemplary representatives of the new young life-style, Françoise Hardy and Johnny Hallyday). Their aesthetic of the 'well-finished' (*soigné*) is one dimension of an ethos of 'conscientiousness' which leads them to appreciate the values of work, order, rigour, care. It is distinct from the taste for the 'sober', frequent among manual workers or members of the promoted petite bourgeoisie who are guided by the concern to pass unnoticed (and also, but with a quite different meaning, among the old bourgeoisie); but it is chiefly opposed to the 'liberated' taste of the new petite bourgeoisie and the eye-catching 'fantasies' it procures for itself from avant-garde boutiques and unisex hairdressers.

The Executant Petite Bourgeoisie

Centrally situated in terms of capital composition, the members of the executant petite bourgeoisie present in their highest degree all the traits, mentioned at the outset, which make them the most complete realization of the petite bourgeoisie, such as the cult of autodidactic effort and the taste for all the activities whose common feature is that they chiefly demand time and cultural goodwill (making collections, for example).[22] Given an intermediate population such as this, it is one and the same thing to show how it differs from the neighbouring fractions and how its members are distributed, in respect of diachronic properties, from the oldest, and especially those of bourgeois or petit-bourgeois origin, who are very close to the most regressive fraction of the declining petite bourgeoisie in their ethical and aesthetic choices, to the youngest, who, especially when possessing high qualifications, are similar to the mobile elements of the new petite bourgeoisie. Everything takes place as if the basic disposition which characterizes the fraction as a whole were systematically transformed as a function of age and social origin, from an optimistic progressivism among the rising young to a pessimistic, regressive conservatism among the oldest.

It is among the youngest members of the occupations offering the most secure future, such as the junior executives and office workers, and more especially among those who originate from the working class and have only moderate qualifications (BEPC or baccalauréat) that one finds the most developed form of the ascetic dispositions and devotion to culture associated with the ambition to pursue by further accumulation of cultural capital a rise made possible by an initial small accumulation. Set on a progressive trajectory by their schooling, they are naturally inclined to a progressivist world view based on faith in enlightenment and a temperate reformism aiming to give to each according to his scholastic merits. As well as owing all they have to education and expecting from it all they aspire to have, they often stand in a relation of *execution* to *conception* vis-à-vis the senior executives, whose instructions they follow, whose plans they implement and whose manuals they use, so that they tend to identify hierarchies with differences in competence or, more simply, in formal qualifications. This is all the more so since, very often, those who have risen by promotion come up against limits (e.g., ignorance of algebra) which the scholastic hurdles they have not crossed arbitrarily place before them, regardless of any technical necessity really entailed by the job. So it is understandable that they distinguish themselves from the declining petite bourgeoisie in that they combine certain features of the popular ethos—such as the taste for 'pot-luck' entertainment and 'bon vivant' or 'amusing' friends—with features which specifically characterize them. These include marks of attachment to ascetic values—'conscientious' or 'well-bred' friends, 'sober and correct' clothes—and numerous indices of a cultural goodwill as intense as it is innocent. Assigned to tasks requiring precision, rigour, seriousness, in short, goodwill and devotion, and richer in cultural goodwill than in cultural capital, they direct their 'preferences' towards typically middle-brow works,[23] such as the *Sabre Dance* or Utrillo, buy their furniture from department stores, prefer 'clean and tidy', 'easy to maintain' interiors, choose Aznavour, Petula Clark or Johnny Hallyday and are very interested in photography and the cinema.[24]

This pure and empty cultural goodwill, entirely defined by the requirements of mobility, has its equivalent in morality. The repressive rigour of the declining fractions, which is based on resentment at social regression, seems to have no other purpose than to provide those who only have a past with the satisfaction of condemning those who have a future, chiefly the young. By contrast the ascetic rigour of the rising fractions, often associated with a prudent reformism in politics, gives rise to a self-discipline and family discipline which is entirely subordinated to social mobility. Proof of this is seen in the fact that the rising petit bourgeois, who are usually much stricter than the other classes (particularly on everything concerned with their children's upbringing—their work, going out alone, reading-matter, sexuality etc.) can, without contradiction, show themselves much less strict than the dominant morality and the class fractions most attached to it (who make it a 'matter of principle'), whenever the practices in question, such as abortion or the availability of contraceptives to young people, can be applied in the interest of mobility. And it can be understood in the same terms why the rising petit bourgeois tend to slip from optimistic austerity to repressive pessimism as they grow older and as the future which made sense of their sacrifices turns sour.

Thus, among junior executives and clerical workers, there are greater differences between the age groups than in other fractions whenever the questions asked offer an outlet for the repressive dispositions. For example, the proportion of this category who reject the idea that teachers are not severe enough declines from 36.2 percent among the under-35s, to 29 percent among the 35- to 50-year-olds, and 26 percent among the over-50s; the proportion who think that teachers are 'too political' rises from 44.6 percent to 47.6 percent and 60.4 percent for the same age groups (IFOP survey, March 1970, secondary analysis).

The whole existence of the rising petit bourgeois is the anticipation of a future which he will, in most cases, only know by proxy, through his children, on whom he projects his ambitions. The future he 'dreams of for his son' eats up his present. Because he is committed to strategies extending over several generations, he is the man of the deferred pleasure, the deferred present that will be taken later, 'when there is time', 'when we've paid off the mortgage', 'when the children are older' or 'when we've retired', in other words, very often when it is too late, when, having given credit on his life, he has no time to collect his 'due' and must 'cut his coat according to his cloth.' There is no compensation for a lost present, especially when (with the break-up of identification with the children, for example) the disproportion between the sacrifices and the satisfactions becomes apparent, retrospectively making nonsense of a past entirely defined by tension towards the future. In the end these altruistic misers who have squandered everything on the alter ego they had hoped to be, either in person, by rising in the social hierarchy, or through a substitute shaped in their own image, the son for whom 'they have done everything', who 'owes them everything', are left with nothing but resentment—the resentment that has always haunted them in the form of the fear of being taken for a ride by a social world which asks so much of them.

As they struggle to the peak of their career and the moment of self-assessment, feeling their values and even their conception of their job threatened by the arrival of new, more highly qualified generations bearing a new ethos, the oldest of the junior executives and office workers are inclined to conservative dispositions in aesthetics, ethics and politics, as is shown by the analysis of the correspondences, which situates them close to the small shopkeepers and traditional craftsmen. To have their revenge, they only have to place themselves on their favourite terrain, that of morality, to make a virtue of *their* necessity, elevate their particular morality into a universal morality. These groups not only have the morality of their interests, as everyone does; they have an interest in morality. For those scourges of privilege, morality is the only title which gives a right to every privilege. Their resentment often leads to fundamentally ambiguous political positions in which verbal fidelity to past convictions is a mask for present disenchantment, when it does not simply serve to justify moral indignation; and the somewhat lachrymose, humanistic anarchism which may outlive adolescence in some elderly, long-haired bohemians can easily veer with age into a fascistic nihilism endlessly ruminating on scandals and plots.

This description of one possible form of the evolution of political dispositions, whereby clerical workers and junior executives move, as they grow older, closer to the attitudes of the declining fractions (small shopkeepers and especially small craftsmen) than to those of younger members of their own class, is intended to counter the typically conservative tendency to establish a transhistorical relation between biological ageing (implicitly associated with a growth in wisdom and reason) and increased conservatism. In fact, changes in political position and dispositions are apparently related to age only through the mediation of changes in social position which occur over time; and there are as many forms of evolution of political opinions as there are forms of social ageing, i.e., social trajectories. The conservative ideology which regards the relationship between a move towards conservatism and growing old as an anthropological law, and which uses this relationship to justify its pessimistic, disabused account of revolutionary ideologies and ideologues, has every appearance on its side. Given that, on the one hand, the countless forms of social ageing available to bourgeois or petit-bourgeois adolescents (the only ones considered by the ideology) can, for the sake of simplicity, be divided into two classes, roughly corresponding to social success and failure, and on the other hand that these two classes of trajectories both lead, by different routes, to conservative dispositions (which differ greatly, of course, in their modality), it can be seen that one only has to ignore the varieties of ideology, and the social principles of variation of the relationship between ideological ageing and social ageing, to turn a sociologically intelligible statistical relationship into a natural law.

Situated on the opposite side from the previous group as regards age and trajectory, the most educated members of the youngest generation of junior executives, technicians and especially primary teachers are close to the new petite bourgeoisie,[25] especially to their competence and preferences in legitimate culture (they equally often choose the *Art of Fugue*, the *Four Seasons, Eine Kleine Nachtmusik* and the *Well-Tempered Clavier*, but more often the *Sabre Dance,* the *Hungarian Rhapsody* and *Rhapsody in Blue,* and less often *L'Enfant et les sortilèges*). They remain apart from them, however, and all the more so, the less they have been exposed to the new mode of scholastic generation, in everything more directly concerned with the daily art of living. Thus, their ideal friend, who for the new petite bourgeoisie is 'dynamic', 'refined', 'stylish' and 'artistic', is more often 'bon vivant', 'conscientious' and 'sociable', and if they include 'artistic' this is no doubt because it is the one dimension of bourgeois values which the ascetic petit bourgeois can find acceptable by virtue of the value he places on legitimate culture. The occupation of primary teacher to some extent shares the characteristics of the new occupations, owing to the changes in academic and social recruitment and in training. These changes, the most visible of which is feminization, no doubt linked to a rise in social origin, have led to the coexistence in the same position of agents who differ in social trajectory and in all the corresponding properties (for example, upwardly mobile men, and women who belong to the upper classes by their origin or by marriage).

The New Petite Bourgeoisie

As this case clearly shows, age differences—increasingly so as one moves towards the cultural pole—mark differences in the scholastic mode of

A Nurse Who 'Lives with Passion'

Elizabeth F. is 25. She obtained the *bac* (with philosophy) and then went to nursing college. For four years she has worked as a nurse at the Cité Universitaire (International Student Residence) in Paris. Her father was a civil servant and her mother is a Post Office clerk. She lives alone in a one-room apartment with a small entrance-hall. It contains no furniture—no table, no chairs, no shelves. Everything—mattress, record-player, books—is on the floor. On the walls she has a Dario Fo poster about Chile, which she bought at a recital of poems and songs about Chile at the Cité Universitaire, a poster for a Yeats play ('very beautiful'), a still from the film *Aphrodite Child* ('very moving'), a photo of her young nephew, an orange mirror ('very functional') and a big crimson board with a whole set of necklaces, made of shells, pearls, enamelware, beans etc., some of which she made herself. She does not expect to buy furniture: 'It's not that I don't like it; I just don't happen to have any—it doesn't seem to be very essential. I admit it's not very convenient for people when I invite them for dinner, but I really don't think it's important.' She bought her Citroën 2CV second-hand, from her godmother ('she let me have it cheap'); she bought her phonograph in her next-to-last year at the lycée, with 'the first money I earned working in a sanatorium in my spare time.' It isn't really 'suitable' for classical music and her records are 'very, very worn out.'

'I love being creative'

She is eager to express her personality and seizes every opportunity to 'create' something personal: 'I love drawing . . . everyone in the family does drawing: my sister draws, my father used to draw.' Mainly, though only episodically, she does black-and-white portraits of people she likes: 'I enjoy colour but for me it's not the important thing in a drawing'; the most important things are 'the curves and then, well, the expression, capturing someone's expression . . . the pleasure comes when I'm doing the drawing, later it's of no significance.' She learnt how to make enamelware: first from books, which her aunt gave her together with a kiln when she was 15; later she made enamelware with her sister and friends at the municipal youth club.

'People who never look outside themselves'

Her only make-up is an invisible foundation cream; her hair is thinned and cut medium-length. The first quality she looks for in her friends 'is joy. I like healthy people, who are glad to be alive.' 'I like people who are at ease with themselves, perhaps because I'm not always at ease wth myself. I think that what makes people carry on living is always being able to hope for something, never accepting things as they are. . . . The people I don't like, I can't accept because they seem to me . . . empty. I mean they're dull, they have no taste, no passion. Perhaps "no passion" is too strong; I mean they don't *want* anything, they don't seem to feel anything, they never look outside themselves. They don't really *live*.

They're imprisoned by a whole environment. They can't get out of it and don't even realize they *could* get out of it. There are quite a lot of them among my patients and the people I work with. People who are perhaps too dependent on material satisfactions, on the material things society can offer them ... I can't say I don't like them, but I'm not interested in them. They don't interest me.'

'Doing something with my body'

She worships 'nature', 'everything that is natural in people, in the street', and loves 'nature in Paris, the woods and flowers.' For a whole year she practised 'physical expression' with the Montreuil theatre group: 'Doing something with my body ... performing movements, gestures, that aren't necessarily theatrical, that express my body—that's something I enjoy.' On holiday, she shuns campsites ('they're too organized nowadays, almost hotels'); she cannot spend more than a week at the seaside 'doing nothing': 'Going to the beach, sun-bathing, the occasional swim ... after two days of that, I'm bored.' She hitch-hikes to Greece, Italy or the Balearic Islands: 'I love travelling that way partly because it's so different from what I do the rest of the year, a different life-style ... but also in order to live with a bit of insecurity—that's exciting—and to meet different people, be able to communicate.' Last year she took part in the restoration of an abbey in the Rouergue region, and in her spare time she has worked with an archaeological team excavating a site in Eure-et-Loire. Every other Wednesday (she works one Wednesday out of two) she attends a course at the Ecole Pratique des Hautes Etudes 'to get a bit of theory' ('it helps to have some notions of history and archaeology').

'We used to choose a theme, talk about it and then create'

For three years she also belonged to an amateur drama group with friends at Bois d'Arcy, near Paris. They put on quite a few cabaret shows based on poetry. 'We did one on Boris Vian's work so as to make it better known.' They have also written their own shows: 'We used to choose a theme, talk about it and then create ... but the people there were too young and it broke down. Everyone went off their own way after the *bac* and we never got together again.' Occasionally with a girl-friend she still does a bit of acting, 'just little sketches that we work on together' ('I wouldn't have wanted to make a living out of it; it's just a hobby').

'I don't go just because it's cheaper'

There are periods when she goes regularly to the theatre. At the theatre in the Cité Universitaire she has recently seen *Ali Baba's Cave* 'by a troupe from the Théâtre Oblique, I think; it wasn't bad', Dario Fo at the Salle Gémier, 'it was very radical, but it was in the form of stories told to people and it was excellent.' She goes to see shows that are not expensive: 'I don't go just because it's cheaper, but the fact is, at the Cité there are very good shows that aren't expensive.... Of course, it isn't very comfortable, but you have a good evening out and it doesn't cost too much, about ten francs ... Afterwards, we normally come back here or visit another friend and we discuss the play if we feel like it.' She went to the Comédie-Française when she was younger, but no longer goes: 'I never disliked it, but it's not my favourite kind of theatre. All the same, it's a very classical theatre, but I don't really know much about it.' On the other hand, boulevard theatre 'isn't theatre at all.... Theatre is something that involves people, brings together the performers and the spectators.... Boulevard theatre doesn't do anything like it. I'm not even sure if people relax, because after all they see their own lives, what they do every day of the week. Theatre shouldn't be about relaxing, it should be about dreaming, inventing.'

'Boris Vian and lots of things about him'

She loves classical music, especially Bach and Beethoven; she often listens to Félix Leclerc, Léo Ferré, Jacques Brel—her 'great love' when she was 15 ('the only singer I've liked all the time for years')—and Georges Brassens: 'I don't like Sheila at all—it's not music, it's commerce, opium, the sort of thing I hate.' Although she does not like him, 'perhaps because of my upbringing' (her family hated him), she thinks that Johnny Hallyday 'does have something'. She likes Pink Floyd—and has one of their records—but 'only superficially'.

She reads *Le Monde* when she has time (but that is not often), the reviews in *Le Nouvel Observateur,* and fairly regularly *Le Canard Enchaîné.* She used to read more when she was at school. She reads novels (recently, 'a book on Nepal by Han Suyin'), all Françoise Sagan's novels, 'Boris Vian and lots of things about him.' She likes to 'discover an author', 'immerse herself in a book and tell herself she's reading something fascinating.' She likes Van Gogh (she went to the exhibition at the Petit Palais), Goya, Buffet, 'everything that's all done in lines' and Impressionism: 'It's a vision that's much deeper than a material object ... you really feel you're given the impression of someone who has seen something and reproduced it.' She recently visited the Rodin Museum, which is 'fantastic': 'I just love his work, it's wonderful.'

---

generation and therefore differences between generations defined in and by their relationship to the educational system. The best qualified of the younger generation of junior executives or clerical workers (mainly originating from the working and middle classes) share with the members of the new occupations—and especially with those of them who do not originate from the bourgeoisie—a relation to culture and, partially at least, to the social world which stems from an interrupted trajectory and the effort to extend or re-establish it. Thus, the new occupations are the natural refuge of all those who have not obtained from the educational system the qualifications that would have enabled them to claim the established positions their original social position promised them; and also of those who have not obtained from their qualifications all they felt entitled to expect by reference to an earlier state of the relationship between qualifications and jobs.

Here too, the complete description of the positions contains an (implicitly normative) description of those who are predisposed to occupy and succeed in them, that is, more precisely, a description of the mediations through which dispositions linked to trajectories are adjusted to these positions—in short, everything that is normally hidden under the word 'vocation'. It can immediately be seen that, precisely by virtue of their actual and potential indeterminacy, positions which offer no guarantees but, in return, ask for no guarantees, which impose no specific condition of entry, especially as regards certificates, but hold out the promise of the highest profits for non-certified cultural capital, which guarantee no particular career prospects (of the type offered by the well-established occupations) but exclude none, not even the most ambitious, are adjusted in advance to the dispositions typical of individuals in decline endowed with a strong cultural capital imperfectly converted into educational capital, or rising individuals who have not obtained all the educational capital which, in the absence of social capital, is needed to escape the most limited of the middle positions.

In the first place, the willingness or capacity to accept the (average) risk resulting from the indeterminacy of the positions no doubt varies, other things being equal, with inherited capital, partly by an effect of the dispositions themselves, which are more self-assured when there is more security, and partly because of the real distance from necessity given by possession of the economic means of persisting in provisionally unprofitable positions.[26] Whereas the personal risk entailed by the riskiest positions declines, both subjectively and objectively, as inherited capital increases, the chances of profit grow as capital increases in all its forms, not only the economic capital which gives the means of waiting for the future of 'coming' occupations, or the cultural capital which helps to make that future by the symbolic violence needed to create and sell new products, but perhaps especially the social capital which, in these informally organized sectors in which recruitment is effected by co-option, enables one to enter the race and stay in it.

Furthermore, these positions, which are ultimately less risky and, at least in the long run, more profitable, the more capital one brings into them, present a further advantage for people seeking an honourable refuge to avoid social decline, perhaps the most important advantage in the short term and in the practical shaping of a 'vocation'. One only has to consider the opposition between the youth leader or cultural organizer and the primary teacher, between the journalist or TV producer and the secondary teacher, between the technician in a public opinion or market research institute and the bank clerk or post office clerk, to see that, unlike the established positions which are situated in a hierarchy and impose the unequivocal image of an occupation defined in its present and future, the new or renovated occupations allow or encourage symbolic rehabilitation strategies, illustrated by the use of noble 'doublets', more or less overtly euphemistic, such as 'personal assistant' for secretary or 'psychotherapeutic' nurse for psychiatric nurse. But this effect is most visible in all those cases in which the agents endeavour to produce jobs adjusted to their ambitions rather than adjust their ambitions to fit already existing jobs, to produce the need for their own product by activities which may be initially voluntary, like a number of 'social' occupations, but aim to be imposed as 'public services' officially recognized and more or less completely State-financed, in accordance with a classic process of professionalization (creation of a specialized training sanctioned by diplomas, a code of ethics and an occupational ideology etc.).

The new petite bourgeoisie comes into its own in all the occupations involving presentation and representation (sales, marketing, advertising, public relations, fashion, decoration and so forth) and in all the institutions providing symbolic goods and services. These include the various jobs in medical and social assistance (marriage guidance, sex therapy, dietetics, vocational guidance, paediatric advice etc.) and in cultural production and organization (youth leaders, play leaders, tutors and monitors, radio and TV producers and presenters, magazine journalists), which have expanded considerably in recent years; but also some established occupations, such as art craftsmen or nurses. Thus, the art craftsmen in the old sense—upholsterers, wrought-iron workers, cabinet-makers, picture-framers, goldsmiths, jewellers, gilders or engravers, trained in technical schools and very close to small craftsmen and their values—have been joined in the last fifteen years or so by makers of jewellery, printed fabrics, ceramics or hand-woven clothes, with a higher level of general education, often Parisian and of bourgeois origin, who are closer in life-style to the cultural intermediaries. Similarly, among the secretaries and nurses, some, originating from the lower or middle classes, are very close to the junior administrative executives, while others, younger, often Parisian and of bourgeois origin, present all the features of the new occupations. In general, the indeterminacy of the new or renovated occupations means that the heterogeneity of the agents' trajectories is particularly marked. One can almost always distinguish two groups separated by social origin and all the associated dispositions, who disagree more or less overtly over the definition of the job and the competences or virtues necessary in order to fill it.

The oppositions which this duality of origins gives rise to within the new petite bourgeoisie are expressed very clearly in the relationship between ethical preferences and refusals. Unlike the declining petite bourgeoisie, which rejects the whole set of values directly opposed to its own, i.e., the very virtues pursued by the new petite bourgeoisie (amusing, refined, stylish, artistic, imaginative), the members of the socio-medical services make contradictory choices which seems to express the antagonisms between the values of their original milieu and the values of their present milieu: some reject the qualities which most of the others put in top place (refined, stylish, amusing) while others reject the qualities most prized by the established petite bourgeoisie (level-headed, classical). These uncertainties or even incoherences no doubt exist in each of the members of the new professions, who have to invent a new life-style, particularly in domestic life, and to redefine their social co-ordinates. If the indeterminacy of a position favours bluffing or euphemizing strategies, there is a price to be paid in terms of the occupant's uncertainty as to his social identity, as we see from the testimony of an industrialist's daughter, aged 35, proprietor of a 'boutique' in Paris selling 'design centre' products, 'contemporary goods' and gifts; she attended a decorative arts school but has no diploma, and conducts her art business as if it were an art: 'When people ask me what I do, and I say "I'm a shopkeeper", I always feel it's someone else answering for me because really I don't see myself as a shopkeeper. But I suppose in the end, when it comes down to it, I must be, I don't know ... All the same, I feel very remote from the preoccupations of my butcher and I feel much closer to someone who works in an advertising agency or to an interior decorator. It's all very complicated. Personally I see myself as rather out on a limb, between two stools, I don't know. For me shopkeeping is like a game; it's always a bit of a gamble, buying and selling.'

Those members of the new petite bourgeoisie who originate from the upper classes and who, for lack (most often) of educational capital, have had to reconvert into the new occupations such as cultural intermediary or art craftsman have had fewer years of schooling than the average for their class of origin but more than the average for the middle classes; they therefore possess a very great cultural capital of familiarity and a social capital of 'connections'. They manifest the highest competence within the middle classes and incline towards a system of choices very similar to that of the bourgeoisie: the *Art of Fugue,* the *Concerto for the Left Hand,* the *Firebird Suite,* the *Four Seasons,* Goya, Braque, Breughel, Jacques Douai, the Modern Art Museum, antique shops and the Flea Market, a 'harmonious', 'discreet', 'studied' interior, 'refined', 'artistic', 'stylish' friends, 'intellectual' films, *Salvatore Giuliano, Exterminating Angel, The Trial,* or, among the comedies, *The Suitor* (see figure 18). Their ambivalent relationship with the educational system, inducing a sense of complicity with every form of symbolic defiance, inclines them to welcome all the forms of culture which are, provisionally at least, on the (lower) boundaries of legitimate culture—jazz, cinema, strip cartoons, science fiction—and to flaunt (for example) American fashions and models—jazz, jeans, rock or the avant-garde underground, which is their monopoly—as a challenge to legitimate culture; but they often bring into these regions disdained by the educational establishment an erudite, even 'academic' disposition which is inspired by a clear intention of rehabilitation, the cultural equivalent of the restoration strategies which define their occupational project.

Thus, the members of the socio-medical services name more film directors than actors, thereby distancing themselves from the clerical workers or the

Figure 18   Films seen (in order of preference): II.

Social and medical services	Junior commercial execs. and secretaries	Office workers	Small shopkeepers and craftsmen
Divorce Italian Style	Divorce Italian Style	Rocco and His Brothers	The Longest Day
The Trial	The Longest Day	Divorce Italian Style	Vice and Virtue
Les dim. de V. d'Avray	Les dim. de V. d'Avray	Vice and Virtue	Divorce Italian Style
The Suitor	Rocco and His Brothers	The Magnificent Seven	Les dim. de V. d'Avray
Salvatore Giuliano	The Suitor	The Longest Day	Rocco and His Brothers
Singing in the Rain	The Magnificent Seven	Imperial Venus	Le glaive et la balance
Rocco and His Brothers	The Trial	Voyage à Biarritz	The Suitor
Exterminating Angel	Salvatore Giuliano	The Trial	The Magnificent Seven
The Longest Day	Vice and Virtue	The Suitor	Imperial Venus
Le glaive et la balance	Singing in the Rain	Le glaive et la balance	Singing in the Rain
Ballade pour un voyou	L'abominable homme	Ballade pour un voyou	L'abominable homme
Voyage à Biarritz	Ballade pour un voyou	Les dim. de V. d'Avray	The Trial
The Leopard	Le glaive et la balance	Le boucanier des îles	Ballade pour un voyou
Vice and Virtue	Voyage à Biarritz	Singing in the Rain	Exterminating Angel
Imperial Venus	Le boucanier des îles	L'abominable homme	55 Days at Peking
L'abominable homme	The Leopard	55 Days at Peking	Voyage à Biarritz
55 Days at Peking	Exterminating Angel	Salvatore Giuliano	Le boucanier des îles
The Magnificent Seven	55 Days at Peking	The Leopard	Salvatore Giuliano
Le boucanier des îles	Imperial Venus	Exterminating Angel	The Leopard

These are the films chosen by the Parisian respondents. Those in the Lille area were offered another list (based on the films then showing); their choices are organized in accordance with an analogous structure.

secretaries, who are mainly interested in actors.[27] Their preference for *The Trial*, a 'prodigious, harrowing' film, or for *Les dimanches de Ville d'Avray* by Serge Bourguignon (who uses 'sometimes questionable' but 'never vulgar' means to retrace with 'unfailing delicacy' the 'very pure and poetic story of a meeting and a friendship between a twelve-year-old girl and a thirty-year-old man'—*Le Monde*, 24 November 1962) no doubt reveals their quasi-professional interest in all psychological explorations;[28] but it is also a sign, among many others, of the high cultural ambitions (also reflected in the frequency with which they say they read works of philosophy) of these transitional, mediating categories, identified in intention and aspiration with the dominant classes whom they serve, often in spatial proximity (secretary and director, nurse and doctor), yet separated from them by an invisible barrier.

The fact that a large proportion of these new positions are occupied by women no doubt contributes to the realization of their potentialities, which express themselves precisely in this recruitment. It would clearly be naive to look to the sex-ratio of the category, which is one of the properties of the category, for the explanation of this or that other property of the category. The socially inculcated dispositions (in particular, the inclination towards the things of taste) which lead especially the women of these fractions towards the adjectives they see as most distinguished ('stylish', 'refined' etc.) are also the basis of the 'vocation' which brings them to the new occupations and of the entirely functional aptitudes they apply in them. Not the least of these are the aesthetic dispositions required both in the production or sale of goods and services and in the self-presentation which is often an essential condition for successful symbolic imposition.

The key to the whole system of preferences of these déclassé petit bourgeois aspiring to recover their lost class is found in the frequency with which they choose adjectives which unambiguously declare an attraction for the most naively aristocratic qualities ('stylish', 'distinguished', 'refined', 'recherché').[29] This systematic pretension to distinction, this quasi-methodical concern to stand aloof from the tastes and values most clearly associated with the established petite bourgeoisie and the working classes, which give to all their practices an air of tension even in relaxation, constraint in the pursuit of a 'liberated' life-style, affectation in simplicity, are indeed the most significant manifestations of this new variant of the petit-bourgeois ethos.

This well-armed pretension, based on a familiarity with culture combined with high social origin, is quite distinct in its means and its modality from the anxious pretension of the promoted petite bourgeoisie. It functions as a sort of social 'flair', allowing its owner to steer through difficult situations when the usual landmarks are missing. Thus, although the members of the new petite bourgeoisie are no more inclined than the others to concede (especially in practice) that photography can transfigure objects such as a pregnant woman, a scrap-yard, a butcher's stall or a car crash, they are more skilful at identifying the 'soppy' objects of popular taste or petit-bourgeois aestheticism—the sunset, the landscape, the little girl playing with a cat, the folk dance (all of which they much more rarely say would make a beautiful photograph). In general, the cultural 'bluff' which relies on this flair—measured by the gap between the tendency to select the rarest painters, composers or works (*L'Enfant et les sortilèges*, the *Firebird Suite*, Kandinsky, Dali, Braque) and the frequency of visits to museums, especially the Modern Art Museum—varies with the proportion of inheritors and parvenus in each category. It is particularly frequent among the cultural intermediaries and commercial executives, very rare among the promoted petit bourgeois (as it is among the public-sector executives and secondary teachers), and is reduced to an empty intention of distinction in the rising fraction of the new occupations (situated on the negative-value side of the second axis).

Of the members of the new petite bourgeoisie who originate from the upper classes, 39.5 percent say they know at least 12 of the works of music, whereas only 25 percent of them can name at least 12 of the composers of the same works. This disparity does not occur with members of this fraction who originate from the working or middle classes: 15 percent of them say they know at least 12 works and 15 percent name at least 12 composers. By the same logic, the former declare much more often (85 percent) than the latter (58 percent): 'All music of quality interests me.'

The dispositions of which the new petite bourgeoisie is the bearer find the conditions for their full development only in Paris (see table 25).[30] Cultural pretension—together with education, of which it reinforces the effects—is no doubt one of the factors conducive to appropriation of the advantages associated with proximity to the centre of cultural values, such as a more intense supply of cultural goods, the sense of belonging and the incentives given by contact with groups who are also culturally favoured.[31] Consequently there is no other category in which the systematic differences between Parisians and provincials are more marked: differences in the intensity of the legitimate practices (museum visits etc.) and the range of competence (in music, for example); differences in the relationship to legitimate culture, with the sense of being an outsider to the world of painting or music ('not my strong point', 'I don't know much about it') always being more marked among provincials, other things being equal; differences, above all, in the ability to recognize—often without knowing them—smart opinions, the Parisians always being more inclined, at all levels of competence, to opt for the most legitimate judgements ('All music of quality interests me') as soon as they are formulated, whereas the provincials more often concur with the judgements expressing a recognition of legitimacy combined with a confession of ignorance ('I don't know much about it') or incompetence ('It's complicated'); differences in the indices of cultural pretension, with, for example, the choice of an 'imaginative' or 'studied' interior, clothes that are 'chic' and 'stylish' (*racé*), two expressions typical of the new art of living promulgated by the mass-circulation women's magazines, and above all the declared preference for the rarest works of music, the *Firebird Suite,* the *Art of Fugue,* the *Well-Tempered Clavier* (instead of the provincials' *Rhapsody in Blue*), through which the new petite bourgeoisie distinguishes itself from the promoted petite bourgeoisie much more decisively in Paris than in the provinces; and differences in all the indices of life-style, in the choice of clothes, in tastes in cooking or ethical preferences, in which the provincials are always more prudent, less audaciously 'liberated'.

Together with the opposition between the Parisians and the provincials, the opposition (strongly marked in cultural competence) between the occupants of the new positions who originate from the dominant class and those who originate from the other classes underlines the conditions of success of the social bluff which always plays a part in the definition of the new occupations. Having acquired only the most visible and least prestigious aspects of the new life-style, the upwardly mobile in-

Table 25 Knowledge and preferences of established and new petite bourgeoisie, in Paris and in the provinces (%).

Type of petite bourgeoisie	Location	Know 0-2 composers	Know 3-6 composers	Paintings don't interest me	Paintings nice but difficult	Jacques Brel	Aznavour	Gilbert Bécaud	Rhapsody in Blue	Sabre Dance	Pragmatic friend	Warm interior
Established[a]	Paris	37.3	34.9	9.3	66.7	53.6	37.7	31.3	21.1	24.5	13.4	27.0
	Provinces	58.5	23.1	19.8	61.4	35.8	42.5	28.3	28.8	20.3	16.6	25.6
New[b]	Paris	10.4	17.9	3.0	20.9	34.3	23.9	13.4	17.7	9.7	12.1	25.8
	Provinces	32.7	26.9	5.7	42.3	50.0	36.5	32.7	35.6	15.6	30.8	43.1

Type of petite bourgeoisie	Location	Know 7-11 composers	Know 12+ composers	Love the Impressionists	Like abstract art	Léo Ferré	Jacques Douai	Firebird Suite	Art of Fugue	Well-Tempered Clavier	Artistic friend	Studied interior
Established[a]	Paris	21.4	6.3	16.3	7.7	32.5	8.7	12.2	5.1	4.2	10.5	3.6
	Provinces	14.2	4.2	8.2	10.6	28.8	4.7	4.0	2.8	2.8	8.1	3.8
New[b]	Paris	43.3	28.4	37.3	38.8	47.8	23.9	21.0	22.6	17.7	39.4	20.9
	Provinces	34.6	5.8	25.0	26.9	36.5	13.5	8.9	2.2	4.4	15.4	15.7

a. Craftsmen, small shopkeepers, clerical employees, junior administrative executives, primary teachers, technicians.

b. Social and medical services, cultural intermediaries, art craftsmen and small art-dealers, secretaries, junior commercial executives.

dividuals who seek in marginal, less strictly defined positions a way of escaping destinies incompatible with the promises implied in their scholastic careers, without possessing the cultural competences, the ethical dispositions and, above all, the social capital and investment sense from which individuals originating from the dominant class expect a recovery of their former position, have every likelihood of being expelled from positions to which they have been led by educationally induced allodoxia, as those positions are progressively revalued (partly through their own elimination) by the activity of the sole legitimate occupants.

From Duty to the Fun Ethic

One can see how inherited dispositions predispose individuals to occupy the positions towards which they orient them. With these 'need merchants', sellers of symbolic goods and services who always sell themselves as models and as guarantors of the value of their products, and who sell so well because they believe in what they sell, the symbolic authority of the honest, trustworthy vendor takes the form of an imposition that is both more violent and more gentle, since the vendor deceives the customer only insofar as he deceives himself and is sincerely 'sold' on the value of what he sells. Because the new 'substitution' industry, which sells fine words instead of things to those who cannot afford the things but are willing to settle for words, finds its ideal clientele in the new petite bourgeoisie, this group is predisposed to collaborate with total conviction in imposing the life-style handed down by the new bourgeoisie, the probable destination of its trajectory and the real goal of its aspirations.[32] In short, this petite bourgeoisie of consumers, which means to acquire on credit, i.e., before its due time, the attributes of the legitimate life-style—'residences' with 'olde-worlde' names and holiday flats at Merlin-Plage, mock luxury cars and mock luxury holidays—is perfectly adapted to act as a transmission belt and pull into the race for consumption and competition those from whom it means to distinguish itself. In fact, one of its distinguishing features is precisely its sense of legitimacy in teaching others the legitimate life-style by a symbolic action which not only produces the need for its own product, and therefore, in the long run, legitimates itself and those who exercise it, but also legitimates the life-style put forward as a model, that is, that of the dominant class, or, more precisely, of the fractions which constitute its ethical avant-garde.

A very different image of themselves and their activity is, of course, held by all those who, in industry or in the great bureaucracies of cultural production—radio, television, research organizations, the major daily or weekly newspapers—and especially in the occupations of 'social work' and 'cultural facilitation', perform the tasks of gentle manipulation assigned to them by the new division of labour. Occupying a dominated position within the hierarchy of the institutions of cultural production and circulation and experiencing a quasi alienation which sometimes provides the basis for an intellectual solidarity with the dominated classes, the new cultural intermediaries are inclined to sympathize with discourses aimed at challenging the cultural order and the hierarchies which the cultural 'hierarchy' aims to maintain, and to return to the themes of all heresies—denunciation of the (technocratic) pretension to the monopoly of competence, hostility to hierarchies and 'the' hierarchy, the ideology of universal creativity. But in fact these occupations condemn their occupants to the essential ambiguity resulting from the discrepancy between the (symbolically) subversive dispositions linked to their position in the division of labour and the manipulative or conservative functions attached to the position, between the subjective image of the occupational project and the objective function of the occupation. The very performance of the function may presuppose this discrepancy, a principle of dissimulation and misrecognition, as in the case of some veteran revolutionaries of May 1968 who have become industrial psychologists: to accept their ambiguous position and to accept themselves doing so, they are forced to invent the skilfully ambiguous discourses and practices that were, so to speak, inscribed in advance in the very definition of the position.[33] Obliged to live out the contradiction between their messianic aspirations and the reality of their practice, to cultivate uncertainty as to their social identity in order to be able to accept it, and therefore condemned to a questioning of the world which masks an anxious self-questioning, these 'intellectual lackeys' are predisposed to experience with particular intensity the existential mood of a whole intellectual generation, which, weary of desperately hoping for a collective hope, seeks in a narcissistic self-absorption the substitute for the hope of changing the social world or even of understanding it.

Thus, in the struggle it wages, within the dominant fractions of the dominant class, to replace old-style conservatism based on an overtly authoritarian image of the hierarchical relations between the classes, generations or sexes with a reconverted conservatism corresponding to the enlightened self-interest of those for whom a rational use of the educational system has provided the means of reconverting themselves in accordance with the new logic of the economy, the new or renovated bourgeoisie finds a natural ally, both economically and politically, in the new petite bourgeoisie. The latter recognizes in the new bourgeoisie the embodiment of its human ideal (the 'dynamic' executive) and, having abandoned the somewhat morose asceticism of the rising petite bourgeoisie, collaborates enthusiastically in imposing the new ethical norms (especially as regards consumption) and the corresponding needs.

Seeking its occupational and personal salvation in the imposition of new doctrines of ethical salvation, the new petite bourgeoisie is predisposed to play a vanguard role in the struggles over everything concerned with the art of living, in particular, domestic life and consumption, relations between the sexes and the generations, the reproduction of the family and its values. It is opposed on almost every point to the repressive morality of the declining petite bourgeoisie whose religious or political conservatism often centres on moral indignation at moral disorder, and especially the disorder of sexual mores—as witness the theme of 'pornocracy' and the anti-feminism which run through a whole current of predominantly petit-bourgeois right-wing thought, from Proudhon to Pareto. But it is equally opposed, by the aristocratic pretension of its fundamental choices and by its subversive representation of the relations between the sexes, to the asceticism of the promoted petite bourgeoisie, whose austere optimism, rigorous but not without a sort of heroism, is opposed to the repressive pessimism of the declining petite bourgeoisie.[34]

Thus, whereas the old morality of duty, based on the opposition between pleasure and good, induces a generalized suspicion of the 'charming and attractive', a fear of pleasure and a relation to the body made up of 'reserve', 'modesty' and 'restraint', and associates every satisfaction of the forbidden impulses with guilt, the new ethical avant-garde urges a morality of pleasure as a duty.[35] This doctrine makes it a failure, a threat to self-esteem, not to 'have fun',[36] or, as Parisians like to say with a little shudder of audacity, *jouir*;[37] pleasure is not only permitted but demanded, on ethical as much as on scientific grounds.[38] The fear of not getting enough pleasure, the logical outcome of the effort to overcome the fear of pleasure, is combined with the search for self-expression and 'bodily expression' and for communication with others ('relating'—*échange*), even immersion in others (considered not as a group but as subjectivities in search of their identity); and the old personal ethic is thus rejected for a cult of personal health and psychological therapy. At the opposite pole from the 'politicization' which depersonalizes personal experiences by presenting them as particular cases of generic experiences common to a class, 'moralization' and 'psychologization' personalize experiences, and are thus perfectly consistent with the more or less secularized forms of the search for religious salvation.[39] As is shown by the use it makes of psychoanalytic jargon, the modernist morality is a psychological vulgate which moralizes under the guise of analysis; and as is shown by the emphasis it places on Erikson's 'utopia of full orgasmic reciprocity', it transmutes a spuriously positive definition of the 'normal' into an imperative of normality and bases the orgasm-duty of its theoretical morality on the findings of a bogus science of mores à la Kinsey, thus introducing the deadly, rational accountancy of equivalences into the area of sexual exchanges, which for most societies is one of the last refuges of collective misrecognition.[40] Invoking the prestige of a false science of sexual behaviour to naturalize a conception and an experience of 'sexuality'—a very recent historical invention which depends on social conditions of possibility that are very unequally distributed[41]—it consigns to the pathology of 'sexual poverty', i.e., to the attentions of the psychoanalyst or the sexologist, sole arbiters of legitimate sexual competence, all those whom the old morality would have consigned to the inferno of 'natural' sexuality. These 'barbarians' who have not caught up with the 'sexual revolution' are once again the victims of a universalization of the definition of competence not accompanied by a universalization of the conditions of acquisition.

Closer in this respect to religious prophecy than to science, whose truths are always partial and provisional, this would-be scientific morality provides a systematic answer to the problems of daily existence. It proposes, for example, a conception of bodily exercise and a representation of childhood and child-rearing which are in perfect harmony with its vision of sexuality. Out goes the asceticism of traditional gymnastics, which measures the value of an exercise by its cost in effort, and even suffering ('il faut souffrir pour être belle'), which sees physical effort as 'character-building' and may even find a form of pleasure in the experience of tension; in its place comes the 'new gymnastics', a self-styled 'anti-gymnastics', with a system of equally imperative and exactly opposite precepts. Aiming to substitute relaxation for tension, pleasure for effort, 'creativity' and 'freedom' for discipline, communication for solitude, it treats the body as the psychoanalyst treats the soul, bending its ear to 'listen ' to a body which has to be 'unknotted', liberated or, more simply, rediscovered and accepted ('feeling at home'). This psychologization of the relation to the body is inseparable from an exaltation of the self, but a self which truly fulfils itself ('growth', 'awareness', 'responsiveness') only when 'relating' to others ('sharing experiences') through the intermediary of the body treated as a sign and not as an instrument (which opens the door to a whole politics of the 'alienated body'). Such are the intentions which lie behind exercises of 'bodily expression', a sort of painless delivery of one's own body.[42]

The same oppositions are found in the area of child-rearing. The puritanical view of the child's nature as a site of dangerous, powerful (essentially auto-erotic) desires leads upbringing to be seen as a 'training', a straightening, and pedagogy as a set of techniques for controlling the child while taming his bad instincts; it gives adults the power to define needs, i.e., legitimate desires, to distinguish, for example, between legitimate cries (of hunger or pain) and illegitimate ones, or between 'good' and 'bad' habits. By contrast, the therapeutic ethic, with its psychobabble of 'liberationist' commonplaces ('father figure', 'Peter Pan complex' etc.), credits the child with a good nature which must be accepted as such, with its legitimate pleasure needs (for attention, affection, maternal care). Child-rearing, which is also a source of legitimate pleasures (so that procreation, which produces this consumer object bringing joy, youth and union to both parents, is also a psychotherapeutic duty), treats the child as a sort of apprentice who must discover his body and the world through exploration; and, blurring the boundaries between work and play, duty and pleasure, it defines play as muscular and mental learning and therefore a necessary pleasure, subjectively agreeable and objectively indispensable, thus making pleasure a duty for children and parents alike.

Psychoanalysis, the rationalizing mystique of the age of science, is freely interpreted to supply the legitimating discourse which gives the appearances of a rational foundation to the arbitrary (but socially necessary) presuppositions of an ethos. And the slide from ethics to therapy produces the need for the therapist of which it is the product; there is no doubt that the search for psychological health through recourse to specialists in the rational cure of souls (psychoanalysts, psychotherapists, marriage guidance counsellors and so on) stands in a dialectical relation to the development of a body of professionals capable of producing the need for their own product, i.e., a market for the goods and services they are equipped to supply.

It would no doubt be a mistake to attribute to this single factor all the changes in domestic ethics which result from the combined impact of a number of (relatively) independent causal series, including the appearance of new psychological theories (psychoanalysis, genetic psychology etc.); the vastly increased number of girls from the bourgeoisie entering higher education and adapting to the associated life-style; the transformation of the mode of social reproduction, which means that scholastic errors tend to count more than moral errors, with academic anxiety, previously more a male concern, replacing ethical anxiety, which used to affect mainly girls; women's increased access to the labour market; and the changes in economic production itself, which, having to place ever greater emphasis on the production of needs and the artificial creation of scarcities, helps in many indirect ways to encourage a consumer morality. The fact remains that the rise of the therapeutic morality is unquestionably linked to the constitution of a corps of professionals (psychoanalysts, sexologists, counsellors, psychologists, specialized journalists and so forth) claiming a monopoly of the legitimate definition of legitimate pedagogic or sexual competence; and that the constitution of a field of production of goods and services called for by the disparity between the competence now demanded in such matters and real competence cannot be understood independently of the whole set of reconversion strategies through which agents, whose domestic or educational training predisposed them to play the role of an ethical vanguard, have been able to find the substitute for the prestigious positions the labour market refused them, in the interstices between the teaching profession and the medical profession. Thus the exemplary history of all those who started by professing a faith and ended up making it a profession, especially of all those associations which, in the areas of social work, adult education, cultural organization or advice on child-rearing and sexuality, have moved, in the space of a generation, from the enthusiastic uncertainties of voluntary evangelism to the security of quasi-civil-servant status, unfolds in time the ambiguous nature of all those professions which are bureaucratized forms of 'exemplary prophecy' and which involve offering (or selling) one's own art of living as an example to others.

If the ethical proselytism of these ethical prophets of bureaucratic societies systematically reverses the ascetic morality of the established petite bourgeoisie, this is because, like the choice, by which they are defined, of making their profession rather than entering ready-made professions, their life-style and ethical and political positions are based on a rejection of everything in themselves that is finite, definite, final, in a word, petit bourgeois, that is, a refusal to be pinned down in a particular site in social space, a practical utopianism which was until then the privilege of intellectuals and which predisposes them to welcome every form of utopia. Classified, déclassé, aspiring to a higher class, they see themselves as unclassifiable, 'excluded', 'dropped out', 'marginal', anything rather than categorized, assigned to a class, a determinate place in social space. And yet all their practices, cultural, sporting, educational, sexual, speak of classification—but in the mode of denial, as one sees from a few headings taken from the index of a 'resource' guide to adolescent counter-culture:[13] aikido, agit-prop, alternative press, anthroposophy, anti-gymnastics, anti-nuclear, anti-psychiatry, anti-radiation, anti-scientism, anti-vaccination, astrology, basket-making, biodynamics, bio-energy, biological farming, body, Charlie Hebdo, childhood, communes, creativity, dance, diet, drugs, ecology, encounters, esoterica, extra-terrestrial, folk, freedom, free flight, futuristics, gays, Gestalt therapy, gliding, go, green, hallucinogens, hiking, grass, homeopathy, imagination, immigrants, independent cinema, invention, judo, kendo, kyudo, Larzac, life, macrobiotics, madness, magnetism, nomads, non-verbal communication, non-violence, one-night stands, ongoing education, oriental medicine, parallel, parapsychology, parascientific popularization, physiotherapy, plants, pottery, prisons, psi-phenomena, regionalism, repression, science fiction, struggles, telepathy, therapy, trailers, transcendental meditation, travel, trekking, vegetarianism, weaving, yoga, Zen. An inventory of thinly disguised expressions of a sort of dream of social flying, a desperate effort to defy the gravity of the social field.

Guided by their anti-institutional temperament and the concern to escape everything redolent of competitions, hierarchies and classifications and, above all, of scholastic classifications, hierarchies of knowledge, theoretical abstractions or technical competences, these new intellectuals are inventing an art of living which provides them with the gratifications and prestige of the intellectual at the least cost; in the name of the fight against 'taboos' and the liquidation of 'complexes' they adopt the most external and most easily borrowed aspects of the intellectual life-style, liberated manners, cosmetic or sartorial outrages, emancipated poses and postures, and systematically apply the cultivated disposition to not-yet-legitimate culture (cinema, strip cartoons, the underground), to everyday life (street art), the personal sphere (sexuality, cosmetics, child-rearing, leisure) and the existential (the relation to nature, love, death). The perfect audience for a new intellectual popularization which is also a popularization of the intellectual life-style, they spontaneously 'relate' to the new spontaneist ideology culled from Freud and Freinet, Rogers and Reich, Fourier and Bakunin.[44] It is scarcely necessary to point out the 'cultivated', even scholastic aspects of this romantic flight from the social world, which, because it exalts the body and nature, sometimes sees itself as a return to the 'wild' and the 'natural': like legitimate culture, the counter-culture leaves its principles implicit (which is understandable since it is rooted in the dispositions of an ethos) and so is still able to fulfil functions of distinction by making available to *almost* everyone the distinctive poses, the distinctive games and other external signs of inner riches previously reserved for intellectuals.

The convergences between the routine themes of advertising—which has long been versed in the language of desire[45]—and the most typical topics of high philosophical popularization, the parallels between the 'social policy' of a dominant class which concedes the better to conserve, and the new child-rearing—specifically bourgeois in its diffusion—which opts for liberalism and indulgence, would be sufficient to show that the new ethic espoused by the vanguard of the bourgeoisie and petite bourgeoisie is perfectly compatible with a form of enlightened conservatism. It may even be wondered if the ethic of liberation is not in the process of supplying the economy with the perfect consumer whom economic theory has always dreamed of, and not only by inducing him to consume and to consume the latest thing. The most important contribution of the new ethic may well be that it produces consumers who are isolated (despite all their associations, which are purely statistical groupings) and therefore free (or forced) to confront in extended order the separate markets ('juniors', 'teenagers', 'senior citizens' etc.) of the new economic order and untrammelled by the constraints and brakes imposed by collective memories and expectations—in short, freed from the temporal structures imposed by domestic units, with their own life-cycle, their long-term 'planning', sometimes over several generations, and their collective defences against the immediate impact of the market.

7 | The Choice of the Necessary

The fundamental proposition that the habitus is a virtue made of necessity is never more clearly illustrated than in the case of the working classes, since necessity includes for them all that is usually meant by the word, that is, an inescapable deprivation of necessary goods. Necessity imposes a taste for necessity which implies a form of adaptation to and consequently acceptance of the necessary, a resignation to the inevitable, a deep-seated disposition which is in no way incompatible with a revolutionary intention, although it confers on it a modality which is not that of intellectual or artistic revolts. Social class is not defined solely by a position in the relations of production, but by the class habitus which is 'normally' (i.e., with a high statistical probability) associated with that position.[1] The *narodniki* of all times and all lands, by identifying with their object to the point of confusing their relation to the working-class condition with the working-class relation to that condition, by speaking and writing as if it were sufficient to occupy the worker's position in the relations of production for a brief while, as observer or even as participant, in order to understand the worker's experience of that position, present an account of the working-class condition that is statistically improbable, since it is not the product of the relation to that condition which is ordinarily associated with the condition, precisely because of the conditionings which it exerts.

It is not a question of the truth or falsity of the insupportable image of the working-class world that the intellectual produces when, putting himself in the place of a worker without having the habitus of a worker, he apprehends the working-class condition through schemes of percep-

tion and appreciation which are not those that the members of the working class themselves use to apprehend it. It is truly the experience that an intellectual can obtain of the working-class world by putting himself provisionally and deliberately into the working-class condition, and it may become less and less improbable if, as is beginning to happen, an increasing number of individuals are thrown into the working-class condition without having the habitus that is the product of the conditionings 'normally' imposed on those who are condemned to this condition. Populism is never anything other than an inverted ethnocentrism, and if descriptions of the industrial working class and the peasantry almost always vacillate between miserabilism and millenarian exaltation, this is because they leave out the relation to class condition which is part of a complete definition of that condition, and because it is less easy to state the actual relation to the condition one is describing (without necessarily being able to feel it) than to put one's own relation to it into the description—if only because this spurious identification and the indignation it inspires have all the appearances of legitimacy to support them.[2]

The Taste for Necessity and the Principle of Conformity

The specific effect of the taste for necessity, which never ceases to act, though unseen—because its action combines with that of necessity—is most clearly seen when it is, in a sense, operating out of phase, having survived the disappearance of the conditions which produced it. One sees examples in the behaviour of some small craftsmen or businessmen who, as they themselves say, 'don't know how to spend the money they've earned', or of junior clerical workers, still attached to their peasant or working-class roots, who get as much satisfaction from calculating how much they have 'saved' by doing without a commodity or service (or 'doing it themselves') as they would have got from the thing itself, but who, equally, cannot ever purchase it without a painful sense of wasting money. Having a million does not in itself make one able to live like a millionaire; and parvenus generally take a long time to learn that what they see as culpable prodigality is, in their new condition, expenditure of basic necessity.[3]

It tends to be forgotten that to appreciate the 'true value' of the purely symbolic services which in many areas (hotels, hairdressing etc.) make the essential difference between luxury establishments and ordinary businesses, one has to feel oneself the legitimate recipient of this bureaucratically personalized care and attention and to display vis-à-vis those who are paid to offer it the mixture of distance (including 'generous' gratuities) and freedom which the bourgeois have towards their servants. Anyone who doubts that 'knowing how to be served' is one component of the bourgeois art of living, need only think of the workers or small clerks who, entering a smart restaurant for some grand occasion, immediately strike up a conversation with the waiters—who realize at once 'whom they are dealing with'—as if to destroy symbolically the servant-master relationship and the unease it creates for them. The worker who sees a watch on sale for two million (old) francs, or who hears that a surgeon has spent three million francs on his son's engagement party, does not envy the watch or the party but the two million, being unable to conceive of the system of needs in which he would have nothing better to do with two million francs than spend it on a watch. When there are 'so many things that come first', as they say, 'you'd have to be crazy' to think of buying a two-million-franc watch. But no one ever really puts himself 'in the place' of those on the other side of the social world. One man's extravagance is another man's prime necessity—and not only because the marginal value of those two million francs varies with the number of millions possessed. Many of the expenditures that are called conspicuous are in no way a squandering and, as well as being obligatory elements in a certain style of life, they are very often—like engagement parties—an excellent investment in social capital.

For a host of reasons—in particular the physical and social separation of the universes of life—these experiences (of the watch and the engagement party) are very *improbable*—although both actually happened. In fact, as Marx observed with some brutality: 'What and how much he can see depends not only on the existing state of affairs in the world, a state of affairs by no means created by him, but also on his purse and on the position in life which falls to his lot owing to the division of labour, which perhaps shuts very much away from him, although he may have very acquisitive eyes and ears.'[4] In general the working classes 'have no idea' of what the system of needs of the privileged classes might be. Their knowledge of upper-class resources is equally abstract and unreal. (Thus, when asked 'the average price of a good meal around the Champs Élysées', 13 percent of the manual workers said they did not know, 35 percent put it at between 15 and 24 francs, 22 percent between 25 and 29, 13 percent between 30 and 39, and 13 percent over 50 francs, as against 2 percent, 11 percent, 20 percent, 33 percent and 14 percent respectively for the executives, industrialists and professionals; the junior executives gave intermediate evaluations.)

What statistics records in the form of systems of needs is nothing other than the coherence of the choices of a habitus. And the inability to 'spend more', or differently, that is, to rise to the system of needs implied in a higher level of resources, is the best illustration of the impossibility of reducing (theoretically) the propensity to consume to the capacity to appropriate or of reducing the habitus to the economic conditions prevailing at a given moment (as represented, for example, by a given level of income). If everything encourages a belief in the existence of a direct relationship between income and consumption, this is because taste is almost always the product of economic conditions identical to those in which it functions, so that income tends to be credited with a causal efficacy which it in fact only exerts in association with the habitus it has produced. The specific efficacy of the habitus is clearly seen when the same income is associated with very different patterns of consumption, which can only be understood by assuming that other selection principles have intervened.

Thus foremen, whose average household income is much greater than that of skilled workers (34,581 francs as against 25,716 francs) devote a very similar proportion of their income to food (35.4 percent, as against 38.3 percent for skilled workers and 30 percent for junior executives), so that their actual spending on food is equal to that of senior executives (12,503 francs as against 12,904 francs). Everything indicates that they remain attached to the popular values of 'eating well' and especially to the popular interpretation of these values. First, spending on the products most typical of popular food—starchy foods, pork, potatoes, poultry—increases; secondly, spending on the expensive products, which manual workers have to restrict although for them they symbolize 'good eating'—*charcuterie,* wine, coffee and especially sugar (which declines sharply in the upper classes)—increases considerably, together with butter (444 francs as against 365 francs, whereas less oil is bought). Thirdly, spending on products which are expensive but characteristic of the bourgeois life-style increases much less or not at all. This is true of veal, lamb, mutton, fish, shellfish, citrus fruit etc.; fresh vegetables increase much more than fresh fruit, and both increase less than *charcuterie.*[5]

Another example: as one moves from the 30,000–50,000 francs income bracket into the higher bracket, the food purchases of senior executives do not change in at all the same way as those of manual workers. Though expenditure on food increases in both cases (relatively more so among the executives), the items which expand are, by order of importance, for senior executives (including teachers and engineers): aperitifs, restaurant meals, non-alcoholic drinks, lamb, cakes and pastries, beef, fresh fruit, fish and shellfish, cheese; and for manual workers: pork, aperitifs, rabbit, fresh fruit, dried vegetables, bread, fresh vegetables.[6]

The principle of the most important differences in the order of lifestyle and, even more, of the 'stylization of life' lies in the variations in objective and subjective distance from the world, with its material constraints and temporal urgencies. Like the aesthetic disposition which is one dimension of it, the distant, detached or casual disposition towards the world or other people, a disposition which can scarcely be called subjective since it is objectively internalized, can only be constituted in conditions of existence that are relatively freed from urgency. The submission to necessity which inclines working-class people to a pragmatic, functionalist 'aesthetic', refusing the gratuity and futility of formal exercises and of every form of art for art's sake, is also the principle of all the choices of daily existence and of an art of living which rejects specifically aesthetic intentions as aberrations.[7]

Thus manual workers say more often than all the other classes that they like interiors that are clean and tidy and easy to maintain,[8] or the

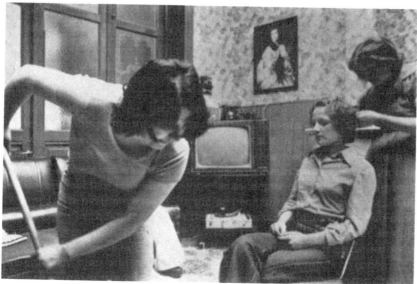

'value for money' clothes which economic necessity assigns to them in any case. The doubly prudent choice of a garment that is both 'simple' ('versatile', 'all-purpose'), i.e., as little marked and as unrisky as possible ('no-nonsense', 'practical'), and 'good value for money', i.e., cheap and long-lasting, no doubt presents itself as the most reasonable strategy, given, on the one hand, the economic and cultural capital (not to mention time) that can be invested in buying clothes and, on the other hand, the symbolic profits that can be expected from such an investment (at least at work—unlike clerical workers, for example).

The proportion of women who say they 'tend not to take account of fashion'—always higher among women who do not work outside the home (59 percent as against 47 percent) and those who never read women's magazines—is distinctly greater in the categories of the craftsmen or small shopkeepers, farm workers and manual workers (62 percent, 61 percent and 55 percent) than among the junior and senior executives, the professionals and the employers (43 percent). Similarly, the concern to 'keep up with fashion' is markedly stronger among the wives of junior executives or clerical workers, whereas the choice of 'whatever is most practical or economical' (rising strongly with age, and much more frequent among housewives) is most pronounced among the wives of farm workers, craftsmen or shopkeepers, and manual workers (the last two categories are those who most often say they are chiefly concerned to 'please their husbands'). The choice of a 'classic' garment (rather than 'refined', 'unconventional' or 'sporty'), which, like 'the most practical and economical', rises strongly with age and varies in inverse ratio to the reading of Elle—an index of investment in the aesthetics of dress—is strongest among the wives of farm workers (67 percent) and manual workers (59 percent), whereas the women of the bourgeoisie, who least often express this choice (39 percent), are the ones who most often choose 'sporty' or 'refined' clothes (C.S. XLII). Further evidence of a low investment in clothing and a low propensity to invest in aesthetic refinement in such matters is seen in the fact that a relatively high proportion of working-class women buy their clothes in the market, by post or in 'popular' department stores, whereas bourgeois women tend to limit their purchases to boutiques and 'up-market' department stores (C.S. XLV). The logic is the same in the area of cosmetics; the numerous market surveys on the subject all show that working-class women reduce their expenditure on make-up and beauty care to the minimum (this item rises strongly as one moves from the wives of farm workers to manual workers, to craftsmen and shopkeepers, to junior executives and to senior executives). They thus represent the zero degree of make-up, of which the complexity (lipstick alone, lipstick plus foundation, plus eyeshadow, plus eyebrow pencil etc.) and the cost in money, and especially in time, increase as one moves up the social hierarchy (in the same order as before), at least up to the level of the clerical workers and junior executives.

Thus, although working-class practices may seem to be deduced directly from their economic conditions, since they ensure a saving of money, time and effort that would in any case be of low profitability, they stem from a choice of the necessary ('That's not for us'), both in the sense of what is technically necessary, 'practical' (or, as others would say, functional), i.e., needed in order to 'get by', to do 'the proper thing and no more', and of what is imposed by an economic and social necessity condemning 'simple', 'modest' people to 'simple', 'modest' tastes. The adjustment to the objective chances which is inscribed in the dispositions constituting the habitus is the source of all the realistic choices which, based on the renunciation of symbolic profits that are in any case inaccessible, reduce practices or objects to their technical function, a 'short back-and-sides' or 'quick trim-up' at the barber's, 'a simple little dress', 'solid' furniture etc. Thus nothing is more alien to working-class women than the typically bourgeois idea of making each object in the home the occasion for an aesthetic choice, of extending the intention of harmony or beauty even into the bathroom or kitchen, places strictly defined by their function, or of involving specifically aesthetic criteria in the choice of a saucepan or cupboard. Festive meals and 'Sunday best' clothes are opposed to everyday meals and clothes by the arbitrariness of a conventional division—'doing things properly'—just as the rooms socially designated for 'decoration', the sitting room, the dining room or living room, are opposed to everyday places, that is, by an antithesis which is more or less that of the 'decorative' and the 'practical', and they are decorated in accordance with established conventions, with knick-knacks on the mantelpiece, a forest scene over the sideboard, flowers on the table, without any of these obligatory choices implying decisions or a search for effect.

This conventionalism, which is also that of popular photography, concerned to fix conventional poses in the conventional compositions,[9] is the opposite of bourgeois formalism and of all the forms of art for art's sake recommended by manuals of graceful living and women's magazines, the art of entertaining, the art of the table, the art of motherhood. In addition to providing a form of basic security in a world in which there can be hardly any assurance, the choice of 'doing the proper thing' or 'the done thing' (the vendors of domestic goods understand the power of 'It's the done thing' over working-class insecurity) has a natural place in an economy of practices based on the search for the 'practical' and the refusal of 'frills' and 'fancy nonsense'.[10]

Even the choices which, from the standpoint of the dominant norms, appear as the most 'irrational' are grounded in the taste of necessity—plus, of course, the entirely negative effect of the absence of information and specific competence which results from the lack of cultural capital. For example, the taste for the trinkets and knick-knacks which adorn mantelpiece and hallways is inspired by an intention unknown to economists and ordinary aesthetes, that of obtaining maximum 'effect' ('It'll make a terrific effect') at minimum cost, a formula which for bourgeois taste is the very definition of vulgarity (one of the intentions of distinction being to suggest with the fewest 'effects' possible the greatest expenditure of time, money and ingenuity). What is the 'gaudy' and the 'tawdry', if not that which creates a big effect for a small price, the 'follies' that are only permissible so long as you can say to yourself, 'They were almost given away'? Street hawkers and sales-promotion specialists know that they must release the brakes and censorships which forbid 'extravagances' by presenting the forbidden goods as 'bargains'—the unfashionable settee which, if you can forget the colour and just think of the price, is exactly the one you had always wanted 'to go in front of the TV', or the unwearable nylon dress you ended up buying because it was reduced in the sale, though you had 'sworn you would never again wear nylon.'

And if it still needed to be proved that resignation to necessity is the basis of the taste of necessity, one only has to consider the waste of time and energy resulting from the refusal to subject the daily management of domestic life to the constraints of rational calculation and formal life-principles ('a place for everything', 'everything in its time' etc.), which only apparently contradicts the refusal to devote time and care to health ('molly-coddling yourself') or beauty ('getting dolled up'). In fact, in these two features of their life-style, working-class women, doubly dominated, show that they do not set sufficient value on their trouble and their time, the only things they can spend (and give) without counting, to be concerned about sparing and saving them, or, to put it another way, that they do not value themselves sufficiently (and they do indeed have a low value on the labour market, unlike bourgeois women with their skilled labour-power and cultivated bodies) to grant themselves a care and attention which always imply a certain indulgence and to devote to their bodies the incessant care, concern and attention that are needed to achieve and maintain health, slimness and beauty.[11]

A whole set of convergent indices tends to show that working-class women set less value on and have less interest in their bodies than women in other classes. For example, 40.2 percent of agricultural workers' wives and 36.0 percent of manual workers' wives consider themselves below average in beauty as against 24.2 percent of upper-class women and 33.2 percent of middle-class women; 13.0 percent and 14.0 percent respectively, as against 10.1 percent and 7.6 percent, say they look old for their age; and working-class women almost always award themselves lower marks (except for skin, nose and hands) than women in other classes. They set less store by beauty and systematically devote less time, money and interest to all personal care (see table 20 in chapter 3).

The calls to order ('Who does she think she is?' 'That's not for the likes of us') which reaffirm the principle of conformity—the only explicit norm of popular taste—and aim to encourage the 'reasonable' choices that are in any case imposed by the objective conditions also contain a warning against the ambition to distinguish oneself by identifying with other groups, that is, they are a reminder of the need for class solidarity. The gaps between the cultural practices and preferences of the different classes are to a large extent due to the fact that the chances of finding in one's milieu the 'market' in which cultural experiences and the discourses to which they give rise can receive a value vary in much the same way as the chances of having such experiences, and no doubt play a part in determining these chances. The low interest which working-class people show in the works of legitimate culture to which they could have access—especially through television—is not solely the effect of a lack of competence and familiarity: just as supposedly vulgar subjects, such as television, are banished from bourgeois conversation (C.S. VI), so the favourite subjects of bourgeois conversation, exhibitions, theatre, concerts or even cinema, are excluded, de facto and de jure, from working-class conversation, in which they could only express the pretension to distinguish oneself. Perhaps the most ruthless call to order, which in itself no doubt explains the extraordinary *realism* of the working classes, stems from the closure effect of the homogeneity of the directly experienced social world. There is no other possible language, no other life-style, no other form of kinship relation; the universe of possibles is closed. Other people's expectations are so many reinforcements of dispositions imposed by the objective conditions.

The ritualization of practices and utterances, which can go as far as stereotyping, is to some extent an effect of the very rigorous application of the principle of conformity. A full-grown man who visits another household is *expected* to have a drink; a middle-aged woman who dresses 'too young for her age' is severely, even cruelly, sanctioned (jibes, remarks behind her back etc.). Whereas great class differences may pass unnoticed and are in any case very well tolerated ('He's a real character' 'He's not like us') because they are seen as based on differences of nature (the doctor's wife will be described as 'made for fine clothes'), not the slightest deviation is permitted to those who belong to the same class (or originate from it), because in this case difference could only arise from the desire to distinguish oneself, that is, from refusal or repudiation of the group (thus the son of a bourgeois who breaks with his family is favourably regarded, whereas a worker's son who does the same thing is condemned). What is objectionable is not difference but the conspicuous intention of aloofness. The 'natural' difference which defines the bourgeois is the more easily accepted because his 'simplicity' proves it is not the product of a negative striving for distinction. Difference is perceived and denounced as such only by people whose awareness has been sharpened by political or trade-union activity, those of whom others say, *'Il fait de la politique'*, implying 'a trouble-maker', 'a rough diamond'. It is clear what advantages the condescension strategies of all forms of paternalism can derive from these deferential dispositions ('a real gentleman' etc.)

Men especially are forbidden every sort of 'pretension' in matters of culture, language or clothing. This is not only because aesthetic refinement, particularly as regards clothing or cosmetics, is reserved for women by a representation, more strict than in any other class, of the sexual division of labour and sexual morality;[12] or because it is more or less clearly associated with dispositions and manners seen as characteristic of the bourgeoisie ('airs and graces', 'la-di-da' etc.) or of those who are willing to submit to bourgeois demands so as to win acceptance, of which the 'toadies', 'lick-spittles' and 'pansies' of everyday invective represent the limit. It is also because a surrender to demands perceived as simultaneously feminine and bourgeois appears as the index of a dual repudiation of virility, a twofold submission which ordinary language, naturally conceiving all domination in the logic and lexicon of sexual domination, is predisposed to express.

It is not only in thoughts that the opposition between the working classes and the dominant class (especially its dominated fractions) is organized by analogy with the opposition between the male and the female, that is, through the categories of the strong and the weak, the fat (and coarse) and the thin (or fine) and so forth. Thus, as regards food, the working classes (and no doubt the men rather than the women) are opposed to the other classes as men are opposed to women. It is known, for example, that a higher proportion of senior executives than of any other class (except farm workers) drink milk for breakfast every day (59 percent, manual workers 42 percent); the same is true of chocolate (executives 12 percent, manual workers 5 percent, farm workers 5 percent, with no difference between the sexes in this case) and tea, in France a typically bourgeois and feminine drink (executives 27 percent, manual workers 3 percent, farm workers 0 percent). But the working class is chiefly distinguished by the inclusion of salty, substantial, clearly masculine foods, such as soup (eaten almost exclusively by farm workers), meat (46 percent of the farm workers, 17 percent of the manual workers, 6 percent of the senior executives say they at least occasionally eat meat for breakfast) and cheese, whereas the senior executives and professionals take first place for sweet foods such as jam or honey (40 percent say they eat them every day, as against 29 percent of the farm workers and 11 percent of the manual workers), which are also clearly marked as feminine (only 38 percent of men eat them occasionally, 63 percent of women; C.S. XLVIII).The same opposition emerges from an older survey, in which the proportion who eat something savoury for breakfast (eggs, ham, sausages, pâté or cheese) declines as one moves from the farm workers to the manual workers, to the clerical workers and senior executives, while the proportion who eat sweet foods (jam, honey or fruit) varies in the opposite way.[13]

It is also known that the whole set of socially constituted differences between the sexes tends to weaken as one moves up the social hierarchy and especially towards the dominated fractions of the dominant class, where women tend to share the most typically male prerogatives such as the reading of 'serious' newspapers and interest in politics, while the men do not

Champion Chomper

'François Bruat, a Bénéjacquois by adoption, last night defended his title of bean-eating champion of France (2.7 kilos in 15 minutes). Would challenger Henri Boiramé wrest his title from him?'

Seconds Out

'The referee bawls their names, they fasten their napkins and . . . they're off! They get stuck into steaming platefuls of kidney beans and bacon. Just watch 'em go down. A spoonful for mummy, a spoonful for daddy. . . .'

Hiccups

'This is no vicarage tea party. They're puffing and blowing all the way as they plough through the beans. Bring on more plates! The spectators yell for another helping, encouraging their favourite, the reigning French champion.'

Jaws

'The champ goes into the lead. A Raymond Poulidor of the spoon and fork, unbeatable against the clock, turning to glance at his rivals every 500 grams, a real glutton for punishment. Two jaws and a Herculean belly. Limbering up like a wrestler between two platefuls, to intimidate the opposition. And a third helping! The champ chomps on. . . .'

La République des Pyrénées, July 1978.

hesitate to express interests and dispositions, in matters of taste, for example, which elsewhere would be regarded as 'effeminate'. The greater tolerance of deviations from the norm of the sexual division of labour no doubt partly explains why the proportion of homosexuals known and acknowledged as such rises strongly with position in the social hierarchy (as also with the size of the town of residence). The proportion of respondents who say they 'know homosexuals among their acquaintances' rises from 10 percent among farm workers to 16 percent among manual workers, 22 percent among small shopkeepers and craftsmen, 25 percent among junior executives and clerical workers, and 37 percent among industrial and commercial employers, senior executives and the professions; it rises from 10 percent in towns of less than 2,000 inhabitants to 38 percent in the Paris conurbation (C.S. XLVII).

Before speaking of cultural inertia or 'cultural lag', with an implicit evolutionism which enables the dominant to perceive their way of being or of doing things as the realized ideal, one needs to ask oneself if the popular valorization of physical strength as a fundamental aspect of virility and of everything that produces and supports it ('strong' food and drink, heavy work and exercise)[14] is not intelligibly related to the fact that both the peasant class and the industrial working class depend on a labour power which the laws of cultural reproduction and of the labour market reduce, more than for any other class, to sheer muscle power;[15] and it should not be forgotten that a class which, like the working class, is only rich in its labour power can only oppose to the other classes— apart from the withdrawal of its labour—its fighting strength, which depends on the physical strength and courage of its members, and also their number, i.e., their consciousness and solidarity or, to put it another way, their consciousness of their solidarity.

Thus it would be a mistake to ignore the specifically political effect of moralization (or 'de-moralization') which is exerted through the vehicles of the new therapeutic morality (women's magazines, the glossy weeklies, radio programmes etc.). As is shown by the limiting case of the peasantry—who, through the imposition of the dominant life-style and the legitimate image of the body, have suffered a blow to their specific conditions of reproduction (with the celibacy of peasant farmers) and to their very existence as a class capable of defining the principles of its own identity—it is perhaps one of the last refuges of the autonomy of the dominated classes, of their capacity to produce their own representation of the accomplished man and the social world, that is being threatened by all the challenges to working-class identification with the values of virility, which are one of the most autonomous forms of their self-affirmation as a class. The most fundamental principles of class identity and unity, those which lie in the unconscious, would be affected if, on the decisive point of relation to the body, the dominated class came to see itself only through the eyes of the dominant class, that is, in terms of the dominant definition of the body and its uses. This having been said, in this area as in so many other and equally important areas which are not politically constituted, there is no realistic chance of any collective resistance to the effect of imposition that would lead either to the valorization of properties stigmatized by the dominant taxonomy (the 'black is beautiful' strategy) or to the creation of new, positively evaluated properties. Thus the dominated have only two options: loyalty to self and the group (always liable to relapse into shame), or the individual effort to assimilate the dominant ideal which is the antithesis of the very ambition of collectively regaining control over social identity (of the type pursued by the collective revolt of the American feminists when it advocates the 'natural look').

The Effects of Domination

Adapting to a dominated position implies a form of acceptance of domination. The effects of political mobilization itself do not easily counterbalance the effects of the inevitable dependence of self-esteem on occupational status and income, signs of social value previously legitimated by the sanctions of the educational market. It would be easy to enumerate the features of the life-style of the dominated classes which, through the sense of incompetence, failure or cultural unworthiness, imply a form of recognition of the dominant values. It was Antonio Gramsci who said somewhere that the worker tends to bring his executant dispositions with him into every area of life. As much as by the absence of luxury goods, whisky or paintings, champagne or concerts, cruises or art exhibitions, caviar or antiques, the working-class life-style is characterized by the presence of numerous cheap substitutes for these rare goods, 'sparkling white wine' for champagne, imitation leather for real leather, reproductions for paintings, indices of a dispossession at the second power, which accepts the definition of the goods worthy of being possessed. With 'mass market' cultural products—music whose simple, repetitive structures invite a passive, absent participation, prefabricated entertainments which the new engineers of cultural mass production design for television viewers, and especially sporting events which establish a recognized division between the spectators and the professionals, virtuosos of an esoteric technique or 'supermen' of exceptional ability—dispossession of the very intention of determining one's own ends is combined with a more insidious form of recognition of dispossession.

The critique of cultural mass production, of which T. W. Adorno long ago provided the formula by establishing a direct, naive analogy between the very form and uses of 'popular' music and the world of alienated labour, which, like a certain critique of sport, no doubt owes much of its credibility to the fact that it enables the nostalgia and revulsion of an amateur to be expressed with populist impeccability, has in fact masked what is essential.[16] It is not only in music or sport that ordinary people are reduced to the role of the 'fan', the militant 'supporter' locked in a passionate, even chauvinistic, but passive and spurious participation which is merely an illusory compensation for dispossession by experts. What the relation to 'mass' (and, a fortiori, 'elite') cultural products reproduces, reactivates and reinforces is not the monotony of the production line or office but the social relation which underlies working-class experience of the world, whereby his labour and the product of his labour, *opus proprium,* present themselves to the worker as *opus alienum,* 'alienated' labour.

Dispossession is never more totally misrecognized, and therefore tacitly recognized, than when, with the progress of automation, economic dispossession is combined with the cultural dispossession which provides the best apparent justification for economic dispossession. Lacking the internalized cultural capital which is the pre-condition for correct appropriation (according to the legitimate definition) of the cultural capital objectified in technical objects, ordinary workers are dominated by the machines and instruments which they serve rather than use, and by those who possess the legitimate, i.e., theoretical, means of dominating them. In the factory as in the school, which teaches respect for useless, disinterested knowledge and establishes relationships invested with the 'natural' authority of scientific and pedagogic reason among simultaneously hierarchized individuals and activities, workers encounter legitimate culture as a principle of order which does not need to demonstrate its practical utility in order to be justified. The experiences which the culturally most deprived may have of works of legitimate culture (or even of many of the prefabricated entertainments offered by 'show business') is only one form of a more fundamental and more ordinary experience, that of the division between practical, partial, tacit *know-how* and theoretical, systematic, explicit *knowledge* (a division which tends to be reproduced even in politics), between science and techniques, theory and practice, 'conception' and 'execution', the 'intellectual' or the 'creator' (who gives his own name to an 'original', 'personal' work and so claims ownership) and the 'manual' worker (the mere servant of an intention greater than himself, an executant dispossessed of the idea of his own practice).[17]

The educational system, an institutionalized classifier which is itself an objectified system of classification reproducing the hierarchies of the social world in a transformed form, with its cleavages by 'level' corresponding to social strata and its divisions into specialities and disciplines which reflect social divisions ad infinitum, such as the opposition between theory and practice, conception and execution, transforms social classifications into academic classifications, with every appearance of neutrality, and establishes hierarchies which are not experienced as purely technical, and therefore partial and one-sided, but as total hierarchies, grounded in nature, so that social value comes to be identified with 'personal' value, scholastic dignities with human dignity. The 'culture' which an educational qualification is presumed to guarantee is one of the basic components in the dominant definition of the accomplished man, so that privation is perceived as an intrinsic handicap, diminishing a person's identity and human dignity, condemning him to silence in all official situations, when he has to 'appear in public', present himself before others, with his body, his manners and his language.[18]

Misrecognition of the social determinants of the educational career— and therefore of the social trajectory it helps to determine—gives the educational certificate the value of a natural right and makes the educational system one of the fundamental agencies of the maintenance of the social order. It is no doubt in the area of education and culture that the members of the dominated classes have least chance of discovering their

Table 26 Awareness of social factors in educational and social success, by class fraction (%), 1971.

Class fraction of respondents	Success at school depends on			Success in life depends on				
	Intelligence	Social background	Don't know	Hard work	Social background	Intelligence	Education	Don't know
Farm workers	65	29	6	51	13	21	15	0
Manual workers	55	42	3	48	11	19	20	2
Craftsmen, shopkeepers	74	25	1	45	9	35	11	0
Junior executives	45	51	4	34	18	28	18	2
Senior executives	52	44	4	34	18	35	8	5

Source: SOFRES, January 1971.

Table 27 Views on ways of reducing inequality, by class fraction (%), 1970.

Question	Class fraction				
	Farm workers	Manual workers	Employers	Clerical, junior executives	Senior executives, professions
The best way to reduce the inequality of opportunity among young people in France is to:					
radically reform laws on inheritance	0	3.0	0	1.0	6.0
thoroughly democratize education	10.5	16.5	0	25.0	29.5
increase State benefits to the most deprived	38.0	50.5	71.0	49.0	23.5
nationalize private firms	0	4.0	0	3.5	0
increase the prosperity of the national economy	24.0	20.0	8.0	18.0	38.0
don't know	27.5	6.0	21.0	3.5	3.0

Source: SOFRES, 1970.

objective interest and of producing and imposing the problematic most consistent with their interests. Awareness of the economic and social determinants of cultural dispossession in fact varies in almost inverse ratio to cultural dispossession (as tables 26 and 27 clearly show). The ideology of charisma, which imputes to the person, to his natural gifts or his merits, entire responsibility for his social destiny, exerts its effects far beyond the educational system; every hierarchical relationship draws part of the legitimacy that the dominated themselves grant it from a confused perception that it is based on the opposition between 'education' and ignorance.

Awareness of the effects of social background is particularly weak among craftsmen and small shopkeepers, farm workers and manual workers. Among the senior executives, recognition of these effects does not exclude belief in the virtues of intelligence (see tables 26 and 27). Everything seems to indicate that in order for the working classes to recognize their educational interest, they at least have to be involved in the educational system: discovering 'schooling as a conservative force' presupposes some experience of 'schooling as a liberating force'. Thus it is students from the middle and working classes who are most sensitive to the problematic of 'democratization', although they often accept the charismatic values which dominate the educational system. But it is above all the experience of relegation to the most devalued courses and sections, as well as the discovery of the devaluation of qualifications already held, that is likely to induce the beginnings of collective awareness.

The most visible principles of the official differences (i.e., those officially recorded in statuses and wages) found within the working class are seniority and education (technical or general); it may be wondered whether these are valued, especially in foremen, as guarantees of competence or as certificates of 'morality', that is, of conformity and even docility. The proportion of individuals who have no educational qualification at all (or whose father had none) declines sharply as one moves from the unskilled labourers, through the semi-skilled and skilled workers, to the foremen. Various indicators of an ascetic disposition often linked to the ambition of upward mobility, such as fertility rate or the practice of sports such as gymnastics and swimming, vary in the same way, and so do indices of cultural good intentions, such as visits to châteaux and monuments, theatres and concerts, or possession of records or use of a public library. This does not mean, however, that the 'aristocracy of labour' merges with the lower strata of the petite bourgeoisie. They differ from the petit bourgeois in a number of ways, not least in the fact that they behave as manual workers even in their spare time (53.9 percent of foremen and 50.8 percent of skilled workers spend some time on 'do-it-yourself' jobs at least once a week). Their solidarity with the working-

A Foreman Who 'Has Always Worked for Other People'

Mr. L., aged 61, started work as an apprentice on the French Railways at the age of fourteen and a half. He became a skilled worker and is now a foreman. He 'deals with passenger rolling-stock.' His wife, aged 52, has never worked. She completed secondary school and would like to find a job. They have had four children; the eldest is a computer programmer, the second a Dominican monk, the third used to be a personal assistant but stopped work when she married, and the youngest is studying for his baccalauréat. They live in a municipal-style flat in Grenoble.

'You have to know what you're doing'

Mr. L. has done a lot of work on the apartment: 'You can see if you look; there used to be a room there and a room here. Because there were so many of us it was really cramped, so I took the wall down, which means we've got more space, we can entertain more people, especially with the whole family.... We need a lot of room, especially when my son has his friends round, all singing and dancing.' Most of their furniture was bought in Tunisia, where they lived for a number of years. Second-hand dealers and antique-dealers 'are all twisters ... con-men', and his wife adds: 'You need to know what you're doing ... but we've no idea what things like that are worth; that's why my husband says they're all twisters, out to cheat you. They can sell us fakes and

tell us they're real, and as for the prices ...'

'I knew how to make good use of it'

Their home is 'no museum'; the ornaments and vases are 'not just dust traps.' The various objects adorning the apartment are mostly presents from the children or friends, or have been 'rescued', and they all have their 'use'. Madame L. will not buy anything until she 'has already found a place for it.' 'That vase now, I needed a vase, I wanted a vase because I wanted flowers, and when I was asked what I wanted, I said "a vase" and they bought it for me because I knew how to make good use of it.' His children 'know perfectly well there's no point in buying things that I won't use or that I'll put away in a sideboard. Everything has to have a place for it ... otherwise, I don't like to have things just to put them away.' They make most of their purchases in supermarkets (Carrefour, Record) or department stores (Nouvelles Galeries): 'I don't like window-shopping, I go straight to a big supermarket and you find everything there; you can choose without going round a dozen shops,' Mr. L. explains. On holiday he always starts by 'checking out the market': 'I'm interested in the price I pay and the quality of what I get. If you buy with your eyes closed, they'll fob you off with anything.'

'Now, I'll be glad to work'

Recently they became the owners of a little house in the mountains outside Grenoble. 'Some friends—he was an engineer'—invited them to take it over several years ago. In the last three years, they have done a lot of work on it: 'Everything was rotten. I was walking around upstairs and I fell through the floor . . . There were no tiles left on the roof; the rain came in on all sides.' Mr. L. has done all the repair work himself: 'You know, I started as an apprentice on the railways, and an apprentice had to learn everything. You got a three-month course on sanitation, three months on electro-welding and so on. And you always remember your trade, to some extent.' They intend to make this house their main home. 'Now, I'll be glad to work, now that it's my house; I'm not working for other people. I'm fed up with working and being exploited.'

'Learning to ski at 42'

He is 'very fond of cold weather, snow, but not skiing': 'I'm afraid of hurting myself. I go tobogganing with my grandchildren. You see, I had an accident in my brother-in-law's car in Tunisia . . . and I injured my wrist. You only have to look at it to see the state it's in. . . . That's why I prefer tobogganing. I can sit up and there's no danger of falling.' (His wife 'started learning to ski at 42, because of the children. . . . We used to go out with them; we didn't want to spend the whole day sitting in a café or freezing in the car.') When he was young, he 'did a lot of sport, especially football.'

'You just have to like them'

He sometimes does the cooking: 'When my wife's away or with her sisters and I'm here on my own, I'd rather do my own cooking than go and eat at my mother's or one of my sisters-in-law's.' When she

'wants to give someone a treat', his wife 'looks up a menu in her recipe books.' 'I don't altogether agree with my children when they say, "You should cook something *you* like." I say, "You often do things in life that you don't like to start with, but you just have to like them."' 'I buy table wine at Carrefour; it's cheaper there. It's eleven proof and it costs one franc forty; by the bottle, it's two francs thirty-five, I think.'

'Always something to keep me busy'

They go camping for their holidays. 'At the seaside, we go swimming. . . . I like looking for shellfish . . . In the mountains, I go looking for mushrooms, or snails. There's always something to keep me busy.' And his wife adds that last summer 'he was a bit disappointed because there was nothing to go looking for . . . He doesn't like being idle, he always has to find something to do. In fact that's why we go camping. He couldn't really see himself sitting around in hotels and restaurants, whereas when we go camping, he can keep himself busy with the shopping, and a bit of swimming, of course, and all the things that have to be done. And then we generally have a look round the surrounding area. . . . When we did Italy, we went all over the place looking at all the old sites, all the archaeological things. My husband doesn't enjoy that as much as I do. Personally, I belong to an adult-education group and so that sort of thing interests me.'

'Circuses, games, quizzes'

On television, he watches 'football matches, cycling, all sorts of sport.

When the World Cup was on, two or three years back, I used to get up at one or two in the morning to watch the matches.' Otherwise he does not watch much: 'I do like a good Western, or a swashbuckling adventure. But if it's a play or something like that, I just drop off.' His wife, who enjoys watching plays on TV, adds that she also likes 'circuses, games—the Guy Lux programme—quizzes ...' He doesn't go to football matches, because he is 'nervous in crowds', but he 'reads the sports results in the papers.' He does not buy a newspaper but sometimes picks up those left by the passengers. The previous day, he 'brought home *Le Figaro, L'Aurore, Le Canard Enchaîné* and *Le Nouvel Observateur.'* 'The one he most reads is *L'Aurore,'* says his wife, 'road accidents, fights, things like that, whereas *Le Monde* is full of politics.' He reads 'detective stories, Maurice Leblanc, Michel Zevaco ... historical adventures. When they turn up, I read them. Otherwise, frankly, I don't pay much attention. I go to bed and pick up a newspaper straight away so as to go to sleep.' His wife, who borrows books from the local library, has recently read Solzhenitsyn's *Cancer Ward,* Michel de Saint-Pierre, Pierre-Henri Simon and the letters of Françoise Parturier. She buys books when she 'thinks them worthwhile.'

'Don't ask me for the names of classical composers'

When he was young, he 'played the clarinet a bit, then I took up football and there wasn't time for both. ... I've always encouraged my children's interest in music because I enjoy it.' 'Vivaldi is nice. Lovely music, really catchy. Beethoven is good because it's soothing. ... Don't ask me for the names of classical composers, apart from Beethoven, Chopin, Bach, people like that ... I can't remember the others.' They have a few records, mainly dance music. His favourite singer is Sheila. 'There are two I can't stand, Sylvie Vartan and that Guy Béart.' (His wife's favourites are Marie Laforêt, Les Compagnons de la Chanson and Moustaki.)

'You can see what they represent'

They rarely go to the cinema: 'Why bother, when you've got TV?' When they visited Paris, they saw *The White Horse* and *The Golden Fleece* at the Théâtre du Châtelet and *Vienna Waltzes* at the Théâtre du Mogador. Since they were married they have not been to the opera; when he was young, he saw and enjoyed *Tosca* and *La Traviata.* On their first trip to Paris, they 'did all the museums': 'even the Musée Grévin, the Louvre, Versailles, the Panthéon; we've been to them all once.' 'I like art but I don't know artists' names. ... I've heard of Goya, and Pirandello, and Michelangelo, people like that.' His wife is somewhat embarrassed by his admission of lack of interest and reminds him: 'Ah, but Michelangelo now, you liked him. You did like the Sistine Chapel.' Then he adds: 'I liked those pictures because you can see what they represent. But when you see half a dozen squiggles and people spending a fortune on it, well, personally, I'd throw that sort of thing in the dustbin if I found it. ... Anyway, I'd be afraid of being swindled.'

class life-style is manifested in every area, in their consumption, their reading, their hobbies and, in particular, in everything concerned with the symbolization of social position, such as clothing, in which, though a little less economy-minded than semi-skilled and unskilled workers, they do not manifest the concern for appearance which characterizes the non-manual occupations, starting with the clerical workers. In short, everything suggests that between the skilled workers and foremen, who remain subject to the principle of conformity, and the office workers, who, at least in thought, are already in the race, there is a real frontier, both in life-style and in political positions.[19]

The former are much less concerned than the latter to mark their distance from the most typically popular amusements and pastimes, such as funfairs or sporting events: 60.4 percent of them (and 58.2 percent of the semi-skilled and unskilled) say they have been to a funfair at least once in the previous year, compared to 49.5 percent of the clerical workers and 49.6 percent of the junior executives. Manual workers in general rather more often watch sport and circuses on TV, whereas junior executives and clerical workers much more often watch scientific, historical or literary programmes (C.S. VII). Out of very similar incomes, the manual workers spend more on food and less on everything concerned with personal appearance and care (clothing, hygiene, hairdressing, pharmaceutical products) (C.S. III); the men's spending on clothing is 85.6 percent, and the women's 83.7 percent, of the corresponding amounts among clerical workers. They buy the same clothes more cheaply (for example, they spend only 83 percent of the amount spent by clerical workers on overcoats, 68.7 percent on jackets, 83.5 percent on shoes—a difference which is much more marked among women) and, above all, different clothes: on the one hand, leather or imitation-leather jackets and lumber jackets (for cold, early-morning travel by scooter), boiler-suits, dungarees and overalls; on the other hand, overcoats (symbols of petit-bourgeois respectability), blouses, aprons, sports jackets and blazers. The skilled workers, the only category isolated in the available statistics, differ from the clerical workers, although they have similar incomes, almost as much as manual workers in general (except on one point, expenditure on films and records).

It is not, however, in the area of culture that one should look for a distance, or a self-distancing, from the dominant class and its values, other than a purely negative one, by default. There is, of course, everything which belongs to the art of living, a wisdom taught by necessity, suffering and humiliation and deposited in an inherited language, dense even in its stereotypes, a sense of revelry and festivity, of self-expression and practical solidarity with others (evoked by the adjective 'bon vivant' with which the working classes identify), in short, everything that is engendered by the realistic (but not resigned) hedonism and sceptical (but not cynical) materialism which constitute both a form of adaptation to

the conditions of existence and a defence against them;[20] there is the effi-
cacity and vivacity of a speech which, freed from the censorship and constraints of quasi-written and therefore de-contextualized speech, bases its
ellipses, short cuts and metaphors on common reference to shared situations, experiences and traditions. There is also everything concerned with
politics, with the tradition of trade-union struggles, which might provide
the one genuine principle of a counter-culture, but where, in fact, the effects of cultural domination never cease to operate. Those who believe in
the existence of a 'popular culture', a paradoxical notion which imposes,
willy-nilly, the dominant definition of culture, must expect to find—if
they were to go and look—only the scattered fragments of an old erudite
culture (such as folk medicine), selected and reinterpreted in terms of
the fundamental principles of the class habitus and integrated into the
unitary world view it engenders, and not the counter-culture they call
for, a culture truly raised in opposition to the dominant culture and consciously claimed as a symbol of status or a declaration of separate existence.

If there is no popular art in the sense of an art of the urban working class,
it is perhaps because this class knows no other hierarchies than the purely
negative ones which are measured by distance from the absolute poverty
and insecurity of the sub-proletariat, and remains fundamentally defined by
the relation of dispossessed to possessor which links it to the bourgeoisie,
in culture as in other areas.[21] What is generally meant by popular art, i.e.,
the art of the peasant classes of capitalist and pre-capitalist societies, is the
product of a stylizing intention which is associated with the existence of a
hierarchy: locally based, relatively autonomous milieux also have their
hierarchies of luxury and necessity, which the symbolic marks, clothing, furniture, jewellery, express and reinforce. Here too, art marks differences
which it presupposes. It is no accident that the only area of working-class
practice in which style in itself achieves stylization is that of language, with
argot, the language of leaders, 'godfathers', which implicitly affirms a
counter-legitimacy with, for example, the intention of deriding and desacralizing the 'values' of the dominant morality and aesthetic.

It tends to be forgotten that the specific logic of cultural domination
means that the fullest recognition of cultural legitimacy can and often
does coexist with the most radical challenging of political legitimacy.
Furthermore, the awakening of political consciousness is often bound up
with a whole process of rehabilitating and rebuilding self-esteem, which,
because it involves a reaffirmation of cultural dignity that is experienced
as (and indeed always is) liberatory, implies a submission to the dominant values and to some of the principles on which the dominant class
bases its domination, such as recognition of the hierarchies linked to
educational qualifications or to the capacities they are supposed to guarantee.

A specific survey would be needed to establish beyond dispute the relationship within the working class between position in the relations of production, political consciousness and relation to culture. But it is known that the rate of unionization rises from 23 percent among unskilled workers to 29 percent among the semi-skilled and 30 percent (of which 24 percent are CGT) among skilled workers, falling back to 18 percent among foremen and technicians, the relationship between educational level and rate of unionization being weakened by the fact that the foremen, while more educated, are also less unionized.[22] It is also clear that, like educational level, knowledge of legitimate culture rises with position in the occupational hierarchy. The skilled workers and foremen, older and having had a slightly longer schooling than the semi-skilled and unskilled workers, manifest a slightly greater cultural competence: only 17.5 percent know (by name) fewer than two of the works of music, as against 48.5 percent of the semi-skilled and unskilled, of whom a very high proportion decline to answer the questions on painting and music. Skilled workers and foremen more often cite the canonical artists, Leonardo (38 percent as against 20 percent), Watteau, Raphael, whereas the semi-skilled and unskilled pick out vaguely familiar names more or less at random, Picasso, Braque, Rousseau (no doubt confusing the 'douanier' with Jean-Jacques).[23] And, above all, whereas the semi-skilled and unskilled readily admit that paintings do not interest them or that classical music is 'complicated', the skilled workers, more under the sway of cultural legitimacy, more often identify with a token of recognition combined with a confession of ignorance ('I love classical music but I don't know much about it' or 'Paintings are nice but difficult').[24]

Thus, everything leads one to believe that the most politically conscious fraction of the working class remains profoundly subject, in culture and language, to the dominant norms and values, and therefore deeply sensitive to the effects of authority imposition which every holder of cultural authority can exert, even in politics, on those in whom the educational system—this is one of the social effects of primary education—has inculcated a recognition without knowledge.

8 | Culture and Politics

Perhaps the most radical approach to the problem of politics is to ask of
it the question that Marx and Engels raise in relation to art. Having analysed the concentration of the capacity for artistic production in the
hands of a few individuals and the correlative (or even consequent) dispossession of the masses, they imagine a (communist) society in which
'there are no painters but at most people who engage in painting among
other things',[1] and in which, thanks to the development of the productive forces, the general reduction of working time (through an overall decrease and an equal distribution) allows 'everyone sufficient free
time to take part in the general affairs of society—*theoretical as well as
practical*.' 'There are no politicians but at most people who engage in politics among other activities': here as elsewhere, a utopia is scientifically
(and, no doubt, politically) justified by the way it demolishes self-evident
appearances and forces one to bring to light the presuppositions of the
usual order. Indeed, although its apparent generosity makes it the
diametric opposite of the élitist denunciations of universal suffrage which
the intellectuals and artists of another age went in for, the indulgent
populism which credits the common people with innate knowledge of
politics equally helps to disguise and so consecrate the 'concentration in a
few individuals' of the capacity to produce discourse about the social
world, and, through this, the capacity for consciously changing that
world. The utopian paradox breaks the doxa: by imagining a social world
in which 'anyone in whom there is a potential Raphael' of painting or
politics could develop without hindrance, it forces one to see that the
concentration of the embodied or objectified instruments of production

is scarcely less in politics than in art, and prevents one forgetting all the potential Raphaels whom the mechanisms responsible for this monopoly keep excluded much more effectively than any 'ideological state apparatuses'.

Even if one only credits the idealized 'people' with a wholly practical knowledge of the social world as such, or at least of its position and interests in that world, one still has to examine whether, and how, this political sense can be expressed in a discourse corresponding to the truth it contains in practical form, and thus become the motor of a conscious and, through the mobilizing power of explicit statement, truly collective action.[2] Staying closer to reality, it has to be asked whether this political sense is really the infallible flair it is sometimes claimed to be, which could at least identify the most appropriate products on the *market* of discourses produced and supplied by the owners of the means of production of legitimate problems and opinions.[3]

Political science long ago began to register the fact that a large proportion of the persons surveyed 'abstained' from answering questions on politics and that these 'non-responses' varied significantly by sex, age, educational level, occupation, place of residence and political tendency. But no conclusions have been drawn, and the psephologists merely deplore this culpable 'abstention'. As soon as one sees that the inert 'don't know' category is largely recruited from what others call 'the masses' or 'the people', one begins to suspect the function it performs in the operation of 'liberal democracy' and the contribution it makes to maintaining the established order. Abstentionism is perhaps not so much a hiccup in the system as one of the conditions of its functioning as a misrecognized—and therefore recognized—restriction on political participation.

What needs to be questioned is the very notion of 'personal opinion'. The opinion poll, by urging all its respondents, without distinction, to produce a 'personal opinion'—an intention underlined by all the 'according-to-yous', 'in-your-views' and 'what-do-you-personally-thinks' in the questionnaires—or to choose, by their own means, unaided, between several pre-formulated opinions, implicitly accepts a political philosophy which makes political choice a specifically political judgement, applying political principles to answer a problem that is presented as political, and which credits everyone with not only the right but also the power to produce such a judgement. A social history of the notion of 'personal opinion' would no doubt show that this eighteenth-century invention is rooted in the rationalist belief that the faculty of 'judging well', as Descartes called it, that is, of discerning good from bad, truth from falsehood, by a spontaneous and immediate inner feeling, is a universal aptitude of universal application (like the faculty of aesthetic judgement according to Kant)—even if it had to be conceded, especially from the nineteenth century on, that universal education is indispensable in order to give this aptitude its full development and to secure a real basis for the universal judgement expressed in universal suffrage. The idea of 'personal opinion' perhaps owes part of its self-evident character to the fact that— being constructed against the Church's claim to a monopoly of the legitimate production of judgements, the means of production of judgements and the producers of judgements, and being inseparable from the idea of tolerance, that is, the challenging of all authority in the name of the conviction that in such matters all opinions, whoever their producer, are equally valid—it expressed from the very beginning the interests of the intellectuals, small, self-employed opinion producers whose role developed parallel to the constitution of a specialized field of production and a market for cultural products, then of a sub-field specializing in the production of political opinions (with the press, the parties and all the representative bodies).

The act of producing a response to a questionnaire on politics, like voting or, at another level of participation, reading a party newspaper (*journal d'opinion*) or joining a party, is a particular case of a supply meeting a demand. On one side is the field of ideological production, a relatively autonomous universe in which amidst competition and conflict, the instruments for thinking the social world are created and where, through this process, the field of the politically thinkable, or, to put it another way, the legitimate problematic, is defined.[4] On the other side are social agents, occupying different positions in the field of class relations and defined by a greater or lesser specific political competence—a greater or lesser capacity to recognize a political question as political and to treat it as such by responding to it politically, i.e., on the basis of specifically political principles (rather than ethical ones, for example). This capacity is inseparable from a more or less strong feeling of being *competent,* in the full sense of the word, that is, socially recognized as entitled to deal with political affairs, to express an opinion about them or even modify their course. In fact, there is reason to suppose that competence in the sense of technical capacity (political culture) is correlated with competence in the sense of a socially recognized capacity, ascribed by and ascribing status—the opposite of which is both impotence and objective and subjective exclusion ('That is none of my business'; 'That doesn't interest me').[5]

Selective Democracy

As soon as one takes seriously the 'don't knows' and their variations, which are the most important information supplied by opinion polls, it is clear that the probability of having a particular opinion that is associated with a given category (which is indicated by the frequency with which members of that category choose one or another of the alternatives offered) is only a *conditional* probability—the probability that an eventuality will occur on condition that another eventuality occurs, in this case the production of an opinion rather than the sheer absence of a response. The opinions recorded, that is, explicitly stated, cannot be interpreted adequately unless it is borne in mind that they depend for their existence and their significance on the (absolute) probability of producing an opinion, which varies (at least as significantly as the conditional probability of producing a particular opinion) according to the properties of the respondents and also the properties of the question, or, more precisely, according to the relationships between these two sets of properties. This probability is greater for men than for women, greater for the young than the old; greater in large towns (especially Paris); and rises with educational capital (measured by qualifications) and economic capital (measured by income) and with social position. The variations linked to these variables are that much more marked when the questions are more remote from experience, more abstract and detached from ordinary realities in their content and phrasing (and also, but secondarily, when they have only recently appeared in the field of ideological production) and when they require more insistently a response produced on the basis of specifically political principles (a demand that is perceived in the very syntax and vocabulary of the question).

Everything takes place as if the most 'legitimate' agents, that is, those most competent in both senses, were and felt that much more legitimated—i.e., inclined and called upon to express an opinion—the more 'legitimate' the problem posed. Thus, one finds that those who cannot reply to the question of their political allegiance or preference (indicating the party to which they feel closest) are those who are also most inclined to leave the other questions unanswered—especially when the question posed is clearly located in the register of professional politics. The interviewees who fall into the non-aligned 'grey area' in the SOFRES survey do not reply much less often (81 percent) than those who identify with the extreme left (91 percent), the left (90 percent), the centre (86 percent), the right (93 percent) or the extreme right (92 percent), when asked whether France should help 'poor countries'. But when asked whether France should favour countries with a 'democratic regime', they reply significantly less often (57 percent) than those identifying with the extreme left (76 percent), the left (67 percent), the centre (75 percent), the right (70 percent), or the extreme right (74 percent) (SOFRES, 1971).

For a complete validation of these propositions, which are based on secondary analysis of the distribution of non-responses and responses to questions asked by several opinion research institutes between 1960 and 1976, one would have to carry out a survey in which the subject and form of the questions were varied systematically. They might range, for example, from foreign policy questions, which are both foreign to concrete experience and seen as outside the scope of any conceivable political action, to the most everyday problems, calling for the ethical responses of ordinary existence, or to the problems most directly rooted in political or union experience, like everything concerned with wages, labour relations, or the unions; and from the most abstract formulations of 'political science' to concrete questions which are sometimes the practical equivalent of these. In practice, the best that could be done to replicate this ideal questionnaire was to juxtapose questions borrowed from different organizations. However, the rate of 'don't knows' varies from one institute to another (other things being equal, SOFRES always seems to find fewer than IFOP) and, independently of the question, from one survey to another, i.e., according to the interviewers' instructions and their inclination to follow them. For a given subject, it also varies over time.[6]

Furthermore, the absence of a reply is not always the product of a negative determination and, alongside the non-responses for lack of competence which are analysed here, one also has to count the elective non-responses, a genuine abstention expressing the effect of a discordance with the legitimate reply, which is censored because it dare not be expressed—an ethical or political conflict with no outcome but silence. In a particularly clear case of censorship, a considerable proportion of the farmers and small employers (17.1 percent and 15.8 percent, as against 4.1 percent of the office workers and junior executives, 5.1 percent of the senior executives and professionals, 8 percent of the manual workers) refrain from answering a question on tax evasion (IFOP, February 1969). In a typical case of conflict accompanied by censorship, senior executives abstain relatively frequently (22 percent—like manual workers—compared with 19 percent for clerical workers and junior executives, 27 percent for the employers and 41 percent for the farmers) from answering a question on the role of the unions (IFOP, April 1969); and the ambiguity of the peasants' relation to the workers and their organizations can surely be read in their high rate of abstention, which cannot be imputed solely to incompetence since, in the same survey, they reply more often (72 percent compared to 59 percent) to a question on the student movements, which they know no better.

A similar unease may express itself in the typical distribution of the members of a group into three fairly equal classes: those who escape by abstention, those who approve and those who disapprove. When asked by IFOP in 1968 about Czecho-Soviet relations ('Do you think that the Moscow agreements signed on August 26 are satisfactory or unsatisfactory for the Czechs?'), 37 percent of the Communist Party (PCF) supporters did not answer, 19 percent said they were satisfactory and 44 percent said they were not. Those who would vote for the other left- or right-wing parties answered more often: only 18 percent of the PSU voters were 'don't-knows', 22 percent of the Centrists, 26 percent of the Socialists and Radicals, 27 percent of the Gaullists (UDR), 32 percent of the Giscardians (RI); and they much more often said the agreements were unsatisfactory (80 percent of the PSU voters, 73 percent of the Centrists, 70 percent of the Socialists and Radicals, 69 percent of the Gaullists, 64 percent of the Giscardians). Similarly, asked whether they 'approved or disapproved of the introduction of sex education into the school curriculum' (IFOP, 1966), 19 percent of the agricultural workers gave no answer (as against 11 percent of the employers, 9 percent of the manual workers, clerical workers and junior executives and 7 percent of the senior executives and professionals), 33 percent of them disapproved and 48 percent approved (whereas 74 percent of the senior executives and professionals, 72 percent of the manual workers, clerical workers and junior executives and 60 percent of the employers were favourable).

It is nonetheless possible to get a fairly precise idea of the specific effect of the relationship between the respondent's competence and the subject and form of the question by examining how the gaps between the rates of non-response—e.g., for men and women—vary in a single survey (a SOFRES survey of February 1971 on France, Algeria and the Third World), that is, in a case where all other things may be considered equal (see table 28). One first finds that though women reply almost as often as men when asked if 'France is or is not doing enough to help immigrant workers find accommodation' (85 percent in each case), 'to give them training' (70 percent as against 75 percent), 'to make them welcome' (80 percent as against 83 percent), 'to give them decent wages' (77 percent as against 83 percent), all of which are problems that can be considered ethically and that, according to the traditional morality, women are competent to deal with, they are much less inclined to reply than men when confronted with a specifically political problem. Only 75 percent of them, compared with 92 percent of the men, answer a question on 'continuing the *policy* of co-operation with Algeria', a problem, as the question itself indicates, of pure politics, foreign policy being more remote from concrete experience than internal politics, especially when approached, as here, without any ethical reference ('As regards Franco-Algerian relations, do you think it desirable that France should continue a *policy* of co-operation with Algeria?'). As soon as the abstract question of co-operation is put back into the realm of ethics, or even the charity which the traditional division of labour assigns to women, specialists of the heart and feelings ('Among the different groups of under-developed countries, in your view should France take a particular interest in the *poorest* countries?'), women reply as often as men (88 percent each). But when the survey returns to specifically political or political-scientific questioning—and an abstract vocabulary which means different things to different groups—by asking if France should be interested in 'countries which have a *democratic regime*', the proportion of women who reply again falls sharply, to 59 percent compared with 74 percent of the men.

We see here a paradigmatic example of the effects of the division of labour between the sexes. Men feel all the more strongly required—not simply authorized—to formulate an opinion, to the extent that women feel dispensed from doing so and freer to delegate this task and to choose by proxy. This is an illustration of the obligation—sometimes an untenable one, as is seen in the situations of a survey on culture—fastened on men in the established

Table 28 'Don't know' responses to political questions, by sex (%), 1971.[a]

Question 1. There are at present a large number of immigrant workers in France. They often do unpleasant work. Do you think that France is or is not doing enough to:

	Sex	Don't know	Enough	Not enough
a. help them find accommodation?	Men	16	30	54
	Women	16	27	57
b. train them?	Men	25	34	41
	Women	30	31	39
c. make them welcome?	Men	17	47	36
	Women	20	40	40
d. give them decent wages?	Men	17	44	39
	Women	23	37	40

Question 2. As regards Franco-Algerian relations, do you think it desirable that France continue a policy of cooperation with Algeria?

Sex	Don't know	Yes	No
Men	8	56	36
Women	25	47	28

Question 3. Among the different groups of under-developed countries, in your view should France take a particular interest in:

	Sex	Don't know	Yes	No
a. the poorest countries?	Men	12	70	18
	Women	12	74	14
b. its former colonies?	Men	13	50	37
	Women	20	41	39
c. countries whose foreign policy is close to that of France?	Men	20	56	24
	Women	32	48	20
d. countries that have a democratic regime?	Men	26	40	34
	Women	41	25	34

Source: SOFRES, *La France, l'Algérie et le Tiers Monde*, February 1971.
a. The distributions by educational level are not available.

view of the sexual division of labour, which is increasingly recognized and binding as one moves down the hierarchies of economic and especially cultural capital.

The effect of sexual status may be reinforced or counteracted by the effect of that other title of political competence, educational qualification (see table 29). Thus, when asked how they would vote in the event of parliamentary elections, women overall reply less often than men, but the gap between the sexes tends to widen as one moves down the social hierarchy: the proportion of 'don't knows' is 21 percent for women and 18 percent for men among senior executives, 22 percent and 17 percent among junior executives, 27 percent and 17 percent among clerical workers, 32 percent and

Table 29 'Don't know' responses to questions on teaching, by educational level (%), 1970.[a]

	'Don't knows' by educational level		
Questions	Primary	Secondary	Higher
Teaching is a good job	10.5	9.8	11.4
Teachers should be admired for doing their job in present-day conditions	11.2	8.3	4.1
Many teachers don't do their job conscientiously	35.5	26.7	17.7
Teachers aren't firm enough with young people	21.6	16.9	8.3
French teachers' holidays are too long	12.0	7.2	3.1
Teachers aren't paid enough	46.4	25.9	19.2
Teachers are too involved in politics	32.3	17.6	12.4
Teachers aren't trained properly to do their job	47.9	24.5	12.5

Source: IFOP, March 1970.

a. The rates of non-response are generally higher than in the realm of ordinary experience, to which the first question still belongs. This is understandable since the survey deals with the educational system, an institution which appears less controllable the less qualified one is. In this intermediate zone between the domestic and the political, the 'don't knows' increase as the questions move from morality (emphasized by such ethically loaded words as: 'should be admired', 'conscientiously', 'aren't firm enough') towards politics. Comparison of the distributions for the last two questions (especially in view of the fact that the 'don't know' rates for men and women are further apart for the penultimate question—18.5% as against 32%—than for the last one—32.5% as against 42%) shows that the propensity to reply or to abstain—social competence—can be based on two principles, which may or may not combine their effects: the status-assigned competence to judge the educational system conferred by qualification, and the status-assigned competence to judge politics, which *also* depends on sex.

24 percent among craftsmen and shopkeepers, 28 percent and 18 percent among manual workers and 38 percent and 26 percent among farm workers.[7]

In fact, analysis by fractions would probably show that, in politics as in aesthetics, the differences between the sexes tend to diminish both when one moves from the dominated classes to the dominant classes and when, within the dominant class and no doubt also the petite bourgeoisie, one moves from the economically dominant fraction to the dominated fractions. Everything suggests that the refusal of sexual status, in political or other matters, tends to increase with educational level. Thus when the sexes have similar secondary or higher education, more women than men consider that membership in a family planning movement is a political act or that sex education is a political problem (the relationship between the sexes on the same questions is inverted at lower levels of education).

More generally, the more the questions deal with problems of daily existence, private life or domestic morality—housing, food, child-rearing, sexuality etc.—the smaller becomes the gap between men and women or between the least educated and the most educated, and sometimes it disappears completely. For example, to a question on girls' upbringing,[8] women reply scarcely less often than men (93.9 percent and 96 percent) and the less educated slightly more often than the more educated (94.5 percent of those with only primary schooling, 92.8 percent of those with higher education). Questioned on cooking, women reply *more often* than men (98 percent, for example, as against 94 percent, to a question on favourite dishes)—except for questions on wines, knowledge of which is a male attribute, or a question in which culinary problems are universalized ('Would you say that, *in general,* the French eat too much, about the right amount, or not enough?'—men 98 percent, women 96 percent; SOFRES, December 1971; C.S. XXXIV).

The same logic explains why manual workers, who normally have a particularly high rate of non-response, are the most eager to answer questions on the government's role in industrial disputes (the level of non-response runs from 13 percent among manual workers to 18 percent among the executives and professions, 19 percent among clerical workers and junior executives, 25 percent among craftsmen and shopkeepers and 31 percent among farmers and farm workers)[9] or on the parties and unions which best defend the interests of wage-earners (manual workers 36.4 percent, employers 37.6 percent, clerical workers and junior executives 38.9 percent, senior executives and the professions 40.1 percent, farmers 49 percent).[10] By contrast, the more specifically political or political-scientific the question, i.e., the more it is constituted as such in both subject and language without direct reference to the experience or interests of the group concerned, the greater the gap between men and women or between the least- and most-educated. Thus, in an extreme case, in an IFOP question on the connection between the 1967 Middle-East 'conflict' and the Vietnam 'war',[11] the level of 'don't knows' rose to 40 percent for women, 21.8 percent for men, 40.6 percent for those with primary education, 8.5 percent for those with higher education. In another question, previously referred to, on Czecho-Soviet relations the corresponding figures are 44.6 percent, 21.1 percent, 39.4 percent and 11 percent.[12] In a sort of experimental reproduction of electoral democracy, the survey shows that the antinomy between democratic spontaneism, which grants everyone the right and duty to have an opinion, regardless of sex and class, and technocratic aristocracy, which restricts opinion to 'experts' elected for their 'intelligence' and 'competence', finds a practical solution in the mechanisms which induce the 'free' self-exclusion of those whom technocratic selection would exclude in any case.

Status and Competence

Thus the probability of replying depends in each case on the relationship between a question (or, more generally, a situation) and an agent (or class of agents) defined by a given competence, a capacity which itself depends on the probability of exercising that capacity. 'Interest' or 'indifference' towards politics would be better understood if it were seen that the propensity to use a political power (the power to vote, or 'talk politics' or 'get involved in politics') is commensurate with the reality of this power, or, in other words, that indifference is only a manifestation of impotence.[13]

This hypothesis is the only one which explains the fact, commonly regarded as self-evident, that, like the propensity to reply, the declared interest in politics is greater among men than women and rises with educational level, position in the social hierarchy, age, and size of town. According to an IFOP survey (*Sondages*, nos. 1–2, 1969), the proportion who say they are 'very interested' in politics rises from 2 percent among those with primary education to 13 percent for those with secondary education and 34 percent for those with higher education. According to Deutsch, Lindon and Weill, the corresponding figures are 6 percent, 14 percent and 32 percent (the proportion for men is 11 percent and for women 5 percent).[14] Similarly, declared interest in political debates on TV (e.g., 'Face à face'), or in programmes on political, economic and social problems, is greater among men than among women, in Paris than in the small towns, among the highly educated than among the less educated (C.S. VII, vol. II, pp. 28–29). By the same logic, men more often than women are 'very interested' in the results of opinion polls (26 percent and 22 percent), the younger more often than the older (under 49, 26 percent; age 50–64, 23

If I Was Better Informed

'What I mean to say is, I'd certainly understand some things more if I was better informed. That's all. If I was better informed, things would be very different. Because I don't go to enough meetings ... There are other ways of finding out, newspapers, TV, debates like "A armes égales", you know. But you have to keep following it, it's always the same, you have to have the time. That's the main problem, I haven't got the time. Now, if I had time, I'd really like to find out about all that, know what's going on and so on. But I really haven't got much time. Now, if I had more time, well, I'd do something about it, I'd try and inform myself, keep more in touch. What I mean is, if you're more informed, you can discuss things with people. When you don't know much, you're a bit left out.'

Charwoman

'Of course, anyone can get involved in politics, that's true. But still, you need a certain education to go in for politics. Need to go to college, don't you, and learn lots of things.'

Municipal clerk

percent; 65 and over, 19 percent), senior executives and professionals (32 percent) more than junior executives and clerical workers (28 percent), craftsmen and shopkeepers (27 percent), manual workers (23 percent) or farmers and farm workers (17 percent) (SOFRES, November 1975). The senior executive and professional categories, according to a SOFRES survey of 1976, also contain the highest proportion of individuals who say they are disposed to discuss a party's programme among themselves, to take part in demonstrations, join a party or donate money to a party 'to help their ideas triumph'.

These regularities have to be compared with those found in the recruitment and promotion of political personnel. Every indication suggests that one has incomparably greater chances of taking an active part in politics and having an important role in a party if one is a man and highly educated. Women make up only 1.8 percent of the Chamber of Deputies and 2.5 percent of the Senate. In all parties there are relatively fewer women in the central decision-making bodies than among the local delegates.[15] In 1977, when 50 percent of potential Socialist voters were women, only 30 percent of the members of the local sections in Paris were women, and only 1.5 percent of the delegates at the party's congress in Nantes. In the Paris Federation of the Communist Party, women constituted 31 percent of the activists present at local conferences, 29 percent of the delegates with party responsibilities and 26 percent of the 'cell' secretaries.

Similarly, manual workers, who represented 31 percent of the UDR electorate and 16 percent of the UDR members (17.6 percent in the Gironde), provided only 2 percent of the officials and only 1 percent of the Deputies elected in 1968. Although, according to voting intentions, they represented 36 percent of the Socialist electorate for the whole of France (40 percent of the whole working population) and 21.9 percent of the members in the Gironde (a department with 34.2 percent manual workers), they were almost absent from the Paris branches (1.7 percent) and provided only 5 percent of the delegates at the Nantes congress and 0 percent of the Socialist Deputies elected in 1968. Manual workers were more represented in the membership of the Communist Party than in the working population (in the Gironde, 53.8 percent as against 34.2 percent), but slightly less represented among the office-holding delegates or cell secretaries (17 percent in Paris, where they constituted 26 percent of the working population) or Communist Deputies (37 percent of those elected in 1968) as against 40 percent in the nation-wide working population.

One finds a strong over-representation of graduates among politicians (although activism offers another way in for those with little education). In 1968, 67.5 percent of the Deputies had higher education, 14 percent secondary education. At the Socialist Party Congress in Grenoble in 1973, 54.6 percent of the delegates had some higher education, 23.3 percent secondary education; and everything suggests that possession of high educational capital is increasingly becoming a necessary condition for selection as a Socialist Party delegate. Two-thirds of the Deputies who joined the party between 1971 and 1973 had higher education, but only 34.6 percent of those who joined before 1968. For Socialist Deputies, access to official positions in the National Assembly group (committee membership etc.) depends either on

Class Consciousness

'To start with, when I got married, I had no definite opinions, I was from Brittany, see, I certainly felt there were problems and, well, I felt it, but I couldn't define them. I married a Communist, without realizing it. At first, you know, when I had just arrived in the house, when I saw *L'Humanité Dimanche*, I was furious. You see, I didn't know the paper, for months and years I didn't know about it. And then, little by little, you see, I was led to recognize, you see, that maybe its attitudes were a little bit hard, but the fact was, they were right. My husband was a trade-union man, so I was dealing with a trade unionist, and then I had one, two, three children, then, you see, I went through the difficulties of life like everyone, little by little. There were some very bad patches, because I had to look after my mother as well as everything else. And my husband's a worker, right, so I knew about the workers' problems. And then I really made up my mind at the time of the Algerian war, you see, I realized that monstrous things were being done that we had always been against. We'd always thought that that war was wrong and that was really when I understood what the Party stood for. Especially when there was the massacre at Charonne, remember? Well, that completely revolted me, because you see, I'd made my husband stay at home that evening, otherwise he might have been there.'

Seamstress, turner's wife, age 42, Communist

the volume of educational capital (64 percent of such 'office holders' have higher education, 31 percent of the rest), or, in parties in which the great majority of Deputies have higher education, on the type of educational capital (law and the humanities are over-represented).

So it would be naive to see the very close relationship between educational capital and the propensity to answer the most specifically political questions as a simple and direct effect of the unequal distribution of specific political competence, defined, in the restricted sense, by possession of the theoretical and practical knowledge needed to produce political actions and judgements and perhaps especially by command of political language, capacities which, one may assume, vary with educational capital.

When the respondents were invited to classify a set of movements, groupings or political parties as they saw fit, in general the higher their social position or the greater their educational capital, the more classes they produced. Most of those educated below the baccalauréat made a maximum of four groups, whereas the better qualified made five or more. A quarter of those with a degree above the *licence* distinguished at least nine groups (a performance rarely achieved by those with the CEP or CAP and never by the unqualified). The ability to make refined classifications, the readiness to comment on them and, especially, to give names or qualifiers to the categories varies even more strongly by social position, educational capital and also social origin.[16]

Such a reading—overemphasizing the unequal distribution of political capital—which would be supported by all the appearances, would do no more than record two contrasting and complementary representations of the division of political labour: the technocratic representation, which makes technical competence (as defined by technocrats) the precondition for access to 'political responsibilities' or 'responsible' political choices, and the complementary representation, based on the sense of incompetence and impotence, which condemns the economically and culturally deprived to reliance on 'experts' or a belief in 'cryptocracy', another way of overestimating the other classes. Like every recording of 'data' at face value, this endorsement of appearances would have the effect of preventing inquiry into the objective bases of these representations, and, more precisely, would prevent one from looking into the reality of the division of political labour for the truth contained in these representations of the division of labour.

In fact, here as elsewhere, the relationship between reality and representations is established through the dispositions which are the internalized form of the probabilities associated with a given position in the division of labour. 'Technical' competence depends fundamentally on social competence and on the corresponding sense of being entitled and required by status to exercise this specific capacity, and therefore to possess it. In other words, to understand the relationship between educational capital and the propensity to answer political questions, it is not sufficient to consider the capacity to understand, reproduce, and even produce political discourse, which is guaranteed by educational qualifications; one also has to consider the (socially authorized and encouraged) sense of being entitled to be concerned with politics, authorized to talk politics, by applying a specific political culture, i.e., explicitly political principles of classification and analysis, instead of replying ad hoc on the basis of ethical principles.[17]

The effect of educational qualifications is not so different as it seems from the effect of sexual status. In each case, what is at stake is as much a status-linked right to politics as a simple political culture, the prerequisite to the exercise of this right which those who feel entitled to exercise it provide for themselves. Technical competence is to social competence what the capacity to speak is to the right to speak, simultaneously a precondition and an effect. The marking produced by the imposition of properties such as educational status or sexual identity impresses itself both on the marked individual, who is called upon to 'live up' to his or her social definition, and on others, who expect him or her to actualize his or her essence. (The psychological translation of this relationship is particularly visible in the relations within couples.) That is why competence in the sense of specific culture is to competence in the sense of status property as existence is to essence: only those who ought to have it can really acquire it and only those who are authorized to have it feel called upon to acquire it.

The beginnings of a proof of this argument are seen in the fact that, other things being equal (in particular, educational capital), women differ from men not so much in strict technical competence as in their manner of affirming it. Thus, at equal educational levels, women define almost the same number of categories within the universe of political movements and parties, and almost as often give them names. It is true that, partly because politics is their business and they invest more in it, the men know more politicians' names, more often know which party they belong to, can more often give the name and party of their local Deputy. But the difference is greatest when it is a matter of socially asserting this competence. At equal educational levels, more women say they do not know whether the various problems mentioned to them are political or not;[18] they more often confess they do not know who 'Philippon' is (see note 16), whereas the men are more often inclined to disguise this ignorance; they are more often content to indicate a general zone in the political scale whereas the men tend to situate themselves precisely. Above all, they are more often prepared to acknowledge that politics is a matter for specialists. Finally, they are much more inclined to confess that at election times they cannot decide whom to vote for. Not only do they tend more to delegate their capacity for political choice to others (in most cases, no doubt, to their husbands), but they seem to have a more local, and more moral and emotional, view of politics. Thus, at all levels, rather more of them say that help for the handicapped is a political problem; and rather fewer of them say this of voting in parliamentary or local elections or of a collection for Vietnam.

Thus, the variations in the rate of non-responses by sex, educational capital or social class, that is, roughly according to the probability of possessing power in any field whatsoever, show that political competence in the sense of a socially recognized capacity is one of the aptitudes a person has insofar as he has a right or duty to have them. And the variations which are also found, other things being equal, according to the saturation of the question with indices of conformity to the norms of depoliticized political discourse (stylistic neutrality, euphemisms etc.), show the contribution which 'political scientists' make to the imposition of the limits of competence when, by bestowing the appearances of science on their inquiry and its analysis, they reinforce the sense of unworthiness in the 'incompetent'.

The Right to Speak

The propensity to speak politically, even in the most rudimentary way, that is, by producing a 'yes' or a 'no', or putting a cross beside a prefabricated answer, is strictly proportionate to the sense of having the right to speak. Nothing shows this more clearly than the composition of the so-called spontaneous sample of people who responded to a 'national consultation' on the educational system, organized, with the aid of the press, after the events of 1968.[19] In so doing they asserted themselves as parties to the debate, entitled to express an authorized, authoritative opinion, to voice the performative utterance of a legitimate pressure group.[20] The opinion mobilized—as if by a petition—about education closely coincides with the population of users of higher education. The probability that an isolated agent, in the absence of any delegation, will form an explicit, coherent opinion on the educational system depends on the extent to which he depends on it for his reproduction and is objectively and subjectively *interested* in its functioning.

As if the propensity to influence the destiny of the institution rose with one's importance within it, the rate of response rises with the sense of legitimacy in speaking about it and with the immediacy of self-interest in its functioning.[21] Thus the probability of responding, which is much greater for men than for women (the latter tending to write in as 'parents' rather than as authorized spokespersons of a group or the general interest) and for Parisians than for provincials, is, for a given social class, very close to its objective chances of getting its children into one of the grandes écoles (i.e., very close to nil for peasants and manual workers—of the order of 0.09 and 0.05 in 10,000—0.7 per 10,000 for craftsmen and shopkeepers, 0.9 for clerical workers, 3 for junior executives, 19 for primary teachers, 5 for industrial and commercial employers, 11 for senior executives, 22 for engineers, 26 for members of the professions, 110 for secondary and higher-education teachers—these figures are obtained by comparing the male population of each class of respondents with the corresponding fraction of the working population). For pupils and students, who respond more often when at higher levels of study and when enrolled in more prestigious establishments (a lycée rather than a comprehensive or technical school, a grande école rather than a faculty) or when living in Paris than in the provinces, the probability of participation is closely linked to social origin. (It is two to three times greater for the son of an industrialist, a senior executive or a professional, in the case of students, and six times greater in the case of pupils.)

Exactly the same tendencies are seen in the responses to various questions the opinion research institutes have asked about the educational system. In general, there are more 'don't knows' among women than men (for example, in a survey on the Government's plans for university reform [IFOP, September 1968], 29.7 percent of women and 25.7 percent of men; in a survey on selection for university entrance [IFOP, September 1968], 16.9 percent and 11.2 percent; but, on the question of Latin in secondary schools

Quantity and Quality

'It would be dangerous, in this area, to allow the notion of *quantity* to prevail over that of quality. A certain *competence* is required, it seems to me, to make an objective judgement of the question.'

Teacher, marginal note to AEERS 'national consultation' questionnaire

[IFOP, September 1968], 26 percent of each sex); there are more 'don't knows' among the less educated than among the more highly educated (32 percent, 19 percent and 35 percent in response to these three questions in the case of those with only primary education, 15 percent, 6 percent and 10 percent respectively in the case of graduates); there are more 'don't knows' among provincials than Parisians, and steadily more as one moves down the social hierarchy. Thus the self-selecting, spontaneous sample in the 'national consultation' is the *limit* towards which the population of respondents in a representative survey tends; or, to put it another way, the answers obtained from a representative sample constitute a spontaneous sample which, although it is not perceived as such, is produced by laws which are fundamentally the same as those described here.

Within the spontaneous sample, the less a category is represented, the less its 'representatives' are typical of the category as a whole, and the principle of the bias is almost always their relationship to the educational system. (Thus, 90.7 percent of the industrial and commercial employers have at least the baccalauréat, compared with only 11.3 percent in the category in the working population, and, for the craftsmen and shopkeepers, 28.7 percent compared with only 2.8 percent.) Similarly, the more remote a fraction is from the educational system, the more those who respond belong to that part of the fraction most interested in the educational system, i.e., those who are of an age to have children in secondary or higher education. Thus 49.7 percent of the teachers in the spontaneous sample are aged 35–54 (38.9 percent in the working population), 69.7 percent of the professionals (53.5 percent in the working population), 77.1 percent of the employers (50.7 percent in the working population).

It follows from this over-selection that the differences between the classes and the fractions (who, within the middle and dominant classes, are represented in accordance with their cultural capital) are reduced to a minimum, so that the degree of agreement over the problems mentioned is no doubt greater than in the population as a whole.[22] If teachers are so strongly over-represented, this is because they are interested and legitimated on several counts. In fact, the hierarchy of chances of participation shows that the effect of legitimacy predominates over the effect of interest due to simple membership. The representation of the different categories of teachers increases as one moves up the hierarchy of institutions (19 per 10,000 for primary teachers, 34 for CET teachers, 60 for CEG teachers,[23] 199 for lycée teachers, 224 for higher-education teachers) and also by rank within each institution (rising from 58 for 'supply' or substitute teachers to 175 for certified teachers and 382 for *agrégés,* and from 164 for *assistants* [junior lecturers, instructors] to 204 for *maîtres-assistants* [senior lecturers, assistant professors] and 320 for *maîtres de conférénces* [readers, associate professors] and full professors). Agrégés in secondary schools, and especially those who teach the 'classic' subjects (Latin, Greek, French, history, geography) thus respond more readily than any other category. This is no doubt because, while being more legitimate than, for example, primary teachers, who are no less linked to the system, they are more *attached* to the system than are university teachers, who can place their investments outside the institution, and not only in research (except for those in the most traditional disciplines, French, Latin, Greek, or history, who are much more inclined to respond than those in other disciplines and other faculties). It is perhaps also because, more than all other categories, agrégés felt themselves personally called into question by the crisis.

If teachers of the disciplines previously dominant in the educational system—Latin, Greek, French, history—were particularly prone to reply (they wrote many books and articles after May 1968), this is also because the redefinition of the legitimate curriculum and legitimate pedagogy, especially in secondary schools, threatened their very existence as producers (or reproducers) of products which had no other market or raison d'être than secondary education and the competitions for recruitment to it.

But the essential lesson of this analysis is that in forcing on everyone, uniformly, problems which only arise for a few, by a procedure as irreproachable as the administration of a questionnaire with pre-formed answers to a representative sample, there is every likelihood of creating a pure artifact out of thin air. Opinions are made to exist which did not pre-exist the questions, and which otherwise would not have been expressed; or which, if they had been otherwise expressed, i.e., through authorized spokesmen, would have been quite different; opinions which, in any case, had little chance of being formulated spontaneously, of being demonstrated—a demonstration being one way of giving strength to opinions by demonstrating the group which they mobilize. Political opinion is not a purely informative judgement which 'catches on' by the intrinsic force of its truth, but an *idée-force,* containing a pretension to become a reality; and the more numerous and powerful the group it mobilizes by its symbolic efficacy, the greater its power of potential enactment. In other words, because it necessarily contains a power to mobilize and a pretension to exist, political opinion is defined, not only by its informative content but also by the social force whereby it exists as a political force, although it is political opinion which helps to make that social force exist by mobilizing the group which contains it in potential form.

The authorized speech of status-generated competence, a powerful speech which helps to create what it says, is answered by the silence of an equally status-linked incompetence, which is experienced as technical incapacity and leaves no choice but delegation—a misrecognized dispossession of the less competent by the more competent, of women by men, of the less educated by the more educated, of those who 'do not know to speak' by those who 'speak well'. The propensity to delegate responsibility for political matters to others recognized as technically competent varies in inverse ratio to the educational capital possessed, because the educational qualification (and the culture it is presumed to guarantee) is tacitly regarded—by its holders but also by others—as a legitimate title to the exercise of authority. On the one side, there are those who admit that politics is not for them and abdicate their formal rights for lack of the means of exercising them; on the other, those who feel entitled to claim a 'personal opinion', or even the authoritative opinion which is the monopoly of the competent. These two opposed but complementary representations of the division of political labour reproduce the objective division of political 'powers' between the classes and the sexes in dispositions, practices and discourses, and so help to reproduce the division itself.[24] And so it is that, by one of the paradoxical reversals that are common in such matters, education, which the nineteenth-century reformers expected above all to ensure the proper functioning of universal suffrage by producing citizens capable of voting ('We must educate our masters') now tends to function as a principle of selection, the more effective for not being officially or even tacitly imposed, which supports and legitimates unequal participation in electoral democracy and, tendentially, the whole division of political labour.

Personal Opinion

Nietzsche somewhere derides the academic cult of the 'personal turn of phrase', and it would be no small undertaking to describe the whole range of institutional mechanisms, especially the intellectual and educational ones, which help to encourage the cult and culture of the 'person', that set of personal properties, exclusive, unique and original, which includes 'personal ideas', 'personal style' and, above all, 'personal opinion'. It could be shown that the opposition between the rare, the distinguished, the chosen, the unique, the exclusive, the different, the irreplaceable, the original, and the common, the vulgar, the banal, the indifferent, the ordinary, the average, the usual, the trivial, with all the associated oppositions between the brilliant and the dull, the fine and the coarse, the refined and the crude, the high (or heightened) and the low is one of the fundamental oppositions (the other being organized around the opposition between ease and poverty) in the language of bourgeois ethics and aesthetics. Those who aim to identify the contribution the educational system may make to the inculcation of a view of the social world, and who, as in so many studies of the content of history manuals, look for it in the most direct and most visible ideological interventions, or even, like the work of the Frankfurt School on the basic elements of the image of history (*Geschichtsbild*), in the élitist philosophy of history which permeates the teaching of that discipline, are probably missing the essential point.[25] In fact, the educational institution as a whole, from its strictly individualist organization of work to the taxonomies it applies in its classifying operations, which always favour the original over the common, not to mention the contents it teaches and the way they are taught, tends to reinforce the propensity to individualism or egoism which the children of the petite bourgeoisie and grande bourgeoisie bring into the system. Literature, in which, as Gide said in his *Journal*, 'only the personal has any value', and the celebration which surrounds it in the literary field and in the educational system, are clearly central to this cult of the self, in which philosophy, often reduced to a lofty assertion of the thinker's distinction, also has a part to play. And there is every reason to predict that psychoanalysis, which, although it describes generic mechanisms, encourages immersion in the uniqueness of formative experiences (unlike sociology, which would not be so resisted if it did not reduce the 'personal' to the generic, the common), will have a place in the modernist variant of this cult.

To explain the petit-bourgeois pretension to 'personal opinion', one has to consider not only the reinforcement by the educational system and the media but also the specific social conditions which produce the 'opinionated' habitus. It can be seen that the claim to the right to 'personal opinion' and distrust of all forms of delegation, especially in politics, have their logical place in the disposition system of individuals whose whole past and whole projected future are oriented towards individual salvation, based on personal 'gifts' and 'merits', on the break-up of oppressive solidarities and even the refusal of onerous obligations, on the

---

A Very Personal Opinion

'Political parties don't interest me. I don't want to vote for a party, I vote for a candidate. A candidate without a party label would be better.

'I haven't got an exact definition of socialism. It's an overused word nowadays, which can mean anything and nothing. So I can't tell you how to construct it or how not to construct it, seeing that I don't know what it is anymore. It's too hackneyed!

'Personally I don't think I could enrol in a party. I'd be incapable of having the same tastes straightaway. Because of my Jansenist origins and my bookseller grandfather, I'm open to everything and I can't get excited about a general idea. What I mean is, I appreciate the good points of several parties. Given that it's one's very personal opinion that counts, I don't think it's possible to find a party that can combine certain elements of several doctrines that personally I don't find incompatible.'

Accountant

An Unclassifiable Professor

'Could you situate yourself on the political spectrum?'

'Look, that's another question I'm incapable of answering. I could tell you I voted for this or that group, at this or that period.'

'Could you define yourself in some other way?'

'In terms of those movements? Look, where do you put Gaullism? It's a question I have to ask you. There are Gaullists who say they are left-wing, and others who say they are right-wing. One of them said it once (laughs). That was brave of him. If I look at the way I've voted since I first started, I've voted for Mendès France, I've fairly often voted for de Gaulle. So you can place me where you like. If someone put a knife to my throat and told me to choose a political party, first of all I wouldn't choose. I'd choose something else so as not to take any of them. No, I don't know, I find the principle of political parties unsatisfactory, if you like. I think it's a necessary evil like a lot of other things. But I don't feel personally concerned. I can eliminate a certain number of things, if you like. By elimination, I'm not Communist. There are certainly leftist, or Mendésist, or left-wing Gaullist ideas, which are ultimately the same thing, that are not foreign to me. And at the same time, paradoxically, I'm in favour of a certain order. I consider that in disorder nothing can be done. In normal circumstances, of course. On the other hand, I'm not a man of the Centre. When I consider it is necessary to choose, I will choose. You see, it's difficult to answer your question. So, right now, you might say I'm slightly Gaullist à la 1940, as I used to be. It isn't a political party. That doesn't prove ... in the Gaullist movement, there are a lot of things I don't approve of, as well. That's why I shall never be enrolled in any political party.'

University professor, Paris

choice of systematically privileging the private and intimate, both at work and 'at home', in leisure and in thought, as against the public, the collective, the common, the indifferent, the borrowed.[26] But the naively 'egoistic' dispositions of the petit bourgeois have nothing in common with the subtle egotism of those who have the means to affirm the uniqueness of their person in all their practices, starting with their profession, a *liberal* activity, freely chosen and freely conducted by a 'personality', irreducible to the anonymous, impersonal, interchangeable roles with which the petit bourgeois must still identify ('rules are rules') in order to exist or, at least, in order to have their social existence recognized, especially in their conflicts with the bourgeois.[27] And the distrustful prudence which shuns delegation and enlistment has nothing in common with the conviction of being the best spokesman for distinguished thoughts and opinions.

'I think politics is a fight. And in a fight there has to be a lot of you. You need a mass.'

Charwoman, Communist

'When they really go on strike, it's because they really need to. People don't go on strike just for the fun of it.'

Charwoman

Senior executives are the category who most often say that, for political information, they rely on daily papers (27 percent of them, and 24 percent of the junior executives and clerical workers, as against 14 percent of the farmers, 11 percent of manual workers, 8 percent of craftsmen and shopkeepers) or on weekly magazines (19 percent of them, as against 7 percent of junior executives and clerical workers, 6 percent of manual workers, 5 percent of craftsmen and shopkeepers and 4 percent of farmers). This may be seen as a manifestation of the concern (which rises with educational level) to 'form an opinion' by resorting to the most specific and most legitimate instrument, the 'journal of opinion', which can be chosen in relation to one's own opinion, as opposed to television or radio—'mass media' offering homogenized products (SOFRES, *Télévision et politique,* May 1976). And one is tempted to see a similarly structured opposition in the fact that, to pursue their demands, senior executives believe in personal representations to a public service, whereas manual and office workers rely on strikes more often than other categories, while artisans, shopkeepers and junior executives prefer a demonstration, a sudden mobilization which does not pre-exist or outlive the event.

But even a rapid reflection on the social conditions of the creation of demand for a 'personal opinion' and of the achievement of this ambition is sufficient to show that, contrary to the naive belief in formal equality before politics, the working-class view is realistic in seeing no choice, for the most deprived, other than simple abdication, a resigned recognition of status-linked incompetence, or total delegation, an unreserved remission of self, a tacit confidence which chooses its speech in choosing its spokesmen.

The Modes of Production of Opinion

In fact not all answers are opinions, and the probability that a given group's responses are only disguised non-responses, polite concessions to the imposed problematic or ethical discourses naively received as 'personal opinions', no doubt varies in the same way as the probability of non-response which characterizes that group. The propensity and ability to raise interests and experiences to the order of political discourse, to seek coherence in opinions and to integrate one's whole set of attitudes around explicit political principles, in fact depends very closely on educational capital and, secondarily, on overall capital composition, increasing with the relative weight of cultural capital as against economic capital.[28]

It is not sufficient to recognize the inequalities in status competence which force attention to the social conditions of possibility of political judgement. The most fundamental political problem, the question of the modes of production of the answer to a political question, is completely masked when one accepts the intellectualist premise that every answer to a political question is the product of an act of political judgement.[29] In fact, an answer to a question which, by the dominant definition of politics, would be classified as political (e.g., a question on abortion or student demonstrations) can be produced by three very different modes of production. The principle of production may be, first, a class ethos, a generative formula not constituted as such which enables objectively coherent responses, compatible with the practical premises of a practical relation to the world, to be generated for all the problems of everyday existence. Secondly, it may be a systematic political 'slant' (*parti*), a system of explicit, specifically political principles, amenable to logical control and reflexive scrutiny, in short, a sort of political 'axiomatics' (in ordinary language, a 'line' or 'programme') which enables the infinity of political acts and judgements implied in the algorithm, and no others, to be generated or foreseen. Thirdly, it may be a two-stage choice, i.e., the identification, in the mode of knowledge, of the answers consistent with the 'line' of a political party, this time in the sense of an organization providing a political 'line' on a set of problems which it constitutes as political. The adherence implied in this tacit or explicit delegation may itself be based on practical recognition by the ethos or on an explicit choice entailed by a 'slant'.[30]

There is every difference between the intentional coherence of the practices and discourses generated from an explicit 'political' principle and the objective systematicity of the practices produced from an implicit principle, below the level of 'political' discourse, that is, from objectively systematic schemes of thought and action, acquired by simple familiarization, without explicit inculcation, and applied in the pre-reflexive mode. Without being mechanically attached to class condition, these two forms of political disposition are closely linked to it, chiefly through the material conditions of existence, whose vital demands are of unequal urgency and therefore unequally easy to 'neutralize' symbolically, and through the educational training which can give the instruments of symbolic mastery of practice, i.e., of verbalization and conceptualization of political experience. The populist inclination to credit the working classes with a 'politics' (as, elsewhere, an 'aesthetic'), spontaneously and naturally endowed with the properties included in the dominant definition of politics, ignores the fact that the practical mastery expressed in everyday choices (which may or may not be capable of being constituted as political in terms of the dominant definition) is based not on the explicit principles

>'I got my politics from the way I
>suffered when I was a kid—know
>what I mean?'
>
>*Municipal clerk, Communist*

of an ever vigilant, universally competent consciousness, but on the implicit schemes of thought and action of a class habitus, in other words—if one must use the simplistic formulae of political discussion—on a class unconscious rather than a class consciousness.

Thus, when confronted with a question of domestic morality such as sex education, which tends to be made a political question through scholastic institutionalization, all social categories except the senior executives and professionals produce responses governed by class ethos and largely independent of declared political opinions. Farmers, for example, are the group which most often say that one should not talk about sex to children, or that no sex education should be given before the age of fifteen; whereas clerical workers and junior executives are once again led by their cultural good intentions to recognize the dominant norm (which is recalled in the question itself) and most often say this education should be given before age eleven; for each category, the variations by political tendency are little marked. By contrast, everything suggests that the responses of the senior executives and professionals express a combination of a class ethos (which inclines them to a certain pedagogic laxity) with explicit political principles. Eighty percent of those who say they are on the left think sex education should be given before age eleven, 50 percent of those who say they are centrist, and 33 percent of those who say they are on the right. It can be seen that, as has been shown for the 'pure' aesthetic disposition, which makes every aesthetic choice the manifestation of an aesthetic 'slant', the propensity to make everyday choices on the basis of political principles, i.e., within the logic of the political 'slant' rather than ethical intuition, is itself a dimension of an ethos which is also expressed in the relation to language, the body, to others and to the world in general.

In fact, the second and third modes of opinion production differ from the first mode in that, in them, the explicitly political principles of the production of political judgement are made explicit and formulated as principles. This may be done either by the institution that is entrusted with the production and management of these principles or by the isolated political agent, who possesses his own means of production of political questions and answers and can provide systematic political responses to problems as different in appearance as a factory occupation, sex education or pollution. In either case, the relationship between social class and political opinion is no longer established directly, solely through the mediation of the class unconscious. To understand political opinions adequately and to explain them fully, one has to bring in a specifically political factor, either the political 'line' or 'programme' of the political party invested with the monopoly of production of the principles of production of political opinions, or the political axiomatics which enables a political opinion to be produced on every problem, whether constituted politically or not.[31]

The fact remains that, for problems that have not been brought into a personal or party 'line', agents are thrown back on their ethos, in which the social conditions of production of that ethos express themselves. This is true not only of ordinary agents but also of professional producers, intellectuals, sociologists, journalists or politicians. In the production of discourse (scientific or otherwise) on the social world, and in the definition of a line of political action on the world, it is class ethos that is called upon to make up for the lacunae in axiomatics or method (or for insufficient mastery of these means of thought and action). The 'workerism' of revolutionary parties no doubt arises from an intuition into the duality of the principles of production of political opinions and actions and from a justified scepticism as to the possibility of answering all the practical questions and challenges of ordinary existence solely on the basis of the principles of a political axiomatics.

At all events, there is every difference in the world between the conscious, quasi-forced systematicity of a political 'line' and the systematicity 'in-itself' of the practices and judgements engendered by the unconscious principles of the ethos; or even between the minimal and yet fundamental consciousness which is necessary to delegate the production of the principles of political-opinion production to a party and the systematic consciousness which can see every situation as political and can bring to it a political solution generated from political principles. If political consciousness without the appropriate dispositions is unreal and uncertain, dispositions without consciousness are self-opaque and always exposed to seduction by false recognitions.[32]

The members of the intellectual occupations (teachers, researchers, artists) declare themselves, more often than all other categories, 'supporters of revolutionary action', opposed to 'authoritarianism' and in favour of 'international class solidarity'. They more often think that 'the crisis of May 1968 was beneficial to the general interest of the population', and say as often as manual workers that 'strike pickets are justified', that 'the Popular Front was a good thing', that they prefer 'socialism' to 'liberalism' and that 'things would be better if the State owned all the major industries.' But their answers often betray an ethos at variance with their discourse: they say more often than manual workers that their 'confidence in the trade unions' has declined since May 1968 or that an individual's most important characteristic is his personality (manual workers more often cite class) or that 'economic progress has benefited the majority' (workers more often think it has only benefited a minority).[33] It may be that the tendency to political hyper-coherence which leads intellectuals to treat every problem as political and to seek perfect coherence in all attitudes in all areas of life is imposed on them by the fundamental discrepancy between their ethos and their discourse, especially when they originate from the dominated fractions of the dominant class.

The dispositions which underlie the production of opinions are chiefly revealed in the manner of expressing them, that is, precisely in all the 'insignificant' nuances which are almost inevitably lost in the ordinary recording of responses (which is generally simplified to the utmost for the sake of rapid, standardized surveying). The result is that opinions which are identical if taken at face value, but which express very different dispositions and imply very different or even opposing actions, are lumped together in the same class. Ordinary intuition, which uses the imponderables of posture and manner, the nuances of argument and hexis, as indices of the different ways of being 'right-wing' or 'left-wing', 'revolutionary' or 'conservative', the principle of every double entendre and political ambiguity, reminds us that the same habitus can espouse apparently different opinions, whereas different habitus can be expressed in superficially (i.e., electorally) similar opinions which nonetheless differ in their modality.

Thus, when Lipset concludes that, in a student population, there is no correlation between the parents' occupation and the children's political position, and attributes all the differences he finds to factors such as type of university and discipline, he not only forgets that differences in university position at a given moment are the scholastic retranslation of differences in social origin, even at the level of aspirations, since the choice of a discipline expresses the ambitions available to individuals of a given social origin with a given level of academic success. Also, and especially, he forgets that, having failed to use adequate questioning to obtain indicators of the modality of political practice and judgements, he has been forced to lump together political stances which, even if identical in their political content, may express opposing dispositions, and which, as the subsequent political realignments show, are less useful predictors of practice, especially in the long run, than the apparently insignificant details of bearing and diction which indicate the modality of 'commitments', not to mention the eloquent silences which may express approval, scepticism, hostility, contempt, resignation etc.[34]

The opposition between first-person production and production by proxy is what is always invoked by the advocates of the established order when, in the case of a strike, for example, they contrast the 'democratic' logic of a vote or an opinion poll with the 'centralist' logic of expression by a trade union, in order to try to break the organic relationship of delegation and to reduce the individual to his own resources by sending him alone to the polling booth. The opinion poll does the same thing when it sets up a mode of opinion production which forces the least competent respondents to produce opinions opposed to those proffered on their behalf by their accredited spokesmen, thus casting doubt on the validity of the delegation.[35] The same opposition between these two modes of production is invoked when, by reference to political clienteles more or less completely devoted to one or the other, those of mass parties on the one hand, and, on the other, those of small parties or 'vanguard' groups, virtually all of whose activists are able to approach politics in terms of an explicit 'line', two conceptions of the relationship between the party and the masses are contrasted. One of these demands a high degree of delegation to the central leadership, generally in the name of 'realism'; the other calls for the 'self-management' of political opinion, unconsciously universalizing the relation to politics characteristic of small owners of their own means of opinion production who have no reason to delegate to others the power to produce opinions for them. The usual image of the relationship between the party apparatuses and their clienteles—in particular, the ideology of imperfect representation, to the effect that 'the political elite does not respond to the demands of its social base' or 'creates the political demand which keeps it in power'—ignores the quite different forms which this relationship may take, depending on the party and on the categories of clientele within a single party.

These variations in the relationship between delegates and their mandators depend, inter alia, on the modes of recruitment, training and promotion of party officers (with, on one side, for example, the Communist Party, which has in a sense to create its politicians from scratch, by a total training almost entirely provided by the party,[36] and, on the other, the conservative parties which can simply incorporate *notables* already furnished with a general training and occupying an established position elsewhere); on the social characteristics of the 'base' (in particular, its level of general education and the modes of political thought it tends to apply); and on the modes of construction of political discourse, or, which amounts to the same thing, the modes of organization of the groups in which this discourse is constructed and circulates.[37]

Morality and Politics

'I've always voted Communist because I think it's the cleanest party. You've never seen Communists involved in financial scandals or anything like that. There've been some who didn't want to go along with it after a few years and slid over to the other side a bit, and they left of their own accord or they were kicked out, but I reckon it's the cleanest party and the only one that defends the working class.'

Carpenter

Analysis of opinion polls provides some indications on the second point (social characteristics of the base). For example, the principle by which Communist Party voters produce their opinions varies according to the terrain, i.e., according to whether they know practically or theoretically, by experience or political apprenticeship (as is the case with everything that concerns struggle in the field of economic relations of production), or whether they have nothing to go on but the dispositions of their ethos, in which case they inevitably appear as the guardians of an outmoded state of bourgeois morality. So it is child's play to demonstrate the contradictions or dissonances between the answers produced by activists and even leaders, in accordance with the two principles (first-person production and production by proxy), and especially between the revolu-

Figure 19 Permissiveness and political preference.

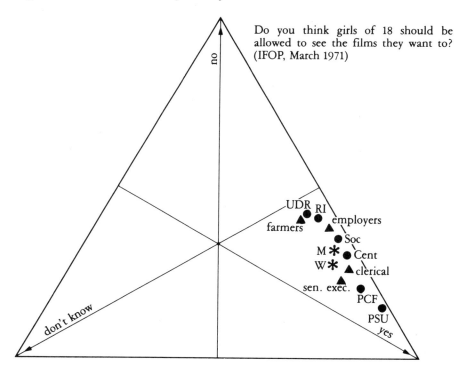

tionary dispositions they manifest in politics and the conservative dispositions they betray in the order of 'ethics'—which may lead, in certain situations, to truly conservative political practices. By contrast, PSU voters,[38] drawn to a large extent from the 'intellectual' occupations, manifest by the high degree of coherence in their responses their aptitude to see everything politically and to provide a system of explicitly compatible answers, more clearly integrated around explicit political principles than those of Communist electors (see figure 19).

All political judgements, including the would-be most enlightened ones, inevitably contain an element of implicit faith, due to the very logic of political choice, which is a choice of spokesmen and representatives and also a choice of ideas, projects, programmes, plans, embodied in 'personalities' and depending for their reality and credibility on the reality and credibility of these 'personalities'. Uncertainty even as to the object of judgement, a person or a set of ideas, is inscribed in the logic of politics, which, whatever the regime, entails entrusting to individuals the task of formulating and imposing political problems or solutions. These individuals may always be chosen either for their (objectified) programme, in the sense of a catalogue of already formulated judgements and predetermined, publicly announced measures (a manifesto), or for their 'personality', i.e., their habitus, an internalized 'program' (in the computing sense) or algorithm, the generative principle of a set of judgements and actions ('political measures') which are not explicitly formulated at the moment of 'choice' by either the candidate or the elector and which have to be intuited through the subtle indices of dispositions revealed only in bodily hexis, diction, bearing, manners. Every political 'choice' takes into account, simultaneously, the guarantor's personality and what he guarantees. The delegate is both a representative who expresses the already expressed opinions of his mandators (he is 'bound' by a programme, a sort of explicit contract of delegation) and an agent who, following his internal programme—or the specific interests associated with his position in the field of ideological production—more than his declared programme, expresses as yet unformulated, implicit or potential opinions which he thereby brings into existence. He may even use the monopoly of speech implied in his spokesman status to credit his mandators, by an unverifiable usurpation, with expectations, intentions and demands which they do not acknowledge (and which, depending on the case, are those of a vanguard or a rear-guard of the group as a whole). In short, the fact tht the delegate is the guarantor of the programme, not only as an *opus operatum* but also as a *modus operandi,* no doubt explains why, to adapt a phrase of Durkheim's, not everything in the contract of political delegation is contractual.

· The advocates of change are forced to spell out their heretical opinions in broad daylight, in defiance of the doxa, the ordinary acceptance of the usual order which goes without saying and therefore usually goes unsaid.

An Eye for Character

'What do you consider in choosing a Deputy?'

'First of all, the party. Then, not his honesty, but the way he fights. Personally I prefer a guy who's a bit rough, even if maybe the results are a bit less good than with someone gentler. I like a guy who doesn't mince his words. Like, right now, I'd rather have Jacques Duclos than Georges Marchais. Because I reckon that when Duclos has something to say, he doesn't beat about the bush. Nor does Marchais, but he's a bit less direct, tends to pussy-foot a bit.'

Manual worker, Communist

'The Radicals are, well they used to be, I don't know what they're like now, but Servan-Schreiber is trying to modernize them, anyway they always used to be a party of old fogies, with a lot of Freemasons I think, and not really any clear ideas. It's not a very frank party, I find.'

Secretary

Trust

'I have confidence in them, I've always had confidence, they've always done what they said, that's why I've always voted for them.'

Municipal clerk, Communist

'On the whole, I always do everything willingly, especially for the Party. So there you are. I've always done what I'm told. There are some things I didn't like, and I've said: I don't like it. But in the end, on the whole, there's no problem, I always agree with what they do.'

Charwoman, Communist

'First and foremost I follow the advice of my party. I take note and I end up voting according to their directives.'

Carpenter, Communist

'A lot of people go and vote because you have to. But not me. Personally I'm not like that at all. I go and vote because I know what I'm voting for. I belong to a party and I vote for my own ideas.'

Typist, Communist

'I'd say that personally I have confidence in the Central Committee, and when they discuss whether so-and-so should be a candidate, they know things I don't. It may be that so-and-so seems very good to me, perhaps even better to my mind than the official candidate, but maybe there's some detail I don't know but they know at the top. So if they've chosen this one rather than that, there must be a good reason.'

Locksmith, Communist

They are thus more acutely exposed to the contradiction between the programme stated by the spokesman and the implicit programme betrayed by his habitus, especially since, by virtue of the hidden conditions of access to political competence (in particular, education), the holders of the monopoly of the production or even the reproduction of the explicit programme are the product of social conditions of production (perceptible in the visible signs of their habitus) which are likely to be different from those of their mandators. By contrast, those who have no other intention than to conserve the established order can spare themselves this effort of making their principles explicit and concentrate on presenting the guarantees of an internalized programme of conservation, in the form of their own person, with its distinction, its elegance, its culture and also its properties (titles of nobility, educational qualifications etc.). They have spontaneously the bodily hexis, diction and pronunciation to suit their words; there is an immediate, perfect, natural harmony between the speech and the spokesman.

Dispossession and Misappropriation

This essential ambiguity of political choice is only one of the reasons why no agent, not even a virtuoso of political consciousness, can in practice avoid having recourse to different modes of production—and the more so, the less the situation to which he has to respond is politically constituted. Other things being equal, the more clearly the problem posed is recognized as political, the more frequent is the use of the two specifically political modes of production, proxy and autonomous production. They are also more frequent, in respect of explicitly political problems, when political consciousness is higher. In other words, they depend on the set of factors (sex, education, social class etc.) which govern the propensity to answer the most specifically political questions (as opposed to the propensity to abstain).

Our survey shows that the proportion who recognize all or virtually all the problems mentioned as political is very low among the educationally unqualified, grows steadily with level of education and rises to two-thirds among those with the baccalauréat or a *licence*. (No doubt because it was a question of 'problems', the variations by education are greater here than for the aptitude to see various *actions* as political.) As might be expected, the variations by educational capital are greater in relation to those 'problems' which have appeared relatively recently in political debates, such as women's liberation, the protection of the environment or sex education, or those which are rarely posed outside the field of ideological production, such as the decline of Latin in secondary education. But there are also significant variations in the capacity to see political problems in unemployment, workers' participation, wage raises or the price of meat.

Figure 20 Opinions on foreign policy and political preference.

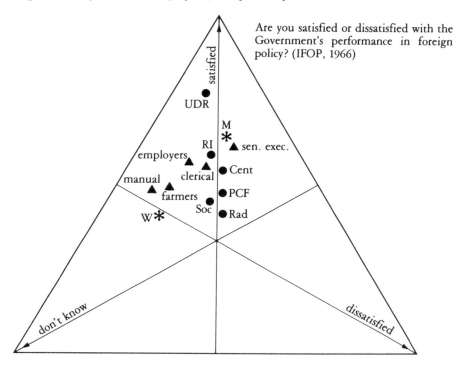

Are you satisfied or dissatisfied with the Government's performance in foreign policy? (IFOP, 1966)

This means that the relationship between social class and political opinions varies by social class, i.e., according to the mode of opinion production most frequent in that class. The probability of producing a political response to a politically constituted question rises as one moves up the social hierarchy (and the hierarchy of incomes and qualifications). Thus, apropos of a typically political problem, such as foreign policy, on which there can only be political opinions, there is a very strong correlation with social class (and also, of course, with sex and education) in the capacity to have an opinion, indicated by the rates of non-response (namely, farmers 37.7 percent, manual workers 38.6 percent, small employers 30.9 percent, office workers and junior executives 25.0 percent, senior executives and professions 16.1 percent). There is a very close correlation with declared political allegiance in the specifically political content of the opinions expressed (proportion of opinions approving the government's foreign policy: Communist Party [PCF] 48.7 percent, Socialists 47.7 percent, Radicals 41.2 percent, Centrists 52.3 percent, Giscardians [RI] 56.8 percent, Gaullists [UDR] 76.3 percent—IFOP 1966).[39] This appears very clearly in figure 20, in which, as happens with most foreign policy questions, the different classes and class fractions are distributed along the axis of non-response, whereas party preferences are distributed along the axis of satisfaction. It can be seen that, in general, the fact of ignoring 'don't knows', as usually happens in the analysis of surveys or elections, and of calculating frequencies solely in relation to the population of respondents, in accordance with electoral logic, has the effect of cancelling out, or at least weakening, the relationship with social class. The greater the proportion of each category which eliminates itself, the less typical the 'survivors' are of the category, precisely in respect of their degree of politicization.

Furthermore, the gap between the capacity to produce a minimal response, a 'yes' or 'no', and the capacity to produce the corresponding question or, at least, to grasp the specifically political significance the question has for those who produce it and ask it (i.e., in the field of production of specifically political problematics) leads to the imposition of a problematic, as a result of which the meaning of the answer given is misappropriated. The respondents are dispossessed of the meaning of their response whenever they choose one of the answers offered to a question which they do not have the means of asking, and so allow an opinion which is totally alien to them (even if it happens to 'express' them) to be treated as their own opinion; or whenever they respond, not to the question asked, but to the one they themselves have had to produce to try to appropriate the initial question. (This work of re-appropriation, which is almost always manifested by a retranslation into another language, so that 'rationalization of budgetary options' becomes 'not wasting money', for example, is almost invariably ignored by political scientists, either at the level of observation or at the time of coding.)

One example (see table 30) will suffice to show the imposition effect—and the allodoxia which results. This is a question on the political influence of 'the business world' (*les affaires*), in which we incidentally see the use of two very common rhetorical devices: the imposition of presuppositions—here, 'in every country', an anodyne phrase which insinuates the whole conservative philosophy of history ('always and everywhere the same')—and the false symmetry which allows a highly improbable, almost absurd answer to exist, under the guise of giving equal chances to all replies. To this should no doubt be added the effect of neutralization and euphemization, tending to discourage any 'indecent' expression of indignation or revolt. The question itself was only devised in order to legitimate (by another false symmetry) the asking of another question, this time definitely part of the dominant problematic: 'And in your view, is the influence of the trade unions too great, about right, or too small?' It can be seen that the proportion who consider the influence of 'the business world' too great rises as one moves up the social hierarchy (and, we may assume, although there are no data on this, the hierarchy of educational levels), that is, in precisely inverse ratio to the proportion who fail to reply. And so we see only 34 percent of manual workers 'judging' the influence of big business excessive

Table 30 The imposition effect: responses to question on the business world and politics, by class fraction (%), 1971.

Question: In every country, the business world exerts a certain influence on political life. In your view, in France is this influence too great, about right, or too small?

Class fraction	Too great	About right	Too small	Don't know
Farmers	28	13	3	56
Manual workers, domestic servants	34	19	14	33
Shopkeepers, craftsmen	39	23	7	31
Junior executives, clerical and commercial employees	44	25	11	20
Senior executives, professions, industrial and commercial employers	55	21	8	16

Source: SOFRES, *La politique et l'argent,* November 1971.

while 52 percent retreat into abstention or neutrality, with a considerable proportion actually 'judging' that influence too small. The retranslation which the least competent respondents have to perform in order to begin to appropriate a long and complex question on a 'political-scientific' issue, often resulting in misunderstandings, is seen in another case (table 31), where the least equipped have no choice but to abstain or to answer in terms of their image of Mitterrand. Here too, a neutralization effect is achieved through stylistic effects as subtle as the 'Mr.' before Mitterrand, or the use of an academic verb such as *préconiser* (advocate); the expression 'socialism of the possible' itself belongs to the register of high politics.

It seems to be proved that, in the survey situation, the least competent agents are almost entirely at the mercy of imposition effects which all result, in the last analysis, from the fact that they have to choose between answers which only take on their meaning in relation to a political problematic. However, this problematic is nothing other than the ideological field itself, i.e., the universe of objective relations, automatically converted into political stances (*prises de position*) defined in their content by the site from which they emanate, among the positions held and defended in this field by the agents and institutions competing for the monopoly of production and imposition of the legitimate representation of the social world and of legitimate action upon this world. The only way fully to appropriate this problematic is to participate in its production, to occupy a position which counts, that is, which others have to take account of, a position whose mere existence modifies all the other positions, forcing their occupants to rethink their own 'positions'. (One only

Table 31 The imposition effect: responses to question on the new socialism, by sex, class fraction and party (%), 1971.

Question: Mr. Mitterrand advocates a new form of socialism, the 'socialism of the possible'—in other words, reforms which take account of international competition and the situation of France in the Common Market. Do you think this new form of socialism can be put into practice (*soit applicable*)?

Sex, class fraction and party	Yes	No	Don't know
Men	37	35	28
Women	24	24	52
Farmers	16	33	51
Manual workers	32	30	38
Craftsmen, shopkeepers	26	31	43
Clerical and commercial employers, junior executives	37	31	32
Professions, senior executives	40	32	28
Communist Party	45	34	21
Non-Communist left	48	22	30
Gaullists	19	37	44
Centre démocrate (Lecanuet)	29	35	36
Centre PDM (Duhamel)	31	28	41
Giscardians	20	42	38
Uncommitted, abstention	18	19	63

Source: SOFRES, *Le socialisme du possible*, June 1971.

has to consider the structural effects resulting from the emergence of ultra-leftism as an *idée-force* in the field.) Political 'problems' (like all those in philosophy, religion etc.) always exist in and through the relationship between two or more antagonistic groups. This means that outsiders, being unable to take an active part in the political game which is de facto reserved for full-time professionals (politicians, permanent officials of the party *apparatuses*—the right word, for once—political journalists, professional ideologues), would only have some chance of picking out the opinions which 'suit' them, from within the universe of ready-made opinions, if the products on offer always bore a trade-mark, the label which is both a marker and a guarantee. By clearly announcing the position in the field of ideological production which is in fact expressed in every authorized statement of position, the label which links an opinion to an authority (a papal encyclical, a Central Committee decision, a canonical author etc.) enables the layman to 'get his bearings', to find the 'right' stance to take, either on the basis of the delegation that he explicitly or tacitly grants to the occupants of a particular position in the field of ideological production, or through his practical grasp of the homologies between the political field (i.e., the field of class struggles,

Reading the Labels

'When there's an election and they all appear on TV, then you can find out and really know the party and everything. But otherwise, between two ... Well, there are some of them speak really well and you can work it out. But still, when he starts with what party he is and all that, you pay more attention.'

Charwoman

ordinary or extra-ordinary, subterranean or overt, individual or collective, spontaneous or organized) in which he can situate and orient himself practically and the field of ideological production which reproduces the structure of the political field in accordance with its own logic.[40]

Misappropriation almost inevitably occurs whenever the question invites two different readings, when the uninitiated cannot answer it without bringing it down from the specifically political plane, where it is situated by the professionals who produce it and who will analyse or comment on the results, to the plane of ordinary experience, to which the unconscious schemes of the ethos can be directly applied. Thus the politically 'incompetent' have every likelihood of placing themselves in the camp of the champions of the moral order and the social order, and even of appearing more conservative in this area than the conscious defenders of the social order, whenever they are led to apply the categories of their class ethos to problems already constituted politically at the level of the field of ideological production. It is known that, so long as one remains in the order of domestic morality, the propensity to liberalism or tolerance tends to increase as one moves up the social hierarchy (which seems to justify the well-known theses about working-class 'authoritarianism'), and it no doubt does so through the mediation of educational level. But this relationship tends to be inverted as soon as the social order, and not solely the moral order, is in question.

Lipset bases his optimistic account ('sociodicy') of American democracy on a similar observation. 'Liberal and leftist' in economic matters, the working class are more 'authoritarian' 'when liberalism is defined in non-economic terms' (e.g., over civil rights) and, incapable of rising to the 'disinterestedness' which defines every genuine culture, in politics as in other matters, show no signs of the 'liberalism' on which the determinedly non-repressive new bourgeoisie centres its life-style.[41] Being authoritarian by nature, the working classes can consciously espouse authoritarian ideologies; because their intolerance inclines them to a simplistic, Manichaean view of politics,

'So if you want to develop commu- nism and achieve socialism, you've got to seize power. Right now, we're too democratic, giving way on too many things. There isn't the violence there was a few years ago. Violence, I don't mean smashing everything, but they're too soft when they go on strike, they don't take a decision. And I tell you, I think it's because the working class isn't miserable enough.'

Carpenter, age 67, Communist

they expect an improvement in their conditions to come only through sud- den, dramatic changes. The 'evolutionist millenarianism' which is the natu- ral culmination of this political theology makes the raising of living standards and the education of the working classes the motor of a universal movement towards American democracy, that is, the abolition of authori- tarianism and of the classes which are its bearers.

It should scarcely be necessary to point out that if the members of the dominant class are more 'innovating' in domestic morality but more 'con- servative' in the area more widely regarded as 'political', i.e., in everything concerned with the economic and political order and with class relations (as shown by their answers on strikes, unions etc.), this is because their propensity to adopt 'innovating' or 'revolutionary' positions varies in in- verse ratio with the degree to which the changes in question affect the basis of their privilege. Thus, to take just one example, senior executives may ap- pear more 'liberal' in their view of immigrant workers than manual work- ers, who are more directly concerned by their competition: these executives much more often say that 'France is not doing enough to help foreign workers find accommodation' (67 percent compared with 48 percent), 'to give them training' (52 percent and 36 percent) or 'make them welcome' (45 percent and 33 percent). But their liberalism is less marked when mea- sures which might have consequences for themselves are mentioned: 41 per- cent of the senior executives and professionals consider that 'France is not doing enough to give decent wages' to immigrant workers, as against 43 percent of the manual workers and 51 percent of the office workers and junior executives; 48 percent consider that 'France should reduce or stop its aid to under-developed countries' as against 31 percent of manual workers and 35 percent of office workers and junior executives (SOFRES, *La France, l'Algérie et le Tiers-Monde*, February 1971).

Moral Order and Political Order

The duality of the principles of discourse production is constantly re- vealed, in the very discourse of activists or the most politicized workers, through the changes of tone and style from one area to another, and even through the permanent tension, within the same discourse, between the two modes of expression. On one side, there are the ready-made formu-

An Assumed Style

Gentlemen:

The present form of contact is an innovation which is advantageous for all, every effort should be made to develop the latter, and team spirit should be vigorously pursued.

It is time for theory to give way to technology, audio-visual methods should be optimized, industrial experience is desirable, and also politicization so long as it is geared to a sufficiently broad overview for stability to be decisively prioritized.

Adult education and updating are now crucially indispensable; basic training is no longer adequate at this point in time; continuous assessment and know-how should maximize social advancement.

Setting aside all sectarian interests, the goal is progress, a major retooling of vocational guidance is called for, education is not synonymous with intelligence, a worthy captain of industry may be found very young, leadership potential is easily spotted . . .

Typesetter, extract from a letter to the AEERS in response to the questionnaire published in the press

lae, indivisible units of prefabricated thought and speech, which give a discourse its colour of conceptual universality but also its air of having been learnt by heart, and the unreality so characteristic of dissertations (a railwayman talks about the 'underprivileged strata' as a schoolboy might write an essay on 'contemporary youth'), the most academic terms of political vocabulary ('mandators', 'revaluation of wages'), which serve to show, at the risk of malapropisms ('c'est contraire à l'intérêt de la masse salariale'),[42] that the speaker is able to stand up to a quasi-scholastic test and defend both the status attribute of a man and the honour of a class, in short, that he is not to be 'soft-soaped', that he has 'got what it takes' to 'deal with those smart-talking politicians.' On the other side, separated by abrupt breaks in tone, are the most concrete references to immediate experience, unique and specific, which give a discourse its reality, its plenitude, its authenticity, while at the same time tending to prevent universalization, the pre-condition of mobilization.[43]

These effects, evident in spoken language, are even more marked in written language. Thus, among the manual workers who responded to the AEERS questionnaire and who are strongly over-selected (they differ from their class in a whole series of ways: they are better educated, their children are more often in lycées, Church schools or higher education, they more often live in Paris or read Paris newspapers), one finds a mechanic who expatiates in the first-person plural on 'the mission of France in the world', a miner who exclaims, 'Poor France! No one gives a damn for her', a typesetter who expounds his vision of an educational system capable of 'enhancing the general well-being' in a style which is a model of the effort to reproduce the grandiloquence of political discourse. But apart from those attempts at generalization which indicate a certain familiarity with trade-union and political discussion of the educational system, most often reduced to key-words or slogans ('pseudo-reform', 'fraud' 'reabsorption of unemployment'—metal worker; 'integrating the dynamic elements of the nation', 'underprivileged strata'—railwayman), the responses are extremely particularized. It is as if the respondents seized this opportunity to formulate a personal grievance not immediately relevant to the questions asked. Often, too, the submission is a way of 'letting people at the top know what is going on', particularly about the teachers' lack of conscientiousness. A farmer writes exactly the same sentence in reply to each question, 'The teachers don't do their job properly, all they think about is their holidays'; another respondent returns, in each of his comments, to the waste of working time; and another (a shorthand-typist married to a coach-builder) leaves half the questions unanswered and replies to each of the others: 'They've got no sense of professional duty, all they talk about is leisure.'

No doubt partly because it is constantly confronted with these interference effects and with the tendency to self-exclusion which flows from dispossession and the sense of impotence, the educational effort of the political or trade-union organizations to inculcate the will to have an opinion and to provide the means of producing it must itself constantly oscillate between the formalism of general principles on the economic and social world and direct reference to immediate experience. For all this, it cannot ever perform the analysis which would truly relate the particular case to its ultimate foundations in political economy, an operation which is no doubt as impossible for the teacher as for the pupil.[44] While attention to the concrete situation is indispensable in order to win credence, it is no less essential to go beyond isolating the particular case in order to achieve collective mobilization around common problems. This dialectic of the general and the particular is at the heart of all politics, but especially of the process of politicization, with the need, for some, whose interests are bound up with the established order, to universalize their particular interests, and, for others, to grasp the universality of their particular conditions.

In political practice, of which opinion surveys indicate the diversity by the variety of areas of existence they deal with, there is an imperceptible gradation from particular, private questions, including those which concern domestic morality (child-rearing, sexuality, parental authority, the sexual division of labour etc.), which may already be political stakes for some vanguard groups, to questions which, though they still concern upbringing or sexuality, are situated at a more general and abstract level, since they involve educational institutions, but also a level more remote from practical experience, such as teaching methods, the recruitment, training or salaries of teachers, sex education and politics in schools, student demonstrations etc., and finally to questions constituted as political by the tradition of trade-union or political struggle, on industrial relations, the role of unions and so forth. The misappropriation of opinion is greatest when, in ambiguous political situations such as all crisis situations, which challenge established guidelines and schemes of thought (in the case in point, just after May 1968), the politically most deprived—who are also, to a large extent, the economically and culturally most deprived—apprehend political problems which for them are still ill-defined, those, for example, posed by student demonstrations, through their everyday schemes of perception and appreciation (in this case, their ethical aversion to 'long-haired students' and the spoilt children of the idle rich). They thus seem to prove their 'authoritarianism' and reinforce the natural defenders of the established order.

Questions on school disorders and student demonstrations or on politics in education are predisposed to function as traps, because they only take on their full meaning in their real context, the dominant problematic, i.e., the set of questions generated from the fundamental question of the maintenance of the established order. As is shown by the inventory of the questions posed by opinion research institutes (see table 32), this problematic marshals the questions which present themselves to those, exclusively, who have to take account of the distribution of opinions about their policy in determining their policy. It only recognizes the questions which the dominant class ask themselves about the groups which are problems for them, and ignores the questions these groups ask (and the problems they have).

The most deprived do not, strictly speaking, know what question they are answering, and do not possess the interests and dispositions that would enable them to reactivate the question by seeing it as a particular form of the question of the conservation or subversion of the established order. They therefore respond not to the question that is actually asked, but to a question they produce from their own resources, i.e., from the practical principles of their class ethos. When the questions posed are in the intermediate area between morality and politics, the contamination of politics by morality and the slippage from moral indignation to political reaction is most clearly seen—especially in those whose position in social space predisposes them to a moral perception of the social world, such as the petite bourgeoisie and especially its declining fractions or individuals. Resentment is clearly the basis of the reactionary or conservative-revolutionary stances of the declining petit bourgeois who are anxious to maintain order on all fronts, in domestic morality and in society, and who invest their revolt against the worsening of their social position in moral indignation against the worsening of morals. But it often also pervades the Jacobin rigour and meritocratic revolt of the as-

Table 32 Views on political order and moral order, by class fraction (%), 1959–1972.[a]

Statements on political order and moral order	Positive responses, by class fraction[b]				
	Farmers, farm workers	Craftsmen, small shopkeepers[c]	Manual workers	Clerical, junior executives	Senior executives, profession
Political order					
Strikes do workers more harm than good (SOFRES, 1970)	58	57	35	33	42
When there is a strike in a firm, those who want to carry on working ought to be able to do so (SOFRES, 1970)	74	62	41	61	82
Employers and workers have the same interests; they should work together in the interest of all (SOFRES, 1970)	72	87	53	60	80
Favour some restriction of the right to strike in the public sector (SOFRES, 1970)	60	54	51	50	57
Labour unions are too powerful at present (IFOP, 1971)	16	26	7	14	20
Disapprove of part played by labour unions (IFOP, 1969)	24	30	19	26	33
Moral order					
Girls under 18 should not be allowed to go out alone (IFOP, 1959)	83	88.5	81.5	82	69.5
Girls of 18 should not be allowed to see any films they want to (IFOP, 1971)	38.5	38.5	31.5	29.5	28
Mixed schools are a bad thing for girls' upbringing (IFOP, 1971)	24	24	20	14.5	8.5
Would be against sex education in schools (IFOP, 1966)	33	29	19	19	19
The pill should only be sold to unmarried minors with parental consent (IFOP, 1967)	74	70	78	76	62

Table 32 (continued)

Statements on political order and moral order	Positive responses, by class fraction[b]				
	Farmers, farm workers	Craftsmen, small shopkeepers[c]	Manual workers	Clerical, junior executives	Senior executives, professions[c]
Parents should tell children what to do and not appear weak-minded (IFOP, 1972)	36	34	*40*	29	25

a. Italic figures indicate the strongest tendency in each row.

b. There are generally fewer 'don't knows' in all classes on all the questions concerned with morality—except those on the sale of the pill to minors and sex education in schools—than for those oncerned with politics.

c. IFOP groups the industrial and commercial employers with the craftsmen and shopkeepers; OFRES groups them with the senior executives and members of the professions.

cendant petit bourgeois, who are convinced of their right to settle scores with a society which has not sufficiently rewarded their merits. This simple reversal of pretension, the disposition of groups condemned to occupy subjectively a position which is not objectively theirs, is characteristic of all those who condemn the established order only because it recognizes them less than they recognize it, in their very revolt, and cannot recognize in them the values it recognizes officially. This is why enlightened conservatism, which is always ready to accept or even initiate changes in every area which does touch the foundations of the social order,[45] finds, on both right and left, the foils it needs in order to present itself as a vanguard.

Class Habitus and Political Opinions

Here as elsewhere, it would be a mistake to seek the explanatory principles of the responses in one factor or in a set of factors combined by addition. The habitus integrates into the biographically synthesizing unity of a generative principle the set of effects of the determinations imposed by the material conditions of existence (whose efficacy is more or less subordinated to the effects of the training previously undergone as one advances in time). It is embodied class (including biological properties that are socially shaped, such as sex or age) and, in all cases of inter- or intra-generational mobility, it is distinguished (in its effects) from class as objectified at a given moment (in the form of property, titles etc.), inasmuch as it perpetuates a different state of the material conditions of existence—those which produced it and which in this case differ to some extent from the conditions of its operation. The determinations which agents undergo throughout their existence constitute a system in which a predominant weight belongs to factors such as the capital possessed (its overall volume and also its composition) and the correlative position in the relations of production (identified through occupation, with all the associated dispositions, such as the influence of working conditions and occupational milieu).

This means that the intrinsic efficacy of a factor taken in isolation can never really be measured by the correlation between this factor and the opinion or practice in question. The same factor may be associated with different effects, depending on the system of factors in which it is inserted. Thus the baccalauréat qualification may be a principle of revolt when possessed by the son of a junior executive or skilled worker who has fallen back into the ranks of the semi-skilled (the regular increase in the number of *bacheliers* among unskilled workers is probably not unconnected with the growth of ultra-leftism in the working class), or a source of integration when possessed by a junior executive whose father was a factory worker or peasant smallholder. It could be shown in the same way that the value of an educational qualification and the associated relation to the social world vary considerably according to the bearer's age (inasmuch as the chances of possessing it are very unequal for the different generations), social origin (inasmuch as inherited social capital—name, family connections etc.—governs its real profitability) and also, no doubt, geographical origin (through embodied properties such as accent and also through the characteristics of the labour market) and sex.

So it is understandable that, through the mediation of the habitus, which defines the relation to the position synchronically occupied and consequently the practical or explicit 'positions' taken vis-à-vis the social world, the distribution of political opinions between right and left should correspond fairly closely to the distribution of the classes and class fractions in the space whose first dimension is defined by overall volume of capital and the second by the composition of this capital: the propensity to vote on the right increases with the overall volume of the capital possessed and also with the relative weight of economic capital in the capital composition, and the propensity to vote on the left increases in the opposite direction in both cases. The homology between the oppositions established in these two respects—the fundamental opposition between the dominant and the dominated, and the secondary opposition between the dominant fractions and the dominated fractions of the dominant class—tends to favour encounters and alliances between the occupants of homologous positions in the different spaces. The most visible of these paradoxical coincidences occurs between the dominated fractions of the dominant class, intellectuals, artists or teachers, and the dominated classes, who each express their (objectively very different) relation to the same dominant fractions in a particular propensity to vote on the left.

If, on the basis of the distributions of voting intentions by socio-occupational category established by G. Michelat and M. Simon,[46] each class fraction is characterized by the algebraic deviation between the percentages of left-wing votes and the percentages of right-wing votes (leaving aside the 'don't knows', which vary relatively little), it can be seen that everything takes place as if the effects of volume and the effects of composition compounded each other. The political space thus appears as a systematic skewing of the social space, with primary teachers (−43) found next to the miners (−44), the secondary and tertiary teachers (−21) next to the skilled workers (−19), the artists (−15) close to the unskilled workers (−15), and the clerical workers (−9) alongside the semi-skilled workers (−10); the other extremity of the political space is occupied by the industrial employers (+61), followed by the professions (+47), the senior administrative executives (+34) and, very close to them, the commercial employers (+32); the technicians (+2) and the foremen (+1) are situated on the frontier between right and left. Everything suggests that a secondary opposition is established between fractions of which a large proportion of the members move towards the most classifying choices of their respective regions of the political space: the industrialists and professionals, on one side, who give a high proportion of votes to the 'liberal right', and the unskilled, semi-skilled and skilled workers, on the other side, who give a high proportion of votes to the Communist Party, thus seem to be opposed to the fractions which combine a high proportion of abstentions and relatively less-classifying choices (non-Communist left or Gaullist), i.e., the artists, teachers and foremen, who perhaps express in this way the contradictions and ambiguities of their social positions.

The classifications used by Michelat and Simon both for the socio-occupational categories and for political opinions (reduced to very broad categories, with no indication of modality) do not make it possible to establish a clear opposition between the established petite bourgeoisie, more attached to the traditional political organizations (although here too, effects of downward mobility have induced new forms of demands and struggle), and the new petite bourgeoisie, which recognizes its image in all the new political forms—from ultra-leftism, through the PSU and the new tendencies in the Socialist Party, to ecology—and in all the participationist and self-management catch-words likely to satisfy the aspirations to autonomy and personal sovereignty of petit bourgeois with intellectual pretensions. However, it may be noted that among all the categories situated in the centre of the political space, the medical and social services (+28) are situated towards the pole marked by the industrialists, whereas the technicians incline more towards the miners' pole (+2); the junior administrative executives (+14) and commercial employees (+16) occupy an intermediate position, with the craftsmen (+13), the engineers (+19) and the farmers (+20).

Political practices or opinions, like other practices, cannot, of course, be fully accounted for if one leaves out everything that is apprehended through the ordinary indicators of social origin. Here it is necessary to distinguish, at least, the effect of the trajectory leading from the original position to the present position, the effect of the conditionings inscribed in a particular socio-economic condition and—especially important when one is trying to understand political 'positions' as explicit 'positions' taken on the social world—the effect of inculcation, since political education, like religious education (which is a disguised form of it) is always partly received from the family, from the earliest days of life.

Before expressing surprise at the intensity of the correlation between religious practice and political opinion, one has to consider whether this is not largely due to the fact that these are simply two different manifestations of the same disposition. This is not only because, both in its content and in the disciplines of inculcation, religious training is a disguised form of political socialization; but also because the imposition of a practice and of a declared belief implies assignment to a class, and therefore the attribution of a social identity which, whatever the content of the corresponding inculcation, is defined relationally by its opposition to the complementary class of 'non-believers' and is thus charged with all the properties excluded from the latter at a given moment (such as the conservative political disposition implied in opposition to the 'reds'). Fidelity to this identity and to those who share it ('I am a Christian') confers a great autonomy on the professed faith with respect to the present conditions of existence. As for the specific effect of the content of the religious message, it may be assumed that it reinforces the propensity to conceive the social world in terms of the 'personalist' logic of 'personal salvation', to see poverty or oppression as personal misfortunes, like illness or death. (By contrast, the political mode of thought tends to exclude from politics everything that personalist thinking and religion constitute as ethics, in particular everything concerned with the domestic economy; it is therefore ill-prepared to politicize domestic matters, such as consumption or the condition of women. The difficulty is aggravated by the fact that the vanguard in politicizing the domestic is often made up of individuals or movements of Christian origin, and it is not easy to determine whether they are politicizing the domestic or domesticating and depoliticizing the political.)

Supply and Demand

To endeavour to specify the relationship between the social classes and the political opinions socially constituted at a given moment, one may be tempted to examine, on the basis of the statistics available, how the different classes and class fractions distribute their choices among the different politically marked newspapers and magazines. However, the inherent fallacies of such a procedure cannot be avoided unless one starts by considering what 'reading a newspaper' means for the different categories of readers, since it may have nothing in common with the functions commonly attributed to it or with those assigned to it by the producers or their backers. Only an ethnocentric faith in the myth of 'personal opinion', an opinion 'formed' by a permanent effort to keep informed, can mask the fact that a newspaper (for those who actually read one) is a 'viewspaper' (*journal d'opinion*) for only a minority.

Thus, the readers of national newspapers such as *France-Soir* and *Le Parisien Libéré* (circulations 510,000 and 360,000 respectively in 1977) are distributed fairly equally between right and left: 41 percent to 36 percent for the former, 33 percent to 33 percent for the latter (and, even more surprisingly, given its more distinctly right-wing content, 27 percent of the readers of *L'Aurore* declare themselves to be left-wing voters); 60 percent and 64 percent of the respective readerships of the first two papers say they would not stop reading them if the papers took political positions contrary to their own; and a high proportion decline to pronounce on their objectivity or their stances in the election campaign. But above all, only a small proportion of their readers (24 percent for *Le Parisien Libéré* and 29 percent for *France-Soir*—as against 37 percent for *Le Figaro* and 42 percent for *L'Aurore*) say they are in complete agreement with the opinions expressed by these papers, whereas a large proportion (40 percent and 50 percent respectively) consider them more right-wing than themselves. It can be seen that the specifically political effect of a newspaper is not measured by the political orientation of its specifically political discourse as evaluated in the field of ideological production, still less by the number of column-inches directly devoted to politics, but by the relationship the readers have to the paper, whose political message they may ignore and whose most important political action may be to give no importance to politics.

It would seem that the lower the readers are situated in the social hierarchy, the more independent their political opinion is of the opinion explicitly professed by their newspaper. Buying a paper like *Le Parisien Libéré* or *France-Soir* (or even *L'Aurore*) is, for manual workers or clerical workers who vote Socialist or Communist (and who no doubt make up the majority of the Communist or Socialist voters among those papers' readerships, i.e., 10 percent and 20 percent of the readership of the former and 9 percent and 29 percent of the readership of the latter), an act which, although it is objectively political, presupposing and no doubt producing 'depoliticization', implies no affiliation, no political delegation. *Le Parisien Libéré,* which devotes 16.3 percent of its space to sport (as against 2.6 percent in *Le Monde*), and to the most popular sports, is regarded by many of its readers as a sports paper which, unlike *L'Equipe,* provides general and anecdotal news as well for the same price.

The relative independence of the readers' political opinions from their newspapers' political tendency thus stems from the fact that, unlike a political party, a newspaper offers information that is not exclusively political (in the narrow sense normally given to this word). It is a multi-purpose product, offering, in very variable proportions, international and national politics, miscellaneous news and sport, so that it can be the object of an interest relatively independent of specifically political interests.[47] Furthermore, consciously endeavouring to maximize their circulation as a direct source of revenue through the cover price, but also as an indirect asset through its value in the eyes of advertisers,[48] what may be called 'omnibus' publications (which include most local papers) must systematically eschew everything which might offend any section of their actual or potential readership, in particular, specifically political pronouncements (just as they are excluded, for the same reasons, from casual conversation between strangers, in favour of safe topics, such as the weather), except for those which can be perceived as least political, i.e., official declarations (this is what gives 'omnibus' newspapers their air of being semi-official or 'governmental' organs).[49] This imperative, which becomes stronger as the clientele expands, necessarily bringing in consumers with increasingly different tastes and opinions, is sufficient to explain the invariant features of all omnibus cultural goods—'family-audience' feature films, best-sellers, the carefully depoliticized political messages of 'catch-all' political parties, the homogenized attractions of Hollywood stars or the professionals of bureaucratic charm, the perfectly polite and polished profile of the model managers who, in the cause of upward mobility, have smoothed away all their social 'rough edges'. The ideal 'wide-audience' product is thus perfectly non-classifying, 'insipid', but, by virtue of this, acceptable to all tastes (this law also applies to material products: one only has to think of the new 'mild' cheeses, such as *Bonbel,* or baby foods).

There is thus every difference between the major omnibus daily and weekly papers, which maximize their clientele by neutralizing their products, and the vanguard grouplets or avant-garde reviews, which testify to their fidelity to their initial programme either by rapid disappearance or by living a precarious existence (dependent on subscriptions, extraordinary efforts by their officials, the devotion of their activists and so on). Their alternative course is to overcome or manage the conflicts arising both in the production unit and in their audience from the pursuit of a wider clientele, the pre-condition for access to power, by making concessions, compromises or attenuations which contradict the initial programme and weaken their links with the oldest and most 'significant' fraction of their audience. Thus, for some major parties (such as the present-day Socialist Party) and some major publications, a rational management of competition within the production unit, which then functions as a field, can be the means of supplying the different fractions of readers or electors (for example, in the case of *Le Monde,* the different fractions of the dominant class) with diversified products adjusted to their different or even opposing expectations, without any conscious intention of doing so.

But in addition, manual and clerical workers—except the most politicized of them, who read *L'Humanité* or another far-left paper—practically never regard the daily newspaper either as that sort of political guide or moral and cultural mentor which it perhaps really is only for a section of the readers of *Le Figaro,* or as the instrument of information, documentation and analysis which it no doubt is only for the pupils of Sciences Po or ENA, for senior civil servants and some teachers, in other words, the target audience of *Le Monde.* As well as the weekend sports results and commentaries, the newspaper is expected to provide 'news', i.e., information on the whole range of events with which one feels concerned because they concern acquaintances (the deaths, marriages, accidents or scholastic successes reported in local papers) or people like oneself, whose misfortunes are experienced vicariously (e.g., the catastrophe in a popular campsite in Spain in 1978). The interest in such 'news', which the so-called 'serious' papers disdainfully relegate to the back page, is perhaps no different in nature from the interest which those members of the dominant class closest to the centres of political decision-making have in so-called 'general news', the appointment of civil servants to ministerial cabinets or of technocrats to 'think-tanks', elections to the Académie française or receptions at the Elysée Palace, the power struggles within the political parties or the wars of succession within a major newspaper or firm, not to mention the diary of social events or the list of admissions to the grandes écoles. Only in bourgeois conditions of existence, around bourgeois dinner tables, do proper names of general interest—the name of the Minister of Finance or his chief adviser, the director of Schlumberger or the chairman of a prize jury and so forth—refer to familiar individuals, known and frequented, belonging, like neighbours and cousins in the space of a village, to the world of mutual acquaintance (which goes a long way to explain why reading *Le Monde* is a sine qua non for entry to the beau monde). One forgets that the dominant class is defined precisely by the fact that it has a particular interest in affairs 'of general interest' because the particular interests of its members are particularly bound up with those affairs.

But this is only one of the many reasons for questioning the semi-scientific opposition between 'news' and 'views', or between the so-called sensational newspaper and the 'journal of reflection'. Behind the reading of these two categories of papers lie in fact two quite different relations to politics. Reading a national newspaper, and especially one of the major, legitimate papers, such as *Le Figaro* or *Le Monde,* is one way among others (like writing *in* the papers, or *to* the papers, signing petitions or answering questionnaires published by them) of showing one's sense of belonging to the 'legal nation', of being a full citizen, entitled and duty-bound to participate in politics and exercise a citizen's rights.

It is not surprising to find that the reading of national newspapers, especially the most legitimate of them, is closely linked to educational level, by virtue of an effect of assignment by status. Educational qualifications strongly contribute to the sense of full membership in the universe of legitimate politics and culture, which includes the sense of the right and duty to read a legitimate newspaper (see tables 33, 34, and 35).

While the probability of reading a national newspaper rises strongly with educational capital (with the probability of reading a regional newspaper varying in the opposite way), the variations are particularly marked in the case of *Le Monde* and *Le Figaro,* the readers of which are to a very large extent drawn from among graduates of higher-education institutions. Through the link with educational capital, the probability of reading a national newspaper is linked to social class (though less closely): it is very low in the working classes, in which reading is almost exclusively limited to the sports papers and omnibus papers (*France-Soir* and *Le Parisien Libéré*), and increases steadily as one moves up the social hierarchy. There is every reason to think that, other things being equal, women are socially more inclined than men to be interested in the 'non-political' content of newspapers (local 'news', anecdotal items, the diary of social events etc.). In politics, unlike cultural practices, the effect of assignment by status exerted by scholastic capital cannot make itself felt in full until the effects of the traditional division of labour between the sexes are weakened or nullified, as is the case in the dominated fractions of the dominant class: thus we find that, except in the dominant class, the rate of readership of a national newspaper is higher among men than women (the relationship is reversed for readership of local newspapers). Whereas the probability of reading at least one daily paper rises steadily with age, the probability of reading a national paper is virtually independent of age—although slightly higher for the 25–49 age group than for older groups, as if ageing were accompanied by a weakening of the sense of needing to keep up to date with politics. (This tendency does not appear in the case of *L'Aurore* and *Le Figaro,* a high proportion of whose readers are industrial and commercial employers who often continue their activity to an advanced age.)

But the difference between the 'sensational' press and the 'informative' press ultimately reproduces the opposition between those who make politics and policy, in deeds, in words or in thought, and those who undergo it, between active opinion and opinion that is acted upon. And it is no accident that the antithesis between understanding and sensibility, reflection and sensation, which is at the heart of the dominant representation of the relationship between the dominant and the dominated, evokes the opposition between two relations to the social world, between the sovereign viewpoint of those who dominate the social world in practice or in thought ('General ideas', said Virginia Woolf, 'are always generals' ideas') and the blind, narrow, partial vision (that of the ordinary soldier lost in the battle) of those who are dominated by this world. Political analysis presupposes distance, height, the overview of the observer who places himself above the hurly-burly, or the 'objectivity' of the historian, who takes and gives the time for reflection by performing a sort of politi-

Table 33 Newspaper reading by men, by educational level, 1975.

Educational level of respondent	Probability (%) of reading daily paper	If respondent does read daily paper, probability (%) of reading:								
		Regional daily	National daily	L'Equipe	L'Aurore	France-Soir	La Croix	Le Figaro	Le Monde	L'Humanité
Primary	64.7	87.3	18.0	3.7	2.7	6.1	0.5	1.3	1.2	3.4
Higher primary	74.2	80.3	25.2	1.2	4.7	7.3	1.6	5.5	3.4	3.1
Technical-commercial	65.5	79.0	15.8	6.9	3.5	8.9	0.3	3.0	3.0	4.4
Secondary	67.2	80.6	28.9	5.6	3.0	7.4	1.0	5.6	8.0	2.7
Higher	73.1	60.0	54.8	7.3	4.3	8.2	4.0	16.0	28.2	6.6

Source: C.S. XXXIX (CESP, 1976).

Table 34 Newspaper reading by men, by age, 1975.

Age of respondent	Probability (%) of reading daily paper	If respondent does read daily paper, probability (%) of reading:								
		Regional daily	National daily	L'Equipe	L'Aurore	France-Soir	La Croix	Le Figaro	Le Monde	L'Humanité
15–25	58.9	84.2	21.3	4.6	1.7	5.1	0.1	1.8	5.3	3.2
25–34	64.6	77.4	32.7	10.4	2.7	8.7	0.6	4.8	10.2	4.3
35–49	66.7	80.0	28.0	6.1	2.7	9.0	0.9	4.9	6.0	5.5
50–64	71.9	81.3	25.4	2.5	3.8	7.7	1.7	3.7	4.3	3.7
65 and over	74.1	82.2	23.7	0.5	5.5	4.7	1.7	6.1	3.3	1.8

Source: C.S. XXXIX (CESP, 1976).

Table 35 Newspaper reading by men and women, by class fraction, 1975.

Class fraction of respondent by sex	Probability (%) of reading daily paper	If respondent does read daily paper, probability (%) of reading:	
		National daily	Regional daily
Men			
Farmers, farm workers	60.2	3.8	98.9
Semi-skilled, domestic	59.3	17.3	92.5
Skilled, foremen	63.0	18.8	89.9
Small employers	70.7	20.2	90.1
Clerical	66.1	33.4	80.5
Junior executives	63.7	40.6	73.3
Business, senior execs.	74.0	49.8	67.6
Women			
Farmers, farm workers	53.3	0	100
Semi-skilled, domestic	46.3	12.8	92.4
Skilled, foremen	40.6	14.6	91.4
Small employers	72.2	13.0	93.4
Clerical	50.2	21.6	83.5
Junior executives	50.3	35.3	70.8
Business, senior execs.	68.9	52.0	61.7

Source: C.S. **XXXIX** (CESP, 1976).

cal 'alienation', which, like aesthetic 'alienation', can neutralize the immediate presence, the urgency and functions of the object, substitute the euphemistic translations of the indirect style for the direct utterance of words or rallying-cries,[50] and subsume under the unifying concepts of political analysis the immediacy, actuality, factuality of ephemeral events, of everything which satisfies the curiosity of the ordinary reader, immersed in events and short-term, 'facile' sensations. Like 'difficult' art as opposed to 'facile' art, or eroticism as opposed to pornography, the so-called quality newspapers call for a relation to the object implying the affirmation of a distance from the object which is the affirmation of a power over the object and also of the dignity of the subject. They give the reader much more than the 'personal' opinions he needs; they acknowledge his dignity as a political subject capable of being, if not a subject of history, then at least the subject of a discourse on history.

Having thus specified the meaning of the relationship of the different social classes to their newspapers, through which we no doubt can grasp one dimension of their objective and subjective relation to 'politics' (which is also seen in the rates of participation in the leaderships of the different parties, and in electoral turn-out rates), we can try to derive some indications as to political positions from the variations in readership of the politically most clearly marked national newspapers (see table 36). First, it is possible to draw fairly precisely the simultaneously political and cultural dividing-line between the working classes—who, apart from local papers, read almost exclusively omnibus papers—and the middle classes. Technicians, whose level of newspaper readership is very close to that of foremen, are opposed to clerical workers, who read more papers but also more right-wing papers (i.e., more often *La Croix, Le Figaro* and *Le Monde,* less often *L'Humanité* or *L'Equipe*). One no doubt sees here the combined effects of very different work milieux, the workshop and the office, and also of types of schooling which tend to reinforce preexisting differences—technical training, which encourages practices and interests close to those of other manual workers, and secondary schooling, which, by at least slightly initiating its pupils into legitimate culture and its values, introduces a break with the popular world view.

To verify this, one only has to observe that foremen, although they have distinctly higher incomes and a geographical distribution very similar to that of the clerical workers (who are only a little more concentrated in Paris), have much lower readership rates for the national dailies and the weeklies (18.5 percent and 28.4 percent respectively, as against the clerical workers' 41.4 percent and 43.2 percent); foremen more often read the omnibus papers and, among the weeklies, *L'Humanité-Dimanche,* whereas the clerical workers slightly more often read *Le Figaro, Le Monde* and *La Croix,* and, among the weeklies, *La Vie* and especially *Le Nouvel Observateur.* There is every reason to think that those whom this dividing-line separates are opposed in other respects, particularly as regards their attitudes to religion, the trade unions and the political parties, with, on the clerical workers' side, a higher proportion of practising Catholics, Force Ouvrière unionists and Socialists (or PSU, or extreme-left) voters, but also Gaullists, and on the manual workers' side, a higher proportion of agnostics or non-practising Catholics, CGT unionists and Communist voters.[51] These oppositions are themselves an integral part of life-styles linked to different social trajectories and different working conditions (for example: differences according to how long the lineage has been urbanized and proletarianized, according to the size of the firm etc.).

The boundary between the industrial working class and the peasantry is also marked by the probability—much higher among industrial workers—of reading a national newspaper, especially *L'Humanité,* and by the fact that agricultural workers almost always read only Catholic weeklies (*Le Pèlerin, La Vie*) whereas industrial workers read a greater variety of papers. As one moves up the occupational hierarchy (which is to some extent linked with seniority in the working class) the Catholic press is increasingly supplanted by the Communist press, which is not surprising when one knows that the tendency to vote on the left varies in the same way.

Except for *L'Humanité,* the newspapers and weekly magazines only really fulfil their role as political markers starting at the level of the middle classes. The space mapped out by the quantity and quality of reading reproduces fairly exactly the ordinary oppositions by volume and compo-

Table 36 Percentage of each class fraction reading each daily and weekly paper.[a]

Fractions of lower, middle and upper classes	Daily							
	L'Equipe (1)	Le Parisien Libéré (2)	L'Aurore (3)	France-Soir (4)	Sum of 2,3,4 (5)	La Croix (6)	Le Figaro (7)	Le Monde (8)
Lower								
Farm workers	0	0.6	0	0	0.6	1.4	0	0
Farmers	0.3	1.4	0.5	0.5	2.4	0.3	0.8	0.3
Fishermen, miners	0	0	0	0	0	0	0	0
Unskilled	0	1.7	0.8	1.7	4.2	0.8	0.8	0.8
Semi-skilled	1.8	2.6	0.4	3.6	6.6	0.2	0.4	0.4
Skilled	2.6	4.0	1.1	4.0	9.1	0.1	0.7	1.6
Foremen	5.0	3.6	2.1	5.7	11.4	0.7	1.4	2.9
Middle								
Domestic servants	8.3	7.3	5.2	14.6	27.1	1.0	3.1	4.2
Craftsmen	5.4	3.6	4.8	4.2	12.6	0.6	1.2	3.6
Small shopkeepers	8.0	3.1	5.6	8.1	16.8	0.6	1.8	5.0
Technicians	8.1	1.0	5.7	7.2	13.9	0	5.0	7.3
Office workers	10.8	7.9	1.9	8.2	18.0	2.5	4.7	7.3
Junior executives	9.7	5.0	6.4	8.8	20.2	2.8	11.1	12.0
Primary teachers	10.4	3.5	4.3	7.7	15.5	4.3	2.6	19.0
Upper								
Commercial employers	7.7	0	2.6	2.6	5.2	0	5.1	5.2
Industrial employers	8.4	0	0	0	0	4.2	12.5	8.3
Professions	2.0	2.0	4.1	8.1	14.2	2.0	18.4	16.3
Senior executives	6.7	1.7	5.9	8.4	16.0	4.2	15.3	22.0
Engineers	8.2	1.4	1.4	10.9	13.7	2.8	23.0	24.3
Higher-ed. and secondary teachers	9.5	0	3.6	6.0	9.6	2.4	8.4	42.9

Source: C.S. **XXXIX** (secondary analysis).

a. Each number represents the percentage of individuals in each class fraction who had read or skimmed the corresponding daily paper either the day before or two days before the survey was made. For the weekly publications, the reading period was the week preceding the survey. Italic

sition of capital, both at the level of the middle classes and at the level of the dominant class. On one side, we find the economically (relatively) rich fractions, craftsmen and small shopkeepers, or industrial and commercial employers, who read little, and mainly omnibus papers; on the other, the culturally (relatively) rich fractions, clerical workers, junior executives and primary teachers at the first level and, at the second level, professionals, engineers, senior executives, secondary and higher-education teachers, who read a lot of national dailies, especially the most 'legitimate' ones, and weekly magazines. In the middle classes as in the dominant class, the proportion of readers of national papers and left-wing

Table 36 (continued)

							Le		
	Total		Le	La	Le		Nouvel	L'Humanité-	Total
L'Humanité	dailies	Minute	Pèlerin	Vie	Point	L'Express	Observateur	Dimanche	weeklies
(9)	(5–9)	(10)	(11)	(12)	(13)	(14)	(15)	(16)	(10–16)
0	2.0	0	9.8	8.4	1.4	0	0	1.4	21.0
0.3	4.1	0.8	12.0	4.8	1.4	2.2	0.3	0.8	21.5
0	0	3.2	6.4	0	3.2	0	0	6.4	19.2
0.8	7.4	0.8	3.4	1.7	0	1.7	3.4	1.6	12.6
2.0	9.6	0.8	7.2	3.0	1.6	2.6	1.4	5.0	21.6
2.0	13.5	1.6	4.3	2.2	2.3	3.0	3.3	5.1	21.8
2.1	18.5	2.1	4.3	1.4	4.2	7.1	2.8	6.5	28.4
2.1	37.5	2.0	2.0	1.0	3.1	6.2	2.0	3.1	19.4
1.2	19.2	3.0	5.4	5.4	5.8	6.6	3.0	5.4	34.6
0.6	24.8	6.2	3.7	6.2	3.1	4.9	1.2	3.0	28.3
4.1	30.3	1.9	6.3	7.7	7.7	14.0	10.0	7.3	54.9
4.5	37.0	3.1	5.0	3.8	7.3	9.8	8.2	6.0	43.2
2.8	48.9	3.7	3.7	5.9	9.2	21.6	11.1	3.7	58.9
5.2	46.6	8.6	7.8	8.6	13.8	25.0	25.8	9.5	99.1
0	15.5	5.2	3.7	0	5.2	12.8	2.6	0	29.5
0	25.0	0	4.2	8.4	16.7	12.5	4.2	0	46.0
0	50.9	8.2	8.2	10.1	20.4	30.7	8.1	0	85.7
2.5	60.0	2.5	3.4	10.2	17.7	26.3	22.9	2.5	85.5
0	63.8	1.4	4.1	8.2	19.0	28.5	13.6	1.4	76.2
6.0	69.3	4.8	4.8	8.2	15.3	21.4	35.8	7.2	97.5

figures indicate the strongest tendency in each column within the middle class and the upper class. The social and medical services and the apprentices were not sufficiently represented to be included.

papers declines, and the proportion of readers of regional papers and right-wing papers increases, as one moves from the primary or secondary teachers to the small or big commercial employers.

Only for the dominant class does the newspaper fully play its role as an attitude-generating principle defined by a certain distinctive position in a field of such institutionalized principles; and the adequacy with which it 'expresses' its readers no doubt depends on the degree of homology between its position in the field of the press and its readers' position in the field of the classes (or class fractions), the basis of their opinion-generating principle. Thus at one pole we find the industrial and commercial employers, reading little, mainly omnibus papers and *Le Figaro;* at the other, the teachers (and, still further away, the intellectuals), reading a lot, mainly *Le Monde* or *L'Humanité* or *Le Nouvel Observateur.* The space of the weekly magazines—no doubt because they have to maintain a greater distance from the daily course of political life, because they devote more space to cultural matters and also because, in order to achieve the high circulation needed to attract advertisers, they must avoid all principles of division and exclusion and seek the most neutral areas, objects and styles—is less clearly marked out, although *Le Nouvel Observateur* is still fairly clearly opposed to *L'Express* and *Le Point.* We should perhaps not read too much into the differences between the fractions defining intermediate positions (especially the most heterogeneous of them, such as the executives or engineers), since surveys in successive years produce divergences attributable to the smallness of the corresponding populations in the representative sample. However, we know from the survey on press readership in the dominant class alone (C.S. V), which separates them out, that private-sector executives much more often read *L'Aurore* and *Le Figaro* (and the economic and financial press: *Les Echos, Entreprise*), much less often *Le Monde* and *Le Nouvel Observateur,* than public-sector executives, and also that the members of the literary and scientific occupations read *Le Nouvel Observateur* more often and *Le Figaro* less often than the teachers. So it would seem that the mode of the distributions of the daily and weekly papers ranked by political content— omnibus papers (with *L'Aurore*), *Le Figaro, Le Monde, Le Nouvel Observateur, L'Humanité*—tends to shift steadily as one moves through the fractions in the following order: commercial and industrial employers, private-sector executives, professions, public-sector executives, teachers, intellectuals (the central categories, especially the professions and engineers, being characterized by a particularly strong dispersion of their choice of reading-matter).

The opposition between the fractions in terms of the composition of their capital is blurred by the effects of the opposition, within each fraction, between 'old' and 'young' or, more precisely, predecessors and successors, the 'old gang' and the 'new wave'. The dominated fractions, who, because of their position in the space of the dominant class, incline towards partial, symbolic subversion, contain their own (temporally) dominant groups who may be pushed towards conservation (partly in response to the subversive dispositions of their own challengers). Similarly, within the dominant fractions, who have an interest in all forms of conservation, the successors (and, to a lesser extent, women), who are temporarily kept away from power, may, up to a point and for a certain time, share the world view put forward by the dominated fractions. Thus the opposition between *Le Figaro* or *L'Express* and *Le Nouvel Observateur* expresses not only the opposition between the dominant and the dominated fractions, between the private and the public, and, more precisely, between, on the one hand, the employers closest to the private pole of the economic field, least rich in educational capital and no doubt most threatened with decline, the oldest private-sector executives, those most linked to the employers, and, on the other hand, the public-sector executives and the teachers; but also the opposition between the predecessors and the successors, the old and the young.[52]

Playing unwittingly on the confusion between class struggles and class-fraction struggles, or, more simply, between right and right-bank or left and left-bank, and also on the classificatory and conceptual fuzziness resulting from the partial overlaps between the different internal divisions of the dominant class, the *Nouvel Observateur* enables all dominant-class members who are dominated in one or another of the possible respects—intellectuals, the young, women—to experience the sum of their necessarily partial challenges as the most radical assault on the established order. Consigning the class struggle to history, it offers its readers as a bonus the means and the gratifications of a simultaneously ethical, aesthetic and political snobbery which can combine, in a sort of anti-bourgeois pessimism, the appearances of intellectual vanguardism, which leads to elitism, and political vanguardism, which leads to populism. If it appears that most of the judgements it delivers on the social world have no other basis than the quarrel between the 'old gang' and the 'new wave', and if its contestation of the established order boils down to a contesting of forms—those of established etiquette, politics or art—this is because the strategies of symbolic subversion which offer themselves in the competitive struggles for succession reach their limits in recognition of the game and of the stakes which they presuppose and produce. More precisely, it is because the internal order of the dominant class depends very directly on everything which regulates the structure of social time, i.e., the order of successions, whether it be the representations which assign to each age its passions and powers, its liberties and duties, or the respect for forms and forms of respect which, better than any rules, guarantee social distances by maintaining temporal distances, the gaps, pauses, delays and expectations which propriety imposes on the impatience of the inheritors.

The Political Space

At this point, it is possible to represent and systematize the set of relations established, in a provisional diagram of the political space (see figure 21). This seeks to show how the different class fractions are distributed in relation to one another (relative positions clearly being easier to verify than distances) and also in relation to the set of political 'products' or 'marques' which function as landmarks or insignia. This space can immediately be seen to be a systematic distortion of the space of the classes and class fractions distributed by the volume and composition of their capital. The set of fractions situated on the left in the political space (and in the figure) are pulled downwards and those on the right are pulled

Figure 21 The political space.

This diagram is a theoretical schema constructed on the basis of a close reading of the available statistics (and various analyses of correspondences). The only newspaper or magazine titles indicated are those which function as political 'marques' or 'markers'.

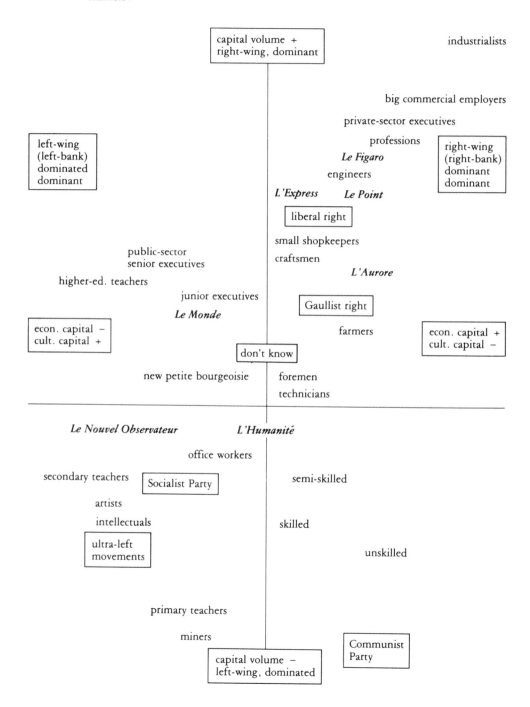

upwards, which is understandable since the effects of the opposition by overall capital volume and the opposition by capital composition (and the associated trajectories) are combined. The positions given to the class fractions or 'marques' only indicate, of course, the central point around which the group or readership in question is more or less widely distributed. The 'social surface' corresponding to each of these points in fact varies considerably with the volume of the population, which is generally linked to its social scatter (although the increased volume of a readership may result as much from more intense penetration in a restricted space as from extension of the space covered).

The Specific Effect of Trajectory

Political choices are much less independent of social class than is generally supposed, even when the latter is synchronically defined by possession of a capital of a given volume and composition. To demonstrate this, one only has to construct the categories adequately—and one could go much further in the direction opened up by Michelat and Simon by taking account of the diachronic properties of each social position and, perhaps above all, by securing the means of describing and understanding what the different political 'trade-marks' and the corresponding products mean for each class or class fraction. It is regrettable that the surveys available (in France) do not make it possible to identify and isolate the effects of trajectory and inculcation (through the parents' occupation and political opinions); even more so, perhaps, that they are equipped with no means of grasping directly—in the way in which they are uttered or justified—the differences which make nominally identical opinions really incommensurable. The fact that electoral logic ignores the differences between the Communist vote of an artist or a university teacher and that of a primary teacher, or a fortiori a clerk, a factory worker or a miner is not an excuse for sociology to do the same thing. If it is to have any chance of producing a scientific explanation, it must uncover the really different ways of being or declaring oneself Communist and the different meanings of a vote for the Communist Party that are hidden under the nominal identity of votes, while at the same time allowing for the politically important fact that electoral logic treats opinions which differ in both their intentions and their reasons as identical.

The fact remains that one cannot truly understand the sometimes immense differences between categories which are nonetheless close in social space, such as craftsmen and small farmers, or foremen and technicians, unless one takes into account not only capital volume and composition but also the historical evolution of these properties, i.e., the trajectory of the group as a whole and of the individual in question and his lineage, which is the basis of the subjective image of the position objectively occupied. One of the most determining characteristics of politi-

cal choices lies in the fact that, more than all other choices, much more than the obscure, deep-rooted choices of the habitus,[53] they involve the more or less explicit and systematic representation an agent has of the social world, of his position within it and of the position he 'ought' to occupy. Political discourse, when it exists as such, is often no more than the more or less euphemized and universalized expression (never perceived as such by those who utter it) of that representation. In other words, between the position really occupied and the political 'positions' adopted, there intervenes a representation of the position which, although determined by the position (so long as the position is defined completely, that is, *also* diachronically), may be at odds with the political 'positions' the position seems to entail for an external observer (this is what is sometimes called 'false consciousness'). The slope of the individual and, above all, the collective trajectory governs, through temporal dispositions, the perception of the position occupied in the social world and the enchanted or disenchanted relation to that position which is one of the principal mediations through which the relationship between social position and political 'position' is established. The degree to which individuals and groups are turned towards the future, novelty, movement, innovation, progress—dispositions which are particularly manifested in liberalism towards 'the young', the bringers and beneficiaries of the new order—and, more generally, inclined towards social optimism, or, on the other hand, oriented towards the past and inclined to social resentment and conservatism depends on their past and potential collective trajectory, i.e., on the extent to which they have succeeded in reproducing the properties of their ascendants and are (or feel) able to reproduce their properties in their descendants.

A class or class fraction is in decline, and therefore turned towards the past, when it is no longer able to reproduce itself with all its properties of condition and position and when a large proportion of its youngest members, in order to reproduce their overall capital and maintain their position in social space, must at the least perform a reconversion of their capital which is accompanied by a change in condition, marked by a horizontal movement in social space; in other words, when the reproduction of class position becomes impossible (*déclassement*) or requires a change of class fraction (reconversion). In this case, the change in the mode of social generation of the agents leads to the appearance of different generations whose conflicts cannot be reduced to what is usually put under the heading of generation conflicts since they arise from the opposition between values and life-styles associated with the predominance of either economic or cultural capital in the asset structure. The liberal conservatism of those fractions of the dominant class whose reproduction can be taken for granted thus contrasts with the reactionary dispositions of the fractions whose collective future is threatened and who can only maintain their value by binding themselves to the past, referring to systems of values, i.e., a logic of the determination of value, corresponding to a superseded state of the structure of the field of class relations.

The repressive dispositions of the small independent craftsmen and shopkeepers and, more especially, of the oldest fractions of these relatively old groups, appear in a whole set of convergent indices. Thus they manifest a suspicion verging on hostility towards modern art and artists, who, in all their practices, and especially in the liberties they take with the linguistic, sartorial, cosmetic or ethical norms, no doubt symbolize all that these groups deplore or detest in 'young people.' Twenty percent of them declare that 'the modern artist takes his audience for a ride', as against 13 percent of both the senior executives and the manual workers, 9 percent of the junior executives and 6 percent of the farm workers; 28 percent of them concur with the view that 'art is just a matter of business', compared to 20 percent of the junior executives, manual and farm workers and 15 percent of the senior executives (C.S. LI). They are the category most inclined to say that teachers do not know how to win respect (62 percent of them, as against 55 percent of the junior executives and clerical workers, 54 percent of the manual workers, 48 percent of the farm workers, 45 percent of the senior executives), to attribute children's failure at school to their 'not working hard enough' (57 percent, as against 47 percent of junior executives and clerical workers, 46 percent of manual and farm workers, 40 percent of senior executives) or to consider that school discipline is too lax (45 percent, as against 38 percent of manual workers, 36 percent of junior executives and clerical workers, 31 percent of farm workers and 30 percent of senior executives) (SOFRES, 1973). They are more often in favour of stricter film censorship than all other groups—in contrast to the manual workers and junior executives (C.S. L). It is not surprising that, like the big commercial employers and the foremen, they devote a significant proportion of their (generally limited) reading to *Minute,* a magazine which specializes in all the themes and social fantasies (such as xenophobia) of petit-bourgeois resentment. There is every reason to suppose that the extreme right recruits strongly in these categories.

Although it is certain that individuals occupying similar positions may have different opinions according to their social origins and their trajectories, everything seems to indicate that the effects of individual trajectory, which are particularly visible in the case of groups occupying less determinate positions in social space and therefore more dispersed in all respects, are exerted within the limits of the inherent effects of class; so that the ethico-political dispositions of the members of the same class appear as transformed forms of the disposition which fundamentally characterizes the whole class.[54] Thus *obsequium,* the deep-rooted respect for the established order which sets limits to petit-bourgeois revolt, is also the basis of the social virtues of the new petite bourgeoisie. When it is a matter of selling goods and services which, like cultural goods or material 'comfort' goods—household equipment, buildings or furniture, clothing or leisure goods—are more or less successful materializations of the dominant life-style, the acquisition of which implies a recognition of the dominant ethical or aesthetic values, nothing succeeds better than the disposition to sell one's own virtues, one's own certainties, one's own values, in a word, the certainty of one's own value, in a sort of *ethical snobbery,* an assertion of exemplary singularity which implies condemnation of all other ways of being and doing. This disposition is particularly called for when endeavouring to convert the working classes, to bring them into the race by foisting on them the latest bourgeois 'must', the latest mode or the latest morality, and when applying the same indignant conviction to repressing the 'repressive' dispositions of the working classes which others applied in the past to repressing their irrepressible laxity and intemperance.

In the political arena, ethical submission to the dominant class and to the 'values' it embodies is revealed in a limited challenging of the established order which, being based on the sense of not occupying one's proper place in that order, conforms to the proprieties of the target class even when challenging that class. Thus, in applying their favourite strategy, which consists in denouncing the established order in the name of the very principles it proclaims, the petit bourgeois bear witness to their recognition of those principles and appeal for recognition of their tireless struggle against scandals and, above all, hypocrisy, the source of all scandals. Their desire for social recognition and their proleptic identification with the dominant class are revealed in the nature of their demands, which give priority to the symbolic aspects of existence, not only because affronts to the dignity of the 'person' are felt more acutely by those who are freed from the most brutal forms of oppression and exploitation, but also because their very concern for dignity inclines them to demands which testify to the dignity of the demander. Thus the fear of losing all they have won, by trying to get all they have been promised (particularly through education and qualifications), does not fully explain the form taken by petit-bourgeois bargaining strategies. The ordinary means of the workers' struggle, strikes or demonstrations, are for them a last resort, which they will consider only when driven to extremities by excessive injustice ('If need be, we'll take to the streets'). They prefer symbolic weapons, starting with campaigns for 'education', which sets up a relation of moral domination, or 'information', in which they have inordinate faith, and that particular form of collective action which is achieved through the 'association', a strictly serial grouping of individuals assembled solely by the same 'cause', the same desire to deliver a sort of ethical summons. Voluntary action, the conspicuous expenditure of goodwill, a pure, disinterested ethical intervention which recognizes no end outside itself, confers, among other privileges, that of righteous indignation, in the name of the impeccability of those who have 'done their bit', done their whole duty and, above all, created a fait accompli which calls for recognition.[55] Strictly 'disinterested', 'clean' activity, free of all 'compromises' with politics, is in fact the pre-condition for the success of the institutionalization, the most perfect form of social recognition, that is more or less secretly pursued by all associations, petit-bourgeois movements par excellence, which, unlike parties, secure the profits of dignity and respectability for undertakings 'of general interest' while promising to satisfy particular interests.

There is every reason to suppose that the petit bourgeois are particularly loath to compromise themselves with the Communist Party—an unseemly party, unappreciative of their specific interests, and above all, unreceptive to the moralizing, edifying, vaguely humanistic phraseology with which they readily identify ('values', 'taking responsibility', 'personal development', 'growth', 'partnership', 'concern' etc.)—when their sense of personal worth and their individualistic reservations have been encouraged by more comfortable conditions of existence and an early upbringing impregnated with religious values conducive to personalism. The higher their social origin, the more probable are these effects of conditioning or inculcation, so that they are very likely to be reinforced by the effects of a declining trajectory. One may also suppose that the petit bourgeois would move towards the PSU and its combination of protest and propriety, if it were less overtly revolutionary or if it 'grew up' to be a 'responsible' party of government, as has now happened with the technocratic-modernist wing of the Socialist Party. But they respond equally well to a reforming, 'intelligent' conservatism. In short, they waver, and at times of crisis they can swing abruptly.

However, if the position occupied in social space at a given moment is not linked to political positions by such simple and direct relations as those observed in other areas, this is not only because individual and collective trajectory orients the perception of the social world, above all of its future, through the experiences linked to social ascent or decline.[56] It is also, and especially, because the chances that political 'choice' will be no more than a politically blind response of class ethos increase as one moves towards the highest age groups, towards the smaller towns and villages, or down the hierarchy of levels of education or of social positions, and are distinctly greater among women than men. The contamination of politics by ethos, although it is less marked among manual workers, who are more 'politicized', than among small farmers and small employers, does not spare the members of the working classes. For those of them who, because of their sex (women), their age (the old), their place of residence (country dwellers), and, associated with this, their occupational milieu (workers in small firms) are more exposed to the threat of social decline, of falling or relapsing into the sub-proletariat, and at the same time are politically the least educated and organized, and therefore less inclined and equipped to grasp problems and situations through political categories of perception and appreciation, there is nothing to counterbalance the tendency to pessimism and even resentment which inclines them to a generalized rejection of 'politics' and 'politicians' of every sort and so to abstention or conservatism.

To understand the dispositions which may, according to the degree of politicization, be expressed in either 'progressive' or 'conservative' political positions, one would have to analyse the deep insecurity engendered by the experience of a whole lifetime lived under the threat of accident, illness, unemployment and the negative career leading to the sub-proletariat; and the corresponding attachment to acquired advantages and to the individual or collective strategies responsible for their acquisition, which has nothing in common with attachment to the established order. One would have to examine how working conditions and, specifically, the disciplines, especially as regards time, imposed by the employer tend, in themselves, quite apart from any ideological inculcation, continuously to reinforce the dispositions inculcated by an early upbringing which (both necessarily and deliberately) reproduces the necessities, harshness and rigidity of the existence for which it prepares. (It goes without saying that 'political education' cannot be reduced—as those who interest themselves in the subject almost always suppose—to the conscious transmission of the representations most directly linked to the sphere of the 'political' in the ordinary sense of the word. It would be at least as absurd to reduce the conditions of production of the dispositions which are the basis of political judgements and practices to specifically political socialization—or, worse, to its institutionalized aspect, 'civic instruction' in schools—as it would be to reduce the social conditions of the production of taste—which is also a political disposition—to specifically artistic training.) One would have to analyse more precisely the universe of practical mediations through which the attachment to an ordered world, starting with an ordered domestic world, i.e., one subordinated to the order imposed by the universe of labour, impresses itself on industrial workers; how the order of the factory—temporal, moral and social—extends even into the sphere of so-called 'private' life, into the schemes of thought and expression which enable it to be thought and expressed and which are often applied outside that sphere. One would have to consider whether the island of security, autonomy and stability which the family represents is not both the last bastion, with, for instance, the memory of past struggles and everything which constitutes the class sense of honour (including, for example, a certain cult of virility, the basis of a whole 'conservative' vision of the division of labour between the sexes), and also the point of least resistance (symbolized in and embodied by women, who are 'depoliticized' by their status and put in charge of consumption) through which the forces of domination penetrate to the heart of practice and the deepest level of the unconscious.

One may assume that individuals are more susceptible to the 'screening' or 'false context' effects of locally based groups (and also fields), that is, more likely to understand their position in social space in terms of a geographically based sub-space (village, neighbourhood etc.), the more they lack the properties which determine the chances of access to opinion or to the means of expressing it (such as reading a national newspaper). Those who are dominant in a space that is dominated overall (the owners of fifty hectares in a region of small holdings, local *notables,* foremen etc.) may thus make political choices which are in harmony with the choices of those who dominate the whole society.[57] The same logic no doubt partly explains why office workers, who are at the bottom of the hierarchy of the civil service and of middle-class wage-earners, more often vote on the left than foremen, who are at the top of the working class. More generally, one may assume that, other things being equal, and whatever the position of these fields in the social space, those dominant in a relatively autonomous field are more inclined to vote on the right than those dominated in the corresponding fields, and that the dominated of all fields are more inclined to vote on the left than the corresponding dominant agents.

Political Language

Thus, the element of discrepancy which remains unexplained so long as the question is looked at in terms of the determinants of ethical dispositions is explained by the relationship that is set up, in each opinion poll or election, between a supply of ready-made opinions and a determinate capacity to choose. The consumers of opinions may make mistakes over the object (allodoxia) and, indeed, the more they rely on the politically uncertain, or even indeterminate, schemes of their class ethos, for lack of specifically political principles of perception and appreciation, the more likely they are to endorse opinions that are not their own. But they may also choose one constituted opinion when, whether they know it or not, they would choose another, more or less different one if it were constituted as such and, above all, if, being professed by a determinate group of professionals, it had some claim to respectability.

The political field puts forward a universe of political possibles which, as such, thus exerts a twofold effect. First, it favours the effect of spurious identification resulting from the fact that the same implicit sense may recognize its political expression in different forms of the 'already-made-explicit'. Secondly, it tends to produce an effect of closure by tacitly presenting the universe of realized possibles as the universe of possible possibles, thus delimiting the universe of the politically thinkable. These two effects are exerted here with particular force because 'demand' hardly ever (at least in the dominated classes) pre-exists a supply of political discourse: unformulated or partially formulated, it only 'knows what it means' when it 'sees what it recognizes', rightly or wrongly, in an offered opinion.

That is why it is necessary to return to the analysis of the logocentrism of the 'politico-scientific' survey which, in its methodological innocence, performs a sort of in vitro replication of the most fundamental effect of the division of political labour. By offering a choice among several utterances and asking for a position to be taken on the already-uttered, the survey—like political consultations—proceeds as if it had already resolved the essential problem of politics, namely, the question of the transmutation of experience into discourse, of the unformulated ethos into a constituted, constituting logos, of a class sense, which may imply a form of adaptation and resignation to the self-evidences of the social order, into a conscious, i.e., explicitly formulated, apprehension of that order. Eliminating the labour of formulation, the survey tacitly presupposes that the person questioned would have been capable of producing or even reproducing the proposition which constitutes the statement of the question, or even of spontaneously adopting the relation to language and to politics which underlies the production of such an inquiry (although the 'yes' or 'no' it can always produce cannot be regarded as an index of that aptitude). At the same time, by unconsciously begging the question, it denies itself the possibility of gathering the information which governs the meaning that can be given to all the information directly gathered. Recognizing only the electoral imperative of formal equality before the questionnaire, which combines with the technical imperative of standardized information-gathering, the pre-condition for the formal comparability of the data and the material and mental automation of the analysis, the survey attributes the operation of *constitution* to the respondent, even when it is in fact a product of the questioning. The effect of questioning is all the stronger, the more completely the 'respondents' are deprived of the means of seeing the questions as 'political' and of giving them an answer—and a 'political' answer—and the further they are from

‾‾‾‾‾‾‾‾‾‾‾‾‾‾‾‾‾‾‾‾‾‾‾‾

'What did the bosses call it—Year
One of the Age of the Worker?
Some crap like that. Anyway, we
were supposed to be having a real
good time. . . .'

  Building worker

‾‾‾‾‾‾‾‾‾‾‾‾‾‾‾‾‾‾‾‾‾‾‾‾

fulfilling the conditions of production of a corpus of coherent, homogeneous opinions, generated from an explicitly constituted principle.

Between ethos and logos, practical mastery and verbal mastery, there is
a radical discontinuity.[58] There is no necessary link between the practical
mastery which can guide everyday practice, including all its (objectively)
political aspects, without ever being made explicit or, still less, systematically conceptualized, and the symbolic mastery of experience which is
expressed in discourse socially recognized as political and which presupposes the bracketing of all direct, exclusive reference to the concrete particularity of a situation. Because this is so, and because the relationship of experience to expression, that is, to consciousness, is relatively undetermined, the same experiences may recognize their images in
very different discourses.[59]

This flexibility is not unlimited, and it would be wrong to credit political language with the power of arbitrarily bringing into being what it
designates. Manipulation tends to be contained within certain limits because one may be able to resist an argument without being capable of ar-
guing resistance, still less of explicitly formulating its principles; and also
because popular language has its own resources which are not those of
analysis but which sometimes find an equivalent in a parable or metaphor
(such as this one, expressing scepticism about 'profit-sharing': 'You lend
me your watch and I'll give you the time'). The fact remains that, even
when recognizing itself in a speech or a spokesman, class habitus is not
infallible. If the members of the dominated classes frequently produce a
discourse that is in contradiction with itself, with the meaning of their
practice and with their objective condition, this is because they have to
talk politics without possessing the instruments of production of their
discourse, without having control over their 'political tongue'.

This crossing-point between experience and expression is where the
professional producers of discourse come in; it is here that the relations
are set up between the experts and the laymen, the signifiers and the signified. The dominated, whose interests are bound up with the raising of
consciousness, i.e., with language, are at the mercy of the discourses that
are presented to them; whenever they emerge from doxa they are liable to
fall into allodoxia, into all the false recognitions encouraged by the domi-

nant discourse. At best, they are at the mercy of their own spokesmen, whose role is to provide them with the means of repossessing their own experience. The essential indeterminacy of the relationship between experience and expression is compounded by the effect of legitimacy imposition and censorship exerted by the dominant use of language, tacitly recognized, even by the spokesmen of the dominated, as the legitimate mode of expression of political opinion. The dominant language discredits and destroys the spontaneous political discourse of the dominated. It leaves them only silence or a borrowed language, whose logic departs from that of popular usage but without becoming that of erudite usage, a deranged language, in which the 'fine words' are only there to mark the dignity of the expressive intention, and which, unable to express anything true, real or 'felt', dispossesses the speaker of the very experience it is supposed to express. It forces recourse to spokesmen, who are themselves condemned to use the dominant language (which is sufficient to introduce a distance from the mandators and, worse, from their problems and their experience of their problems), or at least a routine, routinizing language which, in addition to its functions as a mnemonic and a safety net, constitutes the only system of defence for those who can neither play the game nor 'spoil' it, a language which never engages with reality but churns out its canonical formulae and slogans, and which dispossesses the mandators of their experience a second time.

Through the language and relation to language, bound up with a whole life-style, which foist themselves on anyone who seeks to participate in 'political life', a whole relation to the world is imposed, a relation of denial which (like art) distances and neutralizes, enabling speakers to speak without thinking what they speak. This intrinsically euphemistic language, which presents itself in the guise of universality, de-realizes everything it names (for example, with millions out of work, a minister speaks of 'a certain erosion of full employment'), imposing a total but totally invisible censorship on the expression of the specific interests of the dominated, who can only choose between the sanitized words of official discourse and inarticulate grumblings. Questions which, at best, seem to demand a simple 'yes' or 'no' are in fact addressed, by a tacit privilege, to individuals or groups defined not so much by a particular category of political opinion as by the capacity to sustain the neutralized, quasi-theoretical relation to language which is the pre-condition for the production and reception of discourse 'of general interest' on questions 'of general interest', i.e., the capacity not only to decipher and manipulate the 'technical' terms of political language, but also to situate themselves at the level of quasi abstraction at which political discourse is usually pitched, both in the syntax of its utterances and in the implicit references it contains; or, more precisely, to recognize (in both senses) a 'political' question, to identify it as such and feel called upon to answer it, and to answer it 'politically', i.e., in accordance with the norms of political politeness. In short, a 'politico-scientific' question calls for the expatiating disposition which enables one to manipulate language without reference to any practical situation, rather as one might with an essay topic or examination question, to grant it the conventional seriousness that is applied to scholastic exercises or parlour games.

One only need look at the definition which the 'referee' of the television programme 'Face à face' gives of political debate as he understands it: 'It is perhaps not superfluous to remind you that this is a political debate. I think that, if you will agree, I will start by asking *each of you,* starting with Mr. Habib Deloncle, since we have agreed that he is to speak first, to define your *general position,* your *overall interpretation of the problem,* and to give *examples* from two areas, first education, *in the broad sense,* and then information, again *in the broad sense,* and then, of course, you may sum up.' Like the televised debate, the survey is very close to the scholastic situation in the questions it asks, which are often, to within a word or two, those which furnish ENA dissertation topics, political science lecture themes or the titles of articles in *Le Monde.* Above all, it is very close to the classroom by virtue of the form of the social relation in which the questioning takes place. Only scholastic neutralization and distancing can enable one to respond adequately to a situation in which a perfect stranger comes up and asks political questions (normally excluded from such encounters) without even thinking of invoking the authority of a third party. It has been established empirically that political discussions most often occur between people of identical opinions. If this is so, it is because a whole spontaneous semiology is implemented so as to avoid 'burning issues', the foremost of which are political issues, and to establish the provisional consensus which, in the accidental encounters of everyday life, can only be created by recourse to commonplaces and by constant vigilance.

One is reminded of a remark by Pierre Greco, who pointed out that the question, 'Are your friends' friends your friends?' invites answers which, even if identical, may differ radically as regards their principle, being produced either by a simple logical calculation based on a syntactic rewriting of the utterance itself, or by mental reference to the real world of friends. Like all the discourse of the 'doxosopher', who never teaches anything other than the difficulty of taking sides, the questioning he proposes produces distance: it distances the receiver by reminding him of the complexity and depth of the questions through the very complexity of the formulation; it distances reality by imposing the empty intentionality demanded by the obligatory subjects of scholastic discourse.

The unreality of the most specifically political questions also, and especially, arises from the fact that they only take on their full meaning in relation to the semantic field which is none other than the field of different political positions corresponding to different positions in the field of ideological production. For a complete understanding of the meaning objectively implied in the most summary response ('yes' or 'no' in a referendum) to a question such as, 'Are you in favour of or opposed to a regional reform designed to create regions endowed with extensive powers?'[60] one would have to be able to mobilize the entirely specific competence possessed by political commentators and analysts, which enables them to construct the system of possibles, itemize the set of relevant positions on the question, define the meaning each of these has in the internal and external strategies of the political groups concerned and uncover what each group has at stake. In short, the most genuinely political questions, those which most imperatively demand specific political competence, are those which arise for the professionals who argue about them (such as problems of constitutional law or, in other circles, the question of the dictatorship of the proletariat) or those which, though very directly affecting the most concrete conditions of existence of their addressees, appear in the form they have to take in order to become recognized stakes in the struggles which take place in the field of ideological production.

Nothing more clearly reveals the truth of this self-interested questioning than the ruling fraction's obsession with the 'economic information of the citizens', inspired by their dream of a dominated class possessing just enough economic competence to recognize the economic competence of the dominant class. The information which governments so readily and abundantly supply is of the sort which tends to disqualify (as a doctor does his patient's knowledge) the information the dominated derive in practical form from their ordinary experience (for example, their knowledge of the rise in the cost of living or of inequality in taxation). This leads to a political discourse which, rather than giving understanding, dictates a standpoint, and, far from providing the means of relating particular, practical information to general information, is content to shunt individual experiences into the appropriate general frameworks. Opinion surveys often reproduce the logic of those surveys on the 'economic information of the population' which seek to measure the respondents' knowledge and acknowledgement of official economics and economic information, the simple validating statement of a political economy, and which, with a sovereign ethnocentrism, reduce the practical economics and politics of the agents to a clumsy statement of official economics and political science (in particular through a priori and a posteriori coding operations calculated to obliterate what is essential, namely, the mode of expression).

Everything combines to reinforce the deep distrust—not incompatible with an equally deep form of recognition—which the dominated feel towards political language, broadly identified, like everything symbolic, with the dominant, the masters of the art of packaging and of fobbing off with words. This suspicion of the political 'stage', a 'theatre' whose rules are not understood and which leaves ordinary taste with a sense of helplessness, is often the source of 'apathy' and of a generalized distrust of all forms of speech and spokesmen. And often the only escape from ambivalence or indeterminacy towards language is to fall back on what one *can* appreciate, the body rather than words, substance rather than form, an honest face rather than a smooth tongue.

Conclusion: Classes and Classifications

If I have to choose the lesser of two evils,
I choose neither

Karl Kraus

Taste is an acquired disposition to 'differentiate' and 'appreciate',[1] as Kant says—in other words, to establish and mark differences by a process of distinction which is not (or not necessarily) a distinct knowledge, in Leibniz's sense, since it ensures recognition (in the ordinary sense) of the object without implying knowledge of the distinctive features which define it.[2] The schemes of the habitus, the primary forms of classification, owe their specific efficacy to the fact that they function below the level of consciousness and language, beyond the reach of introspective scrutiny or control by the will. Orienting practices practically, they embed what some would mistakenly call *values* in the most automatic gestures or the apparently most insignificant techniques of the body—ways of walking or blowing one's nose, ways of eating or talking—and engage the most fundamental principles of construction and evaluation of the social world, those which most directly express the division of labour (between the classes, the age groups and the sexes) or the division of the work of domination, in divisions between bodies and between relations to the body which borrow more features than one, as if to give them the appearances of naturalness, from the sexual division of labour and the division of sexual labour. Taste is a practical mastery of distributions which makes it possible to sense or intuit what is likely (or unlikely) to befall—and therefore to befit—an individual occupying a given position in social space. It functions as a sort of social orientation, a 'sense of one's place', guiding the occupants of a given place in social space towards the social positions adjusted to their properties, and towards the practices or goods which befit the occupants of that position. It implies a practical anticipation of what the social meaning and value of the chosen practice or thing will probably be, given their distribution in social space and the practical knowledge the other agents have of the correspondence between goods and groups.

Thus, the social agents whom the sociologist classifies are producers not only of classifiable acts but also of acts of classification which are themselves classified. Knowledge of the social world has to take into account a practical knowledge of this world which pre-exists it and which it must not fail to include in its object, although, as a first stage, this knowledge has to be constituted *against* the partial and interested representations provided by practical knowledge. To speak of habitus is to include in the object the knowledge which the agents, who are part of the object, have of the object, and the contribution this knowledge makes to the reality of the object. But it is not only a matter of putting back into the real world that one is endeavouring to know, a knowledge of the real world that contributes to its reality (and also to the force it exerts). It means conferring on this knowledge a genuinely constitutive power, the very power it is denied when, in the name of an objectivist conception of objectivity, one makes common knowledge or theoretical knowledge a mere reflection of the real world.

Those who suppose they are producing a materialist theory of knowledge when they make knowledge a passive recording and abandon the 'active aspect' of knowledge to idealism, as Marx complains in the *Theses on Feuerbach,* forget that all knowledge, and in particular all knowledge of the social world, is an act of construction implementing schemes of thought and expression, and that between conditions of existence and practices or representations there intervenes the structuring activity of the agents, who, far from reacting mechanically to mechanical stimulations, respond to the invitations or threats of a world whose meaning they have helped to produce. However, the principle of this structuring activity is not, as an intellectualist and anti-genetic idealism would have it, a system of universal forms and categories but a system of internalized, embodied schemes which, having been constituted in the course of collective history, are acquired in the course of individual history and function in their *practical* state, *for practice* (and not for the sake of pure knowledge).

Embodied Social Structures

This means, in the first place, that social science, in constructing the social world, takes note of the fact that agents are, in their ordinary practice, the subjects of acts of construction of the social world; but also that it aims, among other things, to describe the social genesis of the principles of construction and seeks the basis of these principles in the social world.[3] Breaking with the anti-genetic prejudice which often accompanies recognition of the active aspect of knowledge, it seeks in the objective distributions of properties, especially material ones (brought to light by censuses and surveys which all presuppose selection and classification), the basis of the systems of classification which agents apply to every sort of thing, not least to the distributions themselves. In contrast to what is sometimes called the 'cognitive' approach, which, both in its ethnological form (structural anthropology, ethnoscience, ethnosemantics, ethnobotany etc.) and in its sociological form (interactionism, ethnomethodology etc.), ignores the question of the genesis of mental structures and classifications, social science enquires into the relationship between the principles of division and the social divisions (between the generations, the sexes etc.) on which they are based, and into the variations of the use made of these principles according to the position occupied in the distributions (questions which all require the use of statistics).

The cognitive structures which social agents implement in their practical knowledge of the social world are internalized, 'embodied' social structures. The practical knowledge of the social world that is presupposed by 'reasonable' behaviour within it implements classificatory schemes (or 'forms of classification', 'mental structures' or 'symbolic forms'—apart from their connotations, these expressions are virtually interchangeable), historical schemes of perception and appreciation which are the product of the objective division into classes (age groups, genders, social classes) and which function below the level of consciousness and discourse. Being the product of the incorporation of the fundamental structures of a society, these principles of division are common to all the agents of the society and make possible the production of a common, meaningful world, a common-sense world.

All the agents in a given social formation share a set of basic perceptual schemes, which receive the beginnings of objectification in the pairs of antagonistic adjectives commonly used to classify and qualify persons or objects in the most varied areas of practice. The network of oppositions between high (sublime, elevated, pure) and low (vulgar, low, modest), spiritual and material, fine (refined, elegant) and coarse (heavy, fat, crude, brutal), light (subtle, lively, sharp, adroit) and heavy (slow, thick, blunt, laborious, clumsy), free and forced, broad and narrow, or, in another dimension, between unique (rare, different, distinguished, exclusive, exceptional, singular, novel) and common (ordinary, banal, commonplace, trivial, routine), brilliant (intelligent) and dull (obscure, grey, mediocre), is the matrix of all the commonplaces which find such ready acceptance because behind them lies the whole social order. The network has its ultimate source in the opposition between the 'élite' of the dominant and the 'mass' of the dominated, a contingent, disorganized multiplicity, interchangeable and innumerable, existing only statistically. These mythic roots only have to be allowed to take their

course in order to generate, at will, one or another of the tirelessly repeated themes of the eternal sociodicy, such as apocalyptic denunciations
of all forms of 'levelling', 'trivialization' or 'massification', which
identify the decline of societies with the decadence of bourgeois houses,
i.e., a fall into the homogeneous, the undifferentiated, and betray an
obsessive fear of number, of undifferentiated hordes indifferent to difference and constantly threatening to submerge the private spaces of
bourgeois exclusiveness.[4]

The seemingly most formal oppositions within this social mythology
always derive their ideological strength from the fact that they refer back,
more or less discreetly, to the most fundamental oppositions within the
social order: the opposition between the dominant and the dominated,
which is inscribed in the division of labour, and the opposition, rooted in
the division of the labour of domination, between two principles of domination, two powers, dominant and dominated, temporal and spiritual,
material and intellectual etc. It follows that the map of social space previously put forward can also be read as a strict table of the historically
constituted and acquired categories which organize the idea of the social
world in the minds of all the subjects belonging to that world and
shaped by it. The same classificatory schemes (and the oppositions in
which they are expressed) can function, by being specified, in fields organized around polar positions, whether in the field of the dominant class,
organized around an opposition homologous to the opposition constituting the field of the social classes, or in the field of cultural production,
which is itself organized around oppositions which reproduce the structure of the dominant class and are homologous to it (e.g., the opposition
between bourgeois and avant-garde theatre). So the fundamental opposition constantly supports second, third or n^{th} rank oppositions (those
which underlie the 'purest' ethical or aesthetic judgements, with their
high or low sentiments, their facile or difficult notions of beauty, their
light or heavy styles etc.), while euphemizing itself to the point of
misrecognizability.

Thus, the opposition between the heavy and the light, which, in a
number of its uses, especially scholastic ones, serves to distinguish popular or petit-bourgeois tastes from bourgeois tastes, can be used by theatre
criticism aimed at the dominant fraction of the dominant class to express
the relationship between 'intellectual' theatre, which is condemned for
its 'laborious' pretensions and 'oppressive' didacticism, and 'bourgeois'
theatre, which is praised for its tact and its art of skimming over surfaces.
By contrast, 'intellectual' criticism, by a simple inversion of values, expresses the relationship in a scarcely modified form of the same opposition, with lightness, identified with frivolity, being opposed to profundity. Similarly, it can be shown that the opposition between right and
left, which, in its basic form, concerns the relationship between the dominant and the dominated, can also, by means of a first transformation,

designate the relations between dominated fractions and dominant fractions within the dominant class; the words right and left then take on a meaning close to the meaning they have in expressions like 'right-bank' theatre or 'left-bank' theatre. With a further degree of 'de-realization', it can even serve to distinguish two rival tendencies within an avant-garde artistic or literary group, and so on.

It follows that, when considered in each of their uses, the pairs of qualifiers, the system of which constitutes the conceptual equipment of the judgement of taste, are extremely poor, almost indefinite, but, precisely for this reason, capable of eliciting or expressing the sense of the indefinable. Each particular use of one of these pairs only takes on its full meaning in relation to a universe of discourse that is different each time and usually implicit—since it is a question of the system of self-evidences and presuppositions that are taken for granted in the field in relation to which the speakers' strategies are defined. But each of the couples specified by usage has for undertones all the other uses it might have—because of the homologies between the fields which allow transfers from one field to another—and also all the other couples which are interchangeable with it, within a nuance or two (e.g., fine/crude for light/heavy), that is, in slightly different contexts.

The fact that the semi-codified oppositions contained in ordinary language reappear, with very similar values, as the basis of the dominant vision of the social world, in all class-divided social formations (consider the tendency to see the 'people' as the site of totally uncontrolled appetites and sexuality) can be understood once one knows that, reduced to their formal structure, the same fundamental relationships, precisely those which express the major relations of order (high/low, strong/weak etc.) reappear in all class-divided societies. And the recurrence of the triadic structure studied by Georges Dumézil, which Georges Duby shows in the case of feudal society to be rooted in the social structures it legitimates, may well be, like the invariant oppositions in which the relationship of domination is expressed, simply a necessary outcome of the intersection of the two principles of division which are at work in all class-divided societies—the division between the dominant and the dominated, and the division between the different fractions competing for dominance in the name of different principles, *bellatores* (warriors) and *oratores* (scholars) in feudal society, businessmen and intellectuals now.[5]

Knowledge without Concepts

Thus, through the differentiated and differentiating conditionings associated with the different conditions of existence, through the exclusions and inclusions, unions (marriages, affairs, alliances etc.) and divisions (incompatibilities, separations, struggles etc.) which govern the social structure and the structuring force it exerts, through all the hierarchies and classifications inscribed in objects (especially cultural products), in institutions (for example, the educational system) or simply in language, and through all the judgements, verdicts, gradings and warnings imposed by the institutions specially designed for this purpose, such as the family or the educational system, or constantly arising from the meetings and interactions of everyday life, the social order is progressively inscribed in people's minds. Social divisions become principles of division, organizing the image of the social world. Objective limits become a sense of limits, a practical anticipation of objective limits acquired by experience of objective limits, a 'sense of one's place' which leads one to exclude oneself from the goods, persons, places and so forth from which one is excluded.

The *sense* of limits implies *forgetting* the limits. One of the most important effects of the correspondence between real divisions and practical principles of division, between social structures and mental structures, is undoubtedly the fact that primary experience of the social world is that of doxa, an adherence to relations of order which, because they structure inseparably both the real world and the thought world, are accepted as self-evident. Primary perception of the social world, far from being a simple mechanical reflection, is always an act of cognition involving principles of construction that are external to the constructed object grasped in its immediacy; but at the same time it is an act of miscognition, implying the most absolute form of recognition of the social order. Dominated agents, who assess the value of their position and their characteristics by applying a system of schemes of perception and appreciation which is the embodiment of the objective laws whereby their value is objectively constituted, tend to attribute to themselves what the distribution attributes to them, refusing what they are refused ('That's not for the likes of us'), adjusting their expectations to their chances, defining themselves as the established order defines them, reproducing in their verdict on themselves the verdict the economy pronounces on them, in a word, condemning themselves to what is in any case their lot, *ta heautou*, as Plato put it, consenting to be what they have to be, 'modest', 'humble' and 'obscure'. Thus the conservation of the social order is decisively reinforced by what Durkheim called 'logical conformity',[6] i.e., the orchestration of categories of perception of the social world, which, being adjusted to the divisions of the established order (and thereby to the interests of those who dominate it) and common to all minds structured in accordance with those structures, present every appearance of objective necessity.[7]

The system of classificatory schemes is opposed to a taxonomy based on explicit and explicitly concerted principles in the same way that the dispositions constituting taste or ethos (which are dimensions of it) are opposed to aesthetics or ethics. The sense of social realities that is acquired in the confrontation with a particular form of social necessity is what makes it possible to act *as if* one knew the structure of the social world, one's place within it and the distances that need to be kept.

The ideology of the utopian thinker, rootless and unattached, 'free-floating', without interests or profits, together with the correlative refusal of that supreme form of materialistic vulgarity, the reduction of the unique to the class, the explanation of the higher by the lower, the application to the would-be unclassifiable of explanatory models fit only for the 'bourgeois', the petit-bourgeois, the limited and common, scarcely inclines intellectuals to conceptualize the sense of social position, still less their own position and the perverse relation to the social world it forces on them. (The perfect example is Sartre, whose whole work and whole existence revolve around this affirmation of the intellectual's subversive point of honour. This is seen particularly clearly in the passage in *Being and Nothingness* on the psychology of Flaubert, which can be read as a desperate effort to save the person, in the person of the intellectual, an uncreated creator, begotten by his own works, haunted by 'the project of being God', from every sort of reduction to the general, the type, the class, and to affirm the transcendence of the ego against 'what Comte called *materialism,* that is, explaining the higher by the lower.')[8]

The practical mastery of classification has nothing in common with the reflexive mastery that is required in order to construct a taxonomy that is simultaneously coherent and adequate to social reality. The practical 'science' of positions in social space is the competence presupposed by the art of behaving *comme il faut* with persons and things that have and give 'class' ('smart' or 'unsmart'), finding the right distance, by a sort of practical calculation, neither too close ('getting familiar') nor too far ('being distant'), playing with objective distance by emphasizing it (being 'aloof', 'stand-offish') or symbolically denying it (being 'approachable,' 'hobnobbing'). It in no way implies the capacity to situate oneself explicitly in the classification (as so many surveys on social class ask people to do), still less to describe this classification in any systematic way and state its principles.

There is no better opportunity to observe the functioning of this sense of the place one occupies than in condescension strategies, which presuppose both in the author of the strategy and in the victims a practical knowledge of the gap between the place really occupied and the place fictitiously indicated by the behaviour adopted (e.g., in French, use of the familiar *tu*). When the person 'naturally' identified with a Rolls Royce, a top hat or golf (see appendix 4) takes the metro, sports a flat cap (or a polo neck) or plays football, his practices take on their meaning in relation to this attribution by status, which continues to colour the real practices, as if by superimposition. But one could also point to the variations that Charles Bally observed in the style of speech according to the social gap between the interlocutors, or the variations in pronunciation according to the addressee: the speaker may, as appropriate, move closer to the 'accent' of an addressee of (presumed) higher status or move away from it by 'accentuating' his ordinary accent.[9]

The practical 'attributive judgement' whereby one puts someone in a class by speaking to him in a certain way (thereby putting oneself in a class at the same time) has nothing to do with an intellectual operation implying conscious reference to explicit indices and the implementation of classes produced by and for the concept. The same classificatory opposition (rich/poor, young/old etc.) can be applied at any point in the distribution and reproduce its whole range within any of its segments (common sense tells us that one is always richer or poorer than someone, superior or inferior to someone, more right-wing or left-wing than someone—but this does not entail an elementary relativism).

In a series of interviews (n = 30) on the social classes, based on a test which involved classifying thirty occupations (written on cards), the respondents often first asked how many classes the set should be divided into, and then several times modified the number of classes and the criteria of classification, so as to take account of the different dimensions of each occupation and therefore the different respects in which it could be evaluated; or they spontaneously suggested that they could carry on sub-dividing indefinitely. (They thereby exposed the artificiality of the situation created by a theoretical inquiry which called for the adoption of a theoretical attitude to which, as their initial uncertainty indicated, the respondents were quite unaccustomed.) And yet they almost always agreed on the ranks of the different occupations when taken two by two. (Lenski made similar observations in an experiment in which the respondents were asked to rank the families in a small town in New England.)[10]

It is not surprising that it is possible to fault the practical sense of social space which lies behind class-attributive judgement; the sociologists who use their respondents' self-contradictions as an argument for denying the existence of classes simply reveal that they understand nothing of how this 'sense' works or of the artificial situation in which they are making it work. In fact, whether it is used to situate oneself in social space or to place others, the sense of social space, like every practical sense, always refers to the particular situation in which it has to orient practices. This explains, for example, the divergences between surveys of the representation of the classes in a small town ('community studies') and surveys of class on a nation-wide scale.[11] But if, as has often been observed, respondents do not agree either on the number of divisions they make within the group in question, or on the limits of the 'strata' and the criteria used to define them, this is not simply due to the fuzziness inherent in all practical logics. It is also because people's image of the classification is a function of their position within it.

So nothing is further removed from an act of cognition, as conceived by the intellectualist tradition, than this sense of the social structure, which, as is so well put by the word *taste*—simultaneously 'the faculty of perceiving flavours' and 'the capacity to discern aesthetic values'—is social necessity made second nature, turned into muscular patterns and bodily automatisms. Everything takes place as if the social conditionings linked to a social condition tended to inscribe the relation to the social world in a lasting, generalized relation to one's own body, a way of bearing one's body, presenting it to others, moving it, making space for it, which gives the body its social physiognomy. Bodily hexis, a basic dimension of the sense of social orientation, is a practical way of experiencing and expressing one's own sense of social value. One's relationship to the social world and to one's proper place in it is never more clearly expressed than in the space and time one feels entitled to take from others; more precisely, in the space one claims with one's body in physical space, through a bearing and gestures that are self-assured or reserved, expansive or constricted ('presence' or 'insignificance') and with one's speech in time, through the interaction time one appropriates and the self-assured or aggressive, careless or unconscious way one appropriates it.[12]

There is no better image of the logic of socialization, which treats the body as a 'memory-jogger', than those complexes of gestures, postures and words—simple interjections or favourite clichés—which only have to be slipped into, like a theatrical costume, to awaken, by the evocative power of bodily mimesis, a universe of ready-made feelings and experiences. The elementary actions of bodily gymnastics, especially the specifically sexual, biologically pre-constructed aspect of it, charged with social meanings and values, function as the most basic of metaphors, capable of evoking a whole relationship to the world, 'lofty' or 'submissive', 'expansive' or 'narrow', and through it a whole world. The practical 'choices' of the sense of social orientation no more presuppose a representation of the range of possibilities than does the choice of phonemes; these enacted choices imply no acts of choosing. The logocentrism and intellectualism of intellectuals, combined with the prejudice inherent in the science which takes as its object the psyche, the soul, the mind, consciousness, representations, not to mention the petit-bourgeois pretension to the status of 'person', have prevented us from seeing that, as Leibniz put it, 'we are automatons in three-quarters of what we do', and that the ultimate values, as they are called, are never anything other than the primary, primitive dispositions of the body, 'visceral' tastes and distastes, in which the group's most vital interests are embedded, the things on which one is prepared to stake one's own and other people's bodies. The sense of distinction, the *discretio* (discrimination) which demands that certain things be brought together and others kept apart, which excludes all misalliances and all unnatural unions—i.e., all unions contrary to the common classification, to the *diacrisis* (separation) which is the basis of collective and individual identity—responds with visceral, murderous horror, absolute disgust, metaphysical fury, to everything which lies in Plato's 'hybrid zone', everything which passes understanding, that is, the embodied taxonomy, which, by challenging the principles of the incarnate social order, especially the socially constituted principles of the sexual division of labour and the division of sexual labour, violates the mental order, scandalously flouting common sense.

It can be shown that socialization tends to constitute the body as an analogical operator establishing all sorts of practical equivalences between the different divisions of the social world—divisions between the sexes, between the age groups and between the social classes—or, more precisely, between the meanings and values associated with the individuals occupying practically equivalent positions in the spaces defined by these divisions. And it can be shown that it does so by integrating the symbolism of social domination and submission and the symbolism of sexual domination and submission into the same body language—as is seen in etiquette, which uses the opposition between the straight and the curved or, which amounts to the same thing, between raising (oneself) and lowering (oneself), as one of the generative principles of the marks (of respect, contempt etc.) used to symbolize hierarchical relations.

Advantageous Attributions

The basis of the pertinence principle which is implemented in perceiving the social world and which defines all the characteristics of persons or things which can be perceived, and perceived as positively or negatively interesting, by all those who apply these schemes (another definition of common sense), is based on nothing other than the interest the individuals or groups in question have in recognizing a feature and in identifying the individual in question as a member of the set defined by that feature; interest in the aspect observed is never completely independent of the advantage of observing it. This can be clearly seen in all the classifications built around a stigmatized feature which, like the everyday opposition between homosexuals and heterosexuals, isolate the interesting trait from all the rest (i.e., all other forms of sexuality), which remain indifferent and undifferentiated. It is even clearer in all 'labelling judgements', which are in fact accusations, *categoremes* in the original Aristotelian sense, and which, like insults, only wish to know one of the properties constituting the social identity of an individual or group ('You're just a . . .'), regarding, for example, the married homosexual or converted Jew as a 'closet queen' or covert Jew, and thereby in a sense doubly Jewish or homosexual. The logic of the stigma reminds us that social identity is the stake in a struggle in which the stigmatized individual or group, and, more generally, any individual or group insofar as he or it is a potential object of categorization, can only retaliate against the partial perception which limits it to one of its characteristics by highlighting, in its self-definition, the best of its characteristics, and, more generally, by struggling to impose the taxonomy most favourable to its characteristics, or at least to give to the dominant taxonomy the content most flattering to what it has and what it is.

Those who are surprised by the paradoxes that ordinary logic and language engender when they apply their divisions to continuous magnitudes forget the paradoxes inherent in treating language as a purely logical instrument and also forget the social situation in which such a relationship to language is possible. The contradictions or paradoxes to which ordinary language classifications lead do not derive, as all forms of positivism suppose, from some essential inadequacy of ordinary language, but from the fact that these socio-logical acts are not directed towards the pursuit of logical coherence and that, unlike philological, logical or linguistic uses of language—which ought really to be called scholastic, since they all presuppose *schole*, i.e., leisure, distance from urgency and necessity, the absence of vital stakes, and the scholastic institution which in most social universes is the only institution capable of providing all these—they obey the logic of the parti pris, which, as in a court-room, juxtaposes not logical judgements, subject to the sole criterion of coherence, but charges and defences. Quite apart from all that is implied in the oppositions, which logicians and even linguists manage to forget, between the art of convincing and the art of persuading, it is clear that scholastic usage of language is to the orator's, advocate's or politician's usage what the classificatory systems devised by the logician or statistician concerned with coherence and empirical adequacy are to the categorizations and categoremes of daily life. As the etymology suggests, the latter belong to the logic of the trial.[13] Every real inquiry into the divisions of the social world has to analyse the interests associated with membership or non-membership. As is shown by the attention devoted to strategic, 'frontier' groups such as the 'labour aristocracy', which hesitates between class struggle and class collaboration, or the 'cadres', a category of bureaucratic statistics, whose nominal, doubly negative unity conceals its real dispersion both from the 'interested parties' and from their opponents and most observers, the laying down of boundaries between the classes is inspired by the strategic aim of 'counting in' or 'being counted in', 'cataloguing' or 'annexing', when it is not the simple recording of a legally guaranteed state of the power relation between the classified groups.

Leaving aside all cases in which the statutory imposition of an arbitrary boundary (such as a 30-kilo limit on baggage or the rule that a vehicle over two tons is a van) suffices to eliminate the difficulties that arise from the sophism of the heap of grain,[14] boundaries—even the most formal-looking ones, such as those between age-groups—do indeed freeze a particular state of social struggles, i.e., a given state of the distribution of advantages and obligations, such as the right to pensions or cheap fares, compulsory schooling or military service. And if we are amused by Alphonse Allais's story of the father who pulls the communication cord to stop the train at the very moment his child becomes three years old (and so needs a ticket to travel), it is because we immediately see the sociological absurdity of an imaginary variation which is as impeccably logical as those on which logicians base their beloved paradoxes. Here the limits are frontiers to be attacked or defended with all one's strength, and the classificatory systems which fix them are not so much means of knowledge as means of power, harnessed to social functions and overtly or covertly aimed at satisfying the interests of a group.

A number of ethical, aesthetic, psychiatric or forensic classifications that are produced by the 'institutional sciences', not to mention those produced and inculcated by the educational system, are similarly subordinated to social functions, although they derive their specific efficacy from their apparent neutrality. They are produced in accordance with the specific logic, and in the specific language, of relatively autonomous fields, and they combine a real dependence on the classificatory schemes of the dominant habitus (and ultimately on the social structures of which these are the product) with an apparent independence. The latter enables them to help to legitimate a particular state of the classification struggle and the class struggle. Perhaps the most typical example of these semi-autonomous systems of classification is the system of adjectives which underpins scholastic 'appreciations'.[15]

Commonplaces and classificatory systems are thus the stake of struggles between the groups they characterize and counterpose, who fight over them while striving to turn them to their own advantage. Georges Duby shows how the model of the three orders, which fixed a state of the social structure and aimed to make it permanent by codifying it, was able to be used simultaneously and successively by antagonistic groups: first by the bishops, who had devised it, against the heretics, the monks and the knights; then by the aristocracy, against the bishops and the king; and finally by the king, who, by setting himself up as the absolute subject of the classifying operation, as a principle external and superior to the classes it generated (unlike the three orders, who were subjects but also objects, judges but also parties), assigned each group its place in the social order, and established himself as an unassailable vantage-point.[16] In the same way it can be shown that the schemes and commonplaces which provide images of the different forms of domination, the opposition between the sexes and age-groups as well as the opposition between the generations, are similarly manipulated. The 'young' can accept the definition that their elders offer them, take advantage of the temporary licence they are allowed in many societies ('Youth must have its fling'), do what is assigned to them, revel in the 'specific virtues' of youth, *virtù,* virility, enthusiasm, and get on with their own business—knight-errantry for the scions of the mediaeval aristocracy,[17] love and violence for the youth of Renaissance Florence, and every form of regulated, ludic wildness (sport, rock etc.) for contemporary adolescents—in short, allow themselves to be kept in the state of 'youth', that is, irresponsibility, enjoying the freedom of irresponsible behaviour in return for renouncing responsibility.[18] In situations of specific crisis, when the order of successions is threatened, 'young people', refusing to remain consigned to 'youth', tend to consign the 'old' to 'old age'. Wanting to take the responsibilities which define adults (in the sense of socially complete persons), they must push the holders of responsibilities into that form of irresponsibility which defines old age, or rather retirement. The wisdom and prudence claimed by the elders then collapse into conservatism, archaism or, quite simply, senile irresponsibility. The newcomers, who are likely to be also the biologically youngest, but who bring with them many other distinctive properties, stemming from changes in the social conditions of production of the producers (i.e., principally the family and the educational system), escape the more rapidly from 'youth' (irresponsibility) the readier they are to break with the irresponsible behaviour assigned to them and, freeing themselves from the internalized limits (those which may make a 50-year-old feel 'too young reasonably to aspire' to a position or an honour), do not hesitate to push forward, 'leap-frog' and 'take the escalator' to precipitate their predecessors' fall into the past, the outdated, in short, social death. But they have no chance of winning the struggles over the limits which break out between the age-groups when the sense of the limits is lost, unless they manage to impose a new definition of the socially complete person, including in it characteristics normally (i.e., in terms of the prevailing classificatory principle) associated with youth (enthusiasm, energy and so on) or characteristics that can supplant the virtues normally associated with adulthood.

In short, what individuals and groups invest in the particular meaning they give to common classificatory systems by the use they make of them is infinitely more than their 'interest' in the usual sense of the term; it is their whole social being, everything which defines their own idea of themselves, the primordial, tacit contract whereby they define 'us' as opposed to 'them', 'other people', and which is the basis of the exclusions ('not for the likes of us') and inclusions they perform among the characteristics produced by the common classificatory system.

Social psychologists have observed that any division of a population into two groups, however arbitrary, induces discriminatory behaviour favourable to members of the agents' own group and hostile to members of the other group, even if it has adverse effects for the former group.[19] More generally, they describe under the term 'category differentiation' the operations whereby agents construct their perception of reality, in particular the process of accentuating differences vis-à-vis 'outsiders' (dissimilation) and reinforcing similarities with insiders (assimilation).[20] Similarly, studies of racism have shown that whenever different groups are juxtaposed, a definition of the approved, valorized behaviour tends to be contrasted with the despised, rejected behaviour of the other group.[21] Social identity lies in difference, and difference is asserted against what is closest, which represents the greatest threat. Analysis of stereotyping, the propensity to assume a correspondence between membership of a category (e.g., Nordic or Mediterranean, Western or Oriental) and possession of a particular property, so that knowledge of a person's category strongly influences judgements of him, is in line with analysis of that sort of social stereotyping in which all the members of a social formation tend to concur in attributing certain properties to members of the different social classes (see appendix 4).

The fact that, in their relationship to the dominant classes, the dominated classes attribute to themselves strength in the sense of labour power and fighting strength—physical strength and also strength of character, courage, manliness—does not prevent the dominant groups from similarly conceiving the relationship in terms of the scheme strong/weak; but they reduce the strength which the dominated (or the young, or women) ascribe to themselves to brute strength, passion and instinct, a blind, unpredictable force of nature, the unreasoning violence of desire, and they attribute to themselves spiritual and intellectual strength, a self-control that predisposes them to control others, a strength of soul or spirit which allows them to conceive their relationship to the dominated—the 'masses', women, the young—as that of the soul to the body, understanding to sensibility, culture to nature.

The Classification Struggle

Principles of division, inextricably logical and sociological, function within and for the purposes of the struggle between social groups; in producing concepts, they produce groups, the very groups which produce the principles and the groups against which they are produced. What is at stake in the struggles about the meaning of the social world is power over the classificatory schemes and systems which are the basis of the representations of the groups and therefore of their mobilization and demobilization: the evocative power of an utterance which puts things in a different light (as happens, for example, when a single word, such as 'paternalism', changes the whole experience of a social relationship) or which modifies the schemes of perception, shows something else, other properties, previously unnoticed or relegated to the background (such as common interests hitherto masked by ethnic or national differences); a separative power, a distinction, *diacrisis, discretio,* drawing discrete units out of indivisible continuity, difference out of the undifferentiated.

Only in and through the struggle do the internalized limits become boundaries, barriers that have to be moved. And indeed, the system of classificatory schemes is constituted as an objectified, institutionalized system of classification only when it has ceased to function as a sense of limits so that the guardians of the established order must enunciate, systematize and codify the principles of production of that order, both real and represented, so as to defend them against heresy; in short, they must constitute the doxa as orthodoxy. Official systems of classification, such as the theory of the three orders, do explicitly and systematically what the classificatory schemes did tacitly and practically. Attributes, in the sense of predicates, thereby become *attributions,* powers, capacities, privileges, prerogatives, attributed to the holder of a post, so that war is no longer what the warrior does, but the *officium,* the specific function, the raison d'être, of the *bellator.* Classificatory *discretio,* like law, freezes a certain state of the power relations which it aims to fix forever by enunciating and codifying it. The classificatory system as a principle of logical and political division only exists and functions because it reproduces, in a transfigured form, in the symbolic logic of differential gaps, i.e., of discontinuity, the generally gradual and continuous differences which structure the established order; but it makes its own, that is, specifically symbolic, contribution to the maintenance of that order only because it has the specifically symbolic power to make people see and believe which is given by the imposition of mental structures.

Systems of classification would not be such a decisive object of struggle if they did not contribute to the existence of classes by enhancing the efficacy of the objective mechanisms with the reinforcement supplied by representations structured in accordance with the classification. The imposition of a recognized name is an act of recognition of full social existence which transmutes the thing named. It no longer exists merely de facto, as a tolerated, illegal or illegitimate practice, but becomes a *social* function, i.e., a mandate, a mission (*Beruf*), a task, a role—all words which express the difference between authorized activity, which is assigned to an individual or group by tacit or explicit delegation, and mere usurpation, which creates a 'state of affairs' awaiting institutionalization. But the specific effect of 'collective representations', which, contrary to what the Durkheimian connotations might suggest, may be the product of the application of the same scheme of perception or a common system of classification while still being subject to antagonistic social uses, is most clearly seen when the word precedes the thing, as with voluntary associations that turn into recognized professions or corporate defence groups (such as the trade union of the 'cadres'), which progressively impose the representation of their existence and their unity, both on their own members and on other groups.

A group's presence or absence in the official classification depends on its capacity to get itself recognized, to get itself noticed and admitted, and so to win a place in the social order. It thus escapes from the shadowy existence of the 'nameless crafts' of which Emile Benveniste speaks: business in antiquity and the Middle Ages, or illegitimate activities, such as those of the modern healer (formerly called an 'empiric'), bone-setter or prostitute. The fate of groups is bound up with the words that designate them: the power to impose recognition depends on the capacity to mobilize around a name, 'proletariat', 'working class', 'cadres' etc., to appropriate a common name and to commune in a proper name, and so to mobilize the union that makes them strong, around the unifying power of a word.[22]

In fact, the order of words never exactly reproduces the order of things. It is the relative independence of the structure of the system of classifying, classified words (within which the distinct value of each particular label is defined) in relation to the structure of the distribution of capital, and more precisely, it is the time-lag (partly resulting from the inertia inherent in classification systems as quasi-legal institutions sanctioning a state of a power relation) between changes in jobs, linked to changes in the productive apparatus, and changes in titles, which creates the space for symbolic strategies aimed at exploiting the discrepancies between the nominal and the real, appropriating words so as to get the things they designate, or appropriating things while waiting to get the words that sanction them; exercising responsibilities without having entitlement to do so, in order to acquire the right to claim the legitimate titles, or, conversely, declining the material advantages associated with devalued titles so as to avoid losing the symbolic advantages bestowed by more prestigious labels or, at least, vaguer and more manipulable ones; donning the most flattering of the available insignia, verging on imposture if need be—like the potters who call themselves 'art craftsmen', or technicians who claim to be engineers—or inventing new labels, like physiotherapists (*kinésithérapeutes*) who count on this new title to separate them from mere masseurs and bring them closer to doctors. All these strategies, like all processes of competition, a paper-chase aimed at ensuring constant distinctive gaps, tend to produce a steady inflation of titles—restrained by the inertia of the institutionalized taxonomies (collective agreements, salary scales etc.)—to which legal guarantees are attached. The negotiations between antagonistic interest groups, which arise from the establishment of collective agreements and which concern, inseparably, the tasks entailed by a given job, the properties required of its occupants (e.g., diplomas) and the corresponding advantages, both material and symbolic (the name), are an institutionalized, theatrical version of the incessant struggles over the classifications which help to produce the classes, although these classifications are the product of the struggles between the classes and depend on the power relations between them.

The Reality of Representation and the Representation of Reality

The classifying subjects who classify the properties and practices of others, or their own, are also classifiable objects which classify themselves (in the eyes of others) by appropriating practices and properties that are already classified (as vulgar or distinguished, high or low, heavy or light etc.—in other words, in the last analysis, as popular or bourgeois) according to their probable distribution between groups that are themselves classified. The most classifying and best classified of these properties are, of course, those which are overtly designated to function as signs of distinction or marks of infamy, stigmata, especially the names and titles expressing class membership whose intersection defines social identity at any given time—the name of a nation, a region, an ethnic group, a family name, the name of an occupation, an educational qualification, honorific titles and so on. Those who classify themselves or others, by appropriating or classifying practices or properties that are classified and classifying, cannot be unaware that, through distinctive objects or practices in which their 'powers' are expressed and which, being appropriated by and appropriate to classes, classify those who appropriate them, they classify themselves in the eyes of other classifying (but also classifiable) subjects, endowed with classificatory schemes analogous to those which enable them more or less adequately to anticipate their own classification.

Social subjects comprehend the social world which comprehends them. This means that they cannot be characterized simply in terms of material properties, starting with the body, which can be counted and measured like any other object in the physical world. In fact, each of these properties, be it the height or volume of the body or the extent of landed property, when perceived and appreciated in relation to other properties of the same class by agents equipped with socially constituted schemes of perception and appreciation, functions as a symbolic property. It is therefore necessary to move beyond the opposition between a 'social physics'—which uses statistics in objectivist fashion to establish distributions (in both the statistical and economic senses), quantified expressions of the differential appropriation of a finite quantity of social energy by a large number of competing individuals, identified through 'objective indicators'—and a 'social semiology' which seeks to decipher meanings and bring to light the cognitive operations whereby agents produce and decipher them. We have to refuse the dichotomy between, on the one hand, the aim of arriving at an objective 'reality', 'independent of individual consciousnesses and wills', by breaking with common representations of the social world (Durkheim's 'pre-notions'), and of uncovering 'laws'—that is, significant (in the sense of non-random) relationships between distributions—and, on the other hand, the aim of grasping, not 'reality', but agents' representations of it, which are the whole 'reality' of a social world conceived 'as will and representation'.

In short, social science does not have to choose between that form of social physics, represented by Durkheim—who agrees with social semiology in acknowledging that one can only know 'reality' by applying logical instruments of classification[23]—and the idealist semiology which, undertaking to construct 'an account of accounts', as Harold Garfinkel puts it, can do no more than record the recordings of a social world which is ultimately no more than the product of mental, i.e., linguistic, structures. What we have to do is to bring into the science of scarcity, and of competition for scarce goods, the practical knowledge which the agents obtain for themselves by producing—on the basis of their experience of the distributions, itself dependent on their position in the distributions—divisions and classifications which are no less objective than those of the balance-sheets of social physics. In other words, we have to move beyond the opposition between objectivist theories which identify the social classes (but also the sex or age classes) with discrete groups, simple countable populations separated by boundaries objectively drawn in reality, and subjectivist (or marginalist) theories which reduce the 'social order' to a sort of collective classification obtained by aggregating the individual classifications or, more precisely, the individual strategies, classified and classifying, through which agents class themselves and others.[24]

One only has to bear in mind that goods are converted into distinctive signs, which may be signs of distinction but also of vulgarity, as soon as they are perceived relationally, to see that the representation which individuals and groups inevitably project through their practices and properties is an integral part of social reality. A class is defined as much by its *being-perceived* as by its *being*, by its consumption—which need not be conspicuous in order to be symbolic—as much as by its position in the relations of production (even if it is true that the latter governs the former). The Berkeleian—i.e., petit-bourgeois—vision which reduces social being to perceived being, to seeming, and which, forgetting that there is no need to give theatrical performances (*représentations*) in order to be the object of mental representations, reduces the social world to the sum of the (mental) representations which the various groups have of the theatrical performances put on by the other groups, has the virtue of insisting on the relative autonomy of the logic of symbolic representations with respect to the material determinants of socio-economic condition. The individual or collective classification struggles aimed at transforming the categories of perception and appreciation of the social world and, through this, the social world itself, are indeed a forgotten dimension of the class struggle. But one only has to realize that the classificatory schemes which underlie agents' practical relationship to their condition and the representation they have of it are themselves the product of that condition, in order to see the limits of this autonomy. Position in the classification struggle depends on position in the class structure; and social subjects—including intellectuals, who are not those best placed to grasp that which defines the limits of their thought of the social world, that is, the illusion of the absence of limits—are perhaps never less likely to transcend 'the limits of their minds' than in the representation they have and give of their position, which defines those limits.

Postscript: Towards a 'Vulgar' Critique of 'Pure' Critiques

The reader may have wondered why, in a text devoted to taste and art, no appeal is made to the tradition of philosophical or literary aesthetics; and he or she will no doubt have realized that this is a deliberate refusal.

It is certain that the 'high' aesthetic, both that which is engaged in a practical form in legitimate works and that which is expressed in writings intended to make it explicit and present it formally, is fundamentally constituted, whatever the variants, against all that this research may have established—namely, the indivisibility of taste, the unity of the most 'pure' and most purified, the most sublime and most sublimated tastes, and the most 'impure' and 'coarse', ordinary and primitive tastes. This means, conversely, that this project has required, above all, a sort of deliberate amnesia, a readiness to renounce the whole corpus of cultivated discourse on culture, which implies renouncing not only the profits secured by exhibiting signs of recognition but also the more intimate profits of erudite gratification, those Proust refers to when he indicates how much his lucid vision of the pleasures of reading has cost him: 'I have had to struggle here with my dearest aesthetic impressions, endeavouring to push intellectual honesty to its ultimate, cruellest limits'—without being able to ignore that the pleasures of 'lucid vision' may represent the 'purest' and most refined, albeit often somewhat morose, form of enjoyment.[1]

And if we must now allow the 'return of the repressed', having produced the truth of the taste against which, by an immense repression, the whole of legitimate aesthetics has been constructed, this is not only in order to subject the truths won to a final test (though it is not a question of 'comparing and contrasting' rival theories), but also in order to prevent the absence of direct confrontation from allowing the two discourses to coexist peacefully as parallel alternatives, in two carefully separated universes of thought and discourse.

Disgust at the 'Facile'

'Pure' taste and the aesthetics which provides its theory are founded on a refusal of 'impure' taste and of *aisthesis* (sensation), the simple, primitive form of pleasure reduced to a pleasure of the senses, as in what Kant calls 'the taste of the tongue, the palate and the throat', a surrender to immediate sensation which in another order looks like imprudence. At the risk of seeming to indulge in the 'facile effects' which 'pure taste' stigmatizes, it could be shown that the whole language of aesthetics is contained in a fundamental refusal of the *facile,* in all the meanings which bourgeois ethics and aesthetics give to the word;[2] that 'pure taste', purely negative in its essence, is based on the disgust that is often called 'visceral' (it 'makes one sick' or 'makes one vomit') for everything that is 'facile'—facile music, or a facile stylistic effect, but also 'easy virtue' or an 'easy lay'. The refusal of what is easy in the sense of simple, and therefore shallow, and 'cheap', because it is easily decoded and culturally 'undemanding', naturally leads to the refusal of what is facile in the ethical or aesthetic sense, of everything which offers pleasures that are too immediately accessible and so discredited as 'childish' or 'primitive' (as opposed to the deferred pleasures of legitimate art). Thus people speak of 'facile effects' to characterize the obtrusive elegance of a certain style of journalistic writing or the too insistent, too predictable charm of what is called 'light' music (a word whose connotations virtually correspond to those of 'facile'—consider 'easy listening') or certain performances of classical music; thus a critic denounces the 'vulgar sensuality' or 'Casbah orientalism' which reduces one interpretation of the 'Dance of the Seven Veils' in Strauss's *Salome* to 'cabaret music'. 'Vulgar' works, as the words used to describe them indicate—'facile' or 'light', of course, but also 'frivolous', 'futile', 'shallow', 'superficial', 'showy', 'flashy', 'meretricious',[3] or, in the register of oral satisfactions, 'syrupy', 'sugary', 'rose-water', 'schmaltzy', 'cloying'—are not only a sort of insult to refinement, a slap in the face to a 'demanding' (*difficile*) audience which will not stand for 'facile' offerings (it is a compliment to an artist, especially a conductor, to say he 'respects his audience'); they arouse distaste and disgust by the methods of seduction, usually denounced as 'low', 'degrading', 'demeaning', which they try to use, giving the spectator the sense of being treated like any Tom, Dick or Harry who can be seduced by tawdry charms which invite him to regress to the most primitive and elementary forms of pleasure, whether they be the passive satisfactions of the infantile taste for sweet liquids ('syrupy') or the quasi-animal gratifications of sexual desire.[4] One might evoke the Platonic prejudice, endlessly reaffirmed, in favour of the 'noble senses', vision and hearing, or the primacy Kant gives to form, which is more 'pure', over colour and its quasi-carnal seduction.

But it will suffice to quote a quite exemplary text in which Schopenhauer establishes an opposition between the 'sublime' and the 'charming' identical to the one Kant makes in the *Critique of Judgement* between 'pleasure' and 'enjoyment', the 'beautiful' and the 'agreeable', 'that which pleases' and 'that which gratifies'. Schopenhauer defines the 'charming or attractive' as that which 'excites the will by presenting to it directly its fulfilment, its satisfaction', that which 'draws the beholder away from the pure contemplation which is demanded by all apprehension of the beautiful, because it necessarily excites this will, by objects which directly appeal to it'; and, significantly, he condemns simultaneously the two forms of satisfaction, oral and sexual, against which the satisfaction recognized as specifically aesthetic is to be constituted: 'The one species [of the charming], a very low one, is found in Dutch paintings of still life, when they err by representing articles of food, which by their deceptive likeness necessarily excite the appetite for the things they represent, and this is just an excitement of the will, which puts an end to all aesthetic contemplation of the object. Painted fruit is yet admissible, because we may regard it as the further development of the flower, and as a beautiful product of nature in form and colour, without being obliged to think of it as eatable; but unfortunately we often find, represented with deceptive naturalness, prepared and served dishes, oysters, herrings, crabs, bread and butter, beer, wine, and so forth, which is altogether to be condemned. In historical painting and in sculpture the charming consists in naked figures, whose position, drapery, and general treatment are calculated to excite the passions of the beholder, and thus pure aesthetical contemplation is at once annihilated, and the aim of art is defeated.'[5]

Schopenhauer is here very close to Kant,[6] and to all aesthetics in which, in a rationalized form, the ethos of the dominated fraction of the dominant class is expressed; as he so well puts it, the 'charming', which reduces the 'pure knowing subject', 'freed from subjectivity and its impure desires' to a 'willing subject, subject to every desire, every servitude', exerts real violence on the beholder. Indecent and exhibitionist, it captures the body by its rhythm, which is attuned to bodily rhythms, and captivates the mind by the deceptions of its plots, suspense and surprises, forcing on it a real participation which is quite opposed to the 'distance' and 'disinterestedness' of pure taste, and bound to appear as out of place as Don Quixote when, carried away by real anger at a fictitious scandal, he assaults Master Pedro's puppets.[7]

The most radical difference between popular entertainments—from Punch and Judy shows, wrestling or circuses, or even the old neighbourhood cinema, to soccer matches—and bourgeois entertainments is found in audience participation. In one case it is constant, manifest (boos, whistles), sometimes direct (pitch or playing-field, invasions); in the other it is intermittent, distant, highly ritualized, with obligatory applause, and even shouts of enthusiasm, at the end, or even perfectly silent (concerts in churches). Jazz, a bourgeois entertainment which mimics popular entertainment, is only an apparent exception: the signs of participation (hand-clapping or foot-tapping) are limited to a silent sketch of the gesture (at least in free jazz).

The 'Taste of Reflection' and the 'Taste of Sense'

What pure taste refuses is indeed the violence to which the popular spectator consents (one thinks of Adorno's description of popular music and its effects); it demands respect, the distance which allows it to keep its distance. It expects the work of art, a finality with no other end than itself, to treat the spectator in accordance with the Kantian imperative, that is, as an end, not a means. Thus, Kant's principle of pure taste is nothing other than a refusal,[8] a disgust—a disgust for objects which impose enjoyment and a disgust for the crude, vulgar taste which revels in this imposed enjoyment: 'One kind of ugliness alone is incapable of being represented conformably to nature without destroying all aesthetic delight, and consequently artistic beauty, namely, that which excites *disgust*. For, as in this strange sensation, which depends purely on the imagination, the object is represented as insisting, as it were, on our enjoying it, while we still set our face against it, the artificial representation of the object is no longer distinguishable from the nature of the object itself in our sensation, and so it cannot possibly be regarded as beautiful' (pp. 174–175).[9]

Disgust is the paradoxical experience of enjoyment extorted by violence, an enjoyment which arouses horror. This horror, unknown to those who surrender to sensation, results fundamentally from removal of the distance, in which freedom is asserted, between· the representation and the thing represented, in short, from *alienation,* the loss of the subject in the object, immediate submission to the immediate present under the enslaving violence of the 'agreeable'. Thus, in contrast to the inclination aroused by the 'agreeable', which, unlike beauty, is common to humans and animals (p. 49), is capable of seducing 'those who are always intent only on enjoyment' (p. 45; also 47, 117) and 'immediately satisfies the senses'—whereas it is 'mediately displeasing' to reason (p. 47)[10]— 'pure taste', the 'taste of reflection' (p. 54) which is opposed to the 'taste of sense' as 'charms' are opposed to 'form' (pp. 65, 67), must exclude interest and must not 'be in the least prepossessed in favour of the real existence of the object' (p. 43).

Simple grammatical analysis bears out Hegel's complaint that Kant's third *Critique* remains in the register of *Sollen,* 'ought'. The statements on taste are written in the imperative, or rather in that sort of spurious constative which allows the author to remain silent as to the conditions of realization of what is in fact a performative utterance. Some typical examples: 'We say of a man who remains unaffected in the presence of what we consider sublime, that he has no feeling. We *demand* both taste and feeling of every man, and, granted some degree of culture, we give him credit for both' (p. 116); 'Every judgement which is to show the taste of the individual is *required* to be an independent judgement of the individual himself' (p. 137); 'I take my stand on the ground that my judgement *is to be* one of taste, and not one of understanding or reason' (p. 140); 'fine art *must* be free art in a double sense.' (p. 185).

The object which 'insists on being enjoyed', as an image and in reality, in flesh and blood, neutralizes both ethical resistance and aesthetic neutralization; it annihilates the distanciating power of representation, the essentially human power of suspending immediate, animal attachment to the sensible and refusing submission to the pure affect, to simple aisthesis. In the face of this twofold challenge to human freedom and to culture (the anti-nature), disgust is the ambivalent experience of the horrible seduction of the disgusting and of enjoyment, which performs a sort of reduction to animality, corporeality, the belly and sex, that is, to what is common and therefore vulgar, removing any difference between those who resist with all their might and those who wallow in pleasure, who enjoy enjoyment: 'Common human understanding ... has the doubtful honour of having the name of common sense ... bestowed upon it; and bestowed, too, in an acceptation of the word *common* (not merely in our language, where it actually has a double meaning, but also in many others) which makes it amount to what is *vulgar* (*das Vulgare*)—what is everywhere to be met with—a quality which by no means confers credit or distinction upon its possessor' (p. 151). Nature understood as sense equalizes, but at the lowest level (an early version of the 'levelling-down' abhorred by the Heideggerians). Aristotle taught that different things differentiate themselves by what makes them similar, i.e., a common character; in Kant's text, disgust discovers with horror the common animality on which and against which moral distinction is constructed: 'We regard as coarse and low the habits of thought of those who have no feeling for beautiful nature ... and who devote themselves to the mere enjoyments of sense found in eating and drinking' (p. 162).

Elsewhere Kant quite directly states the social basis of the opposition between the 'taste of reflection' and the 'taste of sense': 'In the beginning, the novice must have been guided by instinct alone, that voice of God which is obeyed by all animals. This permitted some things to be used for nourishment, while forbidding others. Here it is not necessary to assume a special instinct which is now lost. It could simply have been the sense of smell, plus its affinity with the organ of taste and the well-known relation of the latter to the organs of digestion; in short an ability, perceivable even now, to sense, prior to the consumption of a certain foodstuff, whether or not it is fit for consumption. It is not even necessary to assume that this sensitivity was keener in the first pair than it is now. For it is a familiar enough fact that men wholly absorbed by their senses have much greater perceptive powers than those who, occupied with thoughts as well as with the senses, are to a degree turned away from the sensuous.'[11] We recognize here the ideological mechanism which works by describing the terms of the opposition one establishes between the social classes as stages in an evolution (here, the progress from nature to culture).

Thus, although it consistently refuses anything resembling an empirical psychological or sociological genesis of taste (e.g., pp. 89, 116), each time invoking the magical division between the transcendental and the empirical,[12] the theory of pure taste is grounded in an empirical social relation, as is shown by the opposition it makes between the agreeable (which 'does not cultivate' and is only an enjoyment—p. 165) and culture,[13] or its allusions to the teaching and educability of taste.[14] The antithesis between culture and bodily pleasure (or nature) is rooted in the opposition between the cultivated bourgeoisie and the people,[15] the imaginary site of uncultivated nature, barbarously wallowing in pure enjoyment: 'Taste that requires an added element of charm and emotion for its delight, not to speak of adopting this as the measure of its approval, has not yet emerged from barbarism' (p. 65).

If one follows through all the implications of an aesthetic which, in accordance with the logic of Kant's 'Essay on Negative Magnitudes', has to measure virtue by the magnitude of the vices overcome and pure taste by the intensity of the impulse denied and the vulgarity refused, then the most accomplished art has to be recognized in those works which carry the antithesis of civilized barbarism, contained impulse, sublimated coarseness, to the highest degree of tension. This criterion would point to Mahler, who went further than any other composer in the dangerous game of facility and every form of high-cultural recuperation of the 'popular arts' or even 'schmaltz'; and, earlier, Beethoven, whose recognized greatness is measured by the negative magnitude of the violences, extravagances and excesses, often celebrated by hagiography, which artistic restraint, a kind of 'mourning', has had to overcome. The inhibition of too immediately accessible pleasure, initially the pre-condition for the experience of 'pure' pleasure, can even become a source of pleasure in itself; refinement can lead to a cultivation, for its own sake, of Freud's 'preliminary pleasure', an ever increasing deferment of the resolution of tension, with, for example, a growing distance between the dissonant chord and its full or conventional resolution. Thus the 'purest' form of the aesthete's pleasure, aisthesis purified, sublimated and denied, may, paradoxically, consist in an asceticism, *askesis*, a trained, sustained tension, which is the very opposite of primary, primitive aisthesis.

Pure pleasure—ascetic, empty pleasure which implies the renunciation of pleasure, pleasure purified of pleasure—is predisposed to become a symbol of moral excellence, and the work of art a test of ethical superiority, an indisputable measure of the capacity for sublimation which defines the truly human man.[16] What is at stake in aesthetic discourse, and in the attempted imposition of a definition of the genuinely human, is nothing less than the *monopoly of humanity*.[17] Art is called upon to mark the difference between humans and non-humans: artistic experience, a free imitation of natural creations, *natura naturans,* whereby the artist (and through him, the beholder) affirms his transcendence of *natura naturata* by producing 'a second nature' (p. 176) subject only to the laws of creative genius (p. 171), is the closest approach to the divine experience of *intuitus originarius,* the creative perception which freely engenders its own object without recognizing any rules or constraints other than its own (p. 168). The world produced by artistic 'creation' is not only 'another nature' but a 'counter-nature', a world produced in the manner of nature but against the ordinary laws of nature—those of gravity in dance, those of desire and pleasure in painting and sculpture etc.—by an act of artistic sublimation which is predisposed to fulfil a function of social legitimation. The negation of enjoyment—inferior, coarse, vulgar, mercenary, venal, servile, in a word, natural—implies affirmation of the sublimity of those who can be satisfied with sublimated, refined, distinguished, disinterested, gratuitous, free pleasures. The opposition between the tastes of nature and the tastes of freedom introduces a relationship which is that of the body to the soul, between those who are 'only natural' and those whose capacity to dominate their own biological nature affirms their legitimate claim to dominate social nature. No wonder, then, that, as Mikhail Bakhtin has pointed out apropos of Rabelais, the popular imagination can only invert the relationship which is the basis of the aesthetic sociodicy: responding to sublimation by a strategy of reduction or degradation, as in slang, parody, burlesque or caricature, using obscenity or scatology to turn arsy-versy, head over heels, all the 'values' in which the dominant groups project and recognize their sublimity, it rides roughshod over difference, flouts distinction, and, like the Carnival games, reduces the distinctive pleasures of the soul to the common satisfactions of food and sex.[18]

A Denied Social Relationship

The theory of beauty as the absolute creation of *artifex deus,* enabling every man (worthy of the name) to mimic the divine act of creation, is no doubt the 'natural' expression of the occupational ideology of those who like to call themselves 'creators', which explains why, even without any direct influence, it has constantly been reinvented by artists, from Leonardo da Vinci, who made the artist 'the master of all things', to Paul

Klee, who aimed to create as nature does.[19] And—quite apart from its clear relationship with the antithesis between the two forms of aesthetic pleasure, and through this, with the opposition between the cultured 'élite' and the barbarous masses—the opposition Kant establishes between 'free art', 'which is agreeable on its own account' and whose product is freedom—since it is agreeable on its *own* account and in no way constrains the beholder[20]—and 'mercenary art', a servile activity 'only attractive by means of what it results in (e.g., the pay), which is consequently capable of being a compulsory imposition' (p. 164), whose product forces itself on the beholder with the enslaving violence of its sensible charms, very directly expresses Kant's conception of the position of 'pure' or 'autonomous' intellectuals in the division of labour, and more precisely in the division of intellectual labour. These 'pure' intellectuals are, according to *The Conflict of the Faculties*, none other than philosophy professors,[21] but artists and writers would no doubt be the purest of all. The *Critique of Judgement* is less remote than it seems from the 'Idea for a Universal History', which has rightly been seen as the expression of the sublimated interests of the bourgeois intelligentsia; this intellectual bourgeoisie, 'whose legitimation', as Norbert Elias puts it, 'consists primarily in its intellectual, scientific or artistic accomplishments', occupies an uncomfortable position in social space, entirely homologous to that of the modern intelligentsia: 'an elite in the eyes of the people, it has a lower rank in the eyes of the courtly aristocracy.'[22]

A number of the oddities of Kant's text are explained once it is seen that the second term of the fundamental opposition between pleasure and enjoyment is twofold; the ethical purity of the pleasure of culture is defined not only against the barbarism of enjoyment but also against the heteronomous enjoyment of Civilization: 'To a high degree we are, through art and science, *cultured*. We are civilized—perhaps too much for our own good—in all sorts of social grace and decorum. But to consider ourselves as having reached *morality*—for that, much is lacking. The ideal of morality belongs to culture; its use for some simulacrum of morality in the love of honour and outward decorum constitutes mere civilization.'[23]

Kant casts into the darkness of the 'empirical' 'the interest indirectly attached to the beautiful by the inclination towards society' that is produced by the process of Civilization, although this 'refined inclination' giving no satisfaction of enjoyment is as close as possible to pure pleasure. The negation of nature leads as much to the perversion of 'unnecessary inclinations' as to the pure morality of aesthetic pleasure: 'Reason has this peculiarity that, aided by the imagination, it can create artificial desires which are not only unsupported by natural instinct but actually contrary to it. These desires, in the beginning called concupiscence, gradually generate a whole host of unnecessary and indeed unnatural inclinations called luxuriousness.'[24]

The 'counter-nature' proves ambiguous: civilization is bad, culture good. The difference between heteronomous, *external, civilized* pleasure and cultivated pleasure, which presupposes 'slow efforts to improve the mind' (*langsame Bemühung der inneren Bildung der Denkungsart*),[25] can only be resolved, for Kant, on the terrain of ethics, i.e., of the determinants of aesthetic pleasure, external and pathological on one side, purely internal on the other.

This pure aesthetic is indeed the rationalization of an ethos: pure pleasure, pleasure totally purified of all sensuous or sensible interest, perfectly free of all social or fashionable interest, as remote from concupiscence as it is from conspicuous consumption, is opposed as much to the refined, altruistic enjoyment of the courtier as it is to the crude, animal enjoyment of the people.[26] Nothing in the content of this typically professorial aesthetic could stand in the way of its being recognized as universal by its sole ordinary readers, the professors of philosophy,[27] who were too concerned with hunting down historicism and sociologism to see the historical and social coincidence which, here as in so many cases, is the basis of their illusion of universality.[28] And the formalization which is required in order for social impulses and interests to be expressed within the limits of the censorship of a particular form of social propriety can only help to encourage this illusion, so that a discourse which makes art a criterion of an ethical and aesthetic distinction which is a misrecognized form of social difference can be read as a universal expression of the universality of art and aesthetic experience.

Totally ahistorical, like all philosophical thought that is worthy of the name (every *philosophia* worth its salt is *perennis*)—perfectly ethnocentric, since it takes for its sole datum the lived experience of a *homo aestheticus* who is none other than the subject of aesthetic discourse constituted as the universal subject of aesthetic experience—Kant's analysis of the judgement of taste finds its real basis in a set of aesthetic principles which are the universalization of the dispositions associated with a particular social and economic condition. But it would be a mistake to see only a formal mask in all the features which the formalized discourse owes to the effort to resolve the problems raised by the theoretical division and conceptual distinctions worked out in the other *Critiques* and to express 'the thinking of Immanuel Kant' in accordance with the discursive schemes constituting what is called 'Kantian thought'.[29] Since we know that the very principle of the symbolic efficacy of philosophical discourse lies in the play between two structures of discourse which the work of formalization seeks to integrate without entirely succeeding, it would be naive to reduce the truth of this double discourse to the subterranean discourse in which the Kantian ideology of the beautiful is expressed and which analysis reconstitutes by reconnecting the web of notations blurred by the interferences of the structures. The *social categories of aesthetic judgement* can only function, for Kant himself and for his readers, in the form of highly sublimated categories, such as the oppositions between beauty and charm, pleasure and enjoyment or culture and civilization, euphemisms which, without any conscious intention of dissimulating, enable social oppositions to be expressed and experienced in a form conforming to the norms of expression of a specific field. What is hidden, that is, the double social relationship—to the court (the site of civilization as opposed to culture) and to the people (the site of nature and sense)—is both present and absent; it presents itself in the text in such a guise that one can in all good faith not see it there and that the naively reductive reading, which would reduce Kant's text to the social relationship that is disguised and transfigured within it, would be no less false than the ordinary reading which would reduce it to the phenomenal truth in which it appears only in disguise.

Parerga and Paralipomena

There is perhaps no more decisive way of manifesting the social mechanisms which lead to the denial of the real principles of the judgement of taste (and their re-denial in all faithful readings) than to see them at work in a commentary intended (apparently, at least) to manifest them, i.e., in the reading of the *Critique of Judgement* offered by Jacques Derrida.[30] Although this reading brings to light some of the hidden presuppositions of Kant's approach to taste by transgressing the most binding rules of orthodox commentary, it remains subject to the censorships of the pure reading.

Derrida does indeed see that what is involved is the opposition between legitimate 'pleasure' and 'enjoyment' or, in terms of objects, between the agreeable arts which seduce by the 'charm' of their sensuous content and the Fine Arts which offer pleasure without enjoyment. He also sees, without explicitly connecting it with the previous opposition, the antithesis between the gross tastes of those who 'are content to enjoy the simple sensations of the senses, at table or over a bottle'—'consumptive orality' seen as 'interested taste'—and pure taste. He indicates that disgust is perhaps the true origin of pure taste, inasmuch as it 'abolishes representative distance' and, driving one irresistibly towards consumption, annihilates the freedom that is asserted in suspending immediate attachment to the sensuous and in neutralizing the affect, that is, 'disinterestedness', a lack of interest as to the existence or non-existence of the thing represented. And one can, no doubt, though Derrida avoids doing so explicitly, relate all the foregoing oppositions, which concern the consumer's relation to the work of art, to the last of the oppositions picked up, the one which Kant establishes, at the level of production, between 'free art', involving free will, and 'mercenary art', which exchanges the value of its labour for a wage.

It goes without saying that such a transcription of Derrida's text, which condenses and tightens, thus making connections excluded from the original, which, by instituting an 'order of reasons', produces links that are only suggested and which, above all, gives to the whole enterprise the air of a demonstration directed towards establishing a truth, constitutes a transformation or distortion. To summarize a discourse which, as is shown by the attention Derrida devotes to the writing and typography, is the product of the intention of putting content into form, and which rejects in advance any summary aiming to separate content from form, to reduce the text to its simplest expression, is in fact to deny the most fundamental intention of the work and, by a sort of transcendental reduction which no critique has any thought of carrying out, to perform the *epochē* of everything by which the philosophical text affirms its existence as a philosophical text, i.e., its 'disinterestedness', its freedom, and hence its elevation, its distinction, its distance from all 'vulgar' discourses.

But Derrida's supremely intellectual game presupposes lucidity in commitment to the game: 'It is a question of pleasure. Of thinking pure pleasure, the being-pleasure of pleasure. Starting out from pleasure, the third *Critique* was written for it, and must be read for it. A somewhat arid pleasure—without concepts and without enjoyment—a somewhat strict pleasure, but we learn here, once again, that there is no pleasure without stricture. Letting myself be led by pleasure, I recognize and, at the same time, I pervert an injunction. *I follow it:* the enigma of pleasure sets the whole book in motion. *I seduce it:* in treating the third *Critique* as a work of art or a beautiful object, which it was not meant simply to be, I act as if the *existence* of the book were indifferent to me (which, Kant explains, is required by every aesthetic experience) and could be considered with imperturbable detachment'.[31]

Thus, Derrida tells us the truth of his text and his reading (a particular case of the experience of pure pleasure), that is, that it implies the epoche of any thesis of existence or, more simply, indifference to the existence of the object in question, but he does so in a text which itself implies that epoche and that indifference. It is an exemplary form of denegation—you tell (yourself) the truth but in such a way that you don't tell it—which defines the objective truth of the philosophical text in its social use; which confers on the philosophical text a social acceptability proportionate to its unreality, its gratuitousness, its sovereign indifference.[32] Because he never withdraws from the philosophical game, whose conventions he respects, even in the ritual transgressions at which only traditionalists could be shocked, he can only philosophically tell the truth about the philosophical text and its philosophical reading, which (apart from the silence of orthodoxy) is the best way of not telling it, and he cannot truly tell the truth about the Kantian philosophy of art and, more generally, about philosophy itself, which his own discourse has helped to produce. Just as the pictorial rhetoric which continues to foist itself on every artist produces an inevitable aestheticization, so the philosophical way of talking about philosophy de-realizes everything that can be said about philosophy.

The radical questionings announced by philosophy are in fact circumscribed by the interests linked to membership in the philosophical field, that is, to the very existence of this field and the corresponding censorships. The field is the historical product of the labour of the successive philosophers who have defined certain topics as philosophical by forcing them on commentary, discussion, critique and polemic; but the problems, theories, themes or concepts which are deposited in writings considered at a given moment as philosophical (books, articles, essay topics etc.) and which constitute *objectified philosophy* impose themselves as a sort of autonomous world on would-be philosophers, who must not only know them, as items of culture, but recognize them, as objects of (prereflexive) belief, failing which they disqualify themselves as philosophers. All those who profess to be philosophers have a life-or-death interest, qua philosophers, in the existence of this repository of consecrated texts, a mastery of which constitutes the core of their specific capital. Thus, short of jeopardizing their own existence as philosophers and the symbolic powers ensuing from this title, they can never carry through the breaks which imply a practical epoche of the thesis of the existence of philosophy, that is, a denouncement of the tacit contract defining the conditions of membership in the field, a repudiation of the fundamental belief in the conventions of the game and the value of the stakes, a refusal to grant the indisputable signs of recognition—references and reverence, *obsequium,* respect for convention even in their outrages—in short, everything which secures recognition of membership.[33]

Failing to be, at the same time, social breaks which truly renounce the gratifications associated with membership, the most audacious intellectual breaks of pure reading still help to preserve the stock of consecrated texts from becoming dead letters, mere archive material, fit at best for the history of ideas or the sociology of knowledge, and to perpetuate its existence and its specifically philosophical powers by using it as an emblem or as a matrix for discourses which, whatever their stated intention, are always, also, symbolic strategies deriving their power essentially from the consecrated texts. Like the religious nihilism of some mystic heresies,[34] philosophical nihilism too can find an ultimate path of salvation in the rituals of liberatory transgression. Just as, by a miraculous dialectical renewal, the countless acts of derision and desacralization which modern art has perpetrated against art have always turned, insofar as these are still artistic acts, to the glory of art and the artist, so the philosophical 'deconstruction' of philosophy is indeed, when the very hope of radical reconstruction has evaporated, the only philosophical answer to the destruction of philosophy.

The strategy of taking as one's object the very tradition one belongs to and one's own activity in order to make them undergo a quasi objectification—

a common practice among artists, since Duchamp—has the effect of turning commentary, a typically scholastic genre, both in its conditions of production (lectures, especially in agrégation classes) and in the docile yet rigorous dispositions it demands, into a personal work suitable for publication in avant-garde reviews, by a further transgression, scandalizing the orthodox, of the sacred frontier between the academic field and the literary field, i.e., between the 'serious' and the 'frivolous'. This entails a dramatization (*mise en scène*), particularly visible in 'parallel-column' production, which aims to draw attention to the philosophical 'gesture', making the very utterance of discourse an 'act' in the sense which avant-garde painters give to the word and placing the person of the philosopher at the centre of the philosophical stage.

Philosophical objectification of the truth of philosophical discourse encounters its limits in the objective conditions of its own existence as an activity aspiring to philosophical legitimacy, that is, in the existence of a philosophical field demanding recognition of the principles which are the very basis of its existence. By means of this semi-objectification one can situate oneself simultaneously inside and outside, in the game and on the touchline, i.e., on the margin, at the frontier, in regions which, like the 'frame', *parergon,* are so many limits, the beginning of the end, the end of the beginning, points from which one can be as distant as possible from the interior without falling into the exterior, into outer darkness, that is, into the vulgarity of the non-philosophical, the coarseness of 'empirical', 'ontic', 'positivist' discourse, and where one can combine the profits of transgression with the profits of membership by producing the discourse that is simultaneously closest to an exemplary performance of philosophical discourse and to an exposure of the objective truth of this discourse.[35]

Whereas the orthodox reading takes literally the overt logic of the sacred text—the 'order of reasons' it puts forward, the plan which it announces and through which it continues to impose its order on its own decoding—the heretical reading takes liberties with the norms and forms imposed by the guardians of the text. On one side, there is the 'right' reading, the one which Kant has designated in advance, by manifesting the apparent architectonics and logic of his discourse, with a whole apparatus of skilfully articulated titles and sub-titles and a permanent display of the external signs of deductive rigour; by basing on his previous writings (with a neat effect of circular self-legitimation) a problematic which is, to a large extent, the artificial product of the divisions and oppositions (between understanding and reason, theory and practice etc.) produced precisely by his own writings, and which have to be known and recognized by anyone (after Hegel and so many others) who seeks to be known and recognized as a philosopher. On the other side, there is a deliberately skewed approach, decentred, liberated and even subversive, which ignores the signposts and refuses the imposed order, fastens on the details neglected by ordinary commentators, notes, examples, parentheses, and thus finds itself obliged—

if only to justify the liberty it takes—to denounce the arbitrariness of the orthodox reading and even of the overt logic of the discourse analysed, to raise difficulties and even to bring to light some of the social slips which, despite all the effort at rationalization and euphemization, betray the denied intentions which ordinary commentary, by definition, overlooks.[36]

The Pleasure of the Text

Although it marks a sharp break with the ordinary ritual of idolatrous reading, this pure reading still concedes the essential point to the philosophical work.[37] Asking to be treated as it treats its object, i.e., as a work of art, making Kant's object its own objective, i.e., cultivated pleasure, cultivating cultivated pleasure, artificially exalting this artificial pleasure by a roué's ultimate refinement which implies a lucid view on this pleasure, it offers above all an exemplary specimen of the pleasure of art, the pleasure of the love of art, of which, like all pleasure, it is not easy to speak. It is a pure pleasure, in the sense that it is irreducible to the pursuit of the profits of distinction and is felt as the simple pleasure of play, of playing the cultural game well, of playing on one's skill at playing, of cultivating a pleasure which 'cultivates' and of thus producing, like a kind of endless fire, its ever renewed sustenance of subtle allusions, deferent or irreverent references, expected or unusual associations.

Proust, who never ceased to cultivate and also analyse cultivated pleasure, is as lucid as ever in describing this. Endeavouring to understand and communicate the idolatrous pleasure he takes in reading a famous page (a passage from Ruskin's *Stones of Venice*), he has to evoke not only the properties of the work itself, but the whole network of criss-crossing references woven around it—reference of the work to the personal experiences it has accompanied, facilitated or produced in the reader, reference of personal experience to the works it has insidiously coloured with its connotations, and references of experience of the work to a previous experience of the same work or experience of other works, each of them enriched with all the associations and resonances it carries with it: 'It is itself mysterious, full of images both of beauty and religion like that same church of St. Mark where all the figures of the Old and New Testaments appear against the background of a sort of splendid obscurity and changing brilliance. I remember *having read it for the first time* in St. Mark's itself, during an hour of storm and darkness when the mosaics shone only with their own material light and with an inner gold, earthy and ancient, to which the Venetian sun, which sets ablaze even the angels on the campaniles, added nothing of itself; the emotion I felt in reading that page there, among all the angels which drew their light from the surrounding shadows, was very great and perhaps not very pure.

As the joy of seeing those beautiful, mysterious figures increased, but was altered by *the pleasure, so to speak, of erudition* which I felt in understanding the texts inscribed in Byzantine characters beside their haloed foreheads, so the beauty of Ruskin's images was intensified and corrupted by the pride of referring to the sacred text. A sort of egoistic self-regard is inevitable in *these mingled joys of art and erudition* in which aesthetic pleasure may become more acute but not remain so pure.'[38]

Cultivated pleasure feeds on these intertwined references, which reinforce and legitimate each other, producing, inseparably, belief in the value of works of art, the 'idolatry' which is the very basis of cultivated pleasure, and the inimitable charm they objectively exert on all who are qualified to enter the game, possessed by their possession. Even in its purest form, when it seems most free of 'worldly' interest, this game is always a 'society' game, based, as Proust again says, on a 'freemasonry of customs and a heritage of traditions': 'True distinction, besides, always affects to address only distinguished persons who know the same customs, and *it does not "explain"*. A book of Anatole France implies a host of learned knowledge, includes *unending allusions* that the vulgar do not perceive there, and these, its other beauties apart, make up its incomparable nobility.'[39] Those whom Proust calls 'the aristocracy of intellect' know how to mark their distinction in the most peremptory fashion by addressing to the 'élite', made up of those who can decipher them, the discreet but irrefutable signs of their membership of the 'élite' (like the loftiness of emblematic references, which designate not so much sources or authorities as the very exclusive, very select circle of recognized interlocutors) and of the discretion with which they are able to affirm their membership.

'Empirical' interest enters into the composition of the most disinterested pleasures of pure taste, because the principle of the pleasure derived from these refined games for refined players lies, in the last analysis, in the denied experience of a social relationship of membership and exclusion. The sense of distinction, an acquired disposition which functions with the obscure necessity of instinct, is affirmed not so much in the manifestos and positive manifestations of self-confidence as in the innumerable stylistic or thematic choices which, being based on the concern to underline difference, exclude all the forms of intellectual (or artistic) activity regarded at a given moment as inferior—vulgar objects, unworthy references, simple didactic exposition, 'naive' problems (naive essentially because they lack philosophical pedigree), 'trivial' questions (Does the *Critique of Judgement* get it right? Is the aim of a reading of the *Critique* to give a true account of what Kant says?), positions stigmatized as 'empiricism' or 'historicism' (no doubt because they threaten the very existence of philosophical activity) and so on. In short, the philosophical sense of distinction is another form of the visceral disgust at vulgarity which defines pure taste as an internalized social relationship, a social relationship made flesh; and a philosophically distinguished reading of the *Critique of Judgement* cannot be expected to uncover the social relationship of distinction at the heart of a work that is rightly regarded as the very symbol of philosophical distinction.

Appendices

Notes

Index

Appendix 1
Some Reflections on the Method

For an earlier version of this text, it was decided to adopt, for once, an order of presentation as close as possible to the actual process of research, and to present progressively, in the order in which they were performed, the operations which led to a systematic explanation of the data collected in various statistical and ethnographic surveys. It was hoped that in this way there might be more ready acceptance of a body of theoretical hypotheses which, if presented at the outset, might have appeared arbitrary or forced; but which could never have been extracted from the material analysed if they had not been present, in the form of heuristic schemes, from the very beginning of the research. Although the present order of exposition, which starts out from the point of arrival of the research, is less favourable to the smug display of data and procedures which is usually regarded as the best guarantee of scientificity, and although the additional rigour it implies is offset by a whole series of ellipses and shortcuts tending to reinforce the suspicions of those who remain attached to a naively empiricist conception of scientific work, it eventually presented itself as the only sequence which allows each fact to be replaced in the system of relations from which it derives its truth-value. For this reason, it is necessary to outline the main operations of the research, without seeking to disguise the artificiality of this retrospective reconstruction.

The survey on which the work was based was carried out in 1963, after a preliminary survey by extended interview and ethnographic observation, on a sample of 692 subjects (both sexes) in Paris, Lille and a small provincial town. To obtain a sample large enough to make it possible to analyse variations in practices and opinions in relation to sufficiently homogeneous social units, a complementary survey was carried out in 1967–68, bringing the total number of subjects to 1,217 (see table A.1). Because the survey measured relatively stable dispositions, this time-lag does not seem to have affected the responses (except perhaps for the question on singers, an area of culture where fashions change more rapidly).[1]

An initial analysis showed that certain categories were extremely

Table A.1 Main characteristics of survey sample: percent in each class fraction, by sex, age, education and social origin.

Class fraction	N	Sex		Age			Highest educational qualification						Social origin (father's class)		
		M	F	<31	31-45	46+	CEP, CAP	BEPC	Bac	Incomplete higher ed.	Licence	>Licence	Working classes	Middle classes	Upper classes
Unskilled, semi-skilled	66	69.7	30.3	45.5	36.4	18.2	100	0	0	0	0	0	70.0	30.0	0
Skilled, foremen	69	73.9	26.1	27.5	36.2	36.2	73.5	26.5	0	0	0	0	59.3	41.7	0
Domestic servants	31	19.4	80.6	38.7	29.0	32.3	96.6	3.4	0	0	0	0	41.2	53.0	5.9
Small shopkeepers	44	48.8	51.2	16.3	30.2	53.5	65.1	18.6	14.0	2.3	0	0	11.8	82.3	5.9
Independent craftsmen	56	71.9	28.1	12.3	42.1	45.7	87.7	7.0	5.3	0	0	0	44.2	53.5	2.3
Commercial employees	40	47.5	52.5	47.5	32.5	20.0	57.5	32.5	10.0	0	0	0	30.3	57.5	12.1
Office workers	200	34.0	66.0	50.0	24.0	26.0	50.0	32.0	16.0	2.0	0	0	12.2	68.3	19.6
Junior administrative executives	47	70.2	29.8	10.6	44.7	44.7	30.5	39.1	30.4	0	0	0	23.8	66.7	9.5
Technicians	38	81.6	18.4	36.8	39.5	21.1	27.8	47.2	22.2	2.8	0	0	19.4	58.1	22.6
Primary teachers	40	37.5	62.5	42.5	37.5	20.0	0	5.0	75.0	20.0	0	0	17.6	70.6	11.8
Junior commercial executives	20	65.0	35.0	30.0	60.0	10.0	20.0	15.0	40.0	20.0	5.0	0	5.0	60.0	35.0
Secretaries	14	0	100.0	50.0	42.9	7.1	7.1	28.6	57.1	7.1	0	0	14.3	50.0	35.7
Medical and social services	45	22.2	77.8	40.0	40.0	20.0	4.7	25.6	46.5	16.3	7.0	0	10.8	40.5	48.6
Art craftsmen	23	60.9	39.1	47.8	30.4	21.7	40.9	13.6	18.2	22.7	4.5	0	10.5	47.9	42.1
Cultural intermediaries	17	76.5	23.5	23.5	52.9	23.5	11.8	11.8	23.5	35.3	17.6	0	18.8	18.8	62.6
Commercial employers	72	66.7	33.3	13.9	30.6	55.6	16.7	25.0	36.1	11.1	2.8	8.3	5.9	47.0	47.0
Industrial employers	30	73.3	26.7	3.3	40.0	56.6	13.8	13.8	37.9	24.1	3.4	6.9	3.6	17.9	78.6
Public-sector executives	80	85.0	15.0	5.3	47.4	47.3	0	0	25.0	10.0	60.0	5.0	11.8	35.3	52.9
Engineers	72	91.7	8.3	27.8	38.9	33.3	8.4	0	2.8	38.9	38.9	11.1	12.5	25.1	62.5
Private-sector executives	80	70.0	30.0	20.0	35.0	45.0	0	11.1	16.7	27.8	44.4	0	5.6	11.1	83.3
Professions	52	69.2	30.8	19.2	36.5	44.2	1.9	0	0	5.8	71.2	21.2	2.2	26.1	71.8
Secondary teachers	48	52.1	47.9	37.5	45.8	16.7	0	0	4.3	4.3	47.8	43.5	12.5	48.0	39.7
Higher-education teachers	19	84.2	15.8	0	47.4	52.6	0	0	0	0	0	100	0	26.3	73.7
Artistic producers	14	78.6	21.4	28.6	42.9	28.6	14.2	7.1	21.4	28.6	21.4	7.1	16.7	0	83.3
Total working classs		62.0	38.0	36.7	34.9	27.1	88.1	11.2	0.6	0	0	0	61.8	37.4	0.8
Total established petite bourgeoisie		49.0	51.0	36.3	32.0	31.6	48.7	27.3	21.0	3.0	0	0	19.7	72.7	7.6
Total new petite bourgeoisie		58.0	42.0	28.7	43.7	17.6	15.5	10.8	37.0	10.8	6.9	0	11.4	43.8	44.8

heterogeneous, as regards both their objective characteristics and their preferences, in particular the independent craftsmen and shopkeepers (*artisans et petits commerçants*), the junior executives (*cadres moyens*), the senior executives (*cadres supérieurs*) and the teachers (*professeurs*). It was decided to isolate, despite their small number, the artistic producers (classed among 'intellectual occupations' by INSEE and grouped with the *professeurs*), the cultural intermediaries (grouped with primary teachers by INSEE) and the art craftsmen and small art-dealers (*artisans et petits commerçants d'art*); and to distinguish, among the *cadres moyens*, between junior administrative executives, junior commercial executives and secretaries; among the *cadres supérieurs*, between private-sector and public-sector senior executives; and, among the *professeurs*, between secondary-school teachers and higher-education teachers (although there were very few of the latter).

The sample contained approximately the same number of Parisians and provincials,[2] and was devised so as to allow analysis of practices and choices by class fraction. The upper and middle classes were therefore over-represented so as to give an adequate sample of each of their fractions without distorting the composition of the class. In particular, this made it possible to study the taste of socio-occupational groups which were very small in number at the time of the survey, but which, like the new petite bourgeoisie, were found to occupy strategic positions and which have in fact grown steadily in number and importance.

In the case of the *classes populaires*, there was under-representation of the most disadvantaged category, that of the semi-skilled workers[3] and unskilled labourers, who are very uniform with regard to the object of the survey, i.e., very uniformly excluded from legitimate culture. And the working class as a whole does not have the weight it would have in a representative sample. This of course implied that not all the data concerning the whole sample would be published (such information is, strictly speaking, always meaningless). Furthermore, the farmers and farm workers were excluded from the analysis, after a preliminary survey which showed that the questionnaire was completely inappropriate and that quite other methods were required to identify the dispositions of a population totally excluded from legitimate culture and even, to a large extent, from 'middle-brow' culture (*la culture moyenne*).[4] This experiment did, however, bring to light the only and most fundamental piece of information which can be derived from putting questions on legitimate culture to a category that is excluded from it, namely, the almost universal recognition of the dominant culture. It also made it possible to observe, at maximum intensity, the effect of imposition of a problematic which any questioning of this sort produces when it forgets to question itself and forces itself authoritatively on agents for whom it would not exist outside of that situation (an effect which, as was subsequently shown by secondary analysis of numerous 'opinion polls', leads to the production of pure artifacts).

For each socio-occupational category, the distribution by sex, age and qualifications was checked against the results of the 1968 census for the whole of France. This verification was not possible in the case of the categories constituting the new petite bourgeoisie, which the censuses do not break down by age and qualification.[5]

The questionnaire was based on the hypothesis of the unity of tastes and included, in addition to a set of questions on personal photography and attitudes to photography which have been analysed in another study,[6] twenty-five questions on tastes in interior decoration, clothing, singers, cooking, reading, cinema, painting, music, photography, radio, pastimes etc. (see the questionnaire, reproduced at the end of this appendix). When endeavouring to grasp systems of tastes, a survey by closed questionnaire is never more than a second best, imposed by the need to obtain a large amount of comparable data on a sample large enough to be treated statistically. It leaves out almost everything to do with the modality of practices; but in an area which is that of art, in the sense of a personal way of being and doing, as in 'art of living', the way things are done and the way they are talked about, blasé or off-hand, serious or fervent, often makes all the difference (at least when dealing with *common* practices, such as viewing TV or cinema). That is the first reason why everything that is said here about differences between the classes or class fractions in fact *applies a fortiori*.

Furthermore, in order to give the systems of dispositions constituting taste as much scope as possible within the limits of a questionnaire, a series of gambles was made, in which the exploration of a whole area (e.g., music, cinema, cooking, clothing) was entrusted to two or three questions (sometimes only one) which often had to stand in for a whole battery of tests and observations. For example, the subjects were asked to choose, from a list of adjectives established a posteriori on the basis of non-directive interviews and tests (showing photographs of socially marked faces, building a composite ['identikit'] picture of the 'ideal' male or female face by adding socially marked features, hairstyle, moustache, whiskers, beard etc.), those which seemed to them best suited to their friends. This could not be expected to yield more than an attenuated, blurred image of the deep dispositions which guide the choice of spouses, friends or colleagues (partly because the list of adjectives, however carefully prepared, was imperfect and forced a number of respondents into the negative choice of the least unacceptable option).[7]

However, the loss of precision and detail in the analysis of particular areas, each of which would require a whole set of surveys, observations and tests, is offset by a gain in systematicity. Just as in a single field, painting for example, the particular configuration of preferences (Renoir does not mean the same thing when combined with Leonardo and Picasso as when linked with Utrillo and Buffet) is a substitute for the indications of manner which would be yielded by direct observation and questioning; so too, the meaning of each particular application of the single system of dispositions emerges in its relationship with all the others. Nothing more clearly manifests the systematicity of the habitus than the systematic redundancy within unlimited invention which defines all its products, judgements or practices.

It is, however, by mobilizing around a systematic survey all the statistical data available on each of the areas directly explored, and also on areas excluded from the initial definition of the object of inquiry, such as knowledge of economics, theatre-going, attitudes to child-rearing or sexuality etc., that one is best able to check and fill out the data provided by the main survey. This makes it possible to compensate for any patchiness or superficiality (depending on the strength of the indicators used) of information gathered directly from such a wide range of fields; and to do so without falling into the abstract unreality of 'secondary analysis' of the disparate data mechanically accumulated by 'data banks' devoid of theoretic capital, positivistic institutions which are the pride and joy of research bureaucracies.[8]

The fact remains that some of the inherent limitations of secondary analysis cannot be overcome. Thus, like the various surveys by INSEE (Institut national de la statistique et des études économiques) the survey conducted by SOFRES (Société française d'enquêtes par sondages) in 1966 at the request of a number of firms, for the strictly limited purpose of discovering consumer intentions (C.S. V), gives little information as to the frequency and occasion of consumption or on the quality of the goods consumed, which often make all the difference (e.g., theatre-going covers both avant-garde and boulevard theatre); it does not distinguish between museum visits and visits to exhibitions, which (as we know from the INSEE survey on leisure, C.S. IV), do not always vary in the same way—museum-going, a more ascetic activity, being more common among teachers, whereas exhibitions attract more members of the professions and a fraction of the old business bourgeoisie—and it gives no indication of how often they are visited. It lumps concerts, opera and ballet together in one question, although one would probably find an opposition between concerts and opera analogous to that between museums and exhibitions.

Similarly, the reading of works of philosophy does not mean much until one knows *which* 'philosophy'. There is reason to think, for example, that each fraction of the dominant class has 'its' philosophers or even its idea of the philosopher and philosophy, and that one group will think of Teilhard de Chardin, or even Saint-Exupéry or Louis Leprince-Ringuet, whereas another will think of Sartre or Michel Foucault. Thus, in 1967 when the arts students of the Ecole Normale Supérieure (ENS), to a large extent drawn from the dominated fractions of the dominant class, were asked whom they would like to see invited to speak in their college, they thought first of Sartre, Claude Lévi-Strauss, Paul Ricoeur and Foucault; whereas the students of the Ecole Nationale d'Administration (ENA), mainly the sons of senior civil servants or members of the professions, named Raymond Aron, François Bloch-Lainé, Pierre Massé or Paul Delouvrier. Sartre, top of the list at ENS, was only fifth at ENA—which put three politicians at the top of its list, Mendès France (second at ENS), Giscard d'Estaing and de Gaulle.

Another limitation of the SOFRES survey (C.S. V) is that it does not provide all the information needed to construct the system of explanatory principles—volume and structure of assets, and social trajectory. There is virtually no information on the respondents' economic wealth (land and property, industrial and commercial profits etc.) or their cultural capital, whether objectified (works of art, antique furniture, piano etc.) or embodied (educational level) or on their social origins and previous careers.

The CESP (Centre d'études des supports de publicité) survey of 1970 (C.S. VI) fills in some of these gaps, but very imperfectly, since only the distribution by newspaper read is available (and not by class or class fraction). The survey carried out for the Ministry of Culture (C.S. VII) contains some very useful information (e.g., on ownership of works of art), but does not allow analysis by fractions (precise information on occupations was not collected).

Finally, the INSEE survey on leisure activities (C.S. IV), although providing the most remarkable set of data ever collected on cultural consumption, is limited by the nature of its classification (the industrialists, for example, end up in a curious position because the category used includes all those employing more than five people); by the fact that it deals with declared practices, which are not related to real practices in the same way in all classes; and by the lack of information on the quality of the activity, which means that the scatter of practices is underestimated. By reducing the different classes of practices and goods to their frequency, i.e., quantity, in areas where almost everything depends on quality, one systematically reduces the difference between the classes (though without affecting the ordinal relations). Thus, differences in the quantity of museum visits are compounded by differences in their quality. The privileged classes, being less subject to collective rhythms, distribute their visits more uniformly through the year and the week and so escape the disenchanting experience of crowds in peak periods. These differences in rhythm are themselves associated with marked differences in the quality of the exhibition areas—different 'levels' of museums, more and less 'distinguished' exhibitions—and in the quality of the genres, styles and authors. But it is, above all, the manner of conducting the visit—in particular, the time devoted to it—and the manner of conducting oneself while visiting which provide inexhaustible material for the games of distinction.

In view of the limits of the data collected and of any information obtained in such an artificial situation as interrogation by questionnaire, recourse was had throughout the analysis—whenever a difficulty arose or a new hypothesis required it—to observations and questionings in real situations (see, for example, the interviews interpolated in part II). But above all there was a rule that had to be unlearnt, the unwritten rule that only data collected in socially defined scientific conditions, i.e., by prepared questioning and observation, may enter into the scientific construction. This rule, which would not be so impressed on the scientific unconscious if it did not have the advantage of putting the sociologist out of the game, and therefore out of reach of the socio-analysis which every analysis properly implies, had to be transgressed in order to bring up all the information which the sociologist, as a social subject, inevitably possesses, and which, when verified by comparing it with the measurable data of observation, has a place in scientific discourse.

Only a research diary could give an adequate idea of the countless choices, all equally humble and derisory, all equally difficult and decisive, and therefore the countless theoretical reflections, often minute and unworthy of the name of theory in the ordinary sense of the word, which had to be made, over several years, when I was faced with a questionnaire difficult to classify, an unexpected curve, a badly phrased question, a distribution that was incomprehensible at first sight, in order to produce a text whose success must be measured by the extent to which it allows the reader to forget the thousands of revisions, alterations, checks and corrections which made it possible, while manifesting at every point the high 'reality content' which distinguishes it from the 'not even wrong' sociological essay. And so I have simply presented, as the argument called for them, the items of information that are needed to understand or check the stages of the statistical analysis, endeavouring to avoid both the methodological flourishes which often mask the absence of any real reflection on the operations and also the theoretical elevation which deprives the reader of every means of verification. (For example, although I have refrained from giving it the air of a formal protocol, I have endeavoured to provide the informed reader—without disconcerting readers less familiar with the technique—with all the information required to check the results of those analyses of correspondences which are presented in detail: the dimensions of the table, the number of questions and total number of corresponding modalities, the number of individuals, the nature and coding of the table, the list of variables, a description of the hypotheses underlying the distinction between active and illustrative variables, a list of the specific values and the rates of inertia, the main absolute contributions and relative contributions.)[9]

There remains one final problem, which would no doubt merit a long discussion: that of writing. The main difficulty, especially on such a subject, is that the language used must signal a *break* with ordinary experience, which is no less necessary in order to appropriate adequately the knowledge produced than to produce it; and at the same time *bring home* the corresponding social experience to those who do not, or do not want, to know about it. The 'concrete' analyses (although there is nothing concrete about them in the ordinary sense of the word, since they pre-suppose construction) are there to assist the return into experience of the product of scientific description, and to make more difficult the distanc-ing and neutralization which the semi-theoretical language of fake sci-ence generally encourages. The same is true of all the documents (facsimiles of books or articles, photographs, extracts from interviews etc.) which have been inserted in the text, in order to discourage absent-minded readings which are abstract in the sense that they have no refer-ent in reality.

Art is one of the major sites of denial of the social world. But the same unconscious intention of disavowal lies behind a number of discourses which overtly set out to speak of the social world, and which, as a result, may be written, and read, schizophrenically. (How many philosophers, sociologists or philologists came to philosophy, sociology or philology because it was one of those obscurely situated areas of the social space which make it possible to avoid definition? All these de facto utopians, who do not want to know where they are, are not in the best position to understand the social space in which they are positioned. Would we oth-erwise have so many readings and *lectores* or 'reproducers', materialists without material, thoughts without instruments of thought and there-fore without an object—and so little observation, so few *auctores* or 'pro-ducers'?) It is not possible to advance the science of the social world, and to make it known, except by forcing the return of the repressed, by neu-tralizing neutralization, denying denial in all its forms, not the least of which is the de-realization through hyperbolic radicalization performed by some revolutionary discourse. Neither true nor false, neither verifiable nor falsifiable, neither theoretical nor empirical, such discourse—like Ra-cine, who never referred to 'cows' but only to 'heifers'—cannot talk of the SMIC (statutory minimum wage) and the vests (undershirts) of working-class men but only of the mode of production and the proletar-iat or of the roles and attitudes of the 'lower middle class'. To break with this genteel abstraction, it is not sufficient to demonstrate: one has to show—but not denounce—things and even people, make them palpable, and take into a working-class café, onto a rugby pitch or a golf course, or into a private club, people who are so used to saying what they think they think that they no longer know how to think what they say.

The subjective and objective difficulty of writing is not solely due to the fact that language is being asked to say what it is normally used to deny or negate. It is not easy to find the right tone, to avoid both celebra-tion and provocation (which is merely its inversion), when the very questions that have to be asked in order to construct the object are re-jected in advance, within the object itself, as barbarisms. Scientific discourse on art and on the social uses of art is bound to appear both vulgar and terroristic. Vulgar, because it transgresses the sacred boundary which distinguishes the pure reign of art and culture from the lower region of the social and of politics, a distinction which is the very source of the effects of symbolic domination exerted by or in the name of culture. Terroristic, because it presumes to reduce to 'uniform' classes everything that is 'liberated' and 'alternative', 'multiple' and 'different', and to confine the supreme experience of 'play' and *jouissance* within the grey propositions of a 'knowledge' which if it aims to be 'positive' must be 'positivist', 'totalizing' and therefore 'totalitarian'. If there is any terrorism, it is in the peremptory verdicts which, in the name of taste, condemn to ridicule, indignity, shame, silence (here one could give examples, taken from everyone's familiar universe), men and women who simply fall short, in the eyes of their judges, of the right way of being and doing; it is in the symbolic violence through which the dominant groups endeavour to impose their own life-style, and which abounds in the glossy weekly magazines: 'Conforama is the Guy Lux of furniture',[10] says *Le Nouvel Observateur,* which will never tell you that the *Nouvel Obs* is the Club Méditerranée of culture. There is terrorism in all such remarks, flashes of self-interested lucidity sparked off by class hatred or contempt. Only the effort required to construct the field of struggles within which the partial viewpoints and antagonistic strategies are defined can give access to a knowledge which differs from the blind insights of the participants without becoming the sovereign gaze of the impartial observer. Objectification is only complete when it objectifies the site of objectification, the unseen standpoint, the blind spot of all theories—the intellectual field and its conflicts of interest, in which sometimes, by a necessary accident, an interest in truth is generated—and also the subtle contributions it makes to the maintenance of the symbolic order, even through the purely symbolic intention of subversion which is usually assigned to it in the division of the labour of domination.

When dealing with such an object, scientific work on the object is inseparable from work on the working subject. It depends above all on the capacity he has to dominate practically, in his practice, the mechanisms he is endeavouring to objectify, which may continue to govern his relation to the object. One might offer for meditation, like 'Parallel Lives' in the past, the history of the Princeton Project, a vast empirical study of the consumption of music, which brought together Adorno and Lazarsfeld, an epistemological couple made flesh. An arrogant theoretician who refuses to sully his hands with empirical trivia and who remains too viscerally attached to the values and profits of Culture to be able to make it an object of science; and a submissive empiricist, ready for every abdication demanded by a scientific order strictly subordinated to the social order. An arrogant positivist who attempts to set up as the norm of all scientific practice a methodology of resentment based on a sort of vengeful fury against any global inquiry; and a submissive Marxist who goes in for vulgar Marxism when refinement is needed and elegant Marxism when vulgarity is called for. Each sees the shortcomings of the other.

The epistemological obstacles which social science has to overcome are initially social obstacles. One of these is the common conception of the hierarchy of the tasks which make up the sociologist's job, which leads so many researchers to disdain humble, easy yet fertile activities in favour of exercises that are both difficult and sterile. Another is an anomic reward system which forces a choice between a safe thesis and a flash in the pan, pedantry and prophecy, discouraging the combination of broad ambition and long patience that is needed to produce a work of science. Unlike the sometimes illuminating *intuitions* of the essay form, the sometimes coherent *theses* of theoreticism and the sometimes valid *observations* of empiricism, provisional systems of scientific propositions which strive to combine internal coherence and adequacy to the facts can only be produced by a slow, difficult labour which remains unremarked by all hasty readings. These will only see repetitive reaffirmations of theses, intuitions or already known facts in the provisional conclusion of a long series of totalizations, because they ignore what is essential, namely, the structure of the relations between the propositions.

The Questionnaire

Sex:

Year of birth:

Marital status:
        single   married
        widowed   divorced

Number and age of children:

Place of residence:

How long have you lived there?
        less than 5 years
        5 to 10 years
        more than 10 years

Previous place of residence:

Highest educational qualification:

Occupation (be as precise as possible):

Highest educational qualification and occupation of your father and paternal grandfather (or last occupation):
        father   qualification   occupation
        paternal grandfather

Approximate annual income of your family:
  less than 10,000 F   20–25,000 F   40–50,000 F
  10–15,000 F   25–30,000 F   50–60,000 F
  15–20,000 F   30–40,000 F   more than 60,000 F

Do you own:
  a record-player   an automobile (indicate make)
  a tape recorder   a TV
  a camera   a movie camera

Do you have a telephone?

---

1. Where did you get your furniture?
     department store   flea market
       (give name)   auction
     antique dealer   inherited
     specialized shop   rented
       (give name)   other (specify)
     craftsman

2. Is your furniture:
     modern
     antique
     country-style

3. If you had the choice, which style of furniture would you rather buy:
     modern
     antique
     country-style

4. Which three adjectives best describe the type of interior you would like to live in:
     clean and tidy   warm   neat (*soigné*)
     comfortable   easy to maintain imaginative (*fantaisie*)
     studied (*composé*) classical   practical and functional
     sober and discreet harmonious   cosy (*intime*)

5. Of the qualities listed above, which three are least important to you?

6. Of the activities listed below, which do you do often, which do you do rarely, and which do you never do?

                               often   rarely   never
     do-it-yourself
     sport (specify)
     camping
     walking
     painting or sculpture

often   rarely   never

playing a musical instrument
  (specify)
parlour games (specify)
watching TV

7. Which are your three favourites among the following singers?
   Charles Aznavour   Edith Piaf   Luis Mariano
   Léo Ferré   Jacques Brel   Petula Clark
   Johnny Hallyday   Georges Guétary   Jacques Douai
   Georges Brassens   Françoise Hardy   Gilbert Bécaud

8. Do you prefer clothes that are:
   classically cut and good value for money
   that reflect fashion and suit your personality
   sober and correct
   daring and out of the ordinary (*recherché*)
   comfortable
   chic and stylish
   other (specify)

9. Are your clothes:

   everyday   best

   home-made, by yourself or one of the
     family
   made up by a small tailor or dressmaker
   made to measure by a large fashion-house
     or tailor
   from a chain-store (*confection*)
   from a boutique (*prêt à porter*)

10. When you have guests for a meal, what kind of meals do you prefer
    to serve:
    simple but well-presented   appetizing and economical
    delicate and exquisite   original and exotic
    plentiful and good   traditional French cuisine
    pot-luck   other (specify)

11. In the following list of adjectives, underline the ones indicating the
    personal qualities you most appreciate:
    bon vivant   refined   conscientious
    level-headed   sociable   amusing (*drôle*)
    artistic   pragmatic   determined
    dynamic   well-bred   stylish

12. Of the qualities listed above, which three are least important to you?

13. Which are your three favourites among the following types of
    books?
    thrillers   poetry
    love stories   political

travel, exploration   philosophical
historical novels   classical authors
scientific   modern authors

14. Which are your three favourite types of films?
    adventure   spectaculars
    war   musicals
    Westerns   comedies
    thrillers   films with a message
    historical   dramas
    nouvelle vague

15. Which films in this list have you seen? For each film, give the names of the director and leading actors, if known. [This list was used in Paris. In the Lille area, another list was used that reflected the films available in local cinemas.]

	seen	director	actors
Divorce Italian Style			
Rocco and His Brothers			
Singing in the Rain			
The Leopard			
The Suitor			
L'abominable homme des douanes			
Exterminating Angel			
Ballade pour un voyou			
55 Days at Peking			
Les dimanches de Ville d'Avray			
Le glaive et la balance			
The Trial			
The Magnificent Seven			
Le voyage à Biarritz			
Le boucanier des îles			
Salvatore Giuliano			
The Longest Day			
Vice and Virtue			
Imperial Venus			

16. What interests you most in a film?
    the actors
    the director
    the plot

17. If you listen to the radio, which programmes do you mainly listen to?
    light music   cultural programmes
    news   classical music
    current affairs   other (specify)

18. If you watch TV, which programmes do you mainly watch?

19. Which of the opinions below is closest to your own view?
    Classical music is complicated.
    Classical music isn't for people like us.
    I love classical music but I don't know much about it.
    I like classical music, Strauss waltzes for example.
    All music of quality interests me.

20. Which of the musical works in this list do you know? In each case,
    name the composer, if you can.

	known	composer
Rhapsody in Blue		
La Traviata		
Concerto for the Left Hand		
Eine Kleine Nachtmusik		
L'Arlésienne		
Sabre Dance		
Firebird Suite		
Scheherazade		
Art of Fugue		
Hungarian Rhapsody		
L'Enfant et les sortilèges		
Blue Danube		
Twilight of the Gods		
Four Seasons		
Well-Tempered Clavier		
Le Marteau sans maître		

21. Which are your three favourites among the above works?

22. Which of the opinions below is closest to your own view?
    Paintings don't interest me.
    Galleries aren't my strong point; I can't appreciate them.
    Paintings are nice but difficult; I don't know enough to talk
       about them.
    I love the Impressionists.
    Abstract painting interests me as much as the classical schools.

23. Which are your three favourites among the painters listed below?

Leonardo	Dali	Kandinsky	Vlaminck
Renoir	Goya	Raphael	Watteau
Buffet	Van Gogh	Braque	Picasso
Utrillo	Breughel	Rousseau	

24. Have you visited the following museums or galleries (if possible, say
    in which year and with whom—school, relatives, friends, alone)?

Louvre	Jacquemart-André
Jeu de Paume	museum of your city (or region)
Modern Art Museum	

25. What do you think of the following opinions:
    Modern painting is just slapped on anyhow; a child could do it.
    I don't need to know who painted it or how.
    I can't appreciate painting because I don't know enough about it.
26. With the following subjects, is a photographer more likely to produce a beautiful, interesting, meaningless or ugly photo?[11]

	beautiful	interesting	meaningless	ugly
a landscape				
a car crash				
a little girl playing with a cat				
a pregnant woman				
a still life				
a woman breastfeeding				
a metal structure				
tramps quarrelling				
cabbages				
a sunset over the sea				
a weaver at his loom				
a folk dance				
a rope				
a butcher's stall				
the bark of a tree				
a famous monument				
a scrapyard				
a first communion				
a wounded man				
a snake				
an 'old master'				

Observation Schedule
(to be completed by interviewer)

Home
    apartment
    house
    suburban detached (single-family) house (*pavillon*)
age:
quality:

municipal (council flat)	old	fairly prestigious
bourgeois	poor	very prestigious

number of rooms:
decoration:

furniture:

predominant style:

floor:

other observations:

Dress

men:

blue overalls	casual (sweat-shirt, jeans ...)
suit	smart 'town' clothes
pullover	tie
shape and colour of shirt:	
cuffs buttoned	double cuffs
rolled-up sleeves	

women:

housework clothes (housedresses)   skirt and blouse   dress
costume (suit)   slacks   very smart
        footwear: high heels   flat heels etc.
                  slippers
make-up and perfume:
well-groomed or not:

Hair

men:

short	medium	crew cut
very short	long	parting (side/middle)
sideburns	moustache (specify type)	beard
brilliantine		

women:

short	medium	frizzy
very short	long	bouffant
bun	bleached	straight
visible perm	dyed	

Speech

refined	standard
slang	mistakes in grammar (specify)

accent:

strong
slight
none

Appendix 2
Complementary Sources[1]

I. The survey on incomes, carried out in 1970 by INSEE (Institut national de la statistique et des études économiques) on a sample of about 45,000 households, was based on the records kept by the tax authorities. It therefore only deals with taxable income, excluding numerous transfers (social security allowances etc.) and also certain types of income from property. Some forms of income, in particular those derived from family-owned businesses, are represented by tax estimates which fall far short of reality. Despite these limitations, the survey provides original data on the structure of the income received by each socio-occupational category, the disparities in average incomes between categories and the dispersion within each category—see G. Banderier and P. Ghigliazza, 'Les revenus des ménages en 1970', *Collections de l'INSEE*, ser. M, no. 40 (December 1974). The data presented in my study (which concern households, not individuals—except for property income)[2] come from tables not published by INSEE (except for the indication of average total taxable income—see Banderier and Ghigliazza, p. 29), but supplied to me by P. Ghigliazza.

II. The 1970 INSEE survey on vocational training and skill was based on a sample of 38,000 individuals. It gives a precise description of the relationship between general and vocational training and occupational situation (occupation, skill, wage level, mobility etc.) and provides data on the subjects' occupational and geographical mobility (changes between 1965 and 1970) and on inter-generational mobility (occupation and qualification of father and subject). The initial findings have been published: R. Pohl, C. Thélot and M. F. Jousset, 'L'enquête formation-qualification professionnelle en 1970', *Collections de l'INSEE*, ser. D, no. 32 (May 1974). The data presented here relate to economically active men born in and after 1918. They result from secondary analysis of tables supplied at my request.

III. INSEE's regular survey on household living conditions and expenditure was based in 1972 on a representative sample of 13,000 households.[3] It consists of a survey by questionnaire dealing with the characteristics of the household (composition, ages, occupation of the head), accommodation and facilities, major expenditure (clothing, fuel etc.), periodic expenditure (rent, service charges etc.), combined with analysis of account books for current expenditure, left with each household for a week, collected and checked by the interviewer. This survey makes it possible to assess the whole range of expenditure (except certain major and infrequent items such as air travel, removal expenses etc.), as well as items of consumption not preceded by purchase (food in the case of farmers, items drawn from their stocks by craftsmen and shopkeepers), which are evaluated at their retail price to allow comparison with the other categories of households. This explains why consumption is considerably higher than income in the case of farmers and small businessmen (categories which are always particularly prone to under-declare their income). For the overall findings, see G. Bigata and B. Bouvier, 'Les conditions de vie des ménages en 1972', *Collections de l'INSEE,* ser. M, no. 32 (February 1972). The data presented here come from secondary analysis of tables by narrow categories produced at my request.

IV. The 1967 INSEE survey on 'leisure activities', based on a random sample of 6,637 individuals representing the whole adult French population, used a questionnaire containing questions on living conditions (household help, child-minding, distance from certain facilities—theatre, swimming pool etc.—possession of a second residence etc.), on the structure of the working week and year, and in particular on the various cultural practices, visits to museums, exhibitions and monuments, reading, attendance at various types of entertainments, use of cafés and restaurants, outings, parties, radio, television, the various pastimes—gardening, do-it-yourself, hunting, fishing, gambling on horses, literary or artistic activities, collecting etc. For the findings, see especially P. Debreu, 'Les comportements de loisir des Français', *Collections de l'INSEE,* ser. M, no. 25 (August 1979). The data presented here (which concern only the male population) are derived from secondary analysis of tables produced at my request.

V. The 1966 survey on 'businessmen and senior executives' was carried out by SOFRES on behalf of the Centre d'études des supports de publicité (CESP). The sample consisted of 2,257 persons aged 15 and over, each living in a household the head of which was a large industrial or commercial employer, a member of the professions, a senior executive, an engineer or a secondary or higher-education teacher. The questionnaire included a set of questions on reading habits and the previous few days' reading of daily, weekly and monthly newspapers and magazines, use of radio and TV, standard of living, household equipment, life-style (holidays, sport, consumption), professional life (conferences, travel, business meals), cultural practices and the principal basic data (educational level, income, population of place of residence etc.). I had access to the whole set of distributions by the socio-occupational category of the head of household or individual.

VI. The survey on readership of the press, conducted by SOFRES in 1970 on behalf of the CESP, used a sample of 2,682 persons, economically active or not, each living in a household the head of which was a large industrial or commercial employer, a member of the professions, an engineer, a senior executive or a secondary or higher-education teacher. At the end of the interview, the respondent was handed a questionnaire to be returned by post. The rate of response was 66 percent. The questionnaire dealt mainly with centres of interest ('subjects you enjoy talking about'), household and leisure equipment, main and second residences, holidays, business trips, cultural practices, reading, records, museums, cinema etc., art collections, sport, cars, economic behaviour etc. I had access to the distributions by daily or weekly paper (but not by socio-occupational category).

VII. The survey on cultural practices was carried out in 1973 on behalf of the Ministry of Culture, on a sample of 1,987 persons aged 15 and over. The questionnaire included a set of questions previously asked in 1967 by the INSEE survey on leisure and some more detailed questions on certain cultural activities (particularly on their content—e.g., the type of TV programmes watched, the type of records owned and listened to, the works of art owned etc.). The way in which the information was gathered (pre-coding of the socio-occupational categories into ten categories) did not permit a more precise analysis by class fraction. The main findings are published in: Secrétariat d'état à la culture, Service des études et de la recherche, *Pratiques culturelles des Français*, 2 vols. (Paris, 1974).

The other surveys consulted are simply listed below.[4] These studies, almost always devoted to a particular area of cultural activity, are generally based on relatively limited samples. They mostly use a classification which groups the occupations into five categories: (1) *agriculteurs* (farmers and farm labourers); (2) *ouvriers* (industrial manual workers); (3) industrial and commercial employers; (4) clerical workers and junior executives; (5) senior executives and the 'liberal professions'.

On the cinema
VIII. 'Cinéma français: Perspectives 1970', *Bulletin d'information du Centre national de la cinématographie,* special issue 91 (February 1965).
IX. IFOP, *Les acteurs et actrices préférés des Français,* October 1968.
X. IFOP, *Les acteurs et actrices préférés des Français,* September 1970.
XI. IFOP, 'La fréquentation et l'image du cinéma en 1970', *Bulletin d'information du Centre national de la cinématographie,* 126 (1970).
XII. 'Le public cinématographique', *Bulletin d'information du Centre national de la cinématographie,* 153–154 (June–August 1975).
XIII. SOFRES, *Les Français et le cinéma en 1975,* March 1975.
XIIIa. CESP, *Étude sur l'audience du cinéma,* XVI (Paris 1975).

On the theatre

XIV. SEMA (Société d'économie et de mathématiques appliquées), *Le théâtre et son public*, 2 vols. (Paris, 1966). (A major survey of Paris theatre audiences in 1964.)

XV. IFOP, *Étude auprès des spectateurs des 'parathéâtrales' au Théâtre de la Ville* (Paris, IFOP, 1969).

On radio and TV

XVI. 'Une enquête par sondage sur l'écoute radiophonique en France', *Études et conjoncture*, 10 (October 1963), 923–1002. (A major study in 1961 of a sample of 12,000 people.)

Of the numerous studies by the opinion research department of the ORTF between 1966 and 1974, the following were particularly used:

XVII. *Les téléspectateurs et les émissions musicales.* (A survey carried out in 1969 and 1970.)

XVIII. *Les dossiers de l'écran.* (A survey carried out in 1971.)

XIX. *Une enquête sur les variétés: traitement des données par l'analyse factorielle des correspondances*, July 1972.

XX. *Les auditeurs de France-musique: attitudes, opinions, habitudes d'écoute des émissions*, July 1972.

XXI. *Les festivals et la radio: phase exploratoire*, July 1974.

On reading habits

XXII. IFOP, *Les lecteurs et acheteurs de livres* (Paris, IFOP, 1967).

XXIII. IFOP, *La clientèle du livre* (Paris, Syndicat national des éditeurs, 1969).

XXIV. IFOP, *Les achats de livres pour la jeunesse* (Paris, IFOP, 1970).

XXV. SOFRES, *Les Français et la lecture* (Paris, SOFRES, 1972).

XXVI. SERVO, *Analyse sectorielle de l'édition*, vol. 1, *Étude des marchés: résultats qualitatifs*, vol. 2, *Étude des marchés: synthèse des résultats du sondage* (Paris, Cercle de la librairie, 1975).

XXVII. SOFRES, *L'image des écrivains dans l'opinion publique*, April 1976.

XXVIII. CESP, *Les lecteurs de la presse.* (Annual surveys on the reading of daily, weekly and monthly newspapers and magazines.)

On drama or music festivals

XXIX. J. Henrard, C. Martin, J. Mathelin, *Étude de trois festivals de musique: La Rochelle 1974, Saintes 1974, Royan 1975* (Paris, Centre d'études des techniques économiques modernes, 1975).

XXX. F.-X. Roussel, *Le public du festival mondial de théâtre de Nancy* (Nancy, Centre d'informations et d'études d'économie, 1975).

XXXI. SEMA, *Données statistiques sur le système musical français* (Paris, SEMA, 1967).

On decoration and furnishing
XXXII. ETMAR, *Le marché de l'ameublement dans les foyers domestiques: importance des dépenses et caractéristiques de la clientèle* (Paris, ETMAR, 1967).

On food and clothing
XXXIII. INSEE, 'La consommation alimentaire des Français', *Collections de l'INSEE.* (The regular INSEE surveys on eating habits.)

In addition to this source, and secondary analysis of the INSEE survey on household living conditions (III above), the following were also consulted:
XXXIV. SOFRES, *Les habitudes de table des Français* (Paris, 1972).
XXXIVa. SOFRES, *Les Français et la gastronomie,* July 1977. (Sample of 1,000.)
XXXV. Thi Nguyen Hun, 'Les dépenses d'habillement des Français en 1971–1972', *Collections de l'INSEE,* ser. M, no. 38 (November 1974).

On sport
In addition to data from secondary analysis of the INSEE survey on leisure (IV) and from the survey on cultural practices (VII), the following were consulted:
XXXVI. SOFRES, *Les Français et le sport,* February 1968.
XXXVII. IFOP, *Les attitudes des Français à l'égard du sport,* December 1972.
XXXVIII. SOFRES, *Les Français et le sport,* June 1975. (Sample of 2,000 people aged 15 and over.)

On the press
In addition to the CESP survey already mentioned (VI):
XXXIX. CESP, *Douzième étude sur les lecteurs de la presse,* 1976. (Sample of 5,562. The data presented in chapter 8 are derived from secondary analysis of tables by narrowly defined categories produced at my request.)
XL. IFOP, *Les lecteurs de quotidiens dans la campagne électorale,* February 1978.

On spending on self-presentation
XLI. SOFRES, *Pourquoi les Françaises veulent-elles maigrir?* March 1974. (Sample of 450 women aged 18–65.)
XLII. SOFRES, *Les femmes et la mode,* October 1974. (Sample of 1,100 women aged 18–50.)
XLIII. IFOP and Groupe d'études de Marie-Claire, *L'art de recevoir,* December 1977–January 1978.
XLIV. IFOP and Groupe d'études de Marie-Claire, *Les Françaises et la beauté,* December 1976. (Sample of 1,016 women aged 18–45.)

XLV. ETMAR, *Achats de vêtements,* 1971. (Sample of 552 women in Paris region.)

On morality

XLVI. IFOP, *Les Français et l'amour,* November 1975.

XLVII. SOFRES, *Attitudes envers l'homosexualité* (*L'Express,* December 7–11, 1973).

XLVIII. IFOP—France-Soir, *Les Français sont comme ça,* August-September 1974. (Sample of 1,217.)

XLIX. SOFRES, *L'image de la justice dans l'opinion publique,* February 1977.

L. SOFRES, *Les Français et la censure au cinéma,* September 1974.

LI. SOFRES, *Les Français et l'art moderne,* April 1972. (Sample of 1,000.)

Appendix 3
Statistical Data

The Survey

Table A.2 Tastes and cultural practices of classes and class fractions (%): I.[a]

					Aesthetic disposition: the following subjects would make a beautiful photo:						
Classes	N	Sunset	First communion	Folk dance	Little girl with cat	Woman breast-feeding	Bark of a tree	Metal frame	Pregnant woman	Cabbages	Car crash
Working classes[b]	166	90	50	63	56	44	17	6	11	7	0
Craftsmen, small shopkeepers	100	91	43	59	58	57	23	9	14	2	1
Clerical, junior executives	287	86	35	57	60	46	25	6	9	8	2
Technicians, primary teachers	78	88	19	51	74	75	49	25	30	13	4
New petite bourgeoisie[c]	119	72	20	36	54	61	45	22	24	24	2
Middle classes[d]	584	84	31	52	60	55	32	12	16	11	1
Industrial and comm. employers	102	80	27	38	47	40	30	10	15	4	2
Executives, engineers	232	59	12	41	50	57	53	20	10	17	1
Professions	52	73	17	36	61	58	54	23	33	19	6
Secondary and higher-ed. teachers, artistic producers	81	53	22	23	48	53	54	49	41	37	17
Upper classes[d]	467	64	18	37	50	53	48	23	19	18	4

a. The percentages exclude 'don't knows'.
b. Excluding farmers and farm labourers.
c. Includes social and medical services, cultural intermediaries, art craftsmen and dealers, secretaries and junior commercial executives.
d. Total for four groups preceding.

Preferred painters

Raphael	Buffet	Utrillo	Vlaminck	Watteau	Renoir	Van Gogh	Dali	Braque	Goya	Breughel	Kandinsky
32	8	20	6	16	49	48	3	5	16	1	0
23	23	26	6	24	53	47	0	8	14	8	0
34	19	18	14	23	56	42	3	5	12	6	0
15	15	18	12	12	49	57	7	1	29	15	3
22	11	16	10	13	42	50	8	12	28	25	6
27	17	18	12	19	51	47	4	7	19	12	2
19	14	21	17	23	59	31	3	12	18	19	6
23	10	24	8	14	47	56	5	6	34	27	2
12	6	16	22	16	61	57	6	8	22	31	10
8	1	10	5	10	30	47	9	13	44	36	6
18	9	20	11	16	48	49	5	9	31	27	4

Table A.3 Tastes and cultural practices of classes and class fractions (%): II.[a]

Classes	Doesn't interest me	Nice but difficult	Love the Impressionists	Like abstract art	Modern art's not just slapped on	Do like to know who painted it	L'Arlésienne	Blue Danube
					Opinions on art[b]			
Working classes	26	62	7	4	32	7	42	66
Craftsmen, small shopkeepers	16	73	5	5	44	2	41	60
Clerical, junior executives	17	65	12	7	35	8	36	53
Technicians, primary teachers	3	50	26	22	53	14	18	18
New petite bourgeoisie	4	30	32	34	64	13	14	22
Middle classes[d]	14	56	16	14	45	9	30	43
Industrial and comm. employers	4	51	27	17	42	6	23	24
Executives, engineers	8	27	39	26	55	11	20	20
Professions	0	31	40	29	58	13	4	17
Secondary and higher-ed. teachers, artistic producers	4	14	39	43	75	21	1	3
Upper classes[d]	5	31	37	27	55	12	15	17

a. The percentages exclude 'don't knows'.
b. Each respondent was invited to say which of several opinions was closest to his own.

					Preferred musical works[c]						
La Traviata	Sabre Dance	Rhapsody in Blue	Hungarian Rhapsody	Twilight of Gods	Eine Kleine Nacht-musik	Four Seasons	Firebird Suite	L'Enfant et les Sortilèges	Art of Fugue	Well-Tempered Clavier	Concerto for Left Hand
28	25	24	33	4	11	7	5	0	2	1	0
30	27	24	34	11	15	15	10	1	1	2	0
23	22	21	40	11	27	22	7	0	3	2	0
18	21	31	38	19	31	46	12	1	10	10	7
10	12	25	25	17	34	47	16	10	14	12	8
21	20	25	36	13	27	29	10	3	6	5	3
28	6	28	50	9	21	30	10	3	15	4	5
11	13	25	42	18	30	39	15	2	13	12	13
6	2	21	32	11	53	55	6	2	13	17	23
9	4	13	21	22	51	51	23	4	31	32	13
14	9	23	39	16	34	41	15	2	17	14	12

c. Each respondent was invited to choose three works from a list of 16.
d. Total for four groups preceding.

Table A.4 Tastes and cultural practices of classes and class fractions (%): III.[a]

Classes	Composers[b]				Film Directors[c]			Love stories	Travel	Thrillers	Books[d]	
	0–2	3–6	7–11	12+	0	1–3	4+				Historical novels	Modern authors
Working classes	77	19	4	0	89	10	2	36	61	57	40	19
Craftsmen, small shop-keepers	65	27	7	1	80	18	2	3	60	3	51	22
Clerical, junior executives	49	31	17	3	59	37	4	28	49	54	47	40
Technicians, primary teachers	17	28	36	19	56	32	11	9	38	38	49	38
New petite bourgeoisie	20	22	39	18	39	44	17	10	25	25	34	56
Middle classes[f]	41	28	22	8	58	35	7	23	45	43	45	40
Industrial and comm. employers	30	28	26	15	61	29	10	10	41	43	68	36
Executives, engineers	16	22	41	21	52	39	9	3	38	38	40	41
Professions	11	13	40	35	42	38	19	8	25	44	48	36
Secondary and higher-ed. teachers, artistic producers	4	11	33	52	22	46	32	7	15	29	24	55
Upper classes[f]	15	22	37	26	47	38	15	6	33	38	41	42

a. The percentages exclude 'don't knows'.
b. Number of composers identified in list of 16 musical works.
c. Number of directors identified in list of 19 films.

			Speech[e]						
Classics	Poetry	Philosophical essays	Slang	Mistakes in grammar	Standard	Refined	Strong accent	Slight accent	No accent
10	8	2	8	50	42	0	33	54	12
11	10	8	4	28	68	0	12	37	50
28	21	5	4	15	77	4	16	56	28
32	17	14	0	0	94	6	0	35	65
41	35	30	5	0	74	21	5	26	68
28	21	12	3	14	78	5	10	44	46
30	6	8	0	0	80	20	0	33	67
36	29	27	0	0	94	6	0	13	87
21	25	38	6	0	81	12	0	12	87
47	35	34	10	0	85	3	0	7	93
35	25	25	5	0	84	11	0	16	84

d. Each respondent was invited to choose three types of books from a list of 10 types.
e. Interviewer's observations.
f. Total for four groups preceding.

Table A.5 Tastes and cultural practices of classes and class fractions (%): IV.[a]

Classes	Activities[b]							
	Do-it-yourself, often	Photography or home movies	Records, often	Painting, sculpture, often	Mus. instr., often	Louvre and Modern Art Gallery	Light music	News
Working classes	63	50	46	4	6	6	52	26
Craftsmen, small shop-keepers	79	59	39	6	5	13	46	22
Clerical, junior executives	51	56	47	7	1	23	50	15
Technicians, primary teachers	61	69	68	10	6	40	13	22
New petite bourgeoisie	52	60	65	24	15	51	14	21
Middle classes[c]	57	59	52	11	5	29	37	18
Industrial and comm. employers	47	59	52	3	8	44	17	40
Executives, engineers	38	66	55	8	9	46	8	29
Professions	44	85	63	14	12	61	14	18
Secondary and higher-ed. teachers, artistic producers	38	54	71	16	16	64	9	15
Upper classes[c]	40	65	58	9	10	51	11	28

a. The percentages exclude 'don't knows'.
b. Each respondent was asked to say whether he never, occasionally or often practised various activities. (Museum-going was measured by at least one visit to the Louvre and Modern Art Gallery.)

Radio[c]		Preferred singers[d]								
Classical music	Light music and cultural or classical	Guétary	Mariano	P. Clark	Aznavour	Hallyday	Brel	Brassens	Ferré	Douai
10	13	31	18	30	52	17	24	41	20	7
17	15	22	20	30	36	2	31	32	20	4
18	16	21	12	25	47	11	48	40	30	6
54	11	4	5	19	19	3	55	72	35	14
56	8	9	11	16	29	5	41	50	13	19
31	13	17	12	23	38	7	45	45	31	9
36	7	13	10	26	33	6	23	61	10	5
54	9	3	7	23	28	5	42	70	37	9
53	15	6	4	15	36	0	50	71	38	21
68	7	1	1	2	12	4	54	85	48	25
53	9	5	6	19	27	5	41	71	33	12

c. Type of radio programme most often listened to.
d. Each respondent was asked to choose three singers from a list of 12.
e. Total for four groups preceding.

Table A.6 Tastes and cultural practices of classes and class fractions (%): V.[a]

Classes	FURNITURE[b]					INTERIOR[c]							
	Dept. store	Special- ized shop	Auc- tion	Flea market	Antique- dealer	Clean, tidy	Easy to main- tain	Cosy	Warm	Studied	Imagi- native	Sober, discreet	Har- mo- nious
Working classes	38	24	4	1	4	41	45	22	25	4	3	8	23
Craftsmen, small shopkeepers	29	27	3	4	8	41	39	45	26	4	5	15	23
Clerical, junior executives	15	35	10	4	4	35	30	45	24	3	2	6	37
Technicians, pri- mary teachers	23	42	5	4	10	22	13	41	32	6	10	10	49
New petite bourgeoisie	15	25	11	14	22	11	12	47	33	19	15	19	47
Middle classes[d]	19	33	9	6	9	30	26	45	27	7	7	11	38
Industrial and comm. employ- ers	10	39	30	18	50	11	17	48	24	5	12	12	47
Executives, engineers	6	28	17	16	42	15	17	48	19	10	11	36	53
Professions	8	31	11	19.	61	10	16	43	25	17	16	10	47
Secondary and higher- ed. teachers, ar- tistic producers	30	27	10	21	32	7	14	36	28	15	12	22	47
Upper classes[d]	11	31	18	18	44	11	16	45	23	11	13	25	50

a. The percentages exclude 'don't knows'.
b. Place (or places) where furniture was purchased.
c. Each respondent was asked to select the three adjectives, from a list of twelve, best describing the interior he or she would like to live in; to select the three statements about clothes (out of six) which best expressed his or

CLOTHES[c]			FRIEND[c]								COOKING[c]		
Value for money	Suit person-ality	Chic and stylish	Bon vivant	Con-scien-tious	Well-bred	Prag-matic	Stylish	Refined	Artistic	Pot-luck	Simple well-presented	Original, exotic delicate
44	28	3	40	63	25	10	5	0	8	23	35	1
29	24	12	22	68	47	5	6	5	9	14	31	6
25	48	6	15	46	55	17	5	7	5	15	34	4
31	42	14	19	45	32	18	10	6	27	16	45	11
17	39	26	9	29	30	20	18	18	29	21	26	14
25	39	12	16	46	44	16	8	9	13	17	35	8
25	43	23	23	45	53	9	18	17	16	17	22	15
15	34	14	12	31	39	18	16	9	27	16	26	9
13	33	21	15	52	38	13	6	17	28	17	27	8
15	35	14	19	27	24	14	12	9	31	20	29	12
17	36	17	16	36	38	16	15	12	25	17	26	11

her tastes; the three qualities (out of twelve) most appreciated in friends; and the type of meal (out of seven) he or she liked to serve to friends.

d. Total for four groups preceding.

Table A.7   Aesthetic disposition by educational capital.[a]

Educational capital	Land-scape	Sunset	Famous monu-ment	Old master	First com-munion	Folk dance	Little girl and cat	Woman breast-feeding	Weaver
No qual., CEP	82.0	88.5	35.5	50.5	51.0	54.5	61.5	46.0	36.0
CAP	88.0	92.5	35.5	47.5	31.0	60.0	57.0	43.0	37.5
BEPC	72.5	85.5	32.5	39.5	32.5	56.0	57.0	55.5	25.5
Baccalauréat	74.5	76.5	20.0	36.5	19.0	37.0	56.5	58.0	44.0
Started higher ed.	68.5	57.5	30.0	23.5	15.0	41.5	46.0	56.0	35.5
Licence	72.0	57.0	19.0	31.5	7.0	36.5	57.0	59.0	44.0
Agrégation, grande école	69.0	65.0	39.5	41.0	25.5	39.5	34.0	49.5	52.0

a. The percentages exclude 'don't knows'. Since it was not possible to reproduce the complete table of distributions among the different responses (ugly, meaningless, interesting, beautiful) for each object, the table indicates the percentage of respondents who consider that a beautiful photo could be made of these objects, which have been ranked, from left to right, from the most 'facile' (i.e., already strongly defined as aesthetic) to the most 'difficult' (i.e., those not defined or scarcely defined as aesthetic objects in terms of the common aesthetic at the time of the survey).

In reading the table, it should be borne in mind that the distribution between the different responses itself varies with the objects and with educational level, so that the structure which I have endeavoured to

Still life	Bark of a tree	Rope	Tramps quarrel-ling	Pregnant woman	Snake	Metal struc-ture	Cabbages	Butcher's stall	Scrap-yard	Wounded man	Car crash
26.5	15.5	6.0	4.0	8.5	13.0	6.5	4.0	5.0	5.5	2.0	0.5
37.5	37.0	8.5	4.5	12.0	18.5	7.5	8.5	6.0	3.0	5.5	0
40.5	27.5	6.5	8.5	13.5	17.5	8.0	13.0	5.0	6.0	5.5	1.0
40.5	42.0	22.0	16.0	21.0	23.5	18.0	13.0	10.5	13.0	12.5	5.0
41.5	45.0	31.0	14.5	19.5	32.0	29.0	18.0	18.0	22.5	9.5	2.5
44.0	56.0	32.5	16.5	22.5	28.5	24.5	22.5	19.5	16.0	17.5	1.5
45.0	60.5	31.0	22.5	29.5	38.0	36.5	27.0	25.5	31.0	22.5	15.5

highlight by emphasizing the strongest tendency in each column would have been much more visible if the respondents had been offered a simple dichotomous choice (between beautiful and ugly). For example, in the case of the famous monument, if the percentage who think it would make a beautiful photo is combined with the percentage who think it would make an interesting photo, one finds that, as for the sunset, the percentages decline steadily as educational level rises (87.5 percent of those with only the CEP or no qualification, 90 percent for the CAP, 78 percent for the BEPC, 74 percent for the baccalauréat, 59 percent for incomplete higher education, 57 percent for the licence, 73 percent for the agrégation and the grandes écoles).

Other Sources

Table A.8 Some indicators of economic capital by socio-occupational category (%

Socio-occupational category	Average total income (francs)	Range of income (C.S. I, 1970)					
		< 10,000F	10 to 20,000F	20 to 30,000F	30 to 60,000F	60 to 100,000F	100,000F+
Farm workers	12,706	43.5	41.3	10.9	4.2	0	0
Farmers	11,339	63.2	22.6	7.1	5.6	1.0	0.4
Unskilled	14,903	34.7	42.4	14.7	7.9	0.3	0
Semi-skilled	18,495	13.7	51.8	23.8	10.4	0.2	0
Skilled	21,289	8.2	44.3	30.4	16.7	0.3	0
Foremen		0.9	17.5	38.0	42.0	1.5	0.1
Craftsmen	25,729	12.3	32.5	25.3	25.8	3.4	0.7
Small shopkeepers	26,864	15.3	27.2	23.2	28.8	3.9	1.5
Commercial employees	22,546	11.5	33.8	27.6	22.2	4.0	0.8
Office workers		5.9	41.7	29.4	21.6	1.1	0.2
Jr. admin executives	32,770	2.1	12.2	26.4	47.9	8.9	2.5
Technicians		1.3	15.1	30.1	48.1	4.8	0.5
Social & medical services		5.7	32.6	29.6	27.8	3.7	0.6
Primary teachers		3.0	19.1	25.4	46.4	5.5	0.5
Commercial employers	61,616	2.2	12.1	11.1	36.9	23.1	14.6
Industrialists	102,222	1.3	2.6	4.1	26.4	31.9	33.6
Sr. admin. executives	57,229	0.5	2.9	11.5	53.3	24.2	7.6
Engineers		0.4	0.8	4.4	51.8	32.8	9.7
Secondary & higher-ed. teachers		1.4	8.6	18.5	43.5	22.3	5.6
Professions	83,309	3.1	4.8	6.5	27.6	33.0	24.9

1 Farm workers 2 Farmers 3 Unskilled 4 Semi-skilled 5 Skilled 6 Foremen 7 Craftsmen 8 Small shopkeepers 9 Commercial employees 10 Office workers 11 Junior administrative executives 12 Technicians 13 Social and medical services 14

	Income sources (C.S. I, 1970)					Nature of home tenure (C.S. III, 1972)			
Wages and salaries	Indust. and comm. profits	Non-comm. profits	Agric. profits	Urban property	Stocks and shares	Owner	Mortgage	Tenant	Free or tied accommodation
86.0	1.5	0.4	5.5	0.8	6.3	16.9	12.8	37.6	32.7
19.3	5.3	0.5	91.9	6.4	16.5	57.3	18.1	17.8	6.8
93.4	1.3	0.1	1.1	2.3	3.3	17.7	10.2	63.2	8.9
97.7	2.2	0.3	1.6	2.4	3.6	15.0	24.6	55.2	5.3
98.2	2.2	0.7	0.5	2.7	3.6	11.4	23.3	57.7	7.5
99.5	1.4	0.8	0.4	4.1	6.7	15.0	35.5	42.2	7.3
34.1	96.9	1.1	3.5	12.9	14.2	32.7	30.9	33.2	3.2
24.3	93.2	4.8	3.8	20.2	19.2	32.2	15.9	46.8	5.1
97.5	3.4	2.6	0.7	8.9	9.5	9.9	13.4	63.2	13.5
98.8	2.1	1.9	1.0	5.1	8.6	14.0	24.1	55.3	6.7
99.3	4.0	5.7	0.5	11.1	17.5	12.8	36.9	43.4	6.9
98.5	2.4	3.9	0.1	5.8	8.7	9.7	35.5	50.1	4.7
84.2	0	24.9	0	10.0	12.4	18.1	20.8	56.9	4.1
96.7	0.9	6.0	0.1	7.6	10.4	10.0	26.0	36.1	27.9
64.0	47.5	9.4	4.9	29.7	30.2	49.8	23.2	27.0	0
83.0	26.0	4.4	3.7	34.7	40.0	32.8	55.6	11.6	0
99.6	3.6	5.3	0.9	15.2	27.7	20.5	33.8	39.1	6.6
98.7	3.1	4.3	0.8	15.5	30.4	12.6	42.6	37.3	7.5
97.6	2.1	14.1	1.8	10.4	21.0	12.2	28.5	49.2	10.1
41.0	17.5	87.2	3.4	30.3	40.6	35.6	22.6	40.0	1.8

Primary teachers 15 Commercial employers 16 Industrialists 17 Senior administrative executives 18 Engineers 19 Secondary and higher education teachers 20 Professions

Table A.9 Some indicators of social trajectory and inherited cultural capital, by socio-occupational category (%).

Socio-occupational category	Farm labourers	Farmers	Unskilled, semi-skilled, miners	Skilled, foremen	Domestic servants	Craftsmen, small shopkeepers	Clerical[c]
Farm workers	29.7	46.9	8.0	5.1	0.8	5.0	3.3
Farmers	3.8	88.6	1.9	1.2	0.2	2.3	0.8
Unskilled	13.6	30.3	23.9	15.0	1.7	5.9	7.6
Semi-skilled	8.8	25.3	25.8	17.7	1.9	9.0	7.2
Skilled	6.1	14.0	25.3	25.8	1.8	10.9	10.0
Foremen	5.5	12.6	23.6	25.6	2.2	10.1	11.3
Craftsmen	6.3	16.7	11.8	13.6	1.9	34.3	8.1
Small shopkeepers	4.9	18.1	7.0	10.7	0.8	39.4	8.1
Commercial employees	4.8	10.3	16.8	18.0	0.9	18.3	15.4
Office workers	5.1	16.8	20.4	17.3	2.7	10.1	15.7
Jr. admin. executives	2.8	10.3	9.9	15.6	3.3	13.7	15.0
Technicians	2.0	7.2	15.6	20.5	2.1	11.4	16.4
Social & medical ⎰ M	3.4	22.2	14.8	16.8	4.8	6.4	13.0
services ⎱ F	1.5	12.7	9.5	12.4	1.3	12.4	12.9
Primary teachers	0.6	6.9	14.8	19.8	1.5	13.1	16.1
Commercial employers	3.4	13.5	5.4	5.2	0.8	27.4	9.1
Industrialists	0.6	19.2	7.7	14.7	1.0	29.2	3.8
Sr. admin. executives	1.3	7.7	7.4	10.3	1.1	14.3	15.2
Engineers	0.6	5.2	6.6	11.7	1.0	11.4	12.6
Secondary & ⎰ M	2.1	7.1	4.6	8.7	0.9	15.4	11.7
higher-ed. ⎱ F	1.6	4.5	2.9	5.2	0	12.0	15.2
teachers							
Professions	0.4	5.5	2.8	1.7	0.5	14.7	9.4

Father's occupation[a] (C.S. II, 1970)

a. For the father's occupation, the calculation excludes non-responses and 'miscellaneous' occupations.

Junior executives	Industrial and comm. employers	Senior executives	Pro-fessions	Father's qualification[b]				
				No qualification, no response	CEP	BEPC	Bac-calauréat	Higher education
0.4	0.3	0.5	0	*81.4*	17.2	0.6	0.6	0.2
0.2	0.2	0.6	0.2	69.8	27.9	1.1	0.7	0.5
1.1	0.4	0.5	0	*84.0*	15.1	0.6	0.3	0
2.1	1.2	0.9	0.1	75.4	22.5	1.3	0.5	0.3
2.9	1.4	1.7	0.1	67.3	29.8	1.5	1.0	0.4
3.7	2.1	3.2	0.1	65.3	30.7	2.0	0.9	1.1
2.4	2.9	1.6	0.4	64.5	32.0	1.9	1.1	0.6
2.1	6.0	2.3	0.6	61.2	31.9	1.2	3.4	2.2
3.7	7.7	3.4	0.7	54.6	37.1	3.3	2.1	2.9
6.4	1.8	3.4	0.3	57.8	34.5	4.1	2.1	1.4
11.9	5.2	9.8	2.4	40.6	41.6	6.7	5.1	6.0
11.5	4.1	8.2	1.0	42.9	*42.9*	5.6	5.0	3.6
8.8	2.0	6.1	1.7	46.8	40.5	5.9	3.1	3.7
12.3	9.1	10.8	5.1	37.2	36.9	6.1	8.6	11.3
15.3	3.2	6.9	1.8	36.1	*43.2*	5.4	9.4	5.9
2.6	*23.7*	5.4	3.4	48.1	38.6	5.3	3.8	4.2
1.5	*18.0*	2.4	1.9	52.9	38.1	2.6	2.2	4.3
11.2	9.7	19.1	2.7	35.1	36.5	7.2	10.0	11.3
14.8	6.7	*25.5*	3.9	32.0	29.4	*8.7*	11.4	18.5
15.7	3.8	23.2	*6.8*	31.6	33.6	7.9	11.6	15.4
20.3	5.9	*26.2*	6.2	23.3	27.1	*12.3*	*14.5*	*22.8*
12.1	11.4	20.7	*20.8*	30.4	23.4	7.4	*12.5*	26.2

b. Excluding technical diplomas.
c. Includes Army and Police.

Table A.10 Educational capital, spare time, fertility and place of residence, by socio-occupational category (%).

Socio-occupational category	Educational capital[a] (C.S. II, 1970)								Works 50 hrs.+ per week (C.S. IV, 1967)
	No qual.	CEP	CAP, BP	BEC, BEH	BEPC	BS, Baccalauréat	Started higher education	Licence +	
Farm workers	67.4	19.6	10.3	1.8	0.6	0.7	0	0	62.9
Farmers	45.1	37.3	13.7	1.0	1.8	0.8	0.2	0.1	68.0
Unskilled	70.0	22.0	7.0	0.1	0.8	0	0	0	21.9
Semi-skilled	51.3	28.4	18.2	0.4	1.3	0.3	0.1	0	23.2
Skilled	29.2	25.1	41.2	1.9	1.7	0.4	0.3	0.1	22.4
Foremen	19.0	31.9	38.8	5.7	2.7	1.0	0.7	0.2	26.4
Craftsmen	23.5	34.5	36.1	2.4	2.1	1.1	0.1	0.2	47.6 ⎫
Small shopkeepers	19.6	43.1	23.9	1.4	6.0	3.8	1.7	0.5	81.1 ⎬
Commercial employees	19.1	39.0	25.6	3.8	5.4	6.5	0.6	0	49.7
Office workers	15.9	40.1	19.9	1.8	17.4	3.8	0.8	0.3	10.9
Jr. admin. executives	8.9	26.0	18.4	9.0	16.0	11.9	5.4	4.4	16.7
Technicians	6.0	21.3	28.4	19.6	11.4	5.8	5.6	1.9 ⎫	
Social & medical services	2.2	10.0	6.4	0.7	0.6	3.2	73.9	3.0 ⎬	14.4
Primary teachers	1.5	5.7	5.1	5.9	6.0	39.3	27.7	8.7	10.3
Commercial employers	17.5	39.2	15.5	5.4	9.7	7.6	3.3	1.8 ⎫	
Industrialists	15.7	36.9	24.1	9.9	4.5	4.0	1.5	3.4 ⎬	45.1
Sr. admin. executives	6.2	16.7	10.9	8.3	11.8	13.7	8.2	24.0	31.5 ⎫
Engineers	3.1	4.7	5.5	6.6	5.0	9.2	10.6	55.3	26.8 ⎪
Secondary & higher-ed. teachers	0.7	2.8	2.6	0.7	0.7	4.6	13.7	74.2	8.3 ⎬
Professions	2.6	4.2	1.8	1.2	1.7	2.8	11.5	74.2	67.1 ⎭

a. The percentages exclude other diplomas.
b. *Economie et Statistique*, 27 October 1971, 28.

Average no. of children	Place of residence (1968 census, economically active men and women, aged 16+)						
	Rural communes	<10,000 pop.	Pop.10 to 50,000	Pop. 50 to 100,000	Pop. 100 to 200,000	Pop. 200,000 to 2,000,000	Paris conurbation
3.00	77.8	9.3	4.9	1.3	1.9	3.0	1.7
2.83	87.5	6.2	3.0	0.8	0.8	1.5	0.3
2.77	28.3	11.6	13.0	6.0	7.7	18.1	15.3
2.42	27.0	12.3	14.3	6.7	8.5	15.7	15.5
2.10	18.2	10.0	13.5	7.4	9.2	19.3	22.3
1.94	12.8	10.1	14.3	7.7	9.7	21.7	23.6
1.92	37.0	12.8	11.8	5.2	5.5	13.9	13.9
	28.1	13.2	13.3	6.1	7.0	17.1	15.1
1.68	13.6	8.1	14.0	8.5	11.1	21.2	23.4
1.97	11.7	7.2	12.3	7.4	9.3	20.5	31.5
1.71	10.6	6.6	11.7	7.1	9.5	20.9	33.7
1.67	8.6	7.1	12.0	7.4	9.6	20.1	35.2
	10.3	7.8	14.3	8.1	11.1	22.0	26.5
1.69	22.4	11.1	14.4	7.8	9.3	17.0	18.0
2.09	15.5	11.8	16.4	7.7	8.6	18.2	21.8
	22.3	14.1	16.0	6.8	7.2	16.5	17.2
	6.3	5.9	11.4	7.0	9.5	20.5	39.3
2.00	5.7	5.7	9.3	6.3	7.9	19.7	45.3
	5.8	5.8	11.6	7.7	11.2	25.4	32.5
2.06	14.4	11.3	13.4	7.3	8.9	20.0	24.8

Table A.11   Consumption and cultural practices, by socio-occupational category (%).

Socio-occupational category	Total consumption (C.S. III, 1972)			Owners of			Spectator sports at least 5 times a year	Car maintenance[a] at least 1¼ hrs. a week
	Per household (francs)	Per capita (francs)	Per unit of consumption (francs)	Second home	Tele-phone	Washing-machine		
Farm workers	22771	5650	7928	1.0	5.8	1.7	b	b
Farmers	26667	6365	8824	2.2	15.8	2.3	12.8	1.3
Unskilled	21840	6170	8578	2.2	0.3	0	41.9	9.5
Semi-skilled	26471	6552	9350	3.4	3.0	0.7	35.3	10.6
Skilled	26988	7476	10392	3.3	4.6	0.6	29.0	14.0
Foremen	35320	9174	12751	10.9	24.2	2.4	39.9	12.6
Craftsmen	28540	8444	11489	14.1	48.0	5.8	37.3	12.6
Small shopkeepers	30861	10118	13360	14.5	57.2	7.1	28.5	4.8
Commercial employees	30455	10324	13818	7.2	28.6	5.2	42.2	8.0
Office workers	27774	9227	12192	9.6	13.2	1.0	32.7	17.8
Jr. admin. executives	36272	11478	15461	11.9	29.4	5.4	23.7	13.1
Technicians	37438	10979	15090	6.5	25.1	5.3	29.9	6.6
Social & medical services	34175	11316	15277	7.8	41.7	3.6	b	b
Primary teachers	32787	11627	15364	18.6	29.9	5.5	29.3	2.8
Commercial employers	41886	10419	14463	29.7	72.3	22.3	64.8	0
Industrialists	47680	15480	19751	25.2	75.1	21.7		
Sr. admin. executives	52166	14694	19835	23.9	67.7	24.5	31.4	3.2
Engineers	49883	13920	19308	22.3	77.6	27.9	29.8	3.1
Secondary & higher-ed. teachers	40853	13136	17708	14.2	39.7	15.4	9.8	0
Professions	57133	16370	22467	25.0	84.5	31.5	20.0	0

a. Percentages calculated for 100 owners of cars or two-wheeled vehicles.

b. The (non-significant) figures for the farm workers and social and medical services (men) are not reproduced.

Cultural practices (C.S. IV, 1967)

Do-it-yourself at least once a week	Stamp collection	Library membership	Evening classes	Château, monument, in the year	Trade-fair in the year	Enter-tain at least once a week	Variety show at least once a year	Theatre at least once a year	Concert at least once a year	Piano
b	b	b	b	b	b	b	b	b	b	b
36.5	0.5	0.2	0.9	23.7	31.6	6.3	16.5	1.3	2.7	1.3
34.8	1.3	1.7	1.0	12.5	21.5	13.8	15.4	1.5	2.7	0
44.4	6.1	4.3	9.3	21.6	26.0	6.5	22.5	0.3	4.7	0.2
50.8	8.6	4.7	6.0	29.2	38.2	8.4	29.0	4.8	4.1	0.4
53.9	9.3	13.6	1.9	40.3	43.9	8.2	26.4	4.7	13.3	3.5
36.8	4.3	0	2.0	30.9	38.8	6.5	16.3	6.6	4.5	2.8
43.7	1.4	4.5	1.9	25.5	43.6	10.6	16.5	5.9	9.0	8.7
29.2	3.7	3.7	5.6	20.5	37.9	12.4	18.0	1.2	9.3	0
37.7	12.9	20.3	10.3	38.8	43.0	12.7	28.2	7.3	13.1	3.8
39.5	14.4	9.8	15.3	58.4	52.9	14.7	38.7	18.3	20.2	12.8
38.7	29.4	15.8	16.5	52.2	58.4	12.9	38.7	6.5	10.8	6.5
b	b	b	b	b	b	b	b	b	b	b
54.3	6.9	59.5	19.0	67.2	53.5	10.3	19.8	21.6	21.6	20.7
14.1	2.8	0	0	38.1	52.1	47.9	43.7	11.3	18.3	7.0
28.9	11.6	13.3	4.8	68.5	62.1	12.1	24.3	21.7	25.9	27.8
34.4	4.5	20.9	17.9	77.6	70.1	26.9	50.8	28.3	49.3	23.9
26.4	2.8	27.8	27.8	38.8	20.9	30.6	13.9	26.4	52.8	50.0
14.1	9.4	4.7	25.8	57.6	33.0	38.9	42.4	25.9	34.1	57.6

Appendix 4
Associations: A Parlour Game

In 1975 a survey was carried out, inviting a sample of the population to associate various objects with various politicians. The originators of the idea, as the comments which accompany the publication of the findings suggest, no doubt saw it simply as an 'entertaining' variant of the periodic surveys on the 'popularity' of public figures. However, the real point of the test they unconsciously produced (and this unconsciousness is part of its value) is not that it shows whether this or that politician is a fox or a crow, an oak or a fir tree, white or black, nor even whether the 'reds' more often assign black to the spokesman of the 'whites' (conservatives) than vice versa.[1]

The interviewer presented lists of six objects or characters (colours, trees, classical heroes, cartoon characters etc.) and asked the subjects to attribute one and only one of these objects to each of the following six politicians: Jacques Chirac, Valéry Giscard d'Estaing, Georges Marchais, François Mitterrand, Michel Poniatowski, Jean-Jacques Servan-Schreiber.[2] The findings of the survey, commissioned in June 1975 by the weekly magazine Le Point, were published in Sondages, 3-4 (1975), 31-47, with the following as sole commentary: 'The findings of this survey are entertaining to read, but they have a deeper interest as well. The set of attributions made for each politician reveals many facets of his public image. Sometimes it is difficult to distinguish with certainty the multiple reasons which have led the subjects to see a politician as one colour rather than another, as an ant rather than a fox, or as a hairdresser rather than a lawyer. However, when a politician is identified with one object by more than a third of the sample, the explanation is generally self-evident, and light is cast on the motivations of the choices by the different results of the other politicians vis-à-vis the same object. Connections are generally made either in terms of the man's physical appearance, or the best-known features of his personality, or his position and political career. We shall not comment further on the findings, but will leave the reader to exercise his imagination.'

With this apparent abdication the analyst gives himself an air of objectivity as he steps aside for the journalist. The latter (in Le Point, 14 July

1975) then only has to observe, with strict neutrality, that a 'majority' associates the left-wing politicians, and especially Marchais, with the most pejorative attributes, and the trick has been pulled off. Guided by the hierarchies they impose, because they take them for granted, the authors of the questionnaire produce a 'datum' which only has to be seen, *as given*, in order to produce a political effect.

This game, in which politicians are at stake, is a political game; but it is so in a much deeper sense than that given to the word in political science institutes and opinion research organizations. The politicians here are only the pretext for a game of attribution, categorization, and the objects offered are attributes, predicates, categoremes (as Aristotle put it, obscuring the original meaning, which is relevant here, of *accusation*). The question of the rules (is that the right word?), principles or schemes which govern these attributions is objectively raised by the fact that where one might have only expected the random associations of the imagination, one finds statistical regularities which cannot be explained unless one assumes that, far from making random individual associations, the people questioned are guided in the connections they make by common principles of vision and division.

Because these principles function implicitly and are not consciously scrutinized as regards either their internal form or their application, agents do not all apply the same scheme to the same object. However, as is shown by the fact that the meanings brought to light for each object are both finite in number (and not as numerous as the respondents, as they would be if the principle of attribution had to be sought in the respondents' individual history) and immediately intelligible (even in the absence of any explicit codification), one is entitled to assume that the schemes which the respondents may apply in each case, thereby selecting different aspects of the same object or person, are both finite in number and common to all the respondents, so that different readings of the same object are intelligible to all of them.

If the meaning that is 'chosen' presents itself unequivocally in each case, despite the polysemy of the objects considered in isolation, that is because the particular scheme of perception (among those objectively applicable) that is actually applied is clearly designated, insofar as it is the only one which enables an intelligible and constant relationship of equivalence or exclusion to be established between the objects, and therefore an intelligible relationship between the aspects (thus constituted) through which the objects, things or persons can enter into the relationship.

Thus, the scheme strong/weak or rigid/supple (which is no doubt virtually co-extensive with the deeply internalized opposition male/female) is clearly the basis of the opposition between the *oak*—majestic, powerful and rigid—and the *reed*—weak, supple, fragile, fickle—and also of the opposition between Giscard (or Poniatowski) and Servan-

Table A.12 Overall survey results.

Politicians	Colours						Trees					
	White	Black	Blue	Orange	Yellow	Green	Oak	Plane	Palm-tree	Reed	Poplar	Fir
Giscard d'Estaing	35%[a]	10%	29%	6%	9%	12%	31%	8%	14%	18%	19%	10%
Poniatowski	16	22	14	16	18	13	21	22	18	7	12	18
Chirac	16	9	25	12	18	18	11	20	18	12	22	17
Servan-Schreiber	14	9	12	23	23	19	6	6	21	26	18	14
Mitterrand	13	10	13	23	18	24	16	16	17	21	15	17
Marchais	6	40	7	20	14	14	15	18	12	16	14	24

Politicians	Flowers						Animals					
	Chrysanthemum	Lily of the valley	Poppy	Narcissus	Lilac	Carnation	Ox	Ant	Grasshopper	Fox	Crow	Tortoise
Giscard d'Estaing	14	23	12	14	18	18	12	29	18	24	9	9
Poniatowski	24	16	8	16	16	20	38	11	8	13	17	12
Chirac	10	21	9	15	25	20	16	22	15	15	16	15
Servan-Schreiber	9	14	13	27	21	17	6	12	28	11	10	33
Mitterrand	16	16	21	17	13	16	9	14	21	22	16	18
Marchais	27	10	37	11	7	9	19	12	10	15	32	13

Politicians	Games						Hats					
	Bridge	Monopoly	Dominoes	Poker	Chess	Roulette	Beret	Cap	Straw boater	Felt hat	Helmet	Top hat
Giscard d'Estaing	39	14	6	12	23	6	11	10	14	10	8	46
Poniatowski	16	17	21	16	14	17	9	5	14	14	41	18
Chirac	15	24	18	18	12	13	12	10	21	26	17	13
Servan-Schreiber	9	14	17	20	13	26	13	12	30	22	11	13
Mitterrand	14	17	15	18	18	18	40	16	15	16	7	6
Marchais	7	14	23	16	20	20	15	47	6	12	16	4

Politicians	Citroën 2cv	Renault 5	Peugeot 504	Rolls Royce	Porsche	Simca 1100	Wardrobe	Louis XVI chair	Empire desk	Four-poster bed	Knoll sofa	Farmhouse table
Giscard d'Estaing	10%	9%	19%	*39%*	18%	6%	7%	*36%*	*33%*	12%	6%	6%
Poniatowski	10	12	*28*	20	10	20	*25*	15	20	17	10	12
Chirac	8	14	23	9	*28*	17	13	19	19	18	22	9
Servan-Schreiber	10	15	12	16	27	21	12	11	10	*28*	*32*	7
Mitterrand	12	*30*	15	7	10	*25*	24	12	11	11	17	24
Marchais	*50*	20	3	9	7	11	19	7	7	14	13	*42*

	Famous women						Family					
Politicians	Brigitte Bardot	Mireille Mathieu	Jane Birkin	Michèle Morgan	Jackie Kennedy	Queen of England	Son	Father-in-law	Brother	Son-in-law	Father	Cousin
Giscard d'Estaing	14	7	10	*26*	15	27	25	12	15	12	24	11
Poniatowski	12	15	11	15	14	*32*	6	*26*	12	12	*27*	16
Chirac	21	14	15	15	21	15	*28*	11	*25*	19	11	8
Servan-Schreiber	*24*	10	19	8	*29*	11	19	13	19	*24*	10	15
Mitterrand	16	18	21	25	13	7	15	18	17	20	20	10
Marchais	13	*36*	*24*	11	8	8	7	20	12	13	8	*40*

	Jobs						Cartoon characters					
Politicians	Lawyer	Concierge	Overseer	Hairdresser	Doctor	Chauffeur	Astérix	Mickey Mouse	Donald Duck	Popeye	Lucky Luke	Tintin
Giscard d'Estaing	28	7	20	9	*24*	13	*26*	14	10	7	*22*	20
Poniatowski	11	19	14	15	22	19	19	14	14	22	13	18
Chirac	12	11	*31*	17	17	10	15	*19*	19	14	20	13
Servan-Schreiber	12	13	13	*29*	14	20	9	18	*22*	14	16	*22*
Mitterrand	*32*	14	10	16	15	14	17	18	15	20	14	16
Marchais	5	*36*	12	14	8	*24*	14	17	20	*23*	15	11

a. The italicized numbers indicate the highest percentage in each column.

Table A.13 Variations in survey responses on the part of Mitterrand and Giscard voters.

Politicians	Colours						Animals						Trees					
	White	Blue	Yellow	Black	Orange	Green	Ox	Grass-hopper	Crow	Ant	Fox	Tortoise	Oak	Palm-tree	Poplar	Plane	Reed	Fir
Mitterrand voters																		
Giscard d'Estaing	36.4%ª	20.6%	9.3%	15.0%	8.4%	10.3%	8.4%	19.6%	10.3%	16.8%	29.9%	14.0%	19.6%	18.7%	20.6%	11.2%	19.6%	9.3%
Poniatowski	15.0	9.3	15.9	39.3	12.1	7.5	42.0	6.5	25.2	8.4	7.5	11.2	15.0	20.6	9.3	28.0	8.4	17.8
Chirac	12.1	22.4	18.7	14.0	16.8	12.1	11.2	16.8	28.0	14.0	12.1	16.8	5.6	18.7	23.4	18.7	15.0	17.8
Servan-Schreiber	15.9	10.3	30.8	7.5	17.8	17.8	7.5	24.3	7.5	15.0	14.0	31.8	5.6	23.4	19.6	7.5	35.5	7.5
Mitterrand	11.2	21.5	13.1	1.9	17.8	33.6	10.3	21.5	9.3	24.3	22.4	12.1	32.7	11.2	12.1	9.3	14.0	19.6
Marchais	8.4	15.0	11.2	21.5	26.2	16.8	21.5	10.3	18.7	20.6	14.0	14.0	20.6	6.5	14.0	24.3	6.5	27.1
Giscard voters																		
Giscard d'Estaing	35.3	36.7	7.2	3.6	4.3	12.9	12.9	14.4	6.5	38.8	18.7	9.4	43.2	10.8	15.1	5.0	18.0	8.6
Poniatowski	18.0	18.0	23.0	8.6	18.0	14.4	42.4	9.4	9.4	12.2	15.8	10.8	28.1	18.7	15.8	18.7	4.3	14.4
Chirac	24.5	28.1	12.2	2.9	8.6	23.7	20.1	15.8	7.9	26.6	18.0	11.5	15.8	15.8	20.1	23.0	7.2	17.3
Servan-Schreiber	7.2	7.9	22.3	10.8	31.7	20.1	4.3	30.2	10.8	7.9	11.5	34.5	2.9	17.3	21.6	20.1	21.6	17.3
Mitterrand	10.8	7.9	22.3	13.7	27.3	18.0	7.2	22.3	20.1	9.4	18.0	23.0	4.3	21.6	14.4	19.4	23.7	16.5
Marchais	4.3	1.4	12.9	60.4	10.1	10.8	12.9	7.9	45.3	5.0	18.0	10.8	5.8	15.8	12.9	13.7	25.2	25.9

Politicians	Famous women						Family						Games					
	Brigitte Bardot	Jane Birkin	Jackie Kennedy	Mireille Mathieu	Michele Morgan	Queen of England	Son	Brother	Father	Father-in-law	Son-in-law	Cousin	Bridge	Dominoes	Chess	Monopoly	Poker	Roulette
Mitterrand voters																		
Giscard d'Estaing	12.1%	15.0%	18.7%	12.1%	14.0%	27.1%	17.8%	10.3%	20.6%	14.0%	18.7%	16.8%	32.7%	6.5%	18.7%	15.9%	16.8%	8.4%
Poniatowski	11.2	13.1	15.0	11.2	6.5	42.1	4.7	5.6	15.0	30.8	16.8	25.2	15.9	17.8	13.1	17.8	18.7	15.9
Chirac	19.6	11.2	19.6	16.8	16.8	15.0	17.8	20.6	9.3	13.1	26.2	11.2	9.3	15.0	13.1	19.6	24.3	17.8
Servan-Schreiber	28.0	22.4	28.0	6.5	8.4	5.6	24.3	25.2	6.5	8.4	15.9	16.8	9.3	15.9	16.8	14.0	15.0	28.0
Mitterrand	15.0	16.8	10.3	13.1	40.2	3.7	24.3	20.6	29.0	12.1	12.1	1.9	25.2	17.8	15.9	16.8	12.1	12.1
Marchais	13.1	20.6	7.5	39.3	13.1	5.6	9.3	16.8	18.7	19.6	9.3	26.2	7.5	26.2	22.4	15.0	12.1	16.8
Giscard voters																		
Giscard d'Estaing	14.4	5.8	10.8	4.3	37.4	26.6	33.8	18.0	29.5	7.9	6.5	4.3	41.7	5.8	28.1	15.8	5.0	2.9
Poniatowski	13.7	7.9	15.8	15.1	18.7	28.1	6.5	16.5	37.4	25.9	8.6	5.0	17.3	26.6	15.1	16.5	11.5	13.7
Chirac	21.6	19.4	18.0	10.8	15.1	15.1	33.1	30.2	10.8	6.5	15.1	4.3	20.1	17.3	9.4	26.6	16.5	10.1
Servan-Schreiber	23.0	16.5	33.8	7.9	4.3	14.4	17.3	15.8	7.9	16.5	29.5	12.9	8.6	17.3	12.2	13.7	23.7	24.5
Mitterrand	15.8	22.3	14.4	20.9	18.0	7.9	5.8	13.7	13.7	23.7	27.3	15.1	7.2	12.9	15.8	12.9	24.5	26.6
Marchais	11.5	28.1	7.2	40.3	5.8	7.2	3.6	5.8	0.7	19.4	12.9	58.3	5.0	20.1	19.4	14.4	18.7	22.3

Hats

Politicians	Beret	Straw boater	Helmet	Cap	Felt hat	Top hat
Mitterrand voters						
Giscard d'Estaing	8.4%	13.1%	8.4%	7.5%	9.3%	52.3%
Poniatowski	4.7	11.2	44.2	5.6	12.1	13.1
Chirac	14.0	15.0	12.1	7.5	33.6	15.0
Servan-Schreiber	12.1	37.4	6.5	9.3	25.2	8.4
Mitterrand	41.1	19.6	4.7	16.8	10.3	7.5
Marchais	18.7	3.7	13.1	53.3	8.4	2.8
Giscard voters						
Giscard d'Estaing	11.5	16.5	7.2	12.9	7.9	43.9
Poniatowski	12.2	15.8	31.7	5.0	15.1	20.1
Chirac	10.1	23.7	23.0	8.6	20.1	14.4
Servan-Schreiber	12.2	24.5	12.9	11.5	23.7	15.1
Mitterrand	41.0	44.4	6.5	15.8	18.0	4.3
Marchais	12.9	5.0	18.7	46.0	15.1	2.2

Cars

Politicians	Citroën 2cv	Peugeot 504	Porsche	Renault 5	Rolls Royce	Simca 1100
Mitterrand voters						
Giscard d'Estaing	7.5%	11.2%	25.2%	7.5%	43.9%	4.7%
Poniatowski	9.3	23.4	6.5	18.7	17.8	22.4
Chirac	11.2	24.3	18.7	14.0	12.1	18.7
Servan-Schreiber	6.5	15.9	34.6	11.2	13.1	17.8
Mitterrand	10.3	22.4	6.5	26.2	7.5	27.1
Marchais	54.2	32.8	7.5	22.4	4.7	8.4
Giscard voters						
Giscard d'Estaing	12.2	23.7	15.8	9.4	33.8	5.8
Poniatowski	8.6	32.4	12.8	8.6	22.3	15.8
Chirac	4.3	25.9	30.2	15.1	6.5	18.0
Servan-Schreiber	9.4	6.5	23.7	15.1	20.1	24.5
Mitterrand	12.2	10.1	12.2	34.5	6.5	24.5
Marchais	53.2	1.4	5.0	17.3	10.8	11.5

Furniture

Politicians	Wardrobe	Louis XVI chair	Empire desk	Four-poster bed	Knoll sofa	Farmhouse table
Mitterrand voters						
Giscard d'Estaing	1.9%	37.4%	30.8%	18.7%	3.7%	5.6%
Poniatowski	24.3	17.8	18.7	15.0	8.4	15.0
Chirac	12.1	21.5	18.7	20.6	19.6	6.5
Servan-Schreiber	8.4	8.4	11.2	29.0	34.6	7.5
Mitterrand	25.2	9.3	15.0	4.7	16.8	28.0
Marchais	20.8	4.7	4.7	11.2	15.9	36.4
Giscard voters						
Giscard d'Estaing	7.2	37.4	37.4	7.9	4.3	5.8
Poniatowski	27.3	15.8	19.4	15.8	13.7	7.9
Chirac	15.1	18.0	21.6	18.7	18.7	7.9
Servan-Schreiber	12.9	12.9	6.5	27.3	33.8	6.5
Mitterrand	24.5	11.5	8.6	13.7	19.4	22.3
Marchais	12.9	4.3	6.5	16.5	10.1	49.6

Jobs

Politicians	Lawyer	Overseer	Doctor	Concierge	Hairdresser	Chauffeur
Mitterrand voters						
Giscard d'Estaing	18.7%	21.5%	15.9%	9.3%	13.1%	20.6%
Poniatowski	0.9	11.2	9.3	31.8	16.8	26.2
Chirac	9.3	20.6	12.1	19.6	21.5	15.0
Servan-Schreiber	14.0	12.1	19.6	11.2	29.9	13.1
Mitterrand	45.8	13.1	26.2	3.7	9.3	0.9
Marchais	10.3	19.6	15.0	22.4	8.4	22.4
Giscard voters						
Giscard d'Estaing	36.7	20.1	32.4	1.4	6.5	2.9
Poniatowski	19.4	17.3	35.3	7.9	12.2	7.9
Chirac	14.4	43.2	19.4	5.8	8.6	7.9
Servan-Schreiber	8.6	9.4	5.0	16.5	33.1	28.1
Mitterrand	20.1	6.5	6.5	20.9	25.2	21.6
Marchais	0.7	3.6	1.4	47.5	14.4	31.7

Flowers

Politicians	Chrysanthemum	Poppy	Lilac	Lily of the valley	Narcissus	Carnation
Mitterrand voters						
Giscard d'Estaing	21.5%	10.3%	13.1%	13.1%	20.6%	20.6%
Poniatowski	38.3	7.5	6.5	15.0	14.0	18.7
Chirac	15.9	10.3	18.7	21.5	19.6	12.1
Servan-Schreiber	2.8	9.3	30.8	12.1	27.1	16.8
Mitterrand	3.7	23.4	19.6	25.2	8.4	13.7
Marchais	16.8	38.3	10.3	12.1	9.3	12.1
Giscard voters						
Giscard d'Estaing	5.8	14.4	21.6	33.1	7.2	18.0
Poniatowski	13.7	8.6	19.4	19.4	17.3	22.3
Chirac	7.2	7.2	28.1	23.7	12.2	20.9
Servan-Schreiber	12.9	15.1	17.3	12.2	26.6	16.5
Mitterrand	24.5	18.0	8.6	5.8	27.3	15.1
Marchais	36.0	36.7	5.0	5.8	9.4	7.2

Cartoon characters

Politicians	Astérix	Donald Duck	Lucky Luke	Mickey Mouse	Popeye	Tintin
Mitterrand voters						
Giscard d'Estaing	14.0%	12.1%	23.4%	23.4%	6.5%	17.8%
Poniatowski	15.9	18.7	10.3	10.3	24.3	18.7
Chirac	12.1	22.4	15.0	19.6	15.0	14.0
Servan-Schreiber	11.2	17.8	15.0	21.5	12.1	21.5
Mitterrand	26.2	14.0	18.7	12.1	15.9	12.1
Marchais	18.7	13.1	15.9	12.1	24.3	15.0
Giscard voters						
Giscard d'Estaing	34.5	8.6	23.7	7.9	6.5	19.4
Poniatowski	25.9	9.4	13.7	13.7	20.9	16.5
Chirac	17.3	12.9	20.9	23.0	11.5	13.7
Servan-Schreiber	5.8	25.2	15.8	12.9	13.7	27.3
Mitterrand	7.2	17.3	12.9	23.7	25.9	12.9
Marchais	9.4	26.6	12.9	18.7	21.6	10.1

a. The italicized numbers indicate the highest percentage in each column.

Schreiber. These two relationships, even if produced successively, determine each other and can be expressed in the form of an analogy: the oak is to the reed as Giscard (or Poniatowski) is to Servan-Schreiber; even if, in the Giscard/Servan-Schreiber opposition, the scheme applies more to political strength, power, designating the oak as king of the forest and Giscard as Head of State, whereas in the Poniatowski/Servan-Schreiber opposition it applies more to physical appearance and the associated 'virtues', designating the oak as big and strong, and Poniatowski, from the point of view of bodily hexis, as powerful and massive. In another case, it is the scheme noble/base, applied to the wood rather than the symbolic value or shape of the tree, which motivates the opposition between oak, a noble material used in fine furniture and ancient houses, and deal (*sapin, fir*), a poor-quality wood, used for coffins, which is strongly linked to Marchais, as are the colour black and the crow, a bird of ill omen.

The most fundamental symbols, such as colours, are of course very strongly over-determined. Black, for example, is firstly the gloomy colour, sinister and, more precisely, in the dominant representation, the symbol of the pessimistic world view (the black thoughts of someone who looks on the dark side), although, through the black flag—which, for some respondents, may have stood in for the absent red flag—it may receive a positive value as a symbol of radical subversion. But black is also poverty (black bread), dirt (particularly associated with certain jobs, e.g., miners—*gueules noires*), ignorance (being in the dark), drink (*être noir*) etc.

The application of secondary schemes, which bring it into other oppositions, will thus cause the oak (like the other objects) to be endowed with a series of properties more or less present in the fundamental properties: the Gaulish roots of druidical oaks (suggesting the cartoon character, Astérix, who is also associated with Giscard) as compared with the exotic palm-tree; noble solidity, as compared with the poplar; and sheer precedence, as compared with the plane, a tall and impressive tree but more vulgar, being associated with public places such as streets and squares.

Because the logic of the game itself and of the objects that were proposed channelled the search for associations in the direction of politics, the respondents invoked analogies in physical appearance (e.g., identifying Chirac with the poplar, a tall, slender tree) only when there was no other way of avoiding a random choice. The same is true of purely verbal associations, as when roulette suggests Marchais, no doubt through Russian roulette. It is also true of the search for coherence, to which social psychologists are so attached: it is only when no other direct relationship springs to mind that there is reference back to choices already made in a different series (e.g., white = Giscard, so Giscard = lily of the valley) or within the same series, so that some 'choices' are defined purely negatively, by elimination. In each series, the first choices, the only ones that are really determined (among the colours, the opposition white/black) limit all the others; for example, if Giscard is associated with the Rolls Royce or the oak, this determines the second choice, which is often a choice of the second, the 'lieutenant' (i.e., Poniatowski or Chirac, who are positionally assigned to the Peugeot 504 or the plane-tree). Everything suggests that the capacity to use all the possibilities offered, in other words, the ability to produce differences, is linked to status-assigned competence, that is, educational level and gender. For example, Giscard is associated with the ant by more men than women, because the idea of hoarding and saving suggested by the ant—through La Fontaine's fable contrasting the ant and the grasshopper—is only connected with Giscard (like Molière's Miser, which varies in the same way) by those who remember him as Minister of Finance. Similarly, more men than women associate chess with Marchais, perhaps because of the popularity of chess in the USSR, whereas women, perhaps seeing chess only as 'an intellectual game', associate it more strongly with Giscard. And again, perhaps because men are more familiar with Mitterrand's background, they more often associate him with the job of lawyer. (These differences are, of course, partly due to the related fact that men tend to be more politicized and more leftish.) Women are more inclined to be guided by analogies with non-political characteristics, such as bodily hexis, especially those indulgently related in women's magazines (e.g., Poniatowski will be seen as a Polish prince rather than as Minister of the Interior).

The source of the coherence of the choices lies not in the intention of coherence but in the self-consistency of a system of classificatory schemes which, though functioning discontinuously, grasps its objects in an objectively consistent way. And so, little by little, through the series of metaphors, there emerges a sociologically coherent social portrait of each 'personality'. All the images associated with Servan-Schreiber are linked by something like the idea of ostentatiousness and flashiness, suggested by the narcissus, a yellow flower, close to the daffodil or cuckoo, and the straw boater (again yellow) of the old music-hall beau, the colours orange and yellow—particularly emphasized by left-wing voters, who, especially in 1975, were probably more sensitive to the connotations;[3] by the grasshopper, spendthrift and strident; by poker and roulette, games of bluff and arriviste impatience (also associated with Chirac); by Don Juan and Jackie Kennedy, the American challenge,[4] or Brigitte Bardot; by the Porsche, the four-poster bed and the Knoll sofa, all essential accoutrements of modernism.[5]

It would be wrong to suppose that such systematic choices could be inspired solely by an intuition into the unique 'personality' of J.-J.S.-S.; what they in fact designate, in a very methodical way, is the life-style of the 'new bourgeoisie', which is seized upon both by the dominated classes and by the well-established fractions of the dominant class, with a hint of racism in the choice of the Middle Eastern palm-tree and the col-

Table A.14 Variations in survey according to income (monthly) group.

	Trees						Games					
Politicians	Oak	Palm-tree	Poplar	Plane	Reed	Fir	Bridge	Dominoes	Chess	Monopoly	Poker	Roulette
>2,499F												
Giscard d'Estaing	33.3%ᵃ	18.2%	10.6%	9.1%	22.7%	6.7%	33.3%	7.6%	19.7%	21.2%	13.6%	4.5%
Poniatowski	21.2	22.7	10.6	19.7	7.6	18.2	19.7	25.8	10.6	7.6	16.7	19.7
Chirac	10.6	21.2	21.2	18.2	15.2	13.6	12.1	21.2	13.6	27.3	10.6	15.2
Servan-Schreiber	4.5	9.1	21.2	22.7	27.3	15.2	9.1	10.6	19.7	9.1	19.7	31.8
Mitterrand	18.2	9.1	25.8	13.6	10.6	22.7	13.6	9.1	13.6	24.2	24.2	15.2
Marchais	12.1	19.7	10.6	16.7	16.7	24.2	12.1	25.8	22.7	10.6	15.2	13.6
2,500 to 6,499F												
Giscard d'Estaing	30.6	12.4	20.2	6.7	18.1	11.9	38.3	6.7	20.7	13.0	13.0	7.3
Poniatowski	19.2	16.6	13.5	23.8	8.3	18.1	14.5	22.3	13.5	18.7	14.0	17.1
Chirac	10.9	18.7	20.7	20.7	12.4	15.5	14.5	19.7	11.9	20.2	22.3	10.4
Servan-Schreiber	5.7	24.9	18.7	13.0	23.8	14.0	11.4	15.5	13.0	15.5	20.7	23.3
Mitterrand	17.6	18.7	11.4	16.1	20.2	15.5	14.5	14.5	19.7	16.6	16.1	19.2
Marchais	15.5	8.3	15.0	19.2	16.6	24.4	6.7	20.7	21.2	15.5	13.5	22.3
6,500F or more												
Giscard d'Estaing	27.8	14.8	27.8	13.0	11.1	5.6	44.4	1.9	35.2	14.8	3.7	0
Poniatowski	35.2	18.5	11.1	18.5	1.9	14.8	13.0	18.5	18.5	18.5	14.8	16.7
Chirac	9.3	13.0	22.2	24.1	9.3	22.2	18.5	7.4	7.4	29.6	16.7	20.4
Servan-Schreiber	3.7	24.1	13.0	13.0	33.3	13.0	5.6	25.9	9.3	18.5	14.8	25.9
Mitterrand	9.3	14.8	11.1	16.7	31.5	16.7	16.7	22.2	11.1	11.1	20.4	18.5
Marchais	14.8	14.8	14.8	14.8	13.0	27.8	1.9	24.1	28.5	7.4	29.6	18.5

Politicians	Hats						Furniture					
	Beret	Straw boater	Helmet	Cap	Felt hat	Top hat	Wardrobe	Empire desk	Sofa	Louis XVI chair	Four-poster bed	Farmhouse table
>2,499F												
Giscard d'Estaing	10.6%	9.1%	12.1%	15.2%	15.2%	37.9%	10.6%	31.8%	4.5%	33.3%	6.1%	13.6%
Poniatowski	6.1	13.6	33.3	7.6	13.6	25.8	16.7	16.7	10.6	15.2	24.2	16.7
Chirac	15.2	27.3	15.2	12.4	16.7	13.6	15.2	15.2	21.2	21.2	15.2	12.1
Servan-Schreiber	13.6	22.7	16.7	15.2	16.7	15.2	15.2	9.1	33.3	10.6	24.2	7.6
Mitterrand	34.8	19.7	4.5	15.2	22.7	3.0	28.8	16.7	19.7	10.6	6.1	18.2
Marchais	19.7	7.6	18.2	34.8	15.2	4.5	13.6	10.6	10.6	9.1	24.2	31.8
2,500 to 6,499F												
Giscard d'Estaing	10.4	15.5	7.8	10.9	7.8	47.2	5.7	32.6	6.7	34.7	15.0	4.7
Poniatowski	8.8	16.1	42.5	4.7	13.5	15.0	27.5	19.7	11.9	17.1	12.4	10.9
Chirac	12.4	18.7	14.5	8.8	30.1	14.0	12.4	17.6	21.8	16.1	22.8	8.3
Servan-Schreiber	11.9	29.0	10.4	11.4	22.3	14.5	11.4	11.4	30.6	11.9	28.0	6.2
Mitterrand	39.9	16.1	7.8	17.1	13.5	5.7	22.3	11.9	15.5	13.0	12.4	24.4
Marchais	16.1	4.7	16.6	47.2	12.4	3.1	20.7	6.2	13.0	6.7	8.8	45.1
6,500F or more												
Giscard d'Estaing	11.1	16.7	3.7	3.7	13.0	51.9	9.3	38.9	3.7	35.2	13.0	0
Poniatowski	9.3	11.1	42.6	3.7	14.8	18.5	29.6	21.2	3.7	14.8	22.2	7.4
Chirac	13.0	24.1	27.8	9.3	14.8	11.1	13.0	24.1	24.1	22.2	9.3	7.4
Servan-Schreiber	13.0	38.9	5.6	5.6	31.5	5.6	7.4	9.3	37.0	9.3	29.6	7.4
Mitterrand	46.3	5.6	7.4	13.0	18.5	9.3	22.2	3.7	16.7	14.8	14.8	27.8
Marchais	7.4	3.7	13.0	64.8	7.4	3.7	18.5	1.9	14.8	3.7	11.1	50.0

a. The italicized numbers indicate the highest percentage in each column.

our yellow, which is also linked to the racist stigma of the yellow star. (Servan-Schreiber is often identified as son-in-law by those with the highest income: perhaps by applying the traditional scheme—one thinks of *Le gendre de Monsieur Poirier*—of the ambitious bourgeois and the ruined aristocrat.)[6] The 'associations' game gives a fairly accurate idea of the everyday class struggle which deploys the quasi concepts of spontaneous sociology ('he's pretentious', 'a show-off' etc.), often closer to insults than judgements, in order to 'catalogue' or 'pin down' adversaries, in short, to imprison them in an essence. This probably explains why, as the interviewers note, the survey was so well received and so well understood (witness the exceptionally low rate of 'don't knows') and why the vision of the social world and politics which it brings to light is ultimately much more real than those constructed from the would-be scientific inquiries of 'political science'.

Because the practical logic governing acts of attribution proceeds piecemeal, successively, and so is not confronted with its own incoherences, and also because, without moving outside a determinate system of classificatory schemes, one can see the same object through different schemes, and therefore relate it to different objects or to the same object seen in other ways, all the meanings which the individual acts of attribution attach to the same object or person are far from being always perfectly coherent. Thus it is not easy to reconcile the properties of the powerful, massive and devoted Poniatowski which evoke the ox or the rugby player Spanghero (known to commentators as a 'dutiful forward'), and the docile strength each symbolizes, or those of the Minister of the Interior, suggesting the helmet, a symbol of repressive violence, with the properties that suggest the Rolls Royce or the Queen of England.

The specificity of practical logic, which I have analysed elsewhere in the case of ritual,[7] perhaps becomes clearer when dealing with a system of schemes of which one is a native user. The native is inclined to accept the immediate, lazy understanding provided by his practical mastery of the schemes of production and interpretation of the symbolism in question, so that an analysis which spells out everything implied in practical, tacit attributions is likely to be seen as fanciful over-interpretation.

Given that the relations observed are produced by the application of schemes which function implicitly and leave undetermined the distinctive features they pick up and the mediating terms on which the analogies are based, each person or thing involved is endowed with a restricted set of more or less coherent, unequally probable meanings. Setting aside the few codified or quasi-codified relationships, such as that between the poppy and Marchais, through the colour red, the recognized symbol of revolutionary parties, which even here is only conditional (since some respondents, no doubt the most anti-Communist, choose the chrysanthemum, the flower of death), a concentration around one dominant meaning reflects the extent to which the different agents agree on the scheme they mobilize to construct the objects and the relationships between them.

Thus, the survey which records the meaning-giving acts produced by the operation of more or less superimposable schemes, and the statistical analysis which aggregates them, reproduce, through a sort of experimental simulation, the process of production of collective representations such as the reputation of a person or the social image of a thing. These representations may be the product of the application of a single scheme of perception or a common system of classification, without ceasing to be subject to antagonistic social uses. While all apperception implies appreciation, the coincidence of schemes of apperception does not imply coincidence of schemes of appreciation; when agents occupying different, and even opposing, positions in social space (or political space) apply the same classificatory schemes, they almost always disagree over the value they give to the signs thereby produced. For example, right and left, rich and poor, make equal use of the opposition between white (or blue— blue blood?) and black (in the absence of red) to express the opposition between Giscard or Poniatowski and Marchais; but this opposition is given diametrically opposed values, depending on whether it is used by Mitterrand supporters or Giscard supporters: the former associate black with Poniatowski (and his helmet) and secondarily with Marchais; the latter associate it with Marchais. The same logic leads the left to associate the crow or chrysanthemum with Poniatowski (and secondarily Chirac and Giscard), while the right associates them with Marchais and secondarily Mitterrand. Giscard's supporters connect him with the oak, 'the king of the forest', Astérix, 'the all-French hero', le Cid, a symbol of courage and honour, or Michèle Morgan, a 'feminine ideal', while left-wing voters associate Mitterrand with the same objects. The right associates the fox, a symbol of perfidious cunning, with Marchais and Mitterrand (also identified with Tartuffe), whereas the left associates it with Giscard. Both sides agree in using the opposition between lineage and marriage as a way of expressing social or political proximity and distance, but Giscard supporters classify Giscard or Chirac as son, brother or father, relegating Marchais or Mitterrand to cousin, son-in-law or father-in-law, whereas Mitterrand supporters keep Poniatowski, Chirac (and secondarily Marchais) at arm's length and make Mitterrand one of the family.

Thus one only has to study common symbols or words in their practical uses, to discover the need to write into their full definition the essential polysemy they derive from these antagonistic uses. Situations of political struggle, of which this 'party game' gives an approximate image, demonstrate—contrary to those who believe in class languages—that words or signs can be common, without ever—despite the illusion of consensus—being perfectly neutral, because they bear within them the potentiality of the antagonistic uses to which they lend themselves.

When it is a matter of classifying objects that are socially classified and classifying, i.e., unequally *distributed* between the social classes and therefore *attributed* to the social classes in the implicit or explicit associations, one finds the same agreement over meaning combined with the same disagreement over the value of the things classified. Thus, whatever their class position (identified by income)[8] and their relation to that position (identified by their preference for Giscard or Mitterrand), the respondents concur in seeing bridge as a bourgeois game (associating it with Giscard and secondarily Poniatowski and Chirac), leaving dominoes (in the absence of belote) to Marchais, that is, to the working class he represents. And they manifest the same practical knowledge of the relationship between objects or practices and the social classes when they attribute skiing (through the skier Killy) to Giscard and boxing or rugby to Marchais; the top hat to Giscard (and then Poniatowski), the cap, emblem of the rowdy urban populace, to Marchais, and the beret, symbol of the placid, provincial working man, to Mitterrand; the Rolls Royce to Giscard (and then Poniatowski), the Peugeot 504 to his 'lieutenants' Poniatowski and Chirac, the Simca 1000 or Renault 5 to Mitterrand, the Citroën 2CV to Marchais, and the Porsche to Servan-Schreiber, who is always credited with the symbols of conspicuous modernism;[9] the Louis XVI chair and Empire desk to Giscard and Poniatowski, the farmhouse table to Marchais and Mitterrand and the wardrobe to Mitterrand and Marchais (and also Poniatowski, with his aristocratic background), and to Servan-Schreiber the attributes of the new bourgeoisie, the Knoll sofa and four-poster; the Queen of England, Rolls Royce of womanhood, to Poniatowski and Giscard (here the Prince comes into his own); Mireille Mathieu, 'popular' in both hexis and repertoire, to Marchais and then Mitterrand; Jackie Kennedy, and then Brigitte Bardot, to Servan-Schreiber. Guided by the sense of social realities which enables them to assess the proprieties and improprieties of social logic, the respondents match people with objects, or people with each other, according to their rank in the distributions, making marriages which are immediately perceived as well-matched by all those who possess the same practical knowledge of the distributions.

In fact, political divergences concern not the (practical) cognition of the objective structures, but their recognition. Those best placed in the distributions (i.e., those with the highest incomes) are also those most inclined to recognize them as right and proper by granting the dominant classes, as personified by Giscard, the attributes they are most likely to possess, that is, the rarest and most valued—bridge, the top hat, the Rolls, skiing (Killy), the Louis XVI chair—and attributing the most common attributes—such as the cap, the 2CV, the farm table or Mireille Mathieu—to the dominated classes, represented by Marchais. By contrast, the proportion who invert the hierarchy, giving Giscard, Chirac or Poniatowski the typically popular, and therefore desacralizing, cap, 2CV or dominoes, or giving Marchais the typically bourgeois bridge or Rolls, increases considerably as one moves down the real hierarchies. Such is the dilemma facing the dominated, which would also arise, perhaps more intensely, when faced with pairs of adjectives such as low and high, clumsy and skilful, laborious and graceful, heavy and light, coarse and fine, rude and polite, common and distinguished—the ordinary instruments of class judgement. Either they betray their recognition of the established order by granting the attributes of the dominant groups, in particular the dominant positions, to the spokesmen of the dominant groups (and they do so much more often, even when they declare themselves supporters of change, than the declared supporters of the established order grant them to the spokesmen of change), in which case they manifest how difficult it is to dissociate recognition of the established order from recognition of the hierarchies it implies (by placing Giscard among the 'good' relatives, father, brother or son, or identifying him with the oak—an increasingly frequent association as one moves down the social hierarchy); or they betray their recognition of the prevailing principles of hierarchy by simply inverting the distribution of the spokesmen of conservation and the spokesmen of change in terms of these principles. The devalued image of the dominated occupations (such as hairdresser or concierge) still has to be recognized in order to seek to *bring down* the dominant by giving them these jobs in symbolic revenge.[10] There is, in any case, only an apparent symmetry between the wish to make a chauffeur or concierge of Poniatowski, Chirac, or, with some hesitation, Giscard, and the restoration of the established order that is performed by the conservatives when they give to Mitterrand or Marchais—especially the latter, with his 'pretentious' airs as the immodest spokesman of 'modest folk'—the places that 'naturally' suit them.

Notes

Preface

1. For an analysis of the values of the 'old bourgeoisie', see P. Bourdieu and M. de Saint Martin, 'Le patronat', *Actes de la Recherche en Sciences Sociales* (subsequently abbreviated to *Actes*), 20–21 (1978), 3–82, and for the basis of a comparison between Germany, England and France, F. K. Ringer, *Education and Society in Modern Europe* (Bloomington and London, Indiana University Press, 1979).
2. This contradicts the belief, held by many intellectuals in every country, that cultural differences are withering away into a common culture. For example: 'Art has become increasingly autonomous, making the artist a powerful taste-maker in his own right: the "social location" of the individual (his social class or other position) no longer determines his life-style and his values. . . . For the majority of the society . . . this general proposition may still hold true. But it is increasingly evident that for the significant proportion of the population, the relation of social position to cultural style—particularly if one thinks in gross dimensions such as working class, middle class and upper class—no longer holds'; D. Bell, 'The Cultural Contradictions of Capitalism', *The Public Interest,* 21 (Fall 1970), 16–43, esp. 19–20. A glance at an evening's TV programmes or the magazine racks of a Boston or Philadelphia newsagent is enough to convince one of the contrary; but one could also point to the work of the pioneers of the sociology of culture (see W. Lloyd Warner and Paul S. Lunt, *The Social Life of a Modern Community* [New Haven, Yale University Press, 1941], esp. ch. 19; and Russell Lynes, *The Tastemakers* [New York, Harper, 1954], esp. ch. 13); not to mention market research, which, being exposed to the sanctions of the market, is infinitely more 'realistic' than most academic studies (see, for example, P. Martineau, 'Social Classes and Spending Behavior', *Journal of Marketing,* 23 [October 1958], 121–130).
3. A. Minton, 'A Form of Class Epigraphy', *Social Forces,* 28 (March 1950), 250–262.
4. Such homologies no doubt underlie international rapprochements and even alliances. For example, William Barrett's penetrating description of the meeting between the envoys of *Les Temps Modernes* and the *Partisan Review* group (see W. Barrett, *The Truants: Adventures among Intellectuals* [New York, Doubleday Anchor Books, 1982], pp. 113–123) gives a fairly accurate picture of the affinities associated with homologous positions in the intellectual and political fields and also the differences due to the specificity of national traditions.
5. See S. Sontag, 'Notes on "Camp" ', *Partisan Review,* 31 (Fall 1964), 515–531.
6. E. A. Poe, 'Philosophy of Furniture', *Selected Prose and Poetry* (New York, Holt, Rinehart and Winston, 1950), p. 386.

7. P. Bourdieu, 'The Economics of Linguistic Exchanges', *Social Science Information*, 16 (December 1977), 645–668, and *Ce que parler veut dire* (Paris, Fayard, 1982).

8. I am grateful to my translator for having been as faithful to the intention of my style as the demands and traditions of English will allow.

9. Readers who may suspect me of a secret indulgence towards the model of the total intellectual are referred to my analyses of the historical conditions of the creation and functioning of this model; P. Bourdieu, 'Sartre', *London Review of Books*, 2 (20 November–3 December 1980), 11–12, and 'The Philosophical Establishment' in A. Montefiore, ed., *Philosophy in France Today* (Cambridge, Cambridge University Press, 1982).

Introduction

1. Bourdieu et al., *Un art moyen: essai sur les usages sociaux de la photographie* (Paris, Ed. de Minuit, 1965); P. Bourdieu and A. Darbel, *L'Amour de l'art: les musées et leur public* (Paris, Ed. de Minuit, 1966).

2. The word *disposition* seems particularly suited to express what is covered by the concept of habitus (defined as a system of dispositions)—used later in this chapter. It expresses first the *result of an organizing action*, with a meaning close to that of words such as structure; it also designates a way of being, a habitual state (especially of the body) and, in particular, a *predisposition, tendency, propensity* or *inclination*. [The semantic cluster of 'disposition' is rather wider in French than in English, but as this note—translated literally—shows, the equivalence is adequate. Translator.] P. Bourdieu, *Outline of a Theory of Practice* (Cambridge, Cambridge University Press, 1977), p. 214, n. 1.

3. E. Panofsky, 'Iconography and Iconology: An Introduction to the Study of Renaissance Art', *Meaning in the Visual Arts* (New York, Doubleday, 1955), p. 28.

4. It will be seen that this internalized code called culture functions as cultural capital owing to the fact that, being unequally distributed, it secures profits of distinction.

5. The sense of familiarity in no way excludes the ethnocentric misunderstanding which results from applying the wrong code. Thus, Michael Baxandall's work in historical ethnology enables us to measure all that separates the perceptual schemes that now tend to be applied to Quattrocento paintings and those which their immediate addressees applied. The 'moral and spiritual eye' of Quattrocento man, that is, the set of cognitive and evaluative dispositions which were the basis of his perception of the world and his perception of pictorial representation of the world, differs radically from the 'pure' gaze (purified, first of all, of reference to economic value) with which the modern cultivated spectator looks at works of art. As the contracts show, the clients of Filippo Lippi, Domenico Ghirlandaio or Piero della Francesca were concerned to get 'value for money'. They approached works of art with the mercantile dispositions of a businessman who can calculate quantities and prices at a glance, and they applied some surprising criteria of appreciation, such as the expense of the colours, which sets gold and ultramarine at the top of the hierarchy. The artists, who shared this world view, were led to include arithmetical and geometrical devices in their compositions so as to flatter this taste for measurement and calculation; and they tended to exhibit the technical virtuosity which, in this context, is the most visible evidence of the quantity and quality of the labour provided; M. Baxandall, *Painting and Experience in Fifteenth-Century Italy: A Primer in the Social History of Pictorial Style* (Oxford, Oxford University Press, 1972).

6. See P. Bourdieu, 'Le marché des biens symboliques', *L'Année Sociologique*, 22 (1973), 49–126; and 'Outline of a Sociological Theory of Art Perception', *International Social Science Journal*, 20 (Winter 1968), 589–612.

7. O. Merlin, 'Mlle. Thibon dans la vision de Marguerite', *Le Monde*, 9 December 1965.
8. F. Chenique, *'Hair* est-il immoral?' *Le Monde*, 28 January 1970.

1. The Aristocracy of Culture

1. The *mondain*, the 'man of the world', is discussed later in this chapter in the section 'Scholars and Gentlemen' (translator).
2. Scholastic terms and abbreviations:
    CEP: Certificat d'études primaires, formerly marking completion of primary schooling.
    CAP: Certificat d'aptitude professionnelle, the lowest trade certificate.
    BEPC: Brevet d'études du premier degré, marking completion of the first part of secondary schooling.
    baccalauréat (*bac*), examination at end of secondary schooling.
    petite école: minor tertiary technical college.
    licence: university degree (three-year course in a *faculté*).
    agrégation: competitive examination to recruit top category of secondary teachers (*agrégés*).
    grandes écoles: set of selective higher-education colleges (parallel, but generally superior, to the *facultés*), awarding their own diplomas or training candidates for the *agrégation*. The academically most prestigious are the Ecole Normale Supérieure (ENS) (in the rue d'Ulm, Paris) and the Ecole Polytechnique (Polytechnique). The former trains *lycée* and university teachers; the latter trains 'engineers' who in fact subsequently work as top technical civil servants or (after fulfilling their obligation to the State, or 'buying themselves out') as top managers in private industry. The 'business schools' form a sub-set of *grandes écoles;* the best known of these is the Ecole des Hautes Etudes Commerciales (HEC). The following are also often classified with the *grandes écoles:* the Institut des Sciences Politiques (Sciences Po), an elite college teaching mainly political science, law etc.; and the Ecole Nationale d'Administration (ENA), which specifically trains its graduates (*énarques*) for the civil service (translator).
3. The clearest manifestation of this effect in the world of legitimate music is the fate of Albinoni's 'famous Adagio' (as the record-jackets call it), or of so many works of Vivaldi which in less than twenty years have fallen from the prestigious status of musicologists' discoveries to the status of jingles on popular radio stations and petit bourgeois record-players.
4. M. Proust, 'Sentiments filiaux d'un parricide' in *Pastiches et mélanges* (Paris, Gallimard, 1970), p. 200.
5. G. Bachelard, *Le rationnalisme appliqué* (Paris, PUF, 1949), p. 106.
6. The word *titre* can mean educational qualification, title, title-deed (translator).
7. The strongest resistance to the survey came from the most highly qualified subjects, who thereby indicate that, being cultured by definition, they are not to be questioned as to their knowledge, but only as to their preferences. (It is well known that writers and artists tend to respond eagerly to 'literary surveys', which they see as acts of homage to the universality of their talent-spotting genius.)
8. This essentialism, which can remain tacit so long as the belief supporting the social value of titles remains intact, necessarily achieves expression, at least in the inverted form of racism, when the capital is threatened (e.g., in declining aristocracies).
9. This legitimate or soon-to-be legitimate culture, in the form of practical and conscious mastery of the means of symbolic appropriation of legitimate or soon-to-be legitimate works, which characterizes the 'cultivated man' (according to the dominant definition at a given moment), is what the questionnaire sought to measure.

10. This effect of assignment by status is also largely responsible for the differences observed between the sexes (especially in the working and middle classes) in all the areas which are assigned to men, such as legitimate culture (especially the most typically masculine regions of that culture, such as history or science) and, above all, politics.

11. One of the most obvious 'advantages' bestowed by high educational capital in intellectual or scientific competition is high self-esteem and high ambition, which may equally be manifested in the breadth of the problems tackled (more 'theoretical' ones, for example), the loftiness of the style adopted etc.; see P. Bourdieu, 'The Specificity of the Scientific Field', *Social Science Information,* 14 (December 1975), 19-47.

12. The initials C.S. followed by a roman numeral refer to an entry in the list of statistical sources given in appendix 2, 'Complementary Sources'.

13. At equal levels, knowledge of film directors is considerably stronger in Paris than in Lille, and the further one moves from the most scholastic and most legitimate areas, the greater the gap between the Parisians and the provincials. In order to explain this, it is no doubt necessary to invoke the constant reinforcements which the cultivated disposition derives from all that is called the 'cultural atmosphere', that is, all the incitements provided by a peer group whose social composition and cultural level, and therefore its cultural dispositions, are defined by its place of residence; and also, inextricably associated with this, from the range of cultural goods on offer.

14. It is among the petite bourgeoisie endowed with cultural capital that one finds most of the devoted 'film-buffs' whose knowledge of directors and actors extends beyond their direct experience of the corresponding films. Some 31 percent of the office workers name actors in films they have not seen and 32 percent of those working in the medical and social services name the directors of films they have not seen. (No craftsman or small shopkeeper is able to do this, and only 7 percent of the skilled workers and foremen name actors in films they have not seen.)

15. E. Panofsky, *Meaning in the Visual Arts* (New York, Doubleday Anchor Books, 1955), p. 12.

16. Ibid., p. 13.

17. For a more extensive analysis of the opposition between the specifically aesthetic disposition and the 'practical' disposition, and the collective and individual genesis of the 'pure' disposition which genesis-amnesia tends to constitute as 'natural', see P. Bourdieu, 'Disposition esthétique et compétence artistique', *Les Temps Modernes,* 295 (1971), 1345-1378, and 'L'invention de la vie d'artiste', *Actes,* 2 (1975), 67-93. For an analysis of the aesthetic *illusio* and of the *collusio* which produces it, see P. Bourdieu, 'The Production of Belief', *Media, Culture and Society,* 2 (July 1980), 261-293.

18. J. Ortega y Gasset, 'La deshumanización del arte' (1925) in *Obras Completas* (Madrid, Revista de Occidente 1966), III, 355-356.

19. S. K. Langer, 'On Significance in Music' in L. A. Jacobus, ed., *Aesthetics and the Arts* (New York, McGraw-Hill, 1968), pp. 182-212; quotation on p. 183. (One recognizes the Kantian theme—endlessly reinvented even without any conscious reference to Kant—of the antinomy of pure pleasure and the pleasure of the senses, which is analysed in the Postscript.)

20. Ortega y Gasset, 'La deshumanización del arte', pp. 356-357.

21. The 'cultivated' spectator's concern with distinction is paralleled by the artist's concern (which grows with the autonomy of the field of production) to assert his autonomy vis-à-vis external demands (of which commissions are the most visible form) and to give priority to form, over which he has full control, rather than function, which leads him, through art for art's sake, i.e., art for artists, to an art of pure form.

22. A number of surveys confirm this hostility towards any kind of formal experiment. One study found a large number of viewers disconcerted by 'Les Perses', a stylized production which was difficult to follow because of the absence of dialogue and of a visible plot—*Les Téléspectateurs en 1967*, Rapport des études de marché de l'ORTF, I, 69ff. Another, which compares reactions to the 'UNICEF gala', classical in style, and the less traditional 'Allegro', establishes that working-class audiences regard unusual camera angles and stylized décor as an impoverishment of reality and often perceive over-exposed shots as technical failures; they applaud what they call 'atmosphere', i.e., a certain quality of the relationship between the audience and the performers, and deplore the absence of a compere (master of ceremonies) as a lack of 'warmth' (ibid., p. 78).

23. The department store is, in a sense, the poor-man's gallery: not only because it presents objects which belong to the familiar world, whose use is known, which could be inserted into the everyday décor, which can be named and judged with everyday words (warm/cold; plain/fancy; gaudy/dull; comfortable/austere etc.); but more especially because, there, people do not feel themselves measured against transcendent norms, that is, the principles of the life-style of a supposedly higher class, but feel free to judge freely, in the name of the legitimate arbitrariness of tastes and colours.

24. Joseph Garat, in his *Mémoires sur la vie de M. Suard*, tells us that Rousseau's *Discours sur le rétablissement des lettres et des arts* provoked 'a sort of terror' in a readership accustomed to take nothing seriously.

25. Virginia Woolf, 'Mr. Bennett and Mrs. Brown', *Collected Essays* (London, Hogarth Press, 1966), I, 326–327.

26. The capacity to designate unremarkable objects as suitable for being transfigured by the act of artistic promotion performed by photography, the most accessible of the means of artistic production, varies in exactly the same way as knowledge of directors. This is understandable since in both cases a relatively scholastic measurement is applied to a competence more remote from formal education than the competence implied in the expression of preference in music or painting.

27. The documents on which these analyses are based will be found in P. Bourdieu et al., *Un art moyen: essai sur les usages sociaux de la photographie* (Paris, Ed. de Minuit, 1965), pp. 113–134.

28. Immanuel Kant, *Critique of Judgement*, trans. J. C. Meredith (London, Oxford University Press, 1952), p. 65.

29. E. H. Gombrich, *Meditations on a Hobby Horse* (London, Phaidon Press, 1963), p. 104.

30. The populist image of the proletarian as an opaque, dense, hard 'in-itself', the perfect antithesis of the intellectual or aesthete, a self-transparent, insubstantial 'for-itself', has a certain basis here.

31. Interest in form, when it is expressed, is still rooted in the schemes of the ethos. It only takes on its true meaning when related to its real principle; the taste for neat, careful work which inspires it stems from the same dispositions as hyper-correction in language, strict correctness of dress and sobriety in interior decoration.

32. The posture of good intentions combined with insecurity which characterizes the rising petite bourgeoisie is expressed in the 'refuge' choice of saying that the objects could make an 'interesting'—as opposed to beautiful, ugly or meaningless—photograph. Thus, 40 percent of the junior executives and clerical workers consider that a snake would make an interesting photo (as against 22.5 percent of the new petite bourgeoisie, who are more inclined to say it could make a beautiful photo).

33. This is seen clearly in literature and in the theatre (e.g., the American 'new wave' of the 1960s).

34. Dickens could also have been cited.

35. P. J. Proudhon, *Contradictions économiques* (Paris, Rivière, 1939), p. 226; italics mine.
36. Ibid., p. 71; italics mine.
37. Ibid., p. 166.
38. Ibid., p. 271.
39. P. J. Proudhon, *Du principe de l'art et de sa destination sociale* (Paris, Rivière, 1939), p. 49.
40. Proudhon, *Contradictions économiques*, p. 256. It is impossible completely to understand the acceptance of the theses of Zdanov, who is very close to Proudhon in several respects, without taking into account the correspondences between his 'aesthetic' and the working-class or petit-bourgeois ethos of a number of the leaders of the French Communist Party.
41. E. H. Gombrich, *Art and Illusion* (London, Phaidon Press, 1960), p. 313.
42. P. Bénichou, *Le sacre de l'écrivain, 1750–1830* (Paris, José Corti, 1973), p. 212.
43. For a similar critique of the application of an empty opposition (between 'soft focus' and 'hard focus') to the German Romantic painters, see E. H. Gombrich, *In Search of Cultural History* (Oxford, Clarendon Press, 1969), p. 33.
44. Proust, *Pastiches et mélanges*, p. 173.
45. Eveline Schlumberger, 'Le charme enivrant de Château-Margaux', *Connaissance des Arts*, November 1973, pp. 101–105.
46. 'Misrecognition' (*méconnaissance*) combines subjective non-recognition (blindness) with objective recognition (legitimation); for example, a teacher who observes his pupils' 'gifts', or lack of them, and who imagines he is indifferent to social class, objectively helps to legitimate the causes and effects of cultural inequality (translator).
47. For an analysis of the relationship between the scholastic environment (a world apart, exercises which are an end in themselves) and the relation to language which is required in all 'official' situations, see P. Bourdieu, 'Les doxosophes', *Minuit*, 1 (1973), 26–45, and P. Bourdieu and L. Boltanski, 'Le fétichisme de la langue', *Actes*, 4 (July 1975), 2–32.
48. Virtually every treatise written in the classical period explicitly makes the link between ease and elegance of style and elegance of life-style. Consider, for example, the doctrine of *sprezzatura*, the nonchalance which, according to Castiglione, distinguishes the perfect courtier and the perfect artist.
49. Two examples, chosen from among hundreds, but paradigmatic, of explicit use of the scheme 'something other than': '*La Fiancée du pirate* is one of those very rare French films that are *really* satirical, *really* funny, because it does not resort to the carefully defused, prudently inoffensive comedy one finds in *la Grande Vadrouille* and *le Petit Baigneur*. . . . In short, it is *something other than* the dreary hackwork of boulevard farce' (J. L. Bory, *Le Nouvel Observateur*, 8 December 1969; italics mine). 'Through distance, or at least, through difference, to endeavour to present a text on pictorial modernity *other than* the hackneyed banalities of *a certain style of art criticism. Between* verbose aphasia, the textual transcription of pictures, exclamations of recognition, *and* the works of specialized aesthetics, perhaps *marking* some of the ways in which conceptual, theoretical work gets to grips with contemporary plastic production' (G. Gassiot-Talabot et al., *Figurations* 1960–1973 [Paris, Union générale des éditions, 1973], p. 7; italics mine).
50. This essential negativity, which is part of the very logic of the constitution of taste and its change, explains why, as Gombrich points out, 'the terminology of art history was so largely built on words denoting some principle of exclusion. Most movements in art erect some new taboo, some new negative principle, such as the banishing from painting by the impressionists of all "anecdotal" elements. The positive slogans and shibboleths which we read in artists' or critics' manifestos past or present are usually much less well defined' (E. H. Gombrich, *Norm*

and Form: Studies in the Art of the Renaissance [London, New York, Phaidon Press, 1966], p. 89).

51. This is seen clearly in the case of the theatre, which touches more directly and more overtly on the implicit or explicit principles of the art of living. Especially in the case of comedy, it presupposes common values or interests or, more precisely, a complicity and connivance based on immediate assent to the same self-evident propositions, those of the *doxa*, the totality of opinions accepted at the level of pre-reflexive belief. (This explains why the institutions supplying the products, and the products themselves, are more sharply differentiated in the theatre than in any other art.)

52. For an analysis of 'art for art's sake' as the expression of the artistic life-style, see P. Bourdieu, 'L'invention de la vie d'artiste,' *Actes,* 2 (1975), 67–93.

53. This is true despite the apparent exception in which some artists return to certain popular preferences, which had a totally different meaning in a cultural configuration dominated by choices which for them would be quite improbable or even impossible. These returns to the 'popular' style, which often pass for a return to the 'people', are determined not by any genuine relationship to the working classes, who are generally spurned—even in idealization, which is a form of refusal—but by the internal relations of the field of artistic production or the field of the dominant class. (This point has a general validity, and one would need to examine what the writings of intellectuals on the working classes owe to the specific interests of intellectuals in struggles in which what is at stake, if not the people, is the legitimacy conferred, in certain conditions, by appearing as the spokesman for popular interests.)

54. It is in these two categories that we encounter the most marked refusal of souvenir photos ('Souvenir photos are stupid and banal'; 'The main point of a photo is to preserve the images of those one loves'), of realism in painting ('A beautiful picture should reproduce what is beautiful in nature') or in photography ('For a photograph to be good, you just have to be able to recognize what it shows'), and the most resolute assertion of faith in modern painting (in refusal of the opinion: 'Modern painting is just slapped on anyhow . . .').

55. One of the major limitations imposed by the list of pre-formed choices is that it does not bring out these 'conflicts' and the strategies aimed at getting around them. A respondent who has, 'against the grain', chosen Georges Brassens or Jacques Douai might have been able to indicate his refusal of song, while showing his 'open-mindedness', by citing (with an implicit redefinition) something by Kurt Weill or an old Neapolitan song. (The France-Musique radio programme of 'personal selections', 'Le concert égoiste', is very revealing in this respect.)

56. Saint-Cloud: second to ENS rue d'Ulm in the hierarchy of the Ecoles normales supérieures (translator).

57. This dogma is still recognized and professed in less advanced sectors of the field of artistic production, as this typical declaration shows: 'However, I will say that these paintings by Gaston Planet are totally incomprehensible. I will say that I like them to be so. Not enigmatic. But entirely mute. Without points of reference. Without distractions' (Paul Rossi, Gaston Planet catalogue).

58. So it is always what is essential that gets left out when, as almost always happens, the survey itself, or the analysis, ignores the modality of practices, tastes or opinions. This modality, which is one of the best indicators of deep-rooted dispositions, is the object of very close attention in all societies. One could enumerate countless cases in which manner, and manner alone, reveals the social truth of dispositions, i.e., the true principle for understanding and predicting practices.

59. That is why the legitimate modality, especially in relation to works of art, which is one of the best practical indices of seniority within the bourgeoisie, remains incomparably more profitable, in the 'high-society' market at least, than the scholas-

tic modality (and the knowledge that is only learnt in school—spelling, grammar or mathematics).

60. It would have seemed somewhat cruel to quote one or another of the texts in which the 'cultivated' express their image of the 'petit-bourgeois' relation to culture and the 'perversions' of the autodidact. The reader's own references (or experience) can no doubt fill the gap.

61. 'A picture is not seen at a glance. This illusion belongs only to those who are incapable of "seeing" and are content to "recognize" an image by connecting it, not with a visual experience, but with intellectualized knowledge'; P. Francastel, 'Problèmes de la sociologie de l'art' in G. Gurvitch, *Traité de sociologie* (Paris, PUF, 1963), II, 278–279.

62. P. de Pressac, *Considerations sur la cuisine* (Paris, NRF, 1931), pp. 23–24. (The italics, which are mine, are intended to bring out more clearly the series of oppositions which are all taken from the tradition of cultural consumption: natural gift and instinct/rules and education; connoisseur/pedant; literary sense/grammar.) One could equally well have quoted Proust (who never fails to relate manners to the manner of acquisition): 'She annoyed me, which was all the more unfair, inasmuch as she did not speak like this to make me think she was an intimate friend of "Mémé", but owing to a too rapid education which made her name these noble lords according to what she believed to be the custom of the country. She had crowded her course into a few months, and had not picked up the rules'; M. Proust, *The Cities of the Plain,* pt. I, trans. C. K. Scott Moncrieff (London, Chatto and Windus, 1941), p. 84.

63. Mystical discourse on the work of art is strictly inexhaustible and there is inevitably a sense of arbitrariness when, to give a concrete illustration of the analysis, one cites a specimen such as the following, which, though it says scarcely less than the profound meditations of Gilson or Heidegger, perhaps owes its exemplary character to its very banality, as is attested by its place of publication: 'Ignorant or initiated, we are each of us disarmed before that mystery, the masterpiece. Uncertainly searching the canvas, we await the moment of grace when the artist's message will come to us. The silent clamour of Rembrandt, the infinite gentleness of Vermeer, no culture will make these things comprehensible to us if we have not restored the calm, created the expectation, prepared within ourselves the void that is propitious to emotion' (*Réalités,* March 1960).

64. Within the dominant class, differences by social trajectory are very closely linked to differences in capital composition; the proportion of newcomers increases as one moves towards the dominated fractions (except for writers and artists). The fact remains that within each fraction (especially the dominant fraction) differences in trajectory are very strongly felt.

65. See R. Bray, *La formation de la doctrine classique en France* (Paris, Nizet, 1951).

66. See M. Magendie, *La politesse mondaine et les théories de l'honnêteté en France, au XVIIe siècle, de 1600 à 1660* (Paris, PUF, 1925).

67. See H. Kantorovitch, *The King's Two Bodies: A Study in Mediaeval Political Theology* (Princeton, Princeton University Press, 1957).

68. G. Post, 'Plena Potestas and Consent' in *Studies in Medieval Legal Thought, Public Law and the State, 1100–1322* (Princeton, Princeton University Press, 1964), pp. 93–162.

69. G. Doncieux. *Un jésuite homme de lettres au XVIIe siècle: le Père Bouhours* (Paris, Hachette, 1886).

70. See P. Bourdieu and M. de Saint Martin, 'Le Patronat', *Actes,* 20–21 (1978), 3–82.

71. N. Elias, *The Civilizing Process* (Oxford, Basil Blackwell, 1978).

72. R. Barthes, 'The Grain of the Voice', in *Image, Music, Text,* trans. S. Heath (London, Fontana, 1977), pp. 179–189; quotation from p. 185.

73. There is a protocol of objects which brings the hierarchy of things into line with the hierarchy of persons. Thus we learn from an article on the Marigny residence,

furnished to accommodate the President's foreign guests: 'The protocol is strict: the hierarchy is measured in space, in the style of furniture and the quality of the drapery. Rare furniture and Lyons silks for the suites reserved for Heads of State; Napoleonic mahogany and velvet for the Prime Minister's first-floor suite; satin and flowered cotton on the second floor for the technical advisers' rooms.' J. Michel, *Le Monde*, 27 January 1975.

74. One only has to recall that appropriated objects, of all sorts, are objectified social (class) relations in order to see how one might be able to develop a sociology of the world of objects that would be something other than the record of a projective test masquerading as a phenomenologico-semiological analysis (I am thinking of J. Baudrillard, *Le système des objets* [Paris, Gallimard, 1968]).

75. Here one might invoke, not so much the erotic theory of rhythm (used, for example, to explain accelerations in rhythm leading to a peak followed by a rest), as the theory which points to a broader concordance or correspondence between musical tempo and inner rhythms, marked for example by the tendency to produce movements in time with music. See, for example, P. Fraisse, *Les structures rythmiques* (Paris, Erasme, 1956), and *Psychologie du temps*, 2nd ed. (Paris, PUF, 1967).

76. For the biographical information, see C. Brunschwig, L. J. Calvet, and J. C. Klein, *100 ans de chanson française* (Paris, Ed. du Seuil, 1972); and *Who's Who in France*.

77. The fact that mathematics and physics have now become the main criteria for exclusion or relegation no doubt helps to reinforce the irrationalism and anti-intellectualism that are encouraged by an ambivalent relationship to the educational system and a declining or spuriously rising trajectory. (This false-trajectory effect impinges on all those who aim for the future which, in an earlier state of the system, was implied in their educational qualification or position.)

78. G. G. Scholem, *On the Kabbalah and Its Symbolism* (London, Routledge and Kegan Paul, 1965), p. 25.

79. As is shown, for example, by the value which the editors and readers of popularizing journals set on highly qualified or high-ranking academic contributors whose rôle is that of institutional guarantors.

80. See G. Razzan, 'Ethnic Dislikes and Stereotypes', *Journal of Abnormal Social Psychology*, 45 (1950), 7–27.

81. Although the legitimate definition of culture, or of the relation to culture, or the hierarchy of the different arts, genres, works or authors is the stake in a permanent struggle, it would be naive to use this as an argument for denying the existence, at every moment, of a legitimate hierarchy. The struggles which aim, for example, to transform or overturn the legitimate hierarchies through the legitimating of a still illegitimate art or genre, such as photography or the strip cartoon, or through the rehabilitation of 'minor' or 'neglected' authors etc., or to impose a new mode of appropriation, linked to another mode of acquisition, are precisely what creates legitimacy, by creating belief not in the value of this or that stake but in the value of the game in which the value of all the stakes is produced and reproduced. It would be no less naive to treat these hierarchies, which reproduce in their own logic, i.e., in a transfigured form, the power relations between the groups, as an absolute order, grounded in nature, although they derive most of their symbolic efficacy, that is, their legitimacy, from the fact that they are seen in this way.

82. The dominant manners, pronunciation, 'ease', 'distinction' tend to impose themselves on the dominated classes themselves, and can only be devalued in the name of entirely 'extra-cultural' principles, such as the values of virility, which constitute the dominant modality as an index of effeminacy.

83. On all these points, and especially on the opposition between ENA and Polytechnique, see Bourdieu and Saint Martin, 'Le patronat', *Actes*, 20–21 (1978), 3–82.

84. It is well known what contempt the members of the dominant class, especially the fractions richest in cultural capital, have for TV or radio quiz shows, which, like

sociological questionnaires, appear to them as parodic negations of the legitimate relation to legitimate culture.

85. See in particular E. Demolins. *A quoi tient la supériorité des anglo-saxons?* (Paris, Firmin-Didot, 1897); *L'éducation nouvelle, l'Ecole des Roches* (Paris, Firmin-Didot, 1898); *L'avenir de l'éducation nouvelle* (Paris, Firmin-Didot, 1899); P. de Coubertin, *L'éducation en Angleterre* (Paris, Hachette, 1888); *L'éducation anglaise en France* (Paris, Hachette, 1889).

86. See Bourdieu and Saint Martin, 'Le patronat'.

87. G. Bachelard, *L'activité rationaliste de la physique contemporaine,* 2nd ed. (Paris, PUF, 1965), p. 60.

88. Everything suggests that this violence increases in proportion to the distance between the persons questioned and legitimate culture—symbolized, rightly or wrongly, by the interviewer and his questionnaire.

89. We know that the division within the business bourgeoisie according to the dominant type of capital (economic or educational) corresponds to the division by seniority.

90. Hoffmann evokes in his *Kreislerbuch* one of the most typical fantasies of all racism in his parable of the 'cultivated young man', an ape who had been taught to speak, read, write and play music, but who could not help betraying his 'exotic origin' in 'a few little details', such as the 'inner movements' which agitated him when he heard nuts being cracked.

2. The Social Space and Its Transformations

1. The extension of the survey to the whole range of material or cultural practices, legitimate or not, which can give rise to judgements of taste—cooking and art, clothing and music, cinema and decoration—was intended to provide the means of examining the relationship between the dispositions generally regarded as aesthetic and the system of dispositions which constitute the habitus.

2. Need it be said that the sociologists who are aware of this pre-condition are not legion, especially among those who profess a concern for methodology?

3. It could no doubt be shown in connection with a number of technical objects, as I have done for photography—P. Bourdieu et al., *Un art moyen: essai sur les usages sociaux de la photographie* (Paris, Ed. de Minuit, 1965)—that apart from what is implied in the negative determinisms, the limits, scarcely anything to do with the social uses of objects can be derived from their technical properties.

4. Economists—and a number of sociologists least burdened by a sense of theoretical inquiry and attention to the complexity of reality—are past masters in the art of formalizing the 'lived experience' or the unconscious of a class. It is difficult to resist the perverse pleasure of evoking a recent study in which Gary S. Becker— who has put his model-making imagination to better use at other times—attempts to account for the paradox whereby the demand for certain goods steadily increases with experience; G. J. Stigler and G. S. Becker, 'De gustibus non est disputandum', *American Economic Review,* 67 (March 1977), 76–90. To account for dispositions such as 'melomania', typical of 'benign manias', Becker invokes in one case the decline in the cost of production of 'musical pleasure' which results from the accumulation of the specific human capital, and in the other the increased cost of production of the 'euphoria' which results from the declining capacity for euphoria. QED.

5. For another example of this paradoxical neglect, see P. Bourdieu, *Travail et travailleurs en Algérie* (Paris, Mouton, 1963), and *Algeria 1960* (Cambridge, Cambridge University Press, 1979).

6. The objective class must not be confused with the mobilized class, the set of individuals brought together, on the basis of the homogeneity of the objectified or embodied properties which define the objective class, for the purpose of the

Notes to Pages 102-111 / 571

struggle to preserve or modify the structure of the distribution of objectified properties.

7. Jean Benzécri puts this well: 'Let us assume individuals $\alpha\beta_1\gamma_1$, $\alpha\beta_2\gamma_2$, ..., $\alpha\beta_n\gamma_n$, each described as possessing three features. Leaving aside the last two elements in each description, we can say that all the individuals belong to a single species defined by feature α, which we can call species α. But although feature α enables us to define this species and recognize its individuals, we cannot study the former without considering features β, γ of the latter. From this standpoint, if we call B the sum of β modalities which the second feature can assume, and C the sum of the γ modalities of the third feature, then studying species α means studying αBC, i.e., in addition to the first, stable feature, every form which the first (B) or the second (C) may take; and also the possible associations between the latter (e.g., β with γ rather than with γ^1 or γ^2).' J. Benzécri, 'Définition logique et définition statistique: notes de lecture sur un chapitre de Ernst Cassirer', *Cahiers de l'Analyse des Données*, 3 (1978), 239-242.

8. To construct the classes and class fractions on which the subsequent analyses are based, systematic account was taken not only of occupation and educational level (which are the basis of INSEE's socio-occupational groups) but also, in each case, of the available indices of the volume of the different sorts of capital, as well as age, sex and place of residence.

9. There are many obstacles to making such a mode of thought accessible and acceptable—including the practical logic of data collection and analysis, and the conception of scientificity which is current in the social sciences. There is every incentive to ask technology to resolve a problem which it merely displaces. This happens, for example, when in an article of unusual rigour for this sort of exercise, Goldberg resorts to the technique of 'causal inference' to test different explanatory models, with the aid of partial correlations expressing the most determinant 'causal relations' for a particular area such as voting behaviour; (see A. S. Goldberg, 'Discerning Causal Pattern among Data on Voting Behavior', *American Political Science Review* 60 (1966) 913-922. And yet perhaps it is not just metaphysical nostalgia to refuse to be satisfied with the countless partial models that have been produced ad hoc to account for religious behaviour, political choices or eating habits, and to wonder whether the fragmentation of the explanatory theories derives from the logic of what is to be explained or the logic of the mode of explanation.

10. Between 1968 and 1975, the proportion of women in the most skilled categories of workers declined even faster than before. In the semi-skilled and unskilled categories, after declining between 1962 and 1968 the proportion of women rose from 24 percent in 1968 to 28 percent in 1975; see L. Thévenot, 'Les catégories sociales en 1975: l'extension du salariat', *Economie et Statistique*, 91 (July-August 1977), 3-31, esp. 6.

11. The fact that the mode of acquisition is especially visible in certain contexts is a particular manifestation of this effect (e.g., mismatch between the scholastic mode of acquisition and 'high society' situations).

12. The directions taken by these 'deviant' trajectories are not entirely random: it seems, for example, that in cases of decline, individuals originating from the professions tend to fall into the new middle-class fractions whereas the children of teachers tend to decline into the established petite bourgeoisie.

13. This effect is itself an essential dimension of the effect of inculcation, since the slope of the father's trajectory helps to shape the initial experience of dynamic insertion in the social universe.

14. It is a mistake to conceive rising groups in terms of simple symmetry. Although for rising groups the educational qualification is a means of defense against exploitation—the more so the more dominated they are—it always tends to function, even in this case, as a means of distinction and legitimation.

15. It may be wondered whether individual decline has the same social effects as collective decline. The latter is no doubt more conducive to collective reactions (such as the Poujadiste movement) than the former.

16. Of course, one does not rule out the use of indicators which combine the essential content of the information contained in a set of factors, such as the indicator of socio-cultural status constructed by Ludovic Lebart and Nicole Tabard to 'summarize' the information supplied on each family by its occupation, the occupation of the paternal and maternal ascendants and the educational level of the two spouses. However, as the authors rightly point out, this synthetic variable cannot be credited with an 'explanatory power' unless the word 'explanatory' is understood in a purely statistical sense; see L. Lebart, A. Morineau and N. Tabard, *Techniques de la description statistique: méthodes et logiciels pour l'analyse des grands tableaux* (Paris, Dunod, 1977), p. 221. Far from assisting research, naive use of such indices would have the effect of excluding the question of the particular configuration of the variables which is operative in each case.

17. A fuller presentation of the fundamental principles of this construction, i.e., the theory of the different sorts of capital, their specific properties and the laws of conversion between these different forms of social energy, which is simultaneously a theory of the classes and class fractions defined by possession of a given volume and structure of capital, is reserved for another book, so as not to overcomplicate the present analysis of the judgement of taste.

18. The gaps are more clear-cut and certainly more visible as regards education than income, because information on incomes (based on tax declarations) is much less reliable than information on qualifications. This is especially true of industrial and commercial employers (who, in the CESP survey—C.S. V—provided, along with doctors, the highest rate of non-response to the questions about income), craftsmen, shopkeepers and farmers.

19. The category 'medical and social services' is characterized by the fact that it contains men mainly drawn from the working classes and women of whom a considerable proportion come from the upper classes (see the two histograms in figure 5).

20. A number of cultural properties are acquired by virtue of position in geographical space, partly through the quality of the social contacts favoured by spatial proximity. One of the most crucial is pronunciation, which unmistakably designates a stigmatized or prestigious origin.

21. The distribution of a class or class fraction in socially ranked geographical space—in particular its distance from the economic and cultural 'centres'—almost always manifests also its internal hierarchies. For example, secondary analysis of the 1967 INSEE survey on leisure activities shows that, in all socio-occupational categories, cultural activity increases with the size of the town (a good indicator of cultural supply): this is no doubt partly because the apparent homogeneity of the categories conceals differences, within the categories themselves, by size of town, especially with respect to cultural capital.

22. In English in the original text (translator).

23. Gerhard Lenski, who, to his credit, sees the problem of discrepancies between the different sorts of capital and points to some of the hidden effects they can produce (in particular, the tendency to 'liberalism' associated with strong 'decrystallization' of status), is no doubt prevented from developing all the consequences of his intuition by the positivist ritual of constructing an index. See G. Lenski, 'Status Crystallization: A Non-Vertical Dimension of Social Status', *American Sociological Review*, 19 (1954), 405–413.

24. Sources: M. Praderie, 'Héritage social et chances d'ascension' in Darras, *Le partage des bénéfices* (Paris, Ed. de Minuit, 1966), p. 348; INSEE, *Recensement général de la population de 1968* (Paris, Imprimerie nationale, 1971).

25. A. Villeneuve, 'Les revenus primaires des ménages en 1975', *Economie et Statistique,* 103 (September 1978), 61.
26. See M. Mangenot, N. Alisé and F. Remoussin, *Les jeunes face à l'emploi* (Paris, Ed. universitaires, 1972), p. 230.
27. These new strategies combine with or replace tried and tested strategies, such as provision of financial aid (a sort of advance inheritance), reconversion of the family's social capital through a profitable marriage, or a move into less competitive markets in which economic, social or cultural capital is better rewarded (e.g., in the past, the colonies; or prestigious—or at least honourable—institutions such as the Army or the Church, which could be entered without economic or even cultural capital).
28. On the evolution of the different socio-occupational categories, see Thévenot, 'Les catégories sociales en 1975', and on the steady development, between 1962 and 1975, of the 'business consultancy' sector—legal, accountancy and financial consultants, advertising agents, architectural advisors etc.—see P. Trogan, 'Croissance régulière de l'emploi dans les activités d'études et de conseils', *Economie et Statistique,* 93 (October 1977), 73-80.
29. See C. Baudelot and R. Establet, *L'Ecole capitaliste en France* (Paris, Maspero, 1971). (Translator's note.)
30. M. Griff, 'Les conflits intérieurs de l'artiste dans une société de masse', *Diogène,* 46 (1964), 61-94. This article gives a very precise description of the devices which advertisers, 'commercial artists', use on their apprentices, who are often would-be artists, so as to induce disinvestment ('running errands' etc.) and reinvestment in a 'lower' field.
31. A proportion of the surplus products of the educational system find employment in managing the social problems and conflicts created by educational 'overproduction' and by the new 'demands' it has created (e.g., the 'need' for continuing education).
32. R. Boudon, 'La crise universitaire française: essai de diagnostic sociologique', *Annales,* 3 (May–June 1969), 747-748.
33. A. Peyrefitte, *Le mal français* (Paris, Plon, 1978), esp. pp. 408-409 and 509-511.
34. See L. Stone, 'The Inflation of Honours, 1558-1641', *Past and Present,* 14 (1958), 45-70.
35. See L. Stone, 'Theories of Revolution', *World Politics,* 18 (January 1966), 159-176.

3. The Habitus and the Space of Life-Styles

1. It follows from this that the relationship between conditions of existence and practices or the meaning of practices is not to be understood in terms either of the logic of mechanism or of the logic of consciousness.
2. J. Rivière in M. Proust and J. Rivière, *Correspondance, 1914-1922* (Paris, Gallimard, 1976), p. 326.
3. In contrast to the atomistic approach of social psychology, which breaks the unity of practice to establish partial 'laws' claiming to account for the products of practice, the opus operatum, the aim is to establish general laws reproducing the laws of production, the modus operandi.
4. Economic theory, which treats economic agents as interchangeable actors, paradoxically fails to take account of the economic dispositions, and is thereby prevented from really explaining the systems of preferences which define incommensurable and independent subjective use-values.
5. An ethic, which seeks to impose the principles of an ethos (i.e., the forced choices of a social condition) as a universal norm, is another, more subtle way of suc-

cumbing to *amor fati,* of being content with what one is and has. Such is the basis of the felt contradiction between ethics and revolutionary intent.

6. 'Bourgeois' is used here as shorthand for 'dominant fractions of the dominant class', and 'intellectual' or 'artist' functions in the same way for 'dominated fractions of the dominant class'.

7. F. Nietzsche, *Der Wille zur Macht* (Stuttgart, Alfred Kröner, 1964), no. 943, p. 630.

8. Bananas are the only fruit for which manual workers and farm workers have higher annual per capita spending (FF 23.26 and FF 25.20) than all other classes, especially the senior executives, who spend most on apples (FF 31.60 as against FF 21.00 for manual workers), whereas the rich, expensive fruits—grapes, peaches and nuts—are mainly eaten by professionals and industrial and commercial employers (FF 29.04 for grapes, 19.09 for peaches and 17.33 for nuts, as against FF 6.74, 11.78 and 4.90 respectively, for manual workers).

9. This whole paragraph is based on secondary analysis of the tables from the 1972 INSEE survey on household expenditure on 39 items by socio-occupational category.

10. A fuller translation of the original text would include: ' "les *nourritures* à la fois les plus *nourrissantes* et les plus *économiques*" (the double tautology showing the reduction to pure economic function).' (Translator's note.)

11. In the French: 'le gros et le gras, gros rouge, gros sabots, gros travaux, gros rire, grosses blagues, gros bon sens, plaisanteries grasses'—cheap red wine, clogs (i.e., obviousness), heavy work, belly laughs, crude common sense, crude jokes (translator).

12. The expression 'tastes of luxury' will be used rather than 'tastes of freedom' so that it is not forgotten that the tastes of freedom are also the product of a social necessity defined by the 'facilities', i.e., the distance from necessity, which it offers.

13. N. Tabard, *Besoins et aspirations des familles et des jeunes* (Paris, CREDOC and CNAF, n.d.), p. 153.

14. J. W. Thibaut and A. W. Riecken, 'Some Determinants and Consequences of the Perception of Social Psychology', *Journal of Personality,* 24 (1956), 113–133.

15. K. Marx, *Capital,* I (Harmondsworth, Penguin, 1976), 482 (translator).

16. One fine example, taken from Böhm-Bawerk, will demonstrate this essentialism: 'We must now consider a *second* phenomenon of human experience—one that is heavily fraught with consequence. That is the fact that we feel less concerned about future sensations of joy and sorrow simply because they do lie in the future, and the lessening of our concern is in proportion to the remoteness of that future. Consequently we accord to goods which are intended to serve future ends a value which falls short of the true intensity of their future marginal utility. *We systematically undervalue our future wants and also the means which serve to satisfy them.'* E. Böhm-Bawerk, *Capital and Interest,* II (South Holland, Ill., 1959), 268, quoted by G. L. Stigler and G. S. Becker, 'De gustibus non est disputandum', *American Economic Review,* 67 (March 1977), 76–90.

17. We may assume that the deep-seated relation to the future (and also to one's own person—which is valued more at higher levels of the social hierarchy) is reflected in the small proportion of manual workers who say that 'there is a new life after death' (15 percent, compared with 18 percent of craftsmen and shopkeepers, office workers and middle managers, and 32 percent of senior executives).

18. It is not superfluous to point out that this art, which has its recognized virtuoso, the 'life and soul of the party', can sink into the caricature of jokes or remarks that are defined as stereotyped, stupid or coarse in terms of the criteria of popular taste.

19. The oppositions are much less clear-cut in the middle classes, although homologous differences are found between primary teachers and office workers on the one hand and shopkeepers on the other.

20. *La bouffe:* 'grub', 'nosh'; *grande bouffe:* 'blow-out' (translator).
21. The preference for foreign restaurants—Italian, Chinese, Japanese and, to a lesser extent, Russian—rises with level in the social hierarchy. The only exceptions are Spanish restaurants, which are associated with a more popular form of tourism, and North African restaurants, which are most favoured by junior executives (C.S. XXXIV).
22. *Les gros:* the rich; *grosse bouffe:* bulk food (cf. *grossiste:* wholesaler; and English 'grocer'). See also note 20 above (translator).
23. That is why the body designates not only present position but also trajectory.
24. In 'The Economics of Linguistic Exchanges', *Social Science Information,* 26 (December 1977), 645–668, Bourdieu develops the opposition between two ways of speaking, rooted in two relations to the body and the world, which have a lexical reflection in the many idioms based on two words for 'mouth': *la bouche* and *la gueule. La bouche* is the 'standard' word for the mouth; but in opposition to *la gueule*—a slang or 'vulgar' word except when applied to animals—it tends to be restricted to the lips, whereas *la gueule* can include the whole face or the throat. Most of the idioms using *la bouche* imply fastidiousness, effeminacy or disdain; those with *la gueule* connote vigour, strength or violence (translator's note).
25. This means that the taxonomies applied to the perceived body (fat/thin, strong/weak, big/small etc.) are, as always, at once arbitrary (e.g., the ideal female body may be fat or thin, in different economic and social contexts) and necessary, i.e., grounded in the specific reason of a given social order.
26. More than ever, the French possessive pronouns—which do not mark the owner's gender—ought to be translated 'his or her'. The 'sexism' of the text results from the male translator's reluctance to defy the dominant use of a sexist symbolic system (translator).
27. Oddly but accurately over-determined in English by droll/drawl (translator).
28. One could similarly contrast the bowl, which is generously filled and held two-handed for unpretentious drinking, and the cup, into which a little is poured, and more later ('Would you care for a little more coffee?'), and which is held between two fingers and sipped from.
29. Formality is a way of denying the truth of the social world and of social relations. Just as popular 'functionalism' is refused as regards food, so too there is a refusal of the realistic vision which leads the working classes to accept social exchanges for what they are (and, for example, to say, without cynicism, of someone who has done a favour or rendered a service, 'She knows I'll pay her back'). Suppressing avowal of the calculation which pervades social relations, there is a striving to see presents, received or given, as 'pure' testimonies of friendship, respect, affection, and equally 'pure' manifestations of generosity and moral worth.
30. Throughout this analysis, it is the whole set of convergent tendencies that should be considered, rather than the scale of the differences, which are in any case minimized by the fact that the dominant class is divided into fractions whose tastes, especially in food, vary in opposite directions.
31. Fish is an exception: it is eaten more at higher social levels, the difference between the classes being particularly marked in the case of sole and salmon, which are associated with luxury, and relatively small in the case of hake and fresh-water fish.
32. This is true for men, but for women the opposition takes a quite different form, because the division of labour between the sexes takes very different forms in the dominated fractions (where it is minimized) and in the dominant fractions (where women's exclusion from economic responsibilities tends to align them with 'young' and 'artistic' roles: bourgeois or aristocratic women—and their salons—have traditionally been mediators between the world of art and the world of business).
33. Cf. J.-P. Sartre, *Being and Nothingness* (London, Methuen, 1969), pp. 339–351.

34. W. D. Dannenmaier and F. J. Thumin, 'Authority Status as a Factor in Perceptual Distortion of Size', *Journal of Social Psychology*, 63 (1964), 361-365.

35. See J. Defrance, 'Esquisse d'une histoire sociale de la gymnastique (1760-1870)', *Actes*, 6 (December 1976), 22-47.

36. The dispositions which practitioners drawn from the working classes or the lower strata of the middle classes bring into these collective sports—in particular, the hope of a miraculous escape from their class—correspond to the demands of rationalized training and playing.

37. See *Collections de l'INSEE*, ser. M, no. 2 (July 1970).

38. Here too there is a hierarchy of legitimacies which defines the value assigned to the different sports in bourgeois conversation. *Le Monde* illustrates this fairly clearly by devoting serious 'critical' articles, often by well-known writers, to tennis and rugby (and secondarily athletics), whereas football and cycling get much more distant and impersonal treatment.

39. M. Proust, *The Captive*, pt. II, trans. C. K. Scott Moncrieff (London, Chatto and Windus, 1941), p. 236. Jean Renoir's film *La Grande Illusion* (1937) depicts the chivalrous code of French and German pilots in the First World War. British readers will remember the motto of the R.A.F., *per ardua ad astra*, 'through difficulties—and the heights—to the stars', which similarly links heroic distinction with height (translator).

40. Another distinctive feature, which sums up the opposition between two relations to the body and to social interactions: two-thirds (59.8 percent) of the teachers say they never dance, whereas dancing is very common in the professions (only 18 percent, the lowest proportion in the whole population, say they never dance) (C.S. IV).

41. More than half the members of the Saint-Nom-la-Bretèche golf club are bankers, industrialists, commercial entrepreneurs or company directors, 26 percent are managing directors, executives or engineers and 16 percent are members of the professions.

42. Equally relevant would be the analysis of the relations between the literary field, as the field of production of a universe of linguistic possibilities, and class habitus—see P. Bourdieu and L. Boltanski, 'Le fétichisme de la langue', *Actes*, 4 (July 1975), 2-32, and Bourdieu, 'Economics of Linguistic Exchanges'—or the relations, examined in chapter 8, between the space of the newspapers or the space of the political parties and the expectations of the different social classes.

4. The Dynamics of the Fields

1. A few examples all the same: 'What is Equality if not the negation of all liberty, all superiority, and nature itself? Equality is slavery. That is why I love art' (Flaubert to Louise Colet, 15-16 May 1852, *Correspondance* (Paris, Conard, 1926-1933). 'In the reign of equality, and it is almost upon us, everything that is not covered with warts will be flayed alive. The masses couldn't give a damn for Art, poetry, style. Give them vaudeville, treatises on prison labour, on housing estates and the material interests of the moment. There is a permanent conspiracy against originality' (20 June 1853, ibid.). 'But it seems to me that one truth has emerged: that we have no need of the vulgar, of the numerous element of majorities, of approval, of consecration; '89 destroyed royalty and the nobility, '48 the bourgeoisie, and '51 the people. There's nothing left, except a loutish, imbecile mob. We are all wading in universal mediocrity. Social equality rules the roost. Books for everyone, Art for everyone, science for everyone, just like railways and warming-rooms. Humanity is furiously intent on moral abasement and I resent being part of it' (28-29 September 1853, ibid.). One could also cite Mallarmé's 'L'Art pour tous'

or 'Le mystère dans les lettres', *Oeuvres complètes* (Paris, Gallimard, 1945), pp. 257–260, 382–387.

2. E. H. Gombrich, *Meditations on a Hobby Horse* (London, Phaidon Press, 1963), pp. 17–18.

3. N. Elias, *Die höfische Gesellschaft* (Darmstadt, Luchterhand, 1975), p. 92.

4. Durkheim, unlike Popper, for example, whose theses he anticipates—cf. K. Popper, *Objective Knowledge An Evolutionary Approach* (Oxford, Oxford University Press, 1972), esp. ch. 3—poses the problem of the relationship between the world of science, 'the result of concentrated, accumulated human existence', and individual reason; but immediately obscures it by answering it in the language of participation, the basis of the illusion of cultural communism: 'Philosophers have often speculated that, beyond the bounds of human understanding, there is a kind of universal and impersonal understanding in which individual minds seek to participate by mystical means; well, this kind of understanding exists, and it exists not in any transcendent world but in this world itself. It exists in the world of science; or at least that is where it progressively realises itself; and it constitutes the ultimate source of logical vitality to which individual human rationality can attain.' E. Durkheim, *The Evolution of Educational Thought* (London, Routledge and Kegan Paul, 1977), pp. 341–342.

5. Because the possession of works of art is supposed to attest not only the owner's wealth but also his good taste, it tends to be perceived as merited and to constitute a guarantee of legitimacy in its own right.

6. The more 'modern' a work of 'high' art is, the rarer is the competence it demands. 'Modernity' is defined in terms of the stages of the relatively autonomous history of the fields of production. This history is quasi-cumulative because belonging in the field and the history of the field ('epoch-making') implies a self-definition by reference to, and generally in opposition to, the immediately previous art. (In the field of music, for example, this leads in certain periods to a constant extension of the field of accepted harmonies or the range of acceptable modulations.) This explains why the history of individual tastes tends to reproduce, with a few deviations, the history of the corresponding art.

7. I am grateful to Jean-Daniel Reynaud for this reference.

8. Thus E. B. Henning has been able to show that the constitution of a relatively autonomous field of artistic production offering stylistically diversified products depends on the existence of two or more patrons with different artistic needs and an equal power to choose works corresponding to their needs. E. B. Henning, 'Patronage and Style in the Arts: A suggestion concerning their Relations', *The Journal of Esthetics and Art Criticism*, 18 (June 1960), 464–471.

9. This system of the ethical, aesthetic or political 'possibles' which are effectively available at a given moment is no doubt an essential dimension of what makes up the historicity of ways of thinking and world views, and the contemporaneity of individuals and groups linked to the same period and place.

10. Advertising for luxury goods systematically exploits the association of a product with a group. In no other field are institutions more overtly defined by their clientele than in the luxury trades, no doubt because here the virtually exclusive function of the products is to classify their owners. The link between the value of emblems and the value of the group which owns them is very clear in the antiques market, in which the value of an object may derive from the social standing of its previous owners.

11. The internalized classifications of taste have to reckon, at every moment, with the classifications objectified in institutions, such as the agencies of cultural consecration and conservation, and with all the objectified hierarchies of which they are always partly the product. But in return, the dominant taxonomies are constantly challenged and revised in the classification struggles through which the different

classes or class fractions endeavour to impose their own taxonomy as legitimate, either directly or through the professionals who compete in the specialized fields of production.

12. Rather than elaborate here all the presuppositions of analysis in terms of field (in particular, the interdependence between specific capital and the field in which it is valid and produced its effects, I shall merely refer the reader to earlier texts in which these ideas are developed. See, in particular: P. Bourdieu, 'Le marché des biens symboliques', *L'Année Sociologique*, 22 (1971), 49–126; 'Genèse et structure du champ religieux', *Revue Française de Sociologie*, 12 (1971), 295–334; 'Champ du pouvoir, champ intellectuel et habitus de classe', *Scolies*, 1 (1971), 7–26; 'Le couturier et sa griffe', *Actes*, 1 (1975), 7–36; 'L'invention de la vie d'artiste', *Actes*, 2 (1975), 67–93; 'L'ontologie politique de Martin Heidegger', *Actes*, 5–6 (1975), 109–156; 'The Specificity of the Scientific Field', *Social Science Information*, 14 (December 1975), 19–47; and especially 'The Production of Belief', *Media, Culture and Society*, 2 (July 1980), 261–293.

13. See Bourdieu, 'Le couturier et sa griffe.'

14. See Bourdieu, 'The Production of Belief.'

15. J.-J. Gautier, *Théâtre d'aujourd'hui* (Paris, Julliard, 1972), pp. 25–26. We may take Gautier at his word when he declares that the efficacy of his reviews stems not from a calculated adjustment to the expectations of his readership but from an objective harmony of view, allowing a perfect sincerity which is essential in order to be believed and therefore effective.

16. See A. Desrosières, 'Marché matrimonial et structure des classes sociales', *Actes*, 20–21 (1978), 97–107.

17. See P. Bourdieu and M. de Saint Martin, "Les catégories de l'entendement professoral', *Actes*, 3 (1975), 87, 90.

18. See Ezra N. Suleiman, *Politics, Power and Bureaucracy in France: The Administrative Elite* (Princeton, Princeton University Press, 1974), p. 69.

19. See J. Marceau, 'The Social Origins, Educational Experience and Career Paths of a Young Business Elite', Final report for SSRC grant of 1973–1975, Paris, 1975.

20. See P. Bourdieu and M. de Saint-Martin, 'Le patronat', *Actes*, 20–21 (1978), 3–82.

21. Before pointing to all the counter-cases of discord and divorce, one needs to consider how strong the cohesive forces constituted by the harmony of habitus have to be in order to counterbalance the contradictions inherent in the matrimonial enterprise as defined by custom and social law.

22. The intuition of the habitus provides an immediate understanding (which would take some time to justify explicitly) of the fact that, when invited to choose from a list of personalities those whom they would like to invite to dinner, the senior executives and professionals choose more often than all other classes Simone Veil, Giscard, Barre, Françoise Giroud and Chirac, but also Gicquel and Mourousi, whereas the working classes most often choose Coluche, Poulidor, Thévenet and Marchais, while the middle classes most often choose Le Luron, Mitterrand, Princess Caroline of Monaco, Platini and Jauffret (C.S. XLIII). (Veil, Barre, Giroud: ministers in the Giscard presidency. For Giscard, Marchais, Mitterrand, see appendix 4. Roger Gicquel and Yves Mourousi: TV and radio personalities; Coluche, Thierry Le Luron: entertainers; Poulidor, Thévenet: cyclists; Platini: footballer; Jauffret: tennis player—translator.)

23. 'The Master's deep gaze has, as he passed, / Calmed the unquiet wonder of Eden, / Whose final shudder, in his voice alone, awakens / For the Rose and the Lily the mystery of a name' (Mallarmé, 'Toast Funèbre', *Oeuvres complètes*, p. 55 [translator]).

24. An inexhaustible discourse of resentment reinforces contentment with what one has; e.g., 'Just think what it must have cost them to rent a villa right by the sea!'

25. The notion of situation, which is central to the interactionist fallacy, enables the objective, durable structure of relationship between officially constituted and

guaranteed positions which organizes every real interaction to be reduced to a momentary, local, fluid order (as in accidental encounters between strangers), and often an artificial one (as in socio-psychological experiments). Interacting individuals bring all their properties into the most circumstantial interactions, and their relative positions in the social structure (or in a specialized field) govern their positions in the interaction. On the opposition between 'situation' and field or market, see P. Bourdieu, 'The Economics of Linguistic Exchanges', *Social Science Information,* 16 (December 1977), 645–668.

26. See F. de Saussure, *Course in General Linguistics* (London, Peter Owen, 1960), p. 121; Saussure's example is a nice one: the distinction between *chaise,* an ordinary chair, and *chaire,* a professorial chair (translator's note).

27. Here too the new petite bourgeoisie distinguishes itself by a particularly frequent choice of the adjectives which most clearly declare the intention of distinction, such as 'studied' for interior decoration or 'chic and stylish' for dress. Similarly, advertisements for the would-be luxury shops of the Faubourg Saint-Antoine declare overtly the 'values' which the luxury shops (Faubourg Saint-Honoré) merely hint at (by references to art, for example), thereby exposing them to the charge of 'vulgarity' in striving for 'effect': 'The furniture of Claude Deco [a shop in the Faubourg Saint-Antoine] has that "je ne sais quoi" which is the soul of elegance and distinction.'

28. The fallacy in the 'trickle-down' model is that it reduces to an intentional pursuit of difference what is in fact an objective, automatic effect of the differentiation of the consumers' conditions and dispositions and the differentiation of the field of production, which may or may not be intentionally reinforced. See B. Barber and L. S. Lobel, 'Fashion in Women's Clothes and the American Social System', *Social Forces,* 31 (1952), 124–31; L. A. Fallers, 'A Note on the "Trickle Effect" ', *Public Opinion Quarterly,* 18 (1954), 314–321.

29. See Bourdieu, 'The Production of Belief.'

30. F. Nietzsche, *Über die Zukunft unserer Bildungsanstalten* in *Werke,* III (Munich, Carl Hanser, 1966), 189.

31. Seen in the smug, joking names given to suburban houses: 'ça m'suffit', 'ça m'plaît' ('good enough for me', 'suits me').

32. In the Conclusion I try to show that such a postulate underlies Erving Goffman's vision of the social world, a sort of social marginalism which reduces the reality of the social order to the sum of the (subjective) representations which agents have of the (theatrical) presentations given to them by other agents.

33. Precisely because of its essential ambivalence, which induces alternating submissiveness and aggression, and also because of the constant risks of humiliation which it entails, the relationship between the pretentious 'pretender' and the self-assured possessor is emotionally charged and generates resentment.

34. Durkheim's celebrated precept that 'social facts should be treated as things' contains its own negation: there would be no need to state this methodological principle with such emphasis if ordinary perception, which is a social fact and which also plays a part in making social fact, treated social facts as science requires them to be treated.

35. The aristocratic ideology of disinterestedness is no doubt the basis of a number of condemnations of 'consumer society' which forget that the condemnation of consumption is itself a consumer's idea.

5. The Sense of Distinction

1. From a whole set of research projects on the different fractions of the dominant class (the findings of some of which have already been published separately), only what is indispensable in order to account for the basic differences in life-styles is included here.

2. On the method of analysis, see L. Lebart, A. Morineau and N. Tabard, *Techniques de la description statistique: méthodes et logiciels pour l'analyse des grands tableaux* (Paris, Dunod, 1977); and for the theoretical foundations and logical conditions of use, J. Benzécri, *L'analyse des données: leçons sur l'analyse factorielle et la reconnaissance des formes et travaux du Laboratoire de statistiques de l'Université de Paris VI*, 2 vols. (Paris, Dunod, 1973).

3. Throughout this paragraph, and in the rest of this book, the figures in parentheses represent the absolute inputs of the variables in question to the corresponding factor.

4. Also in terms of this logic, opinions expressed vis-à-vis pre-formed judgements, such as 'Abstract painting interests me as much as the classical schools', or 'Paintings are nice but difficult', or the choice of singers such as Léo Ferré, Georges Brassens or Jacques Douai, are strongly explained by the first factor.

5. The private-sector and public-sector executives, who are widely dispersed in the plane diagram (figures 11, 12), are not represented by a box.

6. This means that the first factor in the factorial analysis corresponds to the second dimension of the social space and the second factor to the third dimension.

7. In the analyses which were performed successively, either for the same set of indicators (especially the one chosen for the final synthesis) or for the different sets, the first factor proved to be more stable (its significance was not altered by any permutation in the relative position of the factors) than the second; in some areas, seniority in the bourgeoisie was relegated to third rank.

8. In general, it is found that cultural practices vary more strongly as a function of income, within the limits of cultural capital of course, when they have a higher direct cost (e.g., theatre or exhibitions) or when they imply possession of expensive equipment (e.g., listening to records, playing an instrument such as the piano, or amateur filmmaking). Visiting art museums (which are—relatively—more equally distributed geographically than theatres or concert-halls) would depend exclusively on cultural capital (to the extent, of course, that prices are kept low) if tourism, which is closely linked to economic capital, did not intensify this practice (which explains why the representation of the economically richest fractions of the dominant class is higher in museums with high tourist attraction than in 'ordinary' museums).

9. It has been shown that the price of the seats represents only a proportion of the cost of theatre-going (which includes transport costs, the cost in time, the price of dinner and baby-sitting expenses), and that all these expenditures rise with income; see T. Moore, 'The Demand for Broadway Theater Tickets', *The Review of Economics and Statistics*, 48 (February 1966), 79–87. This means that the overall cost of a visit to the theatre must rise very rapidly as one moves from the intellectuals to the professions and the industrial and commercial employers.

10. See P. Martineau, 'Social Classes and Spending Behavior', *Journal of Marketing*, 23 (October 1958), 121–130.

11. The phrases in quotation marks are taken from Jean-Jacques Gautier's ideal-typical review of Françoise Dorin's no less ideal-typical play *Le Tournant* (*Le Figaro*, 12 January 1973).

12. A playwright or his play is said to be 'well served' by the actors.

13. R. Lynes, *The Tastemakers* (New York, Grosset and Dunlap Universal Library, 1954), p. 62.

14. Secondary and higher-education teachers (who represented 16.3 percent of the dominant class in 1968) constitute, respectively, 54.4 percent, 39.5 percent, 34.1 percent, 27.7 percent and 13.5 percent of the dominant-class users of libraries—see 'La lecture publique en France', *Notes et Etudes Documentaires*, no. 3948, 15 December 1972—of theatres of the consecrated avant-garde, the Odéon, TEP, TNP, Montparnasse (C.S. XIV), of museums (cf. our complementary survey, 1965), of

the 'classic' theatres, Atelier, Comédie Française, and of boulevard theatres (C.S. XIV). Secondary analysis of the INSEE 'leisure' survey (C.S. IV) shows that teachers (17.3 percent of the dominant class in the sample) represent, respectively, (a) 40.9 percent, (b) 38 percent, (c) 27.1 percent, (d) 19.4 percent, (e) 16.1 percent and (f) 6 percent of the dominant-class members who *say* (a) they go to a library at least once a month, (b) go to a concert at least five or six times a year, (c) have been to an art exhibition in the last six months, (d) regularly visit a museum, (e) go to the theatre at least five or six times a year, (f) have been to a variety show at least once in the year. The proportion of industrial and commercial employers varies in a systematically opposite way, and they represent, for example, 18.6 percent of the dominant-class members who have been to a variety show.

15. Since the density of the pertinent information seemed no less important than its quality, all the quotations used here are taken from a single issue of *Connaissance des Arts*—November 1971. A close study of two years' issues (1972–73) confirms its representativeness.

16. K. Marx, 'Excerpts from James Mill's Elements of Political Economy' in *Early Writings* (Harmondsworth, Penguin, 1974), p. 266 (translation slightly modified).

17. It can be seen that the inclination to personalism and to all forms of glorification of the uniqueness of the person is deeply rooted in the habitus. What vary between the fractions, i.e., according to the types of capital which are the main determinant of class membership, are the properties constitutive of the person (de facto and de jure)—intellectual value, moral and spiritual value etc.—which are especially exalted.

18. A French equivalent of *Reader's Digest* (translator).

19. The administrative executives (in the very broad INSEE definition), a fairly large proportion of whom are of working-class or middle-class origin, are very close, in the asceticism of their tastes, to the secondary teachers, although, educationally less qualified, they are more inclined to less prestigious cultural practices, such as visiting monuments and châteaux.

20. Some 14.5 percent of the judges and 13.5 percent of the doctors appearing in *Who's Who in France* (as against 9.7 percent of the senior civil servants, 4.2 percent of the employers and company directors) have published at least one non-specialized (political or literary) work.

21. K. Marx, *Capital*, I (Harmondsworth, Penguin, 1976), 741.

22. Centre de recherche économique sur l'épargne, *Enquête sur les comportements patrimoniaux des médecins exerçant une activité libérale* (Paris, CREP, 1971).

23. The same form of disposition, the product of an analagous discrepancy between cultural and economic capital, is found in members of the new-middle-class fractions (see, in chapter 6, the interview with a nurse who 'lives passionately').

24. *Le Quotidien du Médecin*, no. 710, 3–4 May 1974.

25. More strongly than all other fractions, the employers and professionals reject as ugly the photograph of a wounded man.

26. On the essential time-lag between production and consumption which assigns the most advanced producers to posthumous markets and profits, see P. Bourdieu, 'Le marché des biens symboliques', *L'Année Sociologique,* 22 (1973), 49–126, and 'The Production of Belief', *Media, Culture and Society,* 2 (July 1980), 261–293.

27. To designate life-styles, one always has the choice between a neutral, but colourless, terminology (ascetic taste), and the 'native' labels (pedantic taste, bourgeois taste) which are liable to pull one back to the symbolic battlefield on which they were forged.

28. Some interesting indications of the ways in which artists use time are to be found in B. Rosenberg and N. Fliegel, *The Vanguard Artist* (Chicago, Quadrangle Books, 1965), esp. p. 312.

29. The classificatory systems used in the official statistics, which necessarily correspond to an outdated state of the classification struggle, inevitably fail to record the differences resulting from the emergence of new occupations and the decline or redefinition of old ones.

30. In this respect, the teachers occupy an intermediate position between the professions and the engineers or executives. Unable to control the conditions of entry, they have endeavoured, at least in higher education, to control the conditions of promotion. See P. Bourdieu, L. Boltanski and P. Maldidier, 'La défense du corps', *Social Science Information*, 10 (1971), 45–86.

31. The same is true, in the other sector of the field, of a number of big and medium entrepreneurs, who have 'fought their way up' and whose habitus, like a ship continuing on its course under its own momentum, tends to prolong the virtues of asceticism and saving, the tastes and interests of their early days. In other words, the employers are distinguished not only according to the size and status of their firms and their property titles or qualifications, but also, although to a lesser extent, by the trajectories that have led them to their positions. (These analyses have been verified and specified by analysis of the characteristics of the heads of the two hundred largest French firms: see P. Bourdieu and M. de Saint Martin, 'Le patronat', *Actes*, 20–21 [1978], 3–82.)

32. The SOFRES survey shows that 22 percent of the private-sector executives are under 35 and 49 percent are under 49, compared to 14 percent and 40 percent respectively of the public-sector administrative executives (C.S. V). Senior executives in the civil service had, in 1970, an average taxable household income of 47,323 F as against 62,803 F for other senior executives (C.S. I).

33. Partly because it was designed to bring out deep dispositions which are relatively independent of time, the 1963 survey was not the best tool for grasping the variations in practices and systems of preferences linked to historical conditions. This is why recourse was had to secondary analysis of a market survey on 'executives' consumption' (C.S. V), which, aiming to predict the demand for luxury goods, was well adapted to the most distinctive elements of the new life-style.

34. Some 81 percent of the private-sector executives, 80 percent of the engineers, 74 percent of the members of the professions, 69 percent of the public-sector executives, 62 percent of the industrial employers, 60 percent of the commercial employers and 58 percent of the teachers say they always keep a bottle of whisky at home; 80 percent of the industrial employers, 75 percent of the commercial employers and members of the professions, 73 percent of the private-sector executives, 72 percent of the public-sector executives and engineers and 49 percent of the teachers say they keep champagne at home.

35. *Entreprise, caractéristiques professionnelles des lecteurs: résultats de l'enquête IFOP* (Paris, Régie Presse, 1973).

36. J. Marceau, 'The Social Origins, Educational Experience and Career Paths of a Young Business Elite', Final report for SSRC grant of 1973–75, Paris, 1975.

37. In these struggles, in which accounts of the social world—including allegedly scientific ones—are almost always (unconscious) strategies for symbolic imposition, recourse to 'authorities' plays a very important rôle. Hence the high symbolic yield of 'American research', which is spontaneously credited with the objectivity of a 'science' that is in a sense doubly neutral because foreign. Consider the use made of the studies by John MacArthur and Bruce Scott, who argue that the French firm gives priority to technical problems rather than financial management and marketing, to the future of the firm conceived in terms of technological progress and the search for new processes rather than in terms of really profitable mass production.

38. See *L'Expansion*, April and July–August 1975.

39. See P. Bourdieu, 'Le couturier et sa griffe', *Actes*, 1 (January 1975), 7–36.

40. On this world view, see P. Bourdieu and L. Boltanski, 'La production de l'idéologie dominante', *Actes*, 2 (June 1976), 3–8.
41. The dominant fractions are what they are if and only if the economic principle of stratification asserts its real dominance, which it does, in the long run, even in the relatively autonomous field of cultural production, where the divergence between specific value and market value tends to disappear in the course of time.
42. See A. Boime, 'Entrepreneurial Patronage in Nineteenth Century France', in E. Carter II, R. Forster and J. Moody, eds., *Enterprises and Entrepreneurs* (Baltimore and London, Johns Hopkins University Press, 1976), pp. 137–208.

6. *Cultural Goodwill*

1. The opinions expressed on music only have to be compared with the knowledge of works for it to be seen that a high proportion (two-thirds) of those who choose the most 'distinguished' answer ('All music of quality interests me') have little knowledge of classical music.
2. D. Barnes, *Nightwood,* 2nd ed. (London, Faber, 1950), pp. 21–24.
3. J. Frank, *The Widening Gyre* (Bloomington and London, Indiana University Press, 1963), p. 6.
4. Like the very content of these products (with, for example, their conspicuous references to legitimate works), the advertising for middle-brow cultural goods is a permanent encouragement to cultural allodoxia. It emphasizes both the economic and cultural accessibility of the products offered and also their high legitimacy, by invoking cultural authorities (e.g., Academicians or prize juries) whose authority is itself an allodoxia effect, since the recognition it is given tends to vary in inverse ratio to competence.
5. Similar defence mechanisms in which the consumers make themselves the accomplices of the vendors are also found in other areas. Thus a market research specialist suggests that one of the most important functions of advertising may be to provide purchasers with arguments to reassure themselves after the purchase; J. F. Engel, 'The Influence of Needs and Attitudes on the Perception of Persuasion' in S. A. Greyser, ed., *Toward Scientific Marketing* (Chicago, American Marketing Association, 1964), pp. 18–29. These ideological mechanisms of reassurance explain the disparity between the agents' own evaluation of their cultural practices and the objective truth of these practices. Everything takes place as if, at all levels of the hierarchy of degrees of consecration, agents were always inclined to attribute more value to their practices than the structure of the field objectively confers on them.
6. Thus there is no need to invoke censorship or 'political complicity' (although this is not unknown) to explain why the most typically academic products, and also the most typically middle-brow products, have derived considerable reinforcement from television. Partly through the economic effect of the publicity supplied by television and the corresponding changes in publishing and marketing strategies, this tends to modify the relations between the field of restricted production and the field of large-scale production.
7. Felix in Barnes's *Nightwood* (p. 24) shares this taste for oddities: 'Conversant with edicts and laws, folk story and heresy, taster of rare wines, thumber of rarer books and old wives' tales—tales of men who became holy and of beasts that became damned—read in all plans for fortifications and bridges, given pause by all graveyards on all roads, a pedant of many churches and castles, his mind dimly and reverently reverberated to Madame de Sévigné, Goethe, Loyola and Brantôme.'
8. It is no accident that surveys on cultural practices and opinions tend to take the form of an examination in which the respondents, who are and always feel measured against a norm, obtain results that are ranked in accordance with their de-

gree of scholastic consecration and express preferences which always correspond fairly closely to their educational qualifications, both in their content and in their modality.

9. The image which the formally educated have of the self-educated is a fine example of the partial, self-interested truths produced by the partial lucidity of ordinary perception and of the (unconscious) strategies through which each art of living is reinforced in its conviction of its own excellence by comparing itself flatteringly with other arts of living.

10. Need it be said that these two celebrated examples are chosen so as to invite the reader to reason a fortiori?

11. Ferdinand Cheval (1836–1924), a rural postman, built his 'Ideal Palace' single-handed, from 1879 to 1912, with stones which he collected on his round and carried back to his home at Hauterives (Drôme). This extraordinary 'monument' (classified as such by Malraux when Minister of Culture) includes all the features mentioned in the text, and more. *La Veillée des Chaumières* was a magazine which brought serialized historical romances (accompanied by engravings) to a mainly peasant readership. (Translator's note.)

12. 'Though the Wei Bodhisattvas and those of Nara, Khmer and Javanese sculpture and Sung painting do not express the same communion with the cosmos as does a Romanesque tympanum, a Dance of Siva or the horsemen of the Parthenon, all alike express a communion of one kind or another, as does even Rubens in *The Kermesse*. We need but glance at any Greek masterpiece to see at once that its triumph over the mystery-laden East does not stem from any process of the reasoning mind, but from "the innumerable laughter of the waves". Like a muted orchestra the surge and thunder, already so remote, of ancient tragedy accompanies but does not drown Antigone's immortal cry.' A. Malraux, *The Voices of Silence,* trans. S. Gilbert (London, Secker and Warburg, 1954), pp. 635–636.

13. They are by Ferdinand Cheval, among the inscriptions on his Ideal Palace (translator).

14. See P. Bénichou, *Le sacre de l'écrivain* (Paris, José Corti, 1973), pp. 177–178.

15. Harpagon: Molière's *Miser;* Arnolphe: the protagonist of his *Ecole des femmes,* obsessed by marital infidelity (translator).

16. Attributed to the politician Edouard Herriot (translator).

17. What is said here about the middle positions (because it is most obvious in this case) is, of course, equally true of all positions in social space-time.

18. C. Baudelot, R. Establet and J. Malemort, *La petite bourgeoisie en France* (Paris, Maspero, 1974), p. 153.

19. Among the properties of the strongly predetermined positions in the civil service (such as those of the junior administrative executives) the most significant from the point of view considered here is undoubtedly the fact that they offer, through their guaranteed career-structures, the assurance of a relatively predictable individual trajectory.

20. The placement of these positions is understandable since their emergence is to a large extent due to changes in the educational system.

21. The example of the craftsmen provides a good opportunity to re-emphasize that, in treating as a point what is in fact a space (and sometimes a genuine field), one inevitably simplifies. This simplification is entailed by the endeavour to grasp the social space as a whole (and so to avoid the errors almost inevitably incurred, as a direct consequence of autonomization, by monographs devoted to a particular 'occupation').

22. Some 19.5 percent of all the 'junior executives' (administrative executives, technicians, primary teachers) and 20.3 percent of the office workers are enrolled in a library (as against 3.7 percent of the commercial employees and 2.2 percent of the small employers); 18.5 percent and 12.9 percent respectively collect stamps

(as against 3.7 percent and 2.8 percent); 14.2 percent and 10.3 percent follow correspondence courses or evening classes (as against 0 percent and 2 percent) (C.S. IV).

23. The notion of 'preference' in legitimate culture is only appropriate at and above a certain level of competence (corresponding approximately to a certificate of secondary education). This is seen clearly in the fact that, below this level, the respondents treat questions of preference as questions of knowledge, saying they prefer the painters they know, and that the proportion of respondents who know more or as many composers as the number of works they say they know rises with level of education, while the most cultivated respondents refuse to acknowledge value in some of the works they know.

24. The office workers, especially the youngest ones, who have seen a high proportion of the films mentioned (3.5 on average, compared with 2.4 for the skilled manual workers and foremen, 2.3 for the craftsmen and small shopkeepers), are more interested in actors than directors (on average they name 2.8 actors and only 1 director, and often name the actors in films they have not seen). So if they had seen Visconti's *Rocco and His Brothers* more than any other category, it was probably because of the stars, Annie Girardot and Alain Delon.

25. The distinctive feature of the constellation of choices of the technicians (who, as a whole, occupy the positions closest to the centre of gravity) lies in the fact that they read many more scientific or technical books and more often go in for photography and home movies.

26. This law plays an important role in determining the choice of an artistic career rather than a less risky career (or vice versa) and, among the artistic careers, the choice of those which, at the moment in question, are the most risky (genre, manner etc.).

27. Another indication of the ambiguous position of the socio-medical services may be seen in the fact they are much more familiar with the smart sports than the other members of the middle classes (for example, only 41.6 percent of them say they have never played tennis, as against 70.4 percent of the primary teachers; for skiing, the corresponding figures are 41.6 percent and 78.5 percent).

28. The commercial junior executives and the secretaries, who have slightly less cultural capital than the members of the socio-medical services, make more disparate choices. They are interested in the films favoured by the working classes or the small employers (*The Longest Day, The Magnificent Seven, Vice and Virtue*), more than the teachers and the socio-medical services, while also being interested in the favourite films of the latter (*Salvatore Giuliano, The Trial, Les dimanches de Ville d'Avray*).

29. This pursuit of conformity to the ideal of distinction is revealed in the combined choice of 'pot-luck' meals and 'original and exotic' meals—'little Chinese restaurants'—or in series such as Françoise Hardy, Buffet, Van Gogh, which may be combined with the teachers' Kandinsky or the professionals' *Concerto for the Left Hand*.

30. This is true despite the fact that provincials may rely on magazines for a substitute for what they would derive from residence in Paris, i.e., that sense of being 'where the action is' which is the real basis of cultural flair or chutzpah (this is perhaps the chief function of *La Nouvel Observateur*).

31. Because the opportunities offered by the cultural environment are most profitably exploited by those with the highest cultural capital, and because the conformity-inducing pressures of the group on its members also rise with cultural capital, the gaps between the Parisians and the provincials become more pronounced at higher levels of education.

32. Georges Perec's novel *Les choses* (Paris, Julliard, 1965) captures in its own way the relationship which a couple of these mystified mystifiers (social psychologists

working in a market research agency) entertain with things whose whole value lies in the words used about them.

33. See M. Villette, 'La carrière d'un "cadre de gauche" après 1968', *Actes*, 29 (1979), 64–74.

34. One of the many determinants which incline the members of the new occupations to a subversive representation of the relations between the sexes is the fact that it is in the middle class—and especially, no doubt, its new fractions—that women most frequently have higher educational qualifications or occupational status than their husbands, and that the husbands' higher occupational status—given identical qualifications—is, no doubt, most resented.

35. Anticipating the point of view of the old morality on what can only be, in these terms, a sort of 'unthinkable', Kant writes: 'An obligation to enjoyment is a patent absurdity. And the same, then, must also be said of a supposed obligation to actions that have merely enjoyment for their aim, no matter how spiritually this enjoyment be refined in thought (or embellished), and even if it be a mystical, so-called heavenly, enjoyment.' I. Kant, *The Critique of Judgement*, trans. J. C. Meredith (Oxford, Oxford University Press, 1952), p. 48n.

36. M. Wolfenstein, 'The Emergence of Fun Morality' in E. Larrabee and R. Meyersohn, eds., *Mass Leisure* (Glencoe, Ill., Free Press, 1958), pp. 86–97.

37. As readers of avant-garde film criticism well know, *jouir/jouissance* can be eroticized by playing on its colloquial meaning, 'to come' (translator).

38. The endeavour to objectify a social ethic—especially a young and therefore aggressively imposed one—of course entails many dangers; lucidity may be no more than the effect of adherence to a contrary ethic. Each of the words used to characterize two antagonistic moralities can, of course, function as insults for champions of the opposite morality; it is therefore futile to hope to find a perfectly 'neutral' tone (the psychoanalytic vulgate, for example, will identify 'ascetic' with 'masochistic'). In each case, one would need to restore the experiential content of what is sociologically objectified (e.g., the heroic dimension of the ascetic striving for virtue, which takes its pleasure in effort and in the exaltation of self-transcendence, or the generous innocence of the liberationist cult, which is based on an acute sense of the absurdity of social constraints and stakes); and, as has constantly been done here, the dispositions described have to be referred to their conditions of production: repressive dispositions, for example, have to be seen as the product of repression (or social regression).

39. If the opposition between politicization and psychologization is carried too far, it may be forgotten that participation in a community of activists can also offer a solution to existential difficulties—even when these are not the exclusive reason for joining—by providing all the assurances and reassurances of immersion in an integrated, separate, self-contained group, with its own laws, language and ritual, demanding and recognizing devotion and sacrifice; see D. Mothé, *Le métier de militant* (Paris, Seuil, 1973). But reducing the logic of activism to that of group therapy may equally obscure the fact that psychological transactions, in particular the exchange of devotion and recognition ('the comrades' confidence'), are only the experiential (but not on that account negligible) form of much deeper transactions between the 'total institution'—which, demanding total dependence, gives most to those who give it most of what they are and have outside of it—and its members, who give it most (and receive most) when they expect most from it and have or are least outside of it.

40. See P. Bourdieu, *Outline of a Theory of Practice* (Cambridge, Cambridge University Press, 1977), pp. 92–93.

41. See N. Elias, *The History of Manners* (Oxford, Basil Blackwell, 1978), and *State Formation and Civilization* (Oxford, Basil Blackwell, 1982), vols. I and II of *The Civilizing Process*.

42. Though with no more evidence than the observations of ordinary existence and the indirect indications provided by our survey, I am inclined to think that the devotees of the sects organized around the new forms of bodily exercise are mainly recruited among the women of the new petite bourgeoisie, and that the theme of the liberated body takes its place in a problematic with a strong religious colouring (at least in its vocabulary) which also includes the 'problems of the couple', 'women's liberation' etc.

43. It is no surprise that these people should be so horrified by every form of sociological objectification and so fascinated by psychological or psychoanalytical enchantment. Nor that they should be ready to applaud all the fashionable variants of the old personalist denunciation of scientific 'reductionism', the elementary form of intellectual aristocratism, which has received unexpected reinforcement from the identification of every attempt at scientific objectification of practices with an ethical, even political condemnation (with the theme 'science = Gulag', which has enabled some well-worn post-Heideggerian fossils to make an unlooked-for come-back in the intellectual weeklies). Nor that the existence of a scientific sociology is as improbable as ever in times when the position of sociologist is one of the refuges for those intent on escaping classification.

44. Célestin Freinet, educationalist ('active method'); Carl Rogers, inventor of 'group dynamics'; Wilhelm Reich, psychoanalyst (translator's note).

45. See, for example, E. Dichter, *La stratégie du désir: une philosophie de la vente* (Paris, Fayard, 1961).

7. The Choice of the Necessary

1. It is no accident that disregard of the habitus and its effects is common to all bourgeois visions of the people, from the conservative pessimism which naturalizes the properties produced by social conditions to the optimism of the idealist revolutionism which forgets that the working class is shaped by necessity, even in the form of its revolt against necessity.

2. Need it be said that it is not sufficient to originate from these classes in order to produce a true representation of their view of their social world—if only because self-distancing can presuppose or induce relationships towards these classes (such as populist evangelizing) as radically closed as the simple distance of lifelong outsiders?

3. Norbert Elias relates (citing Taine) a gesture by the Duc de Richelieu which shows that the art of spending without counting, which in the seventeenth century marked the distance between the aristocrat and the saving, profit-making bourgeois, just as it now marks the distance between the bourgeois and the petit bourgeois, may, in the limiting case of a class whose very existence depends on the reproduction of its social capital, be the object of an explicit lesson: 'The Duke gave his son a purse full of gold so that the young man would learn to spend it like a *grand seigneur*. When the young man brought the gold back unspent, his father seized the purse and, in front of his son, threw it out of the window.' N. Elias, *Die höfische Gesellschaft* (Darmstadt, Luchterhand, 1975), pp. 103–104.

4. K. Marx and F. Engels, *The German Ideology* in *Collected Works,* V (London, Lawrence and Wishart, 1976), 295.

5. Given that the amount of income devoted to food rises strongly in real terms, the proportions spent on other items decline relatively less, and the structure of expenditure remains much the same as that of skilled workers. Certain items nonetheless rise significantly: small household electrical equipment, maintenance and repairs, hairdressing and beauty care, telephone, books, newspapers and entertainments, school expenses, holidays (C.S. III).

6. C. Roy, 'Les conditions de vie des ménages, exploitation triennale, 1965–66–67', *Collections de l'INSEE*, ser. M, no. 30 (December 1973).

7. It is no doubt the same 'realism' which excludes from political or union action everything which might give it a purely symbolic air as regards the means used (in contrast to the exhibitionism of student demonstrations) and especially the goals pursued.

8. The members of the working classes, like the members of dominated ethnic groups, may make it a point of honour to belie the image that the dominant have of their class. Thus the working-class cult of cleanness or honesty ('poor but honest'), like some forms of conspicuous sobriety, no doubt owes something to the concern to belie bourgeois prejudice. The same intention of rehabilitation underlies the discourse designed to persuade oneself that 'all we lack is money' (and not taste) and that 'if we had the wherewithal, we'd know what to buy' (or 'how to dress properly').

9. See P. Bourdieu et al., *Un art moyen: essai sur les usages sociaux de la photographie* (Paris, Ed. de Minuit, 1965), pp. 54–64.

10. See Y. Delsaut, 'L'économie du langage populaire', *Actes*, 4 (1975), 33–40.

11. This would explain the image that working-class women have of feminist demands.

12. A whole set of indices tends to show that the working classes remain attached to a more strict morality in everything concerned with sexuality and the sexual division of labour. Thus, as regards clothing, while—no doubt for functional reasons—they readily accept that women should wear trousers for work, they reject them much more often than the other classes at home and outside; similarly, they always strongly disapprove of miniskirts, especially at work and outdoors (*Sondages*, 1 [1968], 79). Manual workers and especially farm workers are less inclined (34 percent and 53.5 percent) than junior executives (57 percent) and senior executives (59 percent) to say they attach no importance to virginity; the proportion who consider that physical love has a fairly or very important place in life increases slightly as one moves up the social hierarchy; conversely, the proportion who say they have only loved one person in their lives declines as one moves up the hierarchy, as does the proportion who say one cannot love two people at the same time, or that love chiefly brings tenderness (rather than, say, physical pleasure), or that eroticism and infidelity destroy love (C.S. XLVI).

13. See H. Gournelle and A. Svakvary, 'Enquête sur le petit déjeuner en France', *Annales d'Hygiène de Langue Française*, 3 (May–June 1967), 28.

14. The reference to the division of labour between the sexes which connotes the representation of personal or collective identity (for example, a manual worker, invited to classify a set of occupations, put all the non-manual jobs in a single class, saying, 'All pansies [tous des pédés]!') evokes not so much the specifically sexual dimension of practice as the virtues and capacities associated by status with the two sexes, i.e., strength or weakness, courage or cowardice, rather than potency or impotence, activity or passivity.

15. This fact is underlined by the rapid devaluation of labour power which accompanies ageing.

16. See T. W. Adorno, 'On Popular Music', *Studies in Philosophy and Social Science*, 9 (1941). It would be easy to show, for example, that the most legitimate music is used, through records and radio, no less passively and intermittently than 'popular' music, without thereby being discredited, and without being accused of the alienating effects that are attributed to popular music. As for repetitiveness of form, it is greatest in Gregorian chant (which nonetheless has a high distinctive value), in much mediaeval music now in favour, and in much seventeenth- and eighteenth-century 'divertimento' music originally composed to serve as 'background music'.

17. 'In *Sud-Ouest Dimanche* of 8 August, you publish a photograph of a Renault 5 transformed into a four-seater convertible. An article subtitled "When a coach-builder and a couturier get together to dress a car" presents the coach-builder Lohr as the author of the car. This is quite untrue. I am the one who had the idea of this version of the vehicle, I designed it for Cacharel, and I hold the artistic copyright. I personally supervised its creation in the coach-builder's workshop; his role was purely technical. So a more accurate subtitle would have been: "When an artist and a couturier get together to dress a car"' (Reader's letter, *Sud-Ouest Dimanche*, 22 August 1976).

18. A peasant in the Béarn explained why he had not thought of becoming mayor, although he had won the most votes in the local elections, by saying: 'But I don't know how to talk!'

19. It would be interesting to determine, by a specifically linguistic analysis, precisely how this frontier is defined in the area of language. If one accepts the verdict of the interviewers' 'social sense', a good measure not of the linguistic status of the language used by the respondents but of the social image which educated interlocutors may have of it (the taxonomies used to classify speech and pronunciation are those of scholastic usage), it appears that this difference is in fact very marked between the manual workers (and also the craftsmen and small shopkeepers) and the clerical workers. Of the former, only 42 percent speak a French regarded as 'standard' (*correct*), as against 77 percent of the office workers (to which must be added 4 percent of 'refined' [*châtié*] speech, totally absent among the manual workers); similarly, the proportion judged to have 'no accent' rises from 12.5 percent to 28 percent.

20. Manual workers, the category who most often describe the ideal friend as 'bon vivant', are also those who most often—by far—say they are well-disposed towards someone who eats and drinks well (63 percent of them, as against 56 percent of the farmers and farm workers, 54 percent of the junior executives and clerical workers, 50 percent of the shopkeepers and craftsmen, 48 percent of the employers, senior executives and professionals—C.S. XXXIV). In a similar vein, I have already noted the taste for everything which makes the 'atmosphere' of a show, and also a celebration, a meal, and for those who contribute to it; and also the strongly marked propensity to expect images to immortalize the 'good times' of life and the symbols of festivity.

21. The 'career' available to manual workers is, no doubt, initially experienced as the opposite of the negative career which leads down into the sub-proletariat. What counts in 'promotion' is, together with financial advantages, the additional guarantees it gives against the ever present threat of falling back into insecurity and poverty. The potentiality of a negative career is as important in understanding the dispositions of skilled workers as is the potentiality of promotion for clerical workers and junior executives.

22. See G. Adam, F. Bon, J. Capdevielle and R. Mouriaux, *L'ouvrier français en 1970* (Paris, Armand Colin, 1971). (The CGT is, of the three main labour union organizations, the one most closely linked to a political party, the Communist Party, and strongest in the traditional industries—translator.)

23. Some 10.5 percent of the semi-skilled and unskilled workers and 17 percent of the shopkeepers cite Rousseau among the painters, as against 6 percent of the skilled workers, 3 percent of the primary teachers and technicians and 0 percent of the junior administrative executives. The name Braque, which is cited by 10.5 percent of the semi-skilled and unskilled workers and 4 percent of the skilled workers, had become unusually prominent on radio and TV at the time of the survey, because the artist's death coincided with the survey period.

24. The effects of differences in age and differences in education combine to produce fairly marked differences in tastes in singers. The foremen and skilled workers tend

to prefer the older, more established singers, but also those best placed in the hierarchy of cultural values—Piaf, Bécaud, Brel, Brassens—whereas the semi-skilled and unskilled tend to prefer Johnny Hallyday and Françoise Hardy.

8. Culture and Politics

1. K. Marx and F. Engels, *The German Ideology*, 2nd ed. (London, Lawrence and Wishart, 1974), p. 109.
2. It is the motor of conscious action if one accepts the equation posited by Marx in *The German Ideology* (ibid., p. 50) that 'language is real, practical consciousness'.
3. On the historical genesis of the philosophy of the 'invisible hand' and its function in economic and political thought, see A. Hirschman, *The Passions and the Interests: Political Arguments for Capitalism before Its Triumph* (Princeton, Princeton University Press, 1977).
4. Similarly, the field of artistic production delimits at every moment the field of possible artistic positions.
5. This very general relationship is also found in the area of artistic competence, where subjective exclusion ('That doesn't interest me' or 'That's not for the likes of us') is only the effect of an objective exclusion.
6. It is not possible, in the present state of research, to grasp the logic of the variations in the rates of non-response to identical questions asked by the same organization at different times (a series of IFOP surveys on nuclear energy, undertaken in 1974, 1975, 1976 and 1977). Everything suggests, in any case, that these variations remain smaller than the variations in the different expressed opinions.
7. G. Michelat and M. Simon, 'Catégories socio-professionnelles en milieu ouvrier et comportement politique', *Revue Française de Science Politique*, 25 (April 1975), 291–316.
8. The slightly higher figure for men may well be due to the fact that the question explicitly calls for the appreciation of a principle: 'Do you think that girls of 18 should (*il faut*) be allowed to see the films they want to?' (IFOP, March 1971).
9. 'Do you think that in industrial disputes the Government supports the workers' demands, supports the employers' interests, or is neutral?' (SOFRES, October 1970).
10. 'Among the following trade unions and political parties, who, in your view, best defends employees' interests at the present time—UDR, Centrists, PCF, CFDT, CGT, PS, CGT-FO?' (IFOP, 2 February 1980.)
11. 'In your view, is there or is there not a link between the Middle East conflict and the Vietnam War?' (IFOP, 9 October 1967). (President de Gaulle had just asserted that there was—translator.)
12. Similar distributions (43.4 percent of 'don't knows' among women, 19.6 percent among men, 38.9 percent among the least educated, 9.4 percent among the best educated) are observed on a question on foreign policy: 'Are you satisfied or dissatisfied with the Government's performance in the following areas: . . . foreign policy?' (IFOP 1966).
13. The link between indifference and impotence has been noted by various observers, for example: D. Riesman and N. Glazer, 'Criteria for Political Apathy', in A. W. Gouldner, ed., *Studies in Leadership* (New York, Russell and Russell, 1965), pp. 505–559; E. Kris and N. Leites, 'Trends in Twentieth-Century Propaganda', in G. Roheim, ed., *Psychoanalysis and the Social Sciences* (New York, IUP, 1947), esp. p. 400.
14. E. Deutsch, D. Lindon and P. Weill, *Les familles politiques aujourd'hui en France* (Paris, Ed. de Minuit, 1966), pp. 104–105.
15. On political activists in general, the main sources consulted were as follows: J. Lagroye, G. Lord, L. Monnier-Chazel and J. Palard, *Les militants politiques dans trois partis français: PC, PS, UDR* (Paris, Pedone, 1976); M. Kesselman, 'Système de

pouvoir et cultures politiques au sein des partis politiques français', *Revue Française de Sociologie*, 13 (October-December 1972). On Socialist activists: R. Cayrol, 'Les militants du Parti socialiste, contribution à une sociologie', *Projet*, 88 (September–October 1974); H. Portelle and T. Dumias, 'Militants socialistes à Paris', *Projet*, 101 (January 1976); *L'Unité*, no. 257, 1–6 July 1977; 'Qui sont les cadres du PS?', *Le Point*, no. 249, 27 June 1977. On Communist activists: F. Platone and F. Subileau, *Les militants communistes de la Fédération de Paris* (Paris, Fondation Nationale des Sciences Politiques, 1975). And on the Deputies: R. Cayrol, J.-C. Parodi and C. Ysmal, *Le député français* (Paris, Armand Colin, 1973); and M. Dogan, 'Les filières de la carrière politique', *Revue Française de Sociologie*, 8 (1967), 468–492.

16. These conclusions are based on a summary statistical analysis of the findings of a preliminary survey by extended interview (n = 130), carried out in the Paris region in 1970. (The small sample obviously makes it impossible to see the regularities which emerge as anything more than indications of tendencies, which will be used here as illustrations rather than demonstrations.) In the first stage, the respondents were given a set of 15 cards, each bearing the name of a movement, grouping or party, and were asked to group the cards as they wished (they were not explicitly asked to comment on the categories they applied or to attach names or descriptions to the groups they established). In the second stage, they were given a set of 24 cards, each bearing the name of a politician or trade unionist (one fictitious name, Philippon, was included, so as to measure reactions to an unknown name); they were first asked to say which group or party each individual belonged to, and then to group these cards.

17. At the risk of appearing sacrilegious, it has to be pointed out that it was in the name of the same faith in the legitimacy conferred by cultural competence (or, as it was often put at the time of the Popular Front, 'intelligence') that intellectuals were able to denounce the dangers of universal suffrage or, like Flaubert, to dream of the reign of the mandarins; just as they now feel both entitled and obliged, *by virtue of their essence*, to produce and profess their opinions on the great problems of the day.

18. The respondents were presented with a list of 17 problems and invited to say which they thought were political.

19. This survey was carried out by the publication of a questionnaire in a large number of daily and weekly papers, between 1 and 15 August 1969, at the request of the Association for the Expansion of Scientific Research (AEERS). (The fact that *L'Humanité* and *Le Parisien Libéré* did not publish it undoubtedly contributed to the under-representation of the working classes.) The questionnaire contained 20 questions on the organization of the school year, the situation of education, the changes in curriculum, teaching methods and university organization, the training, selection and salaries of teachers, the relations between teachers, parents and pupils or students, the powers of the different categories of staff, the functions of education (vocational training, 'character-building' etc.), politics in educational establishments, the raising of the school-leaving age, subsidies for Church schools etc. It was preceded by a text of varying length, depending on the newspaper, presenting the survey as a 'full-scale national consultation' on a 'subject of capital importance' organized 'with the kind assistance of the press' by the AEERS, 'an independent, non-profit-making movement'.

The 'events' of May 1968 started with a student uprising in Paris, turned into a general strike and seemed to threaten the whole Gaullist regime. When order was restored, the new Minister of Education initiated reforms of the educational system. (Translator's note.)

20. This population, in which the different groups are represented in proportion to their pretension to influence the educational system, is perfectly representative of the self-legitimated pressure group which has always managed to exert its influ-

592 / Notes to Pages 411-415

ence, at every level of the system. The *idées-forces* it expressed thus foretold what indeed subsequently came to pass: for example, the 'great majority'—for once the term is appropriate—of the respondents desired the continuation of the recruitment competitions (agrégation etc.), the introduction of selection, the maintenance of the grandes écoles, more emphasis on both general culture (for themselves) and vocational training (for other people) etc. On all the points on which comparison was possible (i.e., all the questions except those on the grandes écoles and the agrégation, which no survey institute has ever asked), the tendencies are stronger in the spontaneous sample than in the representative sample.

21. It goes without saying that these capacities and dispositions are linked to those which are needed in order to set pen to paper to answer a questionnaire, which are in turn linked to educational capital. Ethical dispositions exert a specific effect here, which is clearly seen when the respondent is invited to put in regular, prolonged work, as in panel surveys. (Thus the rate of response to the CESP surveys, in which the respondent has to note every quarter of an hour, for a month, the radio stations he has been listening to, varies to some extent with the cultural goodwill that is manifested in scholastic zeal. It is highest among junior executives and foremen, who are characterized by relatively high rates of library use, collecting etc.) One ought also to consider the specific effects of selection by newspaper, and endeavour to determine how far the fact that the enquiry was transmitted through the reader's usual newspaper rather than, for example, through the schools, an association, a union or a party may have affected the make-up of the population of respondents (for example, newspaper subscribers responded more often than occasional readers).

22. The parents who returned their questionnaires to the Cornec Federation of parents' associations (rather than directly to the AEERS) differ overall from the other parents by a lower social and educational level and by the higher proportion of female respondents. This suggests that previous mobilization within an organization and the additional 'authority' conferred by this membership tend to increase the propensity to intervene politically, other things being equal. (This would perhaps explain why, among the teachers, the spontaneous, non-affiliated respondents have very different characteristics from the 'pedagogic' activists, mainly recruited among women agrégées and certified (non-agrégé) men; see J. M. Chapoulie and D. Merllié, *Les déterminants sociaux et scolaires des pratiques professionnelles des enseignants du second degré et leurs transformations* [Paris, CSE, 1974], esp. pp. 120–124.) It is remarkable that the Cornec Federation parents, under-selected in respect of social and cultural capital, are, although more mobilized, generally slightly less inclined to answer the various questions, except (in particular) the one on subsidies for Church education, for which they have a higher rate of response.

23. CET: Collège d'enseignement technique (secondary technical school); CEG: Collège d'enseignement générale ('general secondary school'). (Translator's note.)

24. Every attempt to persuade the members of the working classes to express their vision of the social world (e.g., their image of the class structure) comes up against the difficulty created by this sense of impotence and unworthiness ('I don't see why people like you come and ask blokes like me—you know all that better than I do'). On the other hand, part of the horror aroused by sociology stems from the fact that it questions any Tom, Dick or Harry instead of consulting only the authorized spokesmen.

25. This analysis has the virtue of showing that, by emphasizing the dominant agents ('great men') or personified collective entities, school history conveys a charismatic philosophy of history which leaves no room for social interests or the con-

flicts between antagonistic groups and which calls for moral judgements rather than critical reflection on historical processes and their social conditions.

26. It is not uncommon for the demands of personal salvation (evening classes or docility towards superiors) to come into conflict with the demands of collective salvation (union activities etc.), for practical reasons and also because they spring from two totally opposed visions of the social world. Efforts at retraining or internal promotion (competitions etc.) would not be so positively sanctioned were it not that, in addition to technical improvement, they also guarantee adherence to the institution and to the social order.

27. One could point to a vast literature produced by the champions of the 'medical order' to defend the uniqueness of the medical art, freely performed by a free (and solitary) individual, or the indignant protestations of the university establishment at the call for the recognition of collective student projects.

28. This proposition, which has its equivalent in aesthetics, is a particular case of the more general proposition that the propensity and capacity to subordinate verbal or practical position-takings to explicit principles, which, as such, are subject to an intentional systematization (those of an ethic or aesthetic or a political theory, rather than those of an ethos) rise with cultural capital—this relationship being established as much through the conditions of existence necessary for the acquisition of such capital as through the effect of the specific abilities it gives.

29. To demonstrate the analogy between surveys and voting, one would have to analyse both the political philosophy implied in the questioning itself and that which is implied in the methods of analysis (in particular, the purely aggregative logic of statistics). It would be seen that the survey most overtly reveals its true nature when, aiming to predict the result of an election or referendum, it invites the respondents to give the equivalent of a vote.

30. Suffice it to point out that two-stage choice is very common in the area of taste, where, as has often been shown, consumers choose a producer or distributor (a shop, a theatre, a radio station etc.) and, through this choice, the pre-selected products they offer—when they do not simply delegate this choice to mandated experts, such as decorators, architects, and other vendors of aesthetic services, who play a rôle somewhat similar in such matters to that of the party.

31. Thus party membership or allegiance is only one factor among others, whose effects could be studied in the same way as the effects of sex, age or occupation. Specifically political principles function as factors, relatively autonomous of economic and social determinants, which (although adherence to these principles is not independent of these determinants) make it possible to produce opinions or practices contrary to immediate personal interest.

32. Of all intellectuals, Sartre is no doubt the one who felt most 'authentically' the opposition between the abstract reality of 'commitment', which is always experienced as arbitrary inasmuch as it is the product of a deliberate choice, and the opacity of a choice imposed by the conditions of existence.

33. This analysis is based on the findings of a post-1968 survey of a sample of 3,288 men, including 176 members of the intellectual occupations, presented by Mattéi Dogan to a French Political Science Association colloquium on workers and politics in western Europe.

34. See S. M. Lipset, 'Students and Politics in Comparative Perspective', *Daedalus,* Winter 1968, pp. 1–20. For a critique based on analysis of a survey of French students, see also Y. Delsaut, 'Les opinions politiques dans le système des attitudes: les étudiants en lettres et la politique', *Revue Française de Sociologie,* II (January–March 1970), 3–33.

35. It is no accident that the procuration (or assistance) which is the pre-condition of access to political opinion for those who are deprived of the means of production of 'personal opinion' is one of the more or less skilfully masked targets of conser-

vative or 'revolutionary conservative' thought; see P. Bourdieu, 'L'ontologie poli-tique de Martin Heidegger', *Actes*, 5–6 (November 1975), 109–156.

36. See G. Ansart, *De l'usine à l'Assemblée nationale* (Paris, Éditions Sociales, 1977).

37. As independent producers of their own discourse, intellectuals always tend to de-mand that the institutions claiming a monopoly of the legitimate production of symbolic goods, such as churches or parties, allow them the right to self-manage-ment of opinion. In this respect, the ecological movement, which refuses to be-have as the 'owner' of its electors' votes, declining one of the privileges of party apparatuses, represents the materialized ideal of the intellectual party. (In the present French electoral system, parties less well placed in the first round custom-arily urge their voters to transfer their votes to another party in the second round—translator.)

38. PSU: Parti socialiste unifié, a small left-wing party founded in 1960, characterized by anti-statism and ideas of *autogestion* (translator).

39. In 1966 de Gaulle withdrew French forces from NATO command (translator).

40. Here, too, there is a clear analogy with the cultural market. Could 'taste' function as an internalized system of classification if it were suddenly deprived of all the markers, all the objectified classifications and, in particular, all the indices of posi-tion in the field of production provided by places of publication and exhibition etc. which point the way to what Flaubert called 'the smart opinion'?

41. For a classic statement of these theses, see S. M. Lipset, 'Democracy and Working Class Authoritarianism', *American Sociological Review*, 24 (August 1959), 482–501.

42. He meant, 'It's against the interests of wage-earners (*la masse salariée*)'; *masse sa-lariale* means the total wage bill (translator).

43. This discourse, totally opposed to the homogeneity of the 'pure' products of an ethos or a political axiomatics, takes particular forms which could only be com-pletely accounted for by describing (just as Bachelard describes 'epistemological profiles') the 'political profiles' drawn by practices or discourses generated accord-ing to different principles, in different situations, i.e., in contexts in which the ef-fects of political inculcation or specifically political control are very unequally exerted.

44. What distinguishes these organizations in the universe of educational institutions is no doubt the fact that they perform their educative action within the primary groups, through agents—the activists—belonging to the group itself.

45. This ethical liberalism can be traced back to its basis in the changes in the mode of reproduction of the dominant class, which are recorded in recent changes in fam-ily law. They have the effect of rendering the 'virtues' of the old bourgeoisie un-necessary or even dysfunctional (the very virtues which the traditionalists, condemned to social decline by their inability to reconvert, strive to perpetuate, as if they regarded the reversal of bourgeois values as the cause of the decline of which they are victims and pinned their hopes of social salvation on ethical res-toration).

46. Michelat and Simon, 'Catégories socio-professionnelles en milieu ouvrier', esp. pp. 296–297.

47. The Paris newspapers devote to international affairs, anecdotal news (*faits divers*) and sport, respectively, 14.8 percent, 8.8 percent and 8.9 percent of their space; in the provincial press these proportions are reversed: 7.9 percent, 8.4 percent and 16.5 percent; J. Kayser, *Les quotidiens français* (Paris, Armand Colin, 1963), pp. 125–127. These differences would be even more marked if the national papers whose readership is mainly drawn from the dominant class (like *Le Monde*, *Le Fi-garo*) were separated from the others, which (at least in the case of *Le Parisien Libéré*) give as much space to *faits divers* and sport as the provincial press.

48. In this struggle market research is a weapon—in that it enables the newspaper's 'penetration' to be demonstrated to advertisers, who provide a high proportion of

a newspaper's income—much more than a means of knowledge assisting a better response to the expectations of the readership.

49. As opposed to those publications which are excluded as too 'marked' from places where reading-matter is traditionally supplied—waiting rooms, cafés, hairdressing salons etc.—the 'omnibus' weeklies which are specially designed to offend no section of the potential clientele (*Paris-Match, Jours de France, L'Express*) are perfectly adapted to the situations in which they are asked to perform this very function (*Le Parisien Libéré* and *France-Soir* often fulfil this rôle in barber shops).

50. One of the senior editors of a major 'quality' newspaper, asked if he would have published an interview with a notorious criminal, like the editors of a weekly magazine which had just been prosecuted for doing so, replied, 'Of course, but in indirect speech.'

51. Dogan, 'Les filières de la carrière politique.' (Force Ouvrière is the union organization created in 1947–48 by anti-Communists who split away from the CGT—translator).

52. The proportion of under-25s in the readership, insignificant for *Le Figaro*, is 25 percent in the case of *Le Nouvel Observateur;* and it is remarkable that the papers which have declined most severely in the last ten years are, along with the omnibus papers (*Le Parisien Libéré* and *France-Soir*), *L'Aurore* and *Le Figaro*, with their small proportion of young readers. Their decline and the rise of *Le Monde* and *Le Nouvel Observateur* very directly reflect the morphological changes in the dominant class in favour of the fractions richest in educational capital.

53. Just as what is transmitted through biological heredity is no doubt more stable than what is transmitted through cultural heredity, so the class unconscious inculcated by the conditions of existence is a more stable generative principle of judgements and opinions than explicitly constituted political principles, precisely because it is relatively independent of consciousness.

54. This does not exclude all the essentially ambiguous political positions (the paradigm of which is the 'conservative revolutionary' movement of pre-Nazi Germany), which no doubt reproduce, in their indeterminacy, the contradictions inherent in the revolt against social decline (a sort of contradiction in terms) or in the mismatch between individual trajectory and collective trajectory.

55. This strategy is very common in interpersonal relations, and especially in the economy of domestic exchanges, in which the impeccability acquired by services rendered allows the benefactor the rôle of a living reproach.

56. To understand the political practices and opinions of old people, one has to consider not only the withdrawal effect which, with retirement from the work milieu and the weakening of social relations, tends to reduce collective pressure and support, but also, and especially, the effect of social decline, which is stronger and more rapid in less privileged classes and can no doubt be understood by analogy with the effect of declining social trajectories on individuals or groups.

57. The unification of the economic and symbolic market and the corresponding weakening of locally based social spaces tends to favour the 'politicization' of peasant farmers, who, increasingly affected by the mechanisms of the economy and political decisions, have an increasing interest in being interested in politics. Although 'politicization' is not, as it is for industrial workers, necessarily equivalent to a move to the left, nonetheless the real possibility of this choice appears, and conservatism itself takes on a quite different meaning.

58. On this point, see P. Bourdieu, *Le sens pratique* (Paris, Ed. de Minuit, 1979).

59. This relative indeterminacy of the ethos with respect to the positions expressed no doubt explains the oscillations (e.g., between Gaullism and the Communist Party) of the most deprived fraction of the working class.

60. This is the question de Gaulle put to the nation in a referendum in 1969 (translator).

Conclusion

1. I. Kant, *Anthropology from a Pragmatic Point of View* (Carbondale and Edwardsville, Southern Illinois University Press, 1978), p. 141.
2. G. W. Leibniz, 'Meditationes de cognitione, veritate et ideis' in *Opuscula Philosophical Selecta* (Paris, Boivin, 1939), pp. 1–2 (see also *Discours de Métaphysique*, par. 24). It is remarkable that to illustrate the idea of 'clear but confused' knowledge, Leibniz evokes, in addition to the example of colours, tastes and smells which we can distinguish 'by the simple evidence of the senses and not by statable marks', the example of painters and artists who can recognize a good or bad work but cannot justify their judgement except by invoking the presence or absence of a 'je ne sais quoi.'
3. It would be the task of a genetic sociology to establish how this sense of possibilities and impossibilities, proximities and distances is constituted.
4. Just as the opposition between the unique and the multiple lies at the heart of the dominant philosophy of history, so the opposition, which is a transfigured form of it, between the brilliant, the visible, the distinct, the distinguished, the 'outstanding', and the obscure, the dull, the greyness of the undifferentiated, indistinct, inglorious mass is one of the fundamental categories of the dominant perception of the social world.
5. See G. Duby, *Les trois ordres ou l'imaginaire du féodalisme* (Paris, Gallimard, 1978).
6. E. Durkheim, *Elementary Forms of the Religious Life* (London, Allen and Unwin, 1915), p. 17.
7. A more detailed account of the theoretical context of these analyses will be found in P. Bourdieu, "Symbolic Power" in *Identity and Structure*, ed. D. Gleeson (Driffield, Nafferton Books, 1977), pp. 112–119; also in *Critique of Anthropology*, 4 (Summer 1979), 77–85.
8. Cf. J.-P. Sartre, *Being and Nothingness* (London, Methuen, 1969), pp. 557–565, esp. 562.
9. See H. Giles, 'Accent Mobility: A Model and Some Data', *Anthropological Linguistics*, 15 (1973), 87–105.
10. See G. Lenski, 'American Social Classes: Statistical Strata or Social Groups?', *American Journal of Sociology*, 58 (September 1952), 139–144.
11. These divergences also emerge, in the same survey, when the respondents are first asked to define social classes at the level of their town and then at the level of the whole country; the rate of non-response rises strongly in the latter case, as does the number of classes perceived.
12. Ordinary perception, which applies to practices the scheme of the broad and the narrow, or the expansive and the constrained, anticipates the discoveries of the most refined social psychology, which establishes the existence of a correlation between the room one gives oneself in physical space and the place one occupies in social space. On this point, see S. Fisher and C. E. Cleveland, *Body Image and Personality* (New York, Van Nostrand, 1958).
13. This is true in the ordinary sense but also in the sense of Kafka [*procès* = 'process' but also 'trial'—cf. Kafka's *Die Prozess*, *The Trial*, *Le Procès* in French—translator], who offers an exemplary image of this desperate striving to regain a social identity that is by definition ungraspable, being the infinite limit of all categoremes, all imputations.
14. The sophism of the heap of wheat and all the paradoxes of physical continua mean, as Poincaré observed, that one has simultaneously $A = B$, $B = C$ and $A < C$, or again, $A_1 = A_2$, $A_2 = A_3$, ... $A_{99} = A_{100}$ and $A_1 < A_{100}$. In other words, though it is clear that one grain does not make a heap, nor do two grains, or three, it is not easy to say whether the heap begins at 264 grains or 265; in other words, whether 265 grains make a heap, but not 264.

15. See P. Bourdieu and M. de Saint Martin, 'Les catégories de l'entendement professoral', *Actes*, 3 (1975), 68–93.
16. See Duby, *Les trois ordres*, esp. pp. 422–423.
17. Ibid., pp. 63–64, and 'Les "jeunes" dans la société aristocratique dans la France du Nord-Ouest au XIIème siècle', *Annales*, 19 (September–October 1964), 835–846.
18. Much the same could be said of women, were they not denied most of the advantages of renouncing responsibility, at least outside the bourgeoisie.
19. M. Billing and H. Tajfel, 'Social Categorization and Similarity in Inter-group Behaviour', *European Journal of Social Psychology*, 3 (1973), 27–52.
20. See, for example, H. Tajfel, 'Quantitative Judgement in Social Perception', *British Journal of Psychology*, 50 (1959), 16–21, and H. Tajfel and A. L. Wilkes, 'Classification and Quantitative Judgement', ibid., 54 (1963), 101–104; and for an overview of research in this area, W. Doise, *L'articulation psychosociologique et les relations entre groupes* (Brussels, A. de Boeck, 1976), pp. 178–200.
21. 'Wherever the groups and classes are set in sharp juxtaposition, the values and mores of each are juxtaposed. Out of group opposition there arises an intense opposition of values, which comes to be projected through the social order and serves to solidify social stratification'. L. Copeland, 'The Negro as a Contrast Conception' in E. Thompson, ed., *Race Relations and the Race Problem* (Durham, Duke University Press, 1959), pp. 152–179.
22. '. . . le pouvoir unificateur du nom, du mot d'ordre'—the unifying power of the name/noun, the rallying cry ('order word'). (Translator's note.)
23. One scarcely needs to point out the affinity between social physics and the positivist inclination to see classifications either as arbitrary, 'operational' divisions (such as age groups or income brackets) or as 'objective' cleavages (discontinuities in distributions or bends in curves) which only need to be recorded.
24. Here is a particularly revealing expression (even in its metaphor) of this social marginalism: 'Each individual is responsible for the demeanour image of himself and the deference image of others, so that for a complete man to be expressed, individuals must hold hands in a chain of ceremony, each giving deferentially with proper demeanour to the one on the right what will be received deferentially from the one on the left.' E. Goffmann, 'The Nature of Deference and Demeanour', *American Anthropologist*, 58 (June 1956), 473–502. '. . . routinely the question is that of whose opinion is voiced most frequently and most forcibly, who makes the minor ongoing decisions apparently required for the coordination of any joint activity, and whose passing concerns have been given the most weight. And however trivial some of these *little gains and losses* may appear to be, *by summing them all up* across all the social situations in which they occur, we can see that their total effect is enormous. The expression of subordination and domination through this swarm of situational means is more than a mere tracing or symbol or ritualistic affirmation of the social hierarchy. These expressions *considerably constitute* the hierarchy.' E. Goffmann, 'Gender Display'. (Paper presented at the Third International Symposium, 'Female Hierarchies', Harry Frank Guggenheim Foundation, April 3–5, 1974); italics mine.

Postscript

1. M. Proust, 'En mémoire des églises assassinées' in *Pastiches et mélanges* (Paris, Gallimard, 1970), p. 171.
2. For an aesthetic explicitly based on the antithesis of the beautiful and the facile, see S. Alexander, *Beauty and Other Forms of Value* (London, Macmillan, 1933), esp. pp. 40, 164. (In French, *facile* corresponds to both 'facile' and 'easy'—translator.)

3. Given in English in the text, and described as more distinguished than its French equivalent, *racoleur* (translator).

4. On several occasions, and in particular in an article on the relationship between psychoanalysis and art history—*Meditations on a Hobby Horse* (London, Phaidon Press, 1963), esp. pp. 37–40—E. H. Gombrich refers to the refusal of elementary, vulgar gratifications which is the basis of legitimate taste, or the 'fashionable *don'ts',* as he calls them, 'so easily picked up', which define legitimate taste (ibid., p. 146).

5. A. Schopenhauer, *The World as Will and Idea* (London, Routledge and Kegan Paul, 1883), vol. I, bk. I, pp. 268–269.

6. On the essential points, Schopenhauer's aesthetic can be regarded as a somewhat heavy commentary on Kant's aesthetic, and Fauconnet is quite justified in observing: 'Aesthetic judgement, which is essentially disinterested, is opposed in Kant's work to other, self-interested judgements, exactly as, in Schopenhauer, the voluntary action of the subject who knows only with a view to action is opposed to the contemplation of the pure subject.' A. Fauconnet, *L'esthétique de Schopenhauer* (Paris, Alcan, 1913), p. 108.

7. By the same token, Brecht's 'alienation effect' might be the gap whereby, within popular art itself, the intellectual asserts his distance from popular art, which makes popular art acceptable, i.e., acceptable to intellectuals, and, at a deeper level, his distance from the people, the distance presupposed by the intellectuals' leadership of the people.

8. It was 'refusal', says Kant, which 'brought about the passage from merely sensual to spiritual attractions.' I. Kant, 'Conjectural Beginnings of Human History' in *On History*, ed. L. W. Beck (Indianapolis and New York, Bobbs-Merrill, 1963), p. 57. Having indicated that sexual attraction 'can be prolonged and even increased by means of the imagination' when 'its object is removed from the senses', Kant links the discovery of beauty to sublimation of the sexual instinct and concludes: *'Refusal* was the feat which brought about the passage from merely sensual to spiritual attractions, from mere animal desire gradually to love, and along with this from the feeling of the merely agreeable to a taste for beauty' (ibid.).

9. Here and subsequently in the text, page numbers in parentheses refer to I. Kant, *Critique of Judgement,* trans. J. C. Meredith (London, Oxford University Press, 1952).

10. The specific force of the agreeable is manifested in the fact that it demands an immediate satisfaction of desire, preventing 'the conscious expectation of the future': 'This capacity for facing up in the present to the often very distant future, instead of being wholly absorbed by the enjoyment of the present, is the most decisive mark of the human's advantage.' 'Conjectural Beginnings', pp. 57–58.

11. Ibid., p. 55.

12. Paragraph 41, entitled 'The empirical interest in the beautiful', alludes to what Elias calls 'the process of civilisation'—'Only in society does it occur to him to be not merely a man, but a man more refined after the manner of his kind (the beginning of civilisation) . . . '—but only to cast it into the merely empirical in a single sentence: 'This interest, indirectly attached to the beautiful by the inclination towards society, and, consequently, empirical, is, however, of no importance for us here' (*Critique of Judgement,* pp. 155–156, and also 132). Another example of recognition of the social dimension of taste: 'A judgement upon an object of our delight may be wholly disinterested but withal very interesting, it relies on no interest, but it produces one. Of this kind are all pure moral judgements. But, of themselves, they do not even set up any interest whatsoever. Only in society is it interesting to have taste' (ibid., pp. 43–44, note).

13. Of music, Kant says that 'it is more a matter of enjoyment than of culture' (ibid., p. 194). And later he implicitly identifies the degree to which the arts 'cultivate'

the mind with the 'expansion of the faculties' they call for: 'If, on the other hand, we estimate the worth of the fine arts by the culture they supply to the mind, and adopt for our standard the expansion of the faculties whose confluence in judgement is necessary for cognition, music ... has the lowest place' (ibid., p. 195).

14. 'But as for the beauty ascribed to the object on account of its form, and the supposition that it is capable of being enhanced by charm, this is a *common* error and one very prejudicial to *genuine, uncorrupted, sincere* taste. Nevertheless, charms may be added to beauty to lend to the mind, beyond a bare delight, an adventitious delight in the representation of the object, and thus to advocate taste and its cultivation. This applies *especially where taste is as yet crude and untrained*' (ibid., p. 67; italics mine); 'he may even begin to harbour doubts as to whether he has formed his taste upon an acquaintance with a sufficient number of objects of a particular kind ...' (ibid., p. 139); 'the rectification and extension of our judgements of taste' (ibid., p. 141).

15. Some indices of Kant's inclination to identify the universal with the universe of cultivated people: 'One would scarce think it necessary for a man to have taste to take more delight in a circle than in a scrawled outline, in an equilateral than in one that is all lobsided [*sic*], and, as it were, deformed. *The requirements of common understanding ensure such a preference without the least demand upon taste*' (ibid., p. 87; italics mine); 'We demand both taste and feeling of every man, and, *granted some degree of culture, we give him credit for both*' (ibid., p. 116; italics mine). See also ibid., p. 147n.

16. Pointing out the very early link between still life and the *vanitas* motif—e.g., the timepiece symbolizing temperance—Gombrich acknowledges that the 'Puritan spirit' may find in this reminder an alibi for or antidote to the 'simple pleasures of the senses' offered by 'gorgeous flowers and appealing dishes', an immortalization of sensual enjoyment that 'feasts the eye and stirs up memories and anticipations of feasts enjoyed and feasts to come'; but he observes that 'a painted still life is *ipso facto* also a *vanitas*', because 'the pleasures it stimulates are not real, they are mere illusions' (*Meditations on a Hobby Horse*, p. 104).

17. It is clear what is hidden in the *Sollen* contained in the apparently constative utterances in which Kant presents the definition of pure taste.

18. It follows that the mere intention of speaking scientifically about works of art or aesthetic experience or, more simply, of abandoning the style of the smart essay, which is less concerned with truth than originality, is bound to be seen as one of the sacrilegious degradations which reductive materialism indulges in, and therefore as the expression of a philistinism which denounces what it is incapable of understanding or, worse, of feeling. (On the significance of the Carnival, see appendix 4, note 10—translator.)

19. The most systematic attempt in recent times to formulate this ideology is no doubt that by Malraux. Art, for Malraux, is the realm of freedom, and, as such, it is the symbol of man's power to create a significant, fully human world or, at the very least, of man's eternal struggle to transcend servitude and 'humanize the world.'

20. By treating the work in accordance with its intention, i.e., as a finality without an end, the beholder re-produces the act of creation, in a mimesis of the mimesis of Genesis. (The theory of 'creative reading' is also one of the ideological themes which, because they are indispensable to the reaffirmation of the 'spiritual point of honour' of the literate bourgeoisie, are endlessly reinvented.)

21. In that text, disdained by the commentators (who, because of its apparent triviality, have even wondered if it was not a product of senility), Kant first distinguishes between 'scholars', whether 'incorporated' (in the University guild) or 'independent', and mere 'men of letters' ('businessmen and technicians of scholarship'), 'priests, judges and doctors', who purvey knowledge acquired at the Uni-

600 / Notes to Pages 492-495

versity, and finally the clientele of the latter, 'the people, which is composed of ignoramuses'. He then contrasts the temporally dominant 'higher' faculties, law, medicine and theology, with the temporally dominated but spiritually dominant 'lower' faculty, that of philosophy, which has no temporal power but is 'independent of the orders of government'; perfectly autonomous, knowing only its own laws, those of reason, it is thereby entitled to exercise its *critical* power in total freedom. I. Kant, *The Conflict of the Faculties* (New York, Abaris Books, 1979).

22. N. Elias, *The Civilizing Process,* vol. I, *The History of Manners* (Oxford, Basil Blackwell, 1978), p. 9.
23. I. Kant, 'Idea for a Universal History' in *On History,* p. 21.
24. Kant, 'Conjectural Beginnings', pp. 55-56.
25. Kant, 'Idea for a Universal History', p. 21. Elias shows how the opposition between the court aristocracy and the cultured bourgeoisie was built up around the contrast between, 'on the one hand, superficiality, ceremony, formal conversation, [and] on the other, inwardness, depth of feeling, immersion in books, development of the individual personality'—in short, between the superficial and the deep (*The Civilizing Process,* I, 19). The whole of the second term of the opposition is contained in the 'slow efforts to improve the mind' to which Kant refers.
26. 'But that there is any intrinsic worth in the real existence of a man who merely lives for enjoyment, however busy he may be in this respect, even when in so doing he serves others—all equally with himself intent only on enjoyment—as an excellent means to that end, and does so, moreover, because through sympathy he shares all their gratifications,—this is a view to which reason will never let itself be brought round' (*Critique of Judgement,* p. 47). And in a footnote Kant denounces the 'supposed obligation to actions that have merely enjoyment for their aim, no matter how spiritually this enjoyment be refined in thought (or embellished), and even if it be a mystical, so-called heavenly, enjoyment' (ibid., p. 48n).
27. Another indication of this can be seen in the fact that Kant argues in favour of the *scholastic* teaching of art and the need to submit to *rules.* This is perfectly in accord with the logic of his subterranean discourse in defense of the academic values of *Kultur,* but in contradiction to his refusal of any empirical genesis of taste, which ought to make him subscribe to the theory of untrammelled genius (which he precisely combats—*Critique of Judgement,* p. 183).
28. The invariants of the professorial condition, and more especially of the position of the teaching profession within the dominant class (a dominated fraction) and within the class field as a whole, are sufficiently great, despite differences of epoch and society, to establish affinities of ethos which are the basis of the illusion of universality.
29. Would-be systematic thinking applies its universally applicable schemes to every object. This can lead to some amusing effects, typical of what Schopenhauer calls 'comic pedantry', when these schemes (the same ones that are at work in the *Critique of Judgement,* but there with every appearance of necessity) are too obviously running in neutral: 'I have outlived a good many of my friends or acquaintances who boasted of perfect health and lived by an orderly regimen adopted once and for all, while the seed of death (illness) lay in them unnoticed, ready to develop. They *felt* healthy and did not *know* they were ill; for while the *cause* of natural death is always illness, *causality* cannot be felt. It requires understanding, whose judgment can err. *Feeling,* on the other hand, is infallible; but we do not call a man ill unless he *feels* ill, although a disease which he does not *feel* . . .' etc. Kant, *Conflict of the Faculties,* p. 181.
30. J. Derrida, *La vérité en peinture* (Paris, Flammarion, 1978).
31. Ibid., p. 51.
32. Philosophical denial is here merely a particular form of artistic denial which, as is clearly seen in the case of music, is inseparable from a neutralization or denial of

the political and social: 'If Faust represents the German soul,' writes Thomas Mann, 'then he must be a musician; for the German's relationship to the world is abstract and mystical, in other words, musical.' T. Mann, 'Deutschland und die Deutschen', *Essays*, II (Frankfurt, Fischer Taschenbuch, 1977), 285.

33. Every field of scholarly production has its own 'rules' of propriety, which may remain implicit and only be known to initiates; sometimes, however, scholars endeavour to codify them (for example, Boileau, Rapin, d'Aubignac or Subligny, who exhorted the authors of tragedies to eschew subjects likely to offend the political or moral ideas of the audience, to exclude scenes of bloodshed which might shock, to adapt their characters to the rules of aristocratic etiquette and to avoid crude or vulgar terms).

34. See G. Scholem, 'Der Nihilismus als religioses Phänomen', *Eranos*, 1974; and J. Habermas, 'Die verkleidete Thora' in *Philosophisch-politische Profile*, 2nd ed. (Frankfurt, Suhrkamp, 1981).

35. One would need to make explicit not only the general properties of these borderline positions, such as the double games they allow and the double profits they secure, but also the double vulnerability, the doubling or objective and subjective uncertainty as to personal identity which they impose on their occupants.

36. Thus, Derrida denounces the artificiality and strain of applying the table of categories, established with respect to judgements of knowledge, to aesthetic judgement, which, as Kant constantly points out, is not a judgement of knowledge. Derrida, *La vérité en peinture*, pp. 79–83. By contrast, Louis Guillermit endeavours to show, through a comparison of the three *Critiques*, that Kant rethought his whole theory of sensibility—putting forward a new transcendental definition of feeling which breaks the link between feeling and the faculty of desiring—to make room for a new, disinterested type of pleasure, which he discovers in aesthetic judgement, contemplative pleasure; this pleasure is not linked to desire for the object and, indifferent as to its existence, is solely concerned with its representation. L. Guillermit, 'Esthétique et Critique' in H. Wagner, ed., *Sinnlichkeit und Verstand in der deutschen und französischen Philosophie von Descartes bis Hegel* (Bonn, Bouvier Verlag Herbert Grundmann, 1976), pp. 122–150.

37. By treating the *Critique* as a beautiful object, Derrida no doubt contradicts the deepest intention of Kant, who plays on the opposition between the frivolous and the serious—as is evidenced by the deliberately inaesthetic style—and seeks to place philosophy and the philosopher above art and the artist. But in doing so, Derrida grants the *Critique* the status of an *unconditioned* object, freed from social determinants, which every pure, purely internal reading grants to the work; and which, by the same token, it grants to itself.

38. Proust, 'En mémoire des églises assassinées', p. 170; italics mine. In 'Journées de lecture', Proust further analyses the different perversions of reading—the scholarly perversion, which identifies the search for truth with the discovery of a secret document, demanding 'material trouble', and the perversion of 'the lettered man', who 'reads for the sake of reading and of retaining what he has read'. *Pastiches et mélanges*, pp. 234–240; 'Days of Reading', in J. L. Hevesi, ed., *Essays on Language and Literature* (London, Allan Wingate, 1947), pp. 52–55.

39. *Pastiches et mélanges*, p. 244n; 'Days of Reading', p. 61n.

Appendix 1. Some Reflections on the Method

1. Such effects of fashion are also found in legitimate culture. Thus the social value of some of the works offered may have changed between 1963 and 1967, with the *Four Seasons* and *Eine Kleine Nachtmusik* being pulled towards 'middle-brow' culture by popularization.

2. Within each class and class fraction, a very similar number of interviews was carried out in Paris and the Paris region and in the Nord region. The Nord is characterized by a very different occupational structure from that of the Paris region and by a much lower average level of educational qualification. The 1968 census found many more industrial and commercial entrepreneurs (large and small) and fewer engineers, senior executives, technicians, junior executives and office workers in the Nord than in the Paris region. Except for primary teachers (relatively more numerous in the Nord), the fractions richest in cultural capital seem under-represented in this region.

3. *Ouvriers specialisés:* 'a misleading term, since such workers are specialized in nothing except the execution of one narrow, repetitive task, usually on the assembly-line. For this they require little training; the English term "semi-skilled" would be a very loose equivalent'; D. L. Hanley, A. P. Kerr and N. H. Waites, *Contemporary France: Politics and Society since 1945* (London, Routledge and Kegan Paul, 1979), p. 75 (translator's note).

4. See P. Bourdieu et al., *Un art moyen* (Paris, Ed. de Minuit, 1965), pp. 73-84, and P. and M. C. Bourdieu, 'Le paysan et la photographie', *Revue Française de Sociologie,* (April-June 1965), 164-174. In fact, this exclusion would no doubt be much less justified now, in view of the far-reaching changes which have occurred, inter alia, in the relationship between the peasantry and the educational system, all of them tending to unify the symbolic goods market.

5. It should also be noted that in the sample almost all the socio-occupational categories have a higher average educational level and higher social origin than in the INSEE surveys. It is not possible to establish exactly how far this is due to the high proportion of Parisians (see note 2, above) and how far to the more precise definition of the categories.

6. See Bourdieu, *Un art moyen.*

7. The same would of course apply to the judgements in the areas of interior decoration, clothing or cooking. It is true that the analysis (which was in fact carried out) of some particularly representative interiors might have brought out more clearly the concrete systematicity of these sets of objects and of the relationships (very clearly visible in the non-directive interviews) which link them to other sets, such as clothing or tastes in music. But establishing the statistical regularities presupposed developing the means of systematically grasping the most significant features of each universe, and also entailed sacrificing the power to evoke the whole wealth of each particular realization of the structure.

8. To avoid treating the effect of variations in the measuring conditions as objective differences, all the differences in the nature of the indicators, the phrasing of the questions, the coding of the responses, the conditions of the survey and the structure of the sample, were systematically taken into account. For example, in one survey, hunting and fishing are grouped in a single question, in another separated into two questions; educational level is coded in five categories in one case, in seven categories in another.

9. The economics of publishing made it necessary to exclude many statistical tables (or, at least, to reduce them to synoptic presentation) and many diagrams and documents (interviews, photographs etc.) which made a real contribution to the analyses. For the same reason a bibliography which, even when reduced to the useful and used texts, would have been immense, is not printed here. The list of complementary sources of statistical information (appendix 2) did, however, seem essential, to provide the indispensable means of verification in all the many cases in which the data used in the analysis could be only partially reproduced.

10. Conforama: a chain of cheap furniture stores; Guy Lux: a popular entertainer (translator).

11. Twenty-four further questions on photography are not reproduced here (see Bourdieu, *Un art moyen*).

Appendix 2. Complementary Sources

1. I am particularly grateful to Mme. M. C. de la Godelinais and Mr. C. Thélot for having supplied the (mostly unpublished) tables which were needed for secondary analysis of the INSEE surveys whose findings are used here. My thanks also go to Mr. P. Debreu, Mr. P. Leroux and Mr. P. Ghigliazza for generously supplying data. Use was, of course, also made of earlier surveys by the Centre de sociologie européenne (sometimes with secondary analysis), such as the survey of museum-going (see P. Bourdieu and A. Darbel, *L'amour de l'art* [Paris, Ed. de Minuit, 1966], the survey on students and culture (see P. Bourdieu and J. C. Passeron, *The Inheritors* [Chicago, University of Chicago Press, 1979]) or the survey of the students of the grandes écoles.

2. These are given for each 'tax' household (*foyer*). According to the INSEE definition, a household (*ménage*) consists of all the persons living in the same dwelling occupied as main residence ('usual address'), whatever the number of persons or their relationship to the holder of the tenure. For tax purposes, the *foyer fiscal* is defined more narrowly: it includes the head of the household, his spouse, if any, and the persons recognized as his dependants for tax purposes, i.e., all the persons taxed together.

3. The data given here are for households (*ménages*). For each socio-occupational category, consumption is also indicated per capita and per 'consumption unit'. According to the INSEE definition, the number of consumption units in a household is found by weighting as follows: first adult = 1 unit; each other adult = 0.7 unit; each child (under 14) = 0.5 unit.

4. In reviewing the statistical sources, three bibliographical tools proved particularly useful: C. Guinchat, *Bibliographie analytique du loisir: France, 1966–1973* (Prague, Centre européen pour les loisirs et l'éducation, 1975); A. Willener and P. Béaud, *Nouvelles tendances de la consommation culturelle: vers une troisième culture* (Paris and Cordes, CECMAS, 1972), which brings together quantitative data and survey findings on museums, photography, cinema, TV, music etc.; and the bibliographies of books and articles published each year from 1969 to 1973 on 'cultural development and action', compiled by the research department of the Ministry of Culture.

Appendix 4. Associations: A Parlour Game

1. This sociological test reveals a logic at work in the area of politics and images of the social world that is entirely similar to the logic found operating in the mythico-ritual practices of pre-capitalist societies. It thereby demonstrates that the clear-cut distinction social science makes between 'primitive' or 'savage' thought and 'civilized' thought can only be due to ignorance.

2. In 1975 these politicians occupied the following positions: Giscard d'Estaing, President; Chirac, Prime Minister, Gaullist leader; Marchais, leader of Communist Party; Mitterrand, leader of Socialist Party; Poniatowski, Minister of the Interior; Servan-Schreiber, leader of the Radicals (briefly a minister in 1974; author of *Le défi américain,* published in 1967). (Translator's note.)

3. In France, yellow is the colour of the strike-breaker, the 'scab'; in the 1974 presidential campaign, Servan-Schreiber sided with Giscard against Mitterrand, and was rewarded with a ministry (translator).

4. Servan-Schreiber's *Le défi américain* (translator).

5. To measure the realism of this 'collective representation' one only has to look back at the photograph of the Servan-Schreiber interior, near the end of chapter 5.

6. *Le gendre de Monsieur Poirier* is a play on this theme by Emile Augier and Jules Sandeau, published in 1854 (translator).

7. See P. Bourdieu, *Outline of a Theory of Practice* (Cambridge, Cambridge University Press, 1977).

8. In addition to the tables published in *Sondages,* it was possible to analyse the distributions by sex, age-group and income group, but the distributions by socio-occupational category were not available.

9. It can be seen that the respondents, when the series that is proposed allows them to (as it does here by offering a graduated series of pertinent symbols), make significant connections between *all* the elements in the two series, instead of considering only two or three of them—as they do in most of the other series, in which some of the elements are only defined negatively, by elimination (e.g., lilac and carnation in the flower series, and Chirac, or to a lesser extent Poniatowski, in most of the series). This is an example of the effect inevitably produced by offering a *finite series of products* which excludes possibilities consciously or unconsciously expected (e.g., belote in the game series or red in the colour series) and offers abstract or unreal possibilities which may attract some choices. Another example of the same effect is the attribution of the ant to Giscard, faute de mieux; in a different context of possibilities, the ant—hardworking, modest, thrifty, obstinate and, above all, small and *numerous*—would rather suggest the ascetic virtues of the petite bourgeoisie as opposed to the conspicuous improvidence of the aristocracy and bourgeoisie. (The finite-offer effect also explains why, of the two literary oppositions—the ant and the grasshopper, the fox and the crow—only the first is used with the same logic as in the La Fontaine fable, while in the second, also because of the symbolic charge of the crow, the two elements function separately.)

10. A whole aspect of popular revolt, seen in insults, oaths and especially in truly popular festivity, which has now been ousted by home entertainments (I am thinking of the analyses by Mikhail Bakhtin in his *Rabelais and His World* [Cambridge, Mass., M.I.T. Press, 1968]), works in this way, through the logic of the Saturnalia, in which the usual order is turned upside down symbolically and *temporarily* ('Non semper Saturnalia erunt', said Seneca).

Illustration Credits

Russell Lee, Farm Security Administration, 45; ELF-AQUITAINE, 46; Piet Mondrian, *Broadway Boogie Woogie,* 1942–43. Collection, The Museum of Modern Art, New York, 51; Piet Mondrian, *Painting I,* 1926. Collection, The Museum of Modern Art, New York. Katherine S. Dreier Bequest, 51; Gino Severini, *Dynamic Hieroglyphic of the Bal Tabarin,* 1912. Collection, The Museum of Modern Art, New York. Acquired through the Lillie P. Bliss Bequest, 51; X. Lambours, Viva, 145; H. Gloaguen, Viva, 145; X. Lambours, Viva, 148; F. Hers, Viva, 148; C. Raimond-Dityvon, Viva, 148; C. Raimond-Dityvon, Viva, 149; H. Gloaguen, Viva, 149; P. Guis, Rapho, 166; R. Doisneau, Rapho, 166; Arnaud Legrain, Viva, 166; M. Delluc, Viva, 167; C. Raimond-Dityvon, Viva, 167; P. Michaud, Rapho, 167; Air France, 191; J. P. Verney, Ministère de l'Agriculture, 191; P. Bringe, Ministère de l'Agriculture, 191; C. Raimond-Dityvon, Viva, 191; Chambre de Métiers de la Meuse, 191; R. Doisneau, Rapho, 191; C. Raimond-Dityvon, Viva, 200; Prospectus de *Sculpture humaine,* 210; *Tennis-magazine*/Sygma, 210; M. Delluc, Viva, 242; Esalas Baitel, Viva, 242; A. Dagbert, Viva, 242; D. de Saint-Sauveur, *Le Figaro-Magazine,* 268; Documentation Séminarc, 307; R. Doisneau, Rapho, 313; *Maison et Jardin,* 313; C. Raimond-Dityvon, Viva, 373; C. Raimond-Dityvon, Viva, 377; Y. Jeanmougin, Viva, 377; *La Republique des Pyrenees,* 383; Y. Jeanmougin, Viva, 385; C. Raimond-Dityvon, Viva, 385; C. Raimond-Dityvon, Viva, 455.

Index

Academic market, 13, 23, 88, 91, 93, 96
Acquisition of cultural competence,
2-3, 65-66, 68, 71-72, 80, 85, 95
Adorno, T. W., 386
Aesthetic, 44-50, 485-488; popular aesthetic, 4-5, 32-34, 41; pure aesthetic,
5; dominated aesthetic, 41; anti-
Kantian, 41-42
Aesthetic choices, and ethics, 283;
286-287
Aesthetic disposition, 28-30, 50, 53-56,
263; and photography, 35, 39-40, 42;
and cultural capital, 39
Aesthetic distancing, 34-35, 39-40
Aesthetic-in-itself, 4, 67
Aestheticism, 5, 44, 47, 58; revolu-
tionary, 48
Age, 16, 106; generational conflicts, 1,
296; and cinema-going, 26; bourgeois
adolescents, 55; and income, 104; and
educational capital, 104-105; social
ageing, 110-111; and sports, 212,
219; and political ideology, 353-354
Alienation, 446; and being-for-others,
207; and body image, 207
Allodoxia, 142, 155, 164, 323, 326, 327,
428, 459
Althusser, Louis, 228
Analogy, 53; to male/female differences,
382-383
Analysis of essence, 72
Anti-intellectualism, 93, 293
Appearances, 253-254
Appropriation of cultural products, 23,
227-228, 230, 267, 269-270, 280-281;
material or symbolic, 228, 282-283;
struggles over, 249-250; quality of
goods, 281-282
Appropriation of economic goods,
249-250

Aristocracy, 24, 70, 281
Aristotle, 258, 489
Art, 7, 80, 176, 254
Art dealers, 122
Art galleries, 273
Art museum, 30, 272-273
Art of living, 47-48, 57, 254, 310,
370-371
Artifice, 491
Artists, 3, 62, 176, 228, 239, 267, 295;
appropriation of cultural goods, 282;
and patrons of art, 316-317
Asceticism, 214, 219, 256, 269, 287, 317
Associations, 546-547, 552-553,
556-559
Attributive judgement, 52, 473,
475-476, 479, 556, 558
Authenticity, 74
Autodidacticism, 24, 67, 84-85, 147,
328-329
Autonomy: of production, 3, 226; of
form, 30, 49; of art works, 228
Avant-garde culture, 1, 239, 294
Avant-garde theatre, 19, 234-235, 239

Bakhtin, Mikhail, 491
Bally, Charles, 95, 472
Barbarous taste, and pure taste, 30-32,
43-44, 178
Barthes, Roland, 76
Beauty care. See Health and beauty care
Being and seeming, 252
Body image, 191-193, 380; and foods,
190; and social space, 206-208; alien-
ated body, 207; body-for-others, 207
Body language, 177
Borges, Jorge Luis, 258
Bourgeois, 12, 19, 28, 62, 75, 91, 176,
265; and dominated aesthetic, 41;
shocking the bourgeois, 47-48; semi-

Bourgeois (*Cont.*)
  bourgeois, 150; and survey data, 174;
  meals, 196, 199; entertaining, 197;
  clothing, 201–202; taste, 292–294; fertility strategies, 333. *See also* Petite
  bourgeoisie
Bridge game, 217
Bureaucracies, 370

Cafés, 183
Casualness, 256
Charisma, 31, 208, 390
Charm, 208
Chess game, 217
Child-rearing, 368–369
Cinema, 26–28, 32, 63, 271–272; ethics
  and aesthetics, 45–46
Circus, 34
Civilization, 74
Class habitus. *See* Habitus
Class solidarity, 381, 384, 390, 394
Class struggle, 48, 113, 165, 245–246,
  249–251, 254, 315–317, 451
Classical taste, 65
Classification, 466–467, 471–473,
  477–478; and struggles, 479–481
Clerical workers, 122; ethics and aesthet-
  ics, 46; and food, 180
Clothing, 187; working class use of,
  200–201; bourgeois use of, 201–202;
  and gender, 201–202; and counter-
  culture, 233
Clubs, 162–163
Commercial employers, 115–116, 120,
  122, 124, 263, 266–267; spending by,
  184; clothing of, 202; and sports,
  219; life-style, 305; newspaper reading
  by, 450
Commercial entrepreneurs, 123, 137
Common-sense knowledge, 22, 33, 101
Competence, 2, 13, 23, 50, 52, 63,
  65–66, 86, 96, 263, 281
Competition: in sports, 214; over cul-
  tural goods, 230–231
Condescension strategies, 472–473
Conditions of existence, 53–54, 56;
  classes of, 101, 114; and habitus, 170,
  172; and taste, 178; adaptation to,
  246
Conformity, 331, 381–382
Connoisseurs, 66, 279–280
Conspicuous consumption, 31, 55
Consultancy, 152–153
Consumption of cultural goods, 1–2,

6–7, 13, 100, 280; and social spaces,
  176; and production, 230, 232; manner of, 282
Correspondence analysis, 260–261, 342
Cosmetics. *See* Health and beauty care
Counter-culture, 144, 251; and sports,
  220; and clothing, 233
Craftsmen, 122, 135, 137, 141, 345–346;
  ethics and aesthetics, 46; newspaper
  reading by, 448
Credit, 163–164
Critics, 234–235, 239–240
Cultivated disposition, 13, 24
Cultural capital, 12, 53–54, 70, 114–115,
  261, 264; and cinema-going, 27; and
  aesthetic disposition, 39; and educational capital, 13–14, 18, 80–83, 133;
  and hierarchy of classes, 116, 120; and
  sports, 220; and economic capital,
  303
Cultural competence. *See* Competence
Cultural goodwill, 321, 323; of petite
  bourgeoisie, 352
Cultural nobility, 2
Culture, 1, 74, 99, 250; extra-curricular,
  1, 24–25, 63, 65; general, 23–25; democratization of, 228. *See also* Legitimate culture

Dannenmaier, W. D., 208
Delegation, 72
Democratization: of schooling, 143–144;
  of culture, 228
Derrida, Jacques, 494–495
Detachment, 4, 6
Diachronic properties of positions, 345,
  346, 350, 453, 454
Diplomas, 25
Discriminatory selection, 162
Disenchantment, 144, 146
Disinterestedness, 4, 41, 55–56, 254,
  282; in production of culural prod-
  ucts, 240
Dispossession, 386–387, 390; and politi-
  cal opinion, 428
Distancing, 34–35, 39–40, 54–55, 256,
  394
Doctes, 69, 73–74
Domestic servants, 46, 184
Dominant class, 23–24, 57, 68–69, 114,
  123, 258, 266; generational conflicts
  in, 1; taste in, 16; ethics and aesthet-
  ics, 46; interior decoration, 78–79; or-
  ganisation of, 116; degree of closure,

120, 132; supply and demand in, 232; and symbolic struggles, 254; class fraction, 260; appropriation of cultural products, 270, 282; and producers of cultural goods, 316–317; fertility strategies, 333; and working classes, 382–383; newspaper reading by, 449–450
Dominated aesthetics, 41
Domination, 386, 387, 395, 396
Doxa, 471
Drama. *See* Theatre
Duby, Georges, 470, 477
Dumézil, Georges, 470
Durkheim, Emile, 72, 80, 471

Ease, 55, 71, 176, 255–256, 339
Economic capital, 114–115, 263–264; and hierarchy of classes, 116, 120; and taste, 177–178; and educational capital, 287, 291; and cultural capital, 303
Economic necessity, 54–56, 177; taste for, 374–376, 378–380
Economic power, 55, 56
Economy of practices, 224
Educational capital, 12, 53, 63, 92; and cultural capital, 13–14, 18, 80–83; and competence, 23; and gratuitous knowledge, 26; and cinema-going, 26–28; and occupation, 103–104, 296–297, 301, 303–304, 310, 315, 390; and age, 104–105; and gender, 105; and social origin, 105; and reproduction strategies, 137, 147, 150; and economic capital, 287, 291; and politics, 407–410
Educational function of art, 49–50, 74
Educational system, 13, 23–26, 67; investment in, 120, 122; hierarchy within, 122; and mobile classes, 132–133; and cultural capital, 133; devaluing of academic qualifications, 133–135, 142–143, 147, 150; democratization of schooling, 143–144; changes in, 154–156; uses of, 157, 160; and autodidacts, 328–329; and dispossession, 387, 390; opinions concerning, 411
Elective affinities, 241
Elias, Norbert, 73, 227
Empiricism, 245
Engels, J. F., 177, 397
Engineers, 116, 124, 135, 265; clothing of, 202; ascetic disposition of, 287;

generational conflicts, 296; newspaper reading by, 448
Enjoyment, 490–495
'Enlightened elitism,' 252
Entertaining, 197
Eternity, 72
Ethics, and aesthetics, 44–50, 283, 286–287, 370–371
Executives, 116, 120, 122, 124, 137, 265, 267, 351; ethics and aesthetics, 46; food purchases by, 185; clothing of, 202; and sports, 219; ascetic disposition of, 287; generational conflicts, 296; life-style of, 305; newspaper reading by, 448, 450
Expectations of audiences, 239–240
Experience, 68, 74–76; lived experience, 100
Extra-curricular culture, 1, 24–25, 63; and social origin, 65

Fair play, 215
Family heirlooms. *See* Inheritance
Farm laborers and farmers, 114, 124, 135, 137
Fashion, 378
Females. *See* Gender
Femininity, 191–192
Fertility strategies, 331–332, 337–338
Fetishism, 250
Flaubert, Gustave, 254
Flying, 218
Folk dancing, 58
Foods, 79, 177; attitudes towards eating and drinking, 179–180, 183; expenditures on, 184–185, 187, 190, 199–200; gender and eating habits, 185–187, 190–192, 195; and body image, 190; working-class meals, 194–195, 197; bourgeois meals, 196, 199
Form and substance, 253
Formalism, 33–34; bourgeois, 196–197, 199, 201; in sports, 220
Francastel, Pierre, 68
Freedom, 24, 254–255; working-class, 194–195, 197, 201; in sports, 220
Frivolity, 74
Furnishings, 77–79
Future social ascension, 346
Future, planning for, 180, 183

Games of culture, 12, 54, 250–251, 330
Gastronomy, 68
Gautier, Jean-Jacques, 240

Gender, 107–108; and photogenic object judgements, 39–40; and music recognition, 63; and educational capital, 105; and occupation, 108; and devaluing of academic qualifications, 133–134; and eating habits, 185–187, 190–192, 195; and clothing, 201–202; analogy to male/female differences, 382–383; and personal opinion, 402–405; and politics, 406–407, 410
General culture, 23–25
Genet, Jean, 33
Geographical space, and social distance, 124
Gide, André, 415
Gombrich, E. H., 50, 227
Goodwill, cultural, 321, 323; of petite bourgeoisie, 352
Gramsci, Antonio, 386
Gratuitous knowledge, and educational capital, 26
Greco, Pierre, 463

Habitus, 101–102, 109, 114, 142, 170, 260, 372–374, 466–467; production of, 123; and conditions of existence, 170, 172; and life-styles, 172–173; and political opinions, 437–440
Halbwachs, Maurice, 250
Health and beauty care, 179–180, 184, 202, 378; and foods, 190; of petite bourgeoisie, 206; of working classes, 206
Hedonism, 180, 183, 394; and sports, 219
Hegel, G. W. F., 488
Hierarchies of legitimacy, 86–88, 93
High-society market, 88–89
History of art, 4
Homology: between social spaces, 175, 208; in production/consumption, 232–233, 241
Hosting occupations, 152
Humane and humanitarian tasks and feelings, 40

Idealization, 58
Income. *See* Economic capital
Industrialists, 115–116, 120, 122, 124, 135, 137, 263, 266–267; spending by, 184; clothing of, 202; life-style of, 305; newspaper reading by, 448, 450
Inheritance, 19, 76–78, 80–83, 265; and social class trajectories, 110

Intellectual taste, 292–294
Intellectuals, 12, 62, 176, 228, 239; right-wing and left-wing, 12, 292–293; appropriation of cultural products, 270, 282; and patrons of art, 316–317; art of living, 370–371; and working-class condition, 372–374
Intention, 3; of observer, 30; aesthetic, 47; artistic, 52
Interior decoration, 77–79
Intolerance, 56–57
Intuitionism, 20
Investment sense, 85–88, 142, 249

Kant, Immanuel, 5, 42, 74, 466, 486–490, 492–494, 498; Kantian and anti-Kantian aesthetic, 5, 41–42
Kantarovitch, H., 72
Kitsch, 62, 282
Knowledge, 68, 74–76, 470; gratuitous, 26; of culture, 318–319, 330; and autodidacts, 329

Labour market, 224–225. *See also* Occupations
Langer, Suzanne, 31
Language, 176–177, 194, 226–227, 331, 476; linguistic ease, 255; political, 459–465
Larbaud, Valéry, 228
Legitimate culture, 26, 28
Leibniz, G. W. von, 466
Leisure activities, 179–180
Libraries, 273
Life-style, 101, 124, 170, 193, 208, 258, 283; and habitus, 172–173; and taste, 173–175; indicators of, 263; of new bourgeoisie, 304–305, 309–311, 314–315
Linear thinking, 107, 126
Literary quotation, 73
Lived experience, 100
Love, 243–244
Lower middle class, 44–47
Luxury goods and activities, 55, 278–282, 287

Males. *See* Gender
Manners, 66, 68–72, 91, 95
Manual workers: ethics and aesthetics, 46; and food, 180; clothing of, 201; fertility strategies of, 333
Marital status, and social class, 108–109
Markets, 65, 85–86, 95–96, 113; aca-

demic and non-academic, 13, 23, 88, 91, 93, 96; high-society, 88–89; toy market, 223–224; labour market, 224–225
Married couples, homogeneity of, 241, 243
Marx, Karl, 178–179, 251, 280, 397, 467
Mass production, 386
Materialism, 394
Medical and social services, 123
Melodrama, 34
Méré, Chevalier de, 70
Meritocracy, 291, 303
Michelat, G., 439
Middle class, 111–112, 122–123; taste of, 16; and popular aesthetic, 32; and significance of objects, 43; ethics and aesthetics, 44–47
Middle-brow culture, 323, 325, 327
Middle-brow taste, 16, 58, 60, 267
Misappropriation, 431
Mondains, 69–70, 73–74
Morality: of petite bourgeoisie, 352–353, 367–369; and demoralization, 384; and politics, 432–437
Museums, 30, 272–273
Music, 16, 18–19; knowledge of composers, 13–14, 63, 89; inner music, 19; songs and singers, 60–61, 83; playing of musical instrument, 75–76; concert-going, 272–273

Naivety, 5, 62
Natural feelings, 40
Natural taste, 67, 68, 74
Newcomers, 19
Newspaper reading, 21, 234, 417; and political opinions, 440–444, 446–451
Nietzsche, F. W., 177, 252, 414
Noblesse oblige, 24
Nostalgia, 58

Objectification, 12, 85, 100, 208, 227, 239
Objectified philosophy, 496–497
Objective class, 101
Objectivism, 244
Occupations, 106; and educational capital, 103–104, 296–297, 301, 303–304, 310, 315, 390; and gender, 108; stability of groups, 137, 141; changing nature of, 150–152; representational, 152
Office workers, 104, 114, 135, 345, 351;

food purchases by, 180, 185; clothing of, 201; fertility strategies of, 332–333; newspaper reading by, 447–448
Opera, 272
Opinion. *See* Personal opinion; Questionnaires
Ortega y Gasset, José, 4, 31–32

Painting, 14, 16, 20, 75, 269
Panofsky, Erwin, 2, 29–30
Patrons of art, 316–317
Peer-group pressure, 26
Personal opinion, 398–402, 405, 411, 414–417; and gender, 402–405; production of, 417–426
Personality, 281
Petite bourgeoisie, 14, 40, 48, 57–58, 79, 91, 123, 365; declining, 61, 265–266, 346, 350–351; new, 61, 265–266, 354, 357–363, 365–369, 553; pretensions of, 62, 294, 362; health and beauty care, 206; life-style of new bourgeoisie, 304–305, 309–311, 314–315; reverence for culture, 321, 323; and middle-brow culture, 326–327; seriousness of, 330–331; fertility strategies of, 331, 337–338; upward mobility of, 333, 337–338; taste of, 339, 341–343; executant, 351–354; and personal opinion, 415–416
Philosophy, 496–497
Photography, 32, 58; and aesthetic disposition, 35, 39–40, 42; ethics and aesthetics, 44–47
Physical properties, 384; occupational profit from, 152–153
Piaget, Jean, 80
Pirandello, Luigi, 33
Place of residence, 105, 116
Pleasure, 367–368, 490–495, 498–499
Political space, 451, 453
Politics, 48, 109, 291, 397–398, 411, 414; and social class, 111, 427–428, 440; and age, 353–354; interest or indifference towards, 405–407; and gender, 406–407, 410; and educational capital, 407–410; and dispossession, 428; and morality, 432–437; and habitus, 437–440; and newspapers, 440–444, 446–451; trajectory effect, 453–459; and language, 459–465
Popper, Karl, 228
Popular aesthetic, 32

Popular taste, 16
Popularization, 323, 326
Populism, 374
Pornocracy, 48
Positivism, 20, 94
Practical perceptions, 29
Precocity, 70
Preferences, 13, 19, 261
Presentation, 184, 202, 206; and sports, 214
Pretension, 14, 30, 62, 251–253, 294, 381–382; of petite bourgeoisie, 62, 294, 362
Production of cultural goods, 12, 20, 231; and consumption, 230, 232; and taste, 231, 241; and social class, 233–234; and audience expectations, 239–240; servility in, 240; sincerity in, 240; and dominant class, 316–317
Profane and sacred, 6–7, 19
Professionals, 102–103, 114, 122, 264, 266–267; spending by, 184; food purchases by, 185, 190; and sports, 219; generational conflicts, 296; newspaper reading by, 448
Profundity, 74
Programme of cultivation, 67
Proselytism, 228, 370
Proudhon, P. J., 48–49, 251
Proust, Marcel, 21, 53, 97, 173, 485, 498–499
Psychoanalysis, 367, 369
Pure gaze, 3–4
Pure taste, 486–488; and barbarous taste, 30–32, 43–44, 178
Purity, 176, 254

Questionnaires, 95, 194; and personal opinions, 399–402, 405; methodology of, 503–518

Rapaport, Anatol, 259
Reading matter, 116. *See also* Newspaper reading
Reality of representation, 482–484
Recognition, 319
Reconversion strategies, 125, 131, 133, 135, 137, 147, 150, 157
References, 52–53
Religious opinions, and social class, 111
Representation, 43–44, 72, 184, 253; of reality, 482–484
Representational occupations, 152
Revolutionary aestheticism, 48

Right to speak, 411–414
Rivière, Jacques, 173

Sacred and profane, 6, 7, 19
Sartre, Jean-Paul, 207, 243
Saussure, F. de, 247
Scholastic culture, 23, 65, 68–70, 73
Scholem, Gershom, 85
Schopenhauer, Arthur, 487
Sculpture, 75
Selection, 162
Self-control, 40
Self-employed sector, 264
Self-esteem, 25, 142
Self-image, 25
Seniority, 70
Seriousness, 5, 54, 57, 74, 330–331
Servants, domestic, 46, 184
Servility, in production of cultural products, 240
Sex. *See* Gender
Sexuality, 367–368
Shopkeepers, 123, 135, 137, 141, 345–346; ethics and aesthetics, 46; newspaper reading by, 448
Significance, 22
'Significantness,' 22
Simon, M., 439
Sincerity, 43; in production of cultural products, 240
Skilled and semi-skilled workers, 114–115
Social age, 233
Social capital, 114
Social change, 156
Social class, 103–104, 106–108; and taste, 2, 6; legitimating social differences, 7; and marital status, 108–109; trajectory effect, 109–112, 123–124, 147, 264–265; and religious opinions, 111; and political opinions, 111, 427–428, 440; and geographical distance, 124; downclassing, 147, 150–151, 163–164; upclassing, 163–164; and sports, 214–215, 217–220; and production of cultural goods, 233–234. *See also* Habitus
Social compatibilities and incompatibilities, 241, 243
Social conditioning, 101
Social mobility, 131–133
Social origin, 1, 12–13, 63, 75, 77–78, 92, 265–266; and extra-curricular culture, 65; and educational capital, 105
Social science, 467–468

Social space, 169, 266, 343–345, 473; internalization of, 175; homology between spaces, 175, 208; and cultural consumption, 176; and body image, 206–208; and theatre, 234; as objective space, 244–245
Social structures, 467–471
Social uses, 18, 20–21, 49; and aesthetic judgements, 42–43
Social value, 21
Socialization, 474–475
Soul, 254
Spectacles, 34, 58
Spinoza, Baruch, 228
Spirituality, 19, 317
Sports, 20, 93, 209; functions of, 211–212; and competition, 214; team and individual, 214–215, 217; and fair play, 215; and social class, 215, 217–220; and cultural capital, 220; freedom and formalism, 220
'Stand-in,' 24
Statistical analysis, 22, 40, 94, 103, 557; statistical data, 525–545
Stratification, 245
Stylistic characterizations, 50, 52
Stylization of life, 55, 57, 174, 176, 376
Subjectivism, 244
Substantialism, 22
Substitution industry, 365
Superficiality, 74
Supply and demand, 230–232, 241
Supply side, 223
Survey data, 174, 245–246, 258; methodology, 503–518; complementary sources, 519–524
Symbolic capital, 291
Symbolization, 72
Synchronic properties of positions, 345, 453

Tabard, Nicole, 178
Taste, 1, 7, 99, 174–175, 247, 466, 474; and social class, 2, 6; popular taste, 16; legitimate, 16, 56–57, 71; middle-brow, 16, 58, 60, 267; barbarous and pure tastes, 30–32, 43–44, 178; and distaste, 56–57; classical, 65; and lifestyles, 173–175; and economic capial, 177–178; and conditions of existence, 178; and production of cultural goods, 231, 241; bourgeois taste, 292–294; intellectual taste, 292–294; petit-bourgeois taste, 339, 341–343; for necessity, 374–376, 378–380; pure taste, 486–488; of reflection, 489–491; of sense, 489–491
Taste-maker, 91, 255
Teachers, 115–116, 120, 122–123, 135, 264–265, 267; ethics and aesthetics, 46; spending by, 184; food purchases by, 185; clothing of, 202; and sports, 219; appropriation of cultural products, 272–273; ascetic disposition of, 287; newspaper reading by, 448
Technical objects, 29
Technicians, 83–84, 122, 304; ethics and aesthetics, 46; middle-brow taste of, 58; newspaper reading by, 447
Television, 33
Theatre, 19, 32, 116, 120, 269; and social space, 234; boulevard and experimental, 19, 234–235, 239
Theorists, 245
Thumin, F. J., 208
Time, 71–72, 281–282
Titles, 22–26, 161
Toy market, 223, 224
Travelling space, 169
Trickle-down effect, 232

Ubiquity, 72
Unskilled workers, 114
Utopia, 397

Value of culture, 250
Values, 247
Virility, 192, 384; and foods, 190–192
Visible and invisible, in clothing expenditures, 201

Wealth, indicators of, 116, 127. *See also* Economic capital
Weber, Max, 55, 174
Woolf, Virginia, 35, 444
Working classes, 57, 114; taste in, 16; and popular aesthetic, 32–33; and dominated aesthetic, 41; and significance of objects, 43; ethics and aesthetics, 44–47; and educational system, 143–144; meals, 190, 194–195, 197; entertaining by, 197; clothing of, 200–201; health and beauty care, 206; fertility strategies of, 332; and intellectuals, 372–374; and dominant class, 382–383; newspaper reading by, 447
'Working wives,' 178

Yeats, William Butler, 227